UNIX to Linux® Porting

Prentice Hall
Open Source Software Development Series

Arnold Robbins, Series Editor

"Real world code from real world applications"

Open Source technology has revolutionized the computing world. Many large-scale projects are in production use worldwide, such as Apache, MySQL, and Postgres, with programmers writing applications in a variety of languages including Perl, Python, and PHP. These technologies are in use on many different systems, ranging from proprietary systems, to Linux systems, to traditional UNIX systems, to mainframes.

The **Prentice Hall Open Source Software Development Series** is designed to bring you the best of these Open Source technologies. Not only will you learn how to use them for your projects, but you will learn *from* them. By seeing real code from real applications, you will learn the best practices of Open Source developers the world over.

Titles currently in the series include:

Linux® Debugging and Performance Tuning: Tips and Techniques
Steve Best
0131492470, Paper, 10/14/2005
The book is not only a high-level strategy guide but also a book that combines strategy with hands-on debugging sessions and performance tuning tools and techniques.

Linux Programming by Example: The Fundamentals
Arnold Robbins
0131429647, Paper, 4/12/2004
Gradually, one step at a time, Robbins teaches both high level principles and "under the hood" techniques. This book will help the reader master the fundamentals needed to build serious Linux software.

The Linux® Kernel Primer: A Top-Down Approach for x86 and PowerPC Architectures
Claudia Salzberg, Gordon Fischer, Steven Smolski
0131181637, Paper, 9/21/2005
A comprehensive view of the Linux Kernel is presented in a top down approach—the big picture first with a clear view of all components, how they interrelate, and where the hardware/software separation exists. The coverage of both the x86 and the PowerPC is unique to this book.

UNIX to Linux® Porting

A Comprehensive Reference

Alfredo Mendoza

Chakarat Skawratananond

Artis Walker

PRENTICE
HALL

Upper Saddle River, NJ · Boston · Indianapolis · San Francisco
New York · Toronto · Montreal · London · Munich · Paris Madrid
Cape Town · Sydney · Tokyo · Singapore · Mexico City

The publisher offers excellent discounts on this book when ordered in quantity for bulk purchases or special sales, which may include electronic versions and/or custom covers and content particular to your business, training goals, marketing focus, and branding interests. For more information, please contact:

U.S. Corporate and Government Sales
800-382-3419
corpsales@pearsontechgroup.com

For sales outside the United States, please contact:

International Sales
international@pearsoned.com

This Book Is Safari Enabled

The Safari® Enabled icon on the cover of your favorite technology book means the book is available through Safari Bookshelf. When you buy this book, you get free access to the online edition for 45 days. Safari Bookshelf is an electronic reference library that lets you easily search thousands of technical books, find code samples, download chapters, and access technical information whenever and wherever you need it.

To gain 45-day Safari Enabled access to this book:

- Go to http://www.awprofessional.com/safarienabled
- Complete the brief registration form
- Enter the coupon code D6MB-NTRL-6AC6-ZYL2-GKMV

If you have difficulty registering on Safari Bookshelf or accessing the online edition, please e-mail customer-service@safaribooksonline.com.

Visit us on the Web: www.prenhallprofessional.com

ISBN 0-13-187109-9
Text printed in the United States on recycled paper at R.R. Donnelley & Sons in Crawfordsville, IN.
First printing, April 2006.

Library of Congress Cataloging-in-Publication Data

Mendoza, Alfredo.
Unix to Linux porting : a comprehensive reference / Alfredo Mendoza, Chakarat Skawratananond, Artis Walker.
p. cm.
ISBN 0-13-187109-9 (pbk. : alk. paper) 1. Linux. 2. UNIX (Computer file) 3. Operating systems (Computers) I. Skawratananond, Chakarat. II. Walker, Artis. III. Title.
QA76.76.O63M437 2006
005.4'32—dc22

2006000234

"I would like to dedicate this book to my wife, Lynn, for keeping me straight and honest, and to my son, Justin, who by just being there challenges me every day to test the limits of my abilities."
Freddie Mendoza

"I would like to dedicate this book to my wife, Jaruwan, and my children, Shadt and Padt, for filling my life with joy and for being patient while I took the family time to work on this book. I would also like to dedicate this book to my father and mother for their inspiration and encouragement."
Chakarat Skawratananond

"I would like to thank—first and foremost—God. He has blessed me and created the circle of family and friends that has given me inspiration and strength throughout my life. Speaking of which, I dedicate this book to my family: wife Rose, daughter Bianca, and son Jordan. Your belief in me is what supplied the words in this book."
Artis Walker

Contents

Preface

Having started off as a hacker's exploratory journey to create a free UNIX-like operating system (OS), today Linux represents a viable competitive solution in use worldwide. Being freely redistributed and with all the strengths of UNIX-based operating systems, it is everywhere. People use it to deploy intensive industry solutions such as file servers, Web servers, e-mail, and middleware support. And yet, the operating system is flexible enough to be run as a desktop client on personal computers (PCs). Although the journey to success has been bumpy, it was worth it.

Linux has always been popular within the university setting, but it has really taken off within the corporate world only in the past few years, in part because of the support of and acceptance by large companies. Slowly, over the past few years, Linux has come closer to becoming an enterprise-ready OS for use in such areas as telecom, government, manufacturing, and others.

Recent news of accelerated Linux adoption is all over trade magazines, and studies done by the large research firm Forrester Research report that Linux is the fastest-growing OS (running mission-critical applications in 53 percent of 140 large North American companies[1]). The same Forrester study reports that 52 percent of the same 140 companies run their new applications on Linux, and 44 percent of them use Linux to port their older applications to newer hardware.

---

1 "Linux Crosses Into Mission-Critical Apps," Forrester Research Inc., April 26, 2004

A similar study[2] done by SG Cowen suggests that, more and more, Linux is becoming the OS of choice. Therefore, developers need a structured and concise book that examines the differences between Linux and UNIX operating systems such as Solaris, HP-UX, and AIX. Software programmers familiar with writing applications on UNIX operating systems such as Solaris, HP-UX, and AIX now have to learn how to program on Linux.

This book is written for those tasked with porting applications to the Linux environment (developers, application architects, and project managers):

- For **application developers,** this book identifies the differences between UNIX operating systems used in today's IT infrastructure.
- For **application architects,** this book provides information to help them decide which modules of their applications can best fit the Linux OS.
- For **project managers,** this book gives them a clear understanding of requirements and what it takes to port to the Linux environment.

How This Book Is Organized

Chapter 1, "Porting Project Considerations," supplements existing project management material by pointing out specific tasks that project managers and application architects need to think about before and during a porting project. It introduces you to the porting process and methodology we use in porting projects. Each step in the porting process presented forms the basis of discussion for the chapters that follow.

Chapter 2, "Scoping," discusses the first step in the porting process. Its general presentation of the Linux environment includes an examination of the available compilers, the GNU binutils, the Java environment, shells, and packaging options available on Linux. With the help of the assessment questionnaire in Chapter 1, you can assess the application to be ported to determine the level of work required to port the application. At the end of this chapter, a checklist of project management tasks helps you scope out the preliminary tasks for the project.

2 "Linux and Open Source Gain Momentum," SG Cowen, December 11, 2003

Chapter 3, "Analysis," discusses how to investigate the application architecture at a deeper level. Like Chapter 2, this chapter examines technical features available in Linux. This chapter covers, among other things, what Linux makes available in terms of application programming interfaces (APIs), library functions, library versioning implementation, and system features such as large page support. Each topic invites the porting engineer to ascertain that the application can be ported using Linux functionalities and features. As part of our porting methodology, and to eliminate risk as much as possible, the analysis step exists to uncover any variables (known and unknown) that can come up during the porting phase.

Chapter 4, "Porting Solaris Applications," Chapter 5, "Porting AIX Applications," and Chapter 6, "Porting HP-UX Applications," are the three core chapters of this book. Each comprehensive chapter details differences and similarities between the source (Solaris, AIX, or HP-UX) and the target (Linux) operating system. Topics discussed include standards support, compiler options, linker options, a comparison of system calls, a comparison of library calls, and threads. Each chapter helps porting engineers quickly find answers to questions about porting applications to Linux. These chapters answer common questions such as, "Do the APIs used in my application exist on Linux?" and "How do Linux POSIX threads compare to Solaris threads?"

Chapter 7, "Testing and Debugging," covers Linux debugging and performance tools. As the porting work progresses to the testing and debugging phase, porting engineers will encounter diverse issues from software bugs to performance bottlenecks. This chapter discusses the tools that porting engineers can use to address these issues. Debugging tools such as the GNU debugger, memory leak tools, cscope, and performance tracing tools are discussed. This chapter also identifies Web sites where you can download these tools.

The appendixes include tables of APIs, compilers, and linker options, providing a quick reference when you are porting from the source to the Linux OS. You also learn about Linux on POWER (that is, the porting differences when porting to Linux running on the IBM POWER architecture).

How to Use This Book

You can go through this book in several ways. However, we recommend that you start with Chapter 1 to gain an understanding of our methodology and thinking.

After reading the first chapter, proceed with Chapters 2 and 3. When you get to the porting step, choose the operating system from which the application is being ported, and read that chapter. Then, after you have completed the porting, proceed to Chapter 7. This process is shown in Figure P-1.

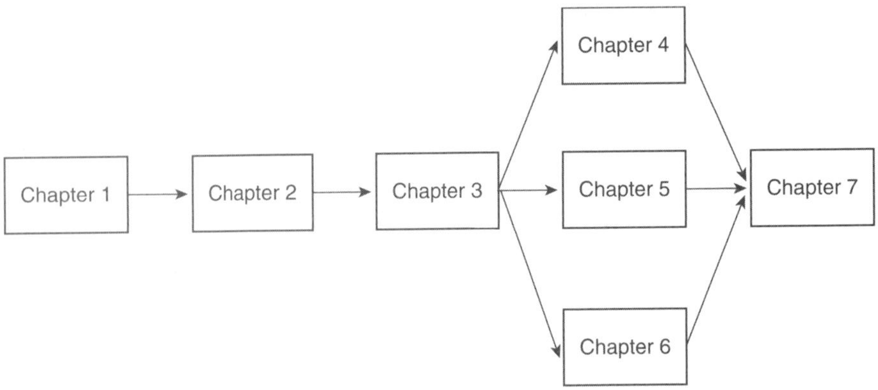

FIGURE P-1
Recommended way to work through this book

Another way to work through this book is to skip Chapters 1, 2, and 3 entirely and jump directly to one of the porting chapters (4, 5, or 6). In this way, you can use this book as reference material for porting projects already under way (rather than as a guide).

Some technical information in Chapters 4, 5, and 6 is intentionally repeated so that those who want to port only from one particular UNIX platform to Linux will have one self-contained chapter to reference.

Although our original intent with this book was to create a porting guide (from UNIX to Linux), it has also become a comprehensive development and troubleshooting reference. As a development reference, it contains code examples to solve specific problems (such as building shared and static archive libraries, using POSIX threads, interprocess communications, and more). And depending on the platform you are porting from, it gives a side-by-side solution comparison of the three popular UNIX platforms (HP, Solaris, and AIX), including what it would take to create the same solution on Linux. In essence, this book is three books in one. Regardless of your porting needs, this book explores solutions to some of the most common coding practices and provides a wide array of solutions (based on experience) to the most common problems Linux porting engineers face. As a troubleshooting reference, this book provides code examples, compiler and linker flags, and alternatives for solving the most common nuances that porting engineers face when porting code to Linux.

We have attempted to cover as much material as possible and believe the information will, at least, provide a starting point for additional research that may be required on your part to address specific needs. For additional assistance on porting, you can research the Internet and some of the following references:

- UNIX Porting Guide (various guides to porting software from one UNIX variant to another), at www.unixporting.com/porting-guides.html
- Guide to Porting from Solaris to Linux on POWER (white paper on porting to Linux on the IBM POWER architecture), at www-128.ibm.com/developerworks/linux/library/l-pow-portsolaris/
- Porting references from Novell (various white papers about porting to Linux), at http://developer.novell.com/wiki/index.php/Porting_and_Migration
- Solaris-to-Linux Porting Guide (by Ulrich Drepper; a white paper on porting from Solaris to Linux on Intel), at www.redhat.com/docs/wp/solaris_port/book1.html

We hope you enjoy reading this book as much as we have enjoyed writing it!

Acknowledgments

First and foremost, we want to thank the technical reviewers, who took the time from their busy schedules to review the book and provide valuable comments to make this book better: Mark Brown, Claudia Salzberg, Mel Gorman, Arnold Robbins, Radhakrishnan Sethuraman, Joe Brazeal, and Alessio Gaspar.

We would like to thank our employer, IBM, and our managers, Karen Slapik and Tayna Fulmer, for supporting us in writing this book. Without their support, we may have still been writing this book.

We would like to give attribution to Wolfgang Gellerich of IBM in Germany for his contribution on porting issues specific to the IBM zSeries mainframe (Appendix F, "Porting Issues Specific to the IBM zSeries Mainframe").

Several folks at IBM also need special mention. They provided us with easy access to lots of technical and nontechnical advice that was helpful in providing us the needed assistance at the right time: Rich Ferri, Craig Cook, Craig Fellenstein, Chris Almond, Gary Hook, Glen Chalemin, Bradford Cobb, Tom Grogan, Hans Dresen, Brian Vicknair, Vandana Kumar, and Calvin Sze.

We would like to thank Mark L. Taub of Prentice Hall for trusting us in our decisions regarding the book content and flow. We want to recognize the guidance that Jennifer Blackwell gave us on how to write a good technical book. Special thanks are also due to Christy Hackerd and the entire copyediting staff at Prentice Hall, who provided us with excellent support and endless patience during the production of this book.

Artis would like to thank Luther and Queen Walker for their guidance and parenting, which taught Artis how to just "do it" when it comes to making decisions.

About the Authors

Alfredo (Freddie) Mendoza is an IT specialist in the Business Strategy and Enablement group within the IBM Systems and Technology division with more than 19 years in application architecture and management. He currently works with independent software vendors to port and migrate their applications into IBM cross-platform operating system offerings. Prior to his current position, Mr. Mendoza worked in IBM's Global Services, for AIX Kernel development organizations, and as an independent consultant for different software development organizations. Mr. Mendoza has authored and coauthored several patent invention publications on thread management and software algorithms. He is the author of the book *Introduction to Utility Computing* and coauthor of "Design of an Enablement Process for On-Demand Applications" in the Utility Computing issue of the *IBM Systems Journal.*

Chakarat Skawratananond, Ph.D., is a technical consultant in the IBM Business Strategy and Enablement organization. He provides technical assistance to software vendors to bring their applications to IBM POWER processor-based systems running AIX and Linux. He has 10 years of experience in UNIX software development and has published several articles related to Linux software migration and performance tuning. He holds a Ph.D. in electrical and computer engineering from the University of Texas at Austin.

Artis Walker is a consultant in the IBM Business Strategy and Enablement group. He provides assistance in porting software vendors' applications and databases to pSeries servers running AIX and Linux on IBM POWER. He has more than 15 years' experience working on both Microsoft Windows and UNIX platforms, including AIX and Sun Solaris. He has extensive software development experience in IBM DB2 Universal Database (DB2 UDB), ORACLE, ODBC, JDBC, C, C++, and Java. He has published numerous tutorials and articles on migration and performance tuning on AIX and DB2. In addition, he is the originator and main author of a series of articles titled "IBM Embraces Open Source," which highlights various open-source solutions and their operability and setup on AIX and Linux on the POWER platform. He holds a BA in computer science from St. Mary's University in San Antonio, Texas.

Chapter 1

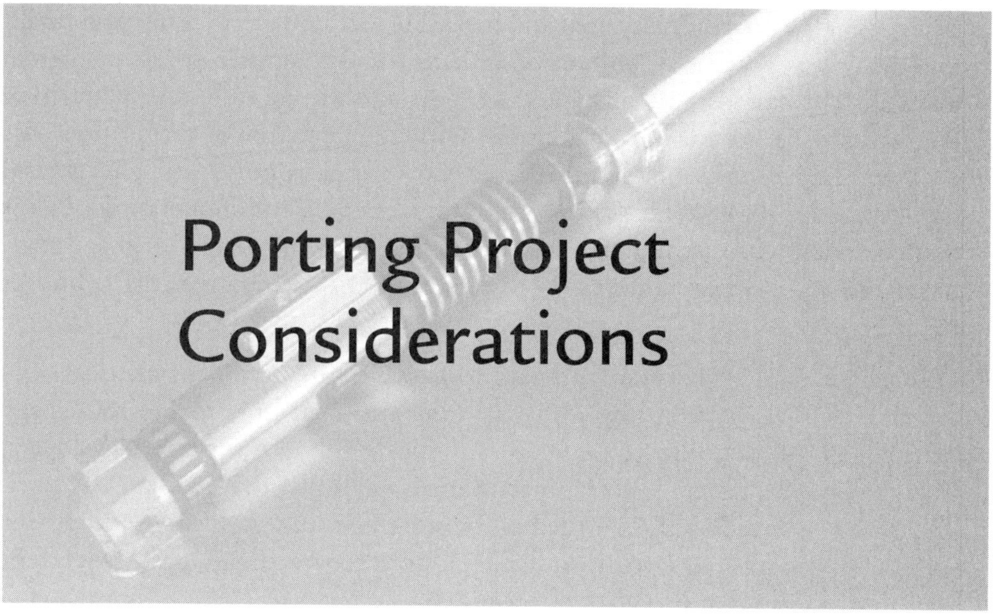

Porting Project Considerations

In this chapter

Application porting refers to the process of taking a software application that runs on one operating system and hardware architecture, recompiling (making changes as necessary), and enabling it to run on another operating system and hardware architecture. In some cases, porting software from one platform to another may be as straightforward as recompiling and running verification tests on the ported application. In other cases, however, it is not as straightforward. Some large applications that were written for older versions of operating systems and compiled with native compilers may not adhere to present language standards and will be more difficult to port, requiring the full attention of project management.

This chapter supplements currently available project management materials and books about application porting projects. Topics such as how to use formalized requirements processes, how to better communicate between software developers, and how to practice extreme project management are topics that modern-day project managers are already well informed of. However, because software development is not exactly the same as porting and migrating software, a gap exists in current publications—a gap that this chapter addresses.

The focus here is on software porting and migration process details and technical risks. All information in this chapter has been collected and gathered through countless porting engagements. This chapter presents best practices and methodologies to achieve high-quality ported applications. This chapter specifically appeals to those involved in software porting and migration projects, especially project managers and application architects.

1.1 Software Application Business Process

Before embarking on a porting project, it is important to note which business processes within the application life cycle will be affected. Business processes currently in place must be modified to accommodate the ported application in terms of having a new platform to support, new test environment, new tools, new documents, and (most important) new customers to support and establish relations with.

The three main areas of the application life cycle to consider that may affect the business process are development and testing, customer support, and software application distribution:

- **Development and testing.** Within the development and testing organization, personnel must be trained to develop and test on Linux in terms of application programming interface (API) differences, development tools, debugging tools, performance tools, third-party applications needed by the application to be ported, and performance tools.
- **Customer support.** Within the customer support organization, support personnel must be trained on Linux system administration, third-party applications needed by the ported application, installation and administration procedures, package maintenance options in the Linux environment, debugging tools and procedures, and anything else that needs to be learned to provide customer support for the ported application.
- **Software application distribution.** Within the software application distribution organization, sales and consultants must be trained in overall Linux features and capabilities.[1] Personnel in the software distribution channels must be trained as trainers of the software application in a Linux environment. From a customer's perspective, they will also look for integration skills to integrate Linux within their IT infrastructure.

Porting an application to Linux means modifying business organization processes that can be affected by a newly ported application. The three main areas should be considered and included in the overall project plan before starting the porting process.

1.2 The Porting Process

Developers involved in porting projects tend to follow similar steps when porting any software application. These steps include scoping, analyzing, porting, and testing. Each step in the process builds a foundation for the next step in the process. Each step, when done properly, makes the next step of the process easier to accomplish. Figure 1-1 shows the high-level steps taken during a porting project.

---

1 Different Linux distributions exist that may require separate training sessions for each.

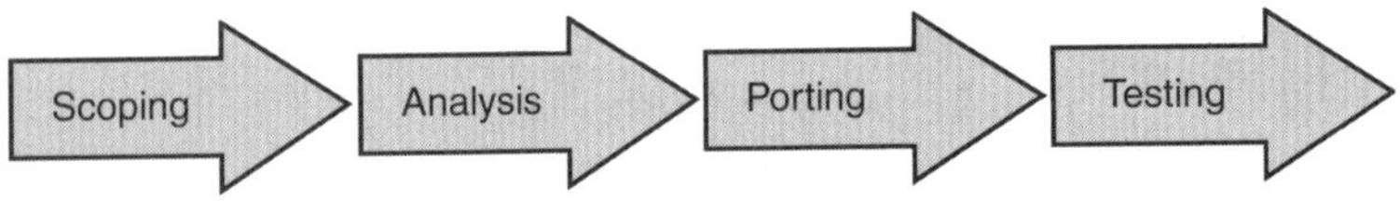

FIGURE 1-1
High-level steps taken during a porting project

1.2.1 Scoping

Scoping is the step in which the project manager asks the porting expert[2] and a domain expert[3] to get together to identify the products, development, and test environment the application to be ported relies on. The key areas to identify during the scoping process include product dependencies, development environment components, build environment components, and test environment components:

- **Product/software dependencies.** Identifying which products the application to be ported relies on means determining which versions of database, middleware, and third-party libraries it uses. By knowing the products and versions, the porting expert can assess whether those products and versions are available for the Linux platform.
- **Development environment components.** Assessing the development environment includes identifying what programming language the application is written in. Applications written in a more recent programming language such as Java tend to port more easily, whereas applications written in C or C++ usually require more analysis and porting effort.
- **Build environment components.** Assessing the build environment includes making sure the build tools are available on Linux. Platform-dependent compiler and link flags used on the source platform must be investigated to determine whether equivalent flags exist on Linux. Some build environments may have dependencies on the source platform that will require a little more effort to port to Linux.

---

2 A software developer who is experienced in porting applications and has knowledge of source and target platforms as well as other third-party products the application uses. We also refer to this person as a porting engineer in this book.

3 A person who is knowledgeable about the application to be ported. This could be the application architect or the chief developer of the application.

- **Test environment components.** Identifying the test environment for the ported application leads to questions pertaining to the ownership of testing after the application is ported. Usually porting engineers do unit testing for the part of the application they port and then hand it off to a testing group for more verification and systems tests. But who is the testing group?

In most cases, the scoping step leads to identifying associated risks that will be assumed by the project as a whole when it begins. Some risks that can be identified in the scoping step are included in the following scenarios:

- Versions of the database, middleware, or third-party libraries are not available for the Linux platform.
- The application has some assembler routines that need to be translated to assembly language instructions on the Linux platform.
- The application was written using a set of APIs or a programming model unique to the source platform. This also includes assumptions about such things as word size or "endian-ness."
- The application was written to draft-standard C++ semantics that relied on the source platform's native compiler framework.
- The test environment requires a complicated client/server framework.
- The development environment requires third-party tools that need to be compiled or ported to the Linux platform.
- The application's distribution or installation method requires facilities or tools unique to the source platform.

Scoping is an involved step in the porting process that takes into account every new piece of information that can be learned from asking the right questions—questions about documentation, packaging, and performance tuning, to name a few. These and others are mentioned in the "sample porting questionnaire" near the end of this chapter.

1.2.2 Analysis

There are two views in the analysis step of the porting process: a project management point of view, and a porting point of view. From a project management point of view, analysis is the step that assesses the various porting issues and risks identified in the preceding step and what impact they bring to the porting project as a whole. The analysis step involves the formulation of the project plan, which includes identifying scope and objectives, creating work schedules, procuring resources needed, and assigning roles within the project.

Identification of scope and objectives defines the boundaries and responsibilities of the project manager and the members of the project team. Boundaries are clearly identified sets of work that need to be done for the project. For example, a simple statement such as "Module A in application XYZ needs to be ported and tested on platform B" can be a good start to defining the boundaries of the work.

After boundaries have been identified, tasks for the porting work can be defined, leading to a work breakdown schedule.[4] The work breakdown schedule helps define which tasks need to be done and whether those tasks can be done in sequence or in parallel. In addition, the work breakdown schedule identifies the resources needed. An overall schedule for the entire porting project results from identifying tasks and resources needed.

From a porting point of view, analysis is a step in the porting process during which a porting engineer examines the application architecture in more detail. The porting engineer begins to identify the APIs and system calls used in the application. In addition, the application is assessed as to its use of dynamic linking and loading, networking, threads, and more. This analysis feeds information back to the project manager that can be used to formulate more detailed tasks and accurate schedules.

1.2.3 Porting

Porting is the step in the process during which the porting engineers perform their assigned tasks. Depending on the application and the work breakdown schedule that resulted from the preceding step, porting engineers may only be able to work their assigned tasks in a serial fashion. Serial tasks are a product of tightly coupled applications. This means that some modules of the application are highly dependent on other parts of the application and that these modules can be worked on only when the part they depend on is ported. A prime example of this is the build

---

4 A project management term used to denote work as an activity arranged in a hierarchical order that has tangible results otherwise referred to as a deliverable.

environment. If the build environment was designed to build the whole application as a monolithic procedure, chances are all modules depend on common configuration files that need to be modified before any porting work can be performed.

If the porting tasks are independent of each other, however, the work effort can be parallelized. Loosely coupled modules can be worked on separately and simultaneously by different porting engineers. A key example of this are shared libraries that can be built independently of each other, do not have common components, and exist for other modules to build on. Identifying which tasks can be done in parallel is important and should be done as part of the analysis step of the process.

The porting engineers' task of compiling the code on the Linux platform includes identifying and removing architectural dependencies and nonstandard practices if possible. Identifying and removing architectural dependencies means heeding compiler errors and warnings produced at compile time and correcting them as needed. Removing architectural dependencies and nonstandard practices involves examining and changing the code to use more portable structures or coding standards. Experienced and quality-conscious porting engineers usually do the latter as they correct compiler errors and warnings.

The porting effort includes porting the build environment to the Linux platform, too. This task should be identified during the scoping step. Although some build environments are portable, some are not. Making sure the build environment does not create any potential problems is a task easily overlooked and needs to be scoped and analyzed with extreme caution.

After the application has been ported—meaning it compiles on the Linux platform without errors—the porting engineer is expected to run unit tests on the application. The unit tests can be as simple as executing the application to determine whether it produces any runtime problems. If runtime problems are detected, they are debugged and fixed before the application is handed to the testing group; the test group then runs more thorough tests on the ported software.

1.2.4 Testing

During testing, the assigned testers run the ported application against a set of test cases, which vary from simple execution of the application to stress-type tests that ensure the application is robust enough when run on the Linux platform. Stress testing the application on the target platform is where most porting problems related to architectural dependencies and bad coding practices are uncovered. Most applications—especially multithreaded applications—behave differently during stress testing on a different platform, in part because of different operating system implementations, especially in the threading area. If problems are found during testing, porting engineers are called in to debug and fix them.

Some application porting may also include porting a test harness to test the application. Porting this test harness is a task that is also identified during scoping and analysis. Most of the time, the testers need to be trained on the application before they can test it. Learning about the application is a task that is independent of the porting tasks and can be performed in parallel.

If bugs are found, they are fixed and the source recompiled; the testing process repeats until the application passes all testing requirements.

1.2.5 Support

When the port is complete, the development phase ends, and the support phase begins. Some of the porting engineers are retained to help answer any porting-specific questions the customer may have. In addition, the developers are expected to train the customer on configuring and running the application on the Linux platform. The typical support phase lasts from 60 to 90 days after the port. During this time, the porting engineers train and answer technical support and sales personnel questions regarding the newly ported application on the Linux environment. After the technical support and sales personnel have been trained in the newly ported product, the porting engineer's task is done.

1.3 Defining Project Scope and Objectives

Project scope is defined as the specific endpoints or boundaries of the project as well as the responsibilities of the project manager and team members.[5] A clearly defined project scope ensures all stakeholders (individuals and organizations that are involved in or that might be affected by project activities—project team, application architect, testing, customer or sponsor, contracts, finance, procurement, contracts and legal) share a common view of what is included as the objectives of the project.

---

5 *Radical Project Management*, Rob Thomsett, 2002, Prentice Hall

Clear project objectives/requirements lead to a better understanding of the scope of the project. During the analysis step in the porting process, customer objectives and requirements are gathered, and these objectives transform themselves into work breakdown structures and eventually project deliverables. Project objectives and requirements provide a starting point for defining the scope of the project. After all project objectives have been laid out, the project scope becomes more defined.

One way to define the scope of a project is to list objectives that will and will *not* be included in the project. A requirements list from the customer is a good start. After the requirements have been gathered, the project manager and the technical leader review the list in detail. If there are questions about the requirements list, they should appear in the "not to be included" list of objectives, at least initially. The list is then reviewed by the customer, who may make corrections to the list. The list is revised until all parties agree that it presents the true objectives of the project.

Again, it should be sufficiently detailed so that it lists requirements that will and will not be included in the project. Yes, it is really that important to include details that are beyond the scope of the project. Objectives that do not provide enough definition to the scope of the project may turn out to be a point of contention as the project draws closer to its release date. An example of this might be listing how pieces of the porting work will be delivered to the porting team—will it be in phases, or will it be in a single delivery? Will each delivery be considered a phase, or will there be smaller pieces of work within a phase? How many phases will make up the entire project? The list not only defines the project itself, it also sets the expectations for all stakeholders in the project.

Here are the basic rules to follow when creating the project objectives list:

1. Define project scopes in as much detail as possible.
2. Confirm that all stakeholders agree to project scopes.
3. List unresolved items on the "not-included/not-in-scope" list until they are resolved.

Table 1-1 shows an example of a simple "in-scope" and "not-in-scope" table for a sample porting project.

TABLE 1-1
In-Scope and Not-in-Scope Objectives

Project: Customer *X* Application Port to Linux	
In Scope	**Not in Scope**
Port Directory, Mail, and Order Entry modules to Linux to be divided up in three phases. Each module will be one phase. Functional verification tests on these modules will be conducted by porting team. Definition of functional verification tests and acceptance criteria will be defined in another section. Provide debugging assistance to customer developers during system verification tests.	System tests of in-scope modules are not included in the porting project. Customer will be responsible for systems test. Packaging of application is not in scope. Fixing bugs found to be present in the original source code are not in scope. External customer documentation of ported modules is not in scope. Customer to produce external customer documentations.

Part of defining the objectives is listing the acceptance or success criteria. A consensus regarding the porting project success criteria must be reached by all stakeholders. Project success may mean passing a percentage of system tests on the Linux platform or passing a level of performance criteria set out by the systems performance group—that is, if the project objectives are to run a specific set of tests or performance analysis, respectively. Regardless of how the project success is defined, all stakeholders must understand and agree on the criteria before the porting effort starts, if possible. Any changes to the criteria during the course of the porting cycle must be communicated to all stakeholders and approved before replacing the existing criteria.

1.4 Estimating

Many porting projects go over budget and miss schedules because risks were not managed properly. Risks play a major part in estimating the schedule as well as resources needed for porting projects. In an application porting project, such risks come from different aspects that relate to application porting, including the following:

- Skill levels and porting experience
- Compiler used
- Programming language used
- Third-party and middleware product availability
- Build environment and tools
- Platform-dependent constructs
- Platform- and hardware-dependent code
- Test environment setup needed
- User interface requirements

Depending on the application to be ported, each of these aspects presents varying levels of complexity and risks to the project. Assessing complexity and risk level help you determine whether they are manageable.

1.4.1 Skill Levels and Porting Experience

The most glaring difference between porting applications and software development is the skill set of the programmers. Although software application developers tend to be more specialized in their knowledge domain, software developers who do porting and migration need broader and more generalized skill sets. An application developer can be someone who is an expert in Java and works on a Windows development environment. Another may be a programmer specializing in database programming on a Sun Solaris operating system environment. On the other hand, engineers who port code are expected to be experts in two or more operating system platforms, programming languages, compilers, debuggers, databases, middleware, and the latest Web-based technologies. They are expected to know how to install and configure third-party database applications and middleware.

Whereas application developers tend to be specialists, porting engineers need to be generalists. Application developers may work on an application for about 18 months (the typical development cycle), whereas porting engineers work on a 3- to 6-month project cycle and are ready to start on a new port as soon as the last one is finished. Finding skilled porting engineers who fit the exact requirements of a porting project may be difficult at times. This is most true when the porting efforts require porting from legacy technologies to newer ones.

1.4.2 Compiler

The compiler and compiler framework used by the source platform make a big difference when porting applications to the Linux environment. If the same compiler is used in both the source and target platforms, the task becomes easier. An example in this case is when the GNU compiler is used in both the source and the target platform. Besides the `-g` and `-c` flags, different brands of compilers use flags differently. Compiler differences become more difficult if the programming language used is C++.

Another thing to consider is the version of the compilers. Source code compiled a few years back with older versions of compilers may have syntax that does not conform to present syntax checking by compilers (because of standards conformity). This makes it more difficult to port on different compilers because these compilers may or may not support backward compatibility for standards. Even if the compilers support older standards, different compilers may implement support for these standards differently.

1.4.3 Third-Party and Middleware Product Availability

The complexity of the port increases when the application to be ported uses third-party and middleware products. Complexity increases even more when the versions of those products are not available for the target platform. In rare cases, some third-party products may not even be available on the target platform. In the past few years, middleware vendors such as IBM, Oracle, Sybase, and many more have ported their middleware products to Linux. They have made efforts to make their products available for companies that are ready and willing to make Linux their enterprise platform. This is partly why we are seeing more and more companies willing to port their applications to Linux.

1.4.4 Build Environment and Tools

The simpler the build environment, the less time the porting team takes to understand how to build the source code. More complicated build environments include multipass builds where objects are built with different compiler flags to get around dependencies between modules. After a first-pass build to build some modules, a second pass compiles yet more modules, but this time builds on top of the previously compiled modules (and so on until the build completes). Sometimes the build scripts call other scripts that automatically generate files on-the-fly based on nonstandard configuration files. Most of these files may be interpreted as ordinary files to be ported, but in fact, it is really the tools and the configuration files that need to be ported to work on the target module. These types of tools are mostly missed during assessment and analysis, which can result in less-than-perfect schedules.

One build environment that came into fashion sometime in the early 1990s was the use of imake. Imake is a makefile generator intended to ease build environment portability issues. Instead of writing makefiles, one writes imakefiles. Imakefiles are files that contain machine-independent descriptions of the application build environment. Imake creates makefiles by reading the imakefile and combining it with machine-dependent configuration files on the target platform. The whole concept of architecting a build environment around the imake facility to make it portable is a noble idea. Of the most recent 50 porting projects done by our porting group, only a few were built around the imake facility. Unfortunately, all of them needed as many modifications to their own environment and imakefiles, negating the ease that imake is intended to provide. And because imake was rarely used, anyone who needed to do a port needed to "relearn" the utility every time.

Nowadays, makefiles are written for the open source make facility called GNU Make (or gmake for short). Most makefile syntax used in different UNIX platforms is syntax that gmake can understand or has an easy equivalent to. Architecting applications around the gmake[6] facility is the most accepted and widely used method in build environments today.

Source code control is another aspect that must be considered. In the Linux environment, CVS is the most frequently used source code control environment. Other source code control environments are Subversion[7] and Arch.[8] A porting project needs to have source code control if there is a possibility of several porting engineers working on the same modules at the same time.

---

6 Some may favor Autoconf even though it had a certain level of complexity compared to using plain old makefiles.

7 http://subversion.tigris.org

8 www.gnu.org/software/gnu-arch/

1.4.5 Platform-Dependent Constructs

When porting from UNIX platforms based on RISC architecture to x86-based platforms, a chance exists that application code needs to be assessed for byte-endian dependencies. For example, the application implements functions that use byte swapping for calculations or data manipulation purposes. Porting the code that uses byte-swapping logic to an Intel-based machine, which is little-endian architecture, requires that code be modified to adhere to little-endian semantics. In cases where byte-swapping logic is not changed between platforms, debugging becomes a chore because it is difficult to track where data corruption takes place. When this happens several instructions before the application fail. Make sure to identify platform-dependent constructs in the scoping and analysis steps.

1.4.6 Platform- and Hardware-Dependent Code

Applications that require kernel extensions and device drivers to operate are the hardest to port. Kernel APIs for all platforms do not follow any standards. In this case, API calls, number of arguments, and even how to load these extensions into the kernel for a specific platform will be different. In most cases, new code that needs to run on Linux must be developed. One thing is for certain: Kernel code will usually, if not always, be written in C or platform-dependent assembler language.

1.4.7 Test Environment and Setup

When the port is done and the project scope includes system tests and verification, equipment required to test the code may contribute to the port's complexity. If the application needs to be tested on specialized devices that need to be ordered or leased, this can add complexity to the project. If the application needs to be tested in a complicated clustered and networked environment, setting up the environment and scheduling the resource adds time to the project.

Testing may also include performance testing. Normally, performance tests require the maximum configuration setup one can afford to be able to load up the application to see how it scales in big installations.

Porting of the application test harness needs to be included in the porting schedule. A test harness that includes both software tests and specialized hardware configurations needs to be assessed as to how much time it will take to port and configure.

1.4.8 User Interface Requirements

Porting user interfaces can range from being easy to complex. User interfaces based on Java technology are easy to port, whereas user interfaces based on X11 technology are more complex. In this type of application, the code may be written in C or C++.

Table 1-2 is a summary of the various aspects involved. Each aspect is ranked as easy, medium, or high complexity, depending on the technology used for each aspect.

TABLE 1-2
Software Porting Risks and Complexities

Aspect	Easy	Medium Complexity	High Complexity
Compiler/ programming language	Java Shell scripts	Use of C, COBOL, Fortran language Use of nonportable syntax Original source code written to other standards of compiler	C++ using compiler-specific framework that supports varying levels of the C++ standard Source code written in languages other than Java or C Use of nonstandard compilers such as ASN or customer-built interpreters Use of assembler language Use of RPG language
Use of third-party products or middleware	None	Supported and available on target platform	Not supported on target platform Use of third-party tools written in C++
Build environment and tools	Simple makefiles	Combination of makefiles and build scripts	Use of noncommon build tools such as imake, multiple-pass builds, on-the-fly-generated code modules
Platform/ hardware-dependent code	No platform- or hardware-dependent code	Platform/hardware-dependent code comes from third-party products already ported to target platform	Extensive use of kernel extensions and device driver code
Test environment and setup	Stand-alone	Client/server setup	Networked, high availability, clustered Needs external peripherals to test such as printers, Fibre Channel-attached disks
User interface	Java-based	Standard-based interface such as X11, CDE	Nonportable user interface such as custom interfaces using proprietary code

Experience shows that real efforts needed to port the application are uncovered during the first two or three weeks of the porting project. This is the time when the code is delivered to the project team and porting engineers get a first glimpse of the software application. In other cases, this is the first time porting engineers work on the application in a Linux environment. They begin to dissect the application components and start preliminary build environment setups. Within the first two to three weeks, the porting engineers will have configured the build environment and started compiling some modules using GNU-based tools and compilers.

After two to three weeks, it is good to revisit the estimated time schedules to determine whether they need to be adjusted based on preliminary real experiences of porting the application into the Linux platform.

1.5 Creating a Porting Project Schedule

When creating the porting schedule, consider all risks, including technical and business-related issues. In terms of technical issues, common things such as resource availability, hardware availability, third-party support, and Linux experience need to be considered. On the business side, issues such as reorganizations, relocations (moving offices), customer release dates, and business objective changes may affect the porting schedule as a whole.

These technical and business issues will create several dependencies external to the porting project that may not be controlled; therefore, it is advisable to consider each external issue to mitigate risks accordingly.

Creating schedules for porting projects is just like creating schedules for software development projects. Figure 1-2 is an adaptation of a diagram from *Radical Project Management* by Rob Thomsett (Prentice Hall, 2002, p. 191). The figure shows that the average estimation error made before the project scopes and objectives are cleared up is +400 percent and –400 percent. As the objectives, scope, risks, and other technical and business issues are clarified, the estimated porting schedule comes closer to the real schedule.

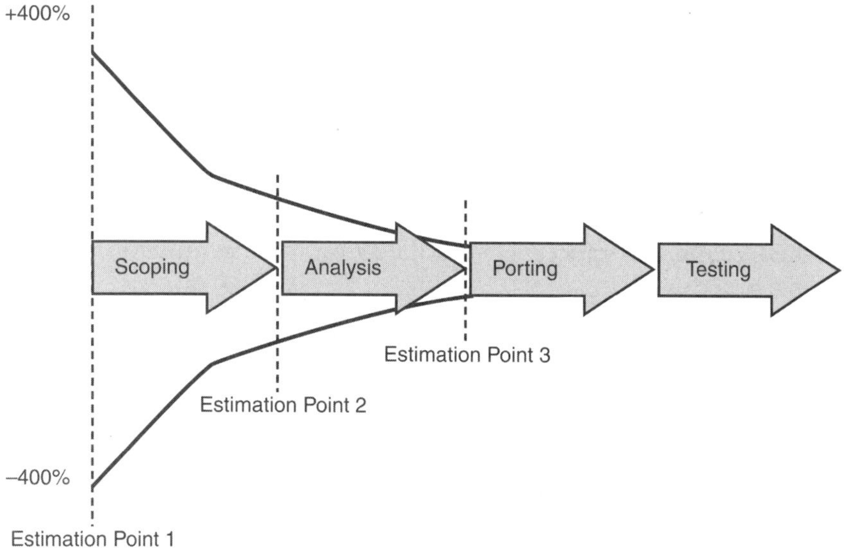

FIGURE 1-2
Average estimation error made before scopes and objectives are cleared

Each transition to the next step in the porting process allows the project team to reassess the project estimates in terms of the schedule and resources. In essence, these transitions can and should serve not only as milestones for the project but also as checkpoints to reexamine the original estimates.

1.6 Porting Process from a Business Perspective

The porting process is not just about porting the software application; the resulting ported application needs the necessary business and support structures to make it a successful business initiative. Although porting efforts are taking place, the stakeholders need to prepare other organizations that will provide support for the application. Organizations such as customer support and software distribution will require documentation and training on the application running on the Linux environment.

Getting the necessary Linux training for personnel in customer support and software distribution should be high on the priority list of objectives. As with any new product, new releases tend to generate the most questions from users and system administrators alike. Expect to answer system administration questions about Linux, too. Our experience shows that newly ported applications on a new operating environment generate questions about system administration and the use of the new operating system in three out of five support line calls.

As system administration and installation questions begin to subside, more technical questions about the application will arise. Support organizations need access to live test machines to duplicate customer problems. These machines may differ from development or porting machines depending on the application and technical problems that will require instances of the application to be running for debugging purposes.

From an overall project perspective, the need to train support personnel and the availability of physical resources to support the ported application will come at later stages of the porting project. As the technical aspects of the porting project near completion, the business aspects of the project pick up.

1.7 Annotated Sample Technical Questionnaire

This questionnaire, based on which other scoping questions can be formed, serves as a guide to the porting technical leader. The customer in this case is an internal or external organization that needs to port its application(s) to the Linux platform.

1.7.1 Platform-Specific Information

1. What is your current development platform for the application?

   This question is about the development platform used to develop the application. It does not assume that the development platform is the same platform the application is deployed on. This is asked in the next question.

2. What platform does the application currently run on?

   Porting engineers need to know which source or reference platform the application to be ported is using.

3. Has this application been deployed on any other platform than the development one? If so, which version of the platform is it running on?

   Asking this question gives you a sense of the portability of the application if it has been ported to other platforms. A word of caution: Although an application may have been ported to other platforms, it may have been done on older versions of the platform.

4. Describe any hardware (that is, graphics adapters or cards) used by your application and whether the required drivers are available on the Linux platform.

   Make sure any platform dependencies are available on Linux.

1.7.2 Application-Specific Information

1. Please describe your application and its architecture in detail.

   This is where the customer describes the application architecture. Have them include an architectural diagram if possible. All components in the application need to be described. This should also tell you what type of application framework, if any, the application runs on. Most Java applications run on product-specific frameworks such as WebSphere or Weblogic. If they are written in C++, they may run on a CORBA framework, which means you may have to deal with a specific CORBA framework that may or may not exist on Linux.

2. What are the different components of your software? Please provide a name and version number for each component.

   This gives you a sense of the breakdown of their applications. Being able to break the application into different discrete components can mean that the porting work can be broken into smaller independent tasks.

3. Which of these pieces needs to be ported or not ported? Please include the version number.

   The customer needs to tell you what is in scope and what is not in scope.

4. What percentage of the application(s) to be ported is/are written in the following programming languages?

   a. Java
   b. C#

c. C
d. C++
e. Assembler
f. Visual Basic (Microsoft)
g. Shells (ksh, csh, perl, awk, others)

Ascertains the complexity of the application by asking what languages they are using and what percentage of those are in use.

5. Please provide a rough estimate of the number of lines of code in the software, listed by language types.

   This is another way of asking Question 4. Asking questions in different ways often brings up data points that contradict each other. This opens the door for open discussions that can result in better project scoping.

6. For Java apps: Does the application use the JNI[9] to link native libraries? Please describe.

   Ascertains the complexity of the application to be ported. Most of the time, Java applications[9] that are not 100 percent pure Java need platform-dependent routines that can only be handled in native language such as C. Be aware of such platform-dependent code, because it takes more time to port.

7. Does the application use kernel modules? If so, please describe.

   Ascertains the complexity of the application to be ported. Kernel modules and routines used by the application are nonportable. These will take more time to convert to equivalent routines in Linux.

8. Is this a 2D/3D graphics application? Please describe.

   Ascertains the complexity of the application to be ported. Make sure compatible graphics toolkits and development tools are available in Linux, whether they are supplied in Linux by default or by other third-party vendors.

9 Java native interface.

9. Does the application use UNIX pipes, message queues, shared memory, signals, or semaphores? Please describe.

   Most of these have standard UNIX interfaces that can be easily ported to Linux. Although the interfaces may be standard, implementation underneath the covers will differ. The catch is to make sure that the intended behavior remains the same when ported to Linux.

10. Is the application, or any of its components, multithreaded? If so, which threads library is currently being used? Does the application rely on any proprietary threading priorities on your development platform?

    Depending on the source platform, multithreading interfaces can vary from standard to nonstandard. Linux supports several threading libraries, but the one that is standard in present and future Linux distributions is the Native Posix Threads Library (NPTL) implementation. NPTL is discussed in other sections of this book. The point is that the closer the source implementation is to NPTL, the easier it is to port.

11. Does the application perform operations that assume specific byte storage order? Is this likely to be an issue during the port?

    This question relates to the "endian-ess" of the application. Most Linux ports will target the Intel platform, which is small-endian, whereas most source platforms will be big-endian. Nonportable code that assumes endian-specific characteristics will break when not ported correctly. Worse yet, the ported code will not exhibit errors during the porting phase. The problem usually crops up during system testing, where it is harder to find.

12. Which compiler(s) and version are used in the development platform?

    a. GNU
    b. Java (what version?)
    c. Platform (HP, AIX, Sun, Microsoft, NCR, AS/400, S390, True64) compiler? Which platform?
    d. Others (please specify)

Ascertains the complexity of the application to be ported. If the source application uses the GNU `gcc` or `g++` compiler, it becomes easier to port to Linux because the native compiler for Linux is GNU `gcc` or `g++`. Applications that are developed on other platforms and are compiled in their native compilers tend to use native compiler semantics, which must be converted to GNU compiler semantics. C++ applications become harder to port than C applications when the application starts to use C++ features such as templates. Because some C++ standards are implemented differently by different compiler vendors, porting this type of code takes more time than simpler C or C++ code.

13. In addition to the development environment, are there any dependencies on debugging tools such as memory leak debuggers, performance analysis tools, exception handling, and so forth?

    This goes back to scoping and dependencies. Third-party tools that may or may not exist in Linux need to be assessed. Who needs to provide for the license? Who is responsible for obtaining the tools? What will be the support structure if third-party support is needed?

14. Is this a socket-based application? If so, does it use RPC? Please describe.

    Although Linux supports standards-based socket and RPC semantics, the intent is to ascertain portability. Asking this question may bring to light nonportable architecture the customer may have implemented in the application. This question can also lead to questions on what setup is needed at the testing phase.

15. Does the application use any third-party software components (database tools, application server, or other middleware)? If so, which ones?

    Every third-party software component adds complexity to the port. If any third-party software components are used, ask what version of the component is used and whether it is available on Linux. Third-party components may require extra time to learn and even to configure or build if necessary.

16. How is the application delivered and installed? Does it use standard packaging? Will the installation scripts need to be ported, too?

    A Linux standard packaging mechanism is RPM. RPM is discussed in other parts of the book. Ascertain whether the customer will need the packaging part of the application ported, too.

17. Is the application or any of its components currently in 64-bit? Will any component need to be migrated to 64-bit?

    With the advent of 64-bit platforms and operating systems, this question pertains to the level at which the application needs to run or be ported. Most 32-bit applications will port to a 64-bit environment without problems through the use of modern compilers. Today's compilers have become efficient at flagging syntax and semantic errors in the application at compile time, allowing the porting engineer to make necessary changes. The one consideration here is that it will require additional time for porting and debugging.

1.7.3 Database Information

1. What databases are currently supported? Please include version numbers.

   Almost all enterprise applications today require a database back end. It's important to make sure that the database for the application is available on Linux. Differences in database products and versions can add substantial porting effort to the project.

2. What database is the ported application expected to run with?

   In addition to Question 1 in this section, what database does the customer expect the ported application to run with on the Linux platform?

3. Does the application use any nonrelational or proprietary databases?

   Any proprietary database needs to be ported to Linux. Make sure the code to run the database is available and is part of the scoped porting work.

4. How does the application communicate with the database?

   a. Programming language(s) (for example, Java, C/C++, other)

   b. Database interface(s) (for example, ODBC, OCI, JDBC)

   Ascertains that programming languages and interfaces are available on Linux, whether or not they are supplied by third-party vendors.

5. Does the application require the use of extended data types (XML, audio, binary, video, and so on)?

   This information can be used to assess the skills needed by the porting group for porting the application.

1.7.4 Porting Project Time Schedule Information

1. What is the desired General Availability date for the application on the target platform?

   This question is asking whether any business objectives need to be considered when creating the porting schedule.

2. Has the porting of the application already started on the target platform?

   This is helpful in assessing complexities and problems that are discovered prior to officially starting the porting project.

3. What is the estimated port complexity level (low, medium, or high)?

   Take the answer to this question with a grain of salt. There may be other factors present today that may not have been fully realized in previous porting efforts.

4. What factors were considered in this complexity ranking?

   Any information from previous porting efforts needs to be assessed and compared to future porting efforts on the Linux platform.

5. If the application has been ported to another platform, how long did that port take? How many resources were dedicated to it? What problems were encountered?

This question attempts to compare previous porting efforts to the Linux port. This is useful only if the porting engineer technical lead has previous porting experience on other platforms as well as Linux.

6. What is your rough estimate of the project porting time and resources required?

   The application or parts of it may have already been ported to other platforms, and knowing the time it took to port to those other platforms may be of some use. Experience and lessons learned from previous ports may come in handy. Knowing some of the lessons learned may help you avoid problems when porting to Linux.

1.7.5 Testing-Specific Information

1. Please describe the acceptance testing setup.
2. What kind of networking and database setup will be required for unit testing?
3. How much testing will be required after porting (number of days, number of resources)?
4. Do you have established test scripts and application performance measurements?
5. Will benchmarks need to be run for comparison testing?
6. Is performance data available on current platforms?
7. When were the performance tests last executed?

All "testing-specific" questions pertain to application software testing on the Linux platform. Asking these questions may bring out other issues related to porting test scripts and the software application test harness, which will add risks and time to the whole project. Pay close attention to the response to Question 1 in this section. Question 1 relates to the type of acceptance criteria that needs to be agreed on before porting starts. An example acceptance criterion is: Module A and B should pass test suites C and D, without failure. When the acceptance criteria are met, the port is considered complete, and formal QA tests can then be performed on the application.

1.7.6 Porting Project Execution Information

1. Please select one or more options, according to how you would like to proceed with this project.

   a. Technical assistance will be provided to the porting engineers as necessary.

   b. Customer will be responsible for acquiring third-party licenses and technical support.

   c. Other (please describe).

   Add other items in this part of the questionnaire that you need the primary customer to consider. Some issues may relate to staff training or testing the application.

2. What kind of hardware will be needed for the project?

   Consider asking this question to ascertain whether existing hardware may be used or whether extra hardware will be needed—for porting, testing, training, and support purposes if necessary.

Although this questionnaire is comprehensive, it should not be the only basis for scoping. Scoping should also include actual examination of application source code when pertinent. Software application documentation needs to be examined to learn more about the application from a customer usage point of view.

1.8 Summary

Project managers and porting technical leads need to consider multiple aspects of a porting project before embarking on the actual port itself. Careful investigation of these aspects has led us to many successful porting projects in the past. Because every porting project is different, these aspects may take on different shapes and forms. Even so, the underlying concepts and descriptions will remain the same. A porting project can be summarized as follows:

- **Scoping.** Ask questions, inspect the code if available, ask more questions and investigate the risks, and develop the schedule.
- **Analysis.** Ask more questions, investigate the risks, and create the schedule based on technical and business issues.
- **Porting.** Set up the build environment, compile, and unit test.
- **Testing.** Set up the test environment, test, and analyze performance. Go back to the porting process if bugs are found.
- **Training.** Train support and sales personnel on the application and operating environment.

Because complexities and risks associated with different technical aspects of the porting project may affect the overall schedule and budget, the transition point between each step of the porting process allows the project team to reassess its original estimates. Reassessing the original estimates helps set the proper expectations of all stakeholders early on before the real work of porting begins. As in all projects, the success of the project is defined not only by the successful delivery of the final product; it is also defined by how well the project was managed to the satisfaction of all parties involved. In the next chapters, we go through each step of the porting process. We present information about Linux that porting engineers can use as they go through the scoping, analysis, porting, and testing phases of a porting project.

Chapter 2

Scoping

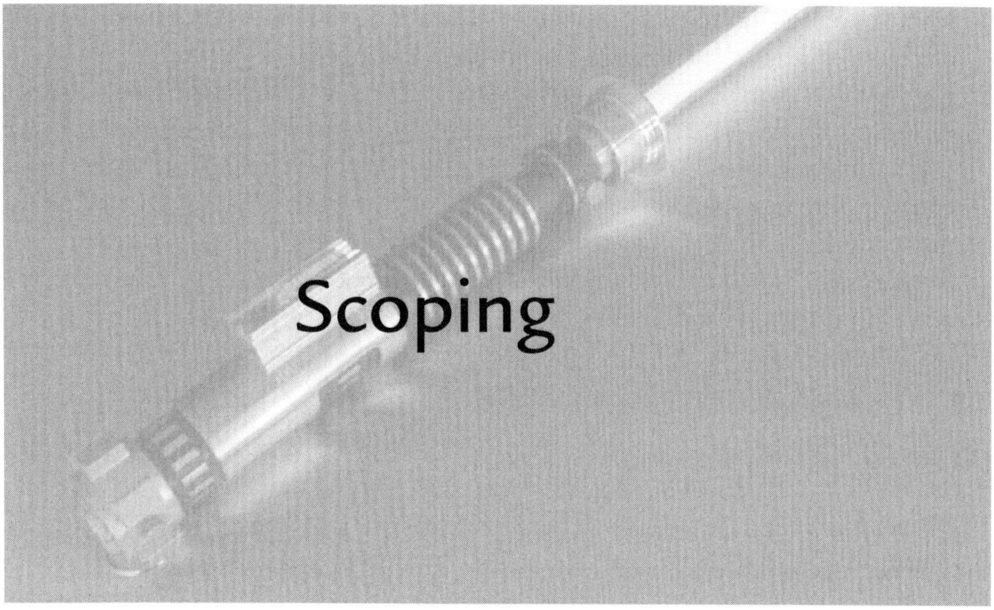

In this chapter

Scoping is the step in the porting project in which preliminary assessment of the application to be ported takes place. You assess the application in terms of the programming language it is written in, the build environment it uses, third-party software dependencies, and more.[1] Each of these areas is examined to make sure the application can be ported to Linux. Based on a positive outcome of this assessment, the porting engineer can then proceed to assess other application components from which information gathered leads to identifying the scope, deliverables, and project tasks. This chapter discusses compilers, build environment tools, shells, and packaging options that exist on Linux to help guide porting personnel as they go through the scoping process.

2.1 Compilers

One of the assessment questions in Chapter 1, "Porting Project Considerations," asks what programming language the application to be ported is written in. The question tries to ascertain whether the application can be compiled by any of the supported[2] compilers on Linux. The most popular compiler in Linux and in the open-source community today is the GNU Compiler Collection (GCC). Initially, when the open-source movement started, the term GCC referred to the GNU C Compiler (`gcc`). Today, because of its overwhelming popularity, GCC is now an integrated distribution of compilers that include several major programming languages, including C, C++, FORTRAN, COBOL, and Java.[3]

2.1.1 GNU gcc C Compiler

`gcc` supports the ANSI C version of the C standard, although support for the most recent version is not yet complete. These standards are as follows:

1 Refer to the assessment questionnaire presented in Chapter 1 and use it during this scoping step.

2 One of the questions we are often asked is this: Does Linux support the RPG language? Unfortunately, the answer is no. The best solution today is to convert RPG applications to Java applications.

3 GCC also includes support for Objective C and Ada.

- ANSI C standard (1990 ISO C and C94/C95)
- C99 ISO C standard (support not complete)[4]

`gcc` has a number of compiler flags to allow the user to select the desired standard. If no standard is specified, the default is `-std=gnu89`; this will change to `-std=gnu99` in some future release when the C99 support is complete.

Most of the compiler support routines used by GCC are present in `libgcc`, with the exception of the `freestanding` environment. When the `-ffreestanding` compiler flag is turned on, users are required to provide their own version of `memcpy`, `memove`, `memset`, and `memcmp`.

For any given input file, the filename suffix determines what kind of compilation is done:

- `file.c`

  C source code that must be preprocessed

- `file.i`

  C source code that should not be preprocessed

- `file.m`

  Objective-C source code (note that you must link with the library `libobjc.a` to make an Objective-C program work)

- `file.mi`

  Objective-C source code that should not be preprocessed

- `file.h`

  C header file (not to be directly compiled or linked)

The command-line options of the GCC family of compilers differ from other proprietary compilers. Many options for GCC compilers have multiletter names; therefore, multiple single-letter options may *not* be grouped: `-dr` is different from `-d-r`. In addition, many options have long names starting with `-f` or `-W` (for

---

4 GCC has incomplete support for C99. See http://gcc.gnu.org/gcc-3.4/c99status.html.

example, `-fforce-mem`, `-fstrength-reduce`, `-Wformat`, and so on). Most of these have both positive and negative forms; the negative form of `-ffoo` would be `-fno-foo`.

More than 100 command-line options can be passed to `gcc`. More than likely, you will use only a few. The following is a typical compile line for `gcc` compiler invocation:

```
gcc <additional flags here> -c main.c -o main.o
```

Here are some examples of `gcc` options controlling the kind of output it produces:

```
-c - compile or assemble source files but do not link.
-S - output is in the form of assembler code.
-E - output is in the form of preprocessed source code.
-v - print the commands executed to run the stages of compilation.
--help - print the description of command-line options.
```

2.1.2 GNU g++ (C++) Compiler

Starting with GNU `g++` version 3.4.0, GNU `g++` claims to be *much* closer to the ISO/ANSI C++ standards.[5] GNU `g++` ships with the standard `libstdc++`. C++ source files conventionally use one of these suffixes: `.C`, `.cc`, `.cpp`, `.c++`, `.cp`, or `.cxx`; preprocessed C++ files use the suffix `.ii`. GCC recognizes files with these names and compiles them as C++ programs even if you call the compiler the same way as for compiling C programs (usually with the name `gcc`).

However, C++ programs often require class libraries as well as a compiler that understands the C++ language. Under some circumstances, you might want to compile programs from standard input, or otherwise without a suffix that flags them as C++ programs. `g++` is a program that calls GCC with the default language set to C++, and automatically specifies linking against the C++ library. On many systems, the executable `g++` is also installed with the name `c++`.

When you compile C++ programs, you may specify many of the same command-line options that you use for compiling programs in any language, or command-line options meaningful for C and related languages, or options that are meaningful only for C++ programs.

---

5 http://gcc.gnu.org/gcc-3.4/changes.html#cplusplus

You can use most of the GNU compiler options when using the `g++` compiler, but some options are meaningful only for C++ programs. Table 2-1 shows a few useful `g++` options.

TABLE 2-1
Sample g++ Options

GNU g++ Options	Description
`-fcheck-new`	Check that the pointer returned by operator `new` is non-null before attempting to modify the storage allocated.
`-fno-elide-constructors`	The C++ standard allows an implementation to omit creating a temporary object that is used only to initialize another object of the same type. Specifying this option disables that optimization and forces g++ to call the copy constructor in all cases.
`-ffor-scope` `-fno-for-scope`	If `-ffor-scope` is specified, the scope of variables declared in a `for-init-statement` is limited to the `for` loop itself, as specified by the C++ standard. If `-fno-for-scope` is specified, the scope of variables declared in a `for-init-statement` extends to the end of the enclosing scope, as was the case in old versions of g++ and other (traditional) implementations of C++. The default if neither flag is given is to follow the standard, but to allow and give a warning for old-style code that would otherwise be invalid or have different behavior.
`-fno-rtti`	Disable generation of information about every class with virtual functions for use by the C++ runtime type identifier features (`dynamic_cast` and `typeid`). If you do not use those parts of the language, you can save some space by using this flag. Note that exception handling uses the same information, but it generates it as needed.

You will use the following command to compile a typical C++ program under GNU:

```
g++ <additional options here> -c firstClass.C -o firstClass.o
```

2.1.3 GNU g77 FORTRAN

GNU FORTRAN consists of a compiler, runtime libraries, and debugger support. It supports ANSI FORTRAN 77 conformance, plus popular extensions to FORTRAN, including some ANSI/ISO FORTRAN 90 features.

The `libf2c` library is distributed with GNU FORTRAN for the convenience of its users but is not part of GNU FORTRAN. It contains the procedures needed by FORTRAN programs while they are running.

GNU FORTRAN, or `g77`, is designed initially as a free replacement for, or alternative to, the UNIX `f77` command and was designed to fit in well with the other GNU compilers and tools. For example, in a GNU FORTRAN installation, `gcc` recognizes FORTRAN source files by name, just like it does with C and C++ source files.[6] It knows to use the FORTRAN compiler named `f771`, instead of `cc1` or `cc1plus`, to compile FORTRAN files. The non-FORTRAN-related operation of `gcc` is generally unaffected by installing the GNU FORTRAN version of `gcc`. However, without the installed version of `gcc` being the GNU FORTRAN version, `gcc` will not be able to compile and link FORTRAN programs—and because `g77` uses `gcc` to do most of the actual work, neither will `g77`!

Because the `g77` command is essentially just a front end for the `gcc` command, FORTRAN users will normally use `g77` rather than `gcc`, because `g77` knows how to specify the libraries needed to link with FORTRAN programs (`libf2c` and `lm`). `g77` can still compile and link programs and source files written in other languages, just like `gcc`.

As of the writing of this book, an effort is underway to replace FORTRAN 77, `g77`, with GNU FORTRAN (`gfortran`) or FORTRAN 95. Although `gfortran`[7]

---

6 `.f`, `.for`, and `.FOR` are file extensions that are recognized as FORTRAN source and must not be preprocessed. `.F`, `.fpp`, and `.FPP` are file extensions that are recognized as FORTRAN source and must be preprocessed.

7 http://gcc.gnu.org/fortran/

is available for download and use, it is still considered to be in (public) beta testing, and has been since February 17, 1995. GNU recommends you continue to use `g77` for all new development until they officially release `gfortran`.

2.1.4 GNU Compiler for Java[8]

GCJ is a portable, optimizing, ahead-of-time compiler for the Java Programming Language. It can compile the following:

- Java source code directly to native machine code
- Java source code to Java bytecode (class files)
- Java bytecode to native machine code

Applications are compiled and linked with the GCJ runtime, `libgcj`. Included within `libgcj` are the core class libraries, a garbage collector, and a bytecode interpreter. One feature of `libgcj` is that it can dynamically load and interpret class files, resulting in a Java application that is a mix of compiled and interpreted objects or classes.

Debugging support for GCJ applications is available using recent versions of the GNU debugger, GDB.[9] A short tutorial on using GDB to debug GCJ-compiled applications is available at http://gcc.gnu.org/java/gdb.html.

2.1.5 GNU Cobol

In 1999, a GNU project named GCC for COBOL was started to create a COBOL 85-compliant compiler for GNU/Linux and other operating systems. At the time of this writing, the compiler was not yet ready for production use. For more information about the GNU COBOL project, refer to www.gnu.org/software/cobol/cobolforgcc.html.

Other open-source and commercially available COBOL compilers support Linux. One open-source COBOL compiler is called TinyCOBOL.[10] For commer-

---

8 http://gcc.gnu.org/java/

9 The latest version as of this writing is version 6.3.

10 http://tiny-cobol.sourceforge.net/index.php

cially available COBOL compilers, there are Acucobol-GT from Acucorp (www.acucorp.com) and Micro Focus Object Cobol Developer Suite from Micro Focus (www.microfocus.com).

2.1.6 Compilers from Other Sources

Several other compilers for Linux are available from different vendors for C++, FORTRAN, COBOL, and Java. Intel offers compilers for C++ and FORTRAN.[11] IBM offers the XL C/C++ compilers for Linux running on POWER.[12] Micro Focus offers a COBOL compiler for Linux.[13]

The porting chapters for Solaris, AIX, and HP-UX cover more of the differences between the respective native platform compilers and the GNU C and C++ compilers.

2.2 Java Environment

More and more applications today are being developed using the Java programming language. One can assume that porting a Java application is relatively easier than porting applications that were developed in other programming languages such as C or C++. However, our experience shows that not all Java Development Kits (JDKs) are created equally, which can make porting Java applications not as easy as first assumed.

All JDKs are expected to follow the Java specifications[14] set forth by Sun. However, implementation specifics are left to the vendor. Most vendors include *helper* classes that provide functionalities to implement specific Java application programming interfaces (APIs). These helper classes are not hidden from the Java developer and hence can be used as if they are part of the JDK specification. This is okay as long as the JDK includes this helper class. When the application is run

---

11 www.intel.com/cd/software/products/asmo-na/eng/compilers/219760.htm

12 www-306.ibm.com/software/awdtools/xlcpp/features/linux/xlcpp-linux.html

13 www.microfocus.com/products/finder/targenvunix.asp

14 http://java.sun.com/reference/api/index.html

on a Java Runtime Environment (JRE) from a different vendor that uses different helper classes, however, the application will fail to find that specific class. This problem can easily escalate to a suspicion of a bug with the Java implementation that does not have the same helper class as the original JDK. The solution here is to not use helper classes included in the JDK that are not part of the Java API specification. Expect this and other similar problems to crop up from time to time when doing a port of a Java application.

Several JVM distributions for Linux can be downloaded from different Web sites:

- JDK from Blackdown (www.blackdown.org/)
- JDK from IBM (www.ibm.com/developerworks/java/jdk/linux/download.html)
- JDK from Sun (www.java.com/en/download/manual.jsp)

When porting Java applications from other platforms to Linux, be aware that some JVM switches used to start the JVM on other platforms may not exist on the JVM available for Linux. These switches are used on the specific platform to make the JVM and the Java application run as optimally as possible on that platform. Use of these specific switches depends on their availability from the JVM distributions just mentioned.

2.3 Build Environment

The assessment of the application continues by examining its build environment. When porting applications, it is important to see what tools are used to build the application. In most circumstances, you will find that the build tools used on other UNIX platforms will have similar counterparts on Linux. When examining the build environment, it is also necessary to take note of the build process. Some build processes are straightforward, and others are complex. Complex build processes add to porting difficulty and should be factored in when creating the schedules for the project.

2.3.1 gmake

The `make` development tool in Linux is the GNU `make` or `gmake`. As of this writing, the latest version of `gmake` is version 3.8, which this section is based on. The `gmake` home page is located at www.gnu.org/software/make/. Note that `gmake` 3.8

is also available on Solaris, AIX, and HP-UX. Porting the build environment from other UNIX platforms to Linux means using `gmake` and making sure the makefiles to build the application are correctly ported to build all necessary application modules.

Because `gmake` conforms to the POSIX standard similarities between other UNIX operating platforms, makefiles and GNU makefiles abound. However, there are still some differences, which are covered in more detail in Chapters 4 through 6.

2.3.2 GNU Binutils

The development tool chain for Linux is made up of other GNU tools known as the GNU binutils. The most commonly used tool in the GNU binutils is the GNU linker, `ld`, and the GNU assembler, `as`.

2.3.2.1 The GNU ld

Running `ld` is usually the last step when compiling source code to produce a program executable. The `ld` command is responsible for combining object and archive files as well as for reconciling symbol references within the program executable. The GNU linker provides more diagnostic information than other linkers. Although other linkers simply abandon execution when an error is encountered, the GNU `ld` tries to continue execution whenever possible to further identify the cause of the error.

Although GNU `ld` has a lot of features to offer, including the use of *linker scripts,* most of the discussion around GNU `ld` focuses on the linker command-line options. A simple command-line option that shows how `ld` links an object file follows:

```
$ ld -o output /lib/crt0.o foo.o -lc
```

This tells `ld` to produce a file called output as the result of linking the file /lib/crt0.o with foo.o and the library `libc.a`, which will come from the standard search directories.

GNU `ld` can also be invoked indirectly through a GNU compiler, such as `gcc`. When invoking indirectly, all command-line options to the linker must be prefixed by the `-Wl` option, as in the following example:

```
$ gcc -Wl,--startgroup foo.o bar.o -Wl,--endgroup
```

GNU `ld` supports many options that are compatible with linker options from other operating systems such as Solaris, AIX, and HP-UX. In each of the main porting chapters for the different operating systems (Chapters 4 through 6), GNU `ld` options are compared side by side so that the porting engineer has a reference of what linker flags to use when porting from other platforms.

For more information about the `ld` options, consult the latest GNU `ld` manual, available from www.gnu.org/software/binutils/manual/ld-2.9.1/ld.html.

2.3.3 The GNU as

GNU `as` is a family of assemblers. If you use (or have used) the GNU assembler on one architecture, you should find a fairly similar environment when you use it on another architecture. Each version has much in common with the others, including object file formats, most assembler directives (often called pseudo-ops), and assembler syntax.

`as` is primarily intended to assemble the output of the GNU C compiler `gcc` for use by the linker `ld`. Nevertheless, GNU has tried to make `as` assemble correctly everything that other assemblers for the same machine would assemble. Any exceptions are documented explicitly in the Machine Dependent Features of the GNU `as` manual.[15] This does not mean that `as` always uses the same syntax as another assembler for the same architecture; for example, GNU is aware of several incompatible versions of the 680x0 assembly language syntax.

Unlike older assemblers, `as` is designed to assemble a source program in one pass of the source file. This has a subtle impact on the `.org` directive.

The GNU assembler can be configured to produce several alternative object file formats. For the most part, this does not affect how you write assembly language programs, but directives for debugging symbols are typically different in different file formats. For instance, on some Intel machines (80960, for example), `as` can be configured to produce either a COFF or an a.out format. On other machines, `as` can be configured to produce either a COFF or a b.out format. On HPPA systems, `as` can be configured to produce either SOM or ELF. The default format on Linux systems is ELF.

---

15 www.gnu.org/software/binutils/manual/gas-2.9.1/html_mono/as.html

After the assembler invocation `as`, the command line may contain options and filenames. Options may appear in any order, and may be before, after, or between filenames. The order of filenames is significant.

A command-line argument that begins with a hyphen (-) is an option. Each option changes the behavior of `as`. No option changes the way another option works. An option is a - followed by one or more letters; the case of the letter is important. The following shows the syntax used by `as`:

```
as -f -o foo.o foo.s
as --help
```

The command-line argument of `--` (two hyphens) by itself names the standard input file explicitly as one of the files for `as` to assemble. The following example shows the syntax for `--`:

```
as -- [files]
```

Some options expect exactly one filename to follow them. The filename may either immediately follow the option's letter (compatible with older assemblers) or it may be the next command argument (GNU standard). These two command lines are equivalent:

```
as -o my-object-file.o mumble.s
as -omy-object-file.o mumble.s
```

For more details on each command-line option, refer to the GNU `as` documentation available from www.gnu.org/software/binutils/manual/gas-2.9.1/as.html.

Another useful feature of GCC is to invoke the GNU assembler from the `gcc` compiler. To do this, you use the following command:

```
gcc -c -g -O -Wa,-alh,-L file.c
```

The assembler arguments must be separated from each other (and the `-Wa`) by commas. The preceding command causes a listing to be emitted to standard output with high-level messaging on an assembly source. Notice that two options (`-alh` and `-L`) are passed on to `as` with one invocation of `-Wa`. Also, the `-c` option is needed so that the file is compiled without linking.

Other tools included in the binutils package are as follows:

- **`addr2line`.** Translates program addresses into filenames and line numbers. Given an address and an executable, it uses the debugging information in the executable to figure out which filename and line number are associated with a given address.

- **ar.** A utility program that creates, modifies, and extracts from archives. An archive is a single file holding a collection of other files in a structure that makes it possible to retrieve the original individual files (called members of the archive). An archive holds libraries of relocatable object files.
- **c++filt.** A program that decodes or demangles low-level names into user-level names so that the linker can keep overloaded functions from clashing. Software developers use `c++filt` to demangle function names when debugging C++ applications.
- **nlmconv.** Converts object code into an NLM (Netware Loadable Module). Not used in Linux.
- **nm.** Lists the symbols from object files.
- **objcopy.** A utility that copies the contents of an object file to another. It can write the destination object file in a format different from that of the source object file.
- **objdump.** A utility that displays information about one or more object files. Information displayed by `objdump` is mostly useful to programmers who are working on the compilation tools, as opposed to programmers who just want their program to compile and work.
- **ranlib.** Generates an index to the contents of an archive and stores it in the archive. The index lists each symbol defined by each member of an archive that is a relocatable object file.
- **readelf.** Displays information from any ELF format object file. This program performs a similar function to `objdump`, but it can display more details.
- **size.** A utility that lists the section[16] sizes—and the total size—for each of the object files' or archive files' `objfile` in its argument list. One line of output is generated for each object file or each module in an archive.

16 A section is a range of addresses within an object file that may contain data that is treated the same for some particular purpose. An object file written by `as` has at least three sections—namely, text, data, and bss.

- **strings.** Prints the printable character sequences that are at least four characters long (or the number given with the options) and are followed by an unprintable character.
- **strip.** Discards symbols from object files. Object files may include archives.
- **windres.** A compiler for Windows resource files (not used in Linux).

For more detailed information about the GNU binutils, refer to www.gnu.org/software/binutils/.

2.3.4 Integrated Development Environment

In some instances, some applications are built using integrated development environments (IDEs). For those who need to use an IDE for C, C++, or Java, an open-source IDE called Eclipse[17] is available. Eclipse is an open-extensible IDE that works well when developing applications. You can download it from www.eclipse.org/. Another open-source IDE for Java that works on Linux is NetBeans. You can download it from www.netbeans.org.

2.4 Linux Shells

Build environments may also use shell scripts to kick off tasks and procedures when building the application. Linux provides support for the most commonly used shells from other UNIX platforms. Depending on the Linux installation, several shells developed for Linux are installed by default. The more popular shells developed for Linux are as follows:

- **bash.** A shell or command language interpreter that is an `sh`-compatible shell incorporating features from the Korn shell (`ksh`) and C shell (`csh`). It is intended to conform to the IEEE POSIX P1003.2/ISO 9945.2 Shell and Tools standard. Most `sh` scripts can be run with `bash` without modification. Refer to www.gnu.org/software/bash/bash.html for more information. `bash` is the default shell on almost all Linux distributions.
- **tcsh.** A shell or command language interpreter that is a completely compatible version of the Berkeley UNIX C shell (`csh`). It can be used as an interac-

17 Eclipse plug-ins for C/C++ are also available.

tive login shell and a shell script command processor. For more detailed information about `csh`, refer to www.tcsh.org.

- **`zsh`.** A shell or command language interpreter that incorporates many of the useful features of `bash`, `ksh`, and `tcsh` as well as its own original features. To get more information about `zsh`, refer to http://zsh.sourceforge.net/.
- **`pdksh`.** A shell or command language interpreter that is a clone of the AT&T Korn shell. It has most of the `ksh88` features as well as some `ksh93` features. For more information about `pdksh`, refer to http://web.cs.mun.ca/~michael/pdksh/.

An excellent reference book about UNIX and Linux shells that can be helpful during the porting process is *UNIX Shells by Example,* 4th Edition, by E. Quigley (Prentice Hall, 2005).

2.5 Packaging

For some applications, you might need to use a package manager to uniformly distribute and install the application on any Linux platform. As an alternative to distributing the application on a tarball image, using a package manager to distribute and install the application on Linux has its advantages. One advantage to using a packaging manager is it allows versions of the application to be managed properly.

The Red Hat Package Manager (RPM) is the most popular package manager available in Linux. It is a command-line utility used to install, uninstall, verify, query, and update software packages in Linux. Before RPM became available, there was no easy and elegant way to manage software application installations on a Linux server. Installation was done through compressed and tar'ed files, and the only way to find out whether an application was dependent on another package was by reading the documentation that came with it or by running the application and hoping it produced a message describing the missing component. The availability of RPM changed all this!

Applications packaged in RPM format made maintaining and managing software applications on a Linux machine easier. Red Hat, the originator of RPM, also became the most popular Linux distribution as a result of the release of RPM. Today, most if not all Linux distributions support RPM as the de facto package manager. It is for this reason that we recommend applications ported to Linux be packaged in an RPM format. More detailed documentations for RPM can be found at www.rpm.org/.

2.5.1 Packaging the Application with RPM

At the heart of RPM is the RPM engine. The engine requires several files as input and builds the packaged application as the output. One of the input files that RPM requires is the spec file. The spec file contains informational and instructional verbiage that will be displayed or acted on by RPM, respectively, during the package build or user installation. The spec file has the following sections:

- **Preamble.** Contains information that displays when information about the package is requested
- **Prep.** Contains a script used by RPM to prepare for the actual build of the package
- **Build.** Contains scripts to actually build the package from source files
- **Install.** Contains commands to install the software application when the build step completes
- **Install and uninstall.** Contains the install and uninstall scripts that are run on the user's system when he or she installs the software application through the RPM command utility
- **Verify.** Contains a script to verify the installation of a package in the user system
- **Clean.** Contains a script to clean up after a package build
- **File list.** Contains the list of files to be packaged, file permissions when files are installed on the user system, documentation, and configuration information

The sections of the spec file used during the build of the package are the prep, build, install, clean, and file list sections. The sections used by RPM when installing the package on the user system are the install and uninstall, verify, and file list sections.

When building a package, a package with RPM follows these steps:

1. Create a build environment that includes the source. This is the environment where the sources will be patched if patches are available and compiled to create the binary distribution.
2. Run the installation script in the install section after the build is complete to install the binaries into the correct directory locations.

3. After the binaries have been installed, create the package using the file list section. Note that RPM does not create the file list automatically. This list needs to be created manually.
4. The final output of the build is the RPM distribution package.

For a complete reference on how to build an RPM package, refer to the Maximum RPM documentation available at www.rpm.org/max-rpm-snapshot/.

2.5.2 Basic RPM Usage

After the software application has been packaged as an RPM file, it can be tested with the command syntax described in the following sections.

2.5.2.1 rpm -i

The command `rpm -i` tells RPM to install a software package. This command also performs dependency checks and pre-installation tasks, unpacks installation files from the package and places them in the proper directories, performs post-installation tasks, and creates a log of what was done.

2.5.2.2 rpm -e

The command `rpm -e` removes or erases one or more packages from the system. This command checks the RPM database for package dependencies, performs pre-uninstall tasks, saves modified configuration files, removes files belonging to this package, and executes post-uninstall tasks.

2.5.2.3 rpm -U

The command `rpm -U` upgrades an old version of the application software. This command removes the previous version of the software and installs a new version. It is basically a combination of the `rpm -i` and `rpm -e` command.

2.5.2.4 rpm -q

The command `rpm -q` provides information about a specific software application. The information may include but is not limited to the version of a package, identifying what file belongs to what package and version of the installed package.

2.5.2.5 rpm -V

The command `rpm -V` verifies an installed package. This command can verify the file attributes of files included in a package. This can give a sense of what may have changed for a particular software installation. Information verified by the `rpm -V` command includes but is not limited to the owner, group, MD5 checksum, and size of the file. These attributes are compared to the RPM database to make sure that they match the original installation results.

2.5.3 Baseline Packaging Format as Recommended by the LSB

The Linux Standard Base 1.2 specification offers a baseline RPM recommendation for Linux packages so that these packages can be installed and used in all Linux distributions. It recommends that applications packaged in the RPM format follow the specifications in the appendix section of the 1997 edition of Maximum RPM (www.rpm.org/max-rpm/) with some restrictions. You can find these restrictions on the LSB website (www.linuxbase.org/spec/refspecs/LSB_1.2.0/gLSB/swinstall.html#FTN.PKG-1).

As a side note, another package manager available for Linux is called DEB.[18,19] DEB is similar to RPM in almost all respects when it comes to packaging features. The main difference between DEB and RPM is the package format. Although RPM packages are most commonly used to package Linux applications for installation on almost all Linux platforms, DEB packages are used to package products for installation on the Debian distribution of Linux.[20] RPM packages can still be installed on Debian Linux, but only after they are converted from an RPM format to a DEB format. A tool that can convert RPM packages to DEB packages and vice versa is `alien`.[21]

---

18 "How to make Debian packages": http://linuxdevices.com/articles/AT8047723203.html

19 "Debian packages": www.tldp.org/HOWTO/Debian-Binary-Package-Building-HOWTO/

20 And other Debian variants, such as Lindows

21 See Linux man pages alien(1).

2.6 Project Management Tasks

After the compiler, build tools, and third-party products used by the application are ascertained to exist or have similar equivalents in Linux, the next step is to scope and identify deliverables and tasks of the project. As the application architecture is examined more closely in terms of lines of code, number of modules, third-party software, testing methodology, packaging, and others, the work required to port the application begins to emerge. The project manager identifies what is in and out of scope for the project at hand. Refer to Chapter 1 to learn why it is important to identify not only what is in scope but also what is out of scope. After the scope has been identified, deliverables, tasks, preliminary schedules, and other factors that are all part of overall project plan are filled in. Each one is briefly discussed in the following list:

- **Deliverables**

  Each porting project has deliverables, and each deliverable has tasks associated with it. Use a form similar to Table 2-2 that associates tasks with each project deliverable. The table clearly states the task's start and due dates as well as its owner.

TABLE 2-2
How to Associate Tasks to Each Identified Deliverable

Activities/ Tasks	Start Date	Due Date	Owner	Status	Comments*
Deliverable 1					
Task 1					
Task 2					
Deliverable 2					
Task 1					
Task 2					

*The Comments column can contain descriptions of issues and dependencies for each deliverable or task.

- **Success criteria**

  The success criteria for each deliverable can be as simple as passing a unit test. Put in place success criteria for each deliverable that will be used to signal the completion of the tasks.

- **Project start and end dates**

  Identify the project start and end dates based on the tasks associated with the deliverables. These start and end dates give the project stakeholders a sense of how long the project will take. Sometimes there may be hard requirements to start or end the project within a certain time frame. In this case, deliverables and tasks need to be revisited to see whether they need to be adjusted to fit the schedule.

- **Required resources**

  After the tasks for each deliverable are identified, the specific skills needed to do these tasks become known. Identify skilled and experienced personnel as well as hardware requirements. In addition to identifying these resources, ascertain when and how long these resources are required.

- **Critical dependencies**

  Identify critical dependencies, including when they are needed and from whom they are coming.

- **Risks**

  Identify the risk factors that can affect the project schedule, cost, or scope. An example of a risk that may affect the schedule can come from a critical dependency where delivery of this dependency may be delayed because of certain unforeseen events. This delayed delivery can then in turn affect the overall schedule.

- **Status communication**

  Last but not least, create a communication process that addresses who, when, and how frequently communication of project status needs to happen.

The collaboration between porting personnel who scope the application and the project manager is crucial. Information gathered from scoping the application affects the project's scope and sometimes even its viability. Identifying key elements such as compilers, build environment, and third-party product dependencies helps fill in the necessary elements that make up the porting project.

2.7 Summary

Using the assessment questionnaire presented in Chapter 1, you should now have a better understanding of the tasks ahead. You may have also noticed that the development environment on Linux is similar to development environments on UNIX platforms. This makes developing or porting applications to Linux a familiar experience to any software developer or porting engineer. Linux comes with a full set of development tools that makes the development and porting experience straightforward:

- Compilers available today in Linux adhere to the same set of standards that compilers from UNIX platforms adhere to. Although not all applications to be ported are expected to be 100 percent portable, many parts of the application that adhere to standards can be easily ported using compilers available on Linux.
- The GNU binutils distribution provides porting engineers with all the utilities needed when porting applications to Linux. These tools are standard in all Linux distributions and are compatible with tools from other platforms. This is especially true of tools such as `size`, `nm`, `ranlib`, and `ar`.
- Ever since the first version of the Java Development Kit was released, Linux developers have kept pace with the Java community to make available a version of Java for Linux. Today, different JDKs that work on Linux are available from different UNIX vendors.
- The packaging environment available in Linux provides application developers and porting engineers an easy environment to package their applications with. It is well documented and supported by the open-source community.
- Creating an overall project plan is also part of the scoping step. Feed information back to the project manager so that tasks, deliverables, success criteria, schedules, resources and dependencies can be discussed and communicated to all members of the porting project.

In the next chapter, we discuss the analysis step of the porting process from the porting personnel point of view. We begin to analyze the application deeper and start to figure out the level of work that needs to be done to port the application. In so doing, the tasks associated with each deliverable are refined and adjusted as necessary.

Chapter 3

Analysis

In this chapter

After the initial scoping work is done, we need to perform a more detailed analysis of the application. The analysis includes but is not limited to examining the application in terms of use of application programming interfaces (APIs), dynamic library loading interfaces, threads, networking interfaces, and other functionalities that the operating system may provide. This chapter assumes that the porting engineer is knowledgeable about the application to be ported or has access to someone who knows the application design.

Each section in this chapter has two purposes. The first one is to help educate the porting personnel as to the standards and features supported in the Linux environment. And the second is to invite the porting engineer to analyze the application to be ported in terms of the topics discussed. For example, take a look at Section 3.5 on library versioning. The porting engineer is expected to know whether the application uses library versioning. If the application uses library versioning, he can then learn how library versioning is implemented on Linux. This knowledge will give him some sense about how much effort it will take to implement library versioning for the application.

Here are the suggested steps to help the porting personnel through this chapter:

1. Read through each section.
2. Ask questions about the application pertaining to the topic discussed in the section. Ask specific questions, such as these: Does the application use these standards? Does the application use this feature? If yes, are there differences in the way Linux implements this standard or feature? If so, based on the information given in this section, what effort will be involved to implement this feature in the application?
3. Note things that come up, such as dependencies, level of difficulty, and risks, that can affect the project schedule. Feed this information back to the project manager.

Remember, analysis from a porting perspective is the step during which we examine the application in more detail. We need to know what the application needs and whether these needs are available on Linux. Let's begin.

3.1 Linux Standards

Almost all Linux distributors acknowledge the values that standardization and portability provide and work with the various Linux implementers/maintainers to meet those standards. The primary Linux industry standard is the Linux Standard Base (LSB), which is a project overseen by the Free Standards Group (FSG). The LSB is based heavily on the IEEE POSIX and Open Group Single UNIX Specification standards, but it also documents places where Linux is not UNIX- or POSIX-compatible. Almost all the major Linux distributors have certified to the LSB.

The LSB, in addition to providing a source code API specification, also provides a binary interface (ABI) specification for each of several common Linux hardware platforms. The goal of the ABI is to ensure binary portability, for LSB-portable applications, between Linux distributions on that hardware platform. Distributors must certify to the ABI as well as the API. Independent software vendors (ISVs) can also certify their applications as "LSB portable" using tools provided by the FSG.

Table 3-1 shows the Linux supported standards based on the LSB specification version 2.0.1.

TABLE 3-1
Supported Standards on Linux

Standard	Linux
IEEE POSIX 1003.1-2001 Base Function	Supported as described in the LSB
IEEE POSIX 1003.1 Threads (Pthreads)	Supported
Single UNIX Specification Base Function (sometimes known as XPG5 or XPG6)	Supported as described in the LSB
IEEE POSIX 1003.1—2001 Real-time scheduler, clocks and timers, asynchronous I/O, semaphores, memory locking, message queues, real-time signals, shared memory	Asynchronous I/O, real-time signals, shared memory, semaphores
IEEE POSIX 1003.1-2001 (commands and utilities)	Supported
System V Interface Definition (SVID3)	Referenced[1]

1 A referenced standard means that not all interfaces within the standard are supported.

Standard	Linux
File System Directory Layout	Filesystem Hierarchy Standard, www.pathname.com/fhs/
X11 Window System, Font Server, and Clients	X11R6.4
OSF/Motif	Supported through third-party libraries (see LessTif, www.lesstif.org)[2]
RPC function interfaces	Supported
NFS+ Diskless and ONC+, NFS+, version 4.2	Referenced standards: SVID Issue 4, SVID Issue 3
OSF/Motif Application Environment Specification (AES)	Supported through third-party products[3]
LP64, 64-bit data model	Supported

Although there is standardization within Linux, Linux itself is not totally compliant to either the IEEE POSIX or Open Group SUS specifications.[4] This means that applications that may be totally portable under these common commercial UNIX standards may still need some work to move successfully to Linux. However, this work will be much less than for an application that meets no standards at all, or one that uses operating system–specific extensions.

3.2 GNU libc

Except for `libc` and `libm`, there are no other standard naming conventions for UNIX system libraries. Some of the system libraries that exist on Linux might not match the names of libraries used on different UNIX platforms. It is important to

2 Not included within the LSB specification

3 See Open Motif, www.opengroup.org/openmotif/faq.html

4 Conflicts between ISO/IEC 9945 (POSIX) and the Linux Standard Base (www.opengroup.org/personal/ajosey/tr01-04-2005.txt)

know which libraries in Linux include and support which functionalities. Table 3-2 shows the Linux system libraries in terms of their functionalities.

TABLE 3-2
Linux System Library Table

Description	Linux
Curses	`libncurses, libform, libmenu, libpanel, libplot`
Database APIs	`libdb*`
Security APIs	`libc(shadow.h)`
Socket APIs	`libc(BSD4.3)`
RPC APIs	`libc`
Math	`libm`
XDR APIs	`libc`
Real-time priority	`libc`

The following lists installed libraries from the GNU `libc` distribution and their respective descriptions:[5]

ld.so is the helper program for shared library executables.

libBrokenLocale.[a,so] is used by programs, such as Mozilla, to solve broken locales.

libSegFault.so is a segmentation fault signal handler. It tries to catch segfaults.

libanl.[a,so] is an asynchronous name lookup library.

libbsd-compat.a provides the portability needed to run certain BSD programs under Linux.

libc.[a,so] is the main C library—a collection of commonly used functions.

libcrypt.[a,so] is the cryptography library.

libdl.[a,so] is the dynamic linking interface library.

libg.a is a runtime library for `g++`.

---

5 Referenced from "Bleeding Edge Linux From Scratch" version CVS 2004-04-06

libieee.a is the IEEE floating-point library.

libm.[a,so] is the mathematical library.

libmcheck.a contains code run at boot.

libmemusage.so is used by memusage to help collect information about the memory usage of a program.

libnsl.a is the network services library.

libnss_compat.so, libnss_dns.so, libnss_files.so, libnss_hesiod.so, libnss_nis.so, libnss_nisplus.so are the Name Service Switch libraries, containing functions for resolving host names, usernames, group names, aliases, services, protocols, and the like.

libpcprofile.so contains profiling functions used to track how much CPU time is spent in which source code lines.

libpthread.[a,so] is the POSIX threads library.

libresolv.[a,so] contains functions for creating, sending, and interpreting packets to the Internet domain name servers.

librpcsvc.a contains functions providing miscellaneous RPC services.

librt.[a,so] contains functions providing most of the interfaces specified by the POSIX.1b real-time extension.

libthread_db.so contains functions useful for building debuggers for multithreaded programs.

libutil.[a,so] contains code for "standard" functions used in many different UNIX utilities.

Most of these libraries are located in the /usr/lib directory; some, such as libSegFault.so, are in the /lib directory.

3.2.1 glibc Conformance

GNU `glibc` distributes a conformance[6] report detailing adherence to various standards. This list also shows where GNU `libc` needs to be improved. As of this writing, the conformance report shows that GNU `libc` passes conformance header checks to FIPS POSIX90, POSIX96, UNIX98, ANSI, C89/99, and ISO9899 standards. All major Linux distributions' `glibc` implementations also support the LSB.

---

6 Available at http://sources.redhat.com/cgi-bin/cvsweb.cgi/libc/CONFORMANCE?cvsroot=glibc

3.3 GNU Scientific Library

High-performance computing applications that need to be ported to Linux require a support library that closely matches scientific libraries from UNIX operating platforms. The equivalent library available on Linux is the GNU Scientific Library (GSL). The GSL is a collection of routines for numeric computing. The routines have been written from scratch in C, and present a modern API for C programmers, allowing wrappers to be written for very high-level languages. The source code is distributed under the GNU General Public License.

The library covers a wide range of topics in numeric computing. Table 3-3 shows the available routines from GNU GSL.

TABLE 3-3
GNU Scientific Library Routines

Complex Numbers	Roots of Polynomials	Quasi-Random Sequences
Special Functions	Vectors and Matrices	Statistics
Permutations	Combinations	N-Tuples
Sorting	BLAS Support	Simulated Annealing
Linear Algebra	CBLAS Library	Interpolation
Fast Fourier Transforms	Eigensystems	Chebyshev Approximations
Random Numbers	Quadrature	Discrete Hankel Transforms
Random Distributions	Differential Equations	Minimization
Histograms	Numerical Differentiation	Physical Constants
Monte Carlo Integration	Series Acceleration	Root-Finding
Least-Squares Fitting	IEEE Floating-Point	

The use of these routines is described in the GSL manual.[7] Each chapter provides detailed definitions of the functions, followed by example programs and references to the articles on which the algorithms are based.

7 swww.gnu.org/software/gss/manual/

3.4 Shared Libraries

Most if not all the applications we have ported use shared libraries. However, different operating systems have differences in creating and naming these shared libraries. In Linux, shared libraries may end with different file extensions. Shared libraries may end with .so or so.1.0 extensions. Shared libraries that end in .so with the extra dot followed by a number and a dot and another number are versioned libraries. The first number stands for the major number; the second number represents the minor number. Sometimes the extension comes with another dot and a number called the release number. The last dot and the release number are optional. Here is the format of the library filename:

```
lib<name>.so.<major>.<minor>.<release>
```

The major, minor, and release numbers signify different changes that are made to the library. Here are some guidelines for incrementing the major, minor, and release numbers:

- The major number is incremented when there is an incompatible change to the interface of the shared library. This major change implies that applications depending on the earlier major version of the library need to be changed to work with the new major version.
- The minor number is incremented when a shared library preserves interfaces but adds new ones.
- The release number is incremented when there is a compatible change that does not involve adding any new interfaces. This usually means that a change is made to the implementation to improve performance or scalability.

To create shared libraries in Linux, use the `-shared` option in the compile arguments; this tells GNU `ld` to create a shared library rather than an application. Here is an example:

```
$ gcc -o libfoo.so -shared -fpic foo.c
```

3.5 Library Versioning[8,9]

Maintaining binary-level compatibility or an ABI between shared libraries and applications using them is an important requirement. An ABI of a shared library is a set of runtime interfaces that an application may depend on; if the ABI evolves in an upward-compatible way from one release to the next, existing applications compiled on a given release will run on all subsequent releases without change. Library versioning is what Linux and other contemporary systems use to achieve binary compatibility.

Some of the applications we have ported in the past required library versioning support. Other UNIX platforms also implement library versioning, and each may be different in its own way. Linux provides two different techniques to use for library versioning: external and symbol versioning.

3.5.1 External Library Versioning

During link time, the linker (`ld`) looks for shared library files that end with .so. Files that end with .so are called linker names because of the way they are used in Linux. When an application that depends on a shared library is built, it is the shared library's *soname* (not the shared library's filename) that is recorded in the application binary as a dependency. It is the library's soname that is used by the runtime linker to locate and load the library depended on by the application. The soname contains only the major number (for example, libfoo.so.1).

When a shared library is updated in such a way that it is not compatible with the older one, the new shared library must have a new external versioned name. In other words, the library's soname needs to be changed. Examples of incompatible updates include the removal of a symbol, the removal of an argument from a function, and the update to the function such that the semantic property no longer matches its original specification and the new version is not binary-compatible with the older one. Consider the following example.

---

8 Refer to the paper "Library Interface Versioning in Solaris and Linux," published in the *Proceedings of the 4th Annual Linux Showcase and Conference*, Atlanta, Oct 10–14, 2000.

9 Refer to the paper "How to Write Shared Libraries" by Ulrich Drepper, located at http://people.redhat.com/~drepper.

foo.c and message.c are files used to create the shared library libfoo.so.1.1 with a soname of libfoo.so.1:

```
/* foo.c v1.1 */
extern const char *_message1;
extern const char *_message2;

void foo1()
{
      (void) printf(_message1);
}

void foo2()
{
      (void) printf(_message2);
}
```

```
/* message.c v1.1 */
const char *_message1 = "this is string message 1\n";
const char *_message2 = "this is string message 2\n";
```

Generate the shared library with a soname of libfoo.so.1:

```
$ gcc -fPIC -c foo.c message.c
$ gcc -shared -Wl,-soname,libfoo.so.1 -o libfoo.so.1.1 foo.o message.o
```

The `-Wl` flag is used to pass the arguments `-soname=libfoo.so.1` to the linker (`ld`), which gives the library a soname of libfoo.so.1.[10] The file libfoo.so.1.1 is generated, and then `ldconfig` is run, specifying the library name:

```
$ /sbin/ldconfig -l libfoo.so.1.1
$ ls
lrwxrwxrwx 1 x users 13 2004-12-24 15:16 libfoo.so.1 -> libfoo.so.1.1
-rwxr-xr-x 1 x users 6539 2004-12-24 15:15 libfoo.so.1.1
```

After running `ldconfig`, a file with the same name as the soname is generated—libfoo.so.1. For applications to be able to use and link to the newly created library, a link to the proper linker name libfoo.so needs to be created:

```
$ ln -s libfoo.so.1 libfoo.so
```

The shared library is now ready for use. The following file, main1.c, is used to link with the shared library:

---

10 In Linux, use the command `objdump -x libfoo.so | grep SONAME` to display the soname.

```
/* main.c */
main()
{
      foo1();
      foo2();
}

$ gcc -L. -lfoo main1.c -o main1
$ ./main
this is string message 1
this is string message 2
```

Using `ldd` to examine the shared library dependencies of main1 shows the following:

```
$ ldd ./main1
    libfoo.so.1 => ./libfoo.so.1 (0xb7ffe000)
    libc.so.6 => /lib/tls/i586/libc.so.6 (0x00b9c000)
    /lib/ld-linux.so.2 (0x00b85000)
```

As you can see from the output, the `ldd` command confirms that the soname libfoo.so.1 is recorded as a dependency of the executable main1.

Let's now assume for a moment that we need to change the internal and interface specifications of one of our library functions, `foo2()`. In this case, we need to create a version 2 of the libfoo.so shared library.

In this example, we change `foo2` to print _message3 and take an argument. This represents an internal change to our specification and interface that alters the behavior of the library in a major way.

foo.c now looks like the following:

```
extern const char * _message1;
extern const char * _message2;
extern const char * _message3;

void foo1()
{
    (void) printf(_message1);
}

void foo2(int x)
{
     int y;

    (void) printf(_message3);     /* change to specification */
        y = x;
}
```

message.c is updated to look like this:

```
const char *_message1 = "this is string message 1\n";
const char *_message2 = "this is string message 2\n";
const char *_message3 = "this is string message 3\n";
```

After making changes to the message.c and foo.c files, recompile and then create the shared library with a different soname, as follows:

```
$ gcc -fPIC -c foo.c message.c
$ gcc -shared -Wl,-soname,libfoo.so.2 -o libfoo.so.2.1 foo.o message.o
```

Notice that we incremented the major number of the soname and the resulting library filename. After creating the shared library with the soname of libfoo.so.2, run `ldconfig`, which creates the link to libfoo.so.2. Link libfoo.so.2 to libfoo.so, and it is ready to use:

```
$ /sbin/ldconfig -l libfoo.so.2.1
$ ln -s libfoo.so.2 libfoo.so
```

Compile a program that uses the new libfoo.so, as in the following example:

```
/* main.c */
main()
{
    foo1();
    foo2(4);
}
```

After compiling a program linked with the new libfoo.so, examine the shared library dependencies and notice the dependency on libfoo.so.2:

```
$ gcc -L. -lfoo main.c -o main2
$ ldd main2
    linux-gate.so.1 => (0xffffe000)
    libfoo.so.2 => ./libfoo.so.2 (0x40018000)
    libc.so.6 => /lib/tls/libc.so.6 (0x4002a000)
    /lib/ld-linux.so.2 => /lib/ld-linux.so.2 (0x40000000)
```

Run the new executable to determine whether it uses the right library:

```
$ ./main2
this is string message 1
this is string message 3
```

Test the original executable to determine whether it still successfully locates the original versioned library:

```
$ ./main1
this is string message 1
this is string message 2
```

Notice that the executable main1 from the previous example still runs even though the link to libfoo.so now points to libfoo.so.2. If main1 is executed in an environment in which there is no libfoo.so.1, you get this error:

```
./main: error while loading shared libraries: libfoo.so.1: cannot open shared
object file: No such file or directory
```

3.5.2 Symbol Versioning

As mentioned earlier, we increment the minor number of a shared library when we make changes to the library that are upward-compatible. This change involves adding some new interfaces while maintaining existing interfaces. However, there is an important issue associated with minor revision change. An application built with a given minor version of a shared library cannot be certain whether it can run with an earlier minor version of the library. This is because the application may have used one or more of the interfaces added to the library at a later minor version, and not present in the earlier one. Symbol versioning is introduced to solve this problem by allowing the shared library to record the information about what has been added in each minor revision.

In Linux, the GNU `ld` permits creation of shared libraries with symbol versioning through the linker switch `-version-script` option. This compiler option `-Wl,--version-script=mapfile` instructs the linker which symbols to export from the generated shared library. Each symbol can belong to one of these two classes: global (exported) or local (not exported). Take, for example, the following program, foo.c. It has one function, `foo1`. This file will be used to create version 1.1 of the shared library.

Example:

```
$cat foo.c
/* foo.c v1.1 */
extern const char *_message1;

void foo1()
{
      (void) printf(_message1);
}

$cat message.c
/* message.c v1.1 */
const char *_message1 = "this is string message 1\n";
```

A script file named scriptfile[11] is created, as shown here:

```
$cat scriptfile
LX_1.1 {
            global:
            foo1;
            local:
                  *;
};
```

In the scriptfile example, symbol foo1 is public and is exported as it is under the global stanza. And all other symbols (matched by the *) within version 1.1 of the library will not be exported.[12]

Build the library:

```
$gcc -o libfoo.so.1 -shared -Wl,--version-script=scriptfile foo.o message.o
```

Run objdump to examine the library:

```
$objdump -x libfoo.so.1 | egrep "foo1|message1"
00001640 l    O .data 00000004        _message1
0000049c g    F .text 0000002b        foo1
```

Notice that the symbol foo1 is the only global symbol (the symbol _message1 is listed as local). `readelf -V` displays the contents of the version sections in the object file:

```
$ readelf -V libfoo.so.1

Version symbols section '.gnu.version' contains 17 entries:
 Addr: 00000000000002c6 Offset: 0x0002c6 Link: 2 (.dynsym)
 000:  0 (*local*)     0 (*local*)     0 (*local*)     0 (*local*)
 004:  0 (*local*)     0 (*local*)     0 (*local*)     0 (*local*)
 008:  0 (*local*)     0 (*local*)     0 (*local*)     2 (LX_1.1)
 00c:  2 (LX_1.1)     3 (GLIBC_2.0)    4 (GLIBC_2.1.3)  0 (*local*)
 010:  0 (*local*)

Version definition section '.gnu.version_d' contains 2 entries:
 Addr: 0x00000000000002e8 Offset: 0x0002e8 Link: 3 (.dynstr)
 000000: Rev: 1 Flags: BASE  Index: 1 Cnt: 1 Name: libfoo.so.1
 0x001c: Rev: 1 Flags: none Index: 2 Cnt: 1 Name: LX_1.1
```

11 Refer to the GNU ld manual at www.gnu.org/manual (and select the `ld` link). Or go directly to www.gnu.org/software/binutils/manual/ld-2.9.1/ld.html.

12 This can be used to prevent symbols from being exported from the library by default.

```
Version needs section '.gnu.version_r' contains 1 entries:
 Addr: 0x0000000000000320 Offset: 0x000320 Link to section: 3 (.dynstr)
 000000: Version: 1 File: libc.so.6 Cnt: 2
 0x0010:  Name: GLIBC_2.1.3 Flags: none Version: 4
 0x0020:  Name: GLIBC_2.0 Flags: none Version: 3
```

A *weak* version definition can be created by updating local objects without introducing new interfaces. Examples of such changes are bug fixes and performance improvements. From the previous example, let's update the symbol _message1:

```
$ cat message.c
/* message.c v1.1 */
const char *_message1 = "this is an updated string message 1\n";
```

Our version script file, scriptfile, has to be changed as follows:

```
$cat scriptfile
LX_1.1 {
        global:
            foo1;
        local:
            *;
};
LX_1.1.1 { } ;
```

Now, rebuild libfoo.so.1:

```
$gcc -fPIC -c foo.c message.c
$gcc -o libfoo.so.1 -shared -Wl,--version-script=scriptfile foo.o message.o
```

The command `readelf -V libfoo.so.1` displays the following:

```
$ readelf -V libfoo.so.1

Version symbols section '.gnu.version' contains 18 entries:
 Addr: 00000000000002e6 Offset: 0x0002e6 Link: 2 (.dynsym)
 000:  0 (*local*)    0 (*local*)    0 (*local*)    0 (*local*)
 004:  0 (*local*)    0 (*local*)    0 (*local*)    0 (*local*)
 008:  0 (*local*)    0 (*local*)    0 (*local*)    3 (LX_1.1.1)
 00c:  2 (LX_1.1)    2 (LX_1.1)    4 (GLIBC_2.0)   5 (GLIBC_2.1.3)
 010:  0 (*local*)    0 (*local*)

Version definition section '.gnu.version_d' contains 3 entries:
 Addr: 0x0000000000000308 Offset: 0x000308 Link: 3 (.dynstr)
 000000: Rev: 1 Flags: BASE  Index: 1 Cnt: 1 Name: libfoo.so.1
 0x001c: Rev: 1 Flags: none Index: 2 Cnt: 1 Name: LX_1.1
 0x0038: Rev: 1 Flags: WEAK  Index: 3 Cnt: 1 Name: LX_1.1.1

Version needs section '.gnu.version_r' contains 1 entries:
 Addr: 0x0000000000000360 Offset: 0x000360 Link to section: 3 (.dynstr)
 000000: Version: 1 File: libc.so.6 Cnt: 2
 0x0010:  Name: GLIBC_2.1.3 Flags: none Version: 5
 0x0020:  Name: GLIBC_2.0 Flags: none Version: 4
```

Note that this time the Version definition section displays the weak version (see text box) definition.

Next, let's update libfoo.so. 1 by adding a function `foo2`:

```
$cat foo.c

/* foo.c v 1.2 */
extern const char * _message1;
extern const char * _message2;

void foo1()
{
        (void) printf(_message1);
}

void foo2()
{
        (void) printf(_message2);
}
```

Update message.c:

```
$cat message.c
/* message.c v1.2 */
const char *_message1 = "this is an updated string message 1\n";
const char *_message2 = "this is a string message 2\n";
```

Update the scriptfile:

```
LX_1.1 {
        global:
            foo1;
        local:
            *;
};
LX_1.1.1 { } ;

LX_1.2 {
        global:
            foo2;
} LX_1.1.1;
```

Build the library:

```
$gcc -fPIC -c foo.c message.c
$gcc -o libfoo.so.1 -shared -Wl,--version-script=scriptfile foo.o message.o
```

The command `readelf -V libfoo.so.1` displays the following:

```
Version symbols section '.gnu.version' contains 20 entries:
 Addr: 0000000000000318 Offset: 0x000318 Link: 2 (.dynsym)
  000:  0 (*local*)    0 (*local*)    0 (*local*)    0 (*local*)
```

```
 004:  0 (*local*)    0 (*local*)    0 (*local*)    0 (*local*)
 008:  0 (*local*)    0 (*local*)    0 (*local*)    4 (LX_1.2)
 00c:  3 (LX_1.1.1)   2 (LX_1.1)     2 (LX_1.1)     5 (GLIBC_2.0)
 010:  6 (GLIBC_2.1.3)  4 (LX_1.2)    0 (*local*)    0 (*local*)

Version definition section '.gnu.version_d' contains 4 entries:
 Addr: 0x0000000000000340 Offset: 0x000340 Link: 3 (.dynstr)
 000000: Rev: 1 Flags: BASE  Index: 1 Cnt: 1 Name: libfoo.so.1
 0x001c: Rev: 1 Flags: none Index: 2 Cnt: 1 Name: LX_1.1
 0x0038: Rev: 1 Flags: WEAK  Index: 3 Cnt: 1 Name: LX_1.1.1
 0x0054: Rev: 1 Flags: none Index: 4 Cnt: 2 Name: LX_1.2
 0x0070: Parent 1: LX_1.1.1

Version needs section '.gnu.version_r' contains 1 entries:
 Addr: 0x00000000000003b8 Offset: 0x0003b8 Link to section: 3 (.dynstr)
 000000: Version: 1 File: libc.so.6 Cnt: 2
 0x0010:  Name: GLIBC_2.1.3 Flags: none Version: 6
 0x0020:  Name: GLIBC_2.0 Flags: none Version: 5
```

The output shows that the version definition LX_1.2 has a dependency on the version definition LX_1.1.1.

Update main.c:

```
$cat main.c
/* main.c v1.2 */
main()
{
      foo1();
      foo2();
}

$ln -s libfoo.so.1 libfoo.so
$gcc -o main main.c -L. -lfoo
```

Examine main using the `ldd -v` command:

```
$ ldd -v main
    libfoo.so => ./libfoo.so (0xb7ffe000)
    libc.so.6 => /lib/tls/i586/libc.so.6 (0x00b9c000)
    /lib/ld-linux.so.2 (0x00b85000)

    Version information:
    ./main:
        libfoo.so (LX_1.1) => ./libfoo.so
        libfoo.so (LX_1.2) => ./libfoo.so
        libc.so.6 (GLIBC_2.0) => /lib/tls/i586/libc.so.6
    ./libfoo.so:
        libc.so.6 (GLIBC_2.1.3) => /lib/tls/i586/libc.so.6
        libc.so.6 (GLIBC_2.0) => /lib/tls/i586/libc.so.6
    /lib/tls/i586/libc.so.6:
        ld-linux.so.2 (GLIBC_2.1) => /lib/ld-linux.so.2
```

```
        ld-linux.so.2 (GLIBC_2.3) => /lib/ld-linux.so.2
        ld-linux.so.2 (GLIBC_PRIVATE) => /lib/ld-linux.so.2
        ld-linux.so.2 (GLIBC_2.0) => /lib/ld-linux.so.2
```

Notice that the main executable references both LX_1.1 and LX_1.2 of the versioned library, as shown in the box.

If main.c looked liked the following:

```
main()
{
        foo1();
}

gcc -o main main.c -L. -lfoo
```

the resulting main executable will still be linked to version 1.2 of libfoo.so but will only show the reference to version 1.1 if examined, because it only needs to resolve symbols from that version of the library:

```
$ ldd -v main
    libfoo.so => ./libfoo.so (0xb7ffe000)
    libc.so.6 => /lib/tls/i586/libc.so.6 (0x00b9c000)
    /lib/ld-linux.so.2 (0x00b85000)

    Version information:
    ./main:
        libfoo.so (LX_1.1) => ./libfoo.so
        libc.so.6 (GLIBC_2.0) => /lib/tls/i586/libc.so.6
    ./libfoo.so:
        libc.so.6 (GLIBC_2.1.3) => /lib/tls/i586/libc.so.6
        libc.so.6 (GLIBC_2.0) => /lib/tls/i586/libc.so.6
    /lib/tls/i586/libc.so.6:
        ld-linux.so.2 (GLIBC_2.1) => /lib/ld-linux.so.2
        ld-linux.so.2 (GLIBC_2.3) => /lib/ld-linux.so.2
        ld-linux.so.2 (GLIBC_PRIVATE) => /lib/ld-linux.so.2
        ld-linux.so.2 (GLIBC_2.0) => /lib/ld-linux.so.2
```

Notice that this time only version LX_1.1 of the versioned library is referenced by the executable.

GNU `ld` also lets you bind a symbol to a version in the source file where the symbol is defined rather than in the versioning script. In addition, GNU `ld` allows multiple versions of the same function to appear in a given shared library. For detailed information, refer to the GNU `ld` manual[13] and the paper "How to Write Shared Libraries" by Ulrich Drepper.

---

13 www.gnu.org/software/binutils/manual/ld-2.9.1/ld.html

Symbol versioning has been implemented in `glibc` since version 2.1. Symbol versioning is also a part of the Linux Standard Base Specification 1.2 and higher.

3.6 Dynamic Linker (or Runtime Linker)

The Linux dynamic linker (/lib/ld.so.1 or /lib64/ld64.so.1) finds and loads the shared libraries needed by a program, prepares the program to run, and then runs it. Linux binaries require dynamic linking unless the `-static` option was given to `ld` during compilation.

On all modern UNIX operating systems, environment variables can be used to affect the operation of the runtime linker. An example is the environment variable `LIBPATH` on AIX, which alters the search path of the runtime linker. The following environment variables affect the operation of the runtime linker on Linux:

- **`LD_LIBRARY_PATH`.** A colon-separated list of directories in which to search for libraries at runtime.
- **`LD_PRELOAD`.** A whitespace-separated list of additional libraries to be loaded before all others. This can be used to selectively override functions in other shared libraries.
- **`LD_BIND_NOW`.** If set to a nonempty string, causes the dynamic linker to resolve all symbols at program startup instead of deferring function call resolution when they are first referenced. This is useful when using a debugger.
- **`LD_TRACE_LOADED_OBJECTS`.** If set to a nonempty string, causes the program to list its dynamic library dependencies, as if run by `ldd`, instead of executing normally.

The Linux dynamic linker loads library dependencies breadth first. That is, first the dependencies of the executable are added in the order listed in its dynamic section. Then the dependencies of the first dependency are added in the same fashion.

Typing the following from a shell prompt gives more information about the Linux dynamic linker:

```
$info ld.so
```

3.6.1 Programming Interface

Linux provides a set of APIs used to dynamically load libraries. The dynamic linking interfaces used by Linux are as follows:

- **dlopen.** Opens a library and prepares it for use
- **dlsym.** Looks up the value of a symbol in the opened library
- **dlclose.** Closes a library
- **dlerror.** Returns a string describing the error from the last call to `dlopen`, `dlsym`, or `dlclose`

C users need to include the header file dlfcn.h to use these APIs. `Glibc` adds two APIs not specified by POSIX:

- **dladdr.** Resolves name and file where a symbol is located from a function pointer
- **dlvsym.** Similar to `dlsym()`, but takes a version string as additional argument

In Linux, a program that uses dynamic linking is linked with the `libdl.so` library, `-ldl`. The libraries it loads do not need to be linked in during the build process. Example 3-1 is a sample program using `dl*` routines in Linux.

Example 3-1 *A Sample Program Illustrating How to Use dl* Routines*

main.c:

```
#include <stdio.h>
#include <stdlib.h>
#include <dlfcn.h>
#include <errno.h>

typedef void (*FP)(void);

int
main( int argc, char** argv )
{
  void*  handle;
  void*  handle1;
  void*  symptr;
  FP   fp;
```

```
/* Load the shared object libdefsym.so containing the
 * definition of the function - defsym.
 */
if ( NULL == ( handle = dlopen( "./libfunc2.so",
                RTLD_NOW|RTLD_GLOBAL)))
{
  perror( dlerror() );
  exit( 1 );
}


/* Load the shared object libcalldefsym.so containing the
 * definition of the function - calldefsym.
 */
if ( NULL == ( handle1 = dlopen( "./libfunc1.so", RTLD_NOW)))
{
  perror( dlerror() );
  exit( 1 );
}

/* Obtain the address to the function - calldefsym. */
if ( NULL == ( symptr = dlsym( handle1, "function1" )))
{
  if ( 0 == errno )
  {
    fprintf( stderr, "Symbol calldefsym not found.
                Exiting\n");
    exit( 1 );
  }
  perror( dlerror() );
  exit( 1 );
}

fp = ( FP )symptr;

/* Call calldefsym which in turn calls defsym
 * via the address obtained above.
 */
fp();

/* Unload the shared library libcalldefsym.so. */
if ( 0 != ( dlclose( handle1 ) ) )
{
  perror( dlerror() );
  exit( 1 );
}

/* Unload the shared library libdefsym.so. */
if ( 0 != ( dlclose( handle ) ) )
{
  perror( dlerror() );
```

```
    exit( 1 );
  }
  exit( 0 );
}
```

function1.c:

```
#include <stdio.h>
#include <stdlib.h>
extern void function2( void );

void
function1( void )
{
    printf( "Calling function2 module function1\n" );
    function2();
}
```

function2.c:

```
#include <stdio.h>
#include <stdlib.h>

void
function2()
{
    printf( "function2 called.\n" );
}
```

Makefile:

```
CC=gcc

all:  main libfunc1.so libfunc2.so

main:  main.o
	$(CC) -o main main.o -g -ldl

main.o: main.c
	$(CC) -c main.c -g

libfunc2.so: function2.o
	$(CC) -o libfunc2.so -shared -fPIC -Wl,-soname=libfunc2.so.1 function2.o -lc

function2.o: function2.c
	$(CC) -c function2.c -fPIC

libfunc1.so:    function1.o
	$(CC) -o libfunc1.so -shared -fPIC -Wl,-soname=libfunc1.so.1 function1.o -lc


function1.o:  function1.c
	$(CC) -c function1.c -fPIC
```

```
.PHONY: clean

clean:
	rm *.o *.so main
```

We can then build the executable:

```
$ make
gcc -c main.c -g
gcc -o main main.o -g -ldl
gcc -c function1.c -fPIC
gcc -o libfunc1.so -shared -fPIC -Wl,-soname=libfunc1.so.1 function1.o
-lc
gcc -c function2.c -fPIC
gcc -o libfunc2.so -shared -fPIC -Wl,-soname=libfunc2.so.1 function2.o
-lc
```

Run the sample program:

```
$ ./main
Calling function2 module function1
function2 called.
```

Using the `ldd` command to inspect the executable gives the following:

```
$ ldd ./main
	linux-gate.so.1 => (0xffffe000)
	libdl.so.2 => /lib/libdl.so.2 (0x40028000)
	libc.so.6 => /lib/tls/libc.so.6 (0x4002b000)
	/lib/ld-linux.so.2 => /lib/ld-linux.so.2 (0x40000000)
```

Notice that the executable main does not reference a dynamically loaded library.

3.6.2 Lazy Relocation

Lazy relocation or loading is a feature that allows the relocations associated with a symbol to be delayed until the symbol is needed. This is used on different UNIX architectures for calls to functions. This feature can prove useful if an application that is linked to a shared library may have the slightest possibility of not calling the function in the shared library. In this case, the library is only loaded if the function is called by the application; otherwise, the shared library is never loaded, thereby saving system resources. However, by setting the environment variable `LD_BIND_NOW` to a nonempty value, all the relocations are performed at the program startup time. Lazy relocation can also be disabled for an individual object by adding the `-z now` option to the linker command line. This setting cannot be undone without relinking the shared objects.

3.6.3 Initializing and Finalizing Routine

Sometimes legacy code may include two special functions, `_init` and `_fini`. The `_init` and `_fini` functions are used to control constructors and destructors when loading and unloading a module,[14] respectively. They have the following C prototypes:

```
void _init(void);
void _fini(void);
```

When a library is opened through `dlopen()` or simply as a shared library, the `_init` function is called if it is exported within the same library.[15] When the library is closed with `dlclose()` or unloaded because no other applications are using symbols from that library, the routine `_fini` is called just before the library is unloaded. When using your own `_init` and `_fini` routines, you may need to avoid linking against the system startup files. To do this, use the GCC option `-nostartfiles`.

However, using these routines or the GCC `-nostartfiles` option is not recommended because it may result in undesired behavior. Instead, libraries should export routines using the `__attribute__((constructor))` and `__attribute__((destructor))` function attributes, as in the following:

```
void __attribute__ ((constructor)) x_init(void);
void __attribute__ ((destructor)) x_fini(void);
```

The constructor routine is called before `dlopen()` returns or when the library is loaded at load time.[16] The destructor routine is called before `dlclose()` returns or after `main()` returns or when `exit()` is called if the library is loaded at load time.

---

14 Objects in a shared library.

15 This is the same as saying the `_init` function is defined as a function within the library.

16 Before `main()` is called.

3.7 System Calls

System calls are interfaces used by user programs to have the kernel perform a specific function on behalf of the calling thread or process. Because some system calls on UNIX platforms are more operating system-specific, they may not be available on Linux. When this happens, a wrapper call may have to be implemented on the Linux side.

A list of system calls in Linux can be located at /usr/include/asm/unistd.h. Tables that give a side-by-side comparison between Linux and a different operating system such as Solaris and HP-UX are also presented in the appendixes of this book.

3.8 Large Page Support

Large page usage is primarily intended to provide performance improvements to applications that allocate a lot of memory and frequently access that memory. The performance improvement is mainly due to the reduced number of misses in the Translation Lookaside Buffer (TLB), a cache of virtual-to-physical translation. The number of misses can be reduced when the TLB is able to map a larger virtual memory range. This is possible due to the multiple page size support provided by most modern architectures. For example, the 32-bit Intel architecture supports 4K and 4MB (2MB in PAE mode) page sizes; Itanium supports multiple page sizes 4K, 8K, 64K, 256K, 1MB, 4MB, 16MB, and 256MB; SUN UltraSPARC supports 8K, 64K, 512K, and 4MB; and the 64-bit PowerPC (ppc64) supports 4K, 64K, 16MB, and 64GB. In this section, we give information for application developers on how to use large page support provided by the Linux kernel.

The 2.6 kernel has built-in support for *hugetlbpage* (a term used by the Linux community for large page). With the kernel configured with hugetlbpage support, the output of the command `cat /proc/meminfo` should display an output having the information about hugetlbpage, as follows:

```
HugePages_Total: 20
HugePages_Free: 20
Hugepagesize: 16384 KB
```

A filesystem of type *hugetlbfs* should also appear in /proc/filesystems. Before the user-space application can use hugetlbpage support, huge pages have to be allocated in the kernel by the administrator. /proc/sys/vm/nr_hugepages indicates the current number of configured huge pages in the kernel. To configure ten huge pages in the system, use this command:

```
echo 10 > /proc/sys/vm/nr_hugepages
```

The allocation will be successful only if there is enough physically contiguous memory in the system at that moment. The deallocation of huge pages is possible only if there are enough huge pages free that can be transferred back to the regular memory pool. Pages that are used as hugetlb pages are reserved inside the kernel and cannot be used for other purposes.

There are two ways for application developers to use the hugetlbpage support:

1. The system V shared memory system call (`shmget`, `shmat`)
2. The `mmap` system call

It is possible for the same application to use a combination of `mmap` and `shm*`.

In the following programming examples, we show how to use these system calls for the hugetlbpage support. These programs originally appeared in /usr/src/linux/Documentation/vm/hugetlbpage.txt.

In Example 3-2, the application uses the System V shared memory system calls to request 256MB of memory backed by huge pages. The SHM_HUGETLB flag is used in the shmget system call to inform the kernel that huge pages are requested.

Example 3-2

Using Huge Page Memory via System V Shared Memory Interfaces

```
/*
 * Example of using huge page memory in a user application using Sys V
 * shared memory system calls. In this example, the app is requesting
 * 256MB of memory that is backed by huge pages. The application
 * uses the flag SHM_HUGETLB in the shmget system call to inform the
 * kernel that it is requesting huge pages.
 *
 * For the ia64 architecture, the Linux kernel reserves Region number 4
 * for huge pages. That means the addresses starting with 0x800000...
 * will need to be specified. Specifying a fixed address is not
 * required on ppc64, i386 or x86_64.
 *
 * Note: The default shared memory limit is quite low on many kernels;
 * you may need to increase it via:
 *
 * echo 268435456 > /proc/sys/kernel/shmmax
 *
```

```
 * This will increase the maximum size per shared memory segment to
 * 256MB. The other limit that you will hit eventually is shmall which
 * is the total amount of shared memory in pages. To set it to 16GB on
 * a system with a 4KB pagesize do:
 *
 * echo 4194304 > /proc/sys/kernel/shmall
*/
#include <stdlib.h>
#include <stdio.h>
#include <sys/types.h>
#include <sys/ipc.h>
#include <sys/shm.h>
#include <sys/mman.h>

#ifndef SHM_HUGETLB
#define SHM_HUGETLB 04000
#endif

#define LENGTH (256UL*1024*1024)

#define dprintf(x) printf(x)

/* Only ia64 requires this */
#ifdef __ia64__
#define ADDR (void *)(0x8000000000000000UL)
#define SHMAT_FLAGS (SHM_RND)
#else
#define ADDR (void *)(0x0UL)
#define SHMAT_FLAGS (0)
#endif

int main(void)
{
    int shmid;
    unsigned long i;
    char *shmaddr;
    if ((shmid = shmget(2, LENGTH,
        SHM_HUGETLB | IPC_CREAT | SHM_R | SHM_W)) < 0) {
        perror("shmget");
        exit(1);
    }
    printf("shmid: 0x%x\n", shmid);

    shmaddr = shmat(shmid, ADDR, SHMAT_FLAGS);
    if (shmaddr == (char *)-1) {
        perror("Shared memory attach failure");
        shmctl(shmid, IPC_RMID, NULL);
        exit(2);
    }
    printf("shmaddr: %p\n", shmaddr);
```

```
    dprintf("Starting the writes:\n");
    for (i = 0; i < LENGTH; i++) {
        shmaddr[i] = (char)(i);
        if (!(i % (1024 * 1024)))
            dprintf(".");
    }
    dprintf("\n");

    dprintf("Starting the Check...");
    for (i = 0; i < LENGTH; i++)
        if (shmaddr[i] != (char)i)
            printf("\nIndex %lu mismatched\n", i);
    dprintf("Done.\n");

    if (shmdt((const void *)shmaddr) != 0) {
        perror("Detach failure");
        shmctl(shmid, IPC_RMID, NULL);
        exit(3);
    }

    shmctl(shmid, IPC_RMID, NULL);

    return 0;
}
```

For ia86 architecture, the kernel reserves a specific region for huge pages. That means a fixed address in the calling process must be specified. A fixed address is not required for i386, x86_64, or ppc64.

You may need to increase the maximum size per shared memory segment to 256MB. This can be done by issuing this command:

```
echo 268435456 > /proc/sys/kernel/shmmax
```

The other limit that you need to be concerned about is /proc/sys/kernel/shmall, which is the total amount of shared memory in pages.

```
mmap system call
```

In this case, it is required that the system administrator mount a filesystem of type hugetlbfs first. Any files created on this mount point will be backed by huge pages.

```
mount none /mnt/huge -t hugetlbfs -o uid=1000,gid=100
```

The preceding command mounts a filesystem of type hugetlbfs on the directory /mnt/huge with the owner and group of the root of the filesystem set to 1000 and 100, respectively. Example 3-3 provides an application using the `mmap` system call to request a memory of size 256MB that is backed by huge pages.

Example 3-3

Using Huge Page Memory via the mmap Routine

```
/*
 * Example of using huge page memory in a user application using the
 * mmap system call. Before running this application, make sure that
 * the administrator has mounted the hugetlbfs filesystem (on some
 * directory like /mnt) using the command mount -t hugetlbfs nodev
 * /mnt. In this example, the app is requesting memory of size 256MB
 * that is backed by huge pages.
 *
 * For ia64 architecture, Linux kernel reserves Region number 4 for
 * huge pages. That means the addresses starting with 0x800000... will
 * need to be specified. Specifying a fixed address is not required
 * on ppc64, i386 or x86_64.
*/
#include <stdlib.h>
#include <stdio.h>
#include <unistd.h>
#include <sys/mman.h>
#include <fcntl.h>

#define FILE_NAME "/mnt/hugepagefile"
#define LENGTH (256UL*1024*1024)
#define PROTECTION (PROT_READ | PROT_WRITE)

/* Only ia64 requires this */
#ifdef __ia64__
#define ADDR (void *)(0x8000000000000000UL)
#define FLAGS (MAP_SHARED | MAP_FIXED)
#else
#define ADDR (void *)(0x0UL)
#define FLAGS (MAP_SHARED)
#endif

void check_bytes(char *addr)
{
    printf("First hex is %x\n", *((unsigned int *)addr));
}

void write_bytes(char *addr)
{
    unsigned long i;

    for (i = 0; i < LENGTH; i++)
        *(addr + i) = (char)i;
}

void read_bytes(char *addr)
```

```
{
    unsigned long i;

    check_bytes(addr);
    for (i = 0; i < LENGTH; i++)
        if (*(addr + i) != (char)i) {
            printf("Mismatch at %lu\n", i);
            break;
        }
}

int main(void)
{
    void *addr;
    int fd;

    fd = open(FILE_NAME, O_CREAT | O_RDWR, 0755);
    if (fd < 0) {
        perror("Open failed");
        exit(1);
    }

    addr = mmap(ADDR, LENGTH, PROTECTION, FLAGS, fd, 0);
    if (addr == MAP_FAILED) {
        perror("mmap");
        unlink(FILE_NAME);
        exit(1);
    }

    printf("Returned address is %p\n", addr);
    check_bytes(addr);
    write_bytes(addr);
    read_bytes(addr);

    munmap(addr, LENGTH);
    close(fd);
    unlink(FILE_NAME);

    return 0;
}
```

Note that read and write system calls are not supported on files residing on a hugetlbfs filesystem. A regular `chown`, `chgrp`, and `chmod` (with the right permissions) could be used to change the file attributes on hugetlbfs.

3.9 The Native POSIX Threads Library (NPTL)

The Linux threading library in all the released versions of Linux prior to kernel version 2.6 is known as *LinuxThreads*. This library has been supported by the GNU C library since `glibc` 2.0, although using the POSIX APIs is not really POSIX-compliant. Starting in the 2.6 kernel, NPTL was introduced. It provides a significant performance improvement over LinuxThreads. NPTL is also far more compliant with the POSIX specification than the LinuxThreads package was. However, simply using the 2.6 kernel does not mean that the NPTL is being used. All modern Linux distributions ship NPTL as the default, even if they ship both NPTL and LinuxThreads.

Issue the following command to see which POSIX implementation you are using:

```
$ getconf GNU_LIBPTHREAD_VERSION
NPTL 0.61                  This was returned from
                      SuSE 9.1 installation


$ getconf GNU_LIBPTHREAD_VERSION
NPTL 2.3.3                 This was returned from
                           Fedora 2.6.9-1.667
                           Installation.
$ getconf GNU_LIBPTHREAD_VERSION
linuxthreads-0.10          This was returned from an old
                           RedHat installation
```

To tell which compiler suite the Linux distribution was compiled and linked with, use the following method.

To find the `libpthreads` library linked with /bin/ls:

```
$ ldd /bin/ls | grep libc.so.6
    libc.so.6 => /lib/tls/i586/libc.so.6 (0x00b9c000)

$ /lib/tls/i586/libc.so.6
GNU C Library stable release version 2.3.3, by Roland McGrath et al.
Copyright (C) 2004 Free Software Foundation, Inc.
This is free software; see the source for copying conditions.
There is NO warranty; not even for MERCHANTABILITY or FITNESS FOR A
PARTICULAR PURPOSE.
Compiled by GNU CC version 3.4.2 20041017 (Red Hat 3.4.2-6.fc3).
Compiled on a Linux 2.4.20 system on 2004-10-27.
Available extensions:
    GNU libio by Per Bothner
    crypt add-on version 2.1 by Michael Glad and others
    Native POSIX Threads Library by Ulrich Drepper et al
```

```
    The C stubs add-on version 2.1.2.
    BIND-8.2.3-T5B
    NIS(YP)/NIS+ NSS modules 0.19 by Thorsten Kukuk
    Glibc-2.0 compatibility add-on by Cristian Gafton
    GNU Libidn by Simon Josefsson
Thread-local storage support included.
For bug reporting instructions, please see:
<http://www.gnu.org/software/libc/bugs.html>.
```

As the preceding output shows, the libc.so.6 is linked with the Native POSIX Threads Library by Ulrich Drepper.

NPTL implements the one-on-one threading model; that is, there is a one-to-one relationship between a user thread and a kernel thread. NPTL also implements the interprocess POSIX synchronization primitives. Specifically, the thread option `PTHREAD_PROCESS_SHARED` is now supported.

3.9.1 Maximum Number of Threads

The maximum number of threads an application can create on a Linux system varies in different Linux distributions. Running SUSE version 9.1 on a two-processor system with 2GB of memory yielded 16,317 pthreads created before `pthread_create` returned an EAGAIN error number. An EGAIN may mean that the application ran into some system-imposed limit. The application was programmed to create threads with a stack size of 16,384, which is the minimum stack size allowed for creating threads. Before setting the stack size to 16,384, the application would fail pthread creation at 1,021 with a return code of ENOMEM. In any case, 8,000 and even 16,000 threads is enough to satisfy any application program needs for creating threads.

To create a large number of threads in Linux, be sure to do the following:

1. Create the right amount of stack size.[17]
2. Examine `ulimit` (an output for memory and stack-size limits).
   Vary it accordingly or edit /etc/security/limits.conf.

Chapters 4, 5, and 6 contain more details on POSIX threads supported and their differences compared to NPTL.

---

17 Use the `pthread_attr_setstacksize` programming interface.

3.10 Internationalization (I18N)[18] and Localization

How I18N affects the porting effort greatly depends on the application. If an application requires simple message catalogue conversions, date and time displays, or simple text string searches using regular expressions, porting these functionalities from UNIX platforms to Linux can be easy. However, if the application does more-complicated text analysis, like ones used in editors, those may be harder to port for the reason mentioned in the next paragraph.

Linux conforms to the ISO naming standard locale names, [locale]_[territory].[codeset], where locale is the two-character language and territory is the two-character territory. Examples of these are en_US.iso885915 and zh_CN.gb18030. However, the locales available on each system and locale contents differ. Porting applications that require complicated use of available locales may require the need to learn language specificity and translation as well as modification of existing locales on Linux to get similar behavior that is expected from the source application running on a different platform.

Table 3-4 shows some of the supported GNU `libc` internationalization functions.

TABLE 3-4
GNU libc I18N Support Table

GNU libc	Functions
`wcscat, wcsncat, wcscmp, wcsncmp, wcscpy, wcsncpy, wcslen, wcschr, wcsrchr, wcsstr, wcspbrk, wcsspn, wcscspn, wcswcs, wcstok, wcscoll, wcwidth, wcswidth, wcsxfrm`	Wide character string functions
`mblen, mbrlen, wcslen, strlen, wcswidth, wcwidth`	Dimension functions
`mbsinit, mbrtowc, wcrtomb mbsrtowcs, wcsrtombs, btowc, wctob, mbtowc, mbstowcs wctomb, wcstombs, wcrtomb, wcsnrtombs, mbsnrtowcs`	Conversion functions
`iconv, iconv_open, iconv_close`	Translation functions
`ngettext, dngettext, dcngettext setlocale, textdomain, bindtextdomain, bind_textdomain_codeset, gettext, dgettext, dcgettext, catgets, gencat, catclose, catopen`	Message catalog functions

18 Refer to www.li18nux.org/ to learn more about the Linux I18N Project.

GNU libc	Functions
getc, getc_unlocked, getchar getchar_unlockec, fgetc, getw, putc, putchar, fputc, putw, fgetc, getw, ungetwc, getwc, getwchar, fgetwc, ungetwc, fgets, ungetc, fputwc, fputws, putwc, putwchar, fputs, fgetws	Input/output functions
fwprintf, wprintf, swprintf, vfwprintf, vwprintf, vswprintf, strftime, strfmon, printf, fprintf, sprintf, wcfstime, vprintf, vfprintf, vsprintf, vsnprintf	String formatting functions
iswalpha, iswupper, iswlower iswdigit, iswxdigit, iswalnum iswspace, iswpunct, iswprint, iswgraph, iswcntrl, wctype, iswctype, isalpha, isupper_, islower, isdigit, isxdigit, isalnum, isspace, ispunct, isprint, isgraph, iscntrl, isascii, isblank, isspace, isupper	Character classifications
strcoll, strxfrm, wcscoll, wcsxfrm	Collation functions
regcomp, regexec, regerror, regfree	Regular expressions
memset, wmemchr, wmemcmp wmemcpy, wmemmove, wmemset_, wcpcpy, wcpncpy, wcscpy, wcsncpy, wcsspn, wmemset, cpcpy, cpncpy, cscpy, csncpy, csspn	String copying and filling functions
towlower, towupper, towctrans, wctrans, tolower, toupper	Conversion functions

On Linux, you can use the command `locale -a` to determine the locales installed on the system, and the decoder file can be found in /usr/share/locale/locale.alias.

3.10.1 Iconv Support

Linux provides the `iconv(1)` utility to convert traditional string encoding to unicode. To get a list of currently implemented encodings in Linux, use the `iconv -list` command at the Linux command prompt.

Sometimes using the `iconv` utilty to translate encodings is not sufficient. Some applications, such as mailers and Web interfaces, need to convert between two different text encodings. The GNU `libc` provides functionalities to programmatically convert string encodings between internal string representation (unicode) and external string representation (a traditional encoding).

Example 3-4 shows how to use the libiconv APIs.

Example 3-4

Listing of iconv_samp.c

```
#include <iconv.h>
#include <errno.h>
#include <unistd.h>
#include <stdio.h>

main(int argc, char *argv[])
{
  int Input = STDIN_FILENO;
  iconv_t cd;                   /* conversion descriptor */
  int bytesread;                /* num bytes read into input buffer */
  unsigned char inbuf[BUFSIZ]; /* input buffer */
  const unsigned char *inchar; /* ptr to input character */
  size_t inbytesleft;           /* num bytes left in input buffer */
  unsigned char outbuf[BUFSIZ];/* output buffer */
  const unsigned char *outchar;/* ptr to output character */
  size_t outbytesleft;          /* num bytes left in output buffer */
  size_t ret_val;               /* number of successful conversions */

  if (argc < 2)
  {
    printf("usage  : iconv_samp <tocode> <fromcode>\n");
    printf("Example : iconv_samp WINDOWS-1256 ISO_8859-16\n");
    printf("Run the command \"iconv --list\" for list of known
                  character sets\n");
    exit(1);
  }
  /* Initiate conversion -- get conversion descriptor */
  if ((cd = iconv_open(argv[1], argv[2])) == (iconv_t)-1) {
    printf("iconv_open failed : %d \n", errno);
    exit(1);
  }

  inbytesleft = 0;          /* no. of bytes converted */
                            /* translate the characters */
  for ( ;; ) {
    /*
     * if any bytes are leftover, they will be in the
     * beginning of the buffer on the next read().
```

```
 */

inchar = inbuf;          /* points to input buffer */
outchar = outbuf;        /* points to output buffer */
outbytesleft = BUFSIZ;  /* no of bytes to be converted */
if ((bytesread = read(Input, inbuf+inbytesleft,
       (size_t)BUFSIZ-inbytesleft)) < 0) {
      perror("prog");
      return 1;
}
if (!(inbytesleft += bytesread)) {
  break;      /* end of conversions */
}

ret_val = iconv(cd, (char **)&inchar, &inbytesleft,
          (char **)&outchar, &outbytesleft);

if (write(1, outbuf, (size_t)BUFSIZ-outbytesleft) < 0) {
  perror("prog");
  return 1;
}

/* iconv() returns the number of non-identical conversions
 * performed. If the entire string in the input buffer is
 * converted, the value pointed to by inbytesleft will be
 * zero. If the conversion stopped due to any reason, the
 * value pointed to by inbytesleft will be nonzero and
 * errno is set to indicate the condition.
 */

switch (ret_val)
{
  case 0:
    /* nothing to do */
    break;
  case -1:
    switch (errno)
    {
      case EINVAL:
        /* Conversion stopped due to an incomplete
         * multibyte sequence encountered in the
         * input buffer.
         */
        /* Copy data left, to the start of buffer */
        memcpy((char *)inbuf, (char *)inchar,
              (size_t)inbytesleft);
        break;
      case EILSEQ:
        /* Conversion stopped due to an invalid
         * multibyte sequence encountered in the
         * input buffer.
```

```
                */
              printf("EILSEQ encountered program exiting\n");
              exit(1);
              break;
            case E2BIG:
              /* Conversion stopped due to lack of space
               * in the output buffer.
               */
              memcpy((char *)inbuf, (char *)inchar,
                  (size_t)inbytesleft);
              break;
            default:
              break;
          }
        default:
        break;
      }
      /* Go back and read from the input file. */
    }

    /* end conversion & get rid of the conversion table */
    if (iconv_close(cd) == (int)-1) {
      printf("iconv_close failed : %d \n", errno);
      exit (1);
    }
    return 0;
}
```

Compile the code:

```
$ gcc iconv_samp.c -o iconv_samp
```

Use the executable to convert an input file:

```
$ ./iconv_samp WINDOWS-1256 ISO 8859-16 < input_file
```

3.10.2 How to Create a Message Catalog[19]

A message catalog is a file used to translate language-dependent output of an application in the language to which the system locale is set. Example 3-5 shows how

19 Refer to *Linux Programming by Example* by Robbins (Prentice Hall, 2004) for more detailed Linux I18N examples.

to create a message catalog on Linux using the GNU `xgettext` and `msgfmt` utilities.

Example 3-5

Sample Listing of message_cat.c

```
#include <locale.h>
#include <stdio.h>
#include <libintl.h>

#define PACKAGE  "my_message"
#define LOCALEDIR "locale"

int
main() {
  setlocale (LC_MESSAGES, "");
  bindtextdomain (PACKAGE, LOCALEDIR);
  textdomain (PACKAGE);

  printf("%s\n", gettext("Linux Porting Guide"));
  printf("%s\n", gettext("Author: Mendoza,Skawratananond,Walker"));
  return(0);
}
```

In this example, we want to output the title and authors of the book in Spanish. To do this, we first run `xgettext` against the sample program:

```
$ xgettext hello.c
```

This produces a file named message.po:

```
$ cat message.po

# SOME DESCRIPTIVE TITLE.
# Copyright (C) YEAR THE PACKAGE'S COPYRIGHT HOLDER
# This file is distributed under the same license as the PACKAGE package.
# FIRST AUTHOR <EMAIL@ADDRESS>, YEAR.
#
#, fuzzy
msgid ""
msgstr ""
"Project-Id-Version: PACKAGE VERSION\n"
"Report-Msgid-Bugs-To: \n"
"POT-Creation-Date: 2005-03-17 12:22-0800\n"
"PO-Revision-Date: YEAR-MO-DA HO:MI+ZONE\n"
"Last-Translator: FULL NAME <EMAIL@ADDRESS>\n"
```

```
"Language-Team: LANGUAGE <LL@li.org>\n"
"MIME-Version: 1.0\n"
"Content-Type: text/plain; charset=ISO-8859-2\n"
"Content-Transfer-Encoding: 8bit\n"

#: hello.c:13
msgid "Linux Porting Guide"
msgstr "Guia de Migracion a Linux"

#: hello.c:14
msgid "Author: Mendoza,Skawratananond,Walker"
msgstr "Autor: Mendoza,Skawratananond,Walker"
```

Edit the file message.po, and change the `msgstr` for *each* of the messages to be translated. Edit the `charset` if it was not set before running `xgettext`. Then run the command msgfmt against the messages.po file. The file named my_messages.mo refers to the domain set in the bindtextdomain with the extension of .mo.

```
$ msgfmt -v -o my_message.mo messages.po
```

For this example, we create a directory for Spanish (Costa Rica) in our local directory (not the default directory /usr/lib/locale, because we do not have root access):

```
$ mkdir -p locale/es_CR/LC_MESSAGES
```

Then move my_messages.mo to the correct directory:

```
$ mv my_message.mo locale/es_CR/LC_MESSAGES
```

Export the correct `LC_MESSAGES` value and run the sample program:

```
$ export LC_MESSAGES=es_CR
$ ./hello
Guia de Migracion a Linux
Autor: Mendoza,Skawratananond,Walker
```

We have just successfully created a message catalogue file on Linux.

3.11 Big/Little-Endian Environment

Although Linux was developed on an Intel platform, which is primarily a little-endian environment, it has been ported to several other hardware platforms that support big-endian environments. Endianness, or byte ordering, refers to how a data element and its individual bytes are stored. In a big-endian (BE) environment, the lowest address is associated with the most-significant or leftmost byte of a multibyte value. In a little-endian (LE) environment, the lowest address is associated with the least-significant or rightmost byte of a multibyte value. In general, bit 0 is associated with the most-significant bit (MSB) for BE, but with the least-significant bit for LE.

Example 3-6 shows a sample program that prints data differently when compiled and run on a BE or LE environment.

Example 3-6

Code Listing of endian_sample.c

```
#include <stdio.h>

main() {
  int i;  /* Loop variable */
  long x = 0xAABBCCDD;
  unsigned char *ptr = (char *) &x;

  /* Print value in host byte order */
  printf("x in hex: %x\n", x);
  printf("x by bytes: ");
  for (i=0; i < sizeof(long); i++)
    printf("%x\t", ptr[i]);
  printf("\n");
}
```

When compiled and run on an Intel server, which is an LE environment, the following is printed:

```
x in hex: aabbccdd
x by bytes: dd cc   bb   aa
```

When compiled and run on an IBM Power server, which is a BE environment, the following is printed:

```
x in hex: aabbccdd
x by bytes: aa bb   cc   dd
```

Note that the preceding example was compiled with `gcc`, which creates a 32-bit executable by default.

Most RISC-based computers, including IBM PowerPC servers, and the Internet Protocol (IP) use a BE layout, whereas Intel and Alpha architectures utilize an LE layout. When porting software, it is recommended to watch out for endian issues, because most if not all of these issues may go undetected, resulting in hard-to-find problems when they occur.

The problems in ported software include the following:

- Nonuniform data reference[20]
- Data sharing across BE and LE platforms
- Data exchange between network devices (for example, IP and PCI)[21]

Nonuniform data reference occurs more often in user space application code, whereas the latter two categories are difficulties encountered at lower code levels (for example, device drivers). Nonuniform data reference arises from improper data type reference with regard to endianness, usually dealing with unions or pointers. Endian-friendly code should incorporate definitions to determine whether the platform is LE or BE. It is considered a good programming habit to never cast a pointer to an int and to explicitly reference data type and byte values during conversion.

3.12 32- to 64-Bit Migration

64-bit Linux platforms are well on their way to replace aging 32-bit servers. A 64-bit application environment can drastically improve the performance of memory addressing and throughput for applications that manipulate very large data

20 Example 3-6 shows nonuniform data reference using a pointer.

21 PCI devices use an LE format, which needs to be accounted for if porting the device driver to a BE platform.

structures. Linux on IBM's PowerPC and AMD's 64-bit architecture provides a unique platform in that 32- and 64-bit applications can be run simultaneously without any performance loss. This advantage can be exploited by compiling applications for 64-bit when a 32-bit environment presents memory limitations for the application.

With `gcc`, use the `-m64` flag to generate 64-bit object files, as in the following example:

```
$ gcc -m64 sample.c -o sample.o
```

Note that on some platforms, such as the IBM PowerPC, the `gcc` compiler produces 32-bit objects even when the Linux platform is a 64-bit platform. On the AMD 64-bit architecture running 64-bit Linux, the `gcc` compiler produces 64-bit objects by default. Also, like UNIX platforms, 64-bit object code works only with other 64-bit object code. 32-bit and 64-bit object code cannot work in the same application space because of address conflicts.

The data type models between a 32-bit and 64-bit compilation environment are different. The C data type model for 32-bit applications is the ILP32 model. The letters stand for the int (I) and long (L) types, and pointers (P). The number 32 denotes that these data types are all 32-bit data types. The data type model for 64-bit applications is the LP64 data model. Except for the int, both the long (L) and pointer (P) types grow to 64 bits. The remaining C integer types and the floating-point types are the same in both data type models.

3.12.1 Common Migration Mistakes

Data type mismatches are common among code incompatibilities due to endianness and 32- to 64-bit issues. It is common to encounter current 32-bit applications that assume that the int type, long type, and pointers are the same size. Because the sizes of long and pointer change in the LP64 data model, this change alone can lead to the principal cause of ILP32-to-LP64 migration problems. Opportunities to isolate the source of these incompatibilities should be exploited as early as the analysis step of the porting process.

3.12.1.1 Assuming int and ptr Are the Same in LP64

In an LP64 environment, pointer (ptr) data types are 64 bits long. Failure to account for this difference from a 32-bit environment will result in at least a compiler warning (or worse, undefined application behavior).

Consider the following example:

```
char *p;
char *q;

p = (char *) malloc(sizeof(long)*4);
q = (char *) ((int)p & 0x4000);
..

$ gcc -m64 1.c -o foo
1.c: In function `main':
1.c:9: warning: cast from pointer to integer of different size
1.c:9: warning: cast to pointer from integer of different size
```

Fix this by changing int to a long, or even better, use `uintptr_t` from `stdint.h`.

3.12.1.2 Overlooking int and long Data Type Size Difference

It is easy to overlook the error created by programmers when they assumed the long and int data types are the same size when they wrote their code in an ILP32 environment.

Consider Example 3-7.

Example 3-7

Listing of bad_1.c

```
main()
{
  long trigger = 1<<31;
  printf("%lx\n", trigger);
}
```

When compiled and run as a 32-bit application:

```
gcc bad_1.c -o foo
$ ./foo
80000000
```

When compiled and run as a 64-bit application:

```
gcc -m64 bad_1.c -o foo
$ ./foo
ffffffff80000000
```

The call `sizeof` returns an integer of type `size_t`. Because `size_t` has changed to 64 bits in an LP64 environment, be careful not to pass this value to a function expecting an int as a parameter. Otherwise, truncation may occur.

3.12.1.3 Ignoring Signed Extensions

Example 3-7 also demonstrates a sign extension problem caused when converting to LP64. ISO C integral promotion rules states that a character, a short integer, or an integer bit field, all either signed or unsigned, or an object of enumeration type, may be used in an expression wherever an integer may be used. If an int can represent all the values of the original type, the value is converted to int; otherwise, the value is converted to unsigned int.

To fix this problem, change 1<<31 to 1L<<31.

3.12.1.4 Not Checking for String Conversions

String functions, such as `printf`, `sprintf`, `scanf`, and `sscanf` use format strings that may need to be prepended by the long size specification, `percentl`, for long arguments and `percentp` for pointer arguments. Failure to use these specifications for an LP64 environment can result in unexpected formatting results.

3.12.2 Best Practices

A best-practice approach for porting a 32-bit application to a 64-bit application suggests that the port be done in two separate phases. The first phase consists of the port from the native platform where the application currently runs (AIX, Solaris, or HP-UX) to Linux. And the second phase consists of *migrating* the ported 32-bit application to a 64-bit application on the Linux platform.

3.13 Summary

Analysis of the application is the most important piece of work that can be done prior to the actual porting step. If done with extreme care, it can uncover hidden gotchas that can help further refine the overall project plan. In some rare cases, the application may use platform-specific features that are not yet supported by Linux. In this case, the porting personnel have to look for a workaround or equivalent functionality in Linux. Fortunately, today's version of Linux supports the most commonly used API standards, such as POSIX threads, large pages, asynchronous I/O, message queues, 64-bit architecture, and many more. Finding equivalent functionality in lieu of the original functionality from the source platform has never been easier.

Here are some of the important highlights discussed in this chapter:

- The document "Conflicts between ISO/IEC 9945 (POSIX) and the Linux Standard Base" elaborates on Linux standards support.[22]
- Linux provides support for three library versioning methods—internal, external, and symbol versioning.
- Through the native POSIX threads library, Linux now supports a more complete implementation of POSIX threads, which makes porting of multi-threaded applications to Linux easier.
- Linux provides large page support for applications that use large page support from UNIX platforms.
- An environment aspect such as endianness affects those applications to be ported on a case-by-case basis. Endianness is a factor only if the application has specific routines that may be affected when coming from platforms that do not have the same bit ordering architecture as the Linux platform the application is being ported to.
- 32- to 64-bit application migration should be treated as a separate port altogether. If the application to be ported is a 32-bit application and the port requires the application to run on Linux as a 64-bit application, treat these as two separate porting projects—the first being the port of the 32-bit application to Linux and the second being the migration from the ported 32-bit application to a 64-bit application on Linux.

Whereas this chapter gives a picture of what Linux 2.6 has to offer in general, the porting chapters for Solaris, AIX, and HP-UX elaborate more on these technical features by citing differences and similarities between Linux and each of these UNIX platforms. The porting chapters are next.

---

22 www.opengroup.org/personal/ajosey/tr01-04-2005.txt

Chapter 4

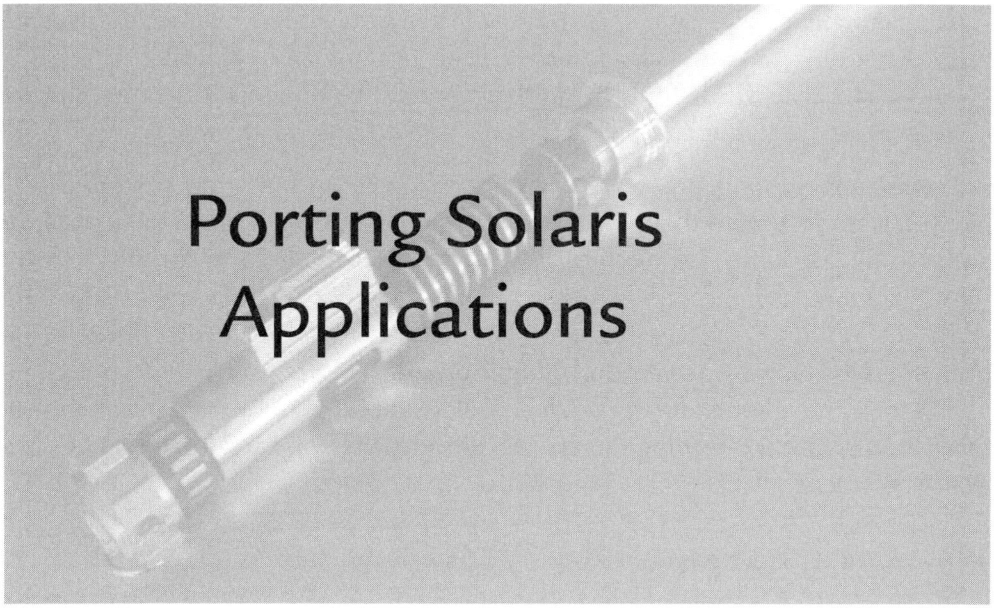

Porting Solaris Applications

In this chapter

Porting is the step of the process during which modifications to the application take place. At this point, most if not all technical aspects and dependencies of the application should have already been uncovered during the scoping and analysis steps. The only thing that needs to be done now is to modify the source code so that it compiles and runs on the Linux platform.

During the porting process, software developers and porting personnel will likely encounter several differences between the UNIX operating system they are used to and the Linux 2.6 platform. For each topic discussed in this chapter, the most common differences are presented to explain what works and what does not work on the Linux 2.6 environment. The Solaris environment described in this chapter is based mostly on version 10 but should also be applicable to older versions of Solaris. Although this chapter discusses Solaris topics in some detail, it is assumed that porting engineers reading this chapter already have software development experience on Solaris.

4.1 Preliminary Tasks

Before the porting work can begin, we need to prepare the environment that we will be working in. Among other things, we need to set up the port, build, and code change systems. Here is a checklist that includes the detailed tasks for each.

4.1.1 Set Up the Porting System

The porting system is used by porting engineers to do the porting work. It includes the porting server running the Linux version the application to be ported is expected to run on. In some instances, the server can be used to run small unit tests that will not affect overall server performance. Here is a list of tasks to set up the porting system:

1. Install the server with the Linux distribution the application to be ported is expected to run on. Set up all necessary home directories and build environment directories.
2. Check for any known patches that need to be installed on the server.
3. Make sure the installation includes the compiler and debugger.
4. Install third-party products and licenses that the application needs. Install any prerequisites or patches needed by these products.

5. Set up access for users and system administrators on the build server.
6. Set up policies using the porting environment as a test machine. These polices must include what can and cannot be tested on the porting server.

Depending on how work is divided among different groups involved in the porting project, the responsibility of doing these tasks may fall on the porting engineer. Even in instances where a separate group in the IT organization sets up the server, the porting engineer still needs to provide the specifications of the environment to the person performing the installation and setup.

4.1.2 Set Up the Code Change Management System

The code change management system consists of a tool that manages code changes to the application. The tool most frequently used is CVS, but other tools such as Subversion[1] and Arch[2] are gaining popularity. Here are the tasks associated with setting up the change management system:

1. Install the code change management tool.
2. Install the scripts that can make using the tool more convenient for the porting engineers.
3. Make sure the HOWTO and FAQs on using the tool and scripts exist and are readily accessible. These documents should include examples of how to use the tool and scripts.
4. Check the application into the code management system.

After the snapshot of the application source code has been checked into the code management system, that code should only be used for porting changes. No outside development changes should be added to this code base during the porting period.

---

1 http://subversion.tigris.org

2 www.gnu.org/software/gnu-arch/

4.1.3 Set Up the Build System

The build system is where automated nightly builds of the ported application take place. Although it may not be needed to begin any porting work, it is good practice to set it up before porting application makefiles. This system needs to be able to check out the source code and start an overnight build of the application. Building the application nightly after the code is stable enough to build with minimum build errors is good practice to make sure all checked-in code that day did not cause anything to break in the build. If something does break, it will be easier to find who and what caused the break. Here are the tasks associated with setting the build system:

1. Develop scripts that can check out the application code and start a nightly build.
2. After the makefiles have been ported, test these scripts. Expect errors, because the porting work may be just getting under way.
3. Add the script to a crontab file to schedule the overnight builds.
4. Write a script that can parse the errors produced so that an automated reporting system can notify responsible parties of any build breaks.

When the port, build, and code change system tasks are complete, the real porting work can begin.

4.2 General Differences

With major operating systems such as HP-UX, Solaris, AIX, and Linux embracing standards set forth by standards bodies such as ISO and POSIX, it seems that porting between platforms should be simple. Indeed, when it comes to application programming interfaces (APIs), these operating systems have a lot in common. If only applications were written strictly to these standards, porting them between platforms would be an easy task. Unfortunately, applications that need to be ported from one platform to another usually do not fit the ideal profile—one that is completely portable. The nonportable nature of applications stems not only from using nonstandard APIs but also from using new and optional standards available on the source platform that the target platform may have yet to implement. Sometimes, interpretations of standards may vary because some standards leave some points open for interpretation, resulting in different implementations on different platforms. This happens a lot when vendors implement standards on their platforms when they are still in the draft stages. This results in applications written or compiled to draft standards. It appears harmless because the application compiles and runs well on the source platform it was written and built on, but the resulting application is not portable.

In this section, we discuss differences and similarities between Solaris and Linux.

4.2.1 C Language

Sun's C compiler supports most of the language features specified in ISO/IEC 9899:1999 (C99) on operating systems earlier than Solaris 10. However, in Solaris 10, the compiler is in full compliance with the C99 standard.

GCC fully supports two versions of the C standard: C90 and the amendment to the 1990 standard published in 1995 (referred to as C95). Support for the C99 is not yet complete. For more details, visit http://gcc.gnu.org/c99status.html. By default, GCC complies with the C90 standard plus GNU extensions (including some C99 features). To select C90 in GCC, use one of the options `-ansi`, `-std=c89`, or `-std=iso9899:1990`. To select C95 in GCC, use the option `-std=iso9899:199409`. To select C99, use the option `-std=c99` or `-std=iso9899:1999`.

4.2.2 C++ Language

Sun's latest C++ compiler supports the 1998 ISO International Standard for C++, ISO IS14882:1998. For Linux, `g++` is a program that calls GCC with the default language set to C++, and automatically specifies linking against the C++ library. GNU `g++` closely conforms to the 1998 ISO/ANSI C++ standard.

Sun's C++ compiler is distributed with a C++ standard library based on the RogueWave Standard C++ Library, version 2, and Tools.h++, version 7.0. On the other hand, GNU `g++` ships with the runtime library `libstdc++`.

4.2.3 GNU C/C++ Language

At the time of this writing, GCC version 3.4.2 is currently available for Solaris 10 (www.sun.com/software/solaris/freeware). If your application can be built successfully using GCC on Solaris, it is most likely that it will be so on Linux. Note that different versions of GCC sometimes conform to different language specifications, especially the C++ standard. Therefore, a recompile with a different version of GCC may not be successful.

4.2.4 Java Language

A Java environment for Linux is available from the Blackdown Java SDK (www.blackdown.org). As of this writing, Blackdown has released Java version 1.4.2 and is working on release version 1.5. Other implementations of the Linux Java SDK are available for download from the Sun and IBM Web sites. Refer to Chapter 2, "Scoping," for more information about the Java environment in Linux.

4.2.5 Threads

Two thread interfaces are supported on Solaris: POSIX threads (commonly known as pthreads) and Solaris threads. Modern Linux distributions support the POSIX thread API standard. If you use Solaris threads, you must change your application when you port it to Linux. Alternatively, you can use the Solaris Compatibility Thread Library (STL) to migrate from the Solaris threads API to the POSIX threads library. For more information on STL, visit http://sourceforge.net/projects/sctl/.

4.2.6 Standards Comparison

Almost all Linux distributors acknowledge the values that standardization and portability provide, and work with the various Linux implementers/maintainers to meet those standards. The primary Linux industry standard is the Linux Standard Base (LSB), which is a project overseen by the Free Standards Group (FSG). The LSB (whose most recent version at this time is LSB 3.0) is based heavily on the IEEE POSIX and Open Group Single UNIX Specification standards, but it also documents those places where Linux is not UNIX- or POSIX-compatible. Most of the major Linux distributors have certified to the LSB.

The LSB, in addition to providing a source code API specification, also provides a binary interface (ABI) specification for each of several common Linux hardware platforms. The goal of the ABI is to ensure binary portability (for LSB-portable applications) between Linux distributions on that hardware platform. Distributors must certify to the ABI as well as to the API. ISVs can also certify their applications as "LSB portable" using tools provided by the FSG.

Although there is standardization within Linux, Linux itself is not totally compliant with either the IEEE POSIX or Open Group SUS specifications.[3] This means applications that may be totally portable under these common commercial UNIX standards may still need some work to move successfully to Linux. However, this work will be much less than for an application that meets no standards at all, or uses Solaris-specific UNIX extensions.

Table 4-1 provides a comparison of standards conformance between Solaris 10 and Linux supported standards based on the LSB specification version 2.0.1.

TABLE 4-1
Solaris and Linux Standards

Standard	Solaris 10[4]	Linux 2.6 (GNU libc)[5]
ISO/IEC 9945-1:2001, the POSIX System API (POSIX.1)	Yes (including many of the real-time extension options)	Partial (minor differences in some APIs and a few of the real-time extensions)
ISO/IEC 9945-2:2001, the POSIX Shell and Utilities standard (POSIX.2)	Yes	Partial (regular expressions and pattern-matching facilities)
X/Open Portability Guide Issue 3 (XPG3) (superset of POSIX.1 containing utilities from SVID)	Yes	No (GNU `libc` defines most of the facilities required by SVID that are not also required by the ISO C or POSIX standards)
X/Open Portability Guide Issue 4 (XPG4)	Yes	Yes
X/Open Portability Guide Issue 4 version 2 (XPG4v2)	Yes	Yes
System V Interface Definition (SVID3)	Yes	Partial
X11 Window System, Font Server, and Clients	Yes	Yes
LP64, 64-bit data model	Yes	Yes

3 Conflicts between ISO/IEC 9945 (POSIX) and the LSB (www.opengroup.org/personal/ajosey/tr01-04-2005.txt)

4 http://docs.sun.com/app/docs/doc/816-5175/6mbba7f3u?a=view

5 www.gnu.org/software/libc/manual/html_mono/ISO%20C

4.3 Compilers

As the porting effort starts, differences in compilers, compiler options, and system libraries between Solaris and Linux become apparent. This section provides information on the GNU compiler available on Linux. It presents comparison tables of compiler options and switches between Sun's Studio and GCC.

4.3.1 C Compiler

Sun's Studio 10 C compiler conforms to the ISO/IEC 9899-1990, Programming language—C (C90). This compiler supports most of the language features specified in the ISO/IEC 9899-1999, Programming Language—C standard (C99) on operating systems earlier than Solaris 10. It is in full compliance with the C99 standard on Solaris 10 when `-xc99=all,lib` is specified.

4.3.2 C Compiler Options

Table 4-2 provides a list of C compiler options for SUN Studio 10 and equivalents for the GNU GCC 3.4.2.

TABLE 4-2
C Compiler Options Comparison

Sun Studio 10	GNU GCC 3.4.2	Description[6]
`-#`	`-v`	Instructs the compiler to report information on the progress of the compilation. The `gcc` equivalent shows the invocation on standard error.
`-###`	`-###`	Traces the compilation without invoking anything.
`-A`*`name`*`(`*`tokens`*`)`	`-A`*`name`*`=`*`tokens`*	Associates *`name`* as a predicate with the specified *`tokens`* as if by an *`#assert`* preprocessing directive.
`-Bstatic`	`-static`	Causes the link editor to look only for files named lib*x*.a.
`-Bdynamic`	Default	Instructs the link editor to look for files named lib*x*.so and then lib*x*.a when given the `-lx` option.

6 http://docs.sun.com/source/819-0494/cc_ops.app.html

Sun Studio 10	GNU GCC 3.4.2	Description
-C	-C	Prevents the C preprocessor from removing comments, except those on the preprocessing directive lines.
-dalign	-malign-double	Obsolete. See -xmemalign=8s.
-d[y|n]	Implicit	-dy specifies dynamic linking. -dn specifies static linking in the link editor. On Linux, if an executable is linked against any shared object, it is a dynamic binary. If it is linked without the use of any shared object, the executable is linked statically.
-errfmt[=[no%]error]	N/A	Prefixes the string "error" to the beginning of error messages so that they are more visible.
-erroff[=t]	N/A	Suppresses C compiler warning messages based on their tag number and has no effect on error messages. There is no direct equivalent in GCC, but you can inhibit all warnings completely with -w.
-errshort=[i]	N/A	Controls the detail of the error message for type mismatch.
-errtags[=a]	N/A	Displays the message tag for each warning message.
-errwarn[=t]	N/A	Causes the compiler to exit with a failure for the specified warning message.
-fast	-O*x*	A macro that enables the compiler to produce optimized executable. GCC does not have this macro, but you can use a combination of -O options and others.
-fd	-Wstrict-prototypes	Reports K&R-style function definition and declaration.
-features=[[no%extinl|%none]	N/A	Generates extern inline functions as global functions or static functions.
-flags	--help, -v	Prints a summary of each available compiler flag.

Sun Studio 10	GNU GCC 3.4.2	Description
`-flteval [={any|2}]`	`-mfpmath=unit` (specific to i386 and x86-64)	Controls how floating-point expression is evaluated.
`-fnonstd`	N/A	A macro for `-fns` and `-ftrap`.
`-fns[={no|yes}]`	N/A	Turns on SPARC nonstandard floating-point mode.
`-fprecision=p`	`-fsingle-precision -constant`	Initializes the rounding-precision mode bits in the floating-point Control Word to single, double, or extended. GCC does not have a direct equivalent, but `-fsingle -precision-constant` forces the compiler to treat a floating-point constant as a single precision instead of converting it to a double precision constant.
`-fround=r`	`-frounding-math`	Sets the IEEE 754 rounding mode. The default IEEE mode is round-to-nearest. This is also the case on Linux, but there is no option to select the mode. Consider `-frounding-math` in GCC.
`-fsimple[=n]`	N/A	Allows the optimizer to make simplifying assumptions about floating-point arithmetic. GCC does not have the exact match. Consider these flags for floating-point optimizations not compliant with IEEE or ISO: `-ffloat-store`, `-ffast-math`, `-fno-math-error`, `-funsafe-math-optimizations`, `-ffinite-math-only`, `-fno-trapping-math`.
`-fsingle`	`-fsingle-precision -constant`	Causes the compiler to evaluate *float* expressions as single precision rather than double precision.
`-fstore`	`-ffloat-store`	Causes floating-point variables not to be stored in registers.

Sun Studio 10	GNU GCC 3.4.2	Description
-ftrap=t[,t...]	-fno-trapping-math	Sets the IEEE trapping mode in effect at startup but does not install a SIGFPE handler. GCC does not have the direct equivalent, but -fno-trapping-math disables all user-visible traps, including division by 0, overflow, underflow, inexact result, and invalid operation.
-G	-shared	Produces a shared object rather than a dynamically linked executable.
-g	-g	Produces additional symbol table information for debugging.
-H	-H	Prints to standard error the path name of each file included during the compilation.
-h*name*	-h*name*, -Wl,-soname,*name*	Gives a name to a shared dynamic library to have different versions of a library.
-I[-|*dir*]	-I[-|*dir*]	Adds *dir* to the list of directories searched for #include files.
-i	N/A	Passes the option to the linker to ignore any LD_LIBRARY_PATH or LD_LIBRARY_PATH64 setting.
-KPIC	-fPIC	Generates position-independent code for use in shared libraries (large model).
-Kpic	-fpic	Same as -fPIC except that the size of the global offset table is limited to 8K on the SPARC and 32K on the m68k and PPC (32,64). This limit does not exist on the 386. Code generated for the IBM PowerPC-based architecture is always position-independent.
-keeptmp	-save-temps	Keeps temporary files created during compilation instead of removing them automatically.

Sun Studio 10	GNU GCC 3.4.2	Description
`-L`*`dir`*	`-L`*`dir`*	Adds directory *`dir`* to the list of directories to be searched for archive libraries by `ld`. The directories are searched in the order in which they are specified on the command line.
`-l`*`name`*	`-l`*`name`*	Adds archive file *`name`* to the list of files to link. `ld` will search a directory for a library with an extension of .so before searching for one with an extension of .a. The linker will search an archive only once, at the location that it is specified on the command line. An undefined symbol in an object appearing later on the command line will not cause the linker to search the archive again.
`-mc`	N/A	Removes duplicate strings from the `.comment` section of the object file.
`-misalign`	Implicit	Obsolete. Look at `-xmemalign=1i`. This option is not necessary for the IA-32 because the processor handles alignment by itself.
`-misalign2`	Implicit	Obsolete. Look at `-xmemalign=2i`. This option is not necessary for the IA-32 because the processor handles alignment by itself.
`-mr[,`*`string`*`]`	N/A	Removes all strings from the `.comment` section.
`-mt`	`-pthread` `-D_REENTRANT`	Macro option that expands to `-D_REENTRANT -lthread`. On Linux, `-pthread` adds support for multithreading with the pthreads library.
`-native`	`-mcpu=`*`cpu_type`*	Synonym for `-xtarget=native`. Produces code that performs best on the host system. GCC does not have the direct equivalent, but you can use `-mcpu` to specify the type of your host system.

Sun Studio 10	GNU GCC 3.4.2	Description
`-nofstore`	Implicit	Has the opposite effect of `-fstore`. GCC has the option `-ffloat-store`, which has the opposite meaning of `-nofstore`.
`-O`	`-O3`	Uses default optimization level `-xO3`.
`-o` *`filename`*	`-o` *`filename`*	Assigns the name *filename* to the output file.
`-P`	`-E`	Runs the source file through the C preprocessor only. This option does not include preprocessor-type line number information in the output.
`-p`	`-p`	Generates extra code to write profile information suitable for the analysis program `prof`.
`-Q[y|n]`	`-Q`	Emits or does not emit identification information to the output file. GCC only has `-Q`.
`-qp`	`-p`	Same as `-p`.
`-R`*`dir[:dir]`*	`-wl,-rpath` *`dir`*	Passes a colon-separated list of directories used to specify library search directories to the runtime linker.
`-S`	`-S`	Directs `cc` to produce an assembly source file but not to assemble the program.
`-s`	`-s`	Removes all symbolic debugging information from the output object file. Passed to `ld`.
`-U`*`name`*	`-U`*`name`*	Undefines the preprocessor symbol *`name`*.
`-V`	`-v, --version`	Prints the name and version ID of each component as the compiler executes.
`-v`	`-Wall`	Directs the compiler to perform stricter semantic checks and to enable other lint-like checks.

Sun Studio 10	GNU GCC 3.4.2	Description
`-Wc,arg`	`-Wc,arg`	Passes the argument `arg` to a specified tool `c`. This option is available on GCC in the same format, but not all tools are supported by `gcc`. The tools that have equivalents in GCC are Assembler, Linker, and Preprocessor.
`-w`	`-w`	Suppresses compiler warning messages.
`-X[c|a|t|s]`	N/A	Specifies varying degrees of compliance to the ISO C standard. There is no exact match in GCC, but the `-pedantic` option issues all the warnings demanded by strict ISO C and ISO C++.
`-x386`	`-mcpu=i386`, `-march=i386`	Obsolete. Use `-xchip=generic`.
`-x486`	`-mcpu=i486`, `-march=i486`	Obsolete. Use `-xchip=generic`.
`-xa`	`-fprofile-arcs` `-ftest-coverage`	Obsolete. Use `-xprofile=tcov`.
`-xalias_level [=l]`	N/A	The compiler uses this option to determine what assumptions it can make to perform optimizations using type-based alias analysis.
`-xarch=isa`	`-march=isa`	Specifies instruction set architecture.
`-xautopar`	N/A	Turns on automatic parallelization for multiple processors.
`-xbuiltin [=(%all| %none)]`	N/A	Substitutes intrinsic functions or inline system functions where profitable for performance.
`-xCC`	N/A	When `-xc99=none` and `-xCC` are specified, the compiler accepts the C++-style comments.

Sun Studio 10	GNU GCC 3.4.2	Description
`-xc99[=o]`	N/A	Controls compiler recognition of the implemented features from the C99 standard. There is no exact match in GCC, but the option `-std=c99` is available.
`-xcache[=c]`	N/A	Defines the cache properties for use by the optimizer.
`-xchar[=o]`	`-funsigned-char` or `-fsigned-char`	Treats the char type as signed or unsigned.
`-xchar_byte_order[=o]`	N/A	Produces an integer constant by placing the characters of a multicharacter character-constant in the specified byte order.
`-xcheck[=o]`	N/A	Adds a runtime check for stack overflow.
`-xchip[=c]`	`-march`	Specifies the target processor for use by the optimizer.
`-xcode[=v]`	N/A	Specifies code address space. There is no exact match in GCC. However, `-xcode=pic13` is equivalent to `-fpic`. `-xcode=pic32` is equivalent to `-fPIC`.
`-xcrossfile[=n]`	`-funit-at-a-time`	Enables optimization and inlining across source files.
`-xcsi`	N/A	Allows the C compiler to accept source code written in locales that do not conform to the ISO C source character code requirements.
`-xdebugformat =[stabs|dwarf]`	`-gstabs`, `-gstab+`, `-gdwarf-2`, `-ggdb`	Allows the C compiler to choose the formats of debugger information.
`-xdepend= [yes|no]`	`-floop-optimize`, `-falign-loops`	Analyzes loops for inter-iteration data dependencies and does loop restructuring.
`-xdryrun`	`-###`	Macro for `-###`.
`-xe`	`-fsyntax-only`	Checks syntax and semantic on the source file, but does not produce any object or executable code.

Sun Studio 10	GNU GCC 3.4.2	Description
`-xexplicitpar`	N/A	Generates parallelized code based on specification of `#pragma` MP directives.
`-xF`	`-freorder-functions`, `-freorder-blocks`, `-freorder-blocks -and-partition`	Enables optimal reordering of functions and variables by the linker.
`-xhelp=`*`f`*	`--help -v`	Displays online help information.
`-xhwcprof`	N/A	Enables compiler support for hardware counter-based profiling.
`-xildoff`	N/A	Turns off the incremental linker and forces the use of `ld`.
`-xildon`	N/A	Turns on the incremental linker and forces the use of `ild` in incremental mode.
`-xinline=`*`list`*	N/A	Attempts to inline only those functions specified in the optional *`list`*.
`-xipo[=a]`	`-funit-at-a-time`	With `-xipo=1`, the compiler performs inlining across all source files. With `-xipo=2`, the compiler performs interprocedural aliasing analysis and optimizations of memory allocation and layout to improve cache performance.
`-xipo_archive=[a]`	N/A	Enables the compiler to optimize object files that are passed to the linker with object files that were compiled with `-xipo` and that reside in the archive `library(.a)` before producing an executable.
`-xjobs=n`	N/A	Sets how many processes the compiler creates to complete its work.
`-xldscope={v}`	N/A	Changes the default linker scoping for the definition of extern symbols.
`-xlibmieee`	N/A	Forces IEEE 754-style return values for math routines in exceptional cases.

Sun Studio 10	GNU GCC 3.4.2	Description
`-xlibmil`	N/A	Inlines some library routines for faster execution.
`-xlibmopt`	N/A	Enables the compiler to use a library of optimized math routines.
`-xlic_lib= sunperf`	N/A	Links in the Sun-supplied performance libraries.
`-xlicinfo`	N/A	Returns information about the licensing system.
`-xlinkopt [=level]`	N/A	Instructs the compiler to perform link-time optimizations on relocatable object files.
`-xloopinfo`	N/A	Shows information about loops that are parallelized.
`-xM`	`-M`	Displays makefile dependencies.
`-xM1`	(`-MM`)	Shows dependencies such as `-xM`, but excludes /usr/include files. The option `-MM` does something similar for GCC, but GCC avoids dependencies for files from the system directories, or header files that are included, directly or indirectly, from such a header.
`-xMerge`	N/A	Merges data segments into text segments.
`xmaxopt[-v]`	N/A	Limits the level of `pragma opt` to the level specified.
`-xmemalign=`*`ab`*	N/A	Specifies max assumed memory alignment and behavior of misaligned data accesses. GCC does not have the exact match, but has multiple options regarding memory alignment for various supported platforms. For i386 and x86-64, GCC provides, for example, `-malign-double`, `-m96bit-long-double`, `m128bit-long-double`, `mpreferred-stack-boundary=`*`num`*.

Sun Studio 10	GNU GCC 3.4.2	Description
`-xnativeconnect =v`	N/A	Enables the shared library to interface with Java code.
`-xnolib`	`-nostdlib`	Does not link any libraries by default.
`-xnolibmil`	N/A	Does not inline math library routines. GCC does not have the exact match, but there are `-fno-default-inline` and `-fno-inline`.
`-xnolibmopt`	N/A	Prevents the use of an optimized math library by the compiler.
`-xO[1|2|3|4|5]`	`-O1`, `-O2`, `-O3`	Selects the optimization levels. GCC does not have the fourth and fifth optimization levels.
`-xopenmp[=i]`	N/A	Enables explicit parallelization with OpenMP directives. The implementation of OpenMP for GNU C, C++, and FORTRAN compilers is under development.
`-xP`	N/A	Prints prototypes for all K&R C functions.
`-xpagesize=n`	N/A	Sets the preferred page size for the stack and the heap.
`-xpagesize_heap=n`	N/A	Sets the page size in memory for the heap.
`-xpagesize_stack=n`	N/A	Sets the page size in memory for the stack.
`-xparallel`	N/A	A macro equivalent to `-xautopar`, `-xdepend`, `-xexplicitpar`.
`-xpch=v`	Default	Activates the precompiled header feature. To create a precompiled header file with GCC, you simply have to compile it as you would any other file. GCC will search for the precompiled header with .gch appended.

Sun Studio 10	GNU GCC 3.4.2	Description
-xpchstop= *[file|<include>]*	N/A	Specifies the last include file of the viable prefix for the precompiled header file.
-xpentium	-mtune=*cpu-type*	Generates code for the Pentium processor.
-xpg	-pg	Prepares the object code to collect data for profiling with gprof.
-xprefetch [=val[,val]]	N/A	Enables prefetch instructions on those architectures that support prefetch.
-xprefetch_auto _type=a	N/A	Determines whether the compiler generates indirect prefetches for the loops indicated by the option -xprefetch_level in the same fashion the prefetches for direct memory accesses are generated.
-xprefetch_ level=l	N/A	Controls the aggressiveness of automatic insert of prefetch instructions as determined with -xprefetch=auto.
-xprofile= collect	-fprofile-generate	Collects and saves execution-frequency data to use in subsequent runs to improve performance.
-xprofile=use	-fprofile-use	Uses the execution-frequency data generated and saved from a previous execution.
-xprofile=tcov	-fprofile-arcs -ftest-coverage	Emits information for the tcov tool. On Linux, use GNU version gcov to process the output.
-xprofile_ ircache [=path]	N/A	Improves compilation time during the *use* phase.
-xprofile_ pathmap	N/A	Locates profile data for an object file that is compiled with -xprofile=use.
-xreduction	N/A	Turns on reduction recognition during automatic parallelization.
-xregs=r[,r ...]	-ffixed-*reg* -fcall-used-*reg* -fcall-saved-*reg*	Specifies the usage of registers for the generated code.

Sun Studio 10	GNU GCC 3.4.2	Description

`-xrestrict[=f]`	`-fargument-alias`
	`-fargument-noalias`
	`-fargument-noalias-global`
		Treats pointer-valued function parameters as restricted pointers. Note that GCC recognizes the ISO C99 keyword *`restrict`* and performs appropriate optimizations.

`-xs`	N/A	Allows debugging by `dbx` without object files. This option causes all the debug information to be copied into the executable.
`-xsafe=mem`	N/A	Grants permission to use the speculative load instruction. The i386 processors do not provide such a feature.
`-xsb`	N/A	Creates extra symbol information for the source browser. This is specific to Sun's IDE.
`-xsbfast`	N/A	Creates the database for the source browser.
`-xsfpconst`	(`-fshort-double`)	Represents unsuffixed floating-point constants as single precision, instead of the default mode of double precision. GCC does not have the exact match, but `-fshort-double` makes double and float the same size.
`-xspace`	`-Os`	Does no optimizations or parallelization of loops that increase code size.
`-xstrconst`	Default	Inserts string literals into the read-only data section of the text segment instead of the default data segment. This is the default with GCC. To get the default behavior of the Sun compiler, use `-fwritable-strings`.
`-xtarget=t`	`-march=`*`cpu_type`* `-mtune=`*`cpu_type`*	Specifies the target system for instruction set and optimization.
`-xtemp=dir`	N/A	Sets the directory for temporary files used by the compiler. GCC uses the environment variable `TMPDIR` to set the directory name for temporary files.

Sun Studio 10	GNU GCC 3.4.2	Description
`-xthreadvar[=o]`	N/A (see comments)	Controls the implementation of thread local variables. GCC supports thread-local storage using keyword `__thread`.
`-xtime`	`-Q`, `-ftime-report`	Reports the time and resources used by each compilation component.
`-xtransition`	N/A	Issues a warning for the differences between K&R C and Sun ISO C.
`-xtrigraphs`	`-trigraphs`	Determines whether the compiler recognizes trigraph sequences as defined by the ISO C standard.
`-xunroll=`*n*	`-funroll-loops` `-funroll-all-loops` `-floop-optimize`	Suggests to the optimizer to unroll loops *n* times.
`-xustr=`*charset*	`-fexec-charset=`*s* `-fwide-exec-charset=`*s* `-finput-charset=`*s*	Supports an internationalized application that uses ISO10646 UTF-16 string literals.
`-xvector [={yes|no}]`	`-maltivec`	Enables automatic generation of calls to the vector library functions. On a PowerPC platform, GCC supports the Altivec instruction set with the option `-maltivec`.
`-xvis`	N/A	Enables the assembly language templates defined in the VIS instruction set software developer kit. This is Sun's specific feature.
`-xvpara`	N/A	Warns about loops that have `#pragma MP` directives specified when the loop may not be parallelization.
`-Y`*c*`,` *dir*	N/A	Specifies a new directory *dir* for the location of component *c*. *c* can consist of any of the characters representing components that are listed under the `-W` option.
`-YA,` *dir*	`-B`*prefix*	Specifies a directory *dir* to search for all compiler components.

Sun Studio 10	GNU GCC 3.4.2	Description
`-YI,` *`dir`*	`-I`*`dir`* `-I-`	Changes the default directory searched for include files.
`-YP,` *`dir`*	`-L`*`dir`*	Changes the default directory for finding library files.
`-YS,` *`dir`*	`-B`	Changes the default directory for startup object files.
`-Zll`	N/A	Creates the program database for `lock_lint`, but does not generate executable code.

4.3.3 C++ Compiler Options

Table 4-3 compares Sun Studio 10's C++ options and G++ 3.4.2's C++ options.

TABLE 4-3
C++ Compiler Options Comparison

Sun Studio 10 C++	GCC C++ 3.4.2	Description[7]
`-386`	`-march=i386`	Same as `-xtarget=386`.
`-486`	`-march=i486`	Same as `-xtarget=486`.
`-a`	N/A	Same as `-xa`.

`-B`*`binding`*	`-Wl,-Bstatic`
	`-Wl,-dn`
	`-Wl,-non-shared`
	`-Wl,-static`
		Specifies whether a library binding for linking is symbolic, dynamic (shared), or static (nonshared).

`-cg{89|92}`	N/A	Same as `-xcg{89|92}`.
`-compat[={4|5}]`	N/A	Sets the major release compatibility mode of the compiler.
`+d`	`-fno-default-inline`	Prevents expansion of C++ inline functions.

7 This description is based on Sun Studio 10 C++ users guide unless otherwise stated.

Sun Studio 10 C++	GCC C++ 3.4.2	Description
`-d{y|n}`	`-Wl,-Bstatic` `-Wl,-static`	Specifies dynamic linking (default) or static linking.
`-dalign`	Several align options available; refer to the GNU GCC manual.[8]	Controls the assumptions the compiler makes about the alignment of data.
`-dryrun`	`-###`	Prints options passed but does not compile.
`+e{0|1}`	N/A	Controls virtual table generation.
`-erroff[=t]`	See `-W` option in GNU GCC for requesting or suppressing warnings.	Suppresses C++ compiler warning messages and has no effect on error messages.
`-errtags[=a]`	See `-W` option in GNU GCC for requesting or suppressing warnings.	Displays the message tag for each warning message of the C++ compiler front end that can be suppressed.
`-errwarn[=t]`	See `-pedantic` option in GNU GCC for requesting or suppressing warnings.	Causes the C++ compiler to exit with a failure status for the given warning messages.
`-fast`	`-Ox`	A starting point for tuning an executable for maximum runtime performance.
`-features=a [,a...]`	N/A	Enables/disables various C++ language features named in a comma-separated list.
`-filt[=filter [,filter..]]`	N/A	Controls the filtering that the compiler normally applies to linker and compiler error messages.
`-flags`	`--help`	Displays a brief description of each compiler option.

8 http://gcc.gnu.org/onlinedocs/

Sun Studio 10 C++	GCC C++ 3.4.2	Description
`-fnonstd`	N/A	Causes hardware traps to be enabled for floating-point overflow, division by 0, and invalid operations exceptions.
`-fns[={yes|no}]`	N/A	Turns on SPARC nonstandard floating-point mode.
`-fprecision=p`	`-fsingle -precision -constant` (see comment)	Initializes the rounding-precision mode bits in the floating-point Control Word to single, double, or extended. GCC does not have a direct equivalent, but `-fsingle-precision-constant` forces the compiler to treat floating-point constant as single precision instead of convert-converting it to double precision constant.
`-fround=r`	`-frounding-math` (see comment)	Sets the IEEE 754 rounding mode. The default IEEE mode is round-to-nearest. This is also the case on Linux, but there is no option to select mode. Consider `-frounding-math` in GCC.
`-fsimple[=n]`	N/A	Allows the optimizer to make simplifying assumptions about floating-point arithmetic. GCC does not have the exact match. Consider these flags for floating-point optimizations not compliant with IEEE or ISO: `-ffloat-store`, `-ffast-math`, `-fno-math-error`, `-funsafe-math-optimizations`, `-ffinite-math-only`, `-fno-trapping-math`.
`-fstore`	`-ffloat-store`	Causes floating-point variables not to be stored in registers.
`-ftrap=t[,t...]`	`-fno-trapping -math` (see comment)	Sets the IEEE trapping mode in effect at startup but does not install a SIGFPE handler. GCC does not have the direct equivalent, but `-fno-trapping-math` disables all user-visible traps, including division by 0, overflow, underflow, inexact result, and invalid operation.

Sun Studio 10 C++	GCC C++ 3.4.2	Description
`-G`	`-Wl,-shared`	Builds a dynamic shared library instead of an executable file.
`-g`	`-g`	Generates debug info, disables inlining.
`-g0`	N/A	Generates debug info, does not disable inlining.
`-H`	`-H`	Prints to standard error the path name of each file included during the compilation.
`-h[ ]`*`name`*	`-h`*`name`*`,` `-Wl,-soname,` *`name`*	Gives a name to a shared dynamic library to have different versions of a library.
`-help`	`--help -v`	Displays online help information.
`-I-`	`-I-`	Changes the include file search rules.
`-i`	N/A	Ignores any `LD_LIBRARY_PATH` setting.
`-inline`	N/A	Same as `-xinline`. Attempts to inline only those specified functions.
`-instances=a`	`-fno-implicit-templates,` `-fno-implicit-inline-templates,` `-frepo`	Controls the placement and linkage of template instances.
`-instlib=`*`filename`*	N/A	Inhibits the generation of template instances that are duplicated in a library.
`-KPIC`	`-fPIC`	Generates position-independent code (large model).
`-Kpic`	`-fpic`	Generates position-independent code (small model).
`-keeptmp`	`-save-temps`	Keeps temporary files created during compilation.
`-libmieee`	N/A	Same as `-xlibmieee`. Forces IEEE 754-style return values for math routines in exceptional cases.
`-libmil`	N/A	Same as `-xlibmil`. Inlines some library routines for faster execution.

Sun Studio 10 C++	GCC C++ 3.4.2	Description
`-library=`*`l[,l...]`*	`-nodefaultlibs`, `-nostdlib` (see comment)	Incorporates specified CC-provided libraries into compilation and linking.
`-mc`	N/A	Removes duplicate strings from the `.comment` section of the object file.
`-migration`	N/A	Explains where to get information about migrating source code that was built for earlier versions of the compiler.
`-misalign`	`(implicit)` (see comment)	Assumes only byte alignment. This option is not necessary for the IA-32 because the processor handles alignment by itself.
`-mr[,`*`string`*`]`	N/A	Removes all strings from the `.comment` section of the object file and, if string is supplied, places string in that section.
`-mt`	`-D_REENTRANT` `-pthread`	Compiles and links for multithreaded code. On Linux, `-pthread` adds support for multithreading with the pthreads library.
`-native`	`-march=`*`cpu-type`*	Optimizes code using host-specific code.
`-noex`	`-fno-enforce -eh-specs` (see comment)	Same as `-features=no%except`. Does not allow C++ exceptions. `g++` does not have the exact match, but consider `-fno-enforce-eh-specs`.
`-nofstore`	`(implicit)` (see comment)	Disables forced precision of an expression. GCC has the option `-ffloat-store`, which has the opposite meaning of `-nofstore`.
`-nolib`	`-nostdlib`	Same as `-xnolib`. Disables linking with default system libraries.
`-nolibmil`	N/A (see comment)	Same as `-xnolibmil`. Cancels `-xlibmil` on the command line. GCC does not have the exact match, but there are `-fno-default-inline` and `-fno-inline`.

Sun Studio 10 C++	GCC C++ 3.4.2	Description
-noqueue	N/A (see comment)	Disables license queuing. This is not necessary for GCC.
-norunpath	N/A (see comment)	Does not build a runtime search path for shared libraries into the executable. In Linux, if -rpath is not used when building an executable, the variable LD_RUN_PATH will be used if it is defined.
-O	-O3	The macro expanding to -xO3.
-O*level*	-O*level*	Optimizes to yield higher application performance.
-o *filename*	-o *filename*	Sets the name of the output file or the executable file to *filename*.
+p	N/A	Ignores nonstandard preprocessor asserts.
-P	-E	Only preprocesses source; does not compile.
-p	-p	Prepares object code to collect data for profiling with prof.
-pentium	-march=*cpu-type*	Replace with -xtarget=Pentium.
-pg	-pg	Compiles self-profiling code to collect data for profiling with gprof.
-PIC	-fPIC	Generates position-independent code (large model).
-pic	-fpic	Generates position-independent code (small model).
-pta	See comment	Same as -template=wholeclass. Instantiates a whole template class, rather than only those functions that are used.
-pti*path*	N/A	Specifies an additional search directory for template source.
-pto	See comment	Same as -instances=static. This option is already deprecated.
-ptr	See comment	Obsolete. Ignored by the compiler.

Sun Studio 10 C++	GCC C++ 3.4.2	Description
`-ptv`	N/A	Same as `-verbose=template`. Turns on the template instantiation verbose mode.
`-Qoption`	N/A	Passes option to the compilation phase.
`-qoption`	N/A	Same as `-Qoption`.
`-qp`	`-p/-profile`	Same as `-p`.
`-Qproduce` *`sourcetype`*	`-E, -c, -S`	Causes the CC driver to produce output of the type *sourcetype* (.i, .o, .s).
`-qproduce` *`sourcetype`*	`-E, -c, -S`	Same as `-Qproduce`.
`-R`*`pathname`* `[:`*`pathname...`*`]`	`-Wl, -rpath`	Builds dynamic library search paths into the executable file. This option is passed to `ld`.
`-readme`	N/A	Same as `-xhelp=readme`.
`-S`	`-S`	Compiles and generates only assembly code.
`-s`	-s	Strips the symbol table from the executable file.
`-sb`	N/A	Replace with `-xsb`. Creates extra symbol for the source browser. This is specific to Sun's IDE.
`-sbfast`	N/A	Same as `-xsbfast`. Produces only source browser info; no compilation.
`-staticlib=`*`l`* `[,`*`l...`*`]`	`-static` (see comment)	Indicates which C++ libraries are to be linked statically. There is no exact match in `g++`, but there is `-static`, which is equivalent to `-staticlib=all`.
`-sync_stdio=` `[yes|no]`	N/A	Turn on/off the synchronization between `iostreams` and `stdio`.
`-temp=`*`path`*	`-save-temps`	Defines the directory for temporary files.
`-template=`*`opt`* `[,`*`opt...`*`]`	N/A (see comment)	Enables/disables various template options. There is no exact match in `g++`, but there are `-frepo`, `-fno-implicit-templates`.

Sun Studio 10 C++	GCC C++ 3.4.2	Description
`-time`	`-Q`, `-ftime-report`	Reports the time and resources used by each compilation component.
`-U`*`name`*	`-U`*`name`*	Deletes initial definition of the preprocessor symbol *`name`*.
`-unroll=`*`n`*	`-funroll-loops` (see comment)	Same as `-xunroll=`*`n`*. Unrolls loop *n* times. `g++` has no exact match, but there is `-funroll-loops`.
`-V`	`--version`	Same as `-verbose=version`. Prints the name and version number.
`-v`	`-v`	Same as `-verbose=diags`. Prints the command line for each compilation pass.
`-vdelx`	N/A	Generates a call to `_vector_deletex_` instead of `_vector_delete_`. This option is deprecated.
`-verbose=`*`v`*`[,`*`v`*`...]`	`--version`, `-v`	Controls compiler verbosity. `g++` does not have the exact match, but `-v` and `--version` partially give the same functionality.
`+w`	`-Wabi`, `-Wctor-dtor-privacy`, `-Wnon-virtual-dtor`, `...` (see comments)	Identifies code that might have unintended consequences. `g++` provides various options for warning specifically for C++.
`+w2`	See comment	Emits warnings by `+w` plus warning about technical violation that reduces portability. See comments in `+w` for `g++`.
`-w`	`-w`	Suppresses most warning messages.
`-Xm`	N/A	Same as `-features=iddollar`. Allow a $ symbol as a noninitial identifier character.
`-xa`	`-fprofile-arcs` `-ftest-coverage`	Emits information for `tcov` tool. On Linux, use GNU version `gcov` to process the output.

Sun Studio 10 C++	GCC C++ 3.4.2	Description
`-xalias_level[=n]`	N/A	Compiler uses this option to determine what assumptions it can make to perform optimizations using type-based alias analysis.
`-xar`	N/A	Creates archive libraries.
`-xarch=isa`	`-march=isa`	Specifies the target instruction set architecture.
`-xautopar`	N/A	Turns on automatic parallelization for multiple processors.
`-xbuiltin [={%all | %none}]`	N/A	Substitutes intrinsic functions or inline system functions where profitable for performance.
`-xcache=c`	N/A	Defines the cache properties for use by the optimizer.
`-xcg89`	N/A	Same as `-xtarget=ss2`.
`-xcg92`	N/A	Same as `-xtarget=ss1000`.
`-xchar[=o]`	`-funsigned-char` or `-fsigned-char`	Treats the char type as signed or unsigned.
`-xcheck[=i]`	N/A	Adds a runtime check for stack overflow.
`-xchip=c`	`-march`	Specifies the target processor for use by the optimizer.
`-xcode=a`	N/A	Specifies code address space. There is no exact match in GCC. However, `-xcode=pic13` is equivalent to `-fpic`. `-xcode=pic32` is equivalent to `-fPIC`.
`-xcrossfile[=n]`	`-funit-at-a-time`	Enables optimization and inlining across source files.
`-xdepend=[yes|no]`	`-floop-optimize`, `-falign-loops`	Analyzes loops for inter-iteration data dependencies and does loop restructuring.
`-xdumpmacros [=value [,value...]]`	`-gvms3`, `-dD`	Provides information such as macro defines, undefines, and instances of usage.

Sun Studio 10 C++	GCC C++ 3.4.2	Description
`-xe`	`-fsyntax-only`	Checks syntax and semantic on the source file, but does not produce any object or executable code.
`-xF[=v[,v...]]`	N/A	Enables optimal reordering of functions and variables by the linker.
`-xhelp=flags`	`--help -v`	Displays online help information.
`-xhelp=readme`	N/A	Displays contents of the online readme file.
`-xia`	N/A	Links the appropriate interval arithmetic libraries and sets a suitable floating-point environment.
`-xildoff`	N/A	Turns the incremental linker off.
`-xildon`	N/A	Turns the incremental linker on.
`-xinline [=func_spec [,func_spec...]]`	N/A	Specifies which user-written routines can be inlined by the optimizer at `-x03` levels or higher.
`-xipo[={0|1|2}]`	`-funit-at-a-time`	Performs interprocedural optimizations.
`-xjobs=n`	N/A	Sets how many processes the compiler creates to complete its work.
`-xlang= [language [,language]]`	N/A	Includes the appropriate runtime libraries and ensures the proper runtime environment for the specified language.
`-xldscope={v}`	N/A	Changes the default linker scoping for the definition of extern symbols.
`-xlibmieee`	N/A	Forces IEEE 754-style return values for math routines in exceptional cases.
`-xlibmil`	N/A	Inlines some library routines for faster execution.
`-xlibmopt`	N/A	Enables the compiler to use a library of optimized math routines.
`-xlic_lib=sunperf`	N/A	Links in the Sun-supplied performance libraries.

Sun Studio 10 C++	GCC C++ 3.4.2	Description
`-xlicinfo`	N/A	Returns information about the licensing system.
`-xlinkopt[=level]`	N/A	Instructs the compiler to perform link-time optimizations on relocatable object files.
`-xM`	`-M`	Displays makefile dependencies.
`-xM1`	`-MM` (see comment)	Shows dependencies like `-xM`, but excludes /usr/include files. The option `-MM` does something similar for GCC, but GCC avoids dependencies for files from the system directories, or header files that are included, directly or indirectly, from such a header.
`-xMerge`	N/A	Merges data segments into text segments.
`-xmaxopt[=v]`	N/A	Limits the level of `pragma opt` to the level specified.
`-xmemalign=ab`	N/A	Specifies max assumed memory alignment and behavior of misaligned data accesses.
`-xnativeconnect [=i]`	N/A	Enables the shared library to interface with Java code.
`-xnolib`	`-nostdlib`	Does not link any default libraries.
`-xnolibmil`	N/A	Does not inline math library routines. GCC does not have the exact match, but there are `-fno-default-inline` and `-fno-inline`.
`-xnolibmopt`	N/A	Prevents the use of an optimized math library by the compiler.
`-xOlevel`	`-O1`, `-O2`, `-O3`	Selects the optimization levels. GCC does not have the fourth and fifth optimization levels.

Sun Studio 10 C++	GCC C++ 3.4.2	Description
`-xopenmp[=i]`	N/A	Enables explicit parallelization with OpenMP directives. The implementation of OpenMP for GNU C, C++, and FORTRAN compilers is under development.
`-xpagesize=n`	N/A	Sets the preferred page size for the stack and the heap.
`-xpagesize_heap=n`	N/A	Sets the page size in memory for the heap.
`-xpagesize_stack=n`	N/A	Sets the page size in memory for the stack.
`-xpch=v`	Default (see comment)	Activates the precompiled header feature. To create a precompiled header file with GCC, you simply have to compile it as you would with any other file. GCC will search for the precompiled header with .gch appended.
`-xpchstop=file`	N/A	Specifies the last include file of the viable prefix for the precompiled header file.
`-xpg`	`-pg`	Prepares the object code to collect data for profiling with `gprof`.
`-xport64[=(v)]`	N/A	Warns against problems common when code is ported from 32-bit to 64-bit architecture.
`-xprefetch [=a[,a...]]`	N/A	Enables prefetch instructions on those architectures that support prefetch.
`-xprefetch _auto_type=a`	N/A	Determines whether the compiler generates indirect prefetches for the loops indicated by the option `-xprefetch_level` in the same fashion the prefetches for direct memory accesses are generated.
`-xprefetch _level[=i]`	N/A	Controls the aggressiveness of automatic insert of prefetch instructions as determined with `-xprefetch=auto`.

Sun Studio 10 C++	GCC C++ 3.4.2	Description
`-xprofile=collect`	`-fprofile -generate`	Collects and saves execution-frequency data to use in subsequent runs to improve performance.
`-xprofile=use`	`-fprofile-use`	Uses the execution-frequency data generated and saved from a previous execution.
`-xprofile _ircache[=`*`path`*`]`	N/A	Improves compilation time during the `use` phase.
`-xprofile_pathmap`	N/A	Locates profile data for an object file that is compiled with `-xprofile=use`.
`-xregs=`*`r`*`[, `*`r`*` ...]`	`-ffixed-`*`reg`* `-fcall-used-`*`reg`* `-fcall-saved-`*`reg`*	Specifies the usage of registers for the generated code.

`-xrestrict[=`*`t`*`]`	`-fargument-alias`
	`-fargument-noalias`
	`-fargument -noalias-global`
		Treats pointer-valued function parameters as restricted pointers. Note that GCC recognizes the ISO C99 keyword `restrict` and performs appropriate optimizations.

`-xs`	N/A	Allows debugging by `dbx` without object files. This option causes all the debug information to be copied into the executable.
`-xsafe=mem`	N/A	Grants permission to use the speculative load instruction. The i386 processors do not provide such a feature.
`-xsb`	N/A	Creates extra symbol information for the source browser. This is specific to Sun's IDE.
`-xsbfast`	N/A	Creates the database for the source browser.
`-xspace`	`-Os`	Does no optimizations or parallelization of loops that increase code size.
`-xtarget=`*`t`*	`-march=`*`cpu-type`* `-mtune=`*`cpu-type`*	Specifies the target platform for instruction set and optimization.

Sun Studio 10 C++	GCC C++ 3.4.2	Description
`-xthreadvar[=o]`	N/A (see comment)	Controls the implementation of thread local variables. GCC supports thread-local storage using keyword `__thread`.
`-xtime`	`-Q`, `-ftime-report`	Reports the time and resources used by each compilation component.
`-xtrigraphs [={yes|no}]`	`-trigraphs`	Determines whether the compiler recognizes trigraph sequences as defined by the ISO C standard.
`-xunroll=n`	`-funroll-loops` `-funroll-all-loops` `-floop-optimize` (see comment)	Suggests to the optimizer to unroll loops *n* times. G++ does not have the exact match, but there are `-funroll-loops`, `-funroll-all-loops`, `-floop-optimize`.
`-xustr={ascii_utf16_ushort|no}`	`-fexec-charset=s` `-fwide-exec-charset=s` `-finput-charset=s`	Supports an internationalized application that uses ISO10646 UTF-16 string literals.
`-xvector [={yes|no}]`	`-maltivec` (see comment)	Enables automatic generation of calls to the vector library functions. On a PowerPC platform, GCC supports the Altivec instruction set with the option `-maltivec`.
`-xvis[={yes|no}]`	N/A	Enables the assembly language templates defined in the VIS instruction set software developer kit. This is Sun's specific feature.
`-xwe`	`-pedantic-errors`	Converts warnings to errors.
`-Yc,path`	N/A	Specifies a new directory `dir` for the location of component `c`. `c` can consist of any of the characters representing components that are listed under the `-W` option.
`-z[ ]arg`	`-Wl, option`, `-Xlinker option`	Link editor option.

4.3.4 Template Instantiation in GNU g++

According to the document "Using the GNU Compiler Collection,"[9] the GNU `g++` compiler provides two automated approaches to template instantiation—the Borland or Cfront model. When used with GNU `ld` version 2.8 or later on an ELF system such as GNU/Linux or Solaris, `g++` supports the Borland model. On other systems, `g++` implements neither automatic instantiation approach. For all applications that use template instantiation, the best approach is to modify the code to include template definitions to make them available at one or more points of instantiation; usually this is a simple as adding `#include <temp_methods.c>` to the end of each template header.

Example 4-1 shows a sample code using this method.

Example 4-1

Template Instantiation in GNU G++

main.C

```
#include "stack.h"

int
main()
{
    Stack<int, 60> s;
    int j;
    int i;

    s >> j;
    s << j;
    i = j;
    return (0);
}
```

stack.h

```
#ifndef STACK_INCLUDED
#define STACK_INCLUDED

typedef enum{tr, fl} Bool;
```

9 http://gcc.gnu.org/onlinedocs/gcc-3.4.4/gcc/Template-Instantiation.html#Template-Instantiation

```
template<class Item, int size> class Stack {
    public:
        int operator << (Item item);
        int operator >> (Item& item);
        Stack(Bool p=fl) {top = 0;}
    private:
        Item stack[size];
        int top;
};

#endif /* STACK_INCLUDED */
```

stack.C

```
#include "stack.h"

template<class Item, int size>
int Stack<Item, size>::operator << (Item item) {
    if (top >= size) return 0;
    stack[top++] = item;
    return 1;
}

template <class Item, int size>
int Stack<Item, size>::operator >> (Item& item)
{
    if(top<=0) return 0;
    item = stack[--top];
    return 1;
}
```

When compiled with the Sun Studio's CC compiler, the files main.C, stack.C, and stack.h produce an executable without any error:

```
$ CC -o main main.C
$ ./main
```

When compiled on Linux using g++, it results in the following compiler error:

```
$ g++ -o main main.C
/tmp/ccicEJmr.o(.text+0x45): In function `main':
: undefined reference to `Stack<int, 60>::operator>>(int&)'
/tmp/ccicEJmr.o(.text+0x5d): In function `main':
: undefined reference to `Stack<int, 60>::operator<<(int)'
collect2: ld returned 1 exit status
```

The preceding g++ compiler error is corrected by modifying stack.h to include stack.C, as in the following code listing:

```
#ifndef STACK_INCLUDED
#define STACK_INCLUDED

typedef enum{tr, fl} Bool;

template<class Item, int size> class Stack {
    public:
        int operator << (Item item);
        int operator >> (Item& item);
        Stack(Bool p=fl) {top = 0;}
    private:
        Item stack[size];
        int top;
};

#include "stack.C"              /* include stack.C */

#endif /* STACK_INCLUDED */
```

Then compile with g++:

```
$ g++ -o main main.C
```

4.3.5 Building 32- or 64-bit Objects

To build a 64-bit object in GCC, use the compiler flag -m64. On the IA-32 platform, GCC produces the 32-bit objects by default. For other platforms, use the -m32 flag to instruct GCC to build the 32-bit object.

4.3.6 Compiler Optimization and Performance Options

Table 4-4 compares compiler optimization and performance options between Solaris and Linux.

TABLE 4-4
Compiler Optimization—Levels and Descriptions

Solaris Level	Solaris Description[10]	GCC Level	GCC Description[11]
`-xO1`	Performs basic local optimization.	`-O` or `-O1`	Tries to reduce code size and execution time, without performing any optimizations that take a great deal of compilation time.
`-xO2`	Does basic local and global optimization. The `-xO2` level does not assign global, external, or indirect references or definitions to registers. It treats these references and definitions as if they were declared `volatile`. In general, the `-xO2` level results in minimum code size.	`-O2`	Performs nearly all supported optimizations that do not involve a space-speed trade-off. The compiler does not perform loop unrolling or function inlining when you specify `-O2`. As compared to `-O`, this option increases both compilation time and the performance of the generated code.
`-xO3` (`-O`)	Performs like `-xO2`, but also optimizes reference or definition for external variables.	`-O3`	Turns on all optimizations specified by `-O2` and also turns on the `-finline-functions`, `-fweb`, and `-frename-registers` options.
`-xO4`	Performs like `-xO3`, but also automatically inline functions contained in the same file.	N/A	N/A
`-xO5`	Attempts to generate the highest level of optimization.	N/A	N/A

10 Sun Studio 10: User's Guide

11 GCC 3.4.2 manual

4.3.7 Name Space Selection on Linux Platform

Linux header files and libraries offer support for several name spaces. They are described in Table 4-5.

TABLE 4-5
Linux Name Space Table

Linux Definitions[12]	Description
`__STRICT_ANSI__`	ISO Standard C.
`_ISOC99_SOURCE`	Extensions to ISO C89 from ISO C99.
`_POSIX_SOURCE`	IEEE Std 1003.1.

`_POSIX_C_SOURCE`	If ==1, like _POSIX_SOURCE;
	if >=2, add IEEE Std 1003.2;
	if >=199309L, add IEEE Std 1003.1b-1993;
	if >=199506L, add IEEE Std 1003.1c-1995;
	if >=200112L, all of IEEE 1003.1-2001.

`_XOPEN_SOURCE`	Includes POSIX and XPG things. Set to 500 if Single UNIX Specification version 2 onformance is wanted, to 600 for the SUSv3.
`_XOPEN_SOURCE_EXTENDED`	XPG things and X/Open UNIX extensions.
`_LARGEFILE_SOURCE`	Some more functions for correct standard I/O.
`_LARGEFILE64_SOURCE`	Additional functionality from LFS for large files.
`_FILE_OFFSET_BITS=N`	Select default filesystem interface.
`_BSD_SOURCE`	ISO C, POSIX, and 4.3BSD things.
`_SVID_SOURCE`	ISO C, POSIX, and SVID things.
`_GNU_SOURCE`	All of the above, plus GNU extensions.
`_REENTRANT`	Select additionally reentrant object.
`_THREAD_SAFE`	Same as `_REENTRANT`; often used by other systems.
`_FORTIFY_SOURCE`	If set to numeric value > 0, additional security measures are defined, according to level.

12 From /usr/include/features.h in Linux

4.4 Linker

The GNU Linker (`ld`) is a major part of the GNU binutils (http://sourceware.org/binutils/), the facility to compile and link programs in Linux. The latest version of the GNU Linker is 2.15. Binutils have been ported to many UNIX variants as well as Windows.

Both the Solaris and Linux linkers work with files that conform to the executable and linking format (ELF). Table 4-6 compares Solaris and GNU `ld` linker options.

TABLE 4-6
Linker Options Comparison

Solaris ld option	GNU ld[13]	Description[14]
`-64`	N/A	Creates a 64-bit object.
`-a`	`-static`	Produces an executable object file in static mode only.
`-b`	N/A (see comment)	With this option, the linker does no special processing for relocations that reference symbols in shared objects. There is no exact match in GNU `ld`, but it can be achieved by not using `-fPIC`/`-fpic` compiler options.
`-B direct`	N/A	Establishes direct binding information by recording the relationship between each symbol reference and the dependency that provides the definition.
`-B dynamic|static`	`-Bdynamic`, `-Bstatic`	Governs library inclusion.
`-B eliminate`	N/A	Causes any global symbols not assigned to a version definition to be eliminated from the symbol table.
`-B group`	`-Bgroup`	Establishes a shared object and its dependencies as a group.

13 http://sources.redhat.com/binutils/docs-2.15/ld/Options.html#Options

14 Sun's `ld` man page (http://docs.sun.com/app/docs/doc/816-5165/6mbb0m9js?a=view)

Solaris ld option	GNU ld	Description
`-B local`	N/A (see comment)	Causes any global symbols not assigned to a version definition to be reduced local. In GNU `ld`, this can only be achieved using the wildcard matching in a version definition file.
`-B reduce`	N/A	When generating a relocatable object, causes the reduction of symbolic information defined by any version definitions.
`-B symbolic`	`-Bsymbolic`	In dynamic mode, when building a shared object, binds references to global symbols to their definitions, if available, within object.
`-c` *name*	`-c`	Records the configuration file name for use at runtime.
`-C`	`--demangle [=`*style*`]`	Demangles C++ symbol names displayed in diagnostic messages.
`-d y|n`	`-dy`, `-dn`	Uses dynamic|static linking.
`-D` *token*, ...	N/A	Prints debugging information, as specified by each token, to the standard error.
`-e` *epsym*	`-e` *entry*, `--entry=`*entry*	Sets the entry point address for the output file to be the symbol *epsym*.
`-f` *name*	`-f` *name*, `--auxiliary` *name*	Specifies that the symbol table of the shared object is used as an auxiliary filter on the symbol table of the shared object specified by *name*.
`-F` *name*	`-F` *name*, `--filter` *name*	Specifies that the symbol table of the shared object is used as a filter on the symbol table of the shared object specified by *name*.
`-G`	`-shared`	Produces a shared object. Undefined symbols are allowed.
`-h` *name*	`-soname` *name*	Records *name* in the object's dynamic section. *name* is recorded in any dynamic objects that are linked with this object rather than the object's file system name.

Solaris ld option	GNU ld	Description
`-i`	N/A	Ignores `LD_LIBRARY_PATH`.
`-l` *name*	`--dynamic-linker` *name*	When building an executable, uses *name* as the path name of the interpreter to be written into the program header.
`-l` *x*	`-l`*x*	Searches a library `libx.so` or `libx.a`.
`-L` *path*	`-L`*path*	Adds *path* to the library search directories.
`-m`	`-M` (see comment)	Produces a memory map or listing of the input/output sections, together with any nonfatal multiply-defined symbols, on the standard output. GNU `ld -M` option outputs similar information but in a different format.
`-M` *mapfile*	`--version -script` *file*	Reads *mapfile* as a text file of directives to `ld`.
`-N` *string*	N/A (see comment)	This option causes a `DT_NEEDED` entry to be added to the `.dynamic` section of the object being built. The value of the `DT_NEEDED` string is the `string` that is specified on the command line. There is no exact match in GNU `ld`. You will have to link against a shared object with this string as the name.
`-o` *outfile*	`-o` *output*	Produces an output object file that is named outfile.
`-p` *auditlib*	N/A	Identifies an audit library, `auditlib`. This audit library is used to audit the object being created at runtime.
`-P` *auditlib*	N/A	Identifies an audit library, `auditlib`. This audit library is used to audit the dependencies of the object being created at runtime.
`-Q y|n`	N/A (see comment)	Under `-Q y`, an `ident` string is added to the `.comment` section of the output file. `-Q n` suppresses version identification. This option is ignored by the GNU `ld`. To achieve this, you could use the `#ident` directive or the linker script.

Solaris ld option	GNU ld	Description
`-r`	`-r`, `--relocatable`	Combines relocatable object files to produce one relocatable object file.
`-R` *path*	`-rpath` *path*	A colon-separated list of directories used to specify library search directories to the runtime linker.
`-s`	`-S`, `-s`	Strips symbolic information from the output file. In GNU `ld`, the `-s` option omits all symbol information, whereas the `-S` option omits only debugger symbol information.
`-S` *supportlib*	N/A	The shared object `supportlib` is loaded with the link-editor and given information regarding the linking process.
`-t`	N/A	Turns off the warning for multiply-defined symbols that have different sizes or different alignments.
`-u` *symname*	`-u` *symname* `--undefined=`*symname*	Enters `symname` as an undefined symbol in the symbol table.
`-V`	`-V`, `--version`, `-v`	Outputs a message giving information about the version of `ld` being used.
`-Y P,` *dirlist*	`-Y` *dirlist*	Changes the default directories used for finding libraries.
`-z absexec`	N/A	Specifies that references to external absolute symbols should be resolved immediately instead of being left for resolution at runtime.
`-z allextract|defaultextract|weakextract`	N/A	Alters the extraction criteria of objects from any archives that follow.
`-z combreloc`	`-z combreloc`	Combines multiple relocation sections.
`-z defs|nodefs`	`-z defs`	`-z defs` forces a fatal error if any undefined symbols remain at the end of the link. The `-z nodefs` option allows undefined symbols.

Solaris ld option	GNU ld	Description
`-z direct|nodirect`	N/A	Enables or disables direct binding to any dependencies that follow on the command line.
`-z endfiltee`	N/A	Marks a filtee so that when processed by a filter, the filtee terminates any further filtee searches by the filter.
`-z finiarray=`*function*	N/A	Appends an entry to the `.finiarray` section of the object being built. If no `.finiarray` section is present, a section is created.
`-z groupperm|nogroupperm`	N/A	Assigns or unassigns each dependency that follows to a unique group.
`-z ignore|record`	N/A	Ignores, or records, dynamic dependencies that are not referenced as part of the link-edit.
`-z initarray=`*function*	N/A	Appends an entry to the `.initarray` section of the object being built. If no `.initarray` section is present, a section is created.
`-z initfirst`	`-z initfirst`	Marks the object so that its runtime initialization occurs before the runtime initialization of any other objects brought into the process at the same time.
`-z interpose`	`-z interpose`	Marks the object as an interposer.
`-z lazyload|nolazyload`	N/A	Enables or disables the marking of dynamic dependencies to be lazily loaded.
`-z ld32=`*arg1,arg2,...* `-z ld64=`*arg1,arg2,...*	N/A	Provides a means of defining any link-editor argument, so that the argument is only interpreted, respectively, by the 32-bit class or 64-bit class of the link-editor.
`-z loadfltr`	`-z loadfltr`	Marks a filter to indicate that filtees must be processed immediately at runtime.

Solaris ld option	GNU ld	Description
`-z muldefs`	`-z muldefs`	Allows multiple symbol definitions.
`-z nocompstrtab`	N/A	Disables the compression of ELF string tables.
`-z nodefaultlib`	`-z nodefaultlib`	Marks the object so that the runtime default library search path, used after any `LD_LIBRARY_PATH` or runpaths, is ignored.
`-z nodelete`	`-z nodelete`	Marks the object as nondeletable at runtime.
`-z nodlopen`	`-z nodlopen`	Marks the object as not available to `dlopen()`, either as the object specified by the `dlopen()`, or as any form of dependency required by the object specified by the `dlopen()`.
`-z nodump`	`-z nodump`	Marks the object as not available to `dldump()`.
`-z nopartial`	N/A	Partially initialized symbols that are defined within the input relocatable object files are expanded in the output file being generated.
`-z noversion`	N/A	Does not record any versioning sections.
`-z now`	`-z now`	Marks the object as requiring non-lazy runtime binding.
`-z origin`	`-z origin`	Marks the object as requiring immediate `$ORIGIN` processing at runtime.
`-z preinitarray=` *`function`*	N/A	Appends an entry to the `.preinitarray` section of the object being built.
`-z redlocsym`	N/A	Eliminates all local symbols except for the *`SECT`* symbols from the symbol table `SHT_SYMTAB`.
`-z rescan`	N/A	Rescans the archive files that are provided to the link-edit.
`-z text`	N/A	Forces a fatal error if any relocations against nonwritable, allocatable sections remain.

Solaris ld option	GNU ld	Description
-z textoff	N/A	Allows relocations against all allocatable sections, including nonwritable ones.
-z textwarn	N/A	Lists a warning if any relocations against nonwritable, allocatable sections remain.
-z verbose	N/A	Provides additional warning diagnostics during a link-edit.

4.4.1 Export Maps

Export maps enable users to tell the linker explicitly which symbols to export from the generated object. Both the Solaris and GNU linkers support export maps. To generate a shared object with this method, the user has to pass the name of the map file with the `-version-script` option of the linker:

```
%gcc -shared -o bar.so bar.c -fPIC -Wl,--version-script=bar.map
```

The file bar.map can contain text like this:

```
{
      global: index;
      local: *;
};
```

4.4.2 Linker Tools

Solaris has various linker tools such as `elfdump`, `lari`, `nm`, `dump`, `ldd`, `pvs`, and `elf`. GNU binutils offer similar tools. Refer to Chapter 2 for more information about GNU binutils.

Table 4-7 provides a comparison of Solaris linker tools and their equivalents on Linux.

TABLE 4-7
Linker Tools

Solaris Tools	Linux Equivalence	Description
`elfdump`	`readelf, objdump`	Dumps selected parts of an object file.
`lari`	N/A	Link analysis of runtime interfaces.
`nm`	`nm`	Prints name list of an object file.
`dump`	`objdump, readelf`	Dumps selected parts of an object file.
`ldd`	`ldd`	Lists dynamic dependencies of executable files or shared objects.
`pvs`	`readelf -V`	Displays the internal version information of dynamic objects.

4.4.3 Shared Libraries

Linux currently uses ELF (Executable Linkage Format) binary format. The only difference between generating an application and a shared library is in the final link command. The option `-shared` for GNU `ld` tells the linker to create a shared library rather than an application.

To create shared libraries in Solaris:

```
cc -o libfoo.so -G -K pic foo.c
```

To create shared libraries in Linux:

```
gcc -o libfoo.so -shared -fpic foo.c
```

In Solaris, when one wants to record a soname to a shared object itself, use the `-h` option:

```
cc -o libfoo.so -G -K pic -h libfoo.so.1 foo.c
```

The equivalent on Linux is this:

```
gcc -o libfoo.so -shared -fpic -Wl,-soname=libfoo.so.1 foo.c
```

or

```
gcc -o libfoo.so -shared -fpic -Wl,-hlibfoo.so.1 foo.c
```

The `dump` command in Solaris is equivalent to the `objdump` command in Linux. The following example shows how the soname recording can be displayed using the `objdump` command in Linux:

```
#objdump -x libGLU.so.1.3 | grep SONAME
        SONAME    libGLU.so.1
```

4.4.4 Library Versioning

In Chapter 3, "Analysis," we provide information about how library versioning is implemented in Linux. Although the external versioning in Solaris is the same as that in Linux, there are some differences in how the symbol versioning works in Solaris and Linux.

Solaris symbol versioning works well in coping with the compatible changes in the shared libraries. When there is an incompatible change, the only way to deal with it in Solaris is to fall back to the external versioning (that is, incrementing the major version number in the soname). Linux symbol versioning can be used to handle incompatible changes. With this, it is not necessary to increase the major version number every time you make an incompatible change to your library. In Linux, it is possible to have multiple definitions of a given symbol (the associated version must differ). Also, the application linked with the versioned shared library contains not only a list of the required version, but also records for each symbol which symbol version was used and from which library the definition came. How to take advantage of this advantage in Linux is, however, beyond the scope of this book. For more information about symbol versioning, refer to the paper by Ulrich Drepper titled "How to Write Shared Libraries," located at http://people.redhat.com/~drepper. In addition, the paper by David J. Brown and Karl Runge titled "Library Interface Versioning in Solaris and Linux" is a good source for the library versioning comparison between Solaris and Linux.

4.4.5 Dynamic Linker (or Runtime Linker)

Both the Solaris dynamic linker and Linux dynamic linker load library dependencies breadth first. That is, first the dependencies of the executable are added in the order listed in its dynamic section. Then the dependencies of the first dependency are added in the same fashion. More information about the Linux dynamic linker is provided in Chapter 3.

4.5 Porting Shell Scripts to Linux

Figure 4-1 shows the Linux shell in relation to the rest of the operating system. The shell, as it is aptly named, sits on the outer edge of the system. It provides users easier ways to interact with system utilities that query or control the operating system, start or stop processes, and list or modify files and directories.

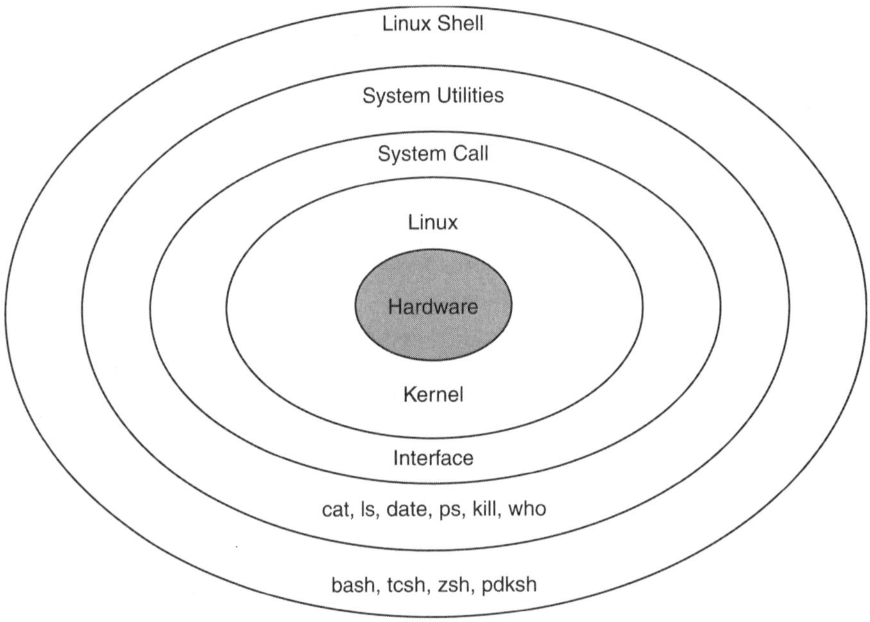

FIGURE 4-1
Linux shell creates an environment to access system interfaces easier.

Depending on the Linux installation, several shells developed for Linux are installed by default. The more popular shells developed for Linux are `bash`, `tcsh`, `zsh`, and `pdksh`. `bash`, however, is considered the default shell on Linux. Chapter 2 contains additional information about Linux shells.

On Solaris, the main shells available are `Bourne shell`, `ksh`, `csh`, `tcsh`, and `bash`. Most applications use these shells to source or check environment variables and kick off processes or daemons. In porting projects that involve porting of test harnesses, however, use of scripting becomes more prevalent.

Table 4-8 compares Solaris and Linux shells.

TABLE 4-8
Solaris and Linux Shell Comparison Table

Shell Name	Solaris Shell Path	Linux Shell Path
Bourne shell	/usr/bin/sh	/bin/sh (linked to bash)
Korn shell	/usr/bin/ksh	/bin/ksh
C shell	/usr/bin/csh	/bin/csh (linked to tcsh)
GNU Bourne Again shell	/usr/bin/bash	/bin/bash
TC shell	/usr/bin/tcsh	/bin/tcsh
Z shell	/usr/bin/zsh	/bin/zsh

4.6 Internationalization and Localization

In Chapter 3, we discussed internationalization (I18N) and localization (L10N) in Linux. In general, steps used to internationalize and localize programs in Solaris and Linux are similar. As you can see, Solaris tools and APIs used for I18N and L10N such as `xgettext`, `msgfmt`, `bindtextdomain()`, `gettext()`, `iconv()`, `dgettext()`, and `dcgettext()` are also available in Linux. Solaris and Linux both support sets of internationalization APIs specified by IEEE POSIX 1003.1-2001 and the SUSv3. The default location for message files in Solaris is also similar to Linux, /usr/lib/locale.

Linux lets the installer choose the default locale during the system installation. Following is the output of the command `locale` showing the current locale environment from one of the author's Linux systems:

```
# locale
LANG=en_US.UTF-8
LC_CTYPE="en_US.UTF-8"
LC_NUMERIC="en_US.UTF-8"
LC_TIME="en_US.UTF-8"
LC_COLLATE="en_US.UTF-8"
LC_MONETARY="en_US.UTF-8"
LC_MESSAGES="en_US.UTF-8"
LC_PAPER="en_US.UTF-8"
LC_NAME="en_US.UTF-8"
LC_ADDRESS="en_US.UTF-8"
LC_TELEPHONE="en_US.UTF-8"
LC_MEASUREMENT="en_US.UTF-8"
LC_IDENTIFICATION="en_US.UTF-8"
LC_ALL=
```

The default locale in Solaris is shown here:

```
$ locale
LANG=
LC_CTYPE="C"
LC_NUMERIC="C"
LC_TIME="C"
LC_COLLATE="C"
LC_MONETARY="C"
LC_MESSAGES="C"
LC_ALL=
```

Table A-1 in Appendix A, "Solaris to Linux Reference Tables," provides a comparison of the internationalization APIs between Solaris and Linux.

4.7 Make

The `make` development tool in Linux is GNU `Make`. As of this writing, the latest version of GNU `Make` is 3.8, which this section is based on. The GNU `Make` home page is located at www.gnu.org/software/make/. Note that GNU `Make` 3.8 is also available on Solaris and can be downloaded from www.istec.org/sunfreeware/. Porting the build environment from Solaris to Linux means using GNU `Make` and making sure that the makefiles used to build the application are correctly ported to build all necessary application modules. Because both Solaris and GNU `Make` conform to the POSIX.2 standard, similarities between Solaris and GNU makefile syntax abound. However, there are still some differences, which are covered in this section. The first difference to take note of is the command-line switches. Table 4-9 shows a comparison between Solaris and GNU `Make` command-line switches.

TABLE 4-9
Make Command-Line Switches

Solaris Flag	GNU Make Equivalent	Description[15]
`-d`	`-d`	Displays the reasons why `Make` chooses to rebuild a target. `Make` displays any and all dependencies that are newer. In addition, `Make` displays options read in from the `MAKEFLAGS` environment variable.

15 Solaris man pages

Solaris Flag	GNU Make Equivalent	Description
`-dd`	N/A	Displays the dependency check and processing in vast detail.
`-D`	N/A	Displays the text of the makefiles read in.
`-DD`	N/A	Displays the text of the makefiles, make.rules file, and all hidden-dependency reports.
`-e`	`-e`	Environment variables override assignments within makefiles.
`-f` *`makefile`*	`-f` *`makefile`*	Uses the specified *makefile.*
`-i`	`-i`	Ignores error codes returned by commands.
`-k`	`-k`	When a nonzero error status is returned by a rule, or when `Make` cannot find a rule, abandons work on the current target, but continues with other dependency branches that do not depend on it.
`-K` *`statefile`*	N/A	Uses the state file *statefile.*
`-n`	`-n`	No execution mode. Prints commands, but does not execute them. Even lines beginning with an `@` are printed. However, if a command line contains a reference to the `$(MAKE)` macro, that line is always executed. When in POSIX mode, lines beginning with a `+` are executed.
`-p`	`-p`	Prints the complete set of macro definitions and target descriptions.
`-P`	N/A	Only reports dependencies, rather than building them.
`-q`	`-q`	Question mode.
`-r`	`-r`	Does not read in the default makefile /usr/share/lib/make/make.rules.
`-s`	`-s`	Silent mode. Does not print command lines before executing them. Equivalent to the special-function target `.SILENT:`.

Solaris Flag	GNU Make Equivalent	Description
`-S`	`-S`	Undoes the effect of the `-k` option. Stops processing when a nonzero exit status is returned by a command.
`-t`	`-t`	Touches the target files (bringing them up to date) rather than performing their rules. Warning: This can be *dangerous* when files are maintained by more than one person. When the `.KEEP_STATE:` target appears in the makefile, this option updates the state file just as if the rules had been performed. When in POSIX mode, lines beginning with a + are executed.
`-V`	N/A	Puts make into SysV mode.

4.7.1 Built-In Makefile Variables for C++

The built-in makefile variable to specify a default C++ compiler in Solaris native `Make` is `CCC`, whereas for the GNU `Make` it is `CXX`. Similarly, the default compiler flag changes from `CCFLAGS` to `CXXFLAGS`.

4.7.2 Library Dependencies

On Solaris, a target name of the form `lib(( `*`symbol`*` ))` refers to the member of a randomized object library that defines the entry point named *`symbol`*. The GNU `Make` equivalent is `lib(`*`file`*`.o)`.

4.7.3 Empty Rules

Empty rules are suffix rules specified without a command. To specify an empty rule in GNU `Make`, put a semicolon immediately after the dependency:

Solaris: `.c.a:`

GNU: `Make: .c.a:;`

4.7.4 Current Targets

In Solaris makefiles, the symbol `$$@` is used in a dependency list to refer to the current target:

Solaris: `$(targets):$$@.o`

In GNU `Make`, you have to use the following:

GNU `Make:` `$(targets):%:%.o`

4.7.5 SCCS and RCS Files

Suffix rules that handle System V makefiles to support SCCS files that contain ~ are not recognized by GNU `Make`. In Solaris, the suffix rule `.c~.o` creates the file x.o from the SCCS file s.n.c. GNU `Make` handles SCCS and RCS files differently by applying two pattern rules for extraction from SCCS or RCS in combination with general rules of rule chaining.

4.7.6 Conditional Macro Assignment

```
$(targets) := special_flags = -g
```

On Solaris, when any target in `$(targets)` is processed, set `$(special_flags)` equal to `-g`. The equivalent on Linux is this:

```
$(targets) : special_flags= -g
```

4.7.7 Pattern-Replacement Macro References

Solaris allows any number of percent metacharacters to appear after the equal sign. On the other hand, Linux only allows one. Here is an example:

```
ORG=one two
NEW=$(ORG:%=integer/%.o integer/%_backup.o)
all:
      @echo ORG is $(ORG)
      @echo NEW is $(NEW)
```

On Solaris, the output from the `make` command is as follows:

```
ORG is one two
NEW is integer/one.o integer/one_backup.o integer/two.o integer/two_backup.o
```

For Linux, you will get this output instead:

```
ORG is one two
NEW is integer/one.o integer/%_backup.o integer/two.o integer/%_backup.o
```

A possible workaround for Linux is this:

```
NEW=$(ORG:%=integer/%.o) $(ORG:%=integer/%_backup.o)
```

4.7.8 VPATH

If a target or a dependency file is found using `VPATH`, any occurrences of the word that is the same as the target name in the subsequent rules will be substituted with the actual name of the target derived from `VPATH`. For example:

```
VPATH=./subdir
foo.o : foo.c
      cc -c foo.c -o foo.o
```

On Solaris, if file.c is located in ./subdir, the following command will be executed:

```
cc -c ./subdir/foo.c -o foo.o
```

However, on Linux, this command will be executed instead:

```
cc -c foo.c -o foo.o
```

4.7.9 Command Execution

Solaris `Make` invokes the shell with the `-e` argument. This flag instructs the shell to exit immediately if any program it runs returns a nonzero status. This is not true for GNU `Make`. However, with the `-S` option in GNU `Make`, we can achieve the same effect.

4.7.10 Special Targets

Special targets are called by different names on various platforms. In Solaris, they are called special-function targets. In GNU `Make`, they are called special built-in targets. When special targets are incorporated in a makefile, they perform special functions. Consult the GNU `Make` manual for the meaning of special targets.

Table 4-10 compares the special targets on Solaris and GNU.

TABLE 4-10
Special Targets

Special Target	Solaris	GNU
.DEFAULT	Yes	Yes
.DELETE_ON_ERROR	No	Yes
.DONE	Yes	No
.EXPORT_ALL_VARIABLES	No	Yes
.FAILED	Yes	No
.GET_POSIX	Yes	No
.IGNORE	Yes	Yes
.INIT	Yes	No
.INTERMEDIATE	No	Yes
.KEEP_STATE	Yes	No
.KEEP_STATE_FILE	Yes	No
.LOW_RESOLUTION_TIME	No	Yes
.MAKE_VERSION	Yes	No
.NOTPARALLEL	No	Yes
.NO_PARALLEL	Yes	No
.PARALLEL	Yes	No
.PHONY	No	Yes
.POSIX	Yes	No
.PRECIOUS	Yes	Yes
.SCCS_GET	Yes	No
.SCCS_GET_POSIX	Yes	No
.SECONDARY	No	Yes
.SILENT	Yes	Yes
.SUFFIXES	Yes	Yes
.WAIT	Yes	No

4.7.11 Environment Variables

Here we list environment variables that affect the execution of GNU `Make` and Solaris `Make`. Table 4-11 compares environment variables between Solaris and Linux.

TABLE 4-11
Make Environment Variables

Variable	Solaris	GNU
`KEEP_STATE`	Yes	No
`USE_SVR4_MAKE`	Yes	No
`MAKEFLAGS`	Yes	Yes
`PROJECTDIR`	Yes	No
`VPATH`	No[16]	Yes

4.7.12 Exit Status

Table 4-12 provides the differences between `Make` exit status on Solaris and Linux.

TABLE 4-12
Make Exit Status

	With -q Solaris	GNU	without -q Solaris	GNU
Successful completion	0	0	0	0
The target was not up-to-date	1	1	—	—
An error occurred	>1	2	>0	2

4.8 Debugger

In Linux systems, the default debugger for non-Java programs is the GNU debugger—GDB for short. GDB has also been ported to Solaris. At the time of this writing, GDB version 6.2.1[17] is available with Solaris 10. You will find more information on GDB in Chapter 7, "Testing and Debugging."

---

16 VPATH is a special-purpose macro in Solaris.

17 www.sun.com/software/solaris/freeware

4.9 Threads

This section addresses issues that developers might face when migrating multithreaded applications from Solaris to Linux. On the Linux side, the material in this section is based on the new implementation of a POSIX thread library (the Native POSIX Thread Library, NPTL for short, developed by Ulrich Drepper). We have provided an introduction to NPTL in Chapter 3. Here we focus on the differences between threading implementations in Solaris and Linux.

4.9.1 Solaris libthread Versus Linux libpthread

Solaris supports two threading implementations: Solaris threads and POSIX threads (pthreads). There are a few functions implemented by the Solaris threads API but not by pthreads API and vice versa. For those functions that do match, the associated arguments might not. The following features are exclusively supported by the Solaris threads API:

- The ability to create *daemon* threads. The process exits when all of its non-daemon threads exit. Daemon threads do not affect its process exit status and are ignored when counting the number of thread exits.
- The ability to suspend or continue the execution of the thread via `thr_suspend()` and `thr_continue()`. Note that `thr_suspend()` suspends the target thread with no regard to the locks that the thread might be holding. This will result in deadlock if the suspending thread calls a function that requires a lock held by the suspended target thread.
- The ability to allow a thread to wait for any undetached thread in the process to terminate. This is achieved when the first argument of `thr_join()` is set to 0. If we set the first argument of `pthread_join()` to 0, the program will be terminated with a segmentation fault.

Table 4-13 compares the Solaris threads APIs with the Linux NPTL APIs.

TABLE 4-13
Solaris Threads and Linux POSIX pthreads Comparison

Solaris Threads API	Linux POSIX Threads API	Description
`thr_create()`	`pthread_create()`	Creates a new thread of control.
`thr_exit()`	`pthread_exit()`	Terminates the execution of the calling thread.
`thr_join()`	`pthread_join()`	Suspends the calling thread until the target thread completes.
`thr_kill()`	`pthread_kill()`	Sends a signal to another thread.
`thr_self()`	`pthread_self()`	Returns the thread ID of the calling process.
`thr_yield()`	`sched_yield()`	Makes the current thread yield to another thread.
`thr_getprio()`	`pthread_getschedparam()`	Retrieves a thread's priority parameters.
`thr_setprio()`	`pthread_setschedparam()`	Modifies a thread's priority parameters.
`thr_getspecific()`	`pthread_getspecific()`	Binds a new thread-specific value to the key.
`thr_setspecific()`	`pthread_setspecific()`	Binds a new thread-specific value to the key.
`thr_getconcurrency()`	`pthread_getconcurrency()`	Gets thread concurrency level.
`thr_setconcurrency()`	`pthread_setconcurrency()`	Sets thread concurrency level.
`thr_sigsetmask()`	`pthread_sigmask()`	Changes or examines the calling thread's signal mask.
`thr_keycreate()`	`pthread_key_create()`	Creates a key that locates data specific to a thread.
N/A	`pthread_key_delete()`	Deletes a key that locates data specific to a thread.

Solaris Threads API	Linux POSIX Threads API	Description
`thr_suspend()`	N/A	Suspends the execution of the specified thread.
`thr_continue()`	N/A	Resumes the execution of a suspended thread.
`mutex_lock()`	`pthread_mutex_lock()`	Locks the given mutex.
`mutex_unlock()`	`pthread_mutex_unlock()`	Unlocks the given mutex.
`mutex_trylock()`	`pthread_mutex_trylock()`	The calling thread not blocked if the mutex is already locked but returns with the error code `EBUSY`.
`mutex_init()`	`pthread_mutex_init()`	Initializes the mutex.
`mutex_destroy()`	`pthread_mutex_destroy()`	Destroys a mutex object.
`cond_wait()`	`pthread_cond_wait()`	Blocks on the conditional variable.
`cond_timedwait()`	`pthread_cond_timedwait()`	Blocks on the conditional variable until the specified absolute time passes.
`cond_reltimedwait()`	N/A	Blocks on the conditional variable until the specified relative time passes.
`cond_signal()`	`pthread_cond_signal()`	Signals a condition.
`cond_broadcast()`	`pthread_cond_braodcast()`	Broadcasts a condition.
`cond_init()`	`pthread_cond_init()`	Initializes condition variables.
`cond_destroy()`	`pthread_cond_destroy()`	Destroys condition variables.
`rwlock_init()`	`pthread_rwlock_init()`	Initializes a read-write lock object.
`rwlock_destroy`	`pthread_rwlock_destroy()`	Destroys a read-write lock object.
`rw_rdlock()`	`pthread_rwlock_rdlock()`	Locks a read-write lock object for reading.

Solaris Threads API	Linux POSIX Threads API	Description
`rw_wrlock()`	`pthread_rwlock_wrlock()`	Locks a read-write lock object for writing.
`rw_unlock()`	`pthread_rwlock_unlock()`	Unlocks a read-write lock object.
`rw_tryrdlock()`	`pthread_rwlock_tryrdlock()`	Tries to lock a read-write lock object for reading.
`rw_trywrlock()`	`pthread_rwlock_trywrlock()`	Tries to lock a read-write lock object for writing.
`sema_init()`	`sem_init()`	Initializes a semaphore.
`sema_destroy()`	`sem_destroy()`	Destroys a semaphore.
`sema_wait()`	`sem_wait()`	Blocks until the semaphore count is greater than 0 and decrements the count.
`sema_post()`	`sem_post()`	Atomically increments the semaphore.
`sema_trywait()`	`sem_trywait()`	Atomically decrements the semaphore.

The behavior of `fork()` in Solaris 9 and earlier releases is different from `fork()` in POSIX threads. In POSIX threads, `fork()` creates a new process, duplicating the complete address space in the child. However, it duplicates only the calling thread in the child process. The Solaris threads API also provides the *replicate all* fork semantics, `forkall()`. This function duplicates the address space and all the threads in the child. This feature is not supported by the POSIX thread standard.

4.9.2 Solaris libpthread Versus Linux libpthread

Although Solaris and Linux both implement the POSIX 1003.1, there are minor differences in platform implementations. In this section, we focus on these differences.

Table 4-14 shows the default values of attributes for POSIX threads on Linux compared to those on Solaris.

TABLE 4-14
Default pthreads Attributes for Solaris and Linux

Attribute	Solaris Default Value	Linux Default Value	Description of Default
Contentionscope	PTHREAD_SCOPE_PROCESS	PTHREAD_SCOPE_SYSTEM	Threads contend for CPU time with all processes running on the machine.
Detachstate	PTHREAD_CREATE_JOINABLE	PTHREAD_CREATE_JOINABLE	Thread created in the joinable state.
Stacksize	NULL[18]	Variable[19]	Minimum stack size (in bytes).
Priority	0	0	Priority of the thread.
Policy	SCHED_OTHER	SCHED_OTHER	The regular scheduling policy.
Inheritsched	PTHREAD_EXPLICIT_SCHED	PTHREAD_INHERIT_SCHED	Indicates how scheduling policy and parameters are determined for the newly created thread.
Guardsize	PAGESIZE	PAGESIZE	Size of guard area for a thread's created stack.

Table 4-15 compares the Solaris pthreads APIs with the Linux NPTL APIs.

18 1MB for 32-bit processes and 2MB for 64-bit processes

19 Dependent on the distribution: 4194304 bytes in SuSE SLES9 and 10485760 bytes in RHEL4

TABLE 4-15
Solaris pthread and Linux pthread Comparison

Routine	Solaris	Linux
pthread_atfork	Yes	Yes[20]
pthread_attr_destroy	Yes	Yes
pthread_attr_getdetachstate	Yes	Yes
pthread_attr_getguardsize	Yes	Yes
pthread_attr_getinheritsched	Yes	Yes
pthread_attr_getschedparam	Yes	Yes
pthread_attr_getschedpolicy	Yes	Yes
pthread_attr_getscope	Yes	Yes
pthread_attr_getstack	Yes	Yes
pthread_attr_getstackaddr	Yes	Yes
pthread_attr_getstacksize	Yes	Yes
pthread_attr_init	Yes	Yes
pthread_attr_getaffinity_np	No	Yes
pthread_attr_setaffinity_np	No	Yes
pthread_attr_setdetachstate	Yes	Yes
pthread_attr_setguardsize	Yes	Yes
pthread_attr_setinheritsched	Yes	Yes
pthread_attr_setschedparam	Yes	Yes
pthread_attr_setschedpolicy	Yes	Yes
pthread_attr_setscope	Yes	Yes
pthread_attr_setstack	Yes	Yes
pthread_attr_setstackaddr	Yes	Yes
pthread_attr_setstacksize	Yes	Yes
pthread_barrierattr_destroy	Yes	Yes

20 In NPTL, thread handlers registered with `pthread_atfork()` are not run if `vfork` is used.

Routine	Solaris	Linux
pthread_barrierattr_getpshared	Yes	Yes
pthread_barrierattr_init	Yes	Yes
pthread_barrierattr_setpshared	Yes	Yes
pthread_barrier_destroy	Yes	Yes
pthread_barrier_init	Yes	Yes
pthread_barrier_wait	Yes	Yes
pthread_cancel	Yes	Yes
pthread_cleanup_pop	Yes	Yes
pthread_cleanup_pop_restore_np	No	Yes
pthread_cleanup_push	Yes	Yes
pthread_cleanup_push_defer_np	No	Yes
pthread_condattr_destroy	Yes	Yes
pthread_condattr_getclock	Yes	Yes
pthread_condattr_getpshared	Yes	Yes
pthread_condattr_init	Yes	Yes
pthread_condattr_setclock	Yes	Yes
pthread_condattr_setpshared	Yes	Yes
pthread_cond_broadcast	Yes	Yes
pthread_cond_destroy	Yes	Yes
pthread_cond_init	Yes	Yes
pthread_cond_reltimedwait_np	Yes	No
pthread_cond_signal	Yes	Yes
pthread_cond_timedwait	Yes	Yes
pthread_cond_wait	Yes	Yes
pthread_create	Yes	Yes
pthread_detach	Yes	Yes
pthread_equal	Yes	Yes
pthread_exit	Yes	Yes

Routine	Solaris	Linux
pthread_getattr_np	No	Yes
pthread_getconcurrency	Yes	Yes
pthread_getschedparam	Yes	Yes
pthread_getspecific	Yes	Yes
pthread_join	Yes	Yes
pthread_key_create	Yes	Yes
pthread_key_delete	Yes	Yes
pthread_kill	Yes	Yes
pthread_kill_other_threads_np	No	Yes[21]
pthread_mutexattr_destroy	Yes	Yes
pthread_mutexattr_getprioceiling	Yes	No
pthread_mutexattr_getprotocol	Yes	No
pthread_mutexattr_getpshared	Yes	Yes
pthread_mutexattr_getrobust_np	Yes	No
pthread_mutexattr_gettype	Yes	Yes
pthread_mutexattr_init	Yes	Yes
pthread_mutexattr_setprioceiling	Yes	No
pthread_mutexattr_setprotocol	Yes	No
pthread_mutexattr_setpshared	Yes	Yes
pthread_mutexattr_setrobust_np	Yes	No
pthread_mutexattr_settype	Yes	Yes
pthread_mutex_consistent_np	Yes	No
pthread_mutex_destroy	Yes	Yes
pthread_mutex_getprioceiling	Yes	No
pthread_mutex_init	Yes	Yes

21 This is a nonportable LinuxThreads extension. It is no longer needed and is not available in the NPTL.

Routine	Solaris	Linux
pthread_mutex_lock	Yes	Yes
pthread_mutex_reltimedlock_np	Yes	No
pthread_mutex_setprioceiling	Yes	No
pthread_mutex_timedlock	Yes	Yes
pthread_mutex_trylock	Yes	Yes
pthread_mutex_unlock	Yes	Yes
pthread_once	Yes	Yes
pthread_rwlockattr_destroy	Yes	Yes
pthread_rwlockattr_getkind_np	No	Yes
pthread_rwlockattr_getpshared	Yes	Yes
pthread_rwlockattr_init	Yes	Yes
pthread_rwlockattr_setkind_np	No	Yes
pthread_rwlockattr_setpshared	Yes	Yes
pthread_rwlock_destroy	Yes	Yes
pthread_rwlock_init	Yes	Yes
pthread_rwlock_rdlock	Yes	Yes
pthread_rwlock_reltimedrdlock_np	Yes	No
pthread_rwlock_reltimedwrlock_np	Yes	No
pthread_rwlock_timedrdlock	Yes	Yes
pthread_rwlock_timedwrlock	Yes	Yes
pthread_rwlock_tryrdlock	Yes	Yes
pthread_rwlock_trywrlock	Yes	Yes
pthread_rwlock_unlock	Yes	Yes
pthread_rwlock_wrlock	Yes	Yes
pthread_self	Yes	Yes
pthread_setcancelstate	Yes	Yes
pthread_setcanceltype	Yes	Yes
pthread_setconcurrency	Yes	Yes

Routine	Solaris	Linux
`pthread_setschedparam`	Yes	Yes
`pthread_setschedprio`	Yes	No
`pthread_setspecific`	Yes	Yes
`pthread_sigmask`	Yes	Yes
`pthread_spin_destroy`	Yes	Yes
`pthread_spin_init`	Yes	Yes
`pthread_spin_lock`	Yes	Yes
`pthread_spin_trylock`	Yes	Yes
`pthread_spin_unlock`	Yes	Yes
`pthread_testcancel`	Yes	Yes
`pthread_timedjoin_np`	No	Yes
`pthread_tryjoin_np`	No	Yes

Although many applications that run on the Linux 2.4 kernel will migrate to the Linux 2.6 kernel without recompilation, the addition of NPTL may require minor modifications in multithreaded applications. Instructions to migrate applications from LinuxThreads to NPTL are beyond the scope of this chapter. Additional information about migrating to use NPTL on the 2.6 kernel is available at http://linuxdevices.com/articles/AT6753699732.html.

4.9.3 Cancellation Points

Thread cancellation allows a thread to terminate the execution of any thread in the process. A cancellation point is a certain point defined by the system at which cancellation can occur. When a thread changes the system or program state just before a cancellation point, and should restore that state before the thread is canceled, you can place a cleanup handler before the cancellation point with `pthread_cleanup_push`. Wherever a thread restores the changed state, you can pop the cleanup handler from the cleanup stack with `pthread_cleanup_pop(3C)`.

Both Solaris and Linux NPTL threads offer the range of cancellation points specified in IEEE POSIX 1003.1-2001 and the Single UNIX Specification.

4.9.4 C++ Exceptions and Linux Threads

Searching the Internet for related topics on C++ exceptions and POSIX threads yields a variety of opinions on how C++ should handle POSIX thread cancellations or vice versa. The fact is that the POSIX thread programming model does not take C++ into account (it is based on C), and the C++ language standard only recently has begun to specify behavior in this area. The sample programs in Example 4-2 involve simple C++ routines mixed within POSIX threads. Compiling and running in both Solaris using the Sun Studio10 C++ compiler and SuSE 9.1 Linux with g++ version 3.3.3 yielded different results.

Example 4-2

Exception_1.c

```
#include <pthread.h>
#include <stdio.h>
#include <stdlib.h>
#include <string.h>

class FooClass {
    public:
    FooClass() {}
    ~FooClass() {
        pthread_cancel(pthread_self());
        pthread_testcancel();
    }
};

void* thread_func(void*) {
    try {
        FooClass cid;
        throw 1;
    }
    catch (int&)
    {}

    return NULL;
}

int main() {
    pthread_t tid;

    pthread_create(&tid, NULL, thread_func, NULL);
    pthread_join(tid, NULL);
    return 0;
}
```

Compiling and running exception _1.c on Linux yields the following:

```
$ g++ exception_1.cc -o exception_1 -lpthread -D_REENTRANT
$ ./exception_1
Aborted (core dumped)
```

Compiling and running exception `_1.c` on Solaris yields the following:

```
$ CC exception_1.cc -o exception_1 -lpthread -D_REENTRANT -g
$ ./exception_1
No core dumped
```

In the preceding case, the `pthread_cancel` within the destructor of FooClass is considered an exception. The book *The C++ Programming Language,* 3rd Edition, by Bjarne Stroustrup (pp. 373, 378) mentions a rule about exceptions in destructors—just don't do it! Dr. Stroustrup explains this in the following manner:

> During stack unwinding, the exception-handling mechanism exits a scope containing an object with a destructor. In this case, an exception may not escape from the destructor itself. If it does, it is considered a failure in the exception handling mechanism and std::terminate is called.

Dr. Stroustrup offers a solution. See the following code snippet to catch the exception (but that solution did not work in our case):

```
~FooClass() {
        try {
      pthread_cancel(pthread_self());
      pthread_testcancel();
        }
    catch (...)
          {

          // do whatever
    throw;
     }
}
```

One solution to try and close the cancellation hole within destructors is to disable cancellation, as in the following code snippet:

```
~FooClass() {
    int oldstate;
    // Disable cancellation at entry
    pthread_setcancelstate(PTHREAD_CANCEL_DISABLE,
                       &oldstate);
    pthread_cancel(pthread_self());
    pthread_testcancel();
    // Enable cancellation before exiting
```

```
        pthread_setcancelstate(PTHREAD_CANCEL_ENABLE,
                               &oldstate);
    }
```

Example 4-3 involves simple throwing of exceptions within threads.

Example 4-3

Exception_2.cc

```
#include <iostream>
#include <cstdio>
#include <cstdlib>
#include <pthread.h>
#include <unistd.h>
using namespace std;

void * thread_func(void *);

int main(int argc, char *argv[]) {
  pthread_t t;
  int i;
  int status;

  try
  {
    if( pthread_create(&t,NULL,thread_func,(void *)i) != 0) {
     cerr << "pthread_create failed" << endl;
     return 1;
    }

    pthread_join(t, NULL);
    cout << "end of thread " << endl;
  }
  catch(...)
  {
    cout << "unexpected exception" << endl;
  }
 }

void * thread_func(void *arg) {
  int i;
  for (i=0; i<4; i++) {
    sleep(1);
    try {
     cout << "throwing exception" << endl;
     throw "exception";
    }
    catch(char *st) {
```

```
      cout << "thread_func caught" << st << endl;
    }
  }
  return 0;
}
```

Compiling and running `exception_2.cc` on Linux yields the following:

```
$ g++ exception_2.cc -o exception_2 -lpthread -D_REENTRANT
$ ./exception_2
throwing check
Aborted (core dumped)
```

Compiling and running `exception_2.cc` on Solaris yields the following:

```
$ CC exception_2.cc -o exception_2 -lpthread -D_REENTRANT -g
$ ./exception_2
throwing exception
Abort (core dumped)
```

Changing `thread_func` to throw an integer instead of a char * changes the behavior of the program to complete its run without aborting:[22]

```
void * thread_func(void *arg) {
  int i;
  for (i=0; i<4; i++) {
    sleep(1);
    try {
     cout << "throwing exception" << endl;
     throw 1;
    }
    catch(int&) {
     cout << "thread_func caught" << endl;
    }
  }
  return 0;
}
```

Another change to make this work is to put a "catchall" catcher:

```
void * thread_func(void *arg) {
  int i;
  for (i=0; i<4; i++) {
    sleep(1);
    try {
     cout << "throwing exception" << endl;
```

22 Note that the sample `exception_2.cc` compiled and ran fine on AIX 5.3 using xlC version 6 compiler.

```
      throw 1;
    }
    catch(...) {
      cout << "thread_func caught" << endl;
    }
  }
  return 0;
}
```

In the case of program listing `exception_2.cc`, the problem seems to be that of uncaught exceptions. Again referring to *The C++ Programming Language,* 3rd Edition, by Bjarne Stroustrup (p. 381), Dr. Stroustrup explains that if an exception is thrown but not caught, the function `std::terminate` is called. Catching the exception prevents the core dump.

The preceding programs clearly show that C++ exceptions and POSIX threads do not mix well. The consensus from porting experience[23] indicates that there is no well-defined standard as to how C++ needs to handle `pthread_cancellations` and exceptions, especially within destructors.[24] The one piece of advice for porting engineers is to be aware of these differences and make sure to test error paths and cleanup handlers as thoroughly as the good path during the testing phase of the porting project.

4.10 Signals

Signals are used to notify a process or thread of a particular event. When the signal is received, that signal is handled through either a default mechanism or a signal handler. POSIX defines a set of signals and signal handling functions that are implemented in Linux. Linux supports both POSIX standard signals and POSIX real-time signals. This section compares and contrasts signal support between Linux 2.6 and Solaris.

4.10.1 Signal Actions

For all possible signals, the system defines a default action to take when a signal occurs:

---

23 Even comments from the comp.programming.threads newsgroup

24 ANSI C++ does not recommend throwing exceptions in the constructor and destructor of a class whose instances may be defined globally (static-globally).

- **Terminate.** Default action is to terminate the process.
- **Ignore.** Default action is to ignore the signal.
- **Core.** Default action is to terminate the process and dump the core.
- **Stop.** Default action is to stop the process.

A process can also install a signal handler to run when a signal is delivered to it. The signal handler takes the place of the default action associated with each signal.

Signals occur as a consequence of an event. Here are some examples that can cause a signal to be sent to a process:

- A program error such as dividing by 0 or accessing an invalid address
- A child process terminating
- A timer expiring
- A user requesting to interrupt or terminate a process

4.10.2 Simple Signals

The simplest signal-handling function Linux supports is the original ISO C standard `signal()` API. It allows the calling process to change the action for a particular signal to either ignore or restore the default signal action or install a function that is called when that particular signal is received by the process.

Although both Linux and Solaris support the `signal()` call, each implementation is different. Example 4-4 provides a sample program demonstrating both behaviors.

Example 4-4

An Example for signal( )

```
#include <string.h>
#include <unistd.h>
#include <signal.h>

void handler (int signum)
{
  char buf[100];
```

```
  strcpy (buf, "In handler\n");
  buf[strlen(buf)+1] = '\0';

  write (2, buf, strlen(buf));
}

int main()
{
  signal(SIGINT, handler);

  for(;;)
    sleep(1);

  return (0);
}
```

Compile and run on Linux:

```
# gcc signal_1.c -o signal_1

# signal_1
In handler                   <- Ctl-c
In handler                   <- Ctl-c
In handler                   <- Ctl-c
Ctl-\ (to kill the process)
Quit (core dumped)
```

The BSD behavior as implemented on Linux reinstalls the signal handler when the signal is received. This is the reason why the handler is always called whenever the user presses Ctrl-C.

Compile and run on Solaris:

```
# cc signal_1.c -o signal_1

# ./signal_1
In handler                   <- Ctl-c
<- Ctl-c
#                       Program is terminated
```

Traditional System V semantics of the `signal()` function returns the signal action to the default action when the signal is handled. Thus, a second `Ctl-c` sent to the process results in process termination. Solaris provides a compatibility function to the BSD signal semantics through the `bsd_signal()` function.

4.10.3 Signal Support in Linux

Every signal has a unique name and a corresponding signal number. Several signal numbers are architecture-dependent. The definition of signal numbers on Linux can be found in /usr/include/bits/signum.h.

To get a list of supported signals in Linux, issue a `kill -l` (the letter *l*) command.

```
# kill -l
 1) SIGHUP        2) SIGINT        3) SIGQUIT       4) SIGILL
 5) SIGTRAP       6) SIGABRT       7) SIGBUS        8) SIGFPE
 9) SIGKILL      10) SIGUSR1      11) SIGSEGV      12) SIGUSR2
13) SIGPIPE      14) SIGALRM      15) SIGTERM      17) SIGCHLD
18) SIGCONT      19) SIGSTOP      20) SIGTSTP      21) SIGTTIN
22) SIGTTOU      23) SIGURG       24) SIGXCPU      25) SIGXFSZ
26) SIGVTALRM    27) SIGPROF      28) SIGWINCH     29) SIGIO
30) SIGPWR       31) SIGSYS       35) SIGRTMIN     36) SIGRTMIN+1
37) SIGRTMIN+2   38) SIGRTMIN+3   39) SIGRTMIN+4   40) SIGRTMIN+5
41) SIGRTMIN+6   42) SIGRTMIN+7   43) SIGRTMIN+8   44) SIGRTMIN+9
45) SIGRTMIN+10  46) SIGRTMIN+11  47) SIGRTMIN+12  48) SIGRTMIN+13
49) SIGRTMIN+14  50) SIGRTMAX-14  51) SIGRTMAX-13  52) SIGRTMAX-12
53) SIGRTMAX-11  54) SIGRTMAX-10  55) SIGRTMAX-9   56) SIGRTMAX-8
57) SIGRTMAX-7   58) SIGRTMAX-6   59) SIGRTMAX-5   60) SIGRTMAX-4
61) SIGRTMAX-3   62) SIGRTMAX-2   63) SIGRTMAX-1   64) SIGRTMAX
```

This particular Linux implementation lists support for 30 non-real-time signals and 30 real-time signals. Table 4-16 compares signals supported by Solaris and Linux 2.6.

TABLE 4-16
Signal Comparison Between Solaris and Linux

Signal	Solaris Default Action	Solaris Signal Number	Linux Default Action[25]	Linux Signal Number[26]	Event
`SIGHUP`	Terminate	1	Terminate	1	Hangup
`SIGINT`	Terminate	2	Terminate	2	Interrupt
`SIGQUIT`	Coredump	3	Coredump	3	Quit
`SIGILL`	Coredump	4	Coredump	4	Illegal instruction

25 This was taken from the comment section in linux/kernel/signal.c version 2.6.10.

26 Signal numbers are for the Linux/i386 architecture.

Signal	Solaris Default Action	Solaris Signal Number	Linux Default Action	Linux Signal Number	Event
SIGTRAP	Coredump	5	Coredump	5	Trace or breakpoint trap
SIGABRT	Coredump	6	Coredump	6[27]	Abort
SIGEMT	Coredump	7	N/A[28]	N/A	Emulation trap
SIGFPE	Coredump	8	Coredump	8	Arithmetic exception
SIGKILL	Terminate	9	Terminate	9	Killed
SIGBUS	Coredump	10	Coredump	7	Bus error
SIGSEGV	Coredump	11	Coredump	11	Segmentation fault
SIGSYS	Coredump	12	Coredump	31	Bad system call
SIGPIPE	Terminate	13	Terminate	13	Broken pipe
SIGALRM	Terminate	14	Terminate	14	Alarm clock
SIGTERM	Terminate	15	Terminate	15	Terminated
SIGUSR1	Terminate	16	Terminate	10	User signal 1
SIGUSR2	Terminate	17	Terminate	12	User signal 2
SIGCHLD	Ignore	18	Ignore	17	Child status changed
SIGPWR	Ignore	19	Terminate	30	Power fail or restart
SIGWINCH	Ignore	20	Ignore	28	Window size change
SIGURG	Ignore	21	Ignore	23	Urgent socket condition
SIGPOLL	Terminate	22	Terminate	29[29]	Pollable event

27 In Linux, SIGABRT and SIGIOT are identical.

28 Not available in Linux/i386, but it is in Linux/Sparc, alpha, and mips.

29 In Linux, SIGPOLL and SIGIO are identical.

Signal	Solaris Default Action	Solaris Signal Number	Linux Default Action	Linux Signal Number	Event
SIGSTOP	Stop	23	Stop	19	Stopped (signal)
SIGTSTP	Stop	24	Stop	20	Stopped (user)
SIGCONT	Ignore	25	Ignore	18	Continued
SIGTTIN	Stop	26	Stop	21	Stopped (tty input)
SIGTTOU	Stop	27	Stop	22	Stopped (tty output)
SIGVTALRM	Terminate	28	Terminate	26	Virtual timer expired
SIGPROF	Terminate	29	Terminate	27	Profiling timer expired
SIGXCPU	Coredump	30	Coredump	24	CPU time limit exceeded
SIGXFSZ	Coredump	31	Coredump	25	File size limit exceeded
SIGWAITING	Ignore	32	N/A	N/A	Reserved for threading support
SIGLWP	Ignore	33	N/A	N/A	Reserved for threading support
SIGFREEZE	Ignore	34	N/A	N/A	Checkpoint freeze
SIGTHAW	Ignore	35	N/A	N/A	Checkpoint thaw
SIGCANCEL	Ignore	36	N/A	N/A	Reserved for threading support
SIGLOST	Terminate	37	N/A	N/A	Resource lost
SIGXRES	Ignore	38	N/A	N/A	Resource control exceeded
SIGJVM1	Ignore	39	N/A	N/A	Reserved for Java Virtual Machine 1
SIGJVM2	Ignore	40	N/A	N/A	Reserved for Java Virtual Machine 2

Signal	Solaris Default Action	Solaris Signal Number	Linux Default Action	Linux Signal Number	Event
SIGRTMIN	Terminate	*	Terminate	34	First real-time signal
(SIGRTMIN+1)	Terminate	*	Terminate	*	Second real-time signal
...					
(SIGRTMAX-1)	Terminate	*	Terminate	*	Second-to-last real-time signal
SIGRTMAX	Terminate	*	Terminate	64	Last real-time signal
SIGSTKFLT	N/A	N/A	Terminate	16	Stack fault on coprocessor (unused)

4.10.4 POSIX Signal-Catching Function

Linux provides the POSIX signal-handling API `sigaction()`. Here is `sigaction` as defined by the POSIX standard:

```
#include <signal.h>

int sigaction(int sig, const struct sigaction *restrict act,
    struct sigaction *restrict oact);
```

The `sigaction` structure defined in signal.h follows the POSIX definition, as follows:

```
typedef struct {
      void (*sa_handler)(int);    /* Pointer to a signal-catching
                  * function or one of the macros.
                                  * SIG_IGN or SIG_DFL.
                                  */

      sigset_t sa_mask;      /* Set of signals to be blocked
                * during execution of the signal
                * handling function.
                */
   int sa_flags;       /* Special flags.
                */
```

```
    void (*sa_sigaction)(int, siginfo_t *, void *);
                  /* Pointer to a signal-catching
                   * function.
                   */
} sigaction_t;
```

The definition of the `sa_sigaction` function pointer within the `sigaction_t` structure uses an argument that is of type `siginfo_t`, which is a structure that can be used to get more information about the signal's context. Here is a simplified version of the `siginfo_t` structure as defined in bits/siginfo.h in Linux:

```
typedef struct {
    int  si_signo;    /* Signal number.  */
    int  si_errno;    /* If non-zero, an errno value is associated
            * with this signal, as defined in <errno.h>.
            */
    int  si_code;     /* Signal code.   */

    pid_t si_pid;     /* Sending process ID. */
    uid_t si_uid ;    /* Real user ID of sending
             * process.
             */
    sigval si_value;  /* Signal value.    */
} siginfo_t;
```

4.10.5 Signal Sets

The data type `sigset_t` in Solaris is defined differently from that in Linux.

In Linux, /usr/include/bits/sigset.h:

```
# define _SIGSET_NWORDS (1024 / (8 * sizeof (unsigned long int)))
typedef struct
 {
  unsigned long int __val[_SIGSET_NWORDS];
 } __sigset_t;
```

In Solaris, /usr/include/sys/signal.h:

```
typedef struct {        /* signal set type */
    unsigned int  __sigbits[4];
} sigset_t;
```

`sigset_t` is used in many POSIX signal-handling interfaces such as `sigemptyset`, `sigfillset`, `sigaddset`, `sigdelset`, `sigismember`, and `sigprocmask`.

4.10.6 Signal Information

Information about how and why a signal was generated is called the signal's context or information. Within the `siginfo_t` structure, the following members, `si_signo` and `si_code`, can be used to obtain more information about the signal. For examples of how to use `siginfo_t`, refer to the code in *Linux Application Development*, by Johnson and Troan, and *Linux Programming by Example*, by Robbins.

The Linux and Solaris implementations of the `si_signo` and `si_code` values are quite close. The only exception is for those signals only supported by Solaris, such as `SIGXRES`. Table 4-17 shows the available `si_code` values.

TABLE 4-17
Values of si_code as Implemented in Linux 2.6 and Solaris 10

Signal	Solaris si_code[30]	Linux si_code[31]	Description
SIGILL	ILL_ILLOPC	ILL_ILLOPC	Illegal opcode
	ILL_ILLOPN	ILL_ILLOPN	Illegal operand
	ILL_ILLADR	ILL_ILLADR	Illegal addressing mode
	ILL_ILLTRP	ILL_ILLTRP	Illegal trap
	ILL_PRVOPC	ILL_PRVOPC	Privileged opcode
	ILL_PRVREG	ILL_PRVREG	Privileged register
	ILL_COPROC	ILL_COPROC	Coprocessor error
	ILL_BADSTK	ILL_BADSTK	Internal stack error
SIGFPE	FPE_INTDIV	FPE_INTDIV	Integer divided by 0
	FPE_INTOVF	FPE_INTOVF	Integer overflow
	FPE_FLTDIV	FPE_FLTDIV	Floating-point divided by 0
	FPE_FLTOVF	FPE_FLTOVF	Floating-point overflow
	FPE_FLTUND	FPE_FLTUND	Floating-point underflow

30 From /usr/include/sys/siginfo.h in Solaris

31 From /usr/include/bits/siginfo.h in Linux

Signal	Solaris si_code	Linux si_code	Description
	FPE_FLTRES	FPE_FLTRES	Invalid floating-point operation
	FPE_FLTINV	FPE_FLTINV	Invalid floating-point operation
	FPE_FLTSUB	FPE_FLTSUB	Subscript out of range
	FPE_FLTDEN	N/A	Floating-point denormalize
SIGSEGV	SEGV_MAPERR	SEGV_MAPERR	Address not mapped to object
	SEGV_ACCERR	SEGV_ACCERR	Invalid permissions for mapped object
SIGBUS	BUS_ADRALN	BUS_ADRALN	Invalid address alignment
	BUS_ADRERR	BUS_ADRERR	Nonexistent physical address
	BUS_OBJERR	BUS_OBJERR	Object-specific hardware error
SIGTRAP	TRAP_BRKPT	TRAP_BRKPT	Process breakpoint
	TRAP_TRACE	TRAP_TRACE	Process trace trap
	TRAP_RWATCH	N/A	Read access watchpoint trap
	TRAP_WWATCH	N/A	Write access watchpoint trap
	TRAP_XWATCH	N/A	Execute access watchpoint trap
	TRAP_DTRACE	N/A	Problem with fasttrap DTrace provider
SIGCHLD	CLD_EXITED	CLD_EXITED	Child exited
	CLD_KILLED	CLD_KILLED	Child killed
	CLD_DUMPED	CLD_DUMPED	Child terminated abnormally
	CLD_TRAPPED	CLD_TRAPPED	Traced child trapped
	CLD_STOPPED	CLD_STOPPED	Child stopped
	CLD_CONTINUED	CLD_CONTINUED	Stopped child continued
SIGPOLL	POLL_IN	POLL_IN	Data input available
	POLL_OUT	POLL_OUT	Output buffers available
	POLL_MSG	POLL_MSG	Input message available
	POLL_ERR	POLL_ERR	I/O error
	POLL_PRI	POLL_PRI	High-priority input available
	POLL_HUP	POLL_HUP	Device disconnected

Signal	Solaris si_code	Linux si_code	Description
SIGEMT	EMT_CPCOVF	N/A	CPU performance counter overflow
SIGXRES	SI_RCTL	N/A	Resource control generated signal

4.10.7 kill()

`kill()` is a traditional UNIX function for sending a signal:

```
int kill(pid_t pid, int sig)
```

There is a slight difference between Solaris and Linux when the first argument `pid` is equal to –1. On a Linux system, the specified signal is sent to every process except the `init` process (PID 1). On a Solaris system, the signal is sent to all processes except the `init` process and other special processes.

4.11 System Calls

System calls are interfaces used by user programs to have the kernel perform a specific function on behalf of the calling thread or process. Some Solaris-proprietary system calls may not be available on Linux. When this happens, a replacement version may have to be implemented on the Linux side.

A list of system calls in Linux can be located at /usr/include/asm/unistd.h.

Table A-2 in Appendix A provides a system call comparison between Solaris and Linux.

In the following subsections, we highlight important system calls that have minor differences, primarily with their flags.

4.11.1 open()

```
int open(const char *pathname, int flags, mode_t mode);
```

The possible values for the argument `flags` are constructed by a `bitwise-inclusive-OR` between one of the following and any combination of the flags provided in:

`O_RDONLY` or

`O_WRONLY` or

`O_RDWR`

Some of these flags are available only on Solaris and some only on Linux (see Table 4-18).

TABLE 4-18
Argument Flags for open()

Solaris	Linux	Description[32]
O_APPEND	O_APPEND	If set, the file offset is set to the end of the file prior to each write.
O_CREATE	O_CREATE	Create the file if it does not exist.
O_DSYNC	O_DSYNC	Write I/O operations on the file descriptor complete as defined by synchronized I/O data-integrity completion.
O_EXCL	O_EXCL	If O_CREATE and O_EXCL are set, open() fails if the file exists. If O_EXCL and O_CREATE are set, and *path* names a symbolic link, open() fails and sets errno to EEXIST, regardless of the contents of the symbolic link. If O_EXCL is set and O_CREATE is not set, the result is undefined.
O_LARGEFILE	O_LARGEFILE	If set, the offset maximum in the open file description is the largest value that can be represented correctly in an object of type off64_t.
O_NOCTTY	O_NOCTTY	If set and *path* identifies a terminal device, open() does not cause the terminal device to become the controlling terminal for the process.
O_NOFOLLOW	O_NOFOLLOW	If the path names a symbolic link, open() fails and sets errno to ELOOP.
O_NOLINKS	N/A	If the link count of the named file is greater than 1, open() fails and sets errno to EMLINK.

32 Solaris and Linux man pages.

Solaris	Linux	Description
O_NONBLOCK or O_NDELAY	O_NONBLOCK or O_NDELAY	The file is open in nonblocking mode.
O_RSYNC	O_RSYNC	Read I/O operations on the file descriptor complete at the same level of integrity as specified by the O_DSYNC and O_SYNC flags.
O_SYNC	O_SYNC	Write I/O operations on the file descriptor complete as defined by synchronized I/O file-integrity completion.
O_TRUNC	O_TRUNC	If the file already exists, it will be truncated.
O_XATTR	N/A	If set in open(), the implied file descriptor is that for the current working directory. Extended attributes must be referenced with a relative path; providing an absolute path results in a normal file reference.
N/A	O_DIRECTORY	If *pathname* is not a directory, cause the open to fail.
N/A	O_DIRECT	File I/O is done directly to/from user space buffers.
N/A	O_ASYNC	Generate a signal (SIGIO, by default) when input or output becomes possible on this file descriptor.

4.11.2 fcntl()

```
int fcntl( int fildes, int cmd, /* arg */ ...) ;
```

This system call is used to perform various control functions as specified by the cmd argument on an open file associated with the fildes file descriptor. The call may require the third argument depending on the value of cmd. The available values of cmd are provided in Table 4-19.

TABLE 4-19
The cmd Flags for fcntl()

Solaris	Linux	Description
F_DUPFD	F_DUPFD	Find the lowest-numbered file descriptor available that is greater than or equal to `arg` and make it a copy of `fildes`.
F_DUP2FD	N/A	Similar to `F_DUPFD`, but always returns `arg`. `F_DUP2FD` closes `arg` if it is open and not equal to `fildes`. `F_DUP2FD` is equivalent to `dup2( fildes, arg)`, which is available on Linux.
F_FREESP	N/A	Free storage space associated with a section of the ordinary file `fildes`. The section is specified by a variable of data type `struct flock` pointed to by `arg`.
F_FREESP64	N/A	Same as `F_FREESP`, but takes a `struct flock64` argument rather than a `struct flock` argument.
F_GETFD	F_GETFD	Get the file descriptor flags that are associated with the file descriptor `fildes`.
F_GETFL	F_GETFL	Get the file status flags and file access modes for the file descriptor specified by `fildes`.
F_GETOWN	F_GETOWN	In Solaris, if the file descriptor refers to a socket, get the process or process group ID specified to receive `SIGURG` signals when out of band data is available. In Linux, it gets the process ID or process group ID specified to receive the `SIGIO` or `SIGURG` signal for events on the file descriptor.
F_GETXFL	N/A	Get the file status flags, file access modes, and file creation and assignment flags for the file descriptor specified by `fildes`.
F_SETFD	F_SETFD	Set the file descriptor flags that are associated with `fildes` to the third argument, `arg`.
F_SETFL	F_SETFL	Set the file status flags part of the descriptor's flag to the value specified by `arg`.

Solaris	Linux	Description
F_SETOWN	F_SETOWN	In Solaris, if fildes refers to a socket, set the process or process group ID specified to receive SIGURG signals when out-of-band data is available, using the value of the third argument, arg. In Linux, it sets the process ID or process group that will receive SIGIO or SIGURG signals for events on file descriptor fd.
F_GETLK	F_GETLK	Return the flock structure that prevents you from getting the lock, or set the l_type field of the lock to F_UNLCK if there is no conflict.
F_GETLK64	F_GETLK64	Equivalent to F_GETLK, but takes a struct flock64 argument instead.
F_SETLK	F_SETLK	Set or clean a file segment lock according to the lock description pointed to by arg.
F_SETLK64	F_SETLK64	Equivalent to F_SETLK, but takes a struct flock64 argument instead.
F_SETLKW	F_SETLKW	Similar to F_SETLK, except that if a shared or exclusive lock is blocked by other locks, the process waits until the request can be satisfied.
F_SETLKW64	F_SETLKW64	Equivalent to F_SETLKW64, but takes a struct flock64 argument instead.
F_SHARE	N/A	Set a share reservation on a file with the specified access mode and designate the types of access to deny.
F_UNSHARE	N/A	Remove an existing share reservation.
F_RDACC	N/A	Set a file share reservation for read-only access.
F_WRACC	N/A	Set a file share reservation for write-only access.
F_RWACC	N/A	Set a file share reservation for read and write access.
F_COMPAT	N/A	Set a file share reservation to compatibility mode.
F_RDDNY	N/A	Set a file share reservation to deny read access to other processes.

Solaris	Linux	Description
F_WRDNY	N/A	Set a file share reservation to deny write access to other processes.
F_RWDNY	N/A	Set a file share reservation to deny read and write access to other process.
F_NODNY	N/A	Do not deny read or write access to any other process.
N/A	F_GETSIG	Get the signal sent when input or output becomes possible.
N/A	F_SETSIG	Set the signal sent when input or output becomes possible.
N/A	F_SETLEASE	Set or remove a file lease according to the values specified in `arg`.
N/A	F_GETLEASE	Indicate what type of lease we hold on the file referred to by `fd`.
N/A	F_RDLCK	Take out a read lease. We will be notified when another process opens the file for writting or truncates it.
N/A	F_WRLCK	Take out a write lease. We will be notified when another process opens the file for reading or writing or truncates it.
N/A	F_UNLCK	Remove our lease from the file.
N/A	F_NOTIFY	Provide notification when the directory referred to by `fd` or any of the files that it contains is changed.

The data type `struct flock` is defined differently in Solaris and Linux. On Solaris, the `flock` structure (defined in /usr/include/sys/fcntl.h) contains at least the following elements:

```
short  l_type;      /* lock operation type */
short  l_whence;    /* lock base indicator */
off_t  l_start;     /* starting offset from base */
off_t  l_len;       /* lock length; l_len == 0 means
 until end of file */
int  l_sysid;       /* system ID running process holding lock */
pid_t  l_pid;       /* process ID of process holding lock */
```

But Linux requires `flock` to have the following fields (`struct flock` is defined in /usr/include/bits/fcntl.h):

```
short l_type;   /* Type of lock: F_RDLCK,
            F_WRLCK, F_UNLCK */
short l_whence; /* How to interpret l_start:
            SEEK_SET, SEEK_CUR, SEEK_END */
off_t l_start;  /* Starting offset for lock */
off_t l_len;    /* Number of bytes to lock */
pid_t l_pid;    /* PID of process blocking our lock
            (F_GETLK only) */
```

4.11.3 dirent

The `dirent` structure in Solaris is different from that in Linux.

On Linux, dirent is defined in /usr/include/bits/dirent.h, as follows:

```
struct dirent
      {
#ifndef __USE_FILE_OFFSET64
        __ino_t d_ino;
        __off_t d_off;
#else
       __ino64_t d_ino;
       _off64_t d_off;
#endif
      unsigned short int d_reclen;
      unsigned char d_type;
      char d_name[256];
      };
```

On Solaris, dirent is defined in /usr/include/sys/dirent.h, as follows:

```
typedef struct dirent {
   ino_t  d_ino;            /* "inode number" of entry */
   off_t  d_off;            /* offset of disk directory entry */
   unsigned short d_reclen; /* length of this record */
   char  d_name[1];         /* name of file */
} dirent_t;
```

4.11.4 CPU Affinity

A process in a multiprocessor system by default bounces among several CPUs. Explicitly binding a process to certain CPUs (assigning CPU affinity) may yield performance gain in some cases. System calls for CPU affinity on Solaris are different from those on Linux. The Linux 2.6 kernel provides `sched_setaffinity()` and `sched_getaffinity()` for CPU affinity. You can find more information about this topic at www.linuxjournal.com/article/6799. Also, `taskset` (http://rlove.org/schedutils) is a nice tool that enables you to manipulate task CPU affinity.

4.11.5 fork()

In Solaris 10, calls to `fork()` or `fork1()` are identical to a call to `fork()` in Linux. That is, only the calling thread is replicated in the child process. Note that this is the POSIX-specified behavior for `fork()`. In the previous release of Solaris, the behavior of `fork()` depends on whether the application is linked with the POSIX thread library. When linked with the Solaris threads (`-lthread`) but not linked with POSIX threads (`-lpthread`), `fork()` is the same as `forkall()`. (All the threads are replicated in the child process.) When linked with POSIX threads, `fork()` is the same as `fork1()`. Linux does not support `forkall()`.

4.12 System Libraries

Some of the system libraries in Solaris may not match the names of libraries used in Linux. Table 4-20 compares Solaris system libraries to Linux system libraries in terms of their function.

TABLE 4-20
Linux and Solaris System Library Comparison

Description	Solaris	Linux
Curses	`libcurses, libform, libmenu, libpanel, libplot`	`libncurses, libform, libmenu, libpanel, libplot`
Database APIs	`libdbm`	`libdb*`
Security APIs	`libbsm`	`libc(shadow.h)`
Socket APIs	`libsocket`	`libc(BSD4.3)`
RPC APIs	`libnsl`	`libc`
Math	`libm`	`libm`
XDR APIs	`librpcsvc`	`libc`
Real-time priority	`rtprio`	`libc`

4.13 Solaris and Linux APIs

Linux 2.6 comes with the latest GNU C library. As of this writing, the latest release of the GNU `glibc` is 2.3.5. As seen in the preceding section, the GNU `libc` distribution installs several libraries, which may come in both archived and shared form. The main objective of this section is to compare Solaris APIs as documented in the Solaris 10 man pages and GNU `libc` as referenced through available online manuals, header files, and Linux man pages.

The C library used on every Linux system is GNU `libc`. Much of the interface of GNU `libc` has been determined by the history of UNIX and various standards. GNU `libc` supports most standards that modern UNIX systems support today, such as ISO C and the POSIX standards. GNU `libc` also supports features of the two major UNIX variants, namely BSD and System V. The list of libraries included in GNU `libc` can be found in Chapter 3. To learn what version of `glibc` you have on your installation, run `/lib/libc.so` (that is, just type the following on the command line):

```
# ./libc.so.6
GNU C Library stable release version 2.3.3 (20040405), by Roland McGrath et al.
Copyright (C) 2004 Free Software Foundation, Inc.
This is free software; see the source for copying conditions.
There is NO warranty; not even for MERCHANTABILITY or FITNESS FOR A
PARTICULAR PURPOSE.
Configured for i686-suse-linux.
Compiled by GNU CC version 3.3.3 (SuSE Linux).
Compiled on a Linux 2.6.4 system on 2004-04-05.
Available extensions:
    GNU libio by Per Bothner
    crypt add-on version 2.1 by Michael Glad and others
    linuxthreads-0.10 by Xavier Leroy
    GNU Libidn by Simon Josefsson
    NoVersion patch for broken glibc 2.0 binaries
    BIND-8.2.3-T5B
    libthread_db work sponsored by Alpha Processor Inc
    NIS(YP)/NIS+ NSS modules 0.19 by Thorsten Kukuk
Thread-local storage support included.
Report bugs using the `glibcbug' script to <bugs@gnu.org>.
```

Table A-3 in Appendix A shows Solaris basic library functions and their equivalents on Linux as implemented through the GNU `libc` distribution.

In the following subsections, we turn our focus to the basic system interfaces, such as memory management and interprocess communication.

4.13.1 Memory Management

Table 4-21 compares library functions that applications use for memory management on Solaris and Linux.

TABLE 4-21
Memory Management APIs

Solaris	Linux	Description
`mlock`	`mlock*`	Locks pages in memory.
`munlock`	`munlock`	Unlocks pages in memory.
`mlockall`	`mlockall*`	Locks address space.
`munlockall`	`munlockall`	Unlocks address space.
`msync`	`msync*`	Synchronizes memory with physical storage.
`malloc`	`malloc`	Returns a pointer to a block of memory at least as large as the amount of requested memory.
`free`	`free`	Returns the memory.
`calloc`	`calloc`	Returns a pointer to a block of memory that is initialized to 0.
`memalign`	`memalign*`	Allocates a specified number of bytes on a specified alignment boundary.
`valloc`	`valloc*`	Allocates a specified number of bytes that are aligned on a page boundary.
`realloc`	`realloc`	Changes the size of the memory block allocated to a process.

*`errno` for this function in Solaris is different from what is used in Linux.

4.13.2 Interprocess Communication (IPC)

Here we provide information about a set of techniques that processes can use to communicate with each other. These techniques are collectively called IPC and include pipes, FIFOs, message queues, shared memory, and semaphores.

4.13.2.1 Pipes

A pipe is a technique used to communicate between two threads in a process or between parent and child processes. When a process calls `fork`, its file descriptors are copied to the new child process. As a result, the parent can communicate with the child. A pipe can be created by calling the `pipe` function:

```
#include <unistd.h>

int pipe (int fildes [2]);
```

Pipes in Linux, however, are half duplex. Pipes in Solaris are full duplex. In Linux, the file descriptor `fildes[0]` is only for reading, and the file descriptor `fildes[1]` is only for writing.

The `popen` and `pclose` functions are both supported in Solaris and Linux:

```
#include <stdio.h>

FILE *popen(const char *command, const char *mode);
int pclose(FILE *stream);
```

The call to `popen` creates a pipe between the calling process and the program specified by *`command`* in the child process. The calling process can either read from or write to the pipe, as specified by the *`mode`* argument. The return value is a stream pointer such that one can write to the standard input of the *`command`*, if the mode is `w`, by writing to the file stream, and one can read from the standard output of the command, if the mode is `r`, by reading from the file stream.

4.13.2.2 FIFOs

A first-in, first-out (FIFO) file (also known as a named pipe) is a pipe that has a name in the filesystem associated with it. This enables the pipe to be open or closed by any process. The processes on either end of the pipe need not be related to each other.

You can create a FIFO programmatically by calling the `mkfifo` function:

```
#include <sys/types.h>
#include <sys/stat.h>

int mkfifo(const char *pathname, mode_t mode);
```

This function works the same way on both Solaris and Linux. A FIFO can have multiple readers and writers. A write request of `PIPE_BUF` bytes or less from a writer is guaranteed not to be interleaved with data from other processes. On Linux, PIPE_BUF is 4096 bytes,[33] whereas it is 5120 bytes on Solaris.[34]

4.13.2.3 POSIX Messages

Messages enable multiple processes to send formatted data streams to arbitrary processes. On Linux, POSIX messages are supported only when the option `_POSIX_MESSAGE_PASSING` is defined. You can determine whether your Linux system has the option `_POSIX_MESSAGE_PASSING` set by issuing the following command:

```
$ getconf _POSIX_MESSAGE_PASSING
200112
```

Table 4-22 compares message queue interfaces in Solaris and Linux.

TABLE 4-22
Comparison Between POSIX Message Queue Interfaces in Solaris and Linux

Solaris Interfaces	Linux Interfaces	Description
mq_close	mq_close	Closes a message queue.
mq_getattr	mq_getattr	Gets message queue attributes.
mq_notify	mq_notify	Notifies the process (or thread) that a message is available on a queue.
mq_open	mq_open	Opens a message queue.
mq_receive	mq_receive	Receives a message from a message queue.
mq_reltimed receive_np	N/A	Receives a message from a message queue and stops waiting if the specified timeout expires. (Timeout is specified as a relative time interval.)
mq_reltimedsend_np	N/A	Sends a message to a message queue and stops blocking on the full message queue if the specified timeout expires. (Timeout is specified as a relative time interval.)

33 /usr/include/linux/limits.h

34 /usr/include/limits.h

Solaris Interfaces	Linux Interfaces	Description
mq_send	mq_send	Sends a message to a message queue.
mq_setattr	mq_setattr	Sets/gets message queue attributes.
mq_timedreceive	mq_timedreceive	Receives a message from a message queue and stops waiting if the specified timeout expires.
mq_timedsend	mq_timedsend	Sends a message to a message queue and stops blocking on the full message queue if the specified timeout expires.
mq_unlink	mq_unlink	Removes a message queue.

4.13.2.4 POSIX Semaphores

Similar to POSIX messages, if your Linux system supports POSIX semaphores, you should see the following output:

```
$getconf _POSIX_SEMAPHORES
200112
```

Table 4-23 compares POSIX semaphore interfaces in Solaris and Linux.

TABLE 4-23
Comparison Between POSIX Semaphore Interfaces in Solaris and Linux

Solaris Interfaces	Linux Interfaces	Description
sem_close	sem_close	Closes a named semaphore.
sem_destroy	sem_destroy	Destroys an unnamed semaphore.
sem_getvalue	sem_getvalue	Gets the value of a semaphore.
sem_init	sem_init	Initializes an unnamed semaphore.
sem_open	sem_open	Initializes/opens a named semaphore.
sem_post	sem_post	Increments the count of a semaphore.
sem_reltimedwait_np	N/A	Locks a semaphore, but stops waiting when the specified timeout expires. (Timeout is specified as relative time interval.)

Solaris Interfaces	Linux Interfaces	Description
sem_timedwait	sem_timedwait	Locks a semaphore, but stops waiting when the specified timeout expires.
sem_trywait	sem_trywait	Acquires or waits for a semaphore.
sem_unlink	sem_unlink	Removes a named semaphore.
sem_wait	sem_wait	Acquires or waits for a semaphore.

4.13.2.5 POSIX Shared Memory

Table 4-24 compares POSIX shared memory interfaces in Solaris and Linux.

TABLE 4-24
Comparison Between POSIX Shared Memory Interfaces in Solaris and Linux

Solaris Interfaces	Linux Interfaces	Description
shm_open	shm_open	Opens a shared memory object. In Linux, using O_TRUNC with O_RDONLY successfully truncates an existing shared memory object, whereas the result of this combination is undefined in Solaris.
shm_unlink	shm_unlink	Removes a shared memory object.

On Linux, these two functions are available in `glibc` version 2.2 and later. To use these functions in your code, you need to use the required real-time library by specifying the `-lrt` flag with the compiler.

4.13.2.6 System V Messages

Table 4-25 compares System V message interfaces in Solaris and Linux.

TABLE 4-25
Comparison Between System V Message Interfaces in Solaris and Linux

Solaris	Linux	Description
msgctl	msgctl	Message control operation
msgget	msgget	Get message queue
msgids	N/A	Discover all message queue identifiers

Solaris	Linux	Description
msgrcv	msgrcv	Message receive operation
msgsnap	N/A	Message queue snapshot operation
msgsnd	msgsnd	Message send operation

The definition of `struct msqid_ds` used in the function `msgctl()` is not the same on Solaris and Linux.

In Solaris, /usr/include/sys/msg.h:

```
struct msqid_ds {
    struct ipc_perm msg_perm;     /* operation permission struct */
    struct msg   *msg_first;      /* ptr to first message on q */
    struct msg   *msg_last;       /* ptr to last message on q */
    msglen_t    msg_cbytes;       /* current # bytes on q */
    msgqnum_t    msg_qnum;        /* # of messages on q */
    msglen_t    msg_qbytes;       /* max # of bytes on q */
    pid_t      msg_lspid;         /* pid of last msgsnd */
    pid_t      msg_lrpid;         /* pid of last msgrcv */
#if defined(_LP64)
    time_t     msg_stime;         /* last msgsnd time */
    time_t     msg_rtime;         /* last msgrcv time */
    time_t     msg_ctime;         /* last change time */
#else
    time_t     msg_stime;         /* last msgsnd time */
    int32_t     msg_pad1;         /* reserved for time_t expansion */
    time_t     msg_rtime;         /* last msgrcv time */
    int32_t     msg_pad2;         /* time_t expansion */
    time_t     msg_ctime;         /* last change time */
    int32_t     msg_pad3;         /* time_t expansion */
#endif
    short      msg_cv;
    short      msg_qnum_cv;
    long      msg_pad4[3];   /* reserve area */
};
```

In Linux, /usr/include/bits/msq.h:

```
struct msqid_ds
{
 struct ipc_perm msg_perm;        /* structure describing operation permission */
 __time_t msg_stime;              /* time of last msgsnd command */
 unsigned long int __unused1;
 __time_t msg_rtime;              /* time of last msgrcv command */
 unsigned long int __unused2;
  __time_t msg_ctime;             /* time of last change */
 unsigned long int __unused3;
```

```
 unsigned long int __msg_cbytes; /* current number of bytes on queue */
 msgqnum_t msg_qnum;             /* number of messages currently on queue */
 msglen_t msg_qbytes;            /* max number of bytes allowed on queue */
 __pid_t msg_lspid;              /* pid of last msgsnd() */
 __pid_t msg_lrpid;              /* pid of last msgrcv() */
 unsigned long int __unused4;
 unsigned long int __unused5;
};
```

The default maximum size of a message queue (`msg_qbytes`) on Linux is set to the system parameter `MSGMNB` (16384 bytes). The `msg_qbytes` value can be raised beyond `MSGMNB` by using the `msgctl` function with the appropriate privileges. On Linux, the maximum size for a message text is set to `MSGMAX` (8192 bytes).

4.13.2.7 System V Semaphores

Table 4-26 compares System V semaphore interfaces in Solaris and Linux.

TABLE 4-26
Comparison Between System V Semaphore Interfaces in Solaris and Linux

Solaris	Linux	Description
`semctl`	`semctl`[35]	Semaphore control operation
`semget`	`semget`	Get set of semaphores
`semids`	N/A	Discover all semaphore IDs
`semop`	`semop`	Semaphore operation
`semtimedop`	`semtimedop`	Semaphore operation with time limit

Here is how Linux defines `struct semid_ds` (which is different from Solaris):

```
struct semid_ds
{
 struct ipc_perm sem_perm;       /* operation permission struct */
 __time_t sem_otime;          /* last semop() time */
 unsigned long int __unused1;
 __time_t sem_ctime;          /* last time changed by semctl() */
 unsigned long int __unused2;
 unsigned long int sem_nsems;     /* number of semaphores in set */
 unsigned long int __unused3;
 unsigned long int __unused4;
};
```

35 See the text following the table.

Linux programmers should define a union like the following to use for the fourth argument of the `semctl` function:

```
union semun
{
 int val;                    /* value for SETVAL */
 struct semid_ds *buf;       /* buffer for IPC_STAT & IPC_SET */
 unsigned short int *array;  /* array for GETALL & SETALL */
 struct seminfo *__buf;      /* buffer for IPC_INFO */
};
```

4.13.2.8 System V Shared Memory

Table 4-27 compares System V shared memory interfaces in Solaris and Linux.

TABLE 4-27
Comparison Between System V Shared Memory Interfaces in Solaris and Linux

Solaris	Linux	Description
`shmat`	`shmat` (see comment following this table)	Attach the shared memory segment to the data segment of the calling process
`shmctl`	`shmctl`	Shared memory control
`shmdt`	`shmdt`	Detach the shared memory segment
`shmget`	`shmget`	Get shared memory segment identifier
`shmids`	N/A	Discover all shared memory identifiers

There is a slight difference in the possible values of the third argument in the function `shmat`.

```
void *shmat(int shmid, const void *shmaddr, int shmflg);
```

Table 4-28 compares the value of `shmflg` available in Solaris and Linux.

TABLE 4-28
Comparison Between shmflg in Solaris and Linux

shmflg in Solaris	shmflg in Linux	Description
`SHM_RDONLY`	`SHM_RDONLY`	Attach read-only (else read-write)
`SHM_RND`	`SHM_RND`	Round attach address to `SHMLBA`
`SHM_SHARE_MMU`	N/A	Share VM resources such as page table
`SHM_PAGEABLE`	N/A	Share VM resources and the dynamic shared memory framework is created
N/A	`SHM_REMAP`	Take over region on attach

In Linux, you can request a shared memory segment to be supported by large page by specifying `SHM_HUGETLB` in the `shmflg` argument of the function `shmget`.

In Solaris, shared memory segments must be explicitly removed (by using the `shmctl` function) when there is no reference to them. In Linux, you can specify that the shared memory segment be removed on last detach.

4.13.3 Memory Placement Optimization (MPO)

Solaris's MPO[36] provides performance improvements on systems in which each CPU accesses some area of memory more quickly than others. This architecture is also known as NUMA (Non-Uniform Memory Access). The essence of the NUMA architecture is the presence of multiple memory subsystems, as opposed to a single one on an SMP system. With MPO, Solaris can recognize the memory locality effects by ensuring that memory is as *close* as possible to the processors that access it while still maintaining balance in the system to avoid bottlenecks. Solaris also provides several APIs[37] for developers who want to further optimize application performance through MPO. Some of those APIs include `getcpuid`, `gethomelgroup`, `lgrp_affinity_get`, `lgrp_affinity_set`, `lgrp_children`, `lgrp_init`, `lgrp_mem_size`, and `lgrp_view`.

The Linux community has made a tremendous effort to make the Linux kernel NUMA-aware. The 2.6 kernel features NUMA awareness in the scheduler so that the majority of processes execute in the *local* memory. With the advent of IBM Power5 and AMD Opteron systems, NUMA is becoming more prevalent in the marketplace, used in many servers, entry-level or high-end. For more information about how NUMA is supported in the kernel, consult "Linux on NUMA Systems" (www.kernel.org/pub/linux/kernel/people/mbligh/presentations/OLS2004-numa_paper.pdf). Enterprise-level Linux distributions such as SuSE SLES9 and Red Hat EL4 are preconfigured with NUMA support. Applications do not require any code changes to take advantage of the NUMA support provided in the Linux kernel. If the application binds its processes to a processor, the kernel attempts to allocate memory *closest* to those processes. However, if programmers would like to

---

36 www.sun.com/software/solaris/performance.jsp

37 http://iforce.sun.com/protected/solaris10/adoptionkit/tech/mpo/mpo_man.html

take an extra step to further optimize the performance of their applications, they can also use the NUMA API to instruct the kernel where memory should be allocated and how. The Linux NUMA API enables applications to assign specific allocation behaviors (*policies*) to regions of their own virtual memory space. There is also a user-space `numactl` utility that controls NUMA policy for processes or shared memory.

4.13.4 vfstab

Solaris filesystem routines employ `vfstab` structures and contain `vfs` in the function name, such as `getvfsent`. Linux provides equivalent interfaces, but the routines use `fstab` structures and contain `fs` in the routine name, such as `getfsent`. `vfstab` on Solaris is defined in /usr/include/sys/vfstab.h. The definition of `fstab` on Linux is in /usr/include/fstab.h.

4.13.5 posix_spawn() and posix_spawnp()

In Solaris 10, these calls are implemented as a `vfork/exec` combination. That is, the fork handlers are not run when `posix_spawn` or `posix_spawnp` is called. These two calls have been available in Linux since `glibc` version 2.2 as user-level implementations. These calls use `vfork` if the `POSIX_SPAWN_USEVFORK` flag is set.[38] You can find more information about `posix_spawn` and `posix_spawnp` at www.opengroup.org/onlinepubs/009695399/functions/posix_spawn.html.

4.13.6 plock()

The Linux equivalent of the `plock` function is `mlock`. The `mlock` function call disables paging for the memory in the range starting at `addr` with length `len` bytes. All pages that contain a part of the specified memory range are guaranteed to be resident in RAM when the `mlock` call returns successfully.

4.13.7 waitpid()

This call suspends execution of the current process until a child as specified by one of the arguments has exited, or until a signal is delivered whose action is to

38 The discussion on using `vfork` in `posix_spawn()` can also be found at http://sources.redhat.com/bugzilla/show_bug.cgi?id=378.

terminate the current process or to call a signal-handling function. Table 4-29 compares the options available for this call in Solaris and Linux.

TABLE 4-29
Comparison of the Option for waitpid() Between Solaris and Linux

Solaris	Linux	Description
`WNOHANG`	`WNOHANG`	Return immediately if status is not immediately available for one of the child processes specified by *`pid`*.
`WUNTRACED`	`WUNTRACED`	The status of any specified child processes that are stopped, and whose status has not yet been reported since they stopped, is also reported to the calling process.
`WCONTINUED`	`WCONTINUED` (since Linux 2.6.10)	Wait for processes continued.
`WNOWAIT`	N/A	Keep the process whose status is returned in a waitable state. The process may be waited for again with the identical result.
N/A	`__WCLONE`	(Linux-specific option) Wait for the clone children only.
N/A	`__WALL`	(Linux-specific option) Wait for all children, regardless of type (clone or nonclone).
N/A	`__WNOTHREAD`	(Linux-specific option) Do not wait for children of other threads in the same thread group.

In Solaris, if the calling process has `SA_NOCLDWAIT` set or has `SIGCHLD` set to `SIG_IGN` and the process has no unwaited children that were transformed into zombie processes, it blocks until all of its children terminate, and `waitpid()` fails and sets `errno` to `ECHILD`. Linux 2.6 conforms to this behavior.

In Linux 2.4, if a `wait()` or `waitpid()` call is made while `SIGCHLD` is being ignored, the call behaves just as though `SIGCHLD` were not being ignored. That is, the call blocks until the next child terminates and then returns the PID and status of that child.

The `waitid()` system call (available since Linux 2.6.9) provides better control over which child state changes to wait for.

4.14 Scientific Library

Solaris provides scientific functionalities through its Sun S3L Toolkit[39] functions. Sun S3L consists of a set of *core* library functions—that is, subroutines that perform linear algebra, Fourier transform, and other scientific computations—plus a set of auxiliary utilities, referred to as the *toolkit* functions.

Table 4-30 shows Sun S3L core routines.

TABLE 4-30
Sun S3L Core Routines

Dense matrix operations	LU-factorization and LU-solve routines	Parallel 1D, 2D, and 3D FFTs
Structured solver	Dense symmetric eigenvalue solver	Dense Singular Value Decomposition
Sparse routines	Iterative solver	Convolution/Deconvolution
Iterative eigensolver	Autocorrelation	Sort and grade
Parallel random number generators	Parallel sort	Parallel transpose
Copy array routine	Zero array elements	PBLAS 1,2,3
Tridiagonal solvers	Banded solvers	Symmetric eigensolver
Singular Value Decomposition	Least Squares Solver	

The GNU Scientific Library (GSL) is a collection of routines for numeric computing. The routines have been written from scratch in C, and they present a modern API for C programmers, allowing wrappers to be written for very high-level languages. The source code is distributed under the GNU General Public License. More information about GSL appears in Chapter 3.

39 http://docs.sun.com/app/docs/doc/805-6275-10/6j5tr68b9?q=scientific+library&a=view

4.15 Large Page Support

Large page usage is primarily intended to provide performance improvements to applications that allocate a lot of memory and frequently access that memory. The performance improvement is mainly due to the reduced number of misses in the Translation Lookaside Buffer (TLB), a cache of virtual-to-physical translation. The number of misses can be reduced when the TLB is able to map a larger virtual memory range. This is possible due to the multiple page size support provided by most modern architectures. For example, the 32-bit Intel architecture supports 4K and 4M (2M in PAE mode) page sizes; Itanium supports multiple page sizes 4K, 8K, 64K, 256K, 1M, 4M, 16M, 256M; SUN UltraSPARC supports 8K, 64K, 512K, 4M; and the 64-bit PowerPC (ppc64) supports 4K, 64K, 16MB, and 16GB.

The Linux 2.6 kernel has built-in support for `hugetlbpage` (the term used by the Linux community for large page). However, how applications can take advantage of the large page support in Solaris and Linux is slightly different. At the time of this writing, Linux applications can only obtain large page support via the `mmap` and System V shared memory system calls. More information on Linux's large page support is provided in Chapter 3.

4.16 Some Solaris Nonportable Programming Practices

As the preceding comparison tables of system and library APIs show, a few Solaris calls are not portable to the Linux platform.Table 4-31 identifies some of the top incompatible APIs that may be encountered when porting Solaris applications to Linux.

TABLE 4-31
Porting Practices on Solaris That May Need Significant Porting Effort on Linux

Solaris	Linux
Use of `nlist`	Look at `lsof` source code for `nlist_private` example
Reading /dev/kmem directly	Port using `/procfs` and `sysinfo` API
Use of System V release 4 streams	Use open source; Linux Streams (LiS) (www.gcom.com/home/linux/lis/)
Use of Service Level Protocol	Use open source; OpenSLP (www.openslp.org)
Use of XTI/TLI	Use open source; OpenSS7 Project (www.openss7.org)

Caution is advised when using the equivalent Linux solutions presented. The list is presented only as a reference and not as officially recommended solutions. Investigate the viability of the solutions before planning to implement them in your applications.

4.17 Summary

The porting work is considered complete when two objectives are met. The first objective is to make sure all the necessary objects and executables of the application are produced. The second objective is to make sure the ported application, including all executables produced, runs and stays up long enough to pass basic unit testing. If the application passes basic unit testing, it is then passed on to the next phase of the project, which is testing and debugging. Here are some important highlights discussed in this chapter:

- Linux 2.6 supports the latest and most common industry standards from POSIX, ISO, and SUS, making it more compatible with UNIX platforms. This allows applications running on other operating systems such as Solaris that adhere to these standards to be ported to Linux with as little change as possible.
- The latest GNU C and C++ compilers offer the same functionalities provided by Solaris compilers. The main task for porting engineers is to find and match the equivalent compiler switches in the GNU compilers to match those used in the Solaris application build environment.
- Library versioning support framework on Solaris is close to that on Linux. Both support external and symbol versioning. GNU `ld` provides a few extensions to that on Solaris.
- Linux 2.6 supports a version of dynamic linking that can easily provide equivalent support for the type of dynamic linking provided on the Solaris platform.
- Linux offers a variety of open-source shells that provide support functionality equivalent to shells on other UNIX platforms. Shell scripts that run on Solaris can be easily ported to run on Linux.
- Some APIs that Linux provides may reside in different libraries. Differences in system library names and locations must be taken into account when linking in Linux.

- Overall the APIs and system calls that exist on Solaris already exist in the standard Linux distribution. For those APIs or system calls supported on Solaris that do not exist in the standard Linux distribution, most have equivalent support through other open-source initiatives referenced in this chapter.

This chapter discussed common issues encountered during a porting project. Although some applications are relatively easy to port because of their inherently portable characteristics, some applications written to use Solaris extensions require a little more porting effort. Overall, Linux 2.6 has improved on its capabiltities to readily accept software applications to run on it. Porting to Linux has never been easier. New features such as a preemptive kernel and support for more-efficient threads scheduling makes Linux an operating system that is truly ready for enterprise use.

Chapter 5

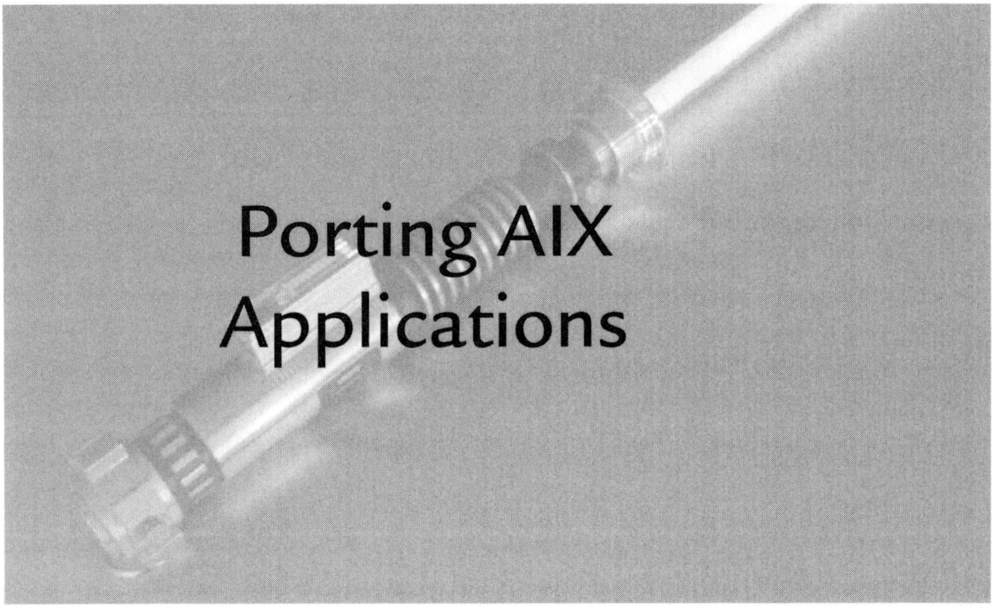

Porting AIX Applications

In this chapter

Porting is the step of the process during which modifications to the application take place. At this point, most if not all technical aspects and dependencies of the application should have already been uncovered during the scoping and analysis steps. The only thing that needs to be done now is to modify the source code so that it compiles and runs on the Linux platform.

During the porting process, software developers and porting personnel will likely encounter several differences between the UNIX operating system they are used to and the Linux 2.6 platform. For each topic discussed in this chapter, the most common differences are presented to explain what works and what does not work on the Linux 2.6 environment. The AIX environment described in this chapter is based mostly on version 5L but should also be applicable to older versions of AIX. Although this chapter discusses AIX topics in some detail, it is assumed that porting engineers reading the chapter already have software development experience on AIX.

5.1 Preliminary Tasks

Before the porting work can begin, we need to prepare the environment that we will be working in. Among other things, we need to set up the port, build, and code change systems. Here is a checklist that includes the detailed tasks for each.

5.1.1 Set Up the Porting System

The porting system includes the porting server running the Linux version that the application to be ported is expected to run on. In some instances, the server can be used to run small unit tests that will not affect overall server performance.

Complete the following steps to set up the porting system:

1. Install the server with the Linux distribution that the application to be ported is expected to run on.
2. Set up all necessary home directories and build environment directories.
3. Check for any known patches that need to be installed on the server.
4. Make sure the installation includes the compiler and debugger.
5. Install third-party products and licenses that the application needs. Install any prerequisites or patches needed by these products.

6. Set up access for users and system administrators on the build server.
7. Set up policies on using the porting environment as a test machine. These polices must include what can and cannot be tested on the porting server.

Depending on how work is divided among different groups involved in the porting project, the responsibility of doing these tasks may fall on the porting engineer. Even in instances where a separate group in the IT organization sets up the server, the porting engineer still needs to provide the specifications of the environment to the person performing the installation and setup.

5.1.2 Set Up the Code Change Management System

The code change management system consists of a tool that manages code changes to the application. CVS is the tool used most frequently, but other tools such as Subversion[1] and Arch[2] are gaining popularity. Complete these steps to set up the change management system:

1. Install the code change management tool.
2. Install scripts that can be used to make using the tool more convenient for the porting engineers.
3. Make sure the HOWTO and FAQs on using the tool and scripts exist and are readily accessible. These documents should include examples of how to use the tool and scripts.
4. Check the application into the code management system.

After the snapshot of the application source code has been checked into the code management system, that code should only be used for porting changes. No outside development changes should be added to this code base during the porting period.

---

1 http://subversion.tigris.org

2 www.gnu.org/software/gnu-arch/

5.1.3 Set Up the Build System

Automated nightly builds of the ported application take place in the build system. Although it may not be needed to begin any porting work, it is good practice to set up the build system before porting application makefiles. This system needs to be able to check out the source code and start an overnight build of the application. Building the application nightly after the code is stable enough to build with minimum build errors is good practice to make sure all checked-in code that day did not cause anything to break in the build. If something does break, it will be easier to determine who and what caused the break. These tasks must be completed when setting up the build system:

1. Develop scripts that can check out the application code and start a nightly build.
2. Test these scripts after the makefiles have been ported. Expect errors, because the porting work may be just getting underway.
3. Add the script to a crontab file to schedule the overnight builds.
4. Write a script that can parse the errors produced so that an automated reporting system can notify responsible parties of any build breaks.

When the port, code change, and build system tasks are complete, the real porting work can begin.

5.2 General Differences

A common misconception is that the more familiar you are with the code you are porting, the more successful the port will be. In fact, first and foremost, your biggest advantage is how familiar you are with the source build environment. Familiarity with the code is second, although not required. On the other hand, not being familiar with the ported code will not hinder the porting effort. Instead, having a good knowledge of ANSI C/C++, ISO, and POSIX standards will give you a greater advantage than knowing the code. These skills are needed to help you assess and troubleshoot the code when you have to make surgical and strategic changes in the existing code. This section will help you build on those analytical skills so that you make the correct changes when necessary.

Although both AIX and GNU claim to adhere to ANSI, ISO, and POSIX standards, there are some differences. This section covers those differences between the two platforms and their development environments. Although some example codes are used to clarify points, most of the material covered in this section relates to differences in system calls, compiler and linker invocation, and library creation.

5.2.1 C Language

Both the AIX C compiler and GCC support the ANSI C (ANSI/ISO 9899-1990) standard, but syntax and semantics differences may still prevent an error-free compilation in Linux. Within GCC other standards can be selected by using the `-ansi`, `-std=89`, or `-std=iso9899:1990` options.

5.2.2 C++ Language

Starting with GNU `g++` version 3.4.0, GNU `g++` claims[3] to be *much* closer to the ISO/ANSI C++ standards. This means, among other things, that a lot of invalid constructs that used to be accepted in previous versions will now be rejected. The AIX `xlC` (C++) compiler implements the latest ANSI C++ standards (including the Standard Template Library, STL) in libC. A GNU `g++` compilers implements the latest ANSI C++ standards and STL in the `libstdc++` library. For both AIX and GNU, to use the STL you just include the appropriate template library. Overall, this means that although some differences do exist between AIX and GNU, there are minimal differences in standards compliance when migrating from the latest version of AIX C++ to GNU `g++`. In short, applications written with standards in mind are easier to migrate than those that are not.

5.2.3 GNU C/C++ Language

The GNU Compiler Collection (`gcc`) is available for AIX. Applications compiled with `gcc` on AIX make porting and migration easier on Linux. You should be careful when using different versions of the GCC compiler when migrating from AIX to Linux. Applications that compile cleanly on older versions of GCC might not compile as well on new versions because of changes in programming standards, specifically in the C++ language.

---

3 http://gcc.gnu.org/gcc-3.4/changes.html#cplusplus

5.2.4 Java Language

The AIX SDK for the Java platform provides the Java 2 (version 1.4) programming tools and runtime environment. The Java environment is available for Linux through the Blackdown Java SDK (www.blackdown.org). As of this writing, Blackdown has released Java version 1.4.2 and is working on release version 1.5. Other Linux Java SDKs are available for download from Sun and IBM Web sites.

5.2.5 Threads

AIX 5L supports the POSIX threads implementation. Previous versions of AIX prior to release 5L supported DCE pthreads. Applications using DCE threads will need some major changes to use POSIX threads on Linux. Refer to Section 5.16, Posix Threads, for more information on differences between AIX and Linux.

5.2.6 Standards Comparison

Almost all Linux distributors acknowledge the values that standardization and portability provide, and work with the various Linux implementers/maintainers to meet those standards. The primary Linux industry standard is the Linux Standard Base (LSB), which is a project overseen by the Free Standards Group (FSG). The LSB (whose most recent version at this time is LSB 3.0) is based heavily on the IEEE POSIX and Open Group Single UNIX Specification standards, but also documents those places where Linux is not UNIX- or POSIX-compatible. Most (and all the major) Linux distributors have certified to the LSB.

The LSB, in addition to providing a source code API specification, also provides a binary interface (ABI) specification for each of several common Linux hardware platforms. The goal of the ABI is to ensure binary portability (for LSB-portable applications) between Linux distributions on that hardware platform. Distributors must certify to the ABI as well as the API. Independent Service Vendors (ISVs) can also certify their applications as "LSB portable" using tools provided by the FSG.

Although there is standardization within Linux, Linux itself is not totally compliant with either the IEEE POSIX or Open Group SUS specifications. This means that applications that may be totally portable under these common commercial UNIX standards may still need some work to move successfully to Linux. Still, considerably less work would be required than for an application that meets no standards at all or that uses AIX-specific UNIX extensions.

Table 5-1 compares AIX supported standards to the Linux supported standards based on the LSB specification version 2.0.1.

TABLE 5-1
Supported Standards on AIX and Linux

Standard	AIX	Linux
IEEE POSIX 1003.1-2001 Base Function	Supported	Supported as described in the LSB
IEEE POSIX 1003.1 Threads (pthreads)	Supported	Supported
Single UNIX Specification Base function (sometimes known as XPG5 or XPG6)	Supported	Supported as described in the LSB
IEEE POSIX 1003.1b Real-time scheduler, clocks and timers, asynchronous I/O, semaphores, memory locking, message queues, real-time signals, shared memory	Supported	Asynchronous I/O, real-time signals, shared memory, semaphores
IEEE POSIX 1003.4a Draft 4 User Threads	On earlier release of AIX prior to 5L only	Not supported
IEEE POSIX 1003.1-2001 (Commands and Utilities)	Supported	Supported
System V Interface Definition (SVID3)	Supported	Referenced[4]
File System Directory Layout	System V.4 (SVR4)	Filesystem Hierarchy Standard, www.pathname.com/fhs/
X11 Window System, Font Server, and Clients	X11R6.3	X11R6.4
OSF/Motif	V2.1	Supported through third-party libraries (see lesstif, www.lesstif.org)[5]

4 A referenced standard means that not all interfaces within the standard are supported.

5 Not included within the LSB specification

Standard	AIX	Linux
RPC function interfaces NFS+ Diskless and ONC+, NFS+, version 4.2	Supported	Supported Referenced standards, SVID Issue 4, SVID Issue 3
OSF/Motif Application Environment Specification (AES)	Supported	Supported through third-party products[6]
LP64, 64-bit data model	Supported	Supported

With the exception of IEEE POSIX 1003.4a Draft 4 user threads, both AIX and Linux fully support standards.[7] Draft 4 user threads are DCE threads, which are an earlier version of POSIX threads. Because over the years AIX has been available longer than Linux, some earlier versions of AIX support DCE threads, whereas Linux support of threads starts with Native POSIX Threads Library (NPTL), which claims to be more compliant with regular POSIX threads. NPTL is discussed in detail in Chapter 3, "Analysis."

5.3 Compilers

IBM VisualAge XL C/C++ and GNU GCC/G++ both are ISO/ANSI standard-compliant, although XL claims to provide a higher level of compliance. In most cases, however, with the exception of a few warnings, applications built with XL C/C++ compile and link with GNU GCC/G++ with minimal effort. In its simplest form, the following syntax shows the similarity in compiler invocation under IBM and GNU. Here's your typical "Hello World" source compiled and linked with both XL and GNU compilers.

C compile and link

Main.c:

```
#include <stdio.h>
int main()
{
printf("Hello World\n");
return 0;
}
```

6 See Open Motif, www.opengroup.org/openmotif/faq.html

7 Conflicts between ISO/IEC 9945 (POSIX) and the LSB

Compile:

```
gcc -c main.c -o main.o (GNU)
xlc -c main.c -o main.o (IBM/AIX)
```

Link:

```
gcc -o main main.o (GNU)
xlc -o main main.o (IBM/AIX)
```

C++ compile and link

Main.cpp:

```
#include <iostream.h>
int main()
{
cout << "Hello World\n"
return 0;
}
```

```
g++ -c main.cpp -o main.o (GNU)[8]
xlC -c main.cpp -o main.o (IBM/AIX)
```

Link:

```
g++ -o main main.o (GNU)
xlC -o main main.o (IBM/AIX)
```

As you can see, the only difference between IBM XL C/C++ and GNU GCC/G++ is the invocation method between the C and C++ compile and link stage. For applications migrating from IBM environments, the equivalent C/C++ invocation under GNU is `gcc/g++`, respectively.

However, some migrations are not so straightforward. There are differences. The extent of those differences depends on the type of output you are trying to build, the code being ported, how well the original developers adhered to ANSI standards, and the number of dependent environment APIs used inside the application being ported.

5.3.1 Invoking the Compiler

One of the many features that IBM tried to build into their compiler is ease of use. Long ago, they recognized that developers used the same distinct parameters to

8 Under AIX, this syntax creates a deprecation warning for `iostream.h` that can be ignored for this source. To suppress this warning, use `-Wno-deprecated`.

build certain applications. For instance, in AIX, to build a multithreaded application, you must include the POSIX threads system library in your executable (`libpthread`). The same holds true for standard AIX system calls such as streams and file manipulations; developers must include the standard system library (`libc.a`) or some variant thereof.

To ease the complexity of trying to remember all the different required parameters and libraries to include when invoking their compiler, IBM introduced distinct compiler invocation methods that in turn turned on certain parameters and included distinct libraries automatically depending on the desired output. For instance, to build a multithreaded C application, the developer merely would have to invoke the `xlc_r` compiler method. The `_r` denotes `REENTRANT`, meaning the resulting executable will be thread-safe. When invoked on the compile line, this method automatically turns the following parameters on and includes the following libraries:

```
xlc_r: use = DEFLT
  crt = /lib/crt0.o
  mcrt = /lib/mcrt0.o
  gcrt = /lib/gcrt0.o
  libraries = -L/usr/lpp/xlopt,-lxlopt,-L/usr/lib/threads,-lpthreads,    -lc
  proflibs = -L/lib/profiled,-L/usr/lib/profiled
  hdlibs = -L/usr/vac/lib,-lhmd_r
  options = -qansialias,-qthreaded,-D_THREAD_SAFE,-D__VACPP_MULTI__
```

The preceding stanza is equivalent to the following ANSI C compiler invocation:[9]

```
cc -o <your desired output > -qansialias,-qthreaded,-D_THREAD_SAFE,
-D__VACPP_MULTI__ -L/usr/lpp/xlopt -L/usr/lib/threads -L/lib/profiled
-L/usr/lib/profiled -L/usr/vac/lib -lxlopt -lpthreads -lc -lhmd_r /lib/crt0.o
/lib/mrt0.o /lib/gcrt0.o <your source ...>
```

GNU GCC/G++ does not provide for this type of shorthand method in building certain types of applications. Depending on your desired output, you must include the appropriate library(s) and parameter(s) on the command line. For instance, the equivalent command in Linux that will replace the IBM XL C `xlc_r` method is as follows:

```
gcc -o <your desired output> -L/usr/lib -lpthreads -D_REENTRANT <your source ...>
```

---

9 For a listing of all the XL C/C++ compiler invocations and the libraries and parameters that are automatically included, refer to the /etc/vac.cfg file on your AIX system.

Table 5-2 provides a GNU reference for each IBM XL C/C++ compiler invocation.

TABLE 5-2
Compiler Invocation on AIX and Linux

IBM XL C/C++ 5.0 or higher	GNU	Description
`xlc_r`, `cc_r`, or (+ `_r4`, `_r7`)	`gcc -L/usr/lib/threads -lpthread -D_REENTRANT`	POSIX 1003.1c threads `_r4` = DCE threads `_r7` = Provided by IBM for AIX 4.3 users to help with migration to POSIX Draft 10
`xlC_r` or (+ `_r4`, `_r7`)	`g++ -L/usr/lib/threads -lpthread -D_REENTRANT`	
`xlc` `cc`	`gcc`	ANSI C compiler usage
`C89`	`gcc -ansi`	Strict ANSI C standard (ISO/IEC 9899:1990)

`xlc128`
`xlC128`
`cc128`
	Not supported	For XL C/C++ increases the length of long double types from 64 to 128 bits

For POSIX threads, depending on the current distribution of Linux you are porting to, additional preprocessor directives may need to be turned on. Refer to the document that came with your distribution.

Both IBM and GCC provide an array of compiler switches that enable the user to control the behavior and the type of output generated. For instance, both have optimization parameters to control the size and performance characteristics of an output, as well as switches to control how the executable is built, such as `-L` and `-I` switches, which control the search path of libraries and include files. In addition, some switches are architecture-specific and are exclusive to either IBM XLC/C++ or GCC. Table 5-3 compares compiler switches between IBM XLC/C++ and gcc/g++. Because some of the -qoption switches for IBM XLC/C++ are architecture-specific, a comparable GCC compiler switch is not available.

TABLE 5-3
XLC/C++ and gcc/g++ Compiler Switches Comparison Table

C/C++ VisualAge for AIX Option[10]	GNU gcc Option[11]	Description (AIX-based)
-+	-x c++	(C++) Compiles any file, *filename.nnn,* as a C++ language file, where *nnn* is any suffix other than .o, .a, or .s.
-#	-###	Traces the compilation without doing anything.
-q32 -q64	-m32[12] -m64[12]	Selects 32- or 64-bit compiler mode. Additional -m options for GCC are available. Refer to GNU Documentation Online.
-qlanglvl=<*option*>	-fstd=<*OPTION*>	Specifies which language level to use when invoking the compiler.
-qaggrcopy	None	Enables destructive copy operations for structures and unions.
-qalias -qansialias	-fstrict-aliasing	Specifies which type-based aliasing is to be used during optimization.
-qalign	-mstrict-align[12]	Specifies what aggregate alignment rules the compiler uses for file compilation.

10 VisualAge C++ for AIX Compiler Reference (SC09-4959-00)

11 GNU Compiler Collections version 3.4.2 (last updated May 23, 2004)

12 These are all part of the GNU -m machine-dependent options. Refer to the following link for specific platform compiler options: http://gcc.gnu.org/onlinedocs/gcc-2.95.3/gcc_2.html.

C/C++ VisualAge for AIX Option	GNU gcc Option	Description (AIX based)
`-qalloca` `-ma`	None	Substitutes inline code for calls to function `alloca` as if `#pragma alloca` directives are in the source code.
`-qarch`	`-mcpu=`*cpu_type*[12]	Specifies the type of IBM architecture on which the executable program will be run. This refers to all the RS6000 and POWER architectures.
`-qnoassert`	None	Asks the compiler to apply aliasing assertions to your compilation unit.
`-qattr`	None	Produces a compiler listing that includes an attribute listing for all identifiers.
`-B`, `-t`	`-B`	`-B`: Determines substitute path names for the compiler, assembler, linkage editor, and preprocessor. `-t`: Adds the prefix specified by the `-B` option to designated programs. `-tE` replaces the CreateExportList script.

`-bdynamic`
`bshared`
	`-shared -fpic`
	(or `-fPIC`)
	`-Bsharable`
	or
	`-Wl -brt -shared`
		Instructs the linker to process subsequent shared objects as either dynamic or shared.

`-bstatic`	`-static`
	`-Bstatic`
	`-dn`
	`-non_shared`
		Links all referenced objects statically although they may be shared objects.

`-qbitfields`	`-fsigned-bitfields` (default)	Specifies whether bitfields are signed.
`-bmaxdata`	Refer to the section, "Large Page Support," in Chapter 3.	Sets the size of the heap in bytes.

C/C++ VisualAge for AIX Option	GNU gcc Option	Description (AIX based)

`-brtl`	`-shared`
	`-Wl`
	Refer Section 5.5, "Linker."
		Enables runtime linking.

`-C`	`-C`	Preserves comments in preprocessed output.
`-c`	`-c`	Instructs the compiler to pass source files to the compiler only.
`-qcache`	None	Specifies a cache configuration for a specific execution machine.
`-qchars=[signed or unsigned]`	`-fsigned-char` `-funsigned-char`	Instructs the compiler to treat all variables of type char as either signed or unsigned.
`-qcheck`	None	Generates code that performs certain types of runtime checking
`-qcinc`	None	(C++) Includes files from specified directories have the tokens `extern " C " {` inserted before the file, and `}` appended after the file.
`-qcompact`	`-Os`	When used with optimization, reduces code size where possible, at the expense of execution speed.
`-qcpluscmt`	C++ syle of comments is turned on automatically in GNU C, unless `-ansi` is turned on.	(C++) Use this option if you want C++ comments to be recognized in C source files.
`-D`	`-D`	Defines the identifier *name,* as in a `#define` preprocessor directive.
`-qdataimported`	None	Marks data as imported. Used to import functions.
`-qdatalocal`	None	Marks data as local.
`-qdbxextra`	None	(C only) Specifies that all `typedef` declarations, `struct`, `union`, and `enum` type definitions are included for debugger processing.

C/C++ VisualAge for AIX Option	GNU gcc Option	Description (AIX based)
`-qdigraph`	None	Allows use of digraph character sequences in your program.
`-qdollar`	`-fdollars-in-identifiers` This is the default behavior of GNU on most platforms.	Allows the $ symbol to be used in the names of identifiers.
`-qdpcl`	None	Generates block scopes to support the IBM Dynamic Probe Class Library.
`-E`	`-E`	Runs the source files named in the compiler invocation through the preprocessor.
`-eLabel`	`-e Label` `--entry=Label` Refer to the "Linker" section.	Specifies the entry name for the shared object. Equivalent to using `ld -e` *name*. See your system documentation for additional information about `ld` options. Used only with `-qmkshrobj`.
`-qeh`	`-fexceptions`	(C++) Controls exception handling.
`-qenum`	Use keyword `__attribute__`[13]	Specifies the amount of storage occupied by the enumerations.
`-qexpfile`	None	Saves all exported symbols in a file.
`-qextchk`	None	Generates bind-time type of checking information and checks for compile-time consistency.
`-F`	None	Names an alternative configuration file for `xlC`.
`-f`	None	Names a file to store a list of object files.

13 Refer to "Specifying Attributes of Types" in the GNU documentation: http://hea-www.harvard.edu/MST/simul/software/docs/pkg/gcc/gcc.html#SEC13.

C/C++ VisualAge for AIX Option	GNU gcc Option	Description (AIX based)
`-qfpdr`	None	Collects program information for use with the AIX `fdpr` performance-tuning utility.
`-qflag`	None	Specifies the minimum severity level of diagnostic messages to be reported.
`-qfloat`	None (Accuracy of floating-point is different on differing platforms.)	Specifies various floating-point options to speed up or improve the accuracy of floating-point operations.
`-qflttrap`	`-mfp-trap-mode=` *`trap mode`*	Generates extra instructions to detect and trap floating-point exceptions.
`-qfold`	None	Specifies that constant floating-point expressions are to be evaluated at compile time.
`-qfullpath`	None	Specifies what path information is stored for files when you use `-g` and the distributed graphical debugger.
`-qfuncsect`	None	Places instructions for each function in a separate object file, control section, or csect.
`-G`	`-shared` `-Bshareable`	Linkage editor (`ld` command) option only. Used to generate a dynamic libary file.
`-g`	`-g`	Generates debugging information used by a debugger such as the Distributed Debugger.
`-qgenproto`	None	Produces ANSI prototypes from K&R function definitions.
`-qhalt`	None	Instructs the compiler to stop after the compilation phase when it encounters errors of specified *severity* or greater.

C/C++ VisualAge for AIX Option	GNU gcc Option	Description (AIX based)
`-qhaltonmsg`	None	Enables debug versions of memory management functions.
`-qhot`	None	Instructs the compiler to perform high-order transformations on loops and array language during optimization, and to pad array dimensions and data objects to avoid cache misses.
`-qhsflt`	None	Speeds up calculations by removing range checking on single-precision `float` results and on conversions from floating-point to integer.
`-qhssngl`	None	Specifies that single-precision expressions are rounded only when the results are stored into `float` memory locations.
`-I`	`-I`	Specifies an additional search path if the filename in the `#include` directive is not specified using its absolute path name.
`-qidirfirst`	None	Specifies the search order for files included with the `#include` *`file_name`* directive.
`-qignerrno`	None	Allows the compiler to perform optimizations that assume `errno` is not modified by system calls.
`-qignprag`	None	Instructs the compiler to ignore certain `pragma` statements.
`-qinfo`	None	Produces informational messages.
`-qinitauto`	None	Initializes automatic storage to a specified two-digit hexadecimal byte value.

C/C++ VisualAge for AIX Option	GNU gcc Option	Description (AIX based)
`-qinlglue`	None	Generates fast external linkage by inlining the pointer glue code necessary to make a call to an external function or a call through a function pointer.
`-qinline`	`-finline-functions`	Attempts to inline functions instead of generating calls to a function.
`-qipa`	None	Turns on or customizes a class of optimizations known as interprocedural analysis (IPA).
`-qisolated_call`	None	Specifies functions in the source file that have no side effects.
`-qkeepinlines`	`-fkeep-inline-functions`	(C++) Instructs the compiler to keep or discard definitions for unreferenced `extern` inline functions.
`-qkeyword`	None	Controls whether a specified string is treated as a keyword or an identifier.
`-L`	`-L`	Searches the specified directory for library files specified by the `-l` option.
`-l`	`-l`	Searches a specified library for linking.
`-qlanglvl`	`-ansi -flang-isoc9x`	Selects the C or C++ language level for compilation.
`-qlargepage`	Refer to the "Large Page Support" section.	Instructs the compiler to exploit large page heaps available on Power4 systems running AIX v5.1D or later.
`-qldbl128`, `-qlongdouble`	None	Increases the size of long double type from 64 bits to 128 bits.

C/C++ VisualAge for AIX Option	GNU gcc Option	Description (AIX based)
`-qlibansi`	None	Assumes that all functions with the name of an ANSI C library function are in fact the system functions.
`-qlinedebug`	None	Generates abbreviated line number and source filename information for the debugger.
`-qlist`	None	Produces a compiler listing that includes an object listing.
`-qlistopt`	None	Produces a compiler listing that displays all options in effect.
`-qlonglit`	None	Makes unsuffixed literals the long type for 64-bit mode.
`-qlonglong`	`-mlong64` (Refer to the `-m` options for your targeted platform.)	Allows long long types in your program.
`-M`	`-M`	Creates an output file that contains targets suitable for inclusion in a description file for the AIX `make` command.
`-ma`	Refer to `alloc`.	(C only) Substitutes inline code for calls to function `alloca` as if `#pragma alloca` directives are in the source code.
`-qmacpstr`	None	(C only) Converts Pascal string literals into null-terminated strings where the first byte contains the length of the string.
`-qmaf`	None	Specifies whether the floating-point multiply-add instructions are to be generated.
`-qmakedep`	`-M`	Creates an output file that contains targets suitable for inclusion in a description file for the AIX `make` command.

C/C++ VisualAge for AIX Option	GNU gcc Option	Description (AIX based)
`-qmaxerr`	None	Instructs the compiler to halt compilation when a specified number of errors of specified or greater severity is reached.
`-qmaxmem`	None	Limits the amount of memory used for local tables of specific, memory-intensive optimizations.
`-qmbcs` `dbcs`	`LANG`[14]	Use the `-qmbcs` option if your program contains multibyte characters.
`-qmkshrobj`	`-shared` or `libtool`[15]	Creates a shared object from generated object files.
`-qnamemangling`	None	Selects the name-mangling scheme for external symbol names generated from C++ source code.
`-O` `-qoptimize`	`-O`	Optimizes code at a choice of levels during compilation.
`-o`	`-o`	Specifies a name or directory for the output executable file(s) created either by the compiler or the linkage editor.
`-qobjmodel`	None	(C++) Sets the type of object model.
`-qoldpassbyvalue`	None	(C++) Specifies how classes containing const or reference members are passed in function arguments.

14 Part of GCC environment variables

15 As an alternative, GNU Libtool could be used. Similar to the `-qmkshrobj` option, Libtool is also a script, but it provides a generic interface for building platform-independent libraries. Refer to http://gnu.mirrors.atn.ro/software/libtool/libtool.es.html for more information about using it.

C/C++ VisualAge for AIX Option	GNU gcc Option	Description (AIX based)
`-P`	`-E`	Preprocesses the C or C++ source files named in the compiler invocation and creates an output preprocessed source file for each input source file.
`-p`	None	Sets up the object files produced by the compiler for profiling.
`-qpascal`	None	(C only) Ignores the word `pascal` in type specifiers and function declarations.
`-qpath`	None	Constructs alternate program and path names.
`-qpdf1` `-qpdf2`	None	Tunes optimizations through Profile-Directed Feedback.
`-pg`	`-fprofile-generate`	Sets up the object files for profiling, but provides more information than is provided by the `-p` option.
`-qphsinfo`	`gcov`[16]	Reports the time taken in each compilation phase.
`-qprint`	None	Suppresses listings.
`-qpriority`	None	(C++) Specifies the priority level for the initialization of static constructors.

`-qproclocal`
`-qprocimported`
`-qprocunknown`
	None	Marks functions as local, imported, or unknown.

`-qproto`	None	(C only) Assumes all functions are prototyped.

16 `gcov` is a tool you can use in conjuction with GNU cc to test and profile code coverage. For more information about `gcov`, refer to the GNU documentation.

C/C++ VisualAge for AIX Option	GNU gcc Option	Description (AIX based)
`-Q`	`-O3`	Attempts to inline functions instead of generating calls to a function.
`-r`	`-mrelocatable`	Produces a relocatable object.
`-qreport`	None	Instructs the compiler to produce transformation reports that show how program loops are parallelized and optimized.
`-qrndflt`	None	Controls the compile-time rounding mode of constant floating-point expressions.
`-qrndsngl`	None	Specifies that the result of each single-precision `float` operation is to be rounded to single precision.
`-qro`	None	Specifies the storage type for string literals.
`-qroconst`	None	Specifies the storage location for constant values.
`-qrrm`	None	Prevents floating-point optimizations that are incompatible with runtime rounding to plus and minus infinity modes.
`-qrtti`	None	(C++) Generates runtime type identification (RTTI) information for the `typeid` operator and the `dynamic_cast` operator.
`-S`	`-S`	Generates an assembly language file (.s) for each source file.
`-s`	None	Strips the symbol table.
`-qshowinc`	None	If used with `-qsource`, all the include files are included in the source listing.

C/C++ VisualAge for AIX Option	GNU gcc Option	Description (AIX based)
`-qsmallstack`	None	Instructs the compiler to reduce the size of the stack frame.
`-qsmp`	None	Enables parallelization of IBM SMP-compliant program code.
`-qsource`	None	Produces a compiler listing and includes source code.
`-qspill`	None	Specifies the size of the register allocation spill area.
`-qspnans`	None	Generates extra instructions to detect signaling NaN on conversion from single precision to double precision.
`-qsrcmsg`	None	(C only) Adds the corresponding source code lines to the diagnostic messages in the `stderr` file.
`-qstaticinline`	None	(C ++) Controls whether inline functions are treated as `static` or `extern`.
`-qstatsym`	None	Adds user-defined, nonexternal names that have a persistent storage class to the name list.
`-qstdinc`	`-nostdinc` (`nostdinc++` for C++ source)	Specifies which files are included with #include <file_name> and #include "file_name" directives.
`-qstrict`	None	Turns off aggressive optimizations of the `-O3` option that have the potential to alter the semantics of your program.
`-qstrict_induction`	None	Disables loop-induction variable optimizations that have the potential to alter the semantics of your program.

C/C++ VisualAge for AIX Option	GNU gcc Option	Description (AIX based)
`-qsuppress`	None	Specifies compiler message numbers to be suppressed.
`-qsymtab`	None	Set symbol tables for unreferenced variables or `xcoff` objects.
`-qsyntaxonly`	`-fsyntax-only`	(C only) Causes the compiler to perform syntax checking without generating an object file.
`-qtabsize`	None	Changes the length of tabs as perceived by the compiler.
`-qtbtable`	None	Sets traceback table characteristics.
`-qtempinc`	`-frepo`	(C++) Generates separate include files for template functions and class declarations, and places these files in a directory, which can be optionally specified.
`-qtemplaterecompile`	`-frepo`	(C ++) Helps manage dependencies between compilation units that have been compiled using the `-qtemplateregistry` compiler option.
`-qtemplateregistry`	`-frepo`	(C++) Maintains records of all templates as they are encountered in the source and ensures that only one instantiation of each template is made.
`-qtempmax`	None	(C++) Specifies the maximum number of template include files to be generated by the `tempinc` option for each header file.
`-qthreaded`	`-lpthread` `-D_REENTRANT`	Indicates that the program will run in a multithreaded environment.
`-qtmplparse`	None	(C++) Controls whether parsing and semantic checking are applied to template definition implementations.

C/C++ VisualAge for AIX Option	GNU gcc Option	Description (AIX based)
`-qtocdata`	None	Marks data as local.
`-qtocmerge`	None	Enables TOC merging to reduce TOC pointer loads and improves the scheduling of external loads.
`-qtune`	`-b`	Specifies the architecture for which the executable program is optimized.
`-qtwolink`	None	(C++) Minimizes the number of static constructors included from libraries.
`-U`	`-U`	Undefines a specified identifier defined by the compiler or by the `-D` option.
`-qunique`	None	(C++) Generates unique names for static constructor/deconstructor file-compilation units.
`-qunroll`	`-funroll-loops`	Unrolls inner loops in the program.
`-qunwind`	None	Informs the compiler that the application does not rely on any program stack unwinding mechanism.
`-qupconv`	None	Preserves the unsigned specification when performing integral promotions.
`-V`	None	Instructs the compiler to report information on the progress of the compilation in a command-like format.
`-v`	`-v`	Instructs the compiler to report information on the progress of the compilation.
`-qvftable`	`-fvtable-thunks`	(C++) Controls the generation of virtual function tables.

C/C++ VisualAge for AIX Option	GNU gcc Option	Description (AIX based)
`-W`	None	Passes the listed words to a designated compiler program.
`-w`	`-w`	Requests that warning messages be suppressed.
`-qwarn64`	None	Enables warning of possible long to integer data truncations.
`-qxcall`	None	Generates code to static routines within a compilation unit as if they were external calls.
`-qxref`	None	Produces a compiler listing that includes a cross-reference listing of all identifiers.
`-y`	None	Specifies the compile-time rounding mode of constant floating-point expressions. See also `rndflt`.

5.4 Make

The `make` utility sorts out dependency relations between files, automatically determines which pieces need to be recompiled, and issues commands to recompile them. It is the biggest contribution to the UNIX development environment dating back to System V enabling easy management of large program projects. Over the years, `make` has been changed and enhanced. AIX still uses a version of the UNIX System V `make`, which is not compatible in Linux. To build code in Linux, you must use the GNU `Make` (`gmake`), which is part of the FSF GNU GCC (GNU Compiler Collection). The GNU `Make` includes enhanced features that are not included in the traditional `make`.

5.4.1 gmake Condition Statements

One of the most useful features that `gmake` has and regular `make` does not is the use of conditional statements. Example 5-1 examines this useful feature.

Example 5-1

GNU Makefile

```
# Gnu Makefile
 CC = gcc
 CXX = g++

 Objects = main.o
 Target = main
 Source = main.c

 main : $(Source)
#22 ifeq ($(Source),main.c)
  $(CC) -o $(Target) $(Source)
#24 else
  $(CXX) -o $(Target) $(Source)
#26 endif
```

The traditional AIX `make` generates the following errors:

```
/: > make
"Makefile", line 22: make: 1254-055 Dependency line needs colon or double colon
operator.
"Makefile", line 24: make: 1254-055 Dependency line needs colon or double colon
operator.
"Makefile", line 26: make: 1254-055 Dependency line needs colon or double colon
operator.
make: 1254-058 Fatal errors encountered -- cannot continue.
```

The same makefile builds fine with GNU `Make`. For a list of other enhancements, visit the official GNU home page (at the time of this writing www.gnu.org/software/make/manual/make.html).

5.5 Linker

Like UNIX, AIX and Linux provide facilities for the creation, development, testing, and debugging of shared libraries and applications that use them. AIX linker utilizes the eXtensible Common Object File Format (XCOFF), and Linux utilizes the Executable and Linkable Format (ELF). Early versions of Linux used a version of the old "a.out" format, but that format had many limitations that ELF corrects. ELF has become the most popular binary file format for UNIX and related operating systems such as Linux.

On both platforms, the default name for an XCOFF and ELF executable file is a.out.

5.5.1 Linker Incompatibilities

Although both AIX and Linux view "static linking" as the technique of defining multiple object files defining global symbols, and containing code and data, which are combined and written to an executable file with all references defined, they have different views on how the linker handles libraries in general. The linker and loader on AIX are designed such that libraries are self-contained entities with well-defined interfaces consisting of sets of imported and exported symbols. The system loader looks up symbols to relocate references, but all symbol resolution is performed at link time, simplifying the work of the loader. Shared objects in AIX are considered fully linked and resolved entities, where symbol references are resolved at link time and cannot be rebound at load time. On the other hand, Linux utilizes a version of linking, whereas it sees libraries as being very similar to ordinary ELF files where resolution of all global symbols is performed at runtime by the loader. In Linux, a dynamically linked file contains a Procedure Linkage Table (PLT). This table contains all the linker information that the runtime linker needs to relocate files and resolve any undefined symbols. The segment within the PLT that the loader examines when it loads a dynamically linked file is the `DYNAMIC` section. The `DYNAMIC` section contains the tagged values and pointers that the loader needs to locate symbols.

A shared module in AIX can be an object file or an archive file member, which can contain shared modules and/or ordinary object files. In Linux, shared libraries are always ordinary ELF object files, created with special options. Because of these differences, on the AIX platform GNU utilizes the native AIX linker rather than the GNU linker to link GNU executables.

In AIX to enable runtime linking (RTL), you must specify the `-brtl` parameter on the link line when building shared objects. The equivalent parameter in Linux is the `-shared` parameter. Both simply tell the loader to defer resolution of certain identified symbols until runtime. On AIX, when used with `-bdynamic`, `-brtl` also changes the search behavior for libraries on the link line. When both switches are turned on in AIX, the `-l` parameter tells the linker to search for libraries with .so and .a extensions (that is, shared objects and archives with precedence on .so). This is why archives can contain shared objects as members in AIX. In Linux, the `ld` command utilizes the standard UNIX behavior for searching for libraries, and the `-l` parameter only searches for archives (.a). For example, in Linux the following `ld` command searches for a `libout.a` library:

```
ld -o output -lout -L/usr/libs
```

The following command builds an RTL shared object in Linux:

```
ld -shared -o libshobj.so -lout -L/usr/libs
```

Additionally, Linux and AIX handle symbol resolution differently. In AIX, when the linker is resolving symbols, it grabs all the code available from the archive whether it needs it or not. In Linux, the linker only grabs what it needs. The downside is in Linux you may have to list archives on the command line more than once (unlike with AIX, in which you only need to list them once). This forces the Linux linker to search the archive more than once for additional symbols found in subsequent object files that are listed further down the link line.

As you can see, if you are accustomed to the AIX linker and loader mechanism for building archives and shared objects, you will have to make a few changes in your build environment before building on the Linux platform. Additional differences that AIX users need to be mindful of when porting to Linux include the following:

- In AIX, because archives can contain shared modules and vice versa, for archives that contain both shared objects and regular archives, the shared objects have to be separated from the link line (`ld` command) and built as separate linkable shared objects with .so extensions. The same goes for .o (object) files that contain shared objects.
- Shared objects that are passed to the Linux linker via the `-l` parameter have to be moved further down the link line (`ld` command) after the object file listing with the fully named shared library specified (for example, `libshobj.so`).
- To resolve symbols, archives may have to be listed more than once on the link line down level from triggering modules.

5.5.2 Linker: AIX to Linux Reference

Although GNU linker (`ld`) has a plethora of parameters, when porting from AIX you only have to concern yourself with a few. Table 5-4 highlights some subtle differences in the most commonly used parameters that are somewhat necessary, depending on your target, when porting to Linux from AIX.

TABLE 5-4
AIX and Linux Linker Switches Comparison Table*

AIX	Linux	Description
-bexpall	-E --export-dynamic	When creating a dynamically linked executable, adds all symbols to the dynamic symbol table.
-bmaxdata:<*size*>	-G*value* --gpsize=*value*	Sets the maximum size of objects to be optimized using the GP register to *size*. This is only meaningful for object file formats such as MIPS ECOFF that support putting large and small objects into different sections. This is ignored for other object file formats.
-e*Label*	-e *entry* --entry=*entry*	Uses *entry* as the explicit symbol for beginning execution of your program, rather than the default entry point.
-bdynamic or -bshared	-Bdynamic -dy -call_shared or -Wl -brt -shared	Links against dynamic libraries. The different variants of this option are for compatibility with various systems. You may use this option multiple times on the command line: It affects library searching for -l options that follow it.
-bM:SRE or -brtl or -G	-shared -Bshareable	Creates a shared library that is reentrant (runtime linkable).
-l	-l*archive*	Adds archive file lib*archive*.a to the list of files to link. This option may be used any number of times. This option also searches for shared objects (.so) for other platforms; however, when running on a Linux platform, only archives are searched.
-Z	-Y	Specifies a search path for library names.
-L	-rpath *path*	Specifies the library search direction for the runtime linker.
-L	-L	Searches the specified directory for library files specified by the -l option.

* Caution is advised when using the equivalent Linux solutions presented. The list is presented only as a reference and not as officially recommended solutions. Please investigate the viability of the solutions before planning to implement them in your applications.

The GNU linker (`ld`) is meant to cover a broad range of situations and to be as compatible as possible with other linkers. As a result, you have many other choices to control its behavior. But if you want your application to remain portable, you can use the GNU libtool for building libraries for Linux. GNU libtool is a generic library support script that hides the complexity of using libraries (for example, creating and installing shared and archived libraries) behind a consistent, portable interface. On Linux, GNU libtool is built on top of the tools and conventions for using the standard GNU Library (`glib`). Refer to the GNU libtool online for additional options and its usage.

5.6 AIX Versus Linux Shared Library Creation

Although all UNIX implementations provide the same general linking and loading functionality, subtle differences do exist in how they are created. In AIX, shared libraries can be an object file or an archived file member. An archived library can contain multiple members, some of which are shared modules and some ordinary object files. In addition, under AIX, after you have built a shared library, the library is ready for use. This is not so in Linux.

In Linux, shared libraries contain only ordinary object files and archives. And a shared library cannot be a member of an archive. In addition, one *major* difference between AIX and Linux is that in Linux after you have your library built, as a final step you must run your library through a versioning tool that links it to a version number. Only then will your library be ready for use.

If you are accustomed to the way AIX builds libraries, Linux library versioning will be a new concept for you. Library versioning is discussed in detail in Chapter 3. AIX users must make sure they fully understand the section in Chapter 3 on Linux library versioning and implement library versioning in all shared libraries to be ported to Linux.

5.7 Dynamic Loading

Dynamically loaded (DL) libraries are libraries that are loaded at times other than during the startup of a program. At runtime, the program allows applications to load new modules into its address space for new functionalities without having to link the required libraries. They are particularly useful for implementing plug-ins or modules. Both AIX and Linux support dynamic loading. Table 5-5 compares the differences in how to dynamically load routines between AIX and Linux.

TABLE 5-5
Dynamically Loading Routines Between AIX and Linux

AIX	Linux	Description

`dlopen`
Flags: `RTLD_LAZY`
`RTLD_NOW`
`RTLD_GLOBAL`
`RTLD_LOCAL`
`RTLD_MEMBER`
`RTLD_NOAUTODEFER`
	`dlopen`
	Flags: `RTLD_LAZY`
	`RTLD_NOW`
	`RTLD_GLOBAL`
	`RTLD_LOCAL`
	`RTLD_NODELETE`
	`RTLD_NOLOAD`
	`RTLD_BINDING_MASK`
	`RTLD_DEEPBIND`
		Dynamically loads a module into the calling process.

`dlsym`
Handles: `RTLD_DEFAULT`
`RTLD_NEXT`
`RTLD_MYSELF`
	`dlsym`
	Handles: `RTLD_DEFAULT`
	`RTLD_NEXT`
		Looks up the location of a symbol in a module that is loaded with `dlsym`.

`dlerror`	`dlerror`	Returns a pointer to information about the last `dlopen`, `dlsym`, or `dlclose` error.
`dlclose`	`dlcloseg`	Closes and unloads a module loaded by the `dlopen` subroutine.

`dladdr`
`DI_info_structure:`
`const char *dli_fname;`
`void *dli_fbase;`
`const char *dli_sname;`
`void *dli_saddr;`
`size_t dli_size;`
`int dli_bind;`
`int dli_type;`
	`dladdr`
	`DI_info_structure:`
	`const char *dli_fname;`
	`void *dli_fbase;`
	`const char *dli_sname;`
	`void *dli_saddr;`
	`size_t dli_size;`
		Translates address to symbolic information.

None	`dlvsym`	(Linux only) Does the same as `dlsym()` but takes a version string as an additional argument.

The basic `dl` functions (`dlopen`, `dlclose`, `dladdr`, and so on) for using DL libraries exhibit the same behavior in Linux as in AIX. The transition from AIX to Linux should be seamless. In Linux, to enable DL functionality, the application must link with the *libld.so* library, `-ldl`. Chapter 3 shows an example of how to use DL on Linux.

5.8 Template Instantiation Differences Between AIX and Linux

C++ templates are the first language feature to require more intelligence from the environment than one usually finds on a UNIX system. Somehow the compiler and linker have to make sure that each template instance occurs exactly once in the executable if it is needed, and not at all otherwise. The most popular method used by compilers today is to use a repository to store template instantiations and compile that code alone with all others as a final step in the compile process prior to linking. This is known as the CFront Model; you let the compiler handle managing and compiling the repository.

AIX handles this style with the `-qtempinc` and `-qtemplateregistry` parameters. The `-qtempinc` parameter creates a `tempinc` directory in the present working directory, and the `-qtemplateregistry` creates a `templateregistry` file in the present working directory. Both areas are used to hold template instantiation methods for the compiler to gather and compile prior to the link stage.

GNU handles this style with the `-frepo` parameter. This parameter creates a file in the present working directory with an .rpo extension. It, too, holds template instantiation methods for the compiler to use as a final step prior to the link stage. It is the simplest and most recommended way to port template code from AIX to Linux. However, in addition to the parameter change, there are a few minor differences in the way you include template code in Linux rather than in AIX. The following subsections examine these differences and address some common concerns.

5.8.1 Using #pragma or #include

In AIX, the source that will be using the template code usually includes just the template header to get the full template implementation. Example 5-2 shows template instantiation under AIX.

Example 5-2

AIX Template

```
stack.h

#ifndef STACK_H
#define STACK_H

#if __TEMPINC__
#pragma implementation ("stack.C")
#endif

template <class T> class stack
{
private:
T* v;
T* p;
int sz;
public:
stack(int s);
~stack();
void push(T a);
T pop();
}; //..end of class Template Stack

#endif //..STACK_H
```

main.cpp

```
#include <iostream>
using namespace std;
#include "stack.h"

int main()
{
stack<char> ch(10);
stack<int> integer(10);

ch.push('d');
ch.push('e');
integer.push(11);
integer.push(12);

cout << "char Stack pop 1 " << ch.pop() << endl;
cout << "char Stack pop 2 " << ch.pop() << endl;
cout << "char Stack pop 3 " << ch.pop() << endl;

cout << "Integer Stack pop 1 " << integer.pop() << endl;
cout << "Integer Stack pop 2 " << integer.pop() << endl;
cout << "Integer Stack pop 3 " << integer.pop() << endl;
} //..end of program
```

In AIX, the template gets included here with an `#include` clause.

The `#pragma implementation ("stack.C")` clause located in the stack.h lets the compiler know where to find the implementation methods for the upcoming stack template class. In other words, it is a fancy `include` for the VisualAge C++ compiler. The AIX stack.C file follows:

stack.C

```
#include "stack.h"
 template <class T> stack<T>::stack(int s)
 {
 p = new T[sz=s];
 v = p;
 } //..end of stack::stack(..)
 template <class T> stack<T>::~stack()
 {
 delete [] v;
 } //..end of stack::~stack(..) destructor
 template <class T> void stack<T>::push(T a )
 {
 *p++ = a;
 } //..end of stack<T>::push(..)
 template <class T> T stack<T>::pop()
 {
 T ret = *p;

 p--;
 return ret;
 } //..end of stack<T>::pop(..)
```

Example 5-3 shows how templates are instantiated under Linux. Note the difference in main.C and stack.C. In Linux, you must include the full template implementation code inside the main.C (whereas in AIX this work in done within the `pragma` clause inside the template .h file).

Example 5-3

Linux Template (AIX Example Modified)

main.C

```
 #include <iostream>
 using namespace std;
 #include "stack.C" // Include the full implementation source here
 int main()
 {

. . . Main body . . .
 } //..end of program
```

For Linux, in the stack.C the `#pragma implementation` identifier must be included as the first line at the top of the file that holds the implementation, as shown in the following syntax:

stack.C

```
#pragma implementation "stack.h"
 #include "stack.h"
 template <class T> stack<T>::stack(int s)
 {
 p = new T[sz=s];
 v = p;
 } //..end of stack::stack(..)

 ...Remainder of code
```

This tells the GNU compiler that this file is an implementation file and the interface to it is located in stack.h. Again, like AIX VisualAge C++, this is a fancy `include` statement for GNU.

Note the difference in syntax when using the `pragma` keyword between AIX and Linux. In addition, the GNU compiler does not require the header to be identified in the `pragma` statement. In such cases, the compiler uses the header filename of the file the `pragma` is being used in. It takes the filename, truncates the prefix (.C, .cpp, and so on), replaces it with an .h extension (stack.C = stack.h), and passes that name to the `pragma` statement. For instance, the preceding `pragma` identifier is rewritten here with a `#pragma implementation` clause:

stack.C

```
#pragma implementation          // Knows to use stack.h
 #include "stack.h"
 template <class T> stack<T>::stack(int s)
 {
 p = new T[sz=s];
 v = p;
 } //..end of stack::stack(..)

 ...Remainder of code
```

As you can see, with the exception of a few minor code changes, the `-frepo` parameter in GNU is your best choice when porting AIX code that utilizes the `-qtempinc` or `-qtemplateregistry`. The nominal required code changes needed are where you must place the `#pragma implementation` identifier within the source. In AIX, this identifier is located in the header. For GNU, you must move this identifier to the top of the template implementation file.

5.8.2 Other Template Options Available Under GNU

If you do not want the burden of managing pragma flags on GNU version 3.2 and older, you can use the `-fno-implicit-templates` parameter as an alternative to the `-frepo` parameter. The `-fno-implicit-templates` parameter gives you more control over what templates are instantiated and when.

5.8.2.1 fno-implicit-templates

`-fno-implicit-templates` disables the implicit generation of template instances, and explicitly instantiates all the ones you use. This approach requires more knowledge of exactly which instances you need, and allows greater control. You can scatter the explicit instantiations throughout your program, perhaps putting them in the translation units where the instances are used or the translation units that define the templates themselves. You can put all the explicit instantiations you need into one big file or create small files such as

```
#include "Foo.h"
#include "Foo.cc"

template class Foo<int>;
template ostream& operator <<
                (ostream&, const Foo<int>&);
```

for each of the instances you need, and create a template instantiation library from those.

As of GNU 3.2, however, the `-fno-implicit-templates` is being deprecated. You should, therefore, only use the `-fno-implicit-templates` flag as a short-term solution. Depending on the GNU compiler version you are using (prior to version 3.2), the GNU compiler can generate a warning if it no longer supports the option.

5.9 C++filt Utility

With C++ polymorphism and templates, functions in different classes or functions with different argument lists may have the same name. For the linker to build the executable or library, it must be able to distinguish between the functions. To facilitate this, the function names in the object code are altered depending on their class or argument list. This is called name mangling. There is no standard implementation for name mangling; as a result, name mangling is different between compiler manufacturers and even between compiler versions. Unfortunately, the behavior is not changed with VACPP and the GNU compilers. Fortunately, however, VACPP and GNU do have something in common that enables you to view mangled function names: the `c++filt` utility. The `c++filt` command returns the demangled function name of a mangled symbol. For more detailed information about the `c++filt` command for the GNU compiler, refer to the man page on your system or to GNU online documentation.

5.10 System APIs: AIX/Linux

AIX System APIs are all implemented in the `libc.a` library, which is automatically included when the VACPP compiler is invoked. Linux has the equivalent `glibc.a`, which houses all of its system calls. One of the most dreaded tasks of a porting engineer is correcting for incompatibility behavior with system APIs between the original and targeted platform. This section tries to ease that burden. It highlights differences in the most widely used System APIs in both AIX and Linux. The following subsection focuses on the I/O service APIs and the differences in *`ERRNO`* return values between AIX and Linux. The subsection after that further compares the system APIs between AIX and Linux by giving you a more in-depth comparison in a man-page format of a selected number of services, including I/O services, file-system services, IPC calls, and memory mapping functions, to name a few.

The information in this section is especially useful for engineers who are at the porting stage of fixing compiler errors. The information here will help you to correct most of the compiler errors that you will encounter when doing a port, errors that will be related to system API incompatibilities. And, for those APIs that are compatible, as far as function calling, you will be able to recognize *`ERRNO`* incompatibilities and correct them early in the porting cycle.

5.10.1 AIX/Linux I/O Service APIs

Since its inception, UNIX has provided services to manipulate files and streams. Over the years, these services have become standard and are part of the operating system low-level I/O services. These services provide a rich set of APIs that can send data to or from either devices or files. Although these APIs are considered standard among all UNIX systems, including AIX and Linux, some information they return is not (for instance, *`ERRNOs`*).

All System APIs store an *ERRNO* value that lets the programmer know the status of a function call (whether a function call went okay or not). This information is vital in anticipating problems and writing good exception-handling routines. Table 5-6 cross-references some of AIX's most popular I/O services with Linux I/O services and examines *ERRNOs* returned from AIX that are not returned in Linux.

TABLE 5-6
AIX and Linux System API Comparison: I/O Services

AIX	Linux	ERRNO(s) in AIX Not Implemented in Linux	Description
access accessx faccessx	access	ESTALE ETIMEDOUT	Check user's permissions for a file.
fclear fclear64	None		Clear space in a file.
fseek ftell rewind fgetpos fsetpos	fseek ftell rewind fgetpos fsetpos	EAGIN EFBIG EINTR EIO ENOSPC	Reposition a stream.
fputc fputs putc putchar puts	fputc fputs putc putchar puts	EPIPE ENOMEM EOVERFLOW ESPIPE	Output character and strings.
scanf fscanf sscanf	scanf fscanf sscanf	EAGIN EBADF EINTR EIO EINVAL EILSEQ ENOMEM	Input format conversion.
fsync	fsync	EINVAL EINTR	Synchronize a file's complete in-core state with that on disk.

AIX	Linux	ERRNO(s) in AIX Not Implemented in Linux	Description
getutent setutent enutent utmptname getutid getutid_r getutline_r pututline_r setutent_r endutent_r utmpname_r	getutent getutent_r getutid getutid_r gututline gututline_r putuline setutent endutent utmpname	None	Provides access user accounting database entries. Entries in database are described by the definitions and data structures in `<utmp.h>`.
lseek lseek64 llseek	lseek llseek lseek64	EOVERFLOW	Move the read-write pointer to within an open file.
lockfx lockf flock	lockf flock fcntl		Controls open file descriptors.
open openx creat	open creat	EAGAIN EDQUOT EFBIG EINTR EIO ENOSR EOVERFLOW ESTALE	The `open()` system call is used to convert a path name into a file descriptor (a small, nonnegative integer for use in subsequent I/O as with `read`, `write`, and so on). When the call is successful, the file descriptor returned is the lowest file descriptor not currently open for the process. This call creates a new open file, not shared with any other process. (But shared open files may arise via the `fork` system call.) The new file descriptor is set to remain open across exec functions (see `fcntl`). The file offset is set to the beginning of the file.

AIX	Linux	ERRNO(s) in AIX Not Implemented in Linux	Description
pathconf fpathconf	pathconf fpathconf	ESTALE ETIMEDOUT	Retrieve file-implementation characteristics.
read readx readv readvx	read readv	EBADMSG EDEADLK EOVERFLOW ENXIO ESPIPE ETIMEDOUT	Read from a file descriptor.
rename	rename	EDQUOT ETIMEDOUT ETXTBSY ESTALE	Change the name or location of a file.
statx stat fstatx fstat fullstat	stat fstat lstat	ESTALE ETIMEDOUT EIO	Get file status.
truncate ftruncate truncate64 ftruncate64	truncate ftrunncate truncate64 ftruncate64	EAGAIN EDQUOT EFBIG EINTR EMFILE ENOSPC ESTALE ETIMEDOUT	Truncate a file to a specified length.
umask	umask		Set file creation mask.
utimes utime	utimes utime	EPERM EACCES EROFS	Change access and/or modification times of an inode.
write writex writev writevx	write, writev	EDQUOT ENXIO EFBIG ERANGE ESPIPE	Write to a file descriptor.
chdir	chdir fchdir	ESTALE ETIMEDOUT	Change working directory.

AIX	Linux	ERRNO(s) in AIX Not Implemented in Linux	Description
chroot	chroot	ESTALE ETIMEDOUT	Change root directory.
getwd getcwd	get_current_ dir_name getwd getcwd	ENOMEM	Get current working directory.
glob globfree	glob globfree		Find path names matching a pattern, free memory from glob().
link	link	EDQUOT ENOSPC ESTALE	Make a new name for a file.
mkdir	mkdir	EDQUOT ETIMEOUT ESTALE	Create a directory.
readdir readdir_r	readdir _syscall3		Return current location in directory stream.
printf fprintf sprintf snprintf vprintf vfprintf vsprintf vsnprintf	printf fprintf sprintf snprintf vprintf vfprintf vsprintf vsnprintf	EAGAIN EABDF EFBIG EINTR EIO ENOSPC EPIPE ELSEQ EINVAL ENOMEM ENXIO	Format output conversion.
rmdir	rmdir	EEXIST EINVAL ETIMEDOUT ESTALE	Remove a directory.

AIX	Linux	ERRNO(s) in AIX Not Implemented in Linux	Description
scandir alphasort	scandir alphasor versionsort		Scan a directory for matching entries.
readlink	readlink	ERANGE ETIMEDOUT	Read value of a symbolic link.
remove	remove	EBUSY ETIMEDOUT ESTALE EEXIST EINVAL	Delete a name and possibly the file it refers to.
symlink	symlink	EDQUOT ETIMEDOUT ESTALE	Make a new name for a file.
unlink	unlink	EBUSY ETIMEDOUT ESTALE	Deletes a name from the filesystem. If that name was the last link to a file and no processes have the file open, the file is deleted and the space it was using is made available for reuse.
tscntl	None		Manipulate filesystem control operations.
getfsent_r getfsspec_r getfsfile_r getfstype_r setfsent_r endfsent_r	getfsent getfsspec getfsfile setfsent endfsent		Gets information about a file system. (In AIX, _r denotes REENTRANT, which means functions are thread-safe. In Linux, you must make your modules that are using the equivalent APIs thread-safe.)

AIX	Linux	ERRNO(s) in AIX Not Implemented in Linux	Description
getvfsent getvfsbytype getvfsbyname getvfsbyflag setvfsent endvfsent	None		Get a (Virtual File System) vfs file entry.
mnctl	None		Return mount status information.
quotacl	quotacl	ELOOP ENAMETOOLONG ENOENT EOPNOTSUPP EROFS EUSERS	Manipulate disk quotas.
statfs fstatfs	statfs fstatfs	ESTALE ETIMEDOUT EIO	Get filesystem statistics.
sysconf	sysconf		Provide a way for the application to determine values for system limits or options at runtime. Functions are compatible, but the information they return is specific to the platform they are running on.
sync	sync		Functions are not compatible. In Linux, sync returns an int, and in AIX this function returns void. Causes all information in memory that should be on disk to be written out. The information returned and its format are different.

AIX	Linux	ERRNO(s) in AIX Not Implemented in Linux	Description
umask	umask		Set the umask to *mask* & 0777.
vmount uvmount	None		AIX-specific; creates what is known as a virtual filesystem (VFS). uvmount removes a VFS. umount can also be used as an alternative to uvmount.
umount	umount	In AIX, ENOBLK is returned. In Linux, ENOTBLK is returned.	Unmount a previously mounted filesystem, directory, or file.
close	close	ETIMEDOUT	Closes a file descriptor that has been previously opened by the open() call.
chmod	chmod	ESTALE ETIMEDOUT	Used to change permissions of a file.
chown fchown lchown	chown fchown lchown	EDQUOT EINVAL ESTALE	Used to change ownership of a file.
setregid setregid	setregid setregid	EINVAL	Sets real and/or effective user ID.

Only pertinent Linux I/O services APIs relating to porting from AIX to Linux are mentioned in this section. You should investigate other API options that Linux has to offer. Table 5-6 should only serve as a guide for you to be able to recognize and identify API differences (in this case, I/O services APIs and their *ERRNO* return values) between Linux and AIX.

5.11 Selected AIX/Linux System API Comparisons

This section takes a selected set of system APIs and compares and contrasts them with AIX and Linux in a man-page format. The APIs were chosen based on how much difference existed between AIX and Linux. Unlike in the previous section, in which the only differences that existed were *ERRNO* returns, the APIs listed in this section show differences that go beyond just *ERRNOs*. In some cases, the information returned by AIX and Linux differs significantly and must be addressed early during the porting cycle.

Like a man page, each API listed in this section lists the API name, prototype for AIX and Linux, parameter listing, and the return value of the routine. In addition, a "Detail Comparison" section is included in each API section explaining the differences in the API between AIX and Linux (with examples and code snippets). If the API is not compatible between AIX and Linux, it is clearly marked with a "**Not compatible**" identifier. In such cases, examples and analytical reasoning are given as to why it is not compatible. Some are identified as "**Compatible**" but with differences, which will also be explained.

In some cases, additional operating system-specific (that is, AIX or Linux) information pertinent to the porting process follows the "Detail Comparison" section.

5.11.1 getfsent(), getfsfile(), getfstype(), getfsspec()

These calls retrieve information about a filesystem. See "Additional Data: Linux-Specific" for Linux-specific information.

5.11.1.1 AIX Prototype

```
#include <fstab.h>
struct fstab *getfsent();
struct fstab *getfsspec ( char *special );
struct fstab *getfsfile( char *file );
struct fstab *getfstype( char* type );
void setfsent( );
void endfsent( );
```

5.11.1.2 Linux Prototype

```
#include <fstab.h>
void endfsent(void);
struct fstab *getfsent(void);
```

```
struct fstab *getfsfile(const char *mount_point);
struct fstab *getfsspec(const char *special_file);
int setfsent(void);
```

5.11.1.3 Detail Comparison

Not Compatible

AIX and Linux implement their filesystem differently, and as a result different information must be returned. Both platforms return an `fstab` struct, but information is different.

AIX

```
struct fstab{
    char  *fs_spec;        /* block special device name */
    char  *fs_file;        /* file system path prefix */
    char  *fs_type;        /* read/write, etc see above defines */
    int   fs_check;        /* true=0, false=-1, else "check" val */
    int   fs_freq;         /* not used */
    int   fs_passno;       /* not used */
};
```

Linux

```
struct fstab {
   char *fs_spec;        /* block device name */
   char *fs_file;        /* mount point */
   char *fs_vfstype;     /* filesystem type */
   char *fs_mntops;      /* mount options */
   const char *fs_type;  /* rw/rq/ro/sw/xx option */
   int fs_freq;          /* dump frequency, in days */
   int fs_passno;        /* pass number on parallel dump */
};
```

5.11.1.4 Additional Data: Linux-Specific

Here the field *`fs_type`* contains (on a *BSD system) one of the five strings: `rw`, `rq`, `ro`, `sw`, `xx` (read-write, read-write with quotas, read-only, swap, ignore).

The function `setfsent()` opens the file when required and positions it at the first line.

The function `getfsent()` parses the next line from the file (after opening it when required).

The function `endfsent()` closes the file when required.

The function `getfsspec()` searches the file from the start and returns the first entry found for which the `fs_spec` field matches the `special_file` argument.

The function `getfsfile()` searches the file from the start and returns the first entry found for which the `fs_file` field matches the `mount_point` argument.

5.11.1.5 Return Value

Upon success, the functions `getfsent()`, `getfsfile()`, and `getfsspec()` return a pointer to a struct `fstab`, whereas `setfsent()` returns 1. Upon failure or end of file, these functions return NULL and 0, respectively.

5.11.2 ioctl()

The `ioctl` function manipulates the underlying device parameters of special files. In particular, many operating characteristics of character special files (for example, terminals) may be controlled with `ioctl` requests. The argument `d` must be an open file descriptor.

An ioctl request has encoded in it whether the argument is an in parameter or out parameter and the size of the argument *argp* in bytes. Macros and defines used in specifying an `ioctl` request are located in the file sys/ioctl.h.

5.11.2.1 AIX Prototype

```
#include <sys/ioctl.h>
#include <sys/types.h>
#include <unistd.h>
int ioctl (int FileDescriptor, int Command, void *Argument);
```

5.11.2.2 Linux Prototype

```
#include <sys/ioctl.h>
int ioctl(int d, int request, ...)
```

5.11.2.3 Detail Comparison

Not Compatible

In Linux, command values are generally driver-specific. This function is not considered portable.

AIX

In AIX, the `ioctl` subroutine performs a variety of control operations on the object associated with the specified open file descriptor. This function is typically used with character or block special files and sockets generic device support such as the termio general terminal interface.

Parameters

- **`FileDescriptor`**. Specifies the open file descriptor for which the control operation is to be performed.
- **`Command`**. Specifies the control function to be performed. The value of this parameter depends on which object is specified by the `FileDescriptor` parameter.
- **`Argument`**. Specifies additional information required by the function requested in the `Command`. The data type of this parameter (a `void` pointer) is object-specific and is typically used to point to an object device-specific data structure. However, in some device-specific instances, this parameter is used as an integer. This parameter is passed on to the object associated with the specified open file descriptor. Although normally of type `int`, this parameter can be used as a pointer to a device-specific structure for some devices.

Linux

The `ioctl` function manipulates the underlying device parameters of special files. In particular, many operating characteristics of character special files (for example, terminals) may be controlled with `ioctl` requests.

- Argument *d*. Must be an open file descriptor.
- *Request*. The second argument is a device-dependent request code.
- Third argument(s). The third argument is an untyped pointer to memory. It is traditionally `char *argp` (from the days before `void *` was valid C).

An `ioctl` request has encoded in it whether the argument is an *in* parameter or *out* parameter, and the size of the argument *argp* in bytes. Macros and defines used in specifying an `ioctl` request are located in the file sys/ioctl.h.

5.11.2.4 Return Value

Usually, on success, 0 is returned. A few `ioctls` use the return value as an output parameter and return a nonnegative value on success. On error, –1 is returned, and *`ERRNO`* is set appropriately.

5.11.2.5 Errors

- **`EBADF`**. *`d`* is not a valid descriptor.
- **`EFAULT`**. *`argp`* references an inaccessible memory area.
- **`ENOTTY`**. *`d`* is not associated with a character special device.
- **`ENOTTY`**. The specified request does not apply to the kind of object that the descriptor *`d`* references.
- **`EINVAL`**. Request or *`argp`* is not valid.

5.11.2.6 ERRNO(s) Not Supported in Linux

- **`EINTR`**. A signal was caught, and the process had not enabled restartable subroutines for the signal.
- **`ENODEV`**. The `FileDescriptor` parameter is associated with a valid character or block special file, but the supporting device driver does not support the `ioctl` function.
- **`ENXIO`**. The `FileDescriptor` parameter is associated with a valid character or block special file, but the supporting device driver is not in the configured state.

5.11.3 read(), write()

To read from a file descriptor into a buffer or to write to a file descriptor from a buffer, use the `read()`/`write()` commands.

5.11.3.1 AIX Prototype

```
#include <unistd.h>
ssize_t read (int FileDescriptor, void *Buffer, size_t NBytes);
ssize_t write(int fd, const void *buf, size_t NBytes);
```

5.11.3.2 Linux Prototype

```
#include <unistd.h>
ssize_t read(int fd, void *buf, size_t NBytes);
ssize_t write(int fd, const void *buf, size_t NBytes;
```

5.11.3.3 Detail Comparison

Compatible

Functions are source-compatible, but `ERROR` return values differ. Refer to the "Errors" section that follows. On most UNIX systems, `O_NONBLOCK` is used on socket descriptors, in which read returns –1 and sets *`ERRNO`* `EAGAIN`, which signifies to the user that additional data is available on the descriptor. Linux, on the other hand, considered current available filesystems and disks to be fast enough and deemed `O_NONBLOCK` unnecessary. As a result, this `O_NONBLOCK` may not be implemented on some flavors of Linux.

5.11.3.4 Additional Info: AIX/Linux

- **`FileDescriptor`**. A file descriptor identifying the object to be read and written to.
- **`Buffer`**. Points to the buffer.
- **`NBytes`**. Specifies the number of bytes associated with the file descriptor for read or write.
- **`FileDescriptor`**. In the case of a write, identifies the size of the buffer.

If *NBytes* is 0, read() returns 0 and has no other results. If *NBytes* is greater than SSIZE_MAX, the result is unspecified.

5.11.3.5 Linux Restrictions

On NFS filesystems, reading small amounts of data updates the timestamp only the first time; subsequent calls may not do so. This is caused by client-side attribute caching, because most if not all NFS clients leave atime updates to the server, and client-side reads satisfied from the client's cache will not cause atime updates on the server because there are no server-side reads. UNIX semantics can be obtained by disabling client-side attribute caching, but in most situations this substantially increases server load and decreases performance.

5.11.3.6 Return Value

On success, the number of bytes read is returned (0 indicates end of file), and the file position is advanced by this number. It is not an error if this number is smaller than the number of bytes requested. This may happen, for example, because fewer bytes are actually available right now (maybe because we were close to end of file, or because we are reading from a pipe or a terminal), or because read() was interrupted by a signal. On error, –1 is returned, and *ERRNO* is set appropriately. In this case, it is left unspecified whether the file position (if any) changes.

5.11.3.7 Errors

- **EINTR**. The call was interrupted by a signal before any data was read.
- **EAGAIN**. Nonblocking I/O has been selected using O_NONBLOCK, and no data was immediately available for reading.
- **EIO**. I/O error. This happens, for example, when the process is in a background process group, tries to read from its controlling tty, and either it is ignoring or blocking SIGTTIN or its process group is orphaned. It may also occur when there is a low-level I/O error while reading from a disk or tape.
- **EISDIR**. *fd* refers to a directory.
- **EBADF**. *fd* is not a valid file descriptor or is not open for reading.
- **EINVAL**. *fd* is attached to an object that is unsuitable for reading.
- **EFAULT**. *buf* is outside your accessible address space.

Other errors may occur, depending on the object connected to `fd`. POSIX allows a read that is interrupted after reading some data to return –1 (with *ERRNO* set to `EINTR`) or to return the number of bytes already read.

Conforming To

SVr4, SVID, AT&T, POSIX, X/OPEN, BSD 4.3

ERRNO(s) Not Supported in Linux

- **EBADMSG**. The file is a STREAM file that is set to control-normal mode, and the message waiting to be read includes a control part.
- **EDEADLK**. A deadlock would occur if the calling process were to sleep until the region to be read was unlocked.
- **EOVERFLOW**. An attempt was made to read from a regular file where *NBytes* was greater than 0 and the starting offset was before the end of file and was greater than or equal to the offset maximum established in the open file description associated with file descriptor.
- **ENXIO**. A request was made of a nonexistent device or the request was outside the capabilities of the device.
- **ESPIPE**. `fd` is associated with a pipe or FIFO.
- **ETIMEDOUT**. The connection timed out.

5.11.4 confstr()

The `confstr()` function provides a method for applications to get configuration-defined string values. Its use and purpose are similar to the `sysconf()` function; however, `confstr()` is used where string values (rather than numeric values) are returned.

5.11.4.1 AIX Prototype

```
#include <unistd.h>
size_t confstr (int name, char * buf, size_t len);
```

5.11.4.2 Linux Prototype

```
#define _POSIX_C_SOURCE 2
or
#define _XOPEN_SOURCE
#include <unistd.h>

size_t confstr(int name, char *buf, size_t len);
```

5.11.4.3 Detail Comparison

Compatible

Functions are source-compatible, but `_POSIX_C_SOURCE` or `_XOPEN_SOURCE` must be turned on in Linux.

5.11.5 opendir()

The `opendir()` function opens a directory stream corresponding to the directory named by the *name* argument.

5.11.5.1 AIX Prototype

```
#include <dirent>
DIR *opendir(const char *name);
struct dirent *readdir (DIR *DirectoryPointer);
```

5.11.5.2 Linux Prototype

```
#include <dirent.h>
DIR *opendir(const char *name);
struct dirent *readdir(DIR *dir);
```

5.11.5.3 Detail Comparison

Compatible

Functions are source-compatible, but there are differences between the dirent structures in the two systems:

Linux	AIX
struct dirent	struct dirent
d_ino	d_ino
d_off	d_offset
d_reclen	d_reclen
d_type	d_namelen
d_name[]	d_name[]

5.11.5.4 ERRNO

When called in AIX, this function can return these *ERRNOs* not documented in Linux:

- **EBADF**. Indicates that the *DirectoryPointer* parameter argument does not refer to an open directory stream (readdir).
- **ENAMETOOLONG**. Indicates that the string length pointed to by the *DirectoryPointer* parameter argument exceeds the PATH_MAX value, or a path name component is longer than the NAME_MAX value while the POSIX_NO_TRUNC value is in effect (opendir).

5.11.6 readdir()

readdir() is a deprecated function. Instead, you should use getdents(). Refer to the Linux documentation for more information on getdents().

5.11.7 fcntl()

The `fcntl` subroutine performs controlling operations on the open file specified by the `FileDescriptor` (*fd*) parameter. If Network File System (NFS) is installed on your system, the open file can reside on another node. The `fcntl` subroutine is used to do the following:

- Duplicate open file descriptors
- Set and get the file-descriptor flags
- Set and get the file-status flags
- Manage record locks
- Manage asynchronous I/O ownership
- Close multiple files

The following commands are supported for all file types and are passed via the *cmd* parameter:

- `F_DUPFD`

  Returns a new file descriptor that is the lowest numbered available (that is, not already open) file descriptor greater than or equal to the specified argument, which is of type `int`. The new file descriptor refers to the same open file description as the original file descriptor and shares any locks. The `FD_CLOEXEC` flag associated with the new file descriptor is cleared to keep the file open across calls to one of the `exec()` family of functions. The return value is the new file descriptor on success or –1 on error.

- `F_SETFD`

  Sets the file descriptor flags for the specified file descriptor. The argument is the new set of flags, as a variable of type `int`. File descriptor flags are associated with a single file descriptor and do not affect other file descriptors that refer to the same file. The return value is 0 on success or –1 on error. The following file descriptor flags may be set. Any additional bits set from the flags specified for `F_GETFD` are ignored. If any bits not defined here are specified, behavior is undefined.

- `FD_CLOEXEC`

  If set, the file descriptor is closed when one of the `exec()` family of functions is called. If not set, the file descriptor is inherited by the new process image.

- `F_GETFD`

  Gets the file descriptor flags for the specified file descriptor. This command takes no argument. File descriptor flags are associated with a single file descriptor and do not affect other file descriptors that refer to the same file. The return value is the current file descriptor flags on success, or –1 on error. In addition to the flags specified for `F_SETFD`, the following flags may be returned:

  `FD_MANDATORYLOCK`

  Mandatory locking is enabled for the file referred to by the specified file descriptor.

  `FD_ADVISORYLOCK`

  Advisory locking is enabled for the file referred to by the specified file descriptor.

  `FD_DIRECTORY`

  The specified file descriptor refers to a directory.

- `F_SETFL`

  Sets the file status flags for the specified file descriptor. The argument is the new set of flags, as a variable of type `int`. These flags are as specified for the `oflag` argument to `open()`, along with the additional values specified later. Bits corresponding to the file access mode and any other `oflag` bits not listed here are ignored. If any bits not defined here or in `open()` are set, behavior is undefined. The return value is 0 on success, or –1 on error. The following file status flags can be changed with `F_SETFL`:

  `O_APPEND`

  Valid only for file descriptors that refer to regular files. The file pointer is moved to the end of the file before each write.

`O_ASYNC`

Valid only for file descriptors that refer to sockets and communications ports. If enabled for a file descriptor, and an owning process/process group has been specified with the `F_SETOWN` command to `fcntl()`, a `SIGIO` signal is sent to the owning process/process group when input is available on the file descriptor.

`O_BINARY`

Sets the file descriptor to binary mode.

`O_LARGEFILE`

Sets the file descriptor to indicate a large-file-aware application.

`O_NDELAY`

Sets the file descriptor to no-delay mode.

`O_NONBLOCK`

Sets the file descriptor to nonblocking mode. The distinction between non-blocking mode and no-delay mode is relevant only for a few types of special files such as pipes and FIFOs. Refer to `read()` and `write()` for more information.

`O_SYNC`

Sets the file descriptor to synchronous-write mode. Writes do not return until file buffers have been flushed to disk.

`O_TEXT`

Sets the file descriptor to text mode.

`FAPPEND`

A synonym for `O_APPEND`.

`FASYNC`

A synonym for `O_ASYNC`.

`FNDELAY`

A synonym for `O_NDELAY`.

- `F_GETFL`

  Gets the file status flags and file access modes for the specified file descriptor. These flags are as specified for the `oflag` argument to `open()`, along with the additional values described for `F_SETFL`. File status flags and file access modes are associated with the file description and do not affect other file descriptors that refer to the same file with different open file descriptions. The return value is the current file status flags and file access modes on success, or –1 on error. The following macros can be used to access fields of the return value:

  `O_ACCMODE`

  Extracts the access-mode field, which is one of `O_RDONLY`, `O_RDWR`, or `O_WRONLY`. Refer to the documentation for `open()` for more information.

The following commands are supported only for sockets and communication ports:

- `F_SETOWN`

  Sets the owning process ID or process group ID for the specified file descriptor. The owning process or process group can receive `SIGURG` signals for out-of-band data or sockets and/or `SIGIO` signals for readable data on sockets or communications ports. The argument is the process ID or the negative of the process group ID for the owner, as a variable of type `pid_t`. The return value is 0 on success or –1 on error.

  To receive `SIGURG` signals, the process should establish a `SIGURG` handler prior to setting ownership of the file descriptor. A `SIGURG` signal is generated whenever out-of-band data is received.

  To receive `SIGIO` signals, the process should establish a `SIGIO` handler prior to setting ownership of the file descriptor, and then must enable `O_ASYNC` with the `F_SETFL` command to `fcntl()`. A `SIGIO` signal is generated whenever there is data to be read on the file descriptor.

- `F_GETOWN`

  Gets the owning process ID or process group ID for the specified file descriptor. The return value is the owner ID on success, or –1 on error. Behavior is undefined if no owner has been established with `F_SETOWN`.

The following commands are used for file locking. Locks may be advisory or mandatory. These command are supported only for regular files.

- `F_GETLK`

  Gets the first lock that blocks a lock description for the file to which the specified file descriptor refers. The argument is a pointer to a variable of type struct `flock`, described later. The structure is overwritten with the returned lock information. If no lock is found that would prevent this lock from being created, the structure is unchanged except for the lock type, which is set to `F_UNLCK`. The return value is 0 on success or –1 or error.

- `F_GETLK64`

  Equivalent to `F_GETLK`, but takes a struct `flock64` argument rather than a struct `flock` argument.

- `F_SETLK`

  Sets or clears a file segment lock for the file to which the specified file descriptor refers. The argument is a pointer to a variable of type struct `flock`, described later. `F_SETLK` is used to establish shared (or read) locks (`F_RDLCK`) or exclusive (or write) locks (`F_WRLCK`), as well as to remove either type of lock (`F_UNLCK`). The return value is 0 on success or –1 on error. If the lock cannot be immediately obtained, `fcntl()` returns –1 with *ERRNO* set to `EACCES`.

- `F_SETLK64`

  Equivalent to `F_SETLK`, but takes a struct `flock64` argument rather than a struct `flock` argument.

- `F_SETLKW`

  This command is the same as `F_SETLK` except that if a shared or exclusive lock is blocked by other locks, the thread waits until the request can be satisfied. If a signal that is to be caught is received while `fcntl()` is waiting for a region, `fcntl()` is interrupted. Upon return from the signal handler, `fcntl()` returns –1 with *ERRNO* set to `EINTR`, and the lock operation is not done.

- `F_SETLKW64`

  Equivalent to `F_SETLKW`, but takes a struct `flock64` argument rather than a struct `flock` argument.

When a shared lock is set on a segment of a file, other processes can set shared locks on that segment or a portion of it. A shared lock prevents any other process from setting an exclusive lock on any portion of the protected area. A request for a shared lock fails if the file descriptor was not opened with read access.

An exclusive lock prevents any other process from setting a shared lock or an exclusive lock on any portion of the protected area. A request for an exclusive lock fails if the file descriptor is not opened with write access.

The `flock` and `flock64` structure contains the following fields:

- `l_type`

  Specifies the type of lock request. Valid settings are as follows:

  `F_RDLCK`

  Creates a shared lock.

  `F_WRLCK`

  Creates an exclusive lock.

  `F_UNLCK`

  Removes a lock.

- `l_whence`

  Specifies the starting offset of the lock segment in the file. Valid settings are as follows:

  `SEEK_SET`

  `l_start` specifies a position relative to the start of the file.

  `SEEK_CUR`

  `l_start` specifies a position relative to the current file offset.

  `SEEK_END`

  `l_start` specifies a position relative to the end of the file.

  On a successful return from an `F_GETLK` or `F_GETLK64` command for which a lock was found, the `l_whence` field is set to `SEEK_SET`.

- `l_start`

  Specifies the relative offset of the start of the lock segment. This setting is used with `l_whence` to determine the actual start position.

- `l_len`

  Specifies the number of consecutive bytes in the lock segment. This value may be negative.

- `l_pid`

  On a successful return from an `F_GETLK` or `F_GETLK64` command for which a lock was found, this field contains the process ID of the process holding the lock.

If `l_len` is positive, the affected area starts at `l_start` and ends at `(l_start + l_len - 1)`. If `l_len` is negative, the area affected starts at `(l_start + l_len)` and ends at `(l_start - 1)`. Locks may start and end beyond the current end of a file but must not be negative relative to the beginning of the file. Setting `l_len` to 0 sets a lock that can extend to the largest possible value of the file offset for that file. If such a lock also has `l_start` set to 0 and `l_whence` set to `SEEK_SET`, the whole file is locked.

There can be at most one type of lock set of each byte in the file. Before a successful return from an `F_SETLK`, `F_SETLK64`, `F_SETLKW`, or `F_SETLKW64` request when the calling process has previously existing locks on bytes in the region specified by the request, the previous lock type for each byte in the specified region is replaced by the new lock type. As specified earlier, an `F_SETLK`, `F_SETLK64`, `F_SETLKW`, or `F_SETLKW64` request fails or blocks, respectively, when another process has existing locks on bytes in the specified region and the type of any of those locks conflicts with the type specified in the request.

All locks associated with a file for a given process shall be removed when a file descriptor for that file is closed by that process or when the process holding that file descriptor terminates. Locks are not inherited by a child process.

A potential for deadlock occurs if a process controlling a locked region is put to sleep by attempting to lock another process's locked region. If the system detects that sleeping until a locked region is unlocked would cause a deadlock, `fcntl()` returns –1 with *ERRNO* set to `EDEADLK`.

5.11.7.1 AIX Prototype

```
#include <fcntl.h>
int fcntl (int FileDescriptor, int cmd, ...);
```

5.11.7.2 Linux Prototype

```
#include <unistd.h>
#include <fcntl.h>
int fcntl(int fd, int cmd);
int fcntl(int fd, int cmd, long arg);
int fcntl(int fd, int cmd, struct flock *lock);
```

5.11.7.3 Detail Comparison

Compatible

The user should take note of the different open modes and command values between AIX and Linux. In the preceding section, the command description is mainly Linux-specific. Refer to the "File Bits" section at the end of this chapter.

5.11.7.4 Return Value

For a successful call, the return value depends on the operation performed:

- **F_DUPFD**. The new descriptor.
- **F_GETFD**. Value of flag.
- **F_GETFL**. Value of flags.
- **F_GETOWN**. Value of descriptor owner.
- **F_GETSIG**. Value of signal sent when read or write becomes possible, or 0 for traditional SIGIO behavior.
- **All other commands**. 0.

On error, –1 is returned, and *ERRNO* is set appropriately.

5.11.7.5 Errors

- **EACCES** or **EAGAIN**. Operation is prohibited by locks held by other processes. Or, operation is prohibited because the file has been memory mapped by another process.

- **EBADF**. *fd* is not an open file descriptor, or the command was F_SETLK or F_SETLKW and the file descriptor open mode does not match the type of lock requested.
- **EDEADLK**. It was detected that the specified F_SETLKW command would cause a deadlock.
- **EFAULT**. The lock is outside your accessible address space.
- **EINTR**. For F_SETLKW, the command was interrupted by a signal. For F_GETLK and F_SETLK, the command was interrupted by a signal before the lock was checked or acquired—most likely when locking a remote file (for example, locking over NFS), but it can sometimes happen locally.
- **EINVAL**. For F_DUPFD, *arg* is negative or is greater than the maximum allowable value. For F_SETSIG, *arg* is not an allowable signal number.
- **EMFILE**. For F_DUPFD, the process already has the maximum number of file descriptors open.
- **ENOLCK**. Too many segment locks are open, the lock table is full, or a remote locking protocol failed (for example, locking over NFS).
- **EPERM**. Attempted to clear the O_APPEND flag on a file that has the append-only attribute set.

5.11.7.6 ERRNOs Not Supported in Linux

- **ESRCH**. The value of the Command parameter is F_SETOWN, and the process ID specified as the Argument parameter is not in use.
- **EOVERFLOW**. The Command parameter was F_GETLK and the block lock could not be represented in the flock structure.
- **ETIMEDOUT**. The connection timed out.

5.11.8 llseek(), lseek(), lseek64()

Sometimes you do not want to start at the beginning of an open file to start reading or writing to it. `llseek()`, `lseek()`, and `lseek64()` reposition the read/write pointer in a file that is associated with a file descriptor (*fd*).

5.11.8.1 AIX Prototype

```
#include <sys/types.h>
#include <unistd.h>
offset_t llseek(int fd, offset_t offset, int whence);
offset_t lseek(int fd, offset_t offset, int whence);
offset_t lseek64(int fd, offset_t offset, int whence);
```

5.11.8.2 Linux Prototype

```
#include <sys/types.h>
#include <unistd.h>
off_t lseek(int fildes, off_t offset, int whence);
_syscall5(int, _llseek, uint, fd, ulong, hi, ulong, lo, loff_t *, res, uint,
wh);
int _llseek(unsigned int fd, unsigned long offset_high, unsigned long
offset_low, loff_t *result, unsigned int whence);
```

5.11.8.3 Detail Comparison

Compatible

Although `llseek` is implemented in Linux, if you are writing new code `lseek` should be used instead of `llseek` for greater portability between UNIX platforms.

5.11.8.4 Additional Info: AIX/Linux, lseek Only

- **fd**. Specifies a file descriptor obtained from a successful `open` or `fcntl` subroutine.
- **offset**. Specifies a value, in bytes, that is used in conjunction with the `Whence` parameter to set the file pointer. A negative value causes seeking in the reverse direction.
- **whence**. Specifies how to interpret the *offset* parameter by setting the file pointer associated with the *fd* parameter to one of the following variables:

  `SEEK_SET`

Sets the file pointer to the value of the `offset` parameter.

`SEEK_CUR`

Sets the file pointer to its current location plus the value of the `offset` parameter.

`SEEK_END`

Sets the file pointer to the size of the file plus the value of the `offset` parameter.

5.11.8.5 Return Value

Upon successful completion, `lseek` returns the resulting offset location as measured in bytes from the beginning of the file. Otherwise, a value of `(off_t)-1` is returned and *ERRNO* is set to indicate the error.

5.11.8.6 Errors

- **EBADF**. *fd* is not an open file descriptor.
- **ESPIPE**. *fd* is associated with a pipe, socket, or FIFO.
- **EINVAL**. *whence* is not a proper value.

5.11.8.7 ERRNOs Not Supported in Linux

- **EOVERFLOW**. The resulting offset is larger than can be returned properly.

Conforming To

SVr4, POSIX, BSD 4.3

5.11.9 uname()

Occasionally, shell programmers as well as application developers need to know information about the system they are running on at runtime. This information could be used to set specific operating system environment variables and could aid in developing install packages for specific systems. To get the name and information about the current kernel and the machine the kernel is running on, use the `uname()` function.

5.11.9.1 AIX Prototype

```
#include <sys/utsname.h>
int uname (struct utsname *Name);
```

5.11.9.2 Linux Prototype

```
#include <sys/utsname.h>
int uname(struct utsname *buf);
```

5.11.9.3 Details Comparison

Not Compatible

AIX does not define `domainname` as part of the *`utsname`* structure. The `domainname` entry is technically not compatible because it is defined in Linux only if the program is compiled with `_GNU_SOURCE`.

5.11.10 syslog(), closelog(), openlog()

These commands provide messaging services to the system logger:

- **`closelog()`** closes the descriptor being used to write to the system logger. The use of `closelog()` is optional.
- **`openlog()`** opens a connection to the system logger for a program. The string pointed to by *`ident`* is prepended to every message and is typically set to the program name. The *`option`* argument specifies flags that control the operation of `openlog()` and subsequent calls to `syslog()`. The *`facility`* argument establishes a default to be used if none is specified in subsequent calls to `syslog()`. Values for *`option`* and *`facility`* are given below. The use of `openlog()` is optional; it is automatically called by `syslog()` if necessary, in which case *`ident`* defaults to NULL.
- **`syslog()`** generates a log message, which is distributed by `syslogd`. The *`priority`* argument is formed by ORing the *`facility`* and the *`level`*

values (explained below). The remaining arguments are a `format`, as in `printf`, and any arguments required by the `format`, except that the two-character sequence `%m` is replaced by the error message string `strerror(errno)`. A trailing newline is added when needed.

5.11.10.1 AIX Prototype

```
#include <syslog.h>
void openlog(const char *ident, int LogOption, int Facility);
void syslog(int Priority, const char *Value,... );
int closelog(void);
```

5.11.10.2 Linux Prototype

```
#include <syslog.h>
void openlog( char *ident, int LogOption, int facility);
void syslog( int priority, char *format, ...);
void closelog( void );
```

5.11.10.3 Details Comparison

Compatible

The facilities will require additional code changes under Linux to make use of the following:

LOG_PERROR

LOG_AUTHPRIV

5.11.11 swapoff(), swapon()

These commands are usually used for device programming for enabling paging on a device. `swapon` sets the swap area to the file or block device specified by `path`. `swapoff` stops swapping to the file or block device specified by `path`.

5.11.11.1 AIX Prototype

```
#include <sys/vminfo.h>
```

```
int swapon (char *PathName);
int swapoff(char *PathName);
```

5.11.11.2 Linux Prototype

```
#include <unistd.h>
#include <asm/page.h>
#include <sys/swap.h>
int swapon(const char *path, int swapflags);
int swapoff(const char *path);
```

5.11.11.3 Details Comparision

Compatible

Functions are compatible, but the `swapflags` must be added for Linux.

5.11.11.4 Return Value

On success, 0 is returned. On error, –1 is returned, and *ERRNO* is set appropriately.

5.11.11.5 Errors

Many other errors can occur if *path* is not valid:

- **EPERM**. The user is not the super user, or more than `MAX_SWAPFILES` (defined to be 8 in Linux 1.3.6) are in use.
- **EINVAL** is returned if *path* exists but is neither a regular path nor a block device.
- **ENOENT** is returned if *path* does not exist.
- **ENOMEM** is returned if there is insufficient memory to start swapping.

5.11.11.6 ERRNO(s) Not Implemented in Linux

- **EINTR**. A signal was received during processing of a request.
- **ENOTBLK**. A block device is required.
- **ENOTDIA**. A component of the *PathName* prefix is not a directory.
- **ENXIO**. No such device address.

5.11.12 acct()

Use this command to switch process accounting on or off.

5.11.12.1 Linux/AIX Prototype

```
#include <unistd.h>
int acct (char *Path);
```

5.11.12.2 Detail Comparison

Compatible

5.11.12.3 Return Value

On success, 0 is returned. On error, –1 is returned, and *ERRNO* is set appropriately.

5.11.12.4 Errors

- **EACCES**. Write permission is denied for the specified file.
- **EACCES**. The argument *filename* is not a regular file.
- **EFAULT**. *filename* points outside your accessible address space.
- **EIO**. Error writing to the file *filename*.
- **EISDIR**. *filename* is a directory.
- **ELOOP**. Too many symbolic links were encountered in resolving *filename*.
- **ENAMETOOLONG**. *filename* was too long.
- **ENOENT**. The specified filename does not exist.
- **ENOMEM**. Out of memory.
- **ENOSYS**. BSD process accounting was not enabled when the operating system kernel was compiled. The kernel configuration parameter controlling this feature is CONFIG_BSD_PROCESS_ACCT.
- **ENOTDIR**. A component used as a directory in *filename* is not in fact a directory.

- **EPERM**. The calling process has no permission to enable process accounting.
- **EROFS**. *filename* refers to a file on a read-only file system.
- **EUSERS**. There are no more free file structures or we ran out of memory.

5.11.12.5 ERRNO(s) Not Implemented in Linux

- **EBUSY**. An attempt is made to enable accounting when it is already enabled.

5.11.13 mmap(), mmap64(),[17] munmap()

These commands are memory-mapping functions. There comes a time when you want to read and write to and from files so that the information is shared between processes. Think of it this way: two processes both open the same file and both read and write from it, thus sharing the information. Wouldn't it be easier if you could just map a section of the file to memory and get a pointer to it? Then you could simply use pointer arithmetic to get (and set) data in the file.

Another great advantage to using memory-mapped files is to speed up performance. It would take a lot of I/O resources if more than one process needs to manipulate a large file. You would have to open, read and write to the file, and close it. If the file is already mapped in memory, access to the file is much quicker, which greatly improves I/O access.

`mmap()`, `mmap64()`, and `munmap()` enable you to map and unmap a file in memory to be shared by two or more processes for I/O processing, and they are really easy to use. A few simple calls, mixed with a few simple rules, and you are mapping like a mad person.

5.11.13.1 AIX Prototype

```
#include <sys/types.h>
#include <sys/mman.h>
void *mmap (void *addr, size_t len, int prot, int flags, int fildes, off_t off);
void *mmap64 (void *addr, size_t len, int prot, int flags, int fildes, off_t off);
int munmap (void *addr, size_t len);
```

17 Used on 64-bit machines and for Large File Support.

5.11.13.2 Linux Prototype

```
#include <unistd.h>
#include <sys/mman.h>
#ifdef _POSIX_MAPPED_FILES
void * mmap(void *start, size_t length, int prot, int flags, int fd, off_t
offset);
void * mmap64(void *start, size_t length, int prot, int flags, int fd, off_t
off);
int munmap(void *start, size_t length);
#endif
```

5.11.13.3 Detail Comparison

Compatible

Values for `prot` are identical to AIX. In AIX, `mmap()` and `munmap()` are system calls.

The `mmap` function asks to map *`length`* bytes starting at *`offset`* from the file (or other object) specified by the file descriptor *`fd`* into memory, preferably at address `start`. If `MAP_FIXED` is used, the start address (*`addr`*) is a hint only and is usually specified as 0. The actual place where the object is mapped is returned by `mmap` and is never 0.

The `prot` argument describes the desired memory protection (and must not conflict with the open mode of the file). It is either `PROT_NONE` or is the bitwise OR of one or more of the other `PROT_*` flags:

- **`PROT_EXEC`**. Pages may be executed.
- **`PROT_READ`**. Pages may be read.
- **`PROT_WRITE`**. Pages may be written.
- **`PROT_NONE`**. Pages may not be accessed.

The *`flags`* parameter specifies the type of the mapped object, mapping options, and whether modifications made to the mapped copy of the page are private to the process or are to be shared with other references. Bits (below) are used to tell the system how the file will be mapped:

- `MAP_FIXED`

  If start address *`addr`* is anything other than 0, do not select a different address than the one specified. If the nonzero specified address cannot be used, `mmap` will fail. If `MAP_FIXED` is specified, *`start`* must be a multiple of the page size. Use of this option is discouraged since it may prevent a system from making the most effective use of its resources.

- `MAP_SHARED`

  Share this mapping with all other processes that map this object. Storing to the region is equivalent to writing to the file. The file may not actually be updated until `msync` or `munmap` is called.

- `MAP_PRIVATE`

  Create a private copy-on-write mapping. Stores to the region do not affect the original file. It is unspecified whether changes made to the file after the `mmap` call are visible in the mapped region.

You must specify exactly one of `MAP_SHARED` and `MAP_PRIVATE`.

The preceding three flags are described in POSIX.1b (formerly POSIX.4) and SUSv2. Linux also is aware of the following nonstandard flags:

- `MAP_DENYWRITE`

  This flag is ignored. (Long ago, it signaled that attempts to write to the underlying file should fail with `ETXTBUSY`, but this was a source of denial-of-service attacks.)

- `MAP_EXECUTABLE`

  This flag is ignored.

- `MAP_NORESERVE`

  (Used together with `MAP_PRIVATE`.) Do not reserve swap space pages for this mapping. When swap space is reserved, you have the guarantee that it is possible to modify this private copy-on-write region. When it is not reserved, you might get `SIGSEGV` upon a write when no memory is available.

- `MAP_LOCKED`

  This flag is ignored.

- `MAP_GROWSDOWN`

  Used for stacks. Indicates to the kernel VM system that the mapping should extend downward in memory.

- `MAP_ANONYMOUS`

  The mapping is not backed by any file; the *`fd`* and *`offset`* arguments are ignored. This flag in conjunction with `MAP_SHARED` has been implemented since Linux 2.4.

- `MAP_ANON`

  Alias for `MAP_ANONYMOUS`. Deprecated.

- `MAP_FILE`

  Compatibility flag. Ignored.

Some systems document the additional flags `MAP_AUTOGROW`, `MAP_AUTORESRV`, `MAP_COPY`, and `MAP_LOCAL`.

`fd` should be a valid file descriptor, unless `MAP_ANONYMOUS` is set, in which case the argument is ignored.

`offset` should be a multiple of the page size as returned by `getpagesize`.

Memory mapped by `mmap` is preserved across `fork()`, with the same attributes.

A file is mapped in multiples of the page size. For a file that is not a multiple of the page size, the remaining memory is zeroed when mapped and writes to that region are not written out to the file. The effect of changing the size of the underlying file of a mapping on the pages that correspond to added or removed regions of the file is unspecified.

The `munmap` system call deletes the mappings for the specified address range and causes further references to addresses within the range to generate invalid memory references. The region is also automatically unmapped when the process is terminated. That said, closing the file descriptor does not unmap the region.

The address *`start`* must be a multiple of the page size. All pages containing a part of the indicated range are unmapped, and subsequent references to these pages will generate `SIGSEGV`. It is not an error if the indicated range does not contain any mapped pages.

For file-backed mappings, the `st_atime` field for the mapped file may be updated at any time between the `mmap()` and the corresponding unmapping; the first reference to a mapped page will update the field if necessary.

The `st_ctime` and `st_mtime` fields for a file mapped with `PROT_WRITE` and `MAP_SHARED` will be updated after a write to the mapped region, and before a subsequent `msync()`, with the `MS_SYNC` or `MS_ASYNC` flag, if one occurs.

5.11.13.4 Return Value

On success, `mmap` returns a pointer to the mapped area. On error, `MAP_FAILED` (–1) is returned, and *`ERRNO`* is set appropriately. On success, `munmap` returns 0, on failure –1, and *`ERRNO`* is set (probably to `EINVAL`).

5.11.13.5 Errors

- **`EBADF`**. *`fd`* is not a valid file descriptor (and `MAP_ANONYMOUS` was not set).
- **`EACCES`**. The file descriptor (*`fd`*) refers to a nonregular file. Or `MAP_PRIVATE` was requested, but *`fd`* is not open for reading. Or `MAP_SHARED` was requested and `PROT_WRITE` is set, but *`fd`* is not open in read/write (`O_RDWR`) mode. Or `PROT_WRITE` is set, but the file is append-only.
- **`EINVAL`**. *`Start`*, *`length`*, or *`offset`* are too large or are not aligned on a `PAGESIZE` boundary.
- **`ETXTBSY`**. `MAP_DENYWRITE` was set, but the object specified by *`fd`* is open for writing.
- **`EAGAIN`**. The file has been locked, or too much memory has been locked.
- **`ENOMEM`**. No memory is available, or the process's maximum number of mappings would have been exceeded.
- **`ENODEV`**. The underlying filesystem of the specified file does not support memory mapping.

Use of a mapped region can result in these signals:

- **`SIGSEGV`**. Attempted write into a region specified to `mmap` as read-only.
- **`SIGBUS`**. Attempted access to a portion of the buffer that does not correspond to the file (for example, beyond the end of the file, including the case where another process has truncated the file).

5.11.13.6 ERRNO(s) Not Implemented in Linux

- **EFBIG**. The mapping requested extends beyond the maximum file size associated with *fildes*.
- **EMFILE**. The application has requested SPEC1170-compliant behavior,[18] and the number of mapped regions would exceed an implementation-dependent limit (per process or per system).
- **ENXIO**. The addresses specified by the range (off, off+len) are invalid for the *fildes* parameter.
- **EOVERFLOW**. The mapping requested extends beyond the offset maximum for the file description associated with *fildes*.

Conforming To

SVr4, POSIX.1b (formerly POSIX.4), 4.4BSD, SUSv2. SVr4 documents additional error codes ENXIO and ENODEV. SUSv2 documents additional error codes EMFILE and EOVERFLOW.

5.11.14 pread(), pwrite()

This command reads from or writes to a file descriptor at a given offset.

5.11.14.1 Linux Prototype

```
b#define _XOPEN_SOURCE 500
#include <unistd.h>
ssize_t pread(int fd, void *buf, size_t count, off_t offset);
ssize_t pwrite(int fd, const void *buf, size_t count, off_t offset);
```

18 SPEC1170-complaint means that *addr* is 0, so let the system allocate a region in memory and return the pointer. If not, use the value specified by *addr*.

5.11.14.2 AIX Prototype

```
#include <unistd.h>
ssize_t pread(int fildes, void *buf, size_t nbyte, off_t offset);
ssize_t pwrite (int FileDescriptor, const void *Buffer, size_t NBytes, off_t
Offset);
```

5.11.14.3 Detail Comparison

Compatible

`pread()` reads up to *`count`* bytes from file descriptor *`fd`* at offset *`offset`* (from the start of the file) into the buffer starting at *`buf`*. The file offset is not changed.

`pwrite()` writes up to *`count`* bytes from the buffer starting at *`buf`* to the file descriptor *`fd`* at offset *`offset`*. The file offset is not changed.

The file referenced by *`fd`* must be capable of seeking.

5.11.14.4 Additional Data: Linux-Specific

Functions are source-compatible, but note the `#define _XOPEN_SOURCE 500` for Linux. `_XOPEN_SOURCE 500` does not have to be explicitly defined by the user for all versions of Linux.

5.11.14.5 Return Value

On success, the number of bytes read or written is returned (0 indicates that nothing was written, in the case of `pwrite`, or end of file, in the case of `pread`), or –1 on error, in which case *`ERRNO`* is set to indicate the error.

5.11.14.6 Errors

`pread` can fail and set *`ERRNO`* to any error specified for `read` or `lseek`. `pwrite` can fail and set *`ERRNO`* to any error specified for `write` or `lseek`.

5.11.14.7 ERRNO(s) Not Implemented in Linux

- **`EBADMSG`**. The file is a `STREAM` file that is set to control-normal mode, and the message waiting to be read includes a control part.
- **`EDEADLK`**. A deadlock would occur if the calling process were to sleep until the region to be read was unlocked.

- **EOVERFLOW**. An attempt was made to read from a regular file where *NBytes* was greater than 0 and the starting *offset* was before the end of file and was greater than or equal to the *offset* maximum established in the open file description associated with `FileDescriptor`.
- **ENXIO**. A request was made of a nonexistent device, or the request was outside the capabilities of the device.
- **ESPIPE**. *fildes* is associated with a pipe or FIFO.
- **ETIMEDOUT**. The connection timed out.

Conforming To

Unix98

5.11.15 stat(), lstat(), fstat()

These functions return information about the specified file. You do not need any access rights to the file to get this information, but you need search rights to all directories named in the path leading to the file.

5.11.15.1 AIX Prototype

```
#include <sys/stat.h>
int stat(const char * Path, struct stat * Buffer);
int lstat (const char * Path, struct stat * Buffer);
int fstat (int FileDescriptor, struct stat * Buffer);
```

5.11.15.2 Linux Prototype

```
#include <sys/types.h>
#include <sys/stat.h>
#include <unistd.h>
int stat(const char *file_name, struct stat * buf);
int fstat(int filedes, struct stat * buf);
int lstat(const char *file_name, struct stat * buf);
```

5.11.15.3 Detail Comparison

Compatible

Functions are source-compatible. Code that references `dev_ts` may not work correctly unless the macros `major()`, `minor()`, and `makedev()` are used. These are found in sys/sysmacros.h.

5.11.15.4 ERRNO(s) Not Implemented in AIX

- **`ESTALE`**. The root or current directory of the process is located in a virtual filesystem that has been unmounted.
- **`ETIMEDOUT`**. The connection timed out.
- **`EIO`**. An input/output (I/O) error occurred while reading from the filesystem.

5.11.16 ptrace()

The `ptrace` system call provides a means by which a parent process may observe and control the execution of another process and examine and change its core image and registers. It is primarily used to implement breakpoint debugging and system call tracing.

5.11.16.1 AIX Prototype

```
#include <sys/reg.h>
#include <sys/ptrace.h>
#include <sys/ldr.h>
int ptrace(int Request, int Identifier, int *Address, int Data, int *Buffer);
```

5.11.16.2 AIX5L Prototype

```
#define _LINUX_SOURCE_COMPAT
#include <sys/ptrace.h>
long int ptrace(enum ptrace_request request, pid_t pid, void *addr, void *data);
```

5.11.16.3 Linux Prototype

```
#include <sys/ptrace.h>
long int ptrace(enum ptrace_request request, pid_t pid, void *addr, void *data);
```

5.11.16.4 Detail Comparison

Not Compatible

Although the service the API provides is similar between AIX and Linux, the way the tracing service is implemented differs. In Linux, kernel-level thread debugging is not possible with the `ptrace` as in AIX. And, in AIX, code built with the `_LINUX_SOURCE_COMPAT` directive is more compatible with the Linux `ptrace`.

The parent can initiate a trace by calling `fork` and having the resulting child do a `PTRACE_TRACEME`, followed (typically) by an `exec`. Alternatively, the parent may commence trace of an existing process using `PTRACE_ATTACH`.

While being traced, the child will stop each time a signal is delivered, even if the signal is being ignored. (The exception is `SIGKILL`, which has its usual effect.) The parent will be notified at its next `wait` and may inspect and modify the child process while it is stopped. The parent then causes the child to continue, optionally ignoring the delivered signal (or even delivering a different signal instead).

When the parent is finished tracing, it can terminate the child with `PTRACE_KILL` or cause it to continue executing in a normal, untraced mode via `PTRACE_DETACH`.

The value of *`request`* determines the action to be performed:

- `PTRACE_TRACEME`

  Indicates that this process is to be traced by its parent. Any signal (except `SIGKILL`) delivered to this process will cause it to stop and its parent to be notified via `wait`. Also, all subsequent calls to `exec` by this process will cause a `SIGTRAP` to be sent to it, giving the parent a chance to gain control before the new program begins execution. A process probably should not make this request if its parent is not expecting to trace it. (*`pid`*, *`addr`*, and *`data`* are ignored.)

  The preceding request is used only by the child process; the rest are used only by the parent. In the following requests, *`pid`* specifies the child process to be acted on. For requests other than `PTRACE_KILL`, the child process must be stopped.

- `PTRACE_PEEKTEXT`, `PTRACE_PEEKDATA`

  Read a word at the location *addr* in the child's memory, returning the word as the result of the `ptrace` call. Linux does not have separate text and data address spaces, so the two requests are currently equivalent. (The argument *data* is ignored.)

- `PTRACE_PEEKUSR`

  Reads a word at offset *addr* in the child's USER area, which holds the registers and other information about the process (see sys/user.h). The word is returned as the result of the `ptrace` call. Typically, the offset must be word-aligned, although this might vary by architecture. (*data* is ignored.)

- `PTRACE_POKETEXT`, `PTRACE_POKEDATA`

  Copy the word *data* to location *addr* in the child's memory. As above, the two requests are currently equivalent.

- `PTRACE_POKEUSR`

  Copies the word *data* to offset *addr* in the child's user area. As above, the offset must typically be word-aligned. To maintain the integrity of the kernel, some modifications to the user area are disallowed.

- `PTRACE_GETREGS`, `PTRACE_GETFPREGS`

  Copy the child's general purpose or floating-point registers, respectively, to location *data* in the parent. See sys/user.h for information on the format of this data. (*addr* is ignored.)

- `PTRACE_SETREGS`, `PTRACE_SETFPREGS`

  Copy the child's general purpose or floating-point registers, respectively, from location *data* in the parent. As for `PTRACE_POKEUSER`, some general-purpose register modifications may be disallowed. (*addr* is ignored.)

- `PTRACE_CONT`

  Restarts the stopped child process. If *data* is nonzero and not `SIGSTOP`, it is interpreted as a signal to be delivered to the child; otherwise, no signal is delivered. Thus, for example, the parent can control whether a signal sent to the child is delivered or not. (*addr* is ignored.)

- `PTRACE_SYSCALL`, `PTRACE_SINGLESTEP`

  Restart the stopped child as for `PTRACE_CONT`, but arrange for the child to be stopped at the next entry to or exit from a system call, or after execution of a single instruction, respectively. (The child will also, as usual, be stopped upon receipt of a signal.) From the parent's perspective, the child will appear to have been stopped by receipt of a `SIGTRAP`. So, for `PTRACE_SYSCALL`, for example, the idea is to inspect the arguments to the system call at the first stop, and then do another `PTRACE_SYSCALL` and inspect the return value of the system call at the second stop. (*addr* is ignored.)

- `PTRACE_KILL`

  Sends the child a `SIGKILL` to terminate it. (*addr* and *data* are ignored.)

- `PTRACE_ATTACH`

  Attaches to the process specified in *pid*, making it a traced "child" of the current process; the behavior of the child is as if it had done a `PTRACE_TRACEME`. The current process actually becomes the parent of the child process for most purposes (for example, it will receive notification of child events and appears in `ps` output as the child's parent), but a `getppid` by the child will still return the `pid` of the original parent. The child is sent a `SIGSTOP`, but will not necessarily have stopped by the completion of this call; use `wait` to wait for the child to stop. (*addr* and *data* are ignored.)

- `PTRACE_DETACH`

  Restarts the stopped child as for `PTRACE_CONT`, but first detaches from the process, undoing the reparenting effect of `PTRACE_ATTACH` and the effects of `PTRACE_TRACEME`. Although perhaps not intended, under Linux a traced child can be detached in this way regardless of which method was used to initiate tracing. (*addr* is ignored.)

5.11.16.5 ERRNO(s) Not Implemented in Linux

- **`ENOTSUP`**. The request is not supported.
- **`EINVAL`**. The debugger and the traced process are the same; or the `Identifier` parameter does not identify the thread that caused the exception.

5.11.17 setgid(), setregid()

These commands are used to set the user and group permission on a particular file or device.

5.11.17.1 AIX/Linux Prototype

```
#include <unistd.h>
int setgid(gid_t gid);
int setregid(gid_t rgid, gid_t egid);
```

5.11.17.2 Detail Comparison

Compatible

Functions are source-compatible, but in AIX `setgid` sets the effective group ID of the current process. In Linux if the caller is the super user, the real and saved group IDs are also set.

`setreuid` sets real and effective user IDs of the current process. Unprivileged users may only set the real user ID to the real user ID or the effective user ID, and may only set the effective user ID to the real user ID, the effective user ID, or the saved user ID.

5.11.17.3 Return Value

On success, 0 is returned. On error, –1 is returned, and *ERRNO* is set appropriately.

5.11.17.4 Errors

- **EPERM**. The user is not the super user (does not have the `CAP_SETGID` capability), and *gid* does not match the effective group ID or saved set-group-ID of the calling process.

5.11.17.5 ERRNO(s) Not Implemented in Linux

- **EINVAL**. Indicates that the value of the *gid* parameter is invalid.

5.11.18 sync()

Reading from a disk is very slow compared to accessing (real) memory. In addition, it is common to read the same part of a disk several times during relatively short periods of time. For example, one might first read an e-mail message, then read the letter into an editor when replying to it, and then make the mail program read it again when copying it to a folder. Or, consider how often the command `ls` might be run on a system with many users. By reading the information from disk only once and then keeping it in memory until no longer needed, one can speed up all but the first read. This is called *disk buffering*, and the memory used for this purpose is called the *buffer cache*. `sync()` commits buffer cache to disk.

5.11.18.1 AIX Prototype

```
#include <unistd.h>
void sync(void);
```

5.11.18.2 Linux Prototype

```
#include <unistd.h>
int sync(void);
```

5.11.18.3 Detail Comparison

Functions are *not quite* compatible. In AIX, `sync()` is a void system call. In Linux, `sync()` always returns 0. Any code that tests or assigns the return value of `sync()` will cause compile errors.

5.11.19 wait3(), wait4()

Often in multiprocess-programming you want to suspend execution of one process until an event of some sort happens either in the current process or in another process. The `wait3` and `wait4` functions control the running of processes.

The `wait3` function suspends execution of the current process until a child has exited, or until a signal is delivered whose action is to terminate the current process or to call a signal handling function. If a child has already exited by the time of the call (a so-called zombie process), the function returns immediately. Any system resources used by the child are freed.

The `wait4` function suspends execution of the current process until a child as specified by the *pid* argument has exited, or until a signal is delivered whose action is to terminate the current process or to call a signal handling function. If a child as requested by *pid* has already exited by the time of the call (a zombie process), the function returns immediately. Any system resources used by the child are freed.

5.11.19.1 AIX Prototype

```
#define _ALL_SOURCE
#include <sys/types.h>
#include <sys/resource.h>
#include <sys/wait.h>
pid_t wait3(int *StatusLocation, int Options, struct rusage *ResourceUsage);
pid_t wait4(pid_t pid, int *status, int options, struct rusage *rusage);
```

5.11.19.2 Linux Prototype

```
#define _USE_BSD
#include <sys/types.h>
#include <sys/time.h>
#include <sys/resource.h>
#include <sys/wait.h>

pid_t wait3(int *status, int options, struct rusage *rusage);
pid_t wait4(pid_t pid, int *status, int options, struct rusage *rusage);
```

5.11.19.3 Detail Comparison

Compatible

The value of *pid* can be one of the following:

- < –1

  Wait for any child process whose process group ID is equal to the absolute value of *pid*.

- –1

  Wait for any child process; this is equivalent to calling `wait3`.

- 0

  Wait for any child process whose process group ID is equal to that of the calling process.

- > 0

  Wait for the child whose process ID is equal to the value of *`pid`*.

The value of *`options`* is a bitwise OR of zero or more of the following constants:

- **`WNOHANG`**, which means to return immediately if no child is there to be waited for.
- **`WUNTRACED`**, which means to also return for children that are stopped and whose status has not been reported.

If *`status`* is not `NULL`, `wait3` or `wait4` stores status information in the location pointed to by *`status`*.

This status can be evaluated with the following macros. (These macros take the stat buffer (an `int`) as an argument, not a pointer to the buffer!)

- **`WIFEXITED(`*`status`*`)`** is nonzero if the child exited normally.
- **`WEXITSTATUS(`*`status`*`)`** evaluates to the least significant 8 bits of the return code of the child that terminated, which may have been set as the argument to a call to `exit()` or as the argument for a return statement in the main program. This macro can only be evaluated if `WIFEXITED` returned nonzero.
- **`WIFSIGNALED(`*`status`*`)`** returns true if the child process exited because of a signal that was not caught.
- **`WTERMSIG(`*`status`*`)`** returns the number of the signal that caused the child process to terminate. This macro can only be evaluated if `WIFSIGNALED` returned nonzero.
- **`WIFSTOPPED(`*`status`*`)`** returns true if the child process that caused the return is currently stopped; this is only possible if the call was done using `WUNTRACED`.
- **`WSTOPSIG(`*`status`*`)`** returns the number of the signal that caused the child to stop. This macro can only be evaluated if `WIFSTOPPED` returned nonzero.

If *rusage* is not NULL, the struct rusage as defined in sys/resource.h or bit/resource.h it points to will be filled with accounting information.

5.11.19.4 Return Value

The process ID of the child that exited is –1 on error (in particular, when no unwaited-for child processes of the specified kind exist) or 0 if WNOHANG was used and no child was available yet. In the latter two cases, *ERRNO* will be set appropriately.

5.11.19.5 Errors

- **ECHILD**. No unwaited-for child process as specified exists.
- **EINTR**. If WNOHANG was not set and an unblocked signal or a SIGCHLD was caught.

5.11.19.6 ERRNO(s) Not Implemented in Linux

- **EFAULT**. The StatusLocation or ResourceUsage parameter points to a location outside of the address space of the process.

5.11.20 getcwd()

The getcwd() function copies the absolute path name of the current working directory to the array pointed to by *buf*, which is of length *size*. If the current absolute path name would require a buffer longer than *size* elements, NULL is returned, and *ERRNO* is set to ERANGE; an application should check for this error and allocate a larger buffer if necessary.

As an extension to the POSIX.1 standard, getcwd() allocates the buffer dynamically using malloc() if *buf* is NULL on call. In this case, the allocated buffer has the length *size* unless *size* is less than 0, when *buf* is allocated as big as necessary. It is possible (and, indeed, advisable) to free() the buffers if they have been obtained this way.

`get_current_dir_name`, which is only prototyped if `__USE_GNU` is defined, will *malloc()* an array big enough to hold the current directory name. If the environment variable `PWD` is set, and its value is correct, that value will be returned.

`getwd`, which is only prototyped if `__USE_BSD` is defined, will *malloc()* an array big enough to hold the absolute path name of the current working directory.

5.11.20.1 AIX Prototype

```
#include <unistd.h>
char *getcwd (char *Buffer, size_t Size);
char *getwd(char *buf);
```

5.11.20.2 Linux Prototype

```
#include <unistd.h>
char *getcwd(char *buf, size_t size);
char *get_current_dir_name(void);
char *getwd(char *buf);
```

5.11.20.3 Detail Comparison

Compatible

AIX does not provide `get_current_dir_name()`.

5.11.20.4 Errors

- **EACCES**. Permission to read or search a component of the filename was denied.
- **EFAULT**. *buf* points to a bad address.
- **EINVAL**. The *size* argument is 0, and *buf* is not a null pointer.
- **ENOENT**. The corrent working directory has been unlinked.
- **ERANGE**. The *size* argument is less than the length of the working directory name. You need to allocate a bigger array (*buf)* and try again.

5.11.20.5 ERRNO(s) Not Implemented in Linux

- **ENOMEM**. Indicates that insufficient storage space is available.

5.11.21 mount(), umount(), vmount()

A file hierarchy is usually made available to the filesystem through the `mount` command. The `umount` command detaches the filesystem(s) mentioned from the file hierarchy. A filesystem is specified by giving the directory where it has been mounted. Giving the special device on which the filesystem lives may also work, but this is obsolete, mainly because it will fail in case this device was mounted on more than one directory.

Note that a filesystem cannot be unmounted when it is "busy"—for example, when there are open files on it, or when some process has its working directory there, or when a swap file on it is in use. The offending process could even be `umount`.

5.11.21.1 AIX Prototype

```
#include <sys/vmount.h>
int vmount (struct vmount *VMount, int size)
int mount(char *Device, char *Path, int Flags)
int umount (char *Device)
```

5.11.21.2 Linux Prototype

```
#include <sys/mount.h>
int mount(const char *specialfile, const char *dir, const char * filesystemtype,
unsigned long rwflag , const void *data);
int umount(const char *specialfile);
int umount(const char *dir);
int umount2(const char *target, int flags);
```

5.11.21.3 Detail Comparison

Not Compatible

Semantics differ between AIX and Linux.

Specifically, AIX users must convert their application usage of this API to that of Linux. Older applications that run on earlier versions of AIX (4.3.3 or before) will have an easier conversion as they most likely would have used an older `mount` subroutine instead of `vmount`. But that comparison is only based on the equal number of arguments. The semantics still differ.

`umount` functions are compatible.

5.11.21.4 Additional Data: Linux-Specific

These functions are Linux-specific and should not be used in programs intended to be portable.

`mount` attaches the filesystem specified by *`source`* (which is often a device name, but can also be a directory name or a dummy) to the directory specified by *`target`*.

`umount` and `umount2` remove the attachment of the (topmost) filesystem mounted on *`target`*.

Only the super user may mount and unmount filesystems. Since Linux 2.4, a single filesystem can be visible at multiple mount points, and multiple mounts can be stacked on the same mount point.

Values for the *`filesystemtype`* argument supported by the kernel are listed in /proc/filesystems (`minix`, `ext2`, `msdos`, `proc`, `nfs`, `iso9660`, and so on). More types may become available when the appropriate modules are loaded.

The *`mountflags`* argument may have the magic number 0xC0ED (`MS_MGC_VAL`) in the top 16 bits (this was required in kernel versions prior to 2.4 but is no longer required and is ignored if specified), and various mount flags (as defined in linux/fs.h for `libc4` and `libc5` and in sys/mount.h for `glibc2`) in the low-order 16 bits:

- `MS_BIND`

  (Linux 2.4 onward) Perform a bind mount, making a file or a directory subtree visible at another point within a file system. Bind mounts may cross file system boundaries and span chroot jails. The *`filesystemtype`*, *`mountflags`*, and *`data`* arguments are ignored.

- `MS_MANDLOCK`

  Permit mandatory locking on files in this filesystem. (Mandatory locking must still be enabled on a per-file basis, as described in `fcntl`.)

- `MS_MOVE`

  Move a subtree. *`source`* specifies an existing mount point, and *`target`* specifies the new location. The move is atomic: At no point is the subtree unmounted. The *filesystemtype*, *mountflags*, and *data* arguments are ignored.

- `MS_NOATIME`

  Do not update access times for (all types of) files on this filesystem.

- `MS_NODEV`

  Do not allow access to devices (special files) on this filesystem.

- `MS_NODIRATIME`

  Do not update access times for directories on this filesystem.

- `MS_NOEXEC`

  Do not allow programs to be executed from this filesystem.

- `MS_NOSUID`

  Do not honor set-UID and set-GID bits when executing programs from this filesystem.

- `MS_RDONLY`

  Mount filesystem read-only.

- `MS_REMOUNT`

  Remount an existing mount. This allows you to change the *mountflags* and *data* of an existing mount without having to unmount and remount the file system. *source* and *target* should be the same values specified in the initial `mount()` call; *filesystemtype* is ignored.

- `MS_SYNCHRONOUS`

  Make writes on this filesystem synchronous (as though the `O_SYNC` flag to `open` were specified for all file opens to this filesystem).

From Linux 2.4 onward, the `MS_NODEV`, `MS_NOEXEC`, and `MS_NOSUID` flags are settable on a per-mount point basis.

The *data* argument is interpreted by the different file systems. Typically, it is a string of comma-separated options understood by this filesystem. See `mount` for details of the options available for each filesystem type.

Linux 2.1.116 added the `umount2()` system call, which, like `umount()`, unmounts a target, but allows additional *flags* controlling the behavior of the operation:

- **`MNT_FORCE`**. Force unmount even if busy (since 2.1.116; only for NFS mounts).
- **`MNT_DETACH`**. Perform a lazy unmount: make the mount point unavailable for new accesses, and actually perform the unmount when the mount point ceases to be busy (since 2.4.11).

5.11.21.5 Return Value

On success, 0 is returned. On error, –1 is returned, and *`ERRNO`* is set appropriately.

5.11.21.6 Errors

The error values given next result from filesystem-type-independent errors. Each filesystem type may have its own special errors and its own special behavior. See the kernel source code for details.

- **`EPERM`**. The user is not the super user.
- **`ENODEV`**. *`Filesystemtype`* is not configured in the kernel.
- **`ENOTBLK`**. *`Source`* is not a block device (and a device was required).
- **`EBUSY`**. *`Source`* is already mounted. Or, it cannot be remounted read-only, because it still holds files open for writing. Or, it cannot be mounted on *`target`* because *`target`* is still busy (it is the working directory of some task, the mount point of another device, has open files, and so on). Or, it could not be unmounted because it is busy.
- **`EINVAL`**. *`Source`* had an invalid superblock. Or, a remount was attempted, whereas *`source`* was not already mounted on *`target`*. Or, a move was attempted, whereas *`source`* was not a mount point, or was /. Or, an umount was attempted, whereas *`target`* was not a mount point.
- **`ENOTDIR`**. The second argument, or a prefix of the first argument, is not a directory.
- **`EFAULT`**. One of the pointer arguments points outside the user address space.

- **ENOMEM**. The kernel could not allocate a free page to copy filenames or data into.
- **ENAMETOOLONG**. A path name was longer than MAXPATHLEN.
- **ENOENT**. A path name was empty or had a nonexistent component.
- **ELOOP**. Too many links encountered during pathname resolution. Or, a move was attempted, whereas *target* is a descendant of *source*.
- **EACCES**. A component of a path was not searchable.

  Or, mounting a read-only filesystem was attempted without giving the MS_RDONLY flag.

  Or, the block device *Source* is located on a filesystem mounted with the MS_NODEV option.
- **ENXIO**. The major number of the block device *source* is out of range.
- **EMFILE**. (In case no block device is required.) Table of dummy devices is full.

Portability

These functions are Linux-specific and should not be used in programs intended to be portable.

5.11.22 readv(), writev()

These commands read and write data into multiple buffers.

readv reads data from file descriptor *filedes* and puts the result in the buffers described by *vector*. The number of buffers is specified by *count*. The buffers are filled in the order specified. It operates just like read except that data is put in *vector* rather than a contiguous buffer.

writev writes data to file descriptor *filedes* and from the buffers described by *vector*. The number of buffers is specified by *count*. The buffers are used in the order specified. It operates just like write except that data is taken from *vector* rather than a contiguous buffer.

5.11.22.1 AIX Prototype

```
#include <sys/uio.h>
ssize_t readv (int FileDescriptor, const struct iovec *iov, int iovCount);
ssize_t writev (int FileDescriptor, const struct iovec *iov, int iovCount);
```

5.11.22.2 Linux Prototype

```
#include <sys/uio.h>
int readv(int filedes, const struct iovec *vector, int count);
int writev(int filedes, const struct iovec *vector, int count);
```

5.11.22.3 Detail Comparison

Not Compatible

Functions return different types. On some systems this may be as simple as casting the return value to an `int`.

Other than return values, semantics are the same.

5.11.22.4 Return Value

On success `readv` returns the number of bytes read. On success `writev` returns the number of bytes written. On error, –1 is returned, and *ERRNO* is set appropriately.

5.11.22.5 Errors

- **EINVAL**. An invalid argument was given. For instance, *count* might be greater than `MAX_IOVEC`, or 0. *filedes* could also be attached to an object that is unsuitable for reading (for `readv`) or writing (for `writev`).
- **EFAULT**. "Segmentation fault." Most likely *vector* or some of the *iov_base* pointers point to memory that is not properly allocated.
- **EBADF**. The file descriptor *filedes* is not valid.
- **EINTR**. The call was interrupted by a signal before any data was read/written.
- **EAGAIN**. Nonblocking I/O has been selected using `O_NONBLOCK`, and no data was immediately available for reading. (Or the file descriptor *filedes* is for an object that is locked.)
- **EISDIR**. *filedes* refers to a directory.

- **EOPNOTSUPP.** `filedes` refers to a socket or device that does not support reading/writing.
- **ENOMEM.** Insufficient kernel memory was available.

Other errors may occur, depending on the object connected to `filedes`.

5.11.22.6 ERRNO(s) Not Implemented in Linux

- **EBADMSG.** The file is a `STREAM` file that is set to control-normal mode, and the message waiting to be read includes a control part.
- **EDEADLK.** A deadlock would occur if the calling process were to sleep until the region to be read was unlocked.
- **EOVERFLOW.** An attempt was made to read from a regular file where `NBytes` was greater than 0 and the starting offset was before the end of file and was greater than or equal to the offset maximum established in the open file description associated with the file descriptor.
- **ENXIO.** A request was made of a nonexistent device or the request was outside the capabilities of the device.
- **ESPIPE.** `fildes` is associated with a pipe or FIFO.
- **ETIMEDOUT.** The connection timed out.

Conforming To

4.4BSD (the `readv` and `writev` functions first appeared in BSD 4.2), Unix98. Linux `libc5` used `size_t` as the type of the `count` parameter.

5.11.23 select()

`select` enables synchronous I/O multiplexing on a file descriptor. It checks the specified file descriptors and message queues (`fd_set`) to see whether they are ready for reading (receiving) or writing (sending).

5.11.23.1 AIX Prototype

```
#include <sys/time.h>
#include <sys/select.h>
#include <sys/types.h>
int select (int Nfdsmsgs, struct sellist *ReadList, struct sellist *WriteList,
struct sellist *ExceptList, struct timeval *TimeOut);
```

5.11.23.2 Linux Prototype

```
#include <sys/time.h>
#include <sys/types.h>
#include <unistd.h>
int select(int n, fd_set *readfds, fd_set *writefds, fd_set *exceptfds, struct
timeval *timeout);
int pselect(int n, fd_set *readfds, fd_set *writefds, fd_set *exceptfds, const
struct timespec *timeout, const sigset_t *sigmask);
```

5.11.23.3 select(), pselect()

Not Compatible

Functions are source-compatible, but semantics differ.

In AIX, the `select` is used for I/O multiplexing as well as exception and event handling. This is not so in Linux. For event and exception notification in Linux, you must use both `select` and `sigprocmask` system calls. Following is a brief example of how to handle the equivalent AIX exception and event notification in Linux:

```
sigprocmask (SIG_BLOCK, &orig_sigmask, 0);
r = select (n, &rd, &wr, &er, 0);
sigprocmask (SIG_BLOCK, &sigmask, 0);
```

In AIX, users call `select` with all three sets empty, *n* zero, and a non-null timeout as a fairly portable way to sleep with subsecond precision.

On Linux, the function `select` modifies timeout to reflect the amount of time not slept, which is different from most other implementations. This causes problems both when porting to Linux from other platforms and vice versa because the timeout is unusable after the call to `select` in Linux. Therefore, in Linux, consider timeout to be undefined after `select` returns.

The file sys/time.h contains compatibility defines for `fd_set` and the prototype for `select()`. The `FD_*` macros are also defined there. The sizes of the `fd_set` types differ, but code is source-compatible. In AIX, `select` is a system call.

In Linux, an `fd_set` is 128 bytes. In AIX, it is 4096 bytes. If your set is larger than 128 bytes in AIX, this will have to be shortened.

5.11.23.4 Return Value

On success, `select` and `pselect` return the number of descriptors contained in the descriptor sets, which may be zero if the timeout expires before anything interesting happens. On error, –1 is returned, and *ERRNO* is set appropriately; the sets and timeout become undefined, so do not rely on their contents after an error.

5.11.23.5 Errors

- **EBADF**. An invalid file descriptor was given in one of the sets.
- **EINTR**. A nonblocked signal was caught.
- **EINVAL**. *n* is negative.
- **ENOMEM**. `select` was unable to allocate memory for internal tables.

5.11.23.6 Example

```
#include <stdio.h>
#include <sys/time.h>
#include <sys/types.h>
#include <unistd.h>

int
main(void) {
 fd_set rfds;
 struct timeval tv;
 int retval;

 /* Watch stdin (fd 0) to see when it has input. */
 FD_ZERO(&rfds);
 FD_SET(0, &rfds);
 /* Wait up to five seconds. */
 tv.tv_sec = 5;
 tv.tv_usec = 0;

 retval = select(1, &rfds, NULL, NULL, &tv);
 /* Don't rely on the value of tv now! */
```

```
 if (retval)
 printf("Data is available now.\n");
 /* FD_ISSET(0, &rfds) will be true. */
 else
 printf("No data within five seconds.\n");

 return 0;
}
```

5.11.23.7 ERRNO(s) Not Implemented in Linux

- **`EAGAIN`**. Allocation of internal data structures was unsuccessful.
- **`EFAULT`**. The `ReadList`, `WriteList`, `ExceptList`, or `TimeOut` parameter points to a location outside of the address space of the process.
- **`ETIMEDOUT`**. The connection timed out.

Conforming To

4.4BSD (the `select` function first appeared in 4.2BSD). Generally portable to/from non-BSD systems supporting clones of the BSD socket layer (including System V variants). However, note that the System V variant typically sets the timeout variable before exit, but the BSD variant does not.

The `pselect` function is defined in IEEE Std 1003.1g-2000 (POSIX.1g) and part of POSIX 1003.1-2001. It is found in `glibc` 2.1 and later. `glibc` 2.0 has a function with this name, but it does not take a *`sigmask`* parameter.

5.11.24 reboot()

Use `reboot` to enable or disable rebooting of a system.

5.11.24.1 AIX Prototype

```
#include <sys/reboot.h>
void reboot (int HowTo, void *Argument)
#define _LINUX_SOURCE_COMPAT
#include <sys/reboot.h>
int reboot (int flag);
```

5.11.24.2 Linux Prototype

Under `glibc`, some of the constants involved have gotten symbolic names `RB_*`, and the library call is a one-argument wrapper around the three-argument system call:

```
#include <unistd.h>
#include <sys/reboot.h>
int reboot (int flag);
```

For `libc4` and `libc5`, the library call and the system call are identical, and since kernel version 2.1.30 there are symbolic names `LINUX_REBOOT_*` for the constants and a fourth argument to the call:

```
#include <unistd.h>
#include <linux/reboot.h>
int reboot(int magic, int magic2, int flag, void *arg);
```

5.11.24.3 Detail Comparison

Not Compatible

In AIX, `reboot` is a system call.

This command is a platform-specific command and is generally not portable for obvious reasons. However, IBM has made this command portable from Linux to AIX by providing the following flags when `_LINUX_SOURCE_COMPAT` is defined (the list also shows the Linux to AIX mapping if enabled [only on AIX5L]):

```
LINUX_REBOOT_CMD_RESTART -> RB_SOFTIPL

LINUX_REBOOT_CMD_HALT -> RB_HALT_POWERED

LINUX_REBOOT_CMD_POWER_OFF -> RB_HALT

LINUX_REBOOT_CMD_RESTART2 -> RB_POWIPL

LINUX_REBOOT_CMD_CAD_ON -> return(ENOSYS)

LINUX_REBOOT_CMD_CAD_OFF -> return(0)
```

AIX did not implement CAD (Ctrl-Alt-Del) for Linux compatibility.

5.11.24.4 Return Value

On success, the system reboots. On error, –1 is returned, and *ERRNO* is set appropriately.

5.11.24.5 Errors

- **EINVAL**. Bad magic numbers or *flag*.
- **EPERM**. A nonroot user attempts to call `reboot`.

5.11.24.6 ERRNO(s) Not Implemented in Linux

- **ENOSYS**. Function not supported (`LINUX_REBOOT_CMD_CAD_ON` only)

5.11.25 chroot()

`chroot()` is a UNIX system call that is often used to provide an additional layer of security when untrusted programs are run. The call to `chroot()` is normally used to ensure that code run after it can only access files at or below a given directory. Generally this is `/`, but the `chroot()` system call can change this. When `chroot()` is successfully called, the calling process has its idea of the root directory changed to the directory given as the argument to `chroot()`. The root directory is inherited by all children of the current process.

Only the super user may change the root directory.

5.11.25.1 AIX/Linux Prototype

```
#include <unistd.h>
int chroot(const char *path);
```

5.11.25.2 Details Comparison

Compatible

In AIX, this is a system call.

5.11.25.3 Return Value

On success, 0 is returned. On error, –1 is returned, and *ERRNO* is set appropriately.

5.11.25.4 Errors

Depending on the filesystem, other errors can be returned. The more general errors are listed here:

- **EPERM**. The effective UID is not 0.
- **EFAULT**. *path* points outside your accessible address space.
- **ENAMETOOLONG**. *path* is too long.
- **ENOENT**. The file does not exist.
- **ENOMEM**. Insufficient kernel memory was available.
- **ENOTDIR**. A component of *path* is not a directory.
- **EACCES**. Search permission is denied on a component of the path prefix.
- **ELOOP**. Too many symbolic links were encountered in resolving *path*.
- **EIO**. An I/O error occurred.

5.11.25.5 ERRNO(s) Not Implemented in Linux

- **ESTALE**. The root or current directory of the process is located in a virtual file system that has been unmounted.
- **ETIMEDOUT**. The connection timed out.

Conforming To

SVr4, SVID, 4.4BSD, X/OPEN. This function is not part of POSIX.1. SVr4 documents additional EINTR, ENOLINK, and EMULTIHOP error conditions. X/OPEN does not document EIO, ENOMEM, or EFAULT error conditions. This interface is marked as legacy by X/OPEN.

5.11.26 fstatfs(), statfs()

`statfs` returns information about a mounted filesystem. `path` is the path name of any file within the mounted filesystem. `buf` is a pointer to a `statfs` structure. Refer to the "Detail Comparison" section for the definition of `statfs` structure

`fstatfs` returns the same information about an open file referenced by descriptor `fd`.

5.11.26.1 AIX/Linux Prototype

```
#include <sys/vfs.h>
int statfs(const char *path, struct statfs *buf);
int fstatfs(int fd, struct statfs *buf);
```

5.11.26.2 Detail Comparison

Functions are compatible. In AIX, the sys/vfs.h file includes sys/statfs.h. Although compatible, the definitions of `struct statfs` are not identical. Refer to the following struct to identify differences.

Linux

```
struct statfs {
 long f_type;      /* type of filesystem (see below) */
 long f_bsize;     /* optimal transfer block size */
 long f_blocks;    /* total data blocks in file system */
 long f_bfree;     /* free blocks in fs */
 long f_bavail;    /* free blocks avail to non-superuser */
 long f_files;     /* total file nodes in file system */
 long f_ffree;     /* free file nodes in fs */
 fsid_t f_fsid;    /* file system id */
 long f_namelen;   /* maximum length of filenames */
 long f_spare[6];  /* spare for later */
};

File system types:

linux/affs_fs.h:
 AFFS_SUPER_MAGIC 0xADFF
linux/efs_fs.h:
 EFS_SUPER_MAGIC 0x00414A53
linux/ext_fs.h:
 EXT_SUPER_MAGIC 0x137D
linux/ext2_fs.h:
 EXT2_OLD_SUPER_MAGIC 0xEF51
 EXT2_SUPER_MAGIC 0xEF53
```

```
linux/hpfs_fs.h:
 HPFS_SUPER_MAGIC 0xF995E849
linux/iso_fs.h:
 ISOFS_SUPER_MAGIC 0x9660
linux/minix_fs.h:
 MINIX_SUPER_MAGIC 0x137F /* orig. minix */
 MINIX_SUPER_MAGIC2 0x138F /* 30 char minix */
 MINIX2_SUPER_MAGIC 0x2468 /* minix V2 */
 MINIX2_SUPER_MAGIC2 0x2478 /* minix V2, 30 char names */
linux/msdos_fs.h:
 MSDOS_SUPER_MAGIC 0x4d44
linux/ncp_fs.h:
 NCP_SUPER_MAGIC 0x564c
linux/nfs_fs.h:
 NFS_SUPER_MAGIC 0x6969
linux/proc_fs.h:
 PROC_SUPER_MAGIC 0x9fa0
linux/smb_fs.h:
 SMB_SUPER_MAGIC 0x517B
linux/sysv_fs.h:
 XENIX_SUPER_MAGIC 0x012FF7B4
 SYSV4_SUPER_MAGIC 0x012FF7B5
 SYSV2_SUPER_MAGIC 0x012FF7B6
 COH_SUPER_MAGIC 0x012FF7B7
linux/ufs_fs.h:
 UFS_MAGIC  0x00011954
linux/xfs_fs.h:
 XFS_SUPER_MAGIC 0x58465342
linux/xia_fs.h:
 _XIAFS_SUPER_MAGIC 0x012FD16D
```

AIX

```
struct statfs {
 int f_version;         /* version/type of statfs, 0 for now */
 int f_type;            /* type of info, zero for now */
 ulong_t f_bsize;       /* optimal file system block size */
 fsblkcnt_t f_blocks;   /* total data blocks in file system */
 fsblkcnt_t f_bfree;    /* free block in fs */
 fsblkcnt_t f_bavail;   /* free blocks avail to non-superuser */
 fsfilcnt_t f_files;    /* total file nodes in file system */
 fsfilcnt_t f_ffree;    /* free file nodes in fs */
#if !defined(_KERNEL) && defined(__64BIT__)
 fsid64_t f_fsid;       /* file system id */
#else
 fsid_t f_fsid;         /* file system id */
#endif
 int f_vfstype;         /* what type of vfs this is */
 ulong_t f_fsize;       /* fundamental file system block size */
 int f_vfsnumber;       /* vfs indentifier number */
 int f_vfsoff;          /* reserved, for vfs specific data offset */
```

```
    int f_vfslen;          /* reserved, for len of vfs specific data */
    int f_vfsvers;         /* reserved, for vers of vfs specific data *
    char f_fname[32];      /* file system name (usually mount pt.) */
    char f_fpack[32];      /* file system pack name */
    int f_name_max;        /* maximum component name length for posix */
};
```

Fields that are undefined for a particular filesystem are set to 0.

5.11.26.3 Return Value

On success, 0 is returned. On error, –1 is returned, and *ERRNO* is set appropriately.

5.11.26.4 Errors

For `statfs`:

- **ENOTDIR**. A component of the path prefix of *path* is not a directory.
- **ENAMETOOLONG**. *path* is too long.
- **ENOENT**. The file referred to by *path* does not exist.
- **EACCES**. Search permission is denied for a component of the path prefix of *path*.
- **ELOOP**. Too many symbolic links were encountered in translating *path*.
- **EFAULT**. *buf* or *path* points to an invalid address.
- **EIO**. An I/O error occurred while reading from or writing to the filesystem.
- **ENOMEM**. Insufficient kernel memory was available.
- **ENOSYS**. The filesystem path does not support `statfs`.

For `fstatfs`:

- **EBADF**. *fd* is not a valid open file descriptor.
- **EFAULT**. *buf* points to an invalid address.
- **EIO**. An I/O error occurred while reading from or writing to the filesystem.
- **ENOSYS**. The filesystem *fd* is open but does not support `statfs`.

5.11.26.5 ERRNO(s) Not Implemented in Linux

- **`ESTALE`**. The root or current directory of the process is located in a virtual filesystem that has been unmounted.
- **`ETIMEDOUT`**. The connection timed out.
- **`EIO`**. An input/output (I/O) error occurred while reading from the filesystem.

Conforming To

The Linux `statfs` was inspired by the 4.4BSD `statfs` (but they do not use the same structure).

5.11.27 poll()

`poll()` (alone with `select()`) indicates when a procedure is safe to execute on an open file descriptor without any delays. For instance, a programmer can use these calls to know when there is data to be read on a socket. By delegating responsibility to `select()` and `poll()`, you do not have to constantly check whether there is data to be read. Instead, `select()` and `poll()` can be placed in the background by the operating system and woken up when the event is satisfied or a specified timeout has elapsed. This process can significantly increase execution efficiency of a program.

5.11.27.1 AIX Prototype

```
#include <sys/poll.h>
int poll(void *ListPointer, unsigned long Nfdsmsgs, long Timeout);
```

5.11.27.2 Linux Prototype

```
#include <sys/poll.h>
int poll(struct pollfd *ufds, unsigned int nfds, int timeout);
```

5.11.27.3 Detail Comparison

Not Compatible

`poll`: wait for some event on a file descriptor.

Functions are source-compatible, but the `pollfd` structs differ.

For maximum performance and scalability, Linux introduced `epoll` in version 2.5, but in Linux 2.6 the function was deprecated and is no longer supported.

AIX

```
struct pollist {
 struct pollfd fds[3];
 struct pollmsg msgs[2];
 } list;
```

Linux

`poll` is a variation on the theme of `select`. It specifies an array of *`nfds`* structures of the following type (and a timeout in milliseconds):

```
struct pollfd {
  int fd;   /* file descriptor */
  short events; /* requested events */
  short revents; /* returned events */
 };
```

A negative value means infinite timeout. The field *`fd`* contains a file descriptor for an open file. The field *`events`* is an input parameter, a bitmask specifying the events the application is interested in. The field *`revents`* is an output parameter, filled by the kernel with the events that actually occurred, either of the type requested, or of one of the types `POLLERR` or `POLLHUP` or `POLLNVAL`. (These 3 bits are meaningless in the *`events`* field and are set in the *`revents`* field whenever the corresponding condition is true.) If none of the events requested (and no error) has occurred for any of the file descriptors, the kernel waits for *timeout* milliseconds for one of these events to occur. The following possible bits in these masks are defined in <sys/poll.h>:

```
#define POLLIN 0x0001 /* There is data to read */
#define POLLPRI 0x0002 /* There is urgent data to read */
#define POLLOUT 0x0004 /* Writing now will not block */
#define POLLERR 0x0008 /* Error condition */
#define POLLHUP 0x0010 /* Hung up */
#define POLLNVAL 0x0020 /* Invalid request: fd not open */
```

In asm/poll.h, too, the values `POLLRDNORM`, `POLLRDBAND`, `POLLWRNORM`, `POLLWRBAND`, and `POLLMSG` are defined.

5.11.27.4 Return Value

On success, a positive number is returned, where the number returned is the number of structures that have nonzero *revents* fields (in other words, those descriptors with events or errors reported). A value of 0 indicates that the call timed out and no file descriptors have been selected. On error, –1 is returned, and *ERRNO* is set appropriately.

5.11.27.5 Errors

- **EBADF**. An invalid file descriptor was given in one of the sets.
- **ENOMEM**. There was no space to allocate file descriptor tables.
- **EFAULT**. The array given as argument was not contained in the calling program's address space.
- **EINTR**. A signal occurred before any requested event.

5.11.27.6 ERRNO(s) Not Implemented in Linux

- **EAGAIN**. Allocation of internal data structures was unsuccessful.
- **EINVAL**. The number of `pollfd` structures specified by the `Nfdsmsgs` parameter is greater than the maximum number of open files, `OPEN_MAX`. This error is also returned if the number of `pollmsg` structures specified by the `Nfdsmsgs` parameter is greater than the maximum number of allowable message queues.

Conforming To

XPG4-UNIX

5.11.28 quotactl()

The `quotactl()` call manipulates disk quotas. *cmd* indicates a command to be applied to UID *id* or GID *id*. To set the type of quota, use the *QCMD(cmd, type)* macro. *special* is a pointer to a null-terminated string containing the path name of the block special device for the filesystem being manipulated. *addr* is the address of an optional, command-specific data structure that is copied in or out of the system. The interpretation of *addr* is given with each of the following commands.

5.11.28.1 AIX Prototype

```
#include <jfs/quota.h>
int quotactl (char *Path, int Cmd, int ID, char *Addr);
```

5.11.28.2 Linux Prototype

```
#include <sys/types.h>
#include <sys/quota.h>
int quotactl(int cmd, const char *special, qid_t id, caddr_t addr);
```

5.11.28.3 Detail Comparison

Not Compatible

The header is in a different location for AIX and Linux. The arguments are in a different order. The Linux *cmd* includes all the AIX commands as a subset plus their own. The remaining documentation is from the Linux man page.

- `Q_QUOTAON`

  Turn on quotas for a filesystem. *addr* points to the path name of the file containing the quotas for the filesystem. The quota file must exist; it is normally created with the *quotacheck* program. This call is restricted to the super user.

- `Q_QUOTAOFF`

  Turn off quotas for a filesystem. *addr* and *id* are ignored. This call is restricted to the super user.

- `Q_GETQUOTA`

  Get disk quota limits and current usage for user or group *id*. *addr* is a pointer to a `mem_dqblk` structure (defined in linux/quota.h). Only the super user may get the quotas of a user other than himself.

- `Q_SETQUOTA`

  Set disk quota limits and current usage for user or group *id*. *addr* is a pointer to a `mem_dqblk` structure (defined in linux/quota.h). This call is restricted to the super user.

- `Q_SETQLIM`

  Set disk quota limits for user or group *id*. *addr* is a pointer to a `mem_dqblk` structure (defined in linux/quota.h). This call is restricted to the super user.

- `Q_SETUSE`

  Set current usage for user or group *id*. *addr* is a pointer to a `mem_dqblk` structure (defined in linux/quota.h). This call is restricted to the super user.

- `Q_SYNC`

  Update the on-disk copy of quota usages for a filesystem. If *special* is null, all filesystems with active quotas are synced. *addr* and *id* are ignored.

- `Q_GETSTATS`

  Get statistics and other generic information about the quota subsystem. *addr* should be a pointer to the `dqstats` structure (defined in linux/quota.h) in which data should be stored. *special* and *id* are ignored.

The new quota format also allows following additional calls:

- `Q_GETINFO`

  Get information (such as grace times) about `quotafile`. *addr* should be a pointer to the `mem_dqinfo` structure (defined in linux/quota.h). *id* is ignored.

- `Q_SETINFO`

  Set information about `quotafile`. *addr* should be a pointer to the `mem_dqinfo` structure (defined in linux/quota.h). *id* is ignored. This operation is restricted to super user.

- `Q_SETGRACE`

  Set grace times in information about `quotafile`. *addr* should be a pointer to the `mem_dqinfo` structure (defined in linux/quota.h). *id* is ignored. This operation is restricted to super user.

- `Q_SETFLAGS`

  Set flags in information about `quotafile`. These flags are defined in linux/quota.h. Note that there are currently no defined flags. *addr* should be a pointer to `mem_dqinfo` structure (defined in linux/quota.h). *`id`* is ignored. This operation is restricted to super user.

For XFS filesystems making use of the XFS Quota Manager (XQM), the preceding commands are bypassed and the following commands are used:

- `Q_XQUOTAON`

  Turn on quotas for an XFS filesystem. XFS provides the ability to turn on/off quota limit enforcement with quota accounting. Therefore, XFS expects the *`addr`* to be a pointer to an unsigned `int` that contains either the flags `XFS_QUOTA_UDQ_ACCT` and/or `XFS_QUOTA_UDQ_ENFD` (for user quota) or `XFS_QUOTA_GDQ_ACCT` and/or `XFS_QUOTA_GDQ_ENFD` (for group quota), as defined in linux/xqm.h. This call is restricted to super user.

- `Q_XQUOTAOFF`

  Turn off quotas for an XFS filesystem. As in `Q_QUOTAON`, XFS filesystems expect a pointer to an unsigned `int` that specifies whether quota accounting and/or limit enforcement needs to be turned off. This call is restricted to the super user.

- `Q_XGETQUOTA`

  Get disk quota limits and current usage for user *`id`*. *`addr`* is a pointer to an `fs_disk_quota` structure (defined in linux/xqm.h). Only the super user may get the quotas of a user other than himself.

- `Q_XSETQLIM`

  Set disk quota limits for user *`id`*. *`addr`* is a pointer to an `fs_disk_quota` structure (defined in linux/xqm.h). This call is restricted to super user.

- `Q_XGETQSTAT`

  Return an `fs_quota_stat` structure containing XFS filesystem-specific quota information. This is useful in finding out how much space is spent to store quota information and to get quota on/off status of a given local XFS filesystem.

- `Q_XQUOTARM`

  Free the disk space taken by disk quotas. Quotas must have already been turned off.

There is no command equivalent to `Q_SYNC` for XFS because *sync* writes quota information to disk (in addition to the other filesystem metadata it writes out).

5.11.28.4 Return Values

`quotactl()` returns 0 on success and –1on failure and sets *ERRNO* to indicate the error.

5.11.28.5 Errors

- **EFAULT**. *addr* and *special* are invalid.
- **EINVAL**. The kernel has not been compiled with the *QUOTA* option. *cmd* is invalid.
- **ENOENT**. The file specified by *special* or *addr* does not exist.
- **ENOTBLK**. *special* is not a block device.
- **EPERM**. The call is privileged and the caller was not the super user.
- **ESRCH**. No disc quota is found for the indicated user. Quotas have not been turned on for this filesystem.
- **EUSERS**. The quota table is full.

If *cmd* is `Q_QUOTAON`, `quotactl()` may set *ERRNO* to the following:

- `EACCES`

  The quota file pointed to by *addr* exists but is not a regular file. The quota file pointed to by *addr* exists but is not on the filesystem pointed to by *special*.

- `EBUSY`

  `Q_QUOTAON` attempted even though another `Q_QUOTAON` has already taken place.

5.12 Some AIX Nonstandard Programming Practices

When developing on any platform, it is sometimes impossible to avoid using platform-specific APIs. For instance, to develop device drivers, you must make use of platform-specific APIs, and these APIs are not portable from one platform to the next. Table 5-7 identifies some nonstandard programming practices that require some programming effort when porting from AIX to Linux.

TABLE 5-7
Nonstandard Programming References

AIX	Linux
Use of Object Data Manager (ODM) APIs: `odm_add_obj`, `odm_change_obj`, `odm_close_class`, and so on	Use www.linux.org and search the documentation for "Linux Device Driver Development."
Use of `nlist`	Look at `lsof` source code for `nlist_private` example.
Reading /dev/kmem directly	Port using /procfs and sysinfo API.
Use of Portable Stream Environment (PSE) and System V release 4 streams: `t_accept`, `t_alloc`, `t_bind`, `t_close`, `t_connect`, and so on	Use open-source Linux Streams (LiS) (www.gcom.com/home/linux/lis/).
Use of /proc	Port using /procfs and sysinfo API.

In short, any low-level programming practices that interact with the kernel directly are all considered nonportable. Additional work will involve reverse engineering to come up with the same behavior and functionality on the targeted platform.

5.13 Signals

A signal is an indication that an event has occurred. Typically, a process that receives a signal handles that signal through either a default mechanism or a signal handler. POSIX defines a set of signals and signal-handling functions that are implemented in Linux. This section compares and contrasts signal support between Linux 2.6 and AIX.

5.13.1 Signal Actions

Each signal has an associated default action associated with it. A default action is what the Linux kernel does for the process when a signal arrives for that process. The default actions are as follows:

- **Process Termination.** Process is terminated.
- **Process Coredump.** Process is terminated and coredump may be produced.[19]
- **Process Stopped.** Process is stopped.
- **Process Ignore Signal.** Process ignores the signal.

A process can also install a signal handler to run when a signal is delivered to it. The signal handler takes the place of the default action associated with each signal.

Signals occur as a consequence of an event. Here are some examples that can cause a signal to be sent to a process:

- A program error such as dividing by 0 or accessing an invalid address
- A child process terminating
- A timer expiring
- A user requesting to interrupt or terminate a process

5.13.2 Simple Signals

The simplest signal-handling function Linux supports is the original ISO C standard `signal()` API. It allows the calling process to change the action for a particular signal, to either ignore or restore the default signal action, or install a function that is called when that particular signal is received by the process.

This section defines the `signal()` APIs available in GNU/Linux and the differences compared to AIX.

---

19 In certain Linux systems, coredumping is turned off by default. To turn it on, use the `ulimit -c` command.

5.13.2.1 AIX Prototype

```
#include <signal.h>
int sigaction (int Signal, struct sigaction *Action, struct sigaction *OAction);
int sigprocmask (int How, const sigset_t *Set, sigset *OSet);
int sigpending (sigset_t *Set);
int sigsuspend (const sigset_t *SignalMask);
int sigpause (int SignalMask);
```

5.13.2.2 Linux Prototype

```
#include <signal.h>
int sigaction(int signum, const struct sigaction *act, struct sigaction
*oldact);
int sigprocmask(int how, const sigset_t *set, sigset_t *oldset);
int sigpending(sigset_t *set);
int sigsuspend(const sigset_t *mask);
int sigpause(int sigmask);
```

5.13.2.3 Detail Comparison

Not Compatible

Signal values are different between AIX and Linux.

The remaining documentation is taken from the Linux man page.

The `sigaction` system call is used to change the action taken by a process on receipt of a specific signal.

`signum` specifies the signal and can be any valid signal except `SIGKILL` and `SIGSTOP`.

If *`act`* is non-null, the new action for signal *`signum`* is installed from *`act`*. If *`oldact`* is non-null, the previous action is saved in *`oldact`*.

The `sigaction` structure is defined as something like this:

```
struct sigaction {
 void (*sa_handler)(int);
 void (*sa_sigaction)(int, siginfo_t *, void *);
 sigset_t sa_mask;
 int sa_flags;
 void (*sa_restorer)(void);
}
```

On some architectures, a union is involved; do not assign to both *`sa_handler`* and *`sa_sigaction`*.

The *sa_restorer* element is obsolete and should not be used. POSIX does not specify an *sa_restorer* element.

sa_handler specifies the action to be associated with *signum* and may be SIG_DFL for the default action, SIG_IGN to ignore this signal, or a pointer to a signal-handling function.

sa_mask gives a mask of signals that should be blocked during execution of the signal handler. In addition, the signal that triggered the handler will be blocked, unless the SA_NODEFER or SA_NOMASK flags are used.

sa_flags specifies a set of flags that modify the behavior of the signal-handling process. It is formed by the bitwise OR of zero or more of the following:

- SA_NOCLDSTOP

  If *signum* is SIGCHLD, do not receive notification when child processes stop (that is, when child processes receive one of SIGSTOP, SIGTSTP, SIGTTIN, or SIGTTOU).

- SA_ONESHOT or SA_RESETHAND

  Restore the signal action to the default state once the signal handler has been called.

- SA_ONSTACK

  Call the signal handler on an alternate signal stack provided by *sigaltstack*. If an alternate stack is not available, the default stack will be used.

- SA_RESTART

  Provide behavior compatible with BSD signal semantics by making certain system calls restartable across signals.

- SA_NOMASK or SA_NODEFER

  Do not prevent the signal from being received from within its own signal handler.

- SA_SIGINFO

  The signal handler takes three arguments, not one. In this case, *sa_sigaction* should be set rather than *sa_handler*. (The *sa_sigaction* field was added in Linux 2.1.86.)

The *siginfo_t* parameter to *sa_sigaction* is a struct with the following elements:

```
siginfo_t {
 int si_signo;       /* Signal number */
 int si_errno;       /* An errno value */
 int si_code;        /* Signal code */
 pid_t si_pid;       /* Sending process ID */
 uid_t si_uid;       /* Real user ID of sending process */
 int si_status;      /* Exit value or signal */
 clock_t si_utime;   /* User time consumed */
 clock_t si_stime;   /* System time consumed */
 sigval_t si_value;  /* Signal value */
 int si_int;         /* POSIX.1b signal */
 void * si_ptr;      /* POSIX.1b signal */
 void * si_addr;     /* Memory location which caused fault */
 int si_band;        /* Band event */
 int si_fd;          /* File descriptor */
}
```

si_signo, *si_errno*, and *si_code* are defined for all signals. The rest of the struct may be a union, so one should only read the fields that are meaningful for the given signal. `Kill`, POSIX.1b signals, and `SIGCHLD` fill in *si_pid* and *si_uid*. `SIGCHLD` also fills in *si_status*, *si_utime*, and *si_stime*. *si_int* and *si_ptr* are specified by the sender of the POSIX.1b signal. `SIGILL`, `SIGFPE`, `SIGSEGV`, and `SIGBUS` fill in *si_addr* with the address of the fault. `SIGPOLL` fills in *si_band* and *si_fd*.

si_code indicates why this signal was sent. It is a value, not a bitmask. Table 5-8 lists the values possible for any signal.

TABLE 5-8
Values of si_code as Implemented in Linux 2.6

Signal	Linux si_code[20]	Description
SIGILL	ILL_ILLOPC	Illegal opcode.
	ILL_ILLOPN	Illegal operand.
	ILL_ILLADR	Illegal addressing mode.
	ILL_ILLTRP	Illegal trap.
	ILL_PRVOPC	Privileged opcode.
	ILL_PRVREG	Privileged register.
	ILL_COPROC	Coprocessor error.
	ILL_BADSTK	Internal stack error.
		Unknown error.
		Break instruction trap.
SIGFPE	FPE_INTDIV	Integer divide by 0.
	FPE_INTOVF	Integer overflow.
	FPE_FLTDIV	Floating-point divide by 0.
	FPE_FLTOVF	Floating-point overflow.
	FPE_FLTUND	Floating-point underflow.
	FPE_FLTRES	Floating-point invalid operation.
	FPE_FLTINV	Subscript out of range.
SIGSEGV	SEGV_MAPERR	Address not mapped to object.
	SEGV_ACCERR	Invalid permissions for mapped object.
SIGBUS	BUS_ADRALN	Bus error.
	BUS_ADRERR	
	BUS_OBJERR	
SIGTRAP	TRAP_BRKPT	Process breakpoint.
	TRAP_TRACE	Process trace trap.

20 Referenced from bits/singingo.h

Signal	Linux si_code	Description
SIGCHLD	CLD_EXITED	Child has exited.
	CLD_KILLED	Child was killed.
	CLD_DUMPED	Child terminated abnormally.
	CLD_TRAPPED	Traced child has trapped.
	CLD_STOPPED	Child has stopped.
	CLD_CONTINUED	Stopped child has continued.
SIGPOLL	POLL_IN	Data input available.
	POLL_OUT	Output buffers available.
	POLL_MSG	Input message available.
	POLL_ERR	I/O error.
	POLL_PRI	High-priority input available.
	POLL_HUP	Device disconnected.

The `sigprocmask` call is used to change the list of currently blocked signals. The behavior of the call is dependent on the value of *`how`*, as follows:

- **`SIG_BLOCK`**. The set of blocked signals is the union of the current set and the *`set`* argument.
- **`SIG_UNBLOCK`**. The signals in *`set`* are removed from the current set of blocked signals. It is legal to attempt to unblock a signal that is not blocked.
- **`SIG_SETMASK`**. The set of blocked signals is set to the argument *`set`*.

If *`oldset`* is non-null, the previous value of the signal mask is stored in *`oldset`*.

The `sigpending` call allows the examination of pending signals (ones that have been raised while blocked). The signal mask of pending signals is stored in *`set`*.

The `sigsuspend` call temporarily replaces the signal mask for the process with that given by *`mask`* and then suspends the process until a signal is received.

5.13.2.4 Return Value

The functions `sigaction`, `sigprocmask`, and `sigpending` return 0 on success and –1 on error. The function `sigsuspend` always returns –1, normally with the error `EINTR`.

5.13.2.5 Errors

- **`EINVAL`**. An invalid signal was specified. This will also be generated if an attempt is made to change the action for `SIGKILL` or `SIGSTOP`, which cannot be caught.
- **`EFAULT`**. *`act`*, *`oldact`*, *`set`*, *`oldset`*, or *`mask`* point to memory that is not a valid part of the process address space.
- **`EINTR`**. System call was interrupted.

5.13.2.6 Signal Values

Signal values are defined differently between Linux and AIX. Linux signals are essentially a fully contained subset of AIX signals. The only exception is `SIGSTKFLT`. No code was found in the Linux kernel to implement the `SIGSTKFLT` signal. Table 5-9 shows the differences in signal values between AIX and Linux.

TABLE 5-9
Linux and AIX Signal Values

Signal	Linux	AIX
`SIGHUP`	1	1
`SIGINT`	2	2
`SIGQUIT`	3	3
`SIGILL`	4	4
`SIGTRAP`	5	5
`SIGABRT`	6	6
`SIGIOT`	6	6
`SIGBUS`	7	10
`SIGFPE`	8	8
`SIGKILL`	9	9

Signal	Linux	AIX
SIGUSR1	10	30
SIGSEGV	11	11
SIGUSR2	12	31
SIGPIPE	13	13
SIGALRM	14	14
SIGTERM	15	15
SIGSTKFLT	16	Undefined
SIGCLD	17	20
SIGCHLD	17	20
SIGCONT	18	19
SIGSTOP	19	17
SIGTSTP	20	18
SIGTTI	21	21
SIGTTOU	22	22
SIGURG	23	16
SIGXCPU	24	24
SIGXFSZ	25	25
SIGVTALRM	26	34
SIGPROF	27	32
SIGWINCH	28	28
SIGPOLL	29	23
SIGIO	29	23
SIGPWR	30	29
SIGSYS	31	12
_NSIG	64	Undefined

Implementation of correct and reliable signals has been in place for many years now, where an installed signal handler remains persistent and is not reset by the kernel. The POSIX standards provided a fairly well-defined set of interfaces for using signals in code, and today the Linux implementation of signals is fully POSIX-compliant.

5.14 Network Programming

Network programming makes it possible for two applications to communicate with each other through a common protocol. A socket is the basic interface that provides this communication link. It provides an end-to-end communications link between a client (requestor) and a server (providing service). AIX and Linux provide support for socket communications, and Table 5-10 compares differences between the two.

TABLE 5-10
AIX and Linux System API Comparison: Network Programming

AIX	Linux Equivalent	Description
`accept`	`Accept`	Accept connection on a socket.
`bind`	`Bind`	Bind an address to a socket.
`connect`	`connect`	Initiate a connection on a socket.
`getdomainname` `setdomainnanme`	`getdomainname` `setdomainname`	Get/set domain name.
`gethostid` `sethostid`	`gethostid` `sethosid`	Get or set the unique identifier of the current host.
`gethostname` `sethostname`	`gethostname` `sethostname`	Get/set host name.
`gethostbyname`	`gethostbyname`	Get network host entry by name.
`gethostbyaddr`	`gethostbyaddr`	Get host entry by address.
`getservbyname`	`getservbyname`	Get service entry by name (according to /etc/services file).
`getservbyport`	`getservbyport`	Get service entry by port (according to /etc/services file).
`getpeername`	`getpeername`	Get name of connected peer socket.
`getsockname`	`getsockname`	Get socket name.

AIX	Linux Equivalent	Description
getsockopt setsockopt	getsockopt setsockoopt	Get/set options on a socket.
listen	listen	Listen for socket connections and limit the backlog of incoming connections.
recv	recv	Receive messages from connected sockets.
recvfrom	recvfrom	Receive messages from a connected or unconnected socket.
recvmsg	recvmsg	Receive messages from any socket. Identical to recvfrom.
send	send	Send a message from a socket.
sendmsg	sendmsg	Send a message from a connected or unconnected socket.
sendto	sendto	Send a message anytime. Identical to sendmsg.
sendfile	sendfile	Send data between file descriptors.
shutdown	shutdown	Shut down part of a full-duplex connection between two sockets.
socket	socket	Create an endpoint for communication.
socketpair	socketpair	Create a pair of connected sockets.

The sockets APIs originated with the 4.2BSD system released in 1983. The final release 4.4BSD at Berkley is widely used today and is considered the Berkley-derived implementation of sockets. The APIs in the preceding table are based on the Berkley-derived socket interface.

5.15 Interprocess Communications

Semaphores, message queues, and shared memory make up the Interprocess Communications (IPC) facility available in AIX. A *semaphore* is synchronization primitive, a *message queue* is a kernel-resident linked list of messages, and *shared memory* is memory that is shared between processes mapped into the address space of the process sharing the memory.

5.15.1 Semaphores

There are two forms of synchronization mechanisms within the UNIX world. One is the System V IPC version, and the other is POSIX 1003.1b. System V semaphores allows for semaphore sets, meaning that a unique semaphore identifier may contain multiple semaphores. Whether a semaphore identifier contains one semaphore or a set of semaphores, each is determined when the semaphore is created with the `semget` system call. The second argument to `semget` determines the number of semaphores that will be associated with the semaphore identifier returned by `semget`. The `semctl()` or `semop()` system allows the programmer to control and operate on the semaphore set as needed.

The POSIX 1003.1b semaphore mechanism allows programmers to create individual named and unnamed semaphores. The basic operation goes like this. The semaphore is created with the `sem_init()`. Once created, the semaphore can be used to synchronize access to shared resources by forcing the calling thread or process to wait on the semaphore before entering the critical section by calling `sem_wait()`. After the calling process is finished with the shared resource, it signals to the other processes or threads waiting that it is finished by posting the semaphore, `sem_post()`. These semaphores are ideal when resources must be shared between either two or more distinct processes (named semaphores) or individual threads within the same process (unnamed semaphore).

AIX and Linux support both mechanisms. Table 5-11 gives a side-by-side comparison between AIX and Linux.

TABLE 5-11
AIX and Linux IPC API Comparison: POSIX Semaphores

AIX	Linux	AIX ERRNO(s)	Linux ERRNO(s)	Description

`sem_init`	`sem_init`	`EFAULT`
		`EINVAL`
		`ENFILE`
		`ENOMEM`
		`ENOSPC`
		`ENOTSUP`
			`EINVAL`
			`ENOSYS`
				Initializes the semaphore object.

AIX	Linux	AIX ERRNO(s)	Linux ERRNO(s)	Description
sem_wait	sem_wait	EACCES EAGAIN (semwait only) EFAULT EIDRM	Does not set *ERRNO*. Always returns 0.	Suspends the calling thread until the semaphore pointed to by `sem` has a nonzero count.
sem_trywait	sem_trywait	EINTR EINVAL ENOMEM ENOTSUP	EAGAIN	
sem_post	sem_post	EACCES EFAULT EIDRM EINVAL ENOMEM ENOTSUP	ERANGE	Unlocks a semaphore.
sem_getvalue	sem_getvalue	EACCES EFAULT EINVAL ENOMEM ENOTSUP	Does not set *ERRNO*. Always returns 0.	Gets the value of a semaphore.
sem_destroy	sem_destroy	EACCES EFAULT EINVAL ENOTSUP	EBUSY	Destroys a semaphore object, freeing the resources it might hold.
sem_timedwait	sem_timedwait	EFAULT EINVAL ETIMEDWAIT EDEADLK ENTR	EENVAL ETIMEDWAIT EDEADLK ENTR	Advanced real-time wait.
sem_unlink	sem_unlink	EACCES EFAULT ENAMETOOLONG ENOENT ENOTSUP	EACCES ENAMETOLONG ENOENT	Removes a named semaphore.

AIX	Linux	AIX ERRNO(s)	Linux ERRNO(s)	Description
sem_close	sem_close	EFAULT EINVAL ENOMEM ENOTSUP	EINVAL	Closes a named semaphore.
sem_open	sem_open	EACCES EEXIST EFAULT EINVAL EMFILE ENAMETOOLONG ENOMEM ENOTSUP ENOSPC	EACCES EEXIST EINTR EENVAL EMFILE ENAMETOOLONG ENFILE ENOENT ENOSPC	Opens a named semaphore.

Semaphores are the primitive synchronization mechanism in many operating systems. The APIs mentioned are standard within the UNIX community. Semaphore sets are also a standard within UNIX, as discussed in detail in the next section.

5.15.2 System V Semaphore sets

The System V version of semaphore functions are `semget()`, `semctl()`, and `semop()`. They perform operations on sets of semaphores associated with a predefined identifier. In Linux, the `semget()`, `semctl()`, and `semop()` functions are completely compatible with AIX versions. The only noticeable difference is in `semop()`. In AIX, the `semop()` sets the `ENOSPC` *ERRNO* and in Linux it does not. However, this *ERRNO* is defined in Linux, which means no coding changes are necessary when migrating to Linux because any code that handles this error in AIX will be ignored in Linux.

5.15.3 Message Queues (mqueue.h)

Both AIX and Linux provide fully POSIX.1b-compliant message queues. On Linux prior to version 2.6.6.rtl, message queues were implemented in a separate required linkable library (libmqueue) that was shipped for certain distributions of Linux. In

Linux kernel version 2.6.6.rtl, the Linux team decided to include the `libmqueue` library in the `glibc` 2.3.4 (04/08/2004 in changelog). Although both AIX and Linux provide support for message queues, the *ERRNO*s they return for certain errors sometimes differ. Minor changes may be necessary in your code if your application takes certain actions based on these *ERRNO*s. Table 5-12 compares the *ERRNO* differences between AIX and Linux.

TABLE 5-12
AIX and Linux IPC API Comparison: Message Queues

AIX->Linux	AIX ERRNO(s)	Linux ERRNO(s)	Description
`mq_close`	EBADF ENOMEM ENOTSUP	EBADF EBUSY	Closes a message queue
`mq_open`	EACCES EEXIST EFAULT EINVAL ENOMEM ENOSPC ENOTSUP ENOENT ENFILE ENAMETOOLONG	EACCES EEXIST EINTR EINVAL EMFILE ENOSPC ENOENT ENFILE ENAMETOOLONG	Opens a message queue
`mq_notify`	EBADF EBUSY EFAULT ENOMEM ENOTSUP EINVAL	EBADF EBUSY	Notifies a process that a message is available
`mq_getattr`	EBADF EFAULT ENOMEM EINVAL ENOTSUP	EBADF	Gets message queue attributes

AIX->Linux	AIX ERRNO(s)	Linux ERRNO(s)	Description
`mq_unlink`	EACCES EFAULT EINVAL ENAMETOOLONG ENOTSUP	EACCES ENOENT ENAMETOOLONG	Removes a message queue
`mq_send`	EAGAIN EFAULT EBADF EIDRM EINTR EINVAL EMSGSIZE ENOMEM ENOTSUP	EAGAIN EBADF EINTR EINVAL EMSGSIZE	Sends a message to the message queue
`mq_setattr`	EBADF EFAULT EINVAL ENOMEM ENOTSUP	EBADF	Sets message queue attributes
`mq_send`, `mq_timedsend`	EAGAIN EBADF EFAULT EIDRM EINTR EINVAL EMSGSIZE ENOTSUP ETIMEDOUT	EAGAIN EBADF EINTR EINVAL EMSCSIZE ETIMEDOUT	Sends a message to a message queue (real time)
`mq_receive`	EAGAIN EBADF EFAULT EIDRM EINTR EINVAL EMSGSIZE ENOMEM ENOTSUP	EAGAIN EBADF EINVAL EMSGSIZE EINTR EINVAL ETIMEOUT	Receives a message from a message queue

AIX->Linux	AIX ERRNO(s)	Linux ERRNO(s)	Description
`msgctl`	EACCES EPERM EFAULT EINVAL	EACCES EPERM EDIRM EFAULT EINVAL	Provides message control operations
`msgget`	EACCES ENOENT EEXIST ENOSPC	ENOMEM EACCES ENOENT EEXIST ENOSPC	Gets a message queue identifier
`msgrcv`	E2BIG EACCES ENOMSG EFAULT EINTR EIDRM EINVAL	E2BIG EACCES ENOMSG EFAULT EINTR EIDRM EINVAL	Reads a message from a queue
`msgsnd`	EAGAIN EACCES EFAULT EIDRM EINTR EINVAL ENOMEM	EAGAIN EACCES EFAULT EIDRM EINTR EINVAL ENOMEM	Sends a message

The default maximum size of a message queue (`msg_qbytes`) on Linux is set to the system parameter `MSGMNB` (16384 bytes). The `msg_qbytes` value can be raised beyond `MSGMNB` by using the `msgctl` function with the appropriate privileges. On Linux, the maximum size for a message text is set to `MSGMAX` (8192 bytes).

5.15.4 Shared Memory

On most UNIX systems, including Linux, the system administrator can edit a master file in the /etc directory to define limits for IPC mechanisms such as shared memory. AIX uses a different method. In AIX, upper limits are defined for IPC mechanisms, which are not configurable. The individual IPC data structures are allocated and deallocated as needed, so memory requirements depend on the current system usage of IPC mechanisms.

In AIX, the maximum size of a shared memory segment for 64-bit processes is 32TB. A 32-bit process cannot attach a shared memory segment larger than 2GB. 32-bit applications can use the `shmat` capability to obtain more than 11 segments when using the very large address space model without having to use extended `shmat`.

In Linux, the default maximum shared memory size is 32MB. For applications that require large address space, this value is often too small. To allow for applications to allocate memory above the 32MB mark (for instance, 512MB), the Linux systems administrator must take the steps listed in the following example (which sets the shared memory maximum to 512MB):

1. Edit the file /etc/sysctl.conf.
2. Set the shared memory size to 512MB (or higher) by adding the two lines listed here to the end of the file:

   ```
   kernel.shmmax = 536870912
   kernel.shmall = 536870912
   ```

3. Run the following command from the UNIX prompt:

   ```
   /sbin/sysctl -p
   ```

Every time the machine reboots, the shared memory will be set to this value. A more permanent solution is to change the value of `SHMMAX` in /usr/src/linux/include/asm/shmparam.h and rebuild your kernel:

```
The maximum value of SHMMAX can be set to 4GB-1
```

Both AIX and Linux define the standard *shmid_ds* and *ipc_perm* structures, and member variable names are the same; however, the Linux version does not contain all the members that AIX has. The following member variables are not defined in the Linux *shmid_ds* structure:

```
__shm_cnattch (shm_cnattch[21]) /* In memory number attachments */
shm_handle   /* segment identifier */
__shm_extshm (shm_extshm[21]) /* page granularity shmat */
```

21 If `_ALL_SOURCE` is defined in AIX.

There are two different shared memory types available for most flavors of UNIX—System V IPC and BSD mmap. AIX and Linux implement both. The functions provide a rich set of APIs that enable two or more processes to share access to a single chunk of memory. Table 5-13 shows there is no difference between AIX and Linux in their implementation of shared memory.

TABLE 5-13
AIX and Linux IPC API Comparison: Shared Memory

AIX	Linux	Description
`shmat`	`shmat`	Attach shared memory to data segment
`shmctl`	`shmctl`	Shared memory control operations
`shmdt`	`shmdt`	Detach shared memory from data segment
`shmget`	`shmget`	Get shared memory segment
`shmop`	`shmop`	Shared memory operations
`mmap, mmap64`	`mmap, mmap64`	Maps a file system object into virtual memory; mmap should be used on 64-bit machines
`munmap`	`munmap`	Unmaps pages of memory

Without IPC programming interfaces, processes and computers cannot share information across the network. A number of platform-independent APIs—including Common Object Request Broker Architecture (CORBA), Distributed Computing Environment (DCE), and Message Bus (MBUS)—use IPC calls to implement their services.

5.16 POSIX Threads

A thread is the most basic independent flow of control that operates within the address space of a process. Although this characteristic is consistent across UNIX systems, the architecture is not, which is why standards have been created. The universal standard for implementing threads within the UNIX world today is POSIX 1003.1, better known as pthreads. POSIX defines a set of strict standardized APIs that operating system vendors must adhere to and provide for application programmers. The idea here is to enable programmers to make their applications portable from one machine to the next. As of the writing of this book, the newest version of the POSIX thread library supported on Linux is the Native POSIX Thread Library (NPTL) developed by Ulrich Drepper.

5.16.1 Linux Versus AIX Thread Models

AIX supports both the *M*:*N* and 1:1 threading models, configurable by the user. The *M*:*N* model means the operating system implements *N* kernel threads to service *M* user threads. The 1:1 model means the system implements one kernel thread for every user thread. Linux NPTL threads only support the 1:1 model. This may affect process scheduling and performance tuning considerations.

Additionally, in AIX and Linux, thread and process characteristics are somewhat obscured. In AIX, a thread is a schedulable entity within a process that has properties that ensure its independent flow of control. These properties include the following:

- Stack
- Scheduling properties (such as policy or priority)
- Set of pending and blocked signals
- Some thread-specific data (such as an `ERRNO`)

In Linux, a thread is considered a "lightweight process" (LWP), which has properties of a process but is not as heavy. Those properties include the following:

- Code (or "text")
- Data
- Stack
- File I/O
- Signal tables

Finally, threads are created architecturally different in AIX than in Linux. Traditionally, to protect the operating system, on most UNIX-like environments, kernel space threads and user space threads are implemented separately within strict processing boundaries.

5.16.2 Kernel Space Threads

Kernel-supported threads fall into two classes. In a "pure" kernel-supported system, the kernel is responsible for scheduling all threads. Systems in which the kernel cooperates with a user-level library to do scheduling are known as *two-level*, or *hybrid*, systems. Typically, the kernel schedules LWPs, and the user-level library schedules threads onto LWPs.

Both AIX and Linux support this thread model. Linux implementation of kernel threads is somewhat less strict than AIX. Linux uses the `clone()` system call to create threads. In the past, this raised questions as to whether these were truly kernel threads. After version 2.6, however, the `clone()` system call was modified under Linux to adhere strictly to the POSIX standards of a kernel thread. Linus Torvalds and other Linux kernel developers consider this model to be more simplistic and have done a pretty good job of making kernel-level context switches between threads efficient.

5.16.3 User-Space Threads

User-space threads live with limited support from the kernel; they maintain all of their state in user space. In addition, user-space threads have their own user scheduler independent of the kernel scheduler. The user scheduler makes it possible for user-space threads to schedule themselves on a kernel thread to execute code. Different implementations of user-space threads exist. On AIX, user-space threads are implemented to run with a ratio of eight user-space threads to one kernel thread by default.

Linux does not support user-space threads and does not anticipate supporting it in the future.

5.16.4 AIX to Linux POSIX Threads Cross-Reference

The POSIX threads implementations of AIX and Linux have little differences. As long as the AIX multithreaded application does not use nonportable POSIX extensions, porting should be straightforward. Tables 5-14 and 5-15 list the POSIX thread attribute, data type, and API differences between AIX and Linux, respectively.

TABLE 5-14
AIX and Linux POSIX Threads Comparison: Attributes

AIX	Linux	Comment
pthread_t	pthread_t	Identifies a thread.
pthread_attr_t	pthread_attr_t	Identifies a thread attribute object.
pthread_cond_t	pthread_cond_t	Identifies a condition variable.
pthread_condattr_t	pthread_condattr_t	Identifies a condition attribute.
pthread_key_t	pthread_key_t	Identifies a thread-specific data key.
pthread_mutex_t	pthread_mutex_t	Identifies a mutex.
pthread_mutexattr_t	pthread_mutexattr_t	Identifies a mutex attributes object.
pthread_once_t	pthread_once_t	Identifies a one-time initialization object.

struct sched_param
{
 int sched_priority;
 int sched_policy;
 int sched_reserved;
}
	struct __sched_param
	{
	 int __sched_priority;
	}
		Used for setting thread attributes.
		AIX: Intended for developer use and contains three member variables.
		Linux: Not intended for developer use and contains one member variable.

TABLE 5-15
AIX and Linux POSIX Threads Comparison: APIs

AIX	Linux	Comment
pthread_atfork	pthread_atfork	Registers fork cleanup handlers.
pthread_attr_destroy	pthread_attr_destroy	Deletes a thread attribute.
pthread_attr_getdetachstate pthread_attr_setdetachstate	pthread_attr_getdetachstate pthread_attr_setdetachstate	Sets and returns the value of the detachstate attribute of a thread attributes object.
pthread_attr_setstackaddr pthread_attr_getstackaddr	pthread_attr_setstackaddr pthread_attr getstackaddr	Returns and sets the value of the stackaddr attribute of a thread attributes object.

AIX	Linux	Comment
pthread_attr_init	pthread_attr_init	Creates a thread attributes object and initializes it with default values.
pthread_attr_setstacksize pthread_attr_getstacksize	pthread_attr_setstacksize pthread_attr_getstacksize	Returns and sets the value of the stacksize attribute of a thread attributes object.
pthread_cancel	pthread_cancel	Request cancellation of a pthread.
pthread_cleanup_pop pthread_cleanup_push	pthread_cleanup_pop pthread_cleanup_push	Activates and deactivates thread cancellation handlers.
pthread_detach	pthread_detach	Used to indicate to the implementation that storage for the thread whose thread ID is in the location thread can be reclaimed when that thread terminates.
pthread_equal	pthread_equal	Compares two thread IDs to determine if they refer to the same thread.
pthread_exit	pthread_exit	Terminates the calling thread and stores the status in the return value.
pthread_getspecific pthread_setspecific	pthread_getspecific pthread_setspecific	Returns and sets the thread-specific data associated with the specified key.
pthread_join	pthread_join	Blocks the calling thread until the specified thread terminates.

AIX	Linux	Comment
`pthread_key_create` `pthread_key_delete`	`pthread_key_create` `pthread_key_delete`	Creates and deletes a thread-specific data key. `pthread_key_create` also accepts a ptr to a function that will be called upon destruction.
`pthread_kill`	`pthread_kill`	The `pthread_kill` subroutine sends the signal signal to the thread thread. It acts with threads like the `kill` subroutine with single-threaded processes.
`pthread_mutex_destroy` `pthread_mutex_init`	`pthread_mutex_destroy` `pthread_mutex_init`	Initializes or destroys a mutex. Passing in NULL initializes all attributes to default values. Behavior is consistent between AIX and Linux.
`pthread_mutexattr_init` `pthread_mutexattr_destroy`	`pthread_mutexattr_init` `pthread_mutexattr_destroy`	Initializes and destroys mutex attributes.
`pthread_mutexattr_getpshared` `pthread_mutexattr_setpshared`	`pthread_mutexattr_getpshared` `pthread_mutexattr_setpshared`	Sets and gets process-shared attribute.
`pthread_once`	`pthread_once`	Executes a routine exactly once in a process.
`pthread_self`	`pthread_self`	Returns the indentifier of the current thread.

Table 5-16 shows APIs that were found to have differences between AIX and Linux and will require some coding changes when porting from AIX to Linux.

TABLE 5-16
AIX and Linux POSIX Threads Comparison: Nonportable

API	Differences
`pthread_attr_init`	Creates a new thread attribute with default values with the following exceptions. AIX: Contention scope = `PTHREAD_SCOPE_PROCESS` `Sched param.sched_prio` = 1 Linux: Contention scope = `PTHREAD_SCOPE_SYSTEM` `Sched param.sched_priority` = 0

`pthread_mutex_lock`
`pthread_mutex_trylock`
`pthread_mutex_unlockj`
	Lock mechanism between AIX and Linux is not compatible. The conditions for deadlocking differ, and the attribute values differ.
	AIX: Possible attribute values
	`PTHREAD_MUTEX_NORMAL`
	`PTHREAD_MUTEX_ERRORCHECKING`
	`PTHREAD_MUTEX_RECURSIVE`
	`PTHREAD_MUTEX_DEFAULT`
	Linux: Possible attribute values
	`#ifdef __USE_GNU`
	`PTHREAD_MUTEX_INITIALIZER`
	`PTHREAD_RECURSIVE_MUTEX_INITIALIZER_NP`
	`PTHREAD_ERRORCHECK_MUTEX_INITIALIZER_NP`
	
	`#ifdef __USE_UNIX98`
	`PTHREAD_MUTEX_NORMAL`
	`PTHREAD_MUTEX_ERRORCHECKING`
	`PTHREAD_MUTEX_RECURSIVE`
	`PTHREAD_MUTEX_DEFAULT`
	
	Refer to the Linux and AIX documentation on the different behavior conditions that could cause a deadlock.

`pthread_mutexattr_gettype`
`pthread_mutexattr_settype`
	Gets or sets a mutex type to the following values:
	AIX: Possible attribute values
	`PTHREAD_MUTEX_NORMAL`
	`PTHREAD_MUTEX_ERRORCHECKING`
	`PTHREAD_MUTEX_RECURSIVE`
	`PTHREAD_MUTEX_DEFAULT`

API	Differences

	Linux: Possible attribute values
	`#ifdef __USE_GNU`
	`PTHREAD_MUTEX_INITIALIZER`
	`PTHREAD_RECURSIVE_MUTEX_INITIALIZER_NP`
	`PTHREAD_ERRORCHECK_MUTEX_INITIALIZER_NP`
	`#ifdef __USE_UNIX98`
	`PTHREAD_MUTEX_NORMAL`
	`PTHREAD_MUTEX_ERRORCHECKING`
	`PTHREAD_MUTEX_RECURSIVE`
	`PTHREAD_MUTEX_DEFAULT`

NPTL—created by Ulrich Drepper—was first released September 20, 2002. With the sponsorship of Red Hat and a collaborative effort among kernel and runtime developers, NPTL quickly replaced the old LinuxThreads library and became part of the GNU C Library distribution. It corrected some shortfalls on POSIX standards in the old LinuxThreads library and, with its thin layer, significantly increased performance. See Chapter 3 for more information about the Linux Native POSIX Threads Library.

5.17 Large Page Support

Large page usage is primarily intended to provide performance improvements to high-performance computing (HPC) applications. Memory-access-intensive applications that use large amounts of virtual memory may obtain performance improvements by using large pages. The large page performance improvements are attributable to reduced translation lookaside buffer (TLB) misses due to the TLB being able to map a larger virtual memory range. Large pages also improve memory prefetching by eliminating the need to restart prefetch operations on 4KB boundaries.

In AIX, large page support[22] for executables can be turned on in four ways:

1. Through the compiler command

```
$ xlC -bmaxdata=0xXXXXXXXX
```

22 AIX support for large pages, http://www-1.ibm.com/servers/aix/whitepapers/large_page.pdf

2. Linker command

```
$ ld -blpdata -o large_exec
```

3. Through the `ldedit` command

```
$ ldedit -blpdata large_exec
```

4. Environment variable

```
$ export LDR_CNTRL=LARGE_PAGE_DATA=Y
```

In Linux, you can enable large page support by reconfiguring the kernel or by using the traditional memory systems calls. Chapter 3 covers how to enable large page support for Linux in more detail.

5.18 Common APIs

AIX and Linux are both UNIX systems with common features. Figure 5-1 presents a list of the remaining common system and library APIs that are compatible between AIX and Linux. Some APIs are implemented in Linux Standard Base (LSB) and are also shown here. Although the list can be used as a reference when porting from AIX to Linux, additional Linux APIs (compatible and noncompatible with AIX) not referenced in this list should be considered. Refer to the book *Building Applications with the Linux Standard Base*, written by core members of the Linux Standard Base Team, and refer to the GNU `glibc` documentation online.

abort	ferror	iswalnum	re_match_2	sighold	strsep
abs	fflush	iswalpha	re_search	sigignore	strsignal
alarm	ffs	iswcntrl	re_search_2	siginterrupt	strspn
alloc	fgetc	iswctype	re_set_registers	sigisemptyset	strstr
asctime	fgets	iswdigit	re_set_syntax	sigismember	strtod
atexit	fileno	iswgraph	realloc recv	siglongjmp	strtof
atof	fopen	iswlower	recvfrom	signal	strtoimax
atoi	fprintf	iswprint	recvmsg	sigorset	strtok
atol	fread	iswpunct	regcomp	sigqueue	strtok_r
bcmp	free	iswspace	regerror	sigrelse	strtol
bcopy	freopen	iswupper	regexec	sigset	strtold
bind	fstat	iswxdigit	regfree	sigsetmask	strtoll
brk	fwrite	isxdigit	remove	sigstack	strtoq
bsearch	getc	jrand48	remque	sigvec	strtoul
bzero	getchar	killpg	res_init	sigwait	strtoull
calloc	getenv	labs	rewinddir	sigwaitinfo	strtoumax
catclose	getfsent	ldiv	rexec	sleep	strtouq
catgets	getfsspec	localtime	rindex	snprintf	strverscmp
catopen	getfsfile	lrand48	sbrk	sprintf	strxfrm
cfgetispeed	getgrent	lstat	scanf	srand	swab
cfgetospeed	getgroups	malloc	sched_yield	srand48	tcdrain
cfsetispeed	getitimer	memchr	seed48	srandom	tcflow
cfsetospeed	gettimeofday	memcmp	seekdir	stime	tcflush
clearerr	gethostid	memcpy	sendmsg	sscanf	tcgetattr
clock	getmsg	memset	sendto	stat	tcgetpgrp
closedir	getpwent	mkfifo	setbuf	statvfs	tcgetsid
confstr	getpwuid	mktime	setgroups	strcasecmp	tcsendbreak
connect	getrlimit	mrand48	setegid	strcasestr	tcsetattr
ctermid	getrusage	nrand48	seteuid	strcat	tcsetpgrp
ctime	gets	opendir	setfsent	strchr	telldir
daylight	getuid	pathconf	setgrent	strcmp	tempnam
difftime	getw	pause	sethostid	strcoll	tmpnam
div	gmtime	pclose	setitimer	strcpy	tmpfile
drand48	index	pipe	setlocale	strcspn	time
dup	initgroups	popen	setpgrp	strdup	times
dup2	initstate	printf	setpwent	strerror	timezone
ecvt	insque	putenv	setrlimit	strerror_r	tolower
endgrent	isalnum	putmsg	settimeofday	strfmon	toupper
endpwent	isalpha	putw	setstate	strfry	tzname
erand48	isascii	qsort	setuid	strftime	tzset
execl	isblank	raise	setvbuf	strlen	ulimit
execle	iscntrl	rand	shutdown	strncasecmp	ustat
execlp	isdigit	random	sigaddset	strncat	ungetc
execv	isgraph	re_comp	sigaltstack	strncmp	vfprintf
execvp	islower	re_compile	sigandset	strncpy	vprintf
fclose	isprint	_fastmap	sigblock	strndup	vsnprintf
fcntl	ispunct	re_compile	sigdelset	strnlen	vsprintf
fcvt	isspace	_pattern	sigemptyset	strpbrk	
fdopen	isupper	re_exec	sigfillset	strptime	
feof	isxdigit	re_match	siggetmask	strrchr	

FIGURE 5-1
AIX/Linux common system and library APIs

5.19 Summary

The porting work is considered complete when two objectives are met. The first objective is to make sure all the necessary objects and executables of the application are produced. The second objective is to make sure the ported application, including all executables produced, runs and stays up long enough to pass basic unit testing. If the application passes basic unit testing, it is then passed on to the next phase of the project, which is testing and debugging. Here are some important highlights discussed in this chapter:

- GNU does not have shorthand methods to invoking their compiler like AIX (`xlC_r`, `xlC`, `xlC128`, and so on) that will automatically include pthreads, DCE threads, or 128-bit libraries. You must include these parameters and libraries separately on the `gcc/g++` and `ld` line when building your executable.
- Both AIX and Linux support the common parameters for building executables, such as the following:

  `-c` Compile only

  `-o` Object name

  `-D` Preprocessor directive name

  `-L` Library search path

  `-I` Library name

  `-l` Include file search path
- But many compiler and link parameters control the behavior and the type of output generated in AIX and Linux. Refer back to Tables 5-3 and 5-4 for an extensive list of AIX compiler and linker parameters and their equivalent Linux compiler and linker parameters.
- To build an executable in Linux, you must use the `gmake` utility. The traditional System V `make` is not compatible in Linux. AIX traditionally uses the System V version of `make`.
- AIX and Linux linkers differ in many ways. AIX uses the XCOFF binary format, whereas Linux uses the ELF format. In addition, AIX and Linux build runtime linkable objects differently, which has an effect on the library search behavior for the `-l` parameter. Linux has library versioning and AIX does not. Users must run their newly created library through the versioning tool under Linux before it can be used.
- For template instantiation, AIX and Linux use a repository to store template instantiations and compile that code along with other code as a final step in

the compile process prior to linking. The AIX equivalent to -qtempinc and -qtemplateregistry is -frepo in Linux.

- AIX and Linux have a long list of compatible system and library APIs. Along with other differences, notable differences are in the return value of *ERRNO*s.
- As of the writing of this book, AIX fully supports POSIX threads and Linux supports Native POSIX Threads Library (NPTL), which has support for POSIX and more. However, both AIX and Linux implement kernel threads and user threads differently.
- Large Page Support can be turned on in AIX in a number of ways:

  Environment variable: LDR_CNTRL

  Compiler flag: -qlargepage

  Linker flag: -bmaxdata=<*value*>

  Relinking the executable with ldedit -blpdata <*filename*>

  To enable Large Page Support in Linux, you need to reconfigure the kernel. Chapter 3 shows you how to enable Large Page Support for Linux.
- Although some applications are relatively easy to port because of their inherently portable characteristics, some applications written to use AIX extensions take a little more porting effort. Overall, Linux 2.6 has improved its capabilities to readily accept software applications to run on it. Porting to Linux has never been easier. New features such as a preemptive kernel and support for better threads scheduling makes Linux an operating system that is truly ready for enterprise use.

Chapter 6

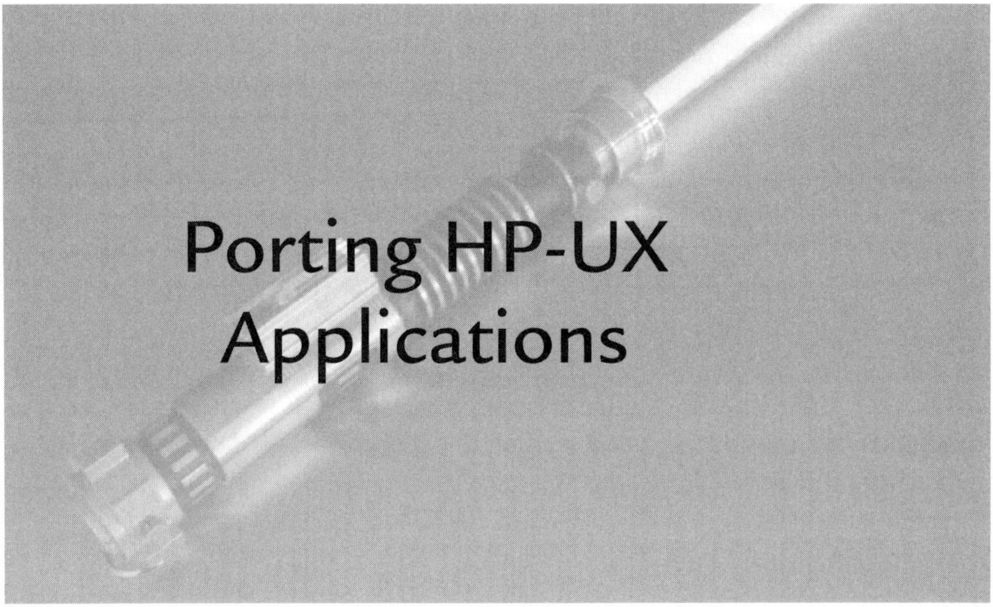

Porting HP-UX Applications

In this chapter

Porting is the step of the process during which modifications to the application take place. At this point, most if not all technical aspects and dependencies of the application should have already been uncovered during the scoping and analysis steps. The only thing that needs to be done now is to modify the source code so that it compiles and runs on the Linux platform.

During the porting process, software developers and porting personnel will likely encounter several differences between the UNIX operating system they are used to and the Linux 2.6 platform. For each topic discussed in this chapter, the most common differences are presented to explain what works and what does not work on the Linux 2.6 environment. The HP-UX environment described in this chapter is based mostly on version 11 but should also be applicable to older versions of HP-UX. Although this chapter discusses topics about HP-UX in some detail, it is assumed that porting engineers reading the chapter already have software development experience on HP-UX.

6.1 Preliminary Tasks

Before the porting work can begin, we need to prepare the environment that we will be working in. Among other things, we need to set up the port, build, and code change systems. Here is a checklist that includes the detailed tasks for each.

6.1.1 Set Up the Porting System

The porting system is used by porting engineers to do the porting work. It includes the porting server running the Linux version that the application to be ported is expected to run on. In some instances, the server can be used to run small unit tests that will not affect overall server performance. Here is a list of tasks to set up the porting system:

1. Install the server with the Linux distribution that the application to be ported is expected to run on. Set up all necessary home directories and build environment directories.
2. Check for any known patches that need to be installed on the server.
3. Make sure the installation includes the compiler and debugger.
4. Install third-party products and licenses that the application needs. Install any prerequisites or patches needed by these products.

5. Set up access for users and system administrators on the build server.
6. Set up policies on using the porting environment as a test machine. These polices must include what can and cannot be tested on the porting server.

Depending on how work is divided among different groups involved in the porting project, the responsibility of doing these tasks may fall on the porting engineer. Even when a separate group in the IT organization sets up the server, the porting engineer still needs to provide the specifications of the environment to the person performing the installation and setup.

6.1.2 Set Up the Code Change Management System

The code change management system consists of a tool that manages code changes to the application. The tool most frequently used is CVS, but other tools such as Subversion[1] and Arch[2] are gaining popularity. Here are the tasks associated with setting up the change management system:

1. Install the code change management tool.
2. Install scripts that can be used to make using the tool more convenient for the porting engineers.
3. Make sure the HOWTO and FAQs on using the tool and scripts exist and are readily accessible. These documents should include examples of how to use the tool and scripts.
4. Check the application into the code management system.

After the snapshot of the application source code has been checked into the code management system, that code should only be used for porting changes. No outside development changes should be added to this code base during the porting period.

---

1 http://subversion.tigris.org

2 www.gnu.org/software/gnu-arch/

6.1.3 Set Up the Build System

The build system is where automated nightly builds of the ported application take place. Although it may not be needed to begin any porting work, it is good practice to set it up before porting application makefiles. This system needs to be able to check out the source code and start an overnight build of the application. Building the application nightly after the code is stable enough to build with minimum build errors is good practice to make sure all checked-in code that day did not cause anything to break in the build. If something does break, it will be easier to find who and what caused the break. Here are the tasks associated with setting the build system:

1. Develop scripts that can check out the application code and start a nightly build.
2. After the makefiles have been ported, test these scripts. Expect errors, because the porting work may be just getting under way.
3. Add the script to a crontab file to schedule the overnight builds.
4. Write a script that can parse the errors produced so that an automated reporting system can notify responsible parties of any build breaks.

When the port, build, and code change system tasks are complete, the real porting work can begin.

6.2 General Differences

With major operating systems such as HP-UX, Solaris, AIX, and Linux embracing standards set forth by standards bodies such as ANSI, ISO, and POSIX, it would seem that porting between platforms should be easy. When it comes to application programming interface (API) implementation, these operating systems have implemented the majority of the standard APIs from the different standards bodies. From a compiler standpoint, these operating systems support the latest compiler standards, too. Unfortunately, other factors such as programming syntax (brought about by the use of old compilers implementing draft standards), use of platform-specific APIs, and use of early releases of third-party libraries, to name a few, may prevent an easy migration of software applications from HP-UX to Linux.

6.2.1 C Language

Both the HP-UX C compiler and GCC support ANSI C, but syntax and semantics differences may still prevent an error-free compilation in Linux. Within GCC, other standards can be selected by using the `-ansi`, `-std=89`, `-std=iso9899:1990`, `-std=c99`,[3] or `-std=iso9899:1999` options.

6.2.2 C++ Language

Starting with GNU `g++` version 3.4.0, GNU `g++` claims[4] to be *much* closer to the ISO/ANSI C++ standards. This means, among other things, that a lot of invalid constructs that used to be accepted in previous versions will now be rejected. HP's `aC++` compiler implements ANSI C++ standards and also claims to implement them more completely. The HP-UX C++ compiler ships with the standard C++ and Roguewave STL library and `Tools.h++`, whereas GNU only ships with `libstdc++`. Overall, there should be minimal differences in standards compliance when migrating from the latest version of HP-UX `aC++` to GNU `g++`.

6.2.3 GNU C/C++ Language

The GNU Compiler Collection (GCC) is available for HP-UX 11i. Applications compiled with GCC on HP-UX will make porting and migration easier on Linux. Take care when using different versions of the GCC compiler when migrating from HP-UX to Linux. Applications that compile cleanly on older versions of GCC might not compile as well on new versions because of changes in programming standards specifically in the C++ language.

6.2.4 Java Language

The HP-UX SDK for the Java platform provides the Java 2 (version 1.4) programming tools and runtime environment. The Java environment is available for Linux through the Blackdown Java SDK (www.blackdown.org). As of this writing, Blackdown has released Java version 1.4.2 and is working on release version 1.5. Other Linux Java SDKs are available for download from the Sun and IBM Web

---

3 GCC has incomplete support for C99. See http://gcc.gnu.org/gcc-3.4/c99status.html.

4 http://gcc.gnu.org/gcc-3.4/changes.html#cplusplus

sites. Refer to Chapter 2, "Scoping," for more information about the Java environment in Linux.

6.2.5 Threads

HP-UX 11i v2 supports the POSIX threads implementation. Previous versions of HP-UX supported what is known as CMA threads, which are also known as DCE pthreads. Applications using HP-UX CMA threads will need some major changes to use POSIX threads on Linux.

6.2.6 Standards Comparison

Almost all Linux distributors acknowledge the value that standardization and portability provide, and they work with the various Linux implementers/maintainers to meet those standards. The primary Linux industry standard is the Linux Standard Base (LSB), which is a project overseen by the Free Standards Group (FSG). The LSB is based heavily on the IEEE POSIX and Open Group Single UNIX Specification standards, but it also documents those places where Linux is not UNIX- or POSIX-compatible. Most and all of the major Linux distributors have certified to the LSB.

The LSB, in addition to providing a source code API specification, provides an Application Binary Interface (ABI) specification for each of several common Linux hardware platforms.[5] The goal of the ABI is to ensure binary portability, for LSB-portable applications, between Linux distributions on that hardware platform. Distributors must certify to the ABI as well as the API. Independent software vendors (ISVs) can also certify their applications as "LSB portable" using tools provided by the FSG.

Table 6-1 compares HP-UX-supported standards to the Linux-supported standards based on the LSB specification version 2.0.1.

---

5 The ABI would also allow the linking of object files even if they are compiled by different compilers.

TABLE 6-1
Supported Standards on HP-UX and Linux

Standard	HP-UX 11i v2	Linux
IEEE POSIX 1003.1-2001 Base Function	Supported	Supported
IEEE POSIX 1003.1 Threads (pthreads)	Supported	Supported
Single UNIX Specification Base function (this is sometimes known as XPG5 or XPG6)	Supported	Supported as described in the LSB
IEEE POSIX 1003.1c-1996 POSIX system calls	Supported	Supported
IEEE POSIX 1003.1-2001 Real-time scheduler, clocks and timers, asynchronous I/O, semaphores, memory locking, message queues, real-time signals, shared memory	Supported	Asynchronous I/O, real-time signals, shared memory, semaphores
IEEE POSIX 1003.4a Draft 4 User Threads	On older HP-UX releases only	Not supported
IEEE POSIX 1003.1-2001 (Commands and Utilities)	Supported	Supported
System V Interface Definition (SVID3)	Supported	Referenced[6]
File System Directory Layout	System V.4 (SVR4)	Filesystem Hierarchy Standard www.pathname.com/fhs/
X11 Window System, Font Server, and Clients	X11R6.3	X11R6.4
OSF/Motif	V2.1	Supported through third-party libraries (see lesstiff, www.lesstif.org)[7]

6 A referenced standard means that not all interfaces within the standard are supported.

7 Not included within the LSB specification

Standard	HP-UX 11i v2	Linux
RPC function interfaces	Supported	Supported
NFS+ Diskless and ONC+, NFS+, version 4.2		Referenced standards: SVID Issue 4, SVID Issue 3
OSF/Motif Application Environment Specification (AES)	Supported	Supported through third-party products[8]
LP64, 64-bit data model	Supported	Supported

Although there is standardization within Linux, Linux itself is not totally compliant with either the IEEE POSIX or Open Group SUS specifications.[9] This means that applications that may be totally portable under these common commercial UNIX standards may still need some work to move successfully to Linux. However, this work will be much less than for an application that meets no standards at all, or that uses HP-UX-specific UNIX extensions.

6.3 The Compilers

As the porting effort starts, differences in compiler locations and compiler options between HP-UX and Linux become apparent. Although the compilers on both HP-UX and Linux claim conformance or close conformance to ANSI and ISO standards, porting personnel may encounter platform-specific programming syntax differences. The use of compiler extensions and platform-specific features are common programming practices that require some effort when porting from HP-UX to Linux.

When starting to work with the build environment, the first thing to check is the location of the compiler binaries. They differ in directory locations, as shown in Table 6-2.

8 See Open Motif, www.opengroup.org/openmotif/faq.html

9 Conflicts between ISO/IEC 9945 (POSIX) and the Linux Standard Base (www.opengroup.org/personal/ajosey/tr01-04-2005.txt)

TABLE 6-2
HP-UX and Linux Compiler Comparison Table

Compiler	HP-UX Path	Linux Path
ANSI C	/opt/ansic/bin/cc	/usr/bin/gcc
C89	/opt/ansic/bin/c89	/usr/bin/gcc -std=c89
C++	/opt/aCC/bin/aCC	/usr/bin/g++

To query the version of the GNU GCC installed on Linux, do one of the following:

```
$ rpm --query -a | grep gcc
gcc-c++-3.4.2-6.fc3
libgcc-3.4.2-6.fc3
gcc-3.4.2-6.fc3
```

To find out the full path to the directory in which gcc resides, run the following:

```
$ type gcc
gcc is hashed (/usr/bin/gcc)
```

To find out what version of gcc is installed, do the following:

```
$ gcc --version
gcc (GCC) 3.3.3 (SUSE Linux)
Copyright (C) 2003 Free Software Foundation, Inc.
This is free software; see the source for copying conditions. There is NO
warranty; not even for MERCHANTABILITY or FITNESS FOR A PARTICULAR PURPOSE.

$ gcc --version (fedora installation)
gcc (GCC) 3.4.2 20041017 (Red Hat 3.4.2-6.fc3)
Copyright (C) 2004 Free Software Foundation, Inc.
This is free software; see the source for copying conditions. There is NO
warranty; not even for MERCHANTABILITY or FITNESS FOR A PARTICULAR PURPOSE.
```

6.3.1 C Compiler Options

By default, both the HP-UX C[10] compilers compile in extended ANSI mode, whereas the GNU C compiler compiles with C89 standards with some GNU extensions.[11] Porting personnel need to watch out for incompatibilities in syntax because there are no guarantees in the standard when the extended mode is used.

10 Starting with HP-UX 10.30 forward

11 This is equivalent to -std=gnu89.

Table 6-3 compares compiler switch options for HP-UX `cc` and its equivalent switch on GNU `gcc`.

TABLE 6-3
HP-UX ANSI cc and gcc Compiler Switches Comparison Table

HP cc Option[12]	GNU gcc Option[13]	Description
`-A[a|c|e]`	`-ansi` `-std=`*`standard`*	Specifies the degree of ANSI compliance.
`-Bextern`	None	Performs the same operation as `+Oextern=sym1,sym2,sym3...`, except that symbols are loaded from an existing file instead of being specified on the command line.
`-Bhidden`	None	Hides all the symbols including references, except for those prefixed with `__declspec(dllexport)`, `__declspec(dllimport)`.
`-Bhidden_def`	None	Hides all the symbols defined in the module except for those prefixed with `__declspec(dllexport)`.
`-c`	`-c`	Compiles only; does not link.
`-C`	`-C`	Prevents the preprocessor from stripping comments.

`-D_POSIX_C_SOURCE=199506L`
`-D_REENTRANT`
`-lpthread`
or use `-lcma`
(for user threads)
	`-D_REENTRANT`
	`-lpthread`
		Compiles with threads.

12 HP C/HP-UX Online Help for HP-UX 11i (HP-UX 11.0, HP-UX 11i v1, HP-UX 11i v2) (http://docs.hp.com/hpux/onlinedocs/dev/C/B3901BA/c_index.html)

13 GNU Compiler Collections version 3.4.2 (last updated May 23, 2004)

HP cc Option	GNU gcc Option	Description
`-Dname`	`-Dname`	Defines the preprocessor variable *name* with a value of 1.
`-Dname=def`	`-Dname=def`	Defines the preprocessor variable *name* with a value of *def*.
`-dynamic`	`-Wl,-Bdynamic`	Enables linking of PIC objects.
`-E`	`-E`	Performs preprocessing only with output to stdout.
`-fast`	None	Expands into a set of compiler options, which results in improved application runtime. Options included are `+O3`, `+Onolooptransform`, `+Olibcalls`, `+FPD`, `+Oentryschedule`, and `+Ofastaccess`. Any of these options can be overridden by placing a subsequent option after `-fast` on the command line.
`-g`	`-g`	Inserts information for the symbolic debugger in the object file.
`-G`	`-pg`	Inserts information required by the `gprof` profiler in the object file.
`-Idir`	`-Idir`	Inserts *dir* in the include file search path.
`-lx`	`-lx`	Links with `libx.a` depending on default library paths.
`-Ldir`	`-Ldir`	Links the libraries in *dir* before the libraries in the default search path. Adds default linker paths to one specified in the `-L` option before searching the default system library directories.
`-Wl,-Lsearchdir`	`-Wl,-Lsearchdir`	`-Wl` specifies a flag to pass on to the linker. In this case, the `-L` flag is passed on. This has the same effect as the `-L` option.
`-n`	`-shared` `-Bshareable`	Generates shareable code.

HP cc Option	GNU gcc Option	Description
-N	None	Generates unshareable code.
-noshared	-static -Bstatic -dn -non_shared	Creates statically bound executables.
-o *outfile*	-o *outfile*	Places object modules in file *outfile*.
-O	-O2	Optimizes at level 2.
-p	-p	Inserts information required by the prof profiler in the object file.
-P	None	Performs preprocessing only with output to the corresponding .i file.
-q	None	Marks the executable as demand-loadable.
-Q	None	Marks the executable as not being demand-loadable.
-s	-s	Strips the symbol table from the executable file.
-S	-S	Generates an assembly language source file.
-t *x,name*	None	Substitutes or inserts subprocess *x* with *name*.
-U*name*	-U*name*	Undefines *name* in the preprocessor.
-v	-v	Enables verbose mode.
None	-###	Shows each invoked component; do not execute.
-V -version	--version	Causes subprocesses to print version information to stderr.
-w	-w	Suppresses warning messages.
-Wd,-a or +a	None	Omits HP-provided prefix files required by the linker.
-W*x*, arg1 [,arg2,..,arg*n*]	-W*x*,*option*	Passes the arguments to the subprocess *x*.

HP cc Option	GNU gcc Option	Description
`-y`	None	Generates information used by the HP SoftBench static analysis tool.
`-Y`	None	Enables Native Language Support (NLS).
`-z`	Default (also see `-fno-delete-null-pointer-checks` `-fdelete-null-pointer-checks`)	Disallows runtime dereferencing of null pointers.
`-Z`	None	Allows dereferencing of null pointers at runtime.
`+DA`*`model`*	`-b` *`machine`* `-m`*`options`* (if `gcc` is set up as a cross-compiler)	Generates object code for a specific version of the PA-RISC architecture. In the case of GCC, whichever platform it is, is set up for cross-compiling.
`+DC`*`apptype`*	None	Generates code for portable or embedded applications.
`+DD32`	`-mpa-risc-1-1`	Generates 32-bit code for PA1.1 architecture.
`+DD64` (64-bit)	`-mpa-risc-2-0` (32-bit)	Generates *x*-bit code for PA2.0 architecture.
`+df`*`name`*	None	Specifies the profile database to use with profile-based optimization.
`+DS`*`model`*	None	Performs instruction scheduling for a specific implementation of PA-RISC.
`+DO`*`osname`*	None	Sets the target operating system for the compiler.
`+e`	None	Enables the following HP value-added features while compiling in ANSI C mode: sized enum, long long, long pointers, compiler-supplied defaults for missing arguments to intrinsic calls, and $ in identifier HP C extensions.

HP cc Option	GNU gcc Option	Description
`+ESfic`	None	Compiles with inline fast indirect calls.
`+ESconstlit`	None	Introduces new default behavior. HP C now stores constant-qualified (const) objects and literals in read-only memory.
`+ESlit`	`default`	Places string literals and constants into read-only data storage.
`+ESnolit`	None	Disables `+ESconstlit`, causing HP C to no longer store literals in read-only memory.
`+ESnoparmreloc`	None	Disables parameter relocation for function calls.
`+ESsfc`	None	Replaces function pointer comparison millicode calls with inline code.
`+f`	None	Inhibits the promotion of float to double, except for function calls and returns.
`+FP`*`flags`* Example: `+FPVZO`	None	Controls floating-point traps.
`+help`	None	Launches a Web browser displaying an HTML version of the HP C/HP-UX online help.
`+hugesize`	None	Lowers the threshold for huge data.
`+I`	`-fprofile-generate`	Prepares the object code for profile-based optimization data collection.
`+k`	None	Generates long-displacement code sequences so that a program can reference large amounts of global data physically located in shared libraries.
`+L`	None	Enables any `#pragma` listing directives and the listing facility.
`+m`	None	Prints identifier maps in the source code listing.
`+o`	None	Prints hexadecimal code offsets in the source code listing.

HP cc Option	GNU gcc Option	Description
`+[no]objdebug`	None	When used with `-g`, `+objdebug` leaves debug information in the object files.
`+O[0|1|2|3|4]`	`-O[0|1|2|3|s]`	Invokes the optimization level.
`+P`	`-fprofile-generate` `-fprofile-use`	Performs profile-based optimization.
`+pgmname`	None	Specifies the execution profile data set to be used by the optimizer.
`+r`	None	Inhibits the automatic promotion of float to double.
`+sb`	`-fsigned-bitfields` `-fno-unsigned-bitfields`	Makes bit fields signed by default in both 32- and 64-bit modes.
`+u`*`bytes`*	`-falign-labels=`*`n`* (align branch targets to a power of 2 boundary)	Controls pointer alignment where *`bytes`* is 1, 2, or 4.
`+uc`	`-funsigned-char`	Makes unqualified char data types unsigned.
`+w`*`n`*	`-W`*`options`* (close equivalent) `-Wall` (turns on all warning messages)	Specifies the level of the warning messages, where *n* is 1–3 (HP-UX).
`+W n1[,n2,...n`*`N`*`]`	`-Wno`*`options`* (close equivalent)	Suppresses the specified warnings.
`+Wen1[,n2,...n`*`N`*`]`	`-Werror` (all warnings, close equivalent) `-pendantic`	Changes the specified warnings to errors.
`+Wwn1[,n2,...n`*`N`*`]`	`-W`*`options`* (close equivalent)	Enables the specified warnings, assuming all other warnings are suppressed with `-w` or `+w3`.
`+z`	`-fpic`	Generates shared library object code (same as `+Z` in 64-bit mode).
`+Z`	`-fPIC`	Generates shared library object code with a large data linkage table (long-form PIC).

6.3.2 C++ Compiler Options

HP-UX `aCC` claims to conform to the ISO/IEC 14882 standard for the C++ programming language, whereas GNU C++ claims to be much closer to full conformance to the ISO/ANSI C++ standard.

Table 6-4 compares compiler switch options for HP-UX `aC++` and its equivalent switch on GNU `g++`.

TABLE 6-4
HP-UX aCC and g++ Compiler Switches Comparison Table

HP aCC Option[14]	GNU g++ Option[15]	Description
`-.suffix`	None	The *suffix* parameter represents the character or characters to be used as the output filename suffix.
`-Aa`	`-ansi` `-std=standard`	Instructs the compiler to use Koenig lookup and strict ANSI for scope rules.
`-AA`	`-std=c++98` (closest option found)	Conforms to the ISO C++ standard.
`-AC89`	`-std=c89`	Invokes the compiler in ANSI C89 compilation mode.
`-AC99`	`-std=c99`[16] (also invoke `-pendantic` flag to receive all diagnostics)	Invokes the compiler in ANSI C99 compilation mode with its features.
`-Ae`	`-std=gnu89`	Invokes as an ANSI C compiler, with additional support for HP C or GNU language extensions.

14 HP aC++ version A.05.50 Programmer's Guide (HP-UX 11i v2) (http://docs.hp.com/hpux/onlinedocs/4310/index.htm)

15 GNU Compiler Collections version 3.4.2 (last updated May 23, 2004)

16 GCC has incomplete support for C99. See http://gcc.gnu.org/gcc-3.4/c99status.html.

HP aCC Option	GNU g++ Option	Description

`-AOa`
`-AOe`
	`-std=iso9899:1990`
	`-std=iso9899:199409`
	(invoke with `-Ox` flag for optimization options)
		In addition to specifying the ANSI C language dialect, allows the optimizer to aggressively exploit the assumption that the source code conforms to the ANSI programming language C standard ISO 9899:1990.

`-AP`	None	Turns off `-AA` mode and uses the older C++ runtime libraries.
`-b`	None	Creates a shared library rather than an executable file.
`-c`	`-c`	Compiles one or more source files but does not enter the linking phase.
`-C`	`-C`	Prevents the preprocessor from stripping comments.
`-dynamic`	`-Wl,-Bdynamic`	Produces dynamically bound executables.
`-D`*`name`*`[=def]`	`-D`*`name`*`=def`	Defines a symbol name (*`name`*) to the preprocessor, as if defined by the preprocessing directive `#define`.

`+d`	`-fno-default-inline`
	(close but not exact)
	`-fno-inline`
		Prevents the expansion of inline functions.

`+dryrun`	`-###`	Displays the options passed, but does not execute.
`-ext` `+e`	None	Enables platform-dependent C++ standards extensions.
`-E`	`-E`	Runs only the preprocessor on the named C++ files and sends the result to standard output (`stdout`).
`-fast`	None	Selects a combination of optimization options for optimum execution speed for reasonable build times.

HP aCC Option	GNU g++ Option	Description
`-fpeval=precision`	None	Specifies the minimum precision to use for floating-point expression evaluation.
`-g[0|1]`	`-g[1|2|3]`	Emits different levels of debug information.
`-G`	`-pg`	Compiles and creates the executable file instrumented for use with `gprof`.
`-Idirs` `-I-`	`-I`	Indicates an optional list of `-Idirectory` specifications.
`-mt`	`-D_REENTRANT` `-lpthread`	Compiles multithreading.
`-n`	`-shared` `-Bshareable`	Causes the program file produced by the linker to be marked as sharable.
`-N`	None	Causes the program file produced by the linker to be marked as unsharable.
`-o` *`outfile`*	`-o` *`outfile`*	Causes the output of the compilation to be placed in *`outfile`*.
`-O`	`-O2`	Invokes the optimizer to perform level 2 optimizations.
`-p`	`-p`	Compiles and creates the executable file instrumented for use with `prof`.
`-P`	None	Only preprocesses the files named on the command line without invoking further phases. Leaves the result in corresponding files with the suffix `.i`.
`-q`	None	Causes the output file from the linker to be marked as demand-loadable.
`-Q`	None	Causes the program file from the linker to be marked as not demand-loadable.
`-r`	`-r`	Retains relocation information in the output file for subsequent relinking.
`-s`	`-Wl,-s`	Causes the executable program file created by the linker to be stripped of symbol table information.

HP aCC Option	GNU g++ Option	Description
`-S`	`-S`	Compiles the named program and leaves the assembly language output in a corresponding file with a `.s` suffix.
`-U`*`name`*	`-u` `-undefined=symbol`	*`name`* is the symbol name whose definition is removed from the preprocessor.
`-v`	`-v`	Enables verbose mode, sending a step-by-step description of the compilation process to `stderr`.
`-V` `-version`	`--version`	Displays the version numbers of the current compiler and linker (if the linker is executed).
`-w`	`-w`	Suppresses all warning messages.
`-Wc,-ansi_for_` `scope,[on][off]`	`-ffor-scope` `-fno-for-scope`	Enables or disables the standard scoping rules for init declarations in `for` statements.
`-Wc,-koenig_` `lookup,[on][off]`	None	Enables or disables standard argument-dependent lookup rules (also known as Koenig lookup).
`-W`*`x`*`,arg1` `[,arg2,..,arg`*`n`*`]`	`-W`*`x`*`,arg1` `[,arg2,..,arg`*`n`*`]`	Passes the arguments `arg1` through `arg`*`n`* to the subprocess *x* of the compilation.
`-Y`	None	Enables Native Language Support (NLS) of 8-bit, 16-bit, and 4-byte EUC characters in comments, string literals, and character constants.
`-z`	Default	Disallows dereferencing of null pointers at runtime.
`-Z`	None	Allows dereferencing of null pointers at runtime.
`+help`	None	Invokes the initial menu window of the HP `aC++` online programmer's guide.
`+ild`	`-Wl,-i`	Specifies incremental linking.
`+noeh`	None	Disables exception handling.

HP aCC Option	GNU g++ Option	Description
`+nostl`	None	Eliminates references to the standard header files and libraries bundled with HP `aC++`.
`+O[no]initcheck`	`-Wuninitialized -O`	The initialization checking feature.
`+sb`	None	Specifies unqualified char/short/int/long/long long bit fields as signed.
`+tls=[static|dynamic]`	`-ftls-model=`*`model`*	Specifies whether references to thread local data items are to be performed according to the mode.
`+ub`	None	Specifies unqualified char/short/int/long/long long bit fields as unsigned.
`+uc`	None	Specifying `+uc` causes an unqualified (plain) char data type to be treated as unsigned char.
`+Warg1 [,arg2,..arg`*`n`*`]`	None	Selectively suppresses any specified warning messages, where `arg1` through `arg`*`n`* are valid compiler warning message numbers.
`+We`	`-Werror`	Interprets all warning and future error messages as errors.
`+Wearg1 [,arg2,..arg`*`n`*`]`	None	Selectively interprets any specified warning or future error messages as errors. `arg1` through `arg`*`n`* are valid compiler warning message numbers.
`+Wwarg1 [,arg2,..arg`*`n`*`]`	None	Selectively treats compiler warnings as warnings. `arg1` through `arg`*`n`* are valid compiler message numbers.
`-Wl,+FPVZO`	None	Hardware trap FPEs.

6.3.3 Template Instantiation in GNU g++

According to the document "Using the GNU Compiler Collection,"[17] the GNU `g++` compiler provides two automated approaches to template instantiation: the Borland and the Cfront model.[18] On platforms other than the Linux on IA, `g++` implements neither automatic instantiation approach. For all applications that use template instantiation to be ported to Linux, the best approach is to modify the code to include template definitions to make them available at one or more points of instantiation; usually this is as simple as adding `#include <temp_methods.c>` to the end of each template header (see Examples 6-1, 6-2, and 6-3).

Example 6-1

Listing of main.C

```
#include "stack.h"

int
main()
{
    Stack<int, 60> s;
    int j;
    int i;

    s >> j;
    s << j;
    i = j;
    return (0);
}
```

---

17 Last updated May 23, 2004, for GCC 3.4.2.

18 Refer to the GCC online manual at http://gcc.gnu.org/onlinedocs/ for definitions of Borland and Cfront models.

Example 6-2

Listing of stack.h

```
#ifndef STACK_INCLUDED
#define STACK_INCLUDED

typedef enum{tr, fl} Bool;

template<class Item, int size> class Stack {
    public:
        int operator << (Item item);
        int operator >> (Item& item);
        Stack(Bool p=fl) {top = 0;}
    private:
        Item stack[size];
        int top;
};

#endif /* STACK_INCLUDED */
```

Example 6-3

Listing of stack.C

```
#include "stack.h"

template<class Item, int size>
int Stack<Item, size>::operator << (Item item) {
    if (top >= size) return 0;
    stack[top++] = item;
    return 1;
}

template <class Item, int size>
int Stack<Item, size>::operator >> (Item& item)
{
    if(top<=0) return 0;
    item = stack[--top];
    return 1;
}
```

When compiled on HP-UX with the `aCC` compiler, the files of main.C, stack.C, and stack.h produce an executable without compile errors when using the `+inst_implicit_include` flag:

```
$ aCC +inst_implicit_include19 -o test main.C
$ ./main
```

When compiled on Linux using `g++`, it results in the following compiler error:

```
$ g++ -o main main.C
/tmp/ccicEJmr.o(.text+0x45): In function `main':
: undefined reference to `Stack<int, 60>::operator>>(int&)'
/tmp/ccicEJmr.o(.text+0x5d): In function `main':
: undefined reference to `Stack<int, 60>::operator<<(int)'
collect2: ld returned 1 exit status
```

The problem here is that when Stack was instantiated, the definitions for operators << and >> could not be found, and thus the error. The preceding `g++` compiler error is corrected by modifying stack.h to include stack.C, as shown in Example 6-4.

Example 6-4

Listing of Modified stack.h

```
#ifndef STACK_INCLUDED
#define STACK_INCLUDED

typedef enum{tr, fl} Bool;

template<class Item, int size> class Stack {
    public:
        int operator << (Item item);
        int operator >> (Item& item);
        Stack(Bool p=fl) {top = 0;}
    private:
        Item stack[size];
        int top;
};

#include "stack.C"              /* include stack.C */

#endif /* STACK_INCLUDED */
```

Then compile with `g++`:

```
$ g++ -o main main.C
```

19 Refer to "Using Templates in HP aC++," September 27, 1997, available from http://docs.hp.com.

As mentioned earlier, modifying the code to include template definitions makes these definitions available at one or more points of instantiation, avoiding the error encountered earlier.

6.3.4 Building 32- or 64-Bit Binaries

Table 6-5 compares compiler switch options for HP-UX compilers and the equivalent switch on GNU for creating 32- and 64-bit binaries.

TABLE 6-5
HP-UX and Linux Compiler Build Switches for Platform-Dependent Builds

HP Option	HP Description	GNU Option	GNU Description
`+DD32`	`32` (generates ILP32 code and is the default)	`-m32` (platforms other than IA32) Default on IA32	`32` (generates ILP32 code)
`+DD64`	`64` (generates LP64 code)	`-m64` (AMD x86-64 code)	`64` (generates LP64 and AMD x86-64 code)

Refer to Chapter 3, "Analysis," for more information about 32-to-64-bit migration.

6.3.5 Compiler Optimization and Performance Options

Table 6-6 compares compiler switch options for HP-UX and its equivalent switch on GNU for optimizing executables.

TABLE 6-6
HP-UX and Linux Compiler Optimization Switches

HP-UX Option	HP-UX Description	GNU Level	GNU Description
`+O0`	Constant folding and simple register assignment. Compiles fastest.	`-O0`	Does not optimize. This is the default.
`+O1`	Performs level 1 optimization only. This includes branch optimization, dead code elimination, faster register allocation, instruction scheduling, and peephole optimization. This is the default optimization level.	`-O` `-O1`	Tries to reduce code size and execution time without performing optimization that takes a great deal of compilation time. Merges constants, optimizes jump instructions, transforms conditional jumps to branchless equivalents, and attempts to reorder instructions to optimize execution stalls.
`+O2` or `-O`	Optimizations performed over entire functions in a single file. Optimizes loops to reduce pipeline stalls. Performs scalar replacement and analysis of data flow, memory usage, loops, and expressions. Can produce faster runtime code than level 1 if programs use loops extensively.	`-O2`	Optimizes better than `-O`. Performs optimization that does not require size-speed trade-off. Increases compilation time and application performance. Turns on all optimization flags specified in `-O`. Forces memory operands to be copied into registers before doing arithmetic on them. Scans jump instructions when target of jump is not reached by any other path. Performs loop optimization. Enables `peephole2` optimization. Aligns start of functions and branch targets.
`+O3`	Full optimization across all subprograms within a single file. Includes subprogram inlining. Can produce faster runtime code than level 2 on code that frequently calls small functions. Links faster than level 4.	`-O3`	Turns on all optimization specified in `-O2`. Integrates simply functions into their callers. Makes use of registers left over after register allocation.

HP-UX Option	HP-UX Description	GNU Level	GNU Description
+O4	Performs level 4 optimization. This includes level 3 optimization. Plus full optimizations across the entire application program. Note: Object files produced at this level are intended to be temporary. Hewlett-Packard reserves the right to change the format of these files without prior notice. There is no guarantee that intermediate object files will be compatible from one revision of the compiler to the next.	-Os	Optimizes for size. Enables -O2 optimization properties that do not increase code size.

6.3.6 Porting and Compiling Using GNU

When compiling an application, several predefines can be used to turn features on or off, depending on the platform and environment that application will run on. The GNU gcc predefines some default definitions, and it is important to know what they are. Be aware that different installations of Linux may have different predefines for the GNU compiler.

To find out what gcc "predefines" during compile time, issue the following command from the command line:

```
$ echo 'main(){printf("hello world\n");}' | gcc -v -E -
Reading specs from /usr/lib/gcc-lib/i586-suse-linux/3.3.3/specs
Configured with: ../configure --enable-threads=posix --prefix=/usr
--with-local-prefix=/usr/local --infodir=/usr/share/info --mandir=/usr/share/man
--enable-languages=c,c++,f77,objc,java,ada --disable-checking --libdir=/usr/lib
--enable-libgcj --with-gxx-include-dir=/usr/include/g++ --with-slibdir=/lib
--with-system-zlib --enable-shared --enable-__cxa_atexit i586-suse-linux
Thread model: posix
gcc version 3.3.3 (SuSE Linux)
 /usr/lib/gcc-lib/i586-suse-linux/3.3.3/cc1 -E -quiet -v -D__GNUC__=3
-D__GNUC_MINOR__=3 -D__GNUC_PATCHLEVEL__=3 -
#include "..." search starts here:
```

```
#include <...> search starts here:
 /usr/local/include
 /usr/lib/gcc-lib/i586-suse-linux/3.3.3/include
 /usr/i586-suse-linux/include
 /usr/include
End of search list.
# 1 "<stdin>"
# 1 "<built-in>"
# 1 "<command line>"
# 1 "<stdin>"
main(){printf("hello world\n");}
```

In this particular example, the predefined variables are as follows:

```
-D__GNUC__=3 -D__GNUC_MINOR__=3 -D__GNUC_PATCHLEVEL__=3
```

To define default variables for this installation, the file usr/lib/gcc-lib/i586-suse-linux/3.3.3/specs can be edited to add more predefined variables. Another way to define variables during compile time is by using the -D<variable_name> switch to the appropriate build flags in the makefiles.

6.3.7 Namespace Selection on Linux Platform

Linux header files and libraries offer support for several namespaces for different types of standards compliance. They are described in Table 6-7.

TABLE 6-7
Linux Namespace Table

Linux Definitions[20]	Description
__STRICT_ANSI__	ISO Standard C.
_ISOC99_SOURCE	Extensions to ISO C89 from ISO C99.
_POSIX_SOURCE	IEEE Std 1003.1.

_POSIX_C_SOURCE	If ==1, like _POSIX_SOURCE;
	if >=2, add IEEE Std 1003.2;
	if >=199309L, add IEEE Std 1003.1b-1993;
	if >=199506L, add IEEE Std 1003.1c-1995;
	if >=200112L, all of IEEE 1003.1-2001.

20 Taken from /usr/include/features.h

Linux Definitions	Description
`_XOPEN_SOURCE`	Includes POSIX and XPG things. Set to 500 if Single UNIX Specification version 2 conformance is wanted, to 600 if SUSv3.
`_XOPEN_SOURCE_EXTENDED`	XPG things and X/Open UNIX extensions.
`_LARGEFILE_SOURCE`	Some more functions for correct standard I/O.
`_LARGEFILE64_SOURCE`	Additional functionality from LFS for large files.
`_FILE_OFFSET_BITS=N`	Select default filesystem interface.
`_BSD_SOURCE`	ISO C, POSIX, and 4.3BSD things.
`_SVID_SOURCE`	ISO C, POSIX, and SVID things.
`_GNU_SOURCE`	All of the above, plus GNU extensions.
`_REENTRANT`	Select additionally reentrant object.
`_THREAD_SAFE`	Same as `_REENTRANT`; often used by other systems.
`_FORTIFY_SOURCE`	If set to numeric value > 0, additional security measures are defined, according to level.

Namespace definitions provide a way to check what level of support is provided on the Linux installation. For example, an application can check to see whether the installation conforms to SUSv3 by checking the value of `_XOPEN_SOURCE`. If it does not conform to SUSv3, it can execute a different path.

6.4 Linker[21]

Both HP-UX and GNU compilers support sending options directly to the linker. This is done by using `-Wl,`*`option`*, which can appear as many times as needed on the command line. Although some command-line switches for HP-UX and GNU `ld` are similar, it is recommended that linker command-line arguments be inspected thoroughly as to their intended purpose.[22]

---

21 Refer to http://people.redhat.com/drepper/dsohowto.pdf for a good reference on writing shared libraries in Linux.

22 Refer to GNU `ld` documentation at www.gnu.org/software/binutils/manual/ld-2.9.1/ld.html.

Table 6-8 compares some HP-UX and GNU `ld` linker options.

TABLE 6-8
HP-UX and Linux Linker Options Comparison Table

HP-UX ld Option	GNU ld Equivalent	Description
Most options starting with +. For example, `+b`, `+vtype`, `+s`.	Not supported	HP-UX `ld` options that start with a +.
`-a {archive | shared | default | archive_shared | shared_archive}`	`-a {archive | shared | default}` `-Bdynamic|-dy|` `-call_shared` `-Bstatic|-dn|` `-non_shared|-static`	Tells the linker what type of library to link to.
`-B [immediate| restricted| symbolic]`	None	Changes binding behavior of application to linked libraries at startup time.
`-e entry`	`-e entry`	Use `entry` as the explicit symbol for beginning execution of your program, rather than the default entry point.
`+e`	`-E|-export-dynamic`	Exports symbols.
`-h`	None[23]	Hides symbols.
`-L`*`dir`*	`-rpath` *`path`*	Specifies the search direction to the runtime linker.
`-L`*`dir`*	`-L`*`dir`*	Augments system default search directories with directories specified with the `-L` flag.
`-l:`	None	In HP-UX, specifies the full base-name of the library to link with. For example, `-l:libfoo.a`.

23 Use the export maps through the `-version-script` option in GNU `ld`.

HP-UX ld Option	GNU ld Equivalent	Description
`-r`	`-r`	Generates relocatable output (that is, generates an output file that can in turn serve as input to `ld`).
`-s`	`-s`	Omits all symbol information from the output file.
`-t`	`-t`	Prints the names of the input files as `ld` processes them.
`-u` *symbol*	`-u` *symbol*	Enters *symbol* as an undefined symbol in the symbol table.
`-v`	None	Displays verbose messages during linking.
`-V`	`-V`, `-v`	Displays the version number for `ld`.
`-G`	`-S`	Strips all unloadable data (such as debug information).
`-x`	`-x`	Deletes all temporary local symbols.
`-y` *symbol*	`-y` *symbol*	Prints the name of each linked file in which *symbol* appears.
`-Z`	None	Allows dereferencing of null pointers (HP-UX only).

Refer to Chapter 3 for information on library versioning available on Linux.

6.4.1 Export Map

Export maps enable users to tell the linker explicitly which symbols to export from the generated object. The GNU linker supports export maps. To generate a shared object with this method, the user has to pass the name of the map file with the `-version-script` option of the linker:

```
$ gcc -shared -o bar.so bar.c -fPIC -Wl,--version-script=bar.map
```

The file bar.map can contain text such as this:

```
{
      global: index;
      local: *;
};
```

Chapter 3 has more information on using export maps on Linux.

6.4.2 Linker Tools

Some application makefiles make use of linker tools that are present in HP-UX. These tools are used to examine object files and manipulate them to create the final object file or executable on HP-UX. Table 6-9 compares other HP-UX linker tools and their equivalents on Linux.

TABLE 6-9
HP-UX and Linux Linker Tools Comparison Table

HP-UX Tool	Linux Equivalent	Description
`chatr`	None	Displays or modifies the internal attributes of an object file.
`elfdump`	`objdump`	Displays the contents of an ELF object file.
`fastbind`	None	Improves startup time of programs that use shared libraries.
`ldd`	`ldd`	Lists dynamic dependencies of executable files and shared libraries.
`lorder`	None	Finds ordering relationship for an object library.
`nm`	`nm`	Displays the symbol table of an object file.
`odump`	`objdump`	Displays the contents of a 32-bit native code object file (HP-UX).
`size`	`size`	Prints sizes of object file elements.
`strip`	`strip`	Strips symbol and debugging information from an object file, executable, or archive library.

See Chapter 2 for more information on the GNU binutils.

6.5 Library Versioning

If the architecture of the application to be ported requires versioning support for libraries, some porting effort will be needed to convert the application to use the Linux library versioning implementation.

6.5.1 Library Versioning on HP-UX

Library versioning support is provided in the HP-UX development environment through the use of the +h linker (ld) option. Take, for example, a library named libmyown. To create a version 0 library for libmyown, the command line will look like this:

```
$ ld -b *.o -o libmyown.0 +h libmyown.0
```

The resulting library, libmyown.0, is produced with an internal name of libmyown.0 represented by the +h flag and its argument. After the shared library, libmyown.0, is produced, it is ready to be placed in its destination directory—in this case, assume /tmp is the destination directory. To install the library to /tmp, copy libmyown.0 to /tmp and use the command ln to link it to a file named libmyown.sl:

```
$ ln -s libmyown.0 libmyown.sl
$ ls -l libmyown.sl
$ libmyown.sl -> libmyown.0
```

To link with the library, use the -l option to specify the library. The linker (ld) searches for the file libmyown.sl. Because the library was created with an internal name, the linker places the internal name of the library in the executable's shared library dependency list. When the application is run, the dynamic loader (dl) loads the library named by this internal name—in this case, libmyown.0.

If another version of libmyown is created and named libmyown.1, the preceding procedure for creating a version library using the +h flag is repeated to produce libmyown.1. The shared library libmyown.1 is linked (using the ln command) with libmyown.sl. Any new programs linked with libmyown .sl will be linked with and use libmyown.1. Old programs that were linked to libmyown.0 will continue using libmyown.0.

6.5.2 Library Versioning on Linux[24]

Two types of versioning exist on Linux—external and symbol versioning. External versioning closely resembles HP-UX semantics; the internal versioning exists to

24 Refer to the paper "Library Versioning in Solaris and Linux" published in the Proceedings of the 4th Annual Linux Showcase and Conference, Atlanta, October 10–14, 2000.

replicate versioning semantics supported by other operating systems such as Solaris. See Chapter 3 for a complete discussion of the library versioning available on Linux.

6.6 Dynamic Linking and Shared Libraries

HP-UX applications that use dynamic linking functions such as `shl_load`, `shl_finsym`, and others need to be ported to use Linux dynamic link functions that begin with `dl`. HP-UX applications that already use the `dl*` functions need to be checked for proper API use because some `dl` functions that HP-UX supports are not supported on Linux.

Table 6-10 shows the HP-UX `dl*` function equivalents to HP-UX `shl_*` calls as well as other `dl*` calls present in HP-UX only.

TABLE 6-10
Dynamic Loading Library Functions Comparison Table

Routine	dl* Routines Present in HP-UX and Linux	Description
`shl_load` and `cxxshl_load`	`dlopen` HP-UX mode: `RTLD_LAZY`, `RTLD_NOW`, `RTLD_GLOBAL`, `RTLD_LOCAL`, `RTLD_GROUP`, `RTLD_WORLD`, `RTLD_PARENT` Linux flags: `RTLD_LAZY`, `RTLD_NOW`, `RTLD_GLOBAL`, `RTLD_LOCAL`, `RTLD_NODELETE`, `RTLD_NOLOAD`, `RTLD_BINDING_MASK`, `RTLD_DEEPBIND`	Loads a shared library.
`shl_findsym`	`dlsym` HP-UX handle: `RTLD_DEFAULT`, `RTLD_NEXT`, `RTLD_SELF` Linux handle: `RTLD_DEFAULT`, `RTLD_NEXT`	Finds the address of a global symbol in a shared library.
`shd_get`	`dlget` (HP-UX only)	Gets information about currently loaded library.

Routine	dl* Routines Present in HP-UX and Linux	Description
shl_gethandle	dlmodinfo (HP-UX only)	Gets descriptor information about a loaded shared library.
shl_definesym	No equivalent	Adds a new symbol to the global shared library symbol table.
shl_getsymbols	No equivalent	Returns a list of symbols in a shared library.
shl_unload	dlclose	Unloads the shared library.
None	dlerror	Returns a pointer to information about the last dlopen, dlsym, or dlclose error.
None	dladdr HP-UX DI_info structure: const char *dli_fname; void *dli_fbase; const char *dli_sname; void *dli_saddr; size_t dli_size; int dli_bind; int dli_type; Linux DI_info structure: const char *dli_fname; void *dli_fbase; const char *dli_sname; void *dli_saddr; size_t dli_size;	Translates address to symbolic information.
	dlgetname (HP-UX only)	Retrieves the name of a loaded module given a load model descriptor.

In Linux, a program that uses dynamic linking is linked with the `libld.so` library, `-ldl`. The libraries it loads do not need to be linked in during the build process. Chapter 3 contains example code that compiles on Linux using `dl*` routines.

6.6.1 GNU libtool

If portability is important to your program, you should consider using GNU `libtool` to build and install libraries. `libtool` masks the complexity of using shared libraries with a consistent, portable interface. For more information, visit www.gnu.org/software/libtool/libtool.html.

6.7 Porting Shell Scripts to Linux

Figure 6-1 shows the Linux shell in relation to the rest of the operating system. The shell, as it is aptly named, sits on the outer edge of the system. It gives users easier ways to interact with system utilities that query or control the operating system, start or stop processes, and list or modify files and directories.

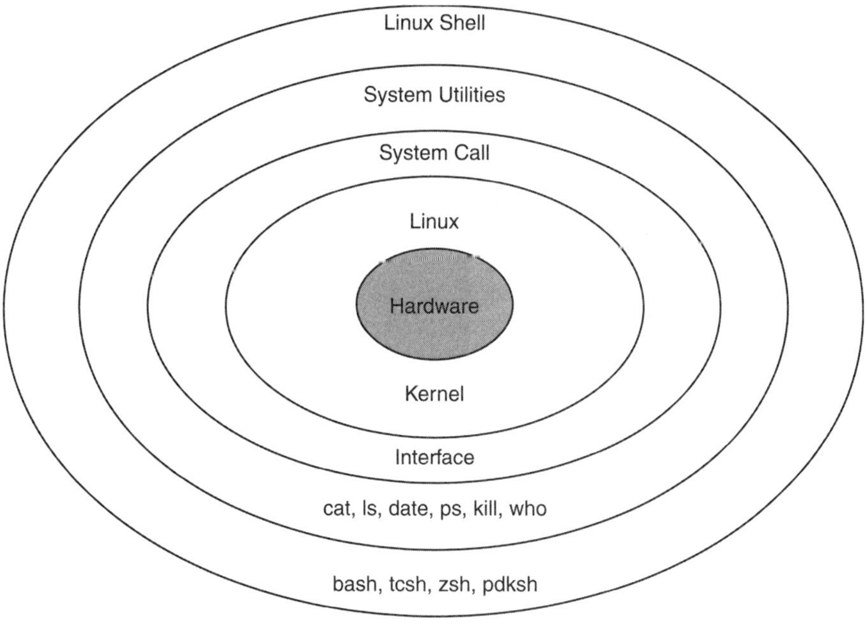

FIGURE 6-1
Linux shell creates an environment to access system interfaces easier.

Depending on the Linux installation, several shells developed for Linux are installed by default. The more popular shells developed for Linux are `bash`, `tcsh`, `zsh`, and `pdksh`. `bash`, however, is considered the default shell on Linux.

On HP-UX, the main shells available are `bsh`, `ksh`, and `csh`. Most applications use these shells to source or check environment variables and kick off processes or deamons. In porting projects that involve porting of test harnesses, however, use of scripting becomes more prevalent.

Table 6-11 compares HP-UX and Linux shells.

TABLE 6-11
HP-UX and Linux Shell Comparison Table

Shell Name	HP-UX Shell Path	Linux Shell Path
Bourne shell	/usr/bin/sh	/bin/sh (linked to bash)
Korn shell	/usr/bin/ksh	/bin/ksh (linked to pdksh)
C shell	/usr/bin/csh	/bin/csh (linked to tcsh)
GNU Bourne Again shell[25]	/opt/OpenSource/bin/bash	/bin/bash
TC shell	/opt/OpenSource/bin/tcsh	/bin/tcsh
Z shell	None	/bin/zsh

Porting scripts is not covered in this book, but an excellent reference book about UNIX and Linux shells that can be helpful is *UNIX Shells by Example,* 4th edition (Prentice Hall, 2005).

6.8 Internationalization (I18N)[26]

How I18N affects the porting effort greatly depends on the application. If an application requires simple message catalogue conversions, date and time displays, or simple text string searches using regular expressions, porting these functionalities from HP-UX to Linux can be easy. However, if the application does more

25 Installed through the Technical Computing Open Source Product bundle

26 Refer to www.li18nux.org/ to learn more about the Linux I18N Project.

complicated text analysis, such as ones used in editors, those may be harder to port for the reason mentioned in the next paragraph.

Both HP-UX and Linux conform to the ISO naming standard locale names, `[locale][_territory].[codeset]`, where `locale` is the two-character language, and `territory` is the two-character territory. Examples of these are `en_US.iso885915` and `zh_CN.gb18030`. However, the locales available on each system, and locale contents, are different. Porting applications that require complicated use of available locales may require the need to learn language specificity and translation as well as modification of existing locales on Linux to get similar behavior as on HP-UX.

Table 6-12 compares HP-UX and GNU `libc` API support related to I18N.

TABLE 6-12
HP-UX and GNU libc I18N Support Comparison Table

HP-UX	GNU libc	Functions
wcscat, wcsncat, wcscmp, wcsncmp, wcscpy, wcsncpy, wcslen, wcschr, wcsrchr, wcsstr, wcspbrk, wcsspn, wcscspn, wcswcs, wcstok, wcscoll, wcwidth, wcswidth, wcsxfrm	wcscat, wcsncat, wcscmp, wcsncmp, wcscpy, wcsncpy, wcslen, wcschr, wcsrchr, wcsstr, wcspbrk, wcsspn, wcscspn, wcswcs, wcstok, wcscoll, wcwidth, wcswidth, wcsxfrm	Wide character string functions
mblen, mbrlen, wcslen, strlen, wcswidth, wcwidth	mblen, mbrlen, wcslen, strlen, wcswidth, wcwidth	Dimension functions
mbsinit, mbrtowc, wcrtomb, mbsrtowcs, wcsrtombs, btowc, wctob, mbtowc, mbstowcs, wctomb, wcstombs	mbsinit, mbrtowc, wcrtomb mbsrtowcs, wcsrtombs, btowc, wctob, mbtowc, mbstowcs wctomb, wcstombs, wcrtomb, wcsnrtombs, mbsnrtowcs	Conversion functions
iconv, iconv_open, iconv_close, genxlt	iconv, iconv_open, iconv_close	Translation functions

HP-UX	GNU libc	Functions
ngettext, dngettext, dcngettext, setlocale, textdomain, bindtextdomain, bind_textdomain_codeset, msgfmt, dumpmsg, findmsg, gencat, catclose, catopen	ngettext, dngettext, dcngettext setlocale, textdomain, bindtextdomain, bind_textdomain_codeset, gettext, dgettext, dcgettext, catgets, gencat, catclose, catopen	Message catalogue functions
getc, getc_unlocked, getchar, getchar_unlocked, fgetc, getw, putc, putchar, fputc, putw, fgetc, getw, ungetwc, getwc, getwchar, fgetwc	getc, getc_unlocked, getchar getchar_unlockec, fgetc, getw, putc, putchar, fputc, putw, fgetc, getw, ungetwc, getwc, getwchar, fgetwc, ungetwc, fgets, ungetc, fputwc, fputws, putwc, putwchar, fputs, fgetws	Input/output functions
fwprintf, wprintf, swprintf, vfwprintf, vwprintf, vswprintf, strftime, strfmon, printf, fprintf, sprintf, wcfstime, vprintf, vfprintf, vsprintf, vsnprintf	fwprintf, wprintf, swprintf, vfwprintf, vwprintf, vswprintf, strftime, strfmon, printf, fprintf, sprintf, wcfstime, vprintf, vfprintf, vsprintf, vsnprintf	String formatting functions
iswalpha, iswupper, iswlower, iswdigit, iswxdigit, iswalnum, iswspace, iswpunct, iswprint, iswgraph, iswcntrl, wctype, iswctype, isalpha, isupper, islower, isdigit, isxdigit, isalnum, isspace, ispunct, isprint, isgraph, iscntrl, isascii	iswalpha, iswupper, iswlower iswdigit, iswxdigit, iswalnum iswspace, iswpunct, iswprint iswgraph, iswcntrl, wctype, iswctype, isalpha, isupper, islower, isdigit, isxdigit, isalnum, isspace, ispunct, isprint, isgraph, iscntrl, isascii, isblank, isspace, isupper	Character classifications

HP-UX	GNU libc	Functions
strcoll, strxfrm, wcscoll, wcwidth, wcswidth, wcsxfrm	strcoll, strxfrm, wcscoll, wcsxfrm	Collation functions
regcomp, regerror, regexec, regfree	regcomp, regexec, regerror, regfree	Regular expressions
memset, wmemchr, wmemcmp, wmemcpy, wmemmove, wmemset	memset, wmemchr, wmemcmp wmemcpy, wmemmove, wmemset, wcpcpy, wcpncpy, wcscpy, wcsncpy, wcsspn, cpcpy, cpncpy, cscpy, csncpy, csspn	String copying and filling functions
towlower, towupper, towctrans, wctrans, tolower, toupper	towlower, towupper, towctrans, wctrans, tolower, toupper	Conversion functions

On HP-UX, the decoder file is located in /usr/lib/nls/config. On Linux, you can find the decoder file in /usr/share/locale/locale.alias. On Linux, you can use the command `locale -a` to determine the locales installed on the system.

6.8.1 iconv Support and Message Catalogs

Linux provides the `iconv(1)` utility to convert traditional string encoding to unicode. To get a list of currently implemented encodings in Linux, use the `iconv -list` command at the Linux command prompt. In HP-UX, the file /usr/lib/nls/iconv/config.iconv lists the implemented encoding. See Chapter 3 for examples of using `libiconv` APIs and how to create a message catalog.

6.9 Software Development Tools

The `make` development tool in Linux is GNU Make. As of this writing, the latest version of GNU Make is version 3.8, which this section is based on. Porting the build environment from HP-UX to Linux means using the GNU Make as well as making sure project makefiles use syntax that the GNU Make understands.

Because both HP-UX[27] and GNU Make conform to the POSIX standard, similarities between HP-UX and GNU makefile syntax abound. However, there are

27 HP-UX make also conforms to SVID2, SVID3, XPG2, XPG3, XPG4.

still some differences, which this section covers. The first differences to take note of are the command-line switches. Table 6-13 shows a comparison between HP-UX and GNU Make command-line switches.

TABLE 6-13
HP-UX Make and GNU Make Comparison Table

HP-UX Flag	HP-UX make Description[28]	GNU Make Equivalents
`-b` (default)	Compatibility mode for version 7 makefiles.	`-b` `-m`
`-B`	Turn off compatibility mode for version 7.	No equivalent
`-d`	Debug mode.	`-d` `--debug[=options]`
`-e`	Environment variable assignments within makefiles.	`-e` `--environment-overrides`
`-f` *`makefile`*	Use *`makefile`* as the makefile target.	`-f` *`makefile`* `--file=`*`file`* `--makefile=`*`file`*
`-i`	Ignore error codes returned by invoked commands.	`-i` `--ignore-errors`
`-k`	When command returns nonzero status, abandon work but continue on other branches that do not depend on abandoned target.	`-k` `--keep-going`

`-n`	No execute mode; print commands, but do not execute.	`-n`
		`--just-print`
		`--dry-run`
		`--recon`

`-p`	Print the complete set of macro definitions and target descriptions.	`-p` `--print-data-base`
`-P`	Update in parallel more than one target at a time.	No equivalent

28 HP-UX `make` man pages

HP-UX Flag	HP-UX make Description	GNU Make Equivalents
`-q`	Question mode. Make returns a zero or nonzero status code depending on whether the target file is or is not up-to-date. Targets are not updated with this option.	`-q` Return: 0 if target is up-to-date 1 if remaking required 2 if error encountered
`-r`	Clear suffix list and do not use built-in rules.	`-r` `--no-builtin-rules`

`-s`	Silent mode.	`-s`
		`--silent`
		`--quiet`

`-S`	Terminate if an error occurs.	`-S`
		`--no-keep-going`
		`--stop`

`-t`	Touch target files.	`-t`
`-u`	Unconditional make, ignoring timestamps.	None
`-w`	Suppress warning messages.	No equivalent `-w` flag used for printing message for current working directory

6.9.1 Makefile Syntax

6.9.1.1 Target for the Form file((entry))

Library dependencies of the form `libname ((entry))` are not supported by GNU Make. GNU Make supports `libname(file.o)`, where file.o is the file containing the symbol. This feature was not put into GNU Make because of the nonmodularity of putting knowledge into `make` of the internal format of archive file symbol tables.

6.9.1.2 Use of :=

Values assigned to a variable can be overridden by a conditional macro definition. A conditional macro definition takes on the form `target :=` *`variable`* `= value`.

When the target line associated with `target` is being processed, the macro value specified in the conditional macro definition is in effect. If *variable* was previously defined, the new value of *variable* overrides the previous definition. The new value of *variable* takes effect when `target` or any dependents of `target` are being processed.

HP-UX Make

Example:

```
CFLAGS = -O
foo_prog := CFLAGS = -g
foo_prog : foo1.o foo2.o bar.o      CFLAGS = -g will be in effect
                                    for foo_prog target and any
                                    dependents of the target
                                    processed.
```

GNU Make

In GNU Make, `:=` is used for variable assignments. To override assigned values in GNU Make for target-specific variables, use the following syntax:

```
target := variable = value
target :  foo1.o foo2.o bar.o      variable = value will be in
                                   effect for target and any
                                   command scripts that create
                                   their prerequisites.
```

6.9.1.3 Use of $$@

HP-UX `make` uses the `$$@` syntax, which is a System V `make` syntax, as part of the dependency list to refer to the current target. The following subsection shows an example of how `$$@` is used in HP-UX makefiles.

HP-UX Make

```
$(targets): $$@.o lib.a
```

GNU Make

The preceding syntax can be replaced in a GNU makefile by using the following syntax:

```
$(target): %: %.o lib.a
```

6.9.1.4 Empty Rules

In HP-UX makefiles, you can specify a suffix rule with no commands (to override an implicit rule). This can be confusing and also meaningless to GNU Make because the command line looks empty (it contains a single tab character). To specify an empty suffix rule with GNU Make, put a semicolon after the dependency, as follows:

```
.c.a: ;
```

6.9.1.5 Suffix Support

HP-UX supports old-fashioned suffix rules, which GNU Make considers obsolete because pattern rules are more general and cleaner (see Table 6-14). GNU Make supports suffix rules for compatibility with older makefile syntax only.

Suffix rules come in two kinds: double-suffix and single-suffix.

A single-suffix rule looks like this:

```
.c  .c~ .cxx .sh
```

The equivalent pattern rule recognized by GNU Make for the `.c` suffix rule is as follows:

```
% : %.c
```

A double-suffix rule looks like this:

```
.c.o .C.o .y.o
```

The equivalent pattern rule for a `.c.o` suffix rule is as follows:

```
%.o : %.c
```

Suffix rules that handle System V makefiles to support SCCS files that contain ~ are not recognized by GNU Make. In HP-UX, the suffix rule `.c~.o` creates the file x.o from the SCCS file s.n.c. GNU Make handles SCCS and RCS files differently by applying two pattern rules for extraction from SCCS or RCS in combination with general rules of rule chaining. For more information, refer to the GNU Make reference.[29]

29 www.gnu.org/software/make/manual/make.html

TABLE 6-14
Summary of Differences Between HP-UX Make and GNU Make

Description	HP-UX[30]	GNU Make
Library dependencies	`libname ((symbol))`	`libname (file.o)`
Current target	`$(targets) : $$@.o`	`$(target) : %: %.o`
Conditional macro	`$(targets) := c_flags = -g`	`$(targets) … :` `c_flags = -g`
Empty rules	`.c.a:`	`.c.a: ;`
Suffix rules	`.c~.o:`	Built in to GNU Make

6.9.2 Debuggers

On all Linux systems, the default application debugger for non-Java programs is the GNU debugger—`gdb` for short. For HP-UX developers, `gdb` is a familiar tool because HP-UX v11 supports a version of `gdb` that has been ported to the HP-UX platform.

Invoking `gdb` on Linux yields the following:

```
$ gdb
GNU gdb 6.1
Copyright 2004 Free Software Foundation, Inc.
GDB is free software, covered by the GNU General Public License, and you are
welcome to change it and/or distribute copies of it under certain conditions.
Type "show copying" to see the conditions. There is absolutely no warranty for
GDB. Type "show warranty" for details.
This GDB was configured as "i586-suse-linux".
```

Invoking `gdb` on HP-UX yields the following:

```
$ gdb
HP gdb 3.2 for PA-RISC 1.1 or 2.0 (narrow), HP-UX 11.00.
Copyright 1986 - 2001 Free Software Foundation, Inc.
Hewlett-Packard Wildebeest 3.2 (based on GDB) is covered by the
GNU General Public License. Type "show copying" to see the conditions to change
it and/or distribute copies. Type "show warranty" for warranty/support.
```

See Chapter 7, "Testing and Debugging," for more information about the GNU debugger.

---

30 Linux Porting guide for HP-UX 11.x on PA platforms and GNU Make manual

6.10 Threads

This section addresses issues that developers might face when migrating multi-threaded applications from HP-UX to Linux. On the Linux side, the material in this section is based on the new implementation of a POSIX thread library (the Native POSIX Thread Library, NPTL for short) developed by Ulrich Drepper.

The Linux threading library in all the released versions of Linux prior to 2.6 is known as *LinuxThreads*. This library has been supported by the GNU C library since `glibc` 2.0 and is largely POSIX-compliant. Starting in the 2.6 kernel, NPTL was introduced. It provides a significant performance improvement over LinuxThreads. NPTL is also far more compliant with the POSIX specification than the LinuxThreads package was. However, just using the 2.6 kernel does not mean that the NPTL is being used. All modern Linux distributions ship NPTL as the default threads package, and many ship both NPTL and LinuxThreads. However, it is recommended that all new applications to be ported to the Linux 2.6 platform use NPTL as the threading library.

Because NPTL is relatively new, it would only be natural for different Linux distributions to support older versions of the LinuxThreads library[31] for backward compatibility. To determine which threading library a system uses, execute the `getconf` command (part of the `glibc` package) to examine the `GNU_LIBPTHREAD_VERSION` environment variable, as in the following command example:

```
$ getconf GNU_LIBPTHREAD_VERSION
linuxthreads-0.10              This was returned from an old
                               Red Hat installation.
```

If your system uses the NPTL, the command returns the value of NPTL that your system is using, as in the following example:

```
$ getconf GNU_LIBPTHREAD_VERSION
NPTL 0.61                      This was returned from
                               SUSE 9.1 installation.


$ getconf GNU_LIBPTHREAD_VERSION
NPTL 2.3.3                     This was returned from
                               Fedora 2.6.9-1.667
                               installation.
```

---

31 LinuxThreads is another library that implements POSIX 1003.1c API specifications.

To tell which compiler suite the Linux distribution was compiled and linked with, use the following method.

To find the `libpthreads` library linked with /bin/ls:

```
$ ldd /bin/ls | grep libc.so.6
    libc.so.6 => /lib/tls/i586/libc.so.6 (0x00b9c000)

$ /lib/tls/i586/libc.so.6
GNU C Library stable release version 2.3.3, by Roland McGrath et al.
Copyright (C) 2004 Free Software Foundation, Inc.
This is free software; see the source for copying conditions.
There is NO warranty; not even for MERCHANTABILITY or FITNESS FOR A
PARTICULAR PURPOSE.
Compiled by GNU CC version 3.4.2 20041017 (Red Hat 3.4.2-6.fc3).
Compiled on a Linux 2.4.20 system on 2004-10-27.
Available extensions:
    GNU libio by Per Bothner
    crypt add-on version 2.1 by Michael Glad and others
    Native POSIX Threads Library by Ulrich Drepper et al
    The C stubs add-on version 2.1.2.
    BIND-8.2.3-T5B
    NIS(YP)/NIS+ NSS modules 0.19 by Thorsten Kukuk
    Glibc-2.0 compatibility add-on by Cristian Gafton
    GNU Libidn by Simon Josefsson
Thread-local storage support included.
For bug reporting instructions, please see:
<http://www.gnu.org/software/libc/bugs.html>.
```

As the preceding output shows, the `libc.so.6` is linked with the Native POSIX Threads Library by Ulrich Drepper.

6.10.1 Threads Support in HP-UX and Linux

HP-UX announced formal support for POSIX 1003.1 threads and discontinued support for new applications written to use DCE threads in version 11 of its HP-UX operating system. Although support for DCE threads has been discontinued, applications written to these standards still exist. Porting these applications to Linux requires them to adhere to the new POSIX 1003.1 standards. Table 6-15 compares DCE threads and POSIX threads on both HP-UX and Linux.

TABLE 6-15
Linux and HP-UX Threads Implementation Comparison

HP-UX DCE	HP-UX POSIX	Linux NPTL
atfork	pthread_atfork	pthread_atfork
hp__pthread_equal	None	None
pthread__cancel_thread	pthread_cancel	pthread_cancel
pthread_attr_create	pthread_attr_init	pthread_attr_init
pthread_attr_delete	pthread_attr_destroy	pthread_attr_destroy
pthread_attr_getguardsize_np	pthread_attr_getguardsize	pthread_attr_getguardsize
pthread_attr_getinheritsched	pthread_attr_getinheritsched	pthread_attr_getinheritsched
pthread_attr_getprio	pthread_attr_getschedparam	pthread_attr_getschedparam
pthread_attr_getsched	pthread_attr_getschedpolicy	pthread_attr_getschedpolicy
pthread_attr_getstacksize	pthread_attr_getstacksize	pthread_attr_getstacksize
pthread_attr_setguardsize_np	pthread_attr_setguardsize	pthread_attr_setguardsize
pthread_attr_setinheritsched	pthread_attr_setinheritsched	pthread_attr_setinheritsched
pthread_attr_setprio	pthread_attr_setschedparam	pthread_attr_setschedparam
pthread_attr_setsched	pthread_attr_setschedpolicy	pthread_attr_setschedpolicy
pthread_attr_setstacksize	pthread_attr_setstacksize	pthread_attr_setstacksize
pthread_cancel	pthread_cancel	pthrhead_cancel
pthread_cond_broadcast	pthread_cond_broadcast	pthread_cond_broadcast
pthread_cond_destroy	pthread_cond_destroy	pthread_cond_destroy
pthread_cond_init	pthread_cond_init	pthread_cond_init

HP-UX DCE	HP-UX POSIX	Linux NPTL
pthread_cond_signal	pthread_cond_signal	pthread_cond_signal
pthread_cond_signal_int_np	None	None
pthread_cond_timedwait	pthread_cond_timedwait	pthread_cond_timedwait
pthread_cond_wait	pthread_cond_wait	pthread_cond_wait
pthread_condattr_create	pthread_condattr_init	pthread_condattr_init
pthread_condattr_delete	pthread_condattr_destroy	pthread_condattr_destroy
pthread_create	pthread_create	pthread_create
pthread_ctxcb_hpux	None	None
pthread_delay_np	nanosleep	nanosleep
pthread_detach	pthread_detach	pthread_detach
pthread_equal	pthread_equal	pthread_equal
pthread_exit	pthread_exit	pthread_exit
pthread_get_expiration_np	get_expiration_time	get_expiration_time
pthread_getprio	pthread_getschedparam	pthread_getschedparam
pthread_getscheduler	pthread_getschedparam	pthread_getschedparam
pthread_getspecific	pthread_getspecific	pthread_getspecific
pthread_is_multithreaded_np	None	None
pthread_join	pthread_join	pthread_join
pthread_keycreate	pthread_key_create	pthread_key_create
pthread_lock_global_np	None	None
pthread_mutex_destroy	pthread_mutex_destroy	pthread_mutex_destroy
pthread_mutex_init	pthread_mutex_init	pthread_mutex_init
pthread_mutex_lock	pthread_mutex_lock	pthread_mutex_lock
pthread_mutex_trylock	pthread_mutex_trylock	pthread_mutex_trylock

HP-UX DCE	HP-UX POSIX	Linux NPTL
pthread_mutex_unlock	pthread_unlock	pthread_unlock
pthread_mutexattr_create	pthread_mutexattr_init	pthread_mutexattr_init
pthread_mutexattr_delete	pthread_mutexattr_destroy	pthread_mutexattr_destroy
pthread_mutexattr_getkind_np	None	None
pthread_mutexattr_setkind_np	None	None
pthread_once	pthread_once	pthread_once
pthread_self	pthread_self	pthread_self
pthread_setasynccancel	pthread_setcanceltype	pthread_setcanceltype
pthread_setcancel	pthread_setcancelstate	pthread_setcancelstate
pthread_setprio	pthread_setschedparam	pthread_setschedparam
pthread_setscheduler	pthread_setschedparam	pthread_setschedparam
pthread_setspecific	pthread_setspecific	pthread_setspecific
pthread_signal_to_cancel_np	None	None
pthread_testcancel	pthread_testcancel	pthread_testcancel
pthread_yield	sched_yield	sched_yield
sigprocmask	pthread_sigmask	pthread_sigmask
sigwait	sigwait	sigwait

Although HP-UX 11 and Linux both implement the POSIX 1003.1, there are minor differences in platform implementations. Tables 6-16 and 6-17 show these differences.

TABLE 6-16
Pthread API Differences Between HP-UX and Linux

API	Difference
`pthread_create`	If called by more than one thread for the same tid: HP: Behavior is undefined. Linux: Returns an error (EINVAL).
`pthread_default_stacksize_np`	HP extension. Linux: Use `pthread_attr_setstacksize`.

`pthread_key_create`	HP:
	`_SC_THREAD_KEYS_MAX = 431`
	`_SC_THREAD_DESTRUCTOR_ITERATIONS = 430`
	Linux:
	`PTHREAD_KEYS_MAX 1024`
	`_POSIX_THREAD_DESTRUCTOR_ITERATIONS 4`

`sched_get_priority_max` `sched_get_priority_min`	Linux does not have any equivalence for HP-UX values `SCHED_RR2`, `SCHED_RTPRIO`, `SCHED_NOAGE`.
`sched_yield`	HP: On error, returns –1 and sets `errno` to `ENOSYS`. Linux: On error, returns –1 and sets `errno` to the appropriate value.
`pthread_sigmask`	HP: If pending unblocked signal, at least one such signal is delivered before the function returns.

`pthread_mutexattr_getspin_np`
`pthread_mutexattr_setspin_np`
`pthread_mutex_getyieldfreq_np`
`pthread_mutex_setyieldfreq_np`
`pthread_attr_getprocessor_np`
`pthread_attr_setprocessor_np`
	HP extensions.

TABLE 6-17
Default Pthreads Attribute Values for HP-UX and Linux

Attribute	HP-UX 11i v2	Linux 2.6
contention scope	PTHREAD_SCOPE_PROCESS	PTHREAD_SCOPE_SYSTEM
detachstate	PTHREAD_CREATE_JOINABLE	PTHREAD_CREATE_JOINABLE
stacksize	256K	Depends on Linux installation: Fedora (2.6.9–1.667): 10MB SUSE 9.1: 2MB
inheritsched	PTHREAD_INHERIT_SCHED	PTHREAD_INHERIT_SCHED
schedpolicy	SCHED_TIMESHARE	SCHED_OTHER
guardsize	PAGESIZE (4K)	PAGESIZE (4K)
processor	PTHREAD_SPUINHERIT_NP	Not applicable
binding type	PTHREAD_BIND_ADVISORY_NP	Not applicable

6.10.2 Differences in HP-UX DCE and POSIX Threads

Linux and HP-UX version 11.0 provide support for POSIX threads as specified by the POSIX.1003.1 standard. Existing HP-UX applications based on DCE pthreads will need to be ported to adhere to the latest POSIX threads standards. This section shows some of the issues porting engineers face when porting from DCE-based applications to the latest POSIX threads standard.

6.10.2.1 Error Returns

All Linux NPTL pthreads functions return the error number as the return value (they also set the errno global variable). In HP-UX DCE pthreads, pthread functions that return on error return a –1 and set the errno global variable to the appropriate value. Applications written to the DCE pthreads API must be changed to handle error returns properly.

HP-UX DCE pthreads:

```
{int ret;
int *per;
ret = pthread_cond_t ( thread, &per ) ;
if ( ret== -1 ) printf ( error =%d\n , errno ) ;
}
```

POSIX pthreads:

```
{int ret;
int *ptr;
ret = pthread_join ( thread, &ptr ) ;
if ( ret ) printf ( error =%d\n , ret ) ;
}
```

6.10.2.2 Threading Model

DCE pthreads are implemented as user threads. This means that thread functionalities such as creating, scheduling, context switching, and terminating (and others) are mainly done in user space as opposed to kernel space. There may be some kernel interaction to attach the user threads to one or more kernel threads to run, but most of the thread activities are done within the pthreads library in user space.

Contrast this to the POSIX threads library, which may implement a 1:1 or M:N model. In 1:1 mode, major thread functionalities such as thread scheduling and dispatching are done within the kernel, whereas in the M:N mode, these functionalities are done within the context of the pthreads library in user space.

Linux only implements the 1:1 threading model as of this writing. There are no plans to support the M:N model in the future.

6.10.2.3 Sigwait() Function

There is a syntax change in `sigwait()` between DCE pthreads and POSIX threads. The following code snippets show how to port between `sigwait` versions.

HP-UX DCE pthreads:

```
{
  ret = sigwait(set);
  if (ret < 0) {
  ret = errno;
  } else {
    *sig = ret;
  ret = 0;
  }
}
```

POSIX pthreads:

```
{
  ret = sigwait(set, sig);
}
```

6.10.2.4 Mutex API Differences

DCE pthreads APIs to create and destroy mutex attributes changed in POSIX.1-1996. DCE pthreads used `pthread_mutexattr_create` and `pthread_mutexattr_delete`, whereas POSIX.1-1996 uses `pthread_mutexattr_init` and `prhread_mutexattr_destroy`, respectively.

POSIX.1003.1c introduces static initialization of mutexes. The following is an example of static initialization:

```
static pthread_mutex_t foo_mutex = PTHREAD_MUTEX_INITIALIZER;
```

6.10.2.5 Condition Variable Differences

DCE pthreads APIs to create and destroy condition variable attributes changed in POSIX.1-1996. DCE pthreads used `pthread_condattr_create` and `pthread_condattr_delete`, whereas POSIX.1-1996 uses `pthread_condattr_init` and `prhread_condattr_destroy`, respectively.

6.10.2.6 Changes in *_r APIs

The POSIX1003.1c standard removed requirements for `libc_r`. Most library functions were made thread-safe without the need to modify the function interface. However, a few functions could not be made such. Read through the GNU `libc` documentation to make sure functions are thread-safe.

6.10.3 Debugging Linux Threads

One of the most asked questions about multithreaded applications is how to analyze and debug the application using a debugger. On HP-UX v11, the main application debugger is `gdb`. HP-UX developers who must port applications to Linux will find that this makes the transistion to Linux a little easier, because like HP-UX, the main debugger used on Linux is `gdb`. Example 6-5 shows a simple multithreaded program, how the program is compiled on a Linux system using `gcc`, and how the program is debugged after it produces a core file in a multithreaded application on Linux.

When using `gdb` to debug multithreaded applications, you need to remember only a few thread-specific commands. The other `gdb` commands to get stack traces and other information remain the same. The thread-specific commands for use in `gdb` are as follows:

- **info threads-**. Inquires about existing threads.
- **thread <threadnumber>**. Switches threads.
- **thread apply [threadnumber] [all] args-**. Applies a command to a list of threads.

Example 6-5 is a multithreaded program that creates four threads. Each thread has its own function to perform—that is, to raise an exception and cause the program to terminate and create a core file. Note that on some Linux systems, a core file is not automatically generated unless the command `ulimit -c <filesize>` is executed from the shell. Only then will it produce a core file in the directory where the executable resides that will be named core.<pid>, where the pid is the process ID of the process that produced the core file.

Example 6-5

Listing of thread_1.c

```
#include <pthread.h>
#include <signal.h>
#include <errno.h>
#include <sched.h>
#include <stdio.h>
#include <stdlib.h>
#include <unistd.h>

#define THREAD_NUM 4

pthread_mutex_t mutex;
pthread_cond_t cond;

static int thread_in_wait = 0;

void *
abort_func(void *arg)
{
  printf("in abort_func\n");
  pthread_mutex_lock(&mutex);
  thread_in_wait++;
  pthread_cond_wait(&cond, &mutex);
  thread_in_wait--;

  while (thread_in_wait != 0)
  {
    pthread_mutex_unlock(&mutex);
```

```
    sched_yield();
    pthread_mutex_lock(&mutex);
  }

  pthread_mutex_unlock(&mutex);
  raise(SIGABRT);
}

void *
segv_func(void *arg)
{
  printf("in segv_func\n");
  pthread_mutex_lock(&mutex);
  thread_in_wait++;
  pthread_cond_wait(&cond, &mutex);
  thread_in_wait--;

  while (thread_in_wait != 0)
  {
    pthread_mutex_unlock(&mutex);
    sched_yield();
    pthread_mutex_lock(&mutex);
  }

  pthread_mutex_unlock(&mutex);

  raise(SIGSEGV);
}

void *
bus_func(void *arg)
{
  printf("in bus_func\n");
  pthread_mutex_lock(&mutex);
  thread_in_wait++;
  pthread_cond_wait(&cond, &mutex);
  thread_in_wait--;

  while (thread_in_wait != 0)
  {
    pthread_mutex_unlock(&mutex);
    sched_yield();
    pthread_mutex_lock(&mutex);
  }

  pthread_mutex_unlock(&mutex);

  raise(SIGBUS);
}

void *
```

```
fpe_func(void *arg)
{
  printf("in fpe_func\n");
  pthread_mutex_lock(&mutex);
  thread_in_wait++;
  pthread_cond_wait(&cond, &mutex);
  thread_in_wait--;

  while (thread_in_wait != 0)
  {
    pthread_mutex_unlock(&mutex);
    sched_yield();
    pthread_mutex_lock(&mutex);
  }

  pthread_mutex_unlock(&mutex);

  raise(SIGFPE);
}

void *(*func_array[THREAD_NUM])(void *) = {
            bus_func,
            segv_func,
            abort_func,
            fpe_func
            };
int
main(void)
{
  pthread_t tid[THREAD_NUM];
  int i = 0;
  int rc = 0;
  void *(*fp[THREAD_NUM])(void *);

  pthread_cond_init(&cond, NULL);
  pthread_mutex_init(&mutex, NULL);

  for (i=0; i<THREAD_NUM; i++)
  {
    fp[i] = func_array[i];
  }

  for (i=0; i<THREAD_NUM; i++)
  {
    if( (rc = pthread_create(&tid[i], NULL, fp[i], NULL )) != 0)
    {
      printf("pthread_create failed: %d\n", errno);
      exit (1);
    }
  }
```

```
  pthread_mutex_lock(&mutex);
  while (thread_in_wait != THREAD_NUM)
  {
    pthread_mutex_unlock(&mutex);
    sched_yield();
    pthread_mutex_lock(&mutex);
  }

  pthread_mutex_unlock(&mutex);
  pthread_cond_broadcast(&cond);

  for (i=0; i<THREAD_NUM; i++)
  {
    pthread_join(tid[i], NULL);
  }

  return (0);
}
```

Compile Linux using gcc:

```
$ gcc thread_1.c -o thread_1 -lpthread -D_REENTRANT -g
```

Run the program:

```
$ ./thread_1
in bus_func
in segv_func
in abort_func
in fpe_func
Floating point exception (core dumped)
```

Analyze the program using gdb:

```
$ gdb thread_1 core.6797          Note that on Linux a core
                                  file is produced with the
                                  process id as the extension.

GNU gdb 6.1
Copyright 2004 Free Software Foundation, Inc.
GDB is free software, covered by the GNU General Public License, and you are
welcome to change it and/or distribute copies of it under certain conditions.
Type "show copying" to see the conditions.
There is absolutely no warranty for GDB. Type "show warranty" for details.
This GDB was configured as "i586-suse-linux"...Using host libthread_db library
"/lib/tls/libthread_db.so.1".
Core was generated by `./thread_1'.
Program terminated with signal 8, Arithmetic exception.

warning: current_sos: Can't read pathname for load map: Input/output error

Reading symbols from /lib/tls/libpthread.so.0...done.
```

```
Loaded symbols for /lib/tls/libpthread.so.0
Reading symbols from /lib/tls/libc.so.6...done.
Loaded symbols for /lib/tls/libc.so.6
Reading symbols from /lib/ld-linux.so.2...done.
Loaded symbols for /lib/ld-linux.so.2
#0 0xffffe410 in ?? ()
(gdb) info thread              Command to display all
                               threads in the process
 5 process 6797 0xffffe410 in ?? ()
 4 process 6798 0xffffe410 in ?? ()
 3 process 6799 0xffffe410 in ?? ()
 2 process 6800 0xffffe410 in ?? ()
* 1 process 6801 0xffffe410 in ?? ()    Notice the asterisk in
                                        front of the thread. This
                                        denotes that the current
                                        thread context is thread
                                        number 1.
```

The command `info threads` displays a summary of all threads currently in the program. In the example output, from left to right, they are as follows:

1. The thread number assigned by `gdb`
2. The target systems thread identifier (`systag`, second and third column)
3. The current stack frame summary for the thread

The asterisk (*) to the left of the `gdb` thread number indicates the current thread.

On an HP-UX machine, the following appears for the same program.

```
#0 0xc020c4b0 in kill+0x10 () from /usr/lib/libc.2
(gdb) info thread
*  5 system thread 1440101 0xc020c4b0 in kill+0x10 () from /usr/lib/libc.2
  4 system thread 1440100 0xc020ed60 in sched_yield+0x10 ()
  from /usr/lib/libc.2
  3 system thread 1440099 0xc020ed60 in sched_yield+0x10 ()
  from /usr/lib/libc.2
  2 system thread 1440098 0xc020ed60 in sched_yield+0x10 ()
  from /usr/lib/libc.2
  1 system thread 1440097 0xc020b318 in __kwakeup+0x10 ()
  from /usr/lib/libc.2
```

Notice that on HP-UX, `systag` denotes a system thread rather than a process on the Linux system from the output when reading a core file.

Continuing with our example:

```
(gdb) bt                    Command to display the
                            stack traceback of the
                            current thread.
#0 0xffffe410 in ?? ()
#1 0x40952a78 in ?? ()
#2 0x00000008 in ?? ()
#3 0x00001a91 in ?? ()
#4 0x400331a1 in raise () from /lib/tls/libpthread.so.0
#5 0x08048997 in fpe_func (arg=0x0) at thread_1.c:98
#6 0x4002d9dd in start_thread () from /lib/tls/libpthread.so.0
#7 0x400efffa in clone () from /lib/tls/libc.so.6
```

At the time of the core dump, the current thread is always the last running thread and would likely have caused the exception. Examining the stack through the `bt` command leads us to the calling function, which was `raise`. `raise` was called from our application in the thread_1.c file and shows the corresponding line number.

We continue with the example by switching to other threads and examining their stack traces:

```
(gdb) thread 2              Command to switch to
                            thread #2.

[Switching to thread 2 (process 6800)]#0 0xffffe410 in ?? ()

(gdb) bt                    Issue command to display
                            the stack of thread #2.
#0 0xffffe410 in ?? ()
#1 0x40751a78 in ?? ()
#2 0x00000006 in ?? ()
#3 0x00001a90 in ?? ()
#4 0x400331a1 in raise () from /lib/tls/libpthread.so.0
#5 0x080487cf in abort_func (arg=0x0) at thread_1.c:35
#6 0x4002d9dd in start_thread () from /lib/tls/libpthread.so.0
#7 0x400efffa in clone () from /lib/tls/libc.so.6

(gdb) thread 5
[Switching to thread 5 (process 6797)]#0 0xffffe410 in ?? ()
(gdb) bt
#0 0xffffe410 in ?? ()
#1 0xbffff528 in ?? ()
#2 0x00001a8e in ?? ()
#3 0x00000000 in ?? ()
#4 0x4002df2f in pthread_join () from /lib/tls/libpthread.so.0
#5 0x08048ad9 in main () at thread_1.c:145


(gdb) quit
```

In most cases when a multithreaded program dumps a core, the most likely thread to have caused the dump is the current running thread. In some cases, however, when the application hangs, you may need to attach `gdb` to the running program. See Chapter 7 or refer to the GNU `gdb` manual[32] online for information about how to attach to a currently running program.

6.10.4 C++ Exceptions and Linux Threads

Searching the Internet for related topics on C++ exceptions and POSIX threads will yield a variety of opinions regarding how C++ should handle POSIX threads cancellations or vice versa. The fact is that the POSIX thread programming model does not take C++ into account (it is based on C), and the C++ language standard only recently has begun to specify behavior in this area.The sample programs that follow involve simple C++ routines mixed with POSIX threads. Compiling and running these programs in both HP-UX using `aCC` (B3910B A.03.50) and SUSE 9.1 Linux with `g++` version 3.3.3 yields different results (see Example 6-6).

Example 6-6

Listing of exception_1.cc

```
#include <pthread.h>
#include <stdio.h>
#include <stdlib.h>
#include <string.h>

class FooClass {
    public:
    FooClass() {}
    ~FooClass() {
        pthread_cancel(pthread_self());
        pthread_testcancel();
    }
};

void* thread_func(void*) {
    try {
        FooClass cid;
        throw 1;
    }
```

32 www.gnu.org/software/gdb/documentation/

```
    catch (int&)
    {}

    return NULL;
}

int main() {
    pthread_t tid;

    pthread_create(&tid, NULL, thread_func, NULL);
    pthread_join(tid, NULL);
    return 0;
}
```

Compiling and running `exception_1.cc` on Linux yields the following:

```
$ g++ exception_1.cc -o exception_1 -lpthread -D_REENTRANT
$ ./exception_1
Aborted (core dumped)
```

Compiling and running `exception_1.cc` on HP-UX yields the following:

```
$ aCC exception_3.cc  -o exception_3 -lpthread -D_REENTRANT -g
$ ./exception_3
No core dumped
```

In this case, the `pthread_cancel` within the destructor of FooClass is considered an exception. *The C++ Programming Language,* 3rd Edition, by Bjarne Stroustrup (pp. 373, 378), mentions a rule about exceptions in destructors—just don't do it ! Dr. Stroustrup explains this in the following manner:

> During stack unwinding, the exception-handling mechanism exits a scope containing an object with a destructor. In this case, an exception may not escape from the destructor itself. If it does it is considered a failure in the exception handling mechanism and std::terminate is called.

Dr. Stroustrup offers a solution to catch the exception in the following code snippet. Unfortunately, this solution did not work in our case:[33]

```
~FooClass() {
             try {
           pthread_cancel(pthread_self());
           pthread_testcancel();
               }
        catch (...)
              {
```

---

33 Not because the solution is wrong for C++ applications, but because the C++ standard does not take into consideration POSIX threads semantics

```
            // do whatever
        throw;
        }
    }
```

One solution to try to close the cancellation hole within destructors is to disable cancellation, as in the following code snippet:

```
~FooClass() {
        int oldstate;
        // Disable cancellation at entry
        pthread_setcancelstate(PTHREAD_CANCEL_DISABLE,
                              &oldstate);
        pthread_cancel(pthread_self());
        pthread_testcancel();
        // Enable cancellation before exiting
        pthread_setcancelstate(PTHREAD_CANCEL_ENABLE,
                              &oldstate);
    }
```

Next, Example 6-7 shows a program that involves canceling a thread from another thread.

Example 6-7

Listing of exception_2.cc

```
#include <stdio.h>
#include <stdlib.h>
#include <unistd.h>
#include <errno.h>
#include <string.h>
#include <pthread.h>

pthread_mutex_t mutex;
static int instance_count;

class  FooBar
{
  public:
    FooBar();
    ~FooBar();
};

FooBar::FooBar()
{
  printf("thr#%u: creating FooBar.\n", pthread_self());
```

```
  {
    pthread_mutex_lock(&mutex);
    ++instance_count;
    pthread_mutex_unlock(&mutex);
  }
}

FooBar::~FooBar()
{
  printf("thr#%u: destroying FooBar.\n", pthread_self());

  {
    pthread_mutex_lock(&mutex);
    --instance_count;
    pthread_mutex_unlock(&mutex);
  }
}

static void* thread_func(void*)
{
  FooBar   f;
  pthread_t this_thread = pthread_self();

  printf("thread#%u: about to sleep...\n", pthread_self());

  sleep(10);
  return 0;
}

int main()
{
  pthread_t tid;
  int rc = 0;

  pthread_mutex_init(&mutex, NULL);

  if ((rc = pthread_create(&tid, NULL, thread_func, NULL)) != 0)
  {
    printf("pthread_create() returned %d. %s\n", errno);
    return 1;
  }

  printf("Main thread cancelling thr#%u\n", tid);

  if ((rc = pthread_cancel(tid)) != 0)
  {
    printf("pthread_cancel() : %s\n", errno);
  }

  pthread_join(tid, NULL);
  printf("Main thread join'ed with thr#%u\n", tid);
```

```
  pthread_mutex_lock(&mutex);
  if (instance_count == 0)
  {
    printf("OK. instance_count = 0\n");
  }
  else
  {
    printf("ERROR! instance_count=%d (expected 0)\n",
                    instance_count);
  }

  pthread_mutex_unlock(&mutex);

  return (0);
}
```

The program in Example 6-7 shows how thread cancellation, even when used outside of destructors, may show different behaviors on different platforms.

Compiling and running `exception_2.cc` on Linux yields the following:

```
$ g++ exception_2.cc -o exception_2 -lpthread -D_REENTRANT
$ ./exception_2
thr#1078156208: creating FooBar.
thread#1078156208: about to sleep...
Main thread cancelling thr#1078156208
thr#1078156208: destroying FooBar.
Main thread join'ed with thr#1078156208
OK. instance_count = 0
```

Compiling and running `exception_2.cc` on HP-UX yields the following:

```
$ aCC exception_2.cc  -o exception_2 -lpthread -D_REENTRANT -g
$ ./exception_2
thr#2: creating FooBar.
thread#2: about to sleep...
Main thread cancelling thr#2
Main thread join'ed with thr#2
ERROR! foobar_instcount=1 (expected 0)
```

The program for listing `exception_2.cc` seems to have been handled well on a Linux system but not on HP-UX. So, it seems Linux handles thread cancellation better in some way.

Example 6-8 involves the simple throwing of exceptions within threads. It also shows how mixing POSIX threads and C++ can yield different results on different platforms.

Example 6-8

Listing of exception_3.cc

```
#include <iostream>
#include <cstdio>
#include <cstdlib>
#include <pthread.h>
#include <unistd.h>
using namespace std;

void * thread_func(void *);

int main(int argc, char *argv[]) {
  pthread_t t;
  int i;
  int status;

  try
  {
    if( pthread_create(&t,NULL,thread_func,(void *)i) != 0) {
     cerr << "pthread_create failed" << endl;
     return 1;
    }

    pthread_join(t, NULL);
    cout << "end of thread " << endl;
  }
  catch(...)
  {
    cout << "unexpected exception" << endl;
  }
 }

void * thread_func(void *arg) {
  int i;
  for (i=0; i<4; i++) {
    sleep(1);
    try {
     cout << "throwing exception" << endl;
     throw "exception";
    }
    catch(char *st) {
     cout << "thread_func caught" << st << endl;
    }
  }
  return 0;
}
```

Compiling and running `exception_3.cc` on Linux yields the following:

```
$ g++ exception_3.cc -o exception_3 -lpthread -D_REENTRANT
$ ./exception_3
throwing check
Aborted (core dumped)
```

Compiling and running `exception_3.cc` on HP-UX yields the following:

```
$ aCC exception_3.cc -o exception_3 -lpthread -D_REENTRANT -g
$ ./exception_3
throwing check
Aborted (core dumped)
```

Changing `thread_func` to throw an integer rather than a char * changes the behavior of the program to complete its run without aborting:[34]

```
void * thread_func(void *arg) {
  int i;
  for (i=0; i<4; i++) {
    sleep(1);
    try {
     cout << "throwing exception" << endl;
     throw 1;
    }
    catch(int&) {
     cout << "thread_func caught" << endl;
    }
  }
  return 0;
}
```

Another change to make this work was to put a "catchall" catcher:

```
void * thread_func(void *arg) {
  int i;
  for (i=0; i<4; i++) {
    sleep(1);
    try {
     cout << "throwing exception" << endl;
     throw 1;
    }
    catch(...) {
     cout << "thread_func caught" << endl;
    }
  }
  return 0;
}
```

---

34 The sample `exception_3.cc` compiled and ran fine on AIX 5.3 using an xlC version 6 compiler.

In the case of a program listing `exception_3.cc`, the problem seems to be that of uncaught exceptions. Again referring to the book *The C++ Programming Language* by Bjarne Stroustrup (p. 381), Dr. Stroustrup explains that if an exception is thrown but not caught, the function `std::terminate` is called. Catching the exception prevents the core dump.

The preceeding program examples clearly show that C++ exceptions and POSIX threads do not mix well. The consensus from porting experience[35] indicates that there is no well-defined standard for how C++ needs to handle `pthread_cancellations` and exceptions, especially within destructors.[36] The one advice for porting engineers is to be aware of these differences and make sure to test error paths and cleanup handlers as thoroughly as the good path during the testing phase of the porting project.

6.10.5 Linking with Thread-Safe Libraries

Sometimes nonthreaded software applications may be linked to thread-safe libraries that call routines that start with `pthread_*`. In HP-UX, nonthreaded libraries that fail because of unresolved symbols such as `pthread_*` can be linked to the threads library `libpthreads` or `libcma` to resolve these symbols. However, linking such libraries to an application may result in overhead because of threading logic that accompanies linking of these threaded libraries. To resolve the performance degradation, HP implemented `pthread_*` calls as stubs in the C language library. Therefore, in HP-UX, nonthreaded applications that reference calls with `pthread_*` call the stubs in `libc`, thus avoiding performance overhead associated when linking with threads libraries.

On Linux, nonthreaded applications that link with thread-safe libraries must be linked with the LinuxThreads or Linux NPTL threads library to resolve symbols referenced within the linked libraries.

---

35 As well as comments from comp.programming.threads newsgroup

36 ANSI C++ does not recommend throwing exceptions in the constructor and destructor of a class whose instances may be defined globally (static-globally).

6.11 Signals

A signal indicates that an event has occurred. Typically, a process that receives a signal handles that signal through either a default mechanism or a signal handler. POSIX defines a set of signals and signal handling functions that are implemented in Linux.

6.11.1 Signal Actions

Every signal has an associated default action associated with it. A default action is what the Linux kernel does for the process when a signal arrives for that process. The default actions are as follows:

- Process termination
- Process core dump[37]
- Process stopped
- Process ignore signal

A process can also *install* a signal handler to run when a signal is delivered to it. The signal handler takes the place of the default action associated with each signal.

Signals occur as a consequence of an event. Here are some examples that can cause a signal to be sent to a process:

- A program error such as dividing by 0 or accessing an invalid address
- A child process terminating
- A timer expiring
- A user requesting to interrupt or terminate a process

6.11.2 Simple Signals

The simplest signal-handling function Linux supports is the original ISO C standard `signal()` API. It allows the calling process to change the action for a

---

37 In certain Linux systems, core dumping is turned off by default. To turn it on, use the `ulimit -c` command.

particular signal to either ignore or restore the default signal action or install a function that is called when that particular signal is received by the process.

Here is the definition of the `signal()` API as defined by the GNU/Linux signal(2) man page:

```
#include <signal.h>
typedef void (*sighandler_t)(int);

sighandler_t signal(int signum, sighandler_t handler);
```
[38]

Here is how the HP-UX man page for signal(2) defines `signal()`:

```
#include <signal.h>
void (*signal(int sig, void (*func)(int)))(int);
```

Although both Linux and HP-UX may seem to support both signal APIs, each implementation is different. Linux implements the BSD behavior; HP-UX implements UNIX V7 or System V behavior.

Example 6-9 demonstrates both behaviors.

Example 6-9

Listing of signal_1.c

```
#include <string.h>
#include <unistd.h>
#include <signal.h>

void handler (int signum)
{
  char buf[100];

  strcpy (buf, "In handler\n");
  buf[strlen(buf)+1] = '\0';

  write (2, buf, strlen(buf));
}

int main()
{
  signal(SIGINT, handler);
```

38 The name `sighandler_t` for this data type is a GNU extension.

```
  for(;;)
    sleep(1);

  return (0);
}
```

Compile and run on Linux:

```
$ c signal_1.c -o signal_1

$ signal_1
In handler                    <- Ctl-c
In handler                    <- Ctl-c
In handler                    <- Ctl-c
Ctl-\ (to kill the process)
Quit (core dumped)
```

The BSD behavior as implemented on Linux reinstalls the signal handler when the signal is received. This is why the handler is always called whenever the user presses Ctrl-c.

Compile and run on HP-UX:

```
$ aCC signal_1.c -o signal_1

$ ./signal_1
In handler                    <- Ctl-c
                              <- Ctl-c
$                             Program is terminated
```

Traditional System V semantics of the signal API returns the signal action to the default action after the signal is handled. Thus, a second Ctl-c sent to the process results in process termination. HP-UX provides a compatibility function to the BSD signal semantics through the `bsd_signal()` API.[39]

6.11.3 Signals Sent

Asynchronous signals sent by the kernel to a process as a result of an event may also differ in Linux compared to HP-UX. Example 6-10 illustrates this.

39 HP-UX man pages say this function may not be supported in the future.

Example 6-10

Listing of coredump_1.c

```
#include <stdio.h>

int func2(void *arg)
{
   return (5);
}

int (*fp)(void *);

int func1()
{
#ifndef _MAKE_CORE
   fp = func2;
#endif

   return (fp(NULL));
}

int
main()
{
   printf ("return from func1 = %d\n", func1());
}
```

Compile and run on Linux:

```
$ gcc coredump_1.c -o coredump_1 -D_MAKE_CORE

$ ./coredump_1
Segmentation fault (core dumped)


Compile and run on HP-UX
$ aCC coredump_1.c -o coredump_1 -D_MAKE_CORE

$ ./coredump_1
Bus error(coredump)
```

Although both programs resulted in process termination, the signal received by both processes differed. The Linux kernel sent a `SIGSEGV`; HP-UX sent a `SIGBUS`.

6.11.4 Signal Support in Linux

To get a list of supported signals in Linux, issue a `kill -l` (the letter *l*) command:

```
$ kill -l
 1) SIGHUP        2) SIGINT        3) SIGQUIT       4) SIGILL
 5) SIGTRAP       6) SIGABRT       7) SIGBUS        8) SIGFPE
 9) SIGKILL      10) SIGUSR1      11) SIGSEGV      12) SIGUSR2
13) SIGPIPE      14) SIGALRM      15) SIGTERM      17) SIGCHLD
18) SIGCONT      19) SIGSTOP      20) SIGTSTP      21) SIGTTIN
22) SIGTTOU      23) SIGURG       24) SIGXCPU      25) SIGXFSZ
26) SIGVTALRM    27) SIGPROF      28) SIGWINCH     29) SIGIO
30) SIGPWR       31) SIGSYS       35) SIGRTMIN     36) SIGRTMIN+1
37) SIGRTMIN+2   38) SIGRTMIN+3   39) SIGRTMIN+4   40) SIGRTMIN+5
41) SIGRTMIN+6   42) SIGRTMIN+7   43) SIGRTMIN+8   44) SIGRTMIN+9
45) SIGRTMIN+10  46) SIGRTMIN+11  47) SIGRTMIN+12  48) SIGRTMIN+13
49) SIGRTMIN+14  50) SIGRTMAX-14  51) SIGRTMAX-13  52) SIGRTMAX-12
53) SIGRTMAX-11  54) SIGRTMAX-10  55) SIGRTMAX-9   56) SIGRTMAX-8
57) SIGRTMAX-7   58) SIGRTMAX-6   59) SIGRTMAX-5   60) SIGRTMAX-4
61) SIGRTMAX-3   62) SIGRTMAX-2   63) SIGRTMAX-1   64) SIGRTMAX
```

This particular Linux implementation lists support for 30 non-real-time signals and 30 real-time signals.

Issuing the same command on an HP-UX v11 machine yields the following:

```
$ kill -l
 1) HUP
 2) INT
 3) QUIT
… other signal output deleted …
37) RTMIN
38) RTMIN+1
39) RTMIN+2
40) RTMIN+3
41) RTMAX-3
42) RTMAX-2
43) RTMAX-1
44) RTMAX
```

Although HP-UX supports most if not all of the POSIX-defined signals, it only supports eight real-time signals.

6.11.5 POSIX Signal-Catching Function

Linux provides the POSIX signal handling API `sigaction()`. Here is `sigaction` as defined by the POSIX standard:

```
#include <signal.h>

int sigaction(int sig, const struct sigaction *restrict act,
    struct sigaction *restrict oact);
```

The `sigaction` structure defined in signal.h follows the POSIX definition, as follows:

```
typedef struct {
void (*sa_handler)(int)        /* Pointer to a signal-catching
                                * function or one of the macros.
                                       * SIG_IGN or SIG_DFL.
                                       */

sigset_t sa_mask               /* Set of signals to be blocked
                                * during execution of the signal
                                * handling function.
                                */

      int sa_flags             /* Special flags.
                                */

      void (*sa_sigaction)(int, siginfo_t *, void *)
                               /* Pointer to a signal-catching
                                * function.
                                */
} sigaction_t;
```

The definition of the `sa_sigaction` function within the `sigaction_t` structure uses an argument that is of type `siginfo_t`, which is a structure that can be used to get more information about the signal's context. Here is a simplified version of the `siginfo_t` structure as defined in `bits/siginfo.h` in Linux:

```
typedef struct {
    int  si_signo    /* Signal number.  */
    int  si_errno    /* If non-zero, an errno value is associated
                      * with this signal, as defined in <errno.h>.
                      */
    int  si_code     /* Signal code.   */

    pid_t si_pid     /* Sending process ID. */
    uid_t si_uid     /* Real user ID of sending
                      * process.
                      */
    sigval si_value  /* Signal value.    */
} siginfo_t;
```

6.11.6 Signal Information

Information about how and why a signal was generated is called the signal's context or information. Within the `siginfo_t` structure, the following members, `si_signo` and `si_code`, can be used to obtain more information about the signal. For code examples that show how to use `siginfo_t`, refer to *Linux Application Development,* by Johnson and Troan.

Table 6-18 compares Linux and HP-UX implementations of the `si_signo` (Signal) and `si_code` values. Blank lines in the HP-UX and Linux columns mean the `si` code is not supported on the platforms.

TABLE 6-18
Values of si_code as Implemented in Linux 2.6 and HP-UX v11

Signal	Linux si_code[40]	HP-UX si_code[41]	Description
SIGILL	ILL_ILLOPC	ILL_ILLOPC	Illegal opcode
	ILL_ILLOPN		Illegal operand
	ILL_ILLADR		Illegal addressing mode
	ILL_ILLTRP		Illegal trap
	ILL_PRVOPC	ILL_PRVOPC	Privileged opcode
	ILL_PRVREG	ILL_PRVREG	Privileged register
	ILL_COPROC		Coprocessor error
	ILL_BADSTK		Internal stack error
		ILL_UNKNOWN	Unknown error
		ILL_ILLBRKINST	Break instruction trap
SIGFPE	FPE_INTDIV		Integer divide by 0
	FPE_INTOVF		Integer overflow
	FPE_FLTDIV		Floating point divide by 0
	FPE_FLTOVF	FPE_FLTOVF	Floating point overflow
	FPE_FLTUND		Floating point underflow

40 Referenced from bits/sigingo.h

41 Referenced from sys/siginfo.h HP-UX v11

Signal	Linux si_code	HP-UX si_code	Description
	FPE_FLTRES		Floating point invalid operation
	FPE_FLTINV		Subscript out of range
		FPE_COND	HP conditional trap
		FPE_ASSISTX	HP assist exception trap
		FPE_ASSISTEM	HP assist exception trap
		FPE_UNKNOWN	Unknown error
SIGSEGV	SEGV_MAPERR		Address not mapped to object
	SEGV_ACCERR		Invalid permissions for mapped object
		SEGV_UNKNOWN	Unknown error
SIGBUS	BUS_ADRALN		Bus error
	BUS_ADRERR		
	BUS_OBJERR		
		BUS_UNKNOWN	Unknown error
SIGTRAP	TRAP_BRKPT		Process breakpoint
	TRAP_TRACE		Process trace trap
		TRAP_UNKNOWN	Unknown error
SIGCHLD	CLD_EXITED		Child has exited
	CLD_KILLED		Child was killed
	CLD_DUMPED		Child terminated abnormally
	CLD_TRAPPED		Traced child has trapped
	CLD_STOPPED		Child has stopped
	CLD_CONTINUED		Stopped child has continued

Signal	Linux si_code	HP-UX si_code	Description
SIGPOLL	POLL_IN		Data input available
	POLL_OUT		Output buffers available
	POLL_MSG		Input message available
	POLL_ERR		I/O error
	POLL_PRI		High-priority input available
	POLL_HUP		Device disconnected

6.11.7 Signal Default Actions

Linux implements both POSIX real-time and non-real-time signals. As discussed earlier in this chapter, each signal has its own default action. Table 6-19 compares the signal default actions and the corresponding signal value as implemented in both Linux 2.6 and HP-UX v11.

TABLE 6-19
Signal Table for HP-UX and Linux Systems

Signal	HP-UX Default Action[42]	HP-UX Signal Number	Linux Default Action[43]	Linux Signal Number
SIGABRT	Abnormal termination of the process. Core dump.	6	Core dump	6
SIGALRM	The process is terminated. Status is made available to `wait()` and `waitpid()`.	14	Terminate	14
SIGFPE	Abnormal termination of the process. Core dump.	8	Core dump	8
SIGHUP	The process is terminated. Status is made available to `wait()` and `waitpid()`.	1	Terminate	1

42 HP-UX signal(5) man pages HP-UX 11i version 2: August 2003

43 This was taken from the comment section in linux/kernel/signal.c version 2.6.10.

Signal	HP-UX Default Action	HP-UX Signal Number	Linux Default Action	Linux Signal Number
`SIGILL`	Abnormal termination of the process. Core dump.	4	Core dump	4
`SIGINT`	The process is terminated. Status is made available to `wait()` and `waitpid()`.	2	Terminate	2
`SIGKILL`	The process is terminated. Status is made available to `wait()` and `waitpid()`.	9	Terminate (always)	9
`SIGPIPE`	The process is terminated. Status is made available to `wait()` and `waitpid()`.	13	Terminate	13
`SIGQUIT`	Abnormal termination of the process. Core dump.	3	Core dump	3
`SIGSEGV`	Abnormal termination of the process. Core dump.	11	Core dump	11
`SIGTERM`	The process is terminated. Status is made available to `wait()` and `waitpid()`.	15	Terminate	15
`SIGUSR1`	The process is terminated. Status is made available to `wait()` and `waitpid()`.	16	Terminate	10
`SIGUSR2`	The process is terminated. Status is made available to `wait()` and `waitpid()`.	17	Terminate	12
`SIGCHLD`	Ignore the signal.	18	Ignore	17
`SIGCONT`	Continue the process if it is stopped; otherwise, ignore the signal.	26	Ignore	18
`SIGSTOP`	Stop the process.	24	Stop (always)	19
`SIGTSTP`	Stop the process.	25	Stop	20
`SIGTTIN`	Stop the process.	27	Stop	21

Signal	HP-UX Default Action	HP-UX Signal Number	Linux Default Action	Linux Signal Number
`SIGTTOU`	Stop the process.	28	Stop	22
`SIGBUS`	Abnormal termination of the process. Core dump.	10	Core dump	7
`SIGPOLL`[44]	The process is terminated. Status is made available to `wait()` and `waitpid()`.	22		29
`SIGPROF`	The process is terminated. Status is made available to `wait()` and `waitpid()`.	21	Terminate	27
`SIGSYS`	Abnormal termination of the process. Core dump.	12	Core dump	31
`SIGTRAP`	Abnormal termination of the process. Core dump.	5	Core dump	5
`SIGURG`	Ignore the signal.	29	Ignore	23
`SIGVTALRM`	The process is terminated. Status is made available to `wait()` and `waitpid()`.	20	Terminate	26
`SIGXCPU`	Abnormal termination of the process. Core dump.	33	Core dump	24
`SIGXFSZ`	Abnormal termination of the process. Core dump.	34	Core dump	25
`SIGRTMIN`	The process is terminated. Status is made available to `wait()` and `waitpid()`.	37	Terminate	35
`SIGRTMAX`	The process is terminated. Status is made available to `wait()` and `waitpid()`.	44	Terminate	64

44 Equivalent to SIGIO in both HP-UX and Linux

> NOTE In HP-UX, a core file is created only if the following conditions are met:
>
> - The real user ID and the effective user ID of the receiving process are equal.
> - The real group ID and the effective group ID of the receiving process are equal.
> - A regular file named core does not exist in the current directory, or if it exists, it is writable.

In Linux, a core file is created in the current directory. On most Linux systems, however, core file creation is disabled by default. To enable core file creation, set a `ulimit` flag `-c` to a specified file size limit, as follows:

```
$ ulimit -c 50000
```

6.12 HP-UX System Calls and Linux Equivalents

The 2.6.x release of Linux continues to offer wider support for POSIX APIs that were not previously supported in older Linux releases. This section and the section on Linux and HP-UX APIs compare HP-UX system calls and library APIs to their Linux equivalents. Linux 2.6 has come a long way in providing the best support for the most common as well as optional POSIX APIs.

6.12.1 Determining POSIX API Support

Depending on the installed version of Linux 2.6 on your platform, some optional POSIX APIs may not be supported. Upgrading to later releases of Linux 2.6 is the only option to get that support. An example of this is the optional POSIX APIs for message queues. Programatically, you can check API support by using the `sysconf` call.

Example 6-11 checks for `_POSIX_MESSAGE_PASSING` to check for message queue support. Note that Linux and HP-UX may return different values for the same POSIX option.

Example 6-11

Listing of samp_conf.c

```
#include <unistd.h>

int
main(int argc, char * argv[])
{
    long ret = 0;

    ret=sysconf(_SC_MESSAGE_PASSING);
    switch (ret)
    {
        case -1:
            printf("Invalid Option: errno %d\n", errno);
            break;
        case 0:
            printf("Option MAY BE supported\n");
            break;
        default:
            printf("Option supported %ld\n", ret);
            break;
    }
}
```

The `samp_conf.c` listing compiled and run on a Linux machine that supports `_POSIX_MESSAGE_PASSING` yields the following:

```
$ make samp_sysconf.c
cc    samp_sysconf.c   -o samp_sysconf
$ ./samp_sysconf
Option supported 200112
```

The same program compiled and run on HP-UX yields the following:

```
$ ./samp_sysconf
Option supported 1
```

The POSIX API `sysconf`[45] allows an application to test at compile time or runtime whether certain options are supported. In the preceding runtime example, the argument to `sysconf` is the `_SC` equivalent of the POSIX option that the programmer is intereseted in finding (whether `_POSIX_MESSAGE_PASSING` is supported on the current Linux installation).

---

45 See sysconf(3) for a more detailed description of the API.

Another programmatic way to check for POSIX options is shown in Example 6-12.

Example 6-12

Listing of test_posix.c

```
#include <unistd.h>
#include <limits.h>
#include <stdio.h>

main()
{
#ifdef _POSIX_MESSAGE_PASSING
     printf("  POSIX.4 Message Queues are supported.\n");
     #ifdef _POSIX_MQ_OPEN_MAX
      printf("    _POSIX_MQ_OPEN_MAX=%d Max # of message queues per
process.\n",_POSIX_MQ_OPEN_MAX);
     #else
      printf("    No _POSIX_MQ_OPEN_MAX value exists.\n");
     #endif
     #ifdef _POSIX_MQ_PRIO_MAX
      printf("    _POSIX_MQ_PRIO_MAX=%d Max # of message
priorities.\n",_POSIX_MQ_PRIO_MAX);
     #else
      printf("    No _POSIX_MQ_PRIO_MAX value exists.\n");
     #endif
#else
     printf("  POSIX.4 Message Queues are not supported.\n");
#endif
}
```

Example 6-12 compiled and run on a Linux machine that supports `_POSIX_MESSAGE_PASSING` yields the following output:

```
$ make test_posix
cc    test_posix.c   -o test_posix
$ ./test_posix
  POSIX.4 Message Queues are supported.
   _POSIX_MQ_OPEN_MAX=8 Max # of message queues per process.
   _POSIX_MQ_PRIO_MAX=32 Max # of message priorities.
```

The same program compiled and run on HP-UX v11 yields the following output:

```
$ ./test_posix
  POSIX.4 Message Queues are supported.
   _POSIX_MQ_OPEN_MAX=8 Max # of message queues per process.
   _POSIX_MQ_PRIO_MAX=32 Max # of message priorities.
```

Table 6-20 shows the different POSIX options[46] and their _SC equivalents along with the corresponding APIs that are affected if the POSIX option is supported.

TABLE 6-20
POSIX Options and Corresponding Affected APIs

POSIX Option	_SC Equivalent	Affected APIs
_POSIX_ADVISORY_INFO	_SC_ADVISORY_INFO	posix_fadvise, posix_fallocate, posix_memalign, posix_madvise
_POSIX_ASYNCHRONOUS_IO	_SC_ASYNCHRONOUS_IO	aio_cancel, aio_error, aio_fsync, aio_read, aio_return, aio_suspend, aio_write, lio_listio
_POSIX_BARRIERS	_SC_BARRIERS	pthread_barrier_destroy, pthread_barrier_init, pthread_barrier_wait, pthread_barrierattr_destroy, pthread_barrierattr_init
POSIX_CHOWN_RESTRICTED		chown, fchown
_POSIX_CLOCK_SELECTION	_SC_CLOCK_SELECTION	pthread_condattr_getclock, pthread_condattr_setclock, clock_nanosleep
_POSIX_FSYNC	_SC_FSYNC	fsync
_POSIX_IPV6	_SC_IPV6	IPV6 is supported
_POSIX_JOB_CONTROL	_SC_JOB_CONTROL	setpgid, tcdrain, tcflush, tcgetpgrp, tcsendbreak, tcsetattr, tcsetpgrp
_POSIX_MAPPED_FILES	_SC_MAPPED_FILES	mmap, msync, munmap
_POSIX_MEMLOCK	_SC_MEMLOCK	mlockall, munlockall
_POSIX_MEMLOCK_RANGE	_SC_MEMLOCK_RANGE	mlock, munlock
_POSIX_MEMORY_PROTECTION	_SC_MEMORY_PROTECTION	mq_close, mq_getattr, mq_notify, mq_open, mq_receive, mq_send, mq_setattr, mq_unlink

46 See posixoptions(7) on the Linux man pages for more information.

POSIX Option	_SC Equivalent	Affected APIs
_POSIX_MONOTONIC_CLOCK	_SC_MONOTONIC_CLOCK	aio_suspend, clock_getres, clock_gettime, clock_settime, timer_create
_POSIX_PRIORITIZED_IO	_SC_PRIORITIZED_IO	aio_read, aio_write
_POSIX_PRIORITY_SCHEDULING	_SC_PRIORITY_SCHEDULING	sched_get_priority_max, sched_get_priority_min, sched_getparam, sched_getscheduler, sched_rr_get_interval, sched_setparam, sched_setscheduler, sched_yield
_POSIX_SPAWN		posix_spawnattr_getschedparam, posix_spawnattr_getschedpolicy, posix_spawnattr_setschedparam, posix_spawnattr_setschedpolicy
_POSIX_RAW_SOCKETS		getsockopt, setsockopt
_POSIX_READER_WRITER_LOCKS	_SC_READER_WRITER_LOCKS	pthread_rwlock_destroy, pthread_rwlock_init, pthread_rwlock_rdlock, pthread_rwlock_tryrdlock, pthread_rwlock_trywrlock, pthread_rwlock_unlock, pthread_rwlock_wrlock, pthread_rwlockattr_destroy, pthread_rwlockattr_init
_POSIX_REALTIME_SIGNALS	_SC_REALTIME_SIGNALS	sigqueue, sigtimedwait, sigwaitinfo
_POSIX_REGEXP	_SC_REGEXP	regcomp, regerror, regexec, regfree
_POSIX_SAVED_IDS	_SC_SAVED_IDS	exec, kill, seteuid, setegid, setgid, setuid
_POSIX_SEMAPHORES	_SC_SEMAPHORES	sem_close, sem_destroy, sem_getvalue, sem_init, sem_open, sem_post, sem_trywait, sem_unlink, sem_wait

POSIX Option	_SC Equivalent	Affected APIs
_POSIX_SHARED_MEMORY_ OBJECTS	_SC_SHARED_MEMORY_ OBJECTS	mmap, munmap, shm_open, shm_unlink
_POSIX_SHELL	_SC_SHELL	system
_POSIX_SPAWN	_SC_SPAWN	posix_spawn, posix_spawn_file_actions_ addclose, posix_spawn_file_actions_ adddup2, posix_spawn_file_actions_ addopen, posix_spawn_file_actions_ destroy, posix_spawn_file_actions_init, posix_spawnattr_destroy, posix_spawnattr_getsigdefault, posix_spawnattr_getflags, posix_spawnattr_getpgroup, posix_spawnattr_getsigmask, posix_spawnattr_init, posix_spawnattr_setsigdefault, posix_spawnattr_setflags, posix_spawnattr_setpgroup, posix_spawnattr_setsigmask, posix_spawnp
_POSIX_SPIN_LOCKS	_SC_SPIN_LOCKS	pthread_spin_destroy, pthread_spin_init, pthread_spin_lock, pthread_spin_trylock, pthread_spin_unlock
_POSIX_SPORADIC_SERVER	_SC_SPORADIC_SERVER	The scheduling policy SCHED_SPORADIC is supported. This option implies the _POSIX_PRIORITY_SCHEDULING option. Affected functions are sched_ setparam, sched_setscheduler.

POSIX Option	_SC Equivalent	Affected APIs
_POSIX_SYNCHRONIZED_IO	_SC_SYNCHRONIZED_IO	open, msync, fsync, fdata, sync
_POSIX_THREAD_ATTR_ STACKADDR	_SC_THREAD_ATTR_ STACKADDR	pthread_attr_getstack, pthread_attr_getstackaddr, pthread_attr_setstack, pthread_attr_setstackaddr
_POSIX_THREAD_ATTR_ STACKSIZE	_SC_THREAD_ATTR_ STACKSIZE	pthread_attr_getstack, pthread_attr_getstacksize, pthread_attr_setstack, pthread_attr_setstacksize
_POSIX_THREAD_CPUTIME	_SC_THREAD_CPUTIME	pthread_getcpuclockid, clock_getres, clock_gettime, clock_settime, timer_create
_POSIX_THREAD_PRIO_ INHERIT	_SC_THREAD_PRIO_ INHERIT	pthread_mutexattr_getprotocol, pthread_mutexattr_setprotocol
_POSIX_THREAD_PRIO_ PROTECT	_SC_THREAD_PRIO_ PROTECT	pthread_mutex_getprioceiling, pthread_mutex_setprioceiling, pthread_mutexattr_ getprioceiling, pthread_mutexattr_getprotocol

6.12.2 Determining Linux Kernel Version

When new Linux versions are announced, sometimes the announcement mentions support for new features or optional standards. At the time of this writing, Linux version 2.6.6 was announced. That announcement mentioned support for message queues (that is, _POSIX_MESSAGE_PASSING).

The easiest way to determine the version of the running Linux kernel is to cat the file /proc/version.

The following is from a SUSE 9.1 installation on IA32:

```
$ cat /proc/version
Linux version 2.6.4-52-smp (geeko@buildhost) (gcc version 3.3.3 (SuSE Linux)) #1
SMP Wed Apr 7 02:11:20 UTC 2004
```

Running Example 6-12 on this Linux server yields the following:

```
$ ./test_posix
POSIX.4 Message Queues are not supported.
```

This version of Linux *does not support* message queues.

The following is from a RHEL4 running on a POWER5:

```
$ cat /proc/version
Linux version 2.6.9-5.EL (bhcompile@sizzler.build.redhat.com) (gcc version 3.4.3
20041212 (Red Hat 3.4.3-9.EL4)) #1 SMP Wed Jan 5 19:23:58 EST 2005
```

Running Example 6-12 on this Linux server yields the following:

```
$ ./test_posix
  POSIX.4 Message Queues are supported.
   _POSIX_MQ_OPEN_MAX=8 Max # of message queues per process.
   _POSIX_MQ_PRIO_MAX=32 Max # of message priorities.
```

This version of Linux *does support* message queues.

During the analysis phase of the porting project, porting engineers may run some tools that look for API incompatibilities between HP-UX and Linux. Some may try to build the application on Linux and look through the build log for errors. However, sometimes tools and build logs are not enough. When an incompatibility is found, you may want to know whether there is an equivalent on Linux (see Table C-3 in Appendix C, "HP-UX to Linux Reference Tables").

6.13 System Libraries

When you are building the source application on Linux, link errors may result because of missing libraries. System libraries may be named differently on Linux or simply don't exist because the APIs are already in the standard `libc` library. Table 6-21 compares HP-UX system libraries to Linux system libraries in terms of their functionalities.

TABLE 6-21
Linux and HP-UX System Library Comparison Table

Description	HP-UX	Linux
Curses	`libxcurses`	`libncurses`
Database APIs	`libc`, `libdbm`	`libdb*`
Security APIs	`libsec (pwd.h)`	`libc (shadow.h)`[47]

Socket APIs	`libxnet (UNIX95/98)`
	`t_accept()`, `t_alloc()`,
	`t_bind()`, `t_close() ...`
	
	`libc (BSD4.3)`
	`endservent()`,
	`gethostbyaddr()`,
	`gethostname()`,
	`getnetbyaddr() ...`
		`libc (BSD4.3)`

RPC APIs	`libnsl`	`libc`

Math	`libm (math.h)`
	`copysign`, `copysignf`
	`ldexp`, `modf`, `scalbn ...`
		`libm`

XDR APIs	`librpcsvc`	`libc`
Real-time priority	`rtprio`	`libc`
Scientific Library	Various (HP MLIB)	`libgsl` (GNU Scientific Library)

GNU `libc` includes a variety of support libraries. See Chapter 3 for a complete listing of the libraries included in the GNU `libc`.

6.14 GNU Scientific Library

HP-UX provides scientific functionalities through its MLIB libraries, which cover BLAS 1, 2, and 3 subroutines, sparse BLAS subroutines, a collection of commonly used dense and sparse linear system solvers, including LAPACK, ScaLAPACK, and SuperLU_DIST; full METIS functionality; Fast Fourier Transforms (FFTs); and

47 PAM for Linux may be another option. See www.linuxdocs.org/HOWTOs/User-Authentication-HOWTO/index.html and www.kernel.org/pub/linux/libs/pam/.

convolutions.[48] Scientific functionality in Linux is supported through the GNU Scientific Library (GSL).

The GSL is a collection of routines for numeric computing. The routines were written from scratch in C and present a modern API for C programmers, allowing wrappers to be written for high-level languages. The source code is distributed under the GNU General Public License.

The library covers a wide range of topics in numeric computing. Routines are available for the following areas:

Complex Numbers	Roots of Polynomials	Quasi-Random Sequences
Special Functions	Vectors and Matrices	Statistics
Permutations	Combinations	N-Tuples
Sorting	BLAS Support	Simulated Annealing
Linear Algebra	CBLAS Library	Interpolation
Fast Fourier Transforms	Eigensystems	Chebyshev Approximations
Random Numbers	Quadrature	Discrete Hankel Transforms
Random Distributions	Differential Equations	Minimization
Histograms	Numerical Differentiation	Physical Constants
Monte Carlo Integration	Series Acceleration	Root Finding
Least-Squares Fitting	IEEE Floating-Point	

The use of these routines is described in the GSL manual;[49] each chapter provides detailed definitions of the functions, followed by example programs and references to the articles on which the algorithms are based.

6.15 HP-UX and Linux APIs

Linux 2.6 comes with the latest GNU C library. As of this writing, the latest release of the GNU `glibc` is 2.3.3. As seen in the preceding section, the GNU `libc`

---

48 http://docs.hp.com/en/B6061-96024/ch01s02.html

49 www.gnu.org/software/gss/manual/

distribution installs several libraries, which may come in both archived and shared form. The main objective of this section is to compare HP-UX APIs as documented in the HP-UX version 11 man pages and GNU `libc` as referenced through available online manuals, header files, and Linux man pages.

Note that APIs that come standard on HP-UX have not been implemented on Linux through the GNU `libc` project but through other open-source projects. An example of this is the **SLP** (Service Location Protocol) library routines, which for Linux are handled by the OpenSLP project.[50]

6.15.1 glibc Version

The C library used on every Linux system is the GNU `libc`. Much of the interface of the GNU `libc` has been determined by the history of UNIX and various standards. The GNU `libc` supports most standards that modern UNIX systems support today, such as ISO C and POSIX standards. The GNU `libc` also supports features of the two major UNIX variants—namely, BSD and System V. To learn what version of `glibc` you have on your installation, run `/lib/libc.so`. Just type the following on the command line:

```
$ ./libc.so.6
GNU C Library stable release version 2.3.3, by Roland McGrath et al.
Copyright (C) 2004 Free Software Foundation, Inc.
This is free software; see the source for copying conditions.
There is NO warranty; not even for MERCHANTABILITY or FITNESS FOR A
PARTICULAR PURPOSE.
Compiled by GNU CC version 3.4.2 20041017 (Red Hat 3.4.2-6.fc3).
Compiled on a Linux 2.4.20 system on 2004-10-27.
Available extensions:
    GNU libio by Per Bothner
    crypt add-on version 2.1 by Michael Glad and others
    Native POSIX Threads Library by Ulrich Drepper et al
    The C stubs add-on version 2.1.2.
    BIND-8.2.3-T5B
    NIS(YP)/NIS+ NSS modules 0.19 by Thorsten Kukuk
    Glibc-2.0 compatibility add-on by Cristian Gafton
    GNU Libidn by Simon Josefsson
Thread-local storage support included.
For bug reporting instructions, please see:
<http://www.gnu.org/software/libc/bugs.html>.
```

50 www.openslp.org

Note that the `libc.so` output uses the Native POSIX Threads library by Ulrich Drepper. On some Linux installations, `libc.so` may still be using the POSIX Threads library by Xavier Leroy, as shown by the following output:

```
$ ./libc.so.6
GNU C Library stable release version 2.3.3 (20040405), by Roland McGrath et al.
Copyright (C) 2004 Free Software Foundation, Inc.
This is free software; see the source for copying conditions.
There is NO warranty; not even for MERCHANTABILITY or FITNESS FOR A
PARTICULAR PURPOSE.
Configured for i686-suse-linux.
Compiled by GNU CC version 3.3.3 (SUSE Linux).
Compiled on a Linux 2.6.4 system on 2004-04-05.
Available extensions:
    GNU libio by Per Bothner
    crypt add-on version 2.1 by Michael Glad and others
    linuxthreads-0.10 by Xavier Leroy
    GNU Libidn by Simon Josefsson
    NoVersion patch for broken glibc 2.0 binaries
    BIND-8.2.3-T5B
    libthread_db work sponsored by Alpha Processor Inc
    NIS(YP)/NIS+ NSS modules 0.19 by Thorsten Kukuk
Thread-local storage support included.
Report bugs using the `glibcbug' script to <bugs@gnu.org>.
```

6.15.2 glibc Conformance

GNU `glibc` distributes a conformance[51] report detailing adherence to various standards. This list also shows where GNU `libc` needs to be improved. As of this writing, the conformance report shows that GNU `libc` passes conformance header checks to FIPS, POSIX90, XPG3, XPG4, POSIX96, UNIX98, ANSI, C89/99, and ISO 9899 standards. All major distributions' `glibc` implementations also support the LSB.

Table C-4 in Appendix C shows HP-UX calls and their equivalent API calls on Linux as implemented through the GNU `libc` distribution.

6.15.3 Some HP-UX Nonportable Programming Practices

As the preceding comparison tables of system and library APIs show, some HP-UX calls and programming practices are not portable to the Linux platform. Table 6-22

---

51 Available at http://sources.redhat.com/cgi-bin/cvsweb.cgi/libc/CONFORMANCE?cvsroot=glibc

highlights some of the top incompatible APIs that may be encountered when porting HP-UX applications to Linux.

TABLE 6-22
Porting Practices on HP-UX That May Need Significant Porting Effort on Linux

HP-UX	Linux
Use of `pstat` API	Port using `/procfs` and `sysinfo` API.
Use of `nlist`	Look at `lsof` source code for `nlist_private` example.
Use of `ttrace`	Port using `ptrace`.
Reading `/dev/kmem` directly	Port using `/procfs` and `sysinfo` API.
Use of System V release 4 streams	Use open source: Linux Streams (LiS) (www.gcom.com/home/linux/lis/).[52]
Sse of Service Level Protocol	Use open-source OpenSLP.
Use of XTI/TLI	Use open-source XTI/TLI library and TLI modules (www.openss7.org/).

Caution is advised when using the equivalent Linux solutions presented. This list is presented only as a reference and not as officially recommended solutions. Investigate the viability of the solutions before planning to implement them in your applications.

6.16 Interprocess Communications

Both HP-UX and Linux support System V and POSIX 1003.1 forms of interprocess communications and synchronization. This section covers pipes, FIFOs, POSIX message queues, POSIX semaphores, POSIX shared memory, System V shared memory, System V messages, and System V semaphores.

52 Use with caution because, at the time of this writing, code may not be maintained.

6.16.1 Pipes

A pipe is a technique used to communicate between two threads in a process or between parent and child processes. When a process calls `fork`, file descriptors are copied to its new child process. As a result, the parent can communication with the child. A pipe can be created by calling the `pipe` function:

```
#include <unistd.h>

int pipe (int fildes [2]);
```

In both Linux and HP-UX, `pipe()` returns two file descriptors: `fildes[0]` and `fildes[1]`, wherein `fildes[0]` is opened for reading and `fildes[1]` is opened for writing.

The `popen` and `pclose` functions are both supported in HP-UX and Linux:

```
#include <stdio.h>

FILE *popen(const char *command, const char *mode);
int pclose(FILE *stream);
```

The call to the `popen` function creates a pipe between the calling process and the program specified by *`command`* in the child process. The calling process can either read from or write to the pipe, as specified by the *`mode`* argument. The return value is a stream pointer such that you can write to the standard input of the *`command`*, if the mode is `w`, by writing to the file stream, and you can read from the standard output of the command, if the mode is `r`, by reading from the file stream.

6.16.2 FIFOs

A first-in, first-out (FIFO) file (also known as *named pipes*) is a pipe that has a name in the filesystem associated with it. This enables the pipe to be open or closed by any processes. The processes on either end of the pipe need not be related to each other.

You can create a FIFO programmatically by calling the `mkfifo` function:

```
#include <sys/types.h>
#include <sys/stat.h>

int mkfifo(const char *pathname, mode_t mode);
```

This function works the same way on both HP-UX and Linux. A FIFO can have multiple readers and writers. A write request of `PIPE_BUF` bytes or less from a writer is guaranteed not to be interleaved with data from other processes. On Linux, PIPE_BUF is 4096 bytes,[53] whereas it is 8192 bytes on HP-UX.[54]

6.16.3 POSIX Message Queues

Messages enable multiple processes to send formatted data streams to arbitrary processes. On Linux, POSIX Message is supported only when the option _POSIX_MESSAGE_PASSING is defined. To determine whether the Linux system has the option _POSIX_MESSAGE_PASSING, issue the following command:

```
$ getconf _POSIX_MESSAGE_PASSING
200112
```

Linux includes:

```
#include <mqueue.h>
```

Using the API sysconf within a program can also determine whether a POSIX option exists on a particular Linux installation.[55]

Table 6-23 compares message queue interfaces between HP-UX and Linux.

TABLE 6-23
Comparison Table of HP-UX and Linux POSIX Message Queue APIs

HP-UX	Linux	Description
mq_close	mq_close	Close a message queue.
mq_getattr	mq_getattr	Get message queue attributes.
mq_notify	mq_notify	Notify process (or thread) that a message is available on a queue.
mq_open	mq_open	Open a message queue.
mq_receive	mq_receive	Receive a message from a message queue.
mq_send	mq_send	Send a message to a message queue.
mq_setattr	mq_setattr	Set/get message queue attributes.

53 /usr/include/linux/limits.h

54 /usr/include/limits.h

55 Refer to the "Determining POSIX API Support" section of this chapter.

HP-UX	Linux	Description
None	`mq_timedreceive`	Receive a message from a message queue; stop waiting if the specified timeout expires.
None	`mq_timedsend`	Send a message to a message queue; stop blocking on full message queue if the specified timeout expires.
`mq_unlink`	`mq_unlink`	Remove a message queue.

6.16.4 POSIX Semaphores

You can determine POSIX semaphore support on a Linux system by using the `genconf` command or the `sysconf` API. To determine whether POSIX semaphore support is present, use the `getconf` command to get the following output:

```
$ getconf _POSIX_SEMAPHORES
200112
```

Linux includes:

```
#include <semaphore.h>
```

Table 6-24 compares POSIX semaphore interfaces in HP-UX and Linux.

TABLE 6-24
Comparison Table of HP-UX and Linux POSIX Semaphore APIs

HP-UX	Linux	Description
`sem_close`	`sem_close`	Close a named semaphore.
`sem_destroy`	`sem_destroy`	Destroy an unnamed semaphore.
`sem_getvalue`	`sem_getvalue`	Get the value of a semaphore.
`sem_init`	`sem_init`	Initialize an unnamed semaphore.
`sem_open`	`sem_open`	Initialize/open a named semaphore.
`sem_post`	`sem_post`	Increment the count of a semaphore.
None	`sem_timedwait`	Lock a semaphore, but stop waiting when the specified timeout expires.
`sem_trywait`	`sem_trywait`	Acquire or wait for a semaphore.
`sem_unlink`	`sem_unlink`	Remove a named semaphore.
`sem_wait`	`sem_wait`	Acquire or wait for a semaphore.

6.16.5 POSIX Shared Memory

HP-UX supports both `shm_open` and `shm_unlink` shared memory functions. On Linux, these two functions are available in `glibc` version 2.2 and later. To use these functions, specify the `-lrt` flag with the compiler.

Linux includes:

```
#include <sys/types>
#include <sys/mman.h>
```

Table 6-25 shows a comparison between HP-UX and Linux supported shared memory APIs.

TABLE 6-25
Comparison Table of HP-UX and Linux POSIX Shared Memory APIs

HP-UX	Linux	Description
`shm_open`	`shm_open`	Open a shared memory object.
`shm_unlink`	`shm_unlink`	Remove a shared memory object.

Sometimes the default shared memory configured on a Linux system may not be enough for applications. To modify shared memory configuration in Linux, use the following methods:

```
sysctl -w kernel.shmmax=[number of bytes]
```
[56]

```
echo [number of bytes] > /proc/sys/kernel/shmmax
```

6.16.6 System V Shared Memory

Both HP-UX and Linux support System V shared memory interfaces. Table 6-26 compares HP-UX and Linux interfaces.

Linux includes:

```
#include <sys/types.h>
#include <sys/shm.h>
```

56 See the man page for `sysctl` or `/etc/sysctl` for more information.

TABLE 6-26
Comparison Between HP-UX and Linux System Memory Interfaces

HP-UX	Linux	Description
`shmat`	`shmat`	Attach the shared memory segment to the data segment of the calling process.
`shmctl`	`shmctl`	Shared memory control.
`shmdt`	`shmdt`	Detach the shared memory segment.
`shmop`	`shmop`	Shared memory operation.
`shmget`	`shmget`	Get shared memory segment identifier.

Note that some flags (`shmflags`) used in `shmget` and `shmat` may have arguments that differ slightly between implementations.

6.16.7 System V Messages

Both HP-UX and Linux support System V messages. The one difference noted is the `msgqid_ds` structure used in the `msgctl` API, which is different on each platform.

Linux includes:

```
#include <sys/types.h>
#include <sys/ipc.h>
#include <sys/msg.h>
```

Table 6-27 compares HP-UX and Linux System V message APIs.

TABLE 6-27
Comparison Table of HP-UX and Linux Messages APIs

HP-UX	Linux	Description
`msgctl`	`msgctl`	Message control operation. The `msgqid_ds` structure on HP-UX and Linux is not the same.
`msgget`	`msgget`	Get message queue.
`msgrcv`	`msgrcv`	Message receive operation.
`msgsnd`	`msgsnd`	Message send operation.

The default maximum size of a message queue (msg_qbytes) on Linux is set to the system parameter MSGMNB (16384 bytes). You can raise the msg_qbytes value beyond MSGMNB by using the msgctl function with the appropriate privileges. On Linux, the maximum size for message text is set to MSGMAX (8192 bytes).

6.16.8 System V Semaphores

Both HP-UX and Linux support System V semaphores. The one difference noted is the semid_ds structure used in the semctl API, which is different on each platform.

Linux includes:

```
#include <sys/types.h>
#include <sys/ipc.h>
#include <sys/sem.h>
```

Table 6-28 compares HP-UX and Linux semaphore APIs.

TABLE 6-28
Comparion Table of HP-UX and Linux Semaphore APIs

HP-UX	Linux	Description
semctl	semctl	Semaphore control operation.
		The semid_ds structure used in semctl is different for HP-UX and Linux.
semget	semget	Get set of semaphores.
semop	semop	Semaphore operation.
semtimedop	semtimedop	Semaphore operation with time limit.

As you can see, Linux provides most if not all interprocess communication facilities available from HP-UX. This makes porting to Linux as easy as just recompiling source code.

6.17 Summary

The porting work is considered complete when two objectives are met. The first objective is to make sure all the necessary objects and executables of the application are produced. The second objective is to make sure the ported application, including all executables produced, runs and stays up long enough to pass basic unit testing. If the application passes basic unit testing, it is then passed on to the next phase of the project, testing and debugging. Here are some important highlights discussed in this chapter:

- Linux 2.6 supports the latest and most common industry standards from POSIX, ISO, and SUS, making it more compatible with other UNIX platforms. This allows applications running on other operating systems (such as HP-UX) that adhere to these standards to be ported to Linux with as little change as possible.
- The latest GNU C and C++ compilers offer the same functionalities provided by HP-UX compilers. The main task for porting engineers is to find and match the equivalent compiler switches in the GNU compilers with those used in the HP-UX application build environment. Also be aware that the C compilers on both platforms by default compile in extended mode, which may cause incompatibilities.
- Library versioning support framework on HP-UX is different from on Linux. Porting engineers must adapt the application to one of the types of library versioning supported on Linux.
- Linux 2.6 supports a version of dynamic linking that can easily provide equivalent support for the type of dynamic linking provided on the HP-UX platform.
- Linux offers a variety of open-source shells that provide support functionality equivalent to shells on UNIX platforms. Shell scripts that run on HP-UX written to use `ksh`, `csh`, or `bsh` can be easily ported to run on Linux.
- Some APIs that Linux provides may reside in different libraries. Differences in systems library names and locations must be taken into account when linking in Linux.
- Overall, the APIs and system calls that exist on HP-UX already exist in the standard Linux distribution. For those APIs or system calls supported on

HP-UX that do not exist in the standard Linux distribution, most have equivalent support through other open-source initiatives referenced in this chapter.

This chapter discussed issues that may be encountered during a porting project. Although some applications are relatively easy to port because of their inherently portable characteristics, some applications written to use HP-UX extensions take a little more porting effort. Overall, Linux 2.6 has improved its capabiltities to readily accept software applications to run on it. Porting to Linux has never been easier. New features such as a preemptive kernel and support for better threads scheduling makes Linux an operating system that is truly ready for enterprise use.

Chapter 7

Testing and Debugging

In this chapter

As the project enters the final stage of the porting process, there is a lot to look forward to. We enter the testing and debugging phase with great anticipation because this is the most interesting part of the process. This is where all the hard work of making sure the build process works and the application compiles and links with all the necessary libraries comes together. This is the moment of truth! You go into the directory where all the executables of the application are located. You have read the user documentation on how to run the application. With mixed feelings of anticipation and trepidation, you type in the executable name on the command line and press Enter.

Like any software application development project, application porting projects need to have the supporting tools available that will enable porting personnel to debug and tune the application. Although GDB is the only popular application debugger in Linux, a multitude of available tools can help make the porting task easier and alleviate the process of finding difficult runtime application problems such as memory leaks and performance bottlenecks.

We present tools that aid application development and porting such as `strace` and `ltrace` as an alternative to the truss facility available on other operating platforms for tracing program execution. To help increase porting productivity by allowing porting engineers to find symbols used within an application more quickly than tools such as `grep`, we describe an underrated tool called `cscope` and discuss how to use it with the Vim editor.

7.1 Using the GNU Debugger

If software applications were bug-free, we would not have any use for debuggers. As software programmers, we all strive to write good programs. As the code gets bigger and more complicated, however, simple programming mistakes can creep in. Like software development, porting an application can introduce bugs in the program. Even if the application is ported without changing any application programming interfaces (APIs) used in the code, a hidden bug in the original code can suddenly expose itself simply by running the application on a different platform. This is one reason why you need to be familiar with the debugger available on Linux.

The GNU debugger, GDB, is a powerful debugger for different applications written in C, C++, Objective-C, FORTRAN, and Ada. This section shows how to use the GDB for multiprocess or multithreaded applications. It serves as a quick how-to guide for anyone new to GDB. The information contained in this section deals with the basics of the GNU debugger; for more definitive information regarding the use of GDB, consult the GNU documentation project for GDB on the Internet.[1]

7.1.1 Compiling a Program for Use with GDB

To get the most effective use out of GDB, the application to be debugged (the debugee) needs to be compiled with the `-g` flag, as follows:

```
$ gcc -g file.c -o file
```

When compiling using makefiles, the `-g` flag may be included in `CFLAGS` or `CPPFLAGS`, as in the following example:

```
DEBUG_FLAG = -g
CFLAGS = $(DEBUG_FLAGS) -D_USING_APA

%.o: %.c
$(CC) -c $(CFLAGS) $< -o $@
```

The `gcc` compiler supports the `-g` flag with `-O` (optimization), making it possible to debug optimized executable programs with GDB. The one thing to remember, though, is that debugging an optimized program may cause some execution path to be rearranged and not match the source files.

7.1.2 Invoking GDB

There are several ways to invoke GDB, as follows:

- Invoking GDB by specifying the executable program as its argument.

  ```
  $ gdb sample_programs/main_program
  ```

- (Optional) Passing arguments to the executable program.

  ```
  $ gdb sample_programs/main_program -a -x
  ```

- Invoking GDB with both an executable program and a core file as its arguments.

  ```
  $ gdb sample_programs/main_program core_file
  ```

1 www.gnu.org/software/gdb/documentation

- Invoking GDB with an executable program name and a process ID.

  ```
  $ gdb sample_programs/main_program 1234
  ```

  In this example, GDB attaches[2] to process 1234, which is assumed to be the process ID of the executable, main_program.

- Invoking GDB with command-line options affects how GDB starts up. An example of invoking GDB without printing the startup message by using the `-silent` flag follows:

  ```
  $ gdb -silent sample_programs/main_program core_file
  ```

7.1.3 GDB Basic Commands

For the most part, commands used inside GDB are intuitive. Once inside GDB, commands to show back traces or source line numbers can easily be remembered. Table 7-1 is a list of the basic GDB commands most widely used when debugging a ported application on Linux.

TABLE 7-1
List of Basic GDB Commands

GDB Commands	Action
`list, show`	List source line number
`break, clear`	Set and delete breakpoints
`bt, where`	List back trace of current thread of execution
`step, next`	Advance program to the next line of execution
`continue`	Continue executing the program
`stepi, nexti`	Execute one machine instruction
`finish`	Continue running until just after the selected stack frame returns
`info`	Return information on various parts of the program
`print`	Examine data
`x`	Examine memory
`directory, dir`	Source directories to use for examining source files

2 Use the command `detach` from the `gdb` prompt to resume execution of the running program.

For commands that are not frequently used, the porting engineer can get help using the `info` command.

7.1.4 Debugging Multiple Processes

On most Linux platforms, GDB has no special support to debug programs that create child processes using the `fork` function. When a program forks, GDB continues to debug the parent process while the child continues to execute in the background, as shown in Example 7-1.

Example 7-1

Code Listing for fork_sample.c

```

#include <sys/types.h>
#include <unistd.h>
#include <sys/wait.h>

main()
{
  pid_t child;
  pid_t child_pid;
  int status;

   if ((child = fork()) < 0)
   {
     printf("fork failed\n");
     exit(1);
   }
   else if (child == 0)
   {
     /* child */
     child_pid = getpid();
     printf("I am the child %d\n", child_pid);
   }
   else
   {
     /* parent */
     printf("I am the parent %d\n", getpid());
     waitpid(child_pid, &status, WNOHANG);
   }

   exit(0);
}
```

Compile fork_sample.c:

```
$ gcc fork_sample. c -o fork_sample -g     compile code with -g
```

Run GDB against the compiled code:

```
$ gdb fork_sample

(gdb) break printf              put a breakpoint in printf
Breakpoint 1 at 0xfecadf0
(gdb) run
Starting program: fork_sample
Detaching after fork from child process 8012.

I am the child 8012
Breakpoint 1, 0x0fecadf0 in printf () from /lib/tls/libc.so.6
(gdb) where
#0 0x0fecadf0 in printf () from /lib/tls/libc.so.6
#1 0x10000548 in main () at fork.c:26
```

In the sample GDB session, we placed a breakpoint at a `printf` statement. But how do we know which `printf` statement the debugger will stop at—the child's or the parent's? The session shows GDB stopped at the `printf` invocation inside the parent process (line 26). GDB does not have any special provisions to create a separate GDB session to debug the child process. To follow the child process using GDB, use the command `set follow-fork-mode` within GDB. The following GDB session shows how to follow a child using GDB:

```
$ gdb fork_sample
(gdb) set follow-fork-mode child    Set GDB to follow the child
(gdb) break printf
Breakpoint 1 at 0x10010aa8
(gdb) run
Starting program: fork_sample
Breakpoint 1 at 0xfecadf0
Attaching after fork to child process 8019.
I am the parent 8016
[Switching to process 8019]

Breakpoint 1, 0x0fecadf0 in printf () from /lib/tls/libc.so.6
(gdb) where
#0 0x0fecadf0 in printf () from /lib/tls/libc.so.6
#1 0x10000528 in main () at fork.c:21
```

Notice that after setting `follow-fork-mode` to follow the child, GDB stopped at line 21, where the `printf` function was about to be invoked by the child process.

7.1.5 Debugging Multithreaded Applications

You need to remember only a few thread-specific commands when using GDB to debug multithreaded applications. The rest of the GDB commands to get stack traces and other program information remain the same. The thread-specific commands for use in GDB are as follows:

- **`info threads`**—A command to inquire about existing threads
- **`thread <`*`thread number`*`>`**—A command to switch threads
- **`thread apply [`*`thread number`*`] [all] args`**—A command to apply a command to a list of threads

The program and debugging session shown in Example 7-2 is an example of how to debug a multithreaded application with GDB.

Example 7-2

Listing of thread_sample.c

```

#include <pthread.h>
#include <signal.h>
#include <errno.h>
#include <sched.h>
#include <stdio.h>
#include <stdlib.h>
#include <unistd.h>

#define THREAD_NUM 3


int
common_func(int x)
{
  sleep(x);
}

void *
func1(void *arg)
{
  common_func(5);
  printf("thread func1 exiting\n");
}

void *
```

```
func2(void *arg)
{
  common_func(10);
  printf("thread func2 exiting\n");
}

void *
func3(void *arg)
{
  common_func(15);
  printf("thread func3 exiting\n");
}

void *(*func_array[THREAD_NUM])(void *) = {
            func1,
            func2,
            func3
            };

int
main(void)
{
  pthread_t tid[THREAD_NUM];
  int i = 0;
  int rc = 0;
  void *(*fp[THREAD_NUM])(void *);

  for (i=0; i<THREAD_NUM; i++)
  {
    fp[i] = func_array[i];
  }

  for (i=0; i<THREAD_NUM; i++)
  {
    if( (rc = pthread_create(&tid[i],NULL,fp[i],NULL))!= 0)
    {
      printf("pthread_create failed: %d\n", errno);
      exit (1);
    }
  }

  for (i=0; i<THREAD_NUM; i++)
  {
    pthread_join(tid[i], NULL);
  }

  return (0);
}

```

Compile the sample multithreaded application:

```
$ gcc thread_sample.c -o thread_sample -g -lpthread -D_REENTRANT
```

Run GDB against the sample program:

```
$ gdb thread_sample

(gdb) run
Starting program: thread_sample
[Thread debugging using libthread_db enabled]
[New Thread 4160589856 (LWP 8051)]
[New Thread 4160586976 (LWP 8054)]
[New Thread 4150101216 (LWP 8055)]
[New Thread 4139615456 (LWP 8056)]

ctl-c                ctl-c to break into the debugger

Program received signal SIGINT, Interrupt.
[Switching to Thread 4160589856 (LWP 8051)]
0x0fc268a8 in pthread_join () from /lib/tls/libpthread.so.0
(gdb) info thread
 4 Thread 4139615456 (LWP 8056) 0x0ff15a64 in __nanosleep_nocancel ()
  from /lib/tls/libc.so.6
 3 Thread 4150101216 (LWP 8055) 0x0ff15a64 in __nanosleep_nocancel ()
  from /lib/tls/libc.so.6
 2 Thread 4160586976 (LWP 8054) 0x0ff15a64 in __nanosleep_nocancel ()
  from /lib/tls/libc.so.6
* 1 Thread 4160589856 (LWP 8051) 0x0fc268a8 in pthread_join ()
  from /lib/tls/libpthread.so.0
```

Notice the output of the `info thread` command: One of the lines has an asterisk. The asterisk signifies this thread is the current thread about which GDB will display information:

```
(gdb) where                 display stack trace
#0 0x0fc268a8 in pthread_join () from /lib/tls/libpthread.so.0
#1 0x1000079c in main () at thread_sample.c:70
```

To make GDB switch to a different thread, issue the command `thread <num>` where *num* is the thread number taken from the `info thread` output:

```
(gdb) thread 3
[Switching to thread 3  (Thread 4150101216 (LWP 8059))]#0 0x0ff15a64 in
__nanosleep_nocancel () from /lib/tls/libc.so.6
(gdb) where
#0 0x0ff15a64 in __nanosleep_nocancel () from /lib/tls/libc.so.6
#1 0x0ff157e8 in sleep () from /lib/tls/libc.so.6
#2 0x10000564 in common_func (x=10) at thread_sample.c:16
#3 0x100005e8 in func2 (arg=0x0) at thread_sample.c:29
#4 0x0fc25a58 in start_thread () from /lib/tls/libpthread.so.0
```

```
#5 0x0ff51c5c in clone () from /lib/tls/libc.so.6
#6 0x0ff51c5c in clone () from /lib/tls/libc.so.6
```

To cause a GDB command to apply to all threads, issue the `thread apply all` command. The following example applies the `where` (display back trace) command to all threads:

```
(gdb) thread apply all where

Thread 4 (Thread 4139615456 (LWP 8060)):
#0 0x0ff15a64 in __nanosleep_nocancel () from /lib/tls/libc.so.6
#1 0x0ff157e8 in sleep () from /lib/tls/libc.so.6
#2 0x10000564 in common_func (x=15) at thread_sample.c:16
#3 0x10000630 in func3 (arg=0x0) at thread_sample.c:36
#4 0x0fc25a58 in start_thread () from /lib/tls/libpthread.so.0
#5 0x0ff51c5c in clone () from /lib/tls/libc.so.6
#6 0x0ff51c5c in clone () from /lib/tls/libc.so.6
Previous frame identical to this frame (corrupt stack?)

Thread 3 (Thread 4150101216 (LWP 8059)):
#0 0x0ff15a64 in __nanosleep_nocancel () from /lib/tls/libc.so.6
#1 0x0ff157e8 in sleep () from /lib/tls/libc.so.6
#2 0x10000564 in common_func (x=10) at thread_sample.c:16
#3 0x100005e8 in func2 (arg=0x0) at thread_sample.c:29
#4 0x0fc25a58 in start_thread () from /lib/tls/libpthread.so.0
#5 0x0ff51c5c in clone () from /lib/tls/libc.so.6
#6 0x0ff51c5c in clone () from /lib/tls/libc.so.6
Previous frame identical to this frame (corrupt stack?)

Thread 2 (Thread 4160586976 (LWP 8058)):
#0 0x0ff15a64 in __nanosleep_nocancel () from /lib/tls/libc.so.6
#1 0x0ff157e8 in sleep () from /lib/tls/libc.so.6
#2 0x10000564 in common_func (x=5) at thread_sample.c:16
#3 0x100005a0 in func1 (arg=0x0) at thread_sample.c:22
#4 0x0fc25a58 in start_thread () from /lib/tls/libpthread.so.0
#5 0x0ff51c5c in clone () from /lib/tls/libc.so.6
#6 0x0ff51c5c in clone () from /lib/tls/libc.so.6
Previous frame identical to this frame (corrupt stack?)

Thread 1 (Thread 4160589856 (LWP 8057)):
#0 0x0fc268a8 in pthread_join () from /lib/tls/libpthread.so.0
#1 0x1000079c in main () at thread_sample.c:70
```

7.1.6 Stopping Multithreaded Programs

If the application being debugged is a multithreaded program, as in the preceding example, it is possible to set breakpoints on a particular thread by using the following GDB commands:

```
(gdb) break <line> thread <thread number>
```

or

```
(gdb) break <line> thread <thread number> if <qualifier>
```

where *line* is a particular line number in the specified module used in the program and *thread number* is the thread number taken from the `info thread` output. The following is a sample invocation of the command:

```
(gdb) break thread_sample.c:14 thread 2
```

To conditionally stop a thread, use a conditional qualifier as follows:

```
(gdb) break thread_sample.c:14 thread 2 if foo < bar
```

Remember that whenever GDB stops a particular thread, all threads in the program are stopped, too. Threads that are in the middle of a system call are interrupted and may return from the system call without completing the system call. It is therefore suggested that programs check system call return values so that the proper action can be taken if the call is interrupted.

When the multithreaded program is restarted, all threads are started, too. When doing a `step` or `next` command, GDB does not guarantee that all threads will be stopped after executing a line or instruction in the program. Some threads may execute more than a single line or instruction depending on where the threads are in their current state of execution.

7.1.7 GDB Initialization File

During startup, GDB reads an initialization file if it exists. This file is read from the user's home directory and/or the current working directory and is normally named .gdbinit. The .gdbinit file is useful for customizing a GDB session. GDB reads commands from the .gdbinit file and executes them for the particular GDB session.

An example of where .gdbinit can prove useful is when specifying source directories so that GDB can find source file information. Another example is setting the child `follow-fork-mode` before starting GDB, as in the following example:

```
$ cat .gdbinit
dir /home/user1/src/lib:/home/user1/src/unix
set follow-fork-mode child
```

7.1.8 GDB and Signals

Like any normal application executing outside of GDB, applications under the control of GDB (debuggee) may receive signals from external sources. GDB can control the signals directed at the debuggee by either passing them to the debuggee or ignoring them. The commands to control signal behavior under GDB are as follows:

- **`info signals`** or **`info handle`**—Prints a table of all the kinds of signals and how GDB has been told to handle each one. You can use this command to see the signal numbers of all the defined types of signals.
- **`handle`** ***`signal keywords`*** **`. . .`**—Changes the way GDB handles a specific signal. The *`signal`* can be the number of a signal or its name (with or without the SIG at the beginning); a list of signal numbers of the form low-high; or the word `all`, meaning all the known signals. The *`keywords`* say what changes to make.

  Keywords:

  `nostop` GDB should not stop your program when this signal happens. It may still print a message telling you that the signal has come in.

  `stop` GDB should stop your program when this signal happens. This implies the `print` keyword, too.

  `print` GDB should print a message when this signal happens.

  `noprint` GDB should not mention the occurrence of the signal at all. This implies the `nostop` keyword, too.

  `pass` or `noignore` GDB should allow your program to see this signal; your program can handle the signal, or else it may terminate if the signal is fatal.

Example 7-3 shows a GDB session using a sample program that invokes some signals.

Example 7-3

Listing of signal_sample.c

```
#include <stdio.h>
#include <signal.h>
#include <errno.h>

void sig_handler(int signo)
{
  printf("in alarm_handler()\n");
  alarm(5); /* reset alarm */
}

int main()
{
  sigset_t sigmask;
  struct sigaction sigact;

  sigact.sa_handler=sig_handler;
  sigact.sa_flags=0;

  if (sigaction(SIGALRM, &sigact, NULL) < 0)
  {
    perror("sigaction()");
    return 1;
  }

  alarm(6);

  while (1)
  {
    sleep(1);
    fprintf(stdout, ".");
    fflush(stdout);
  }
}
```

Compile the sample program with the `-g` flag:

```
$ gcc signal_sample.c -o signal_sample -g
```

Invoke GDB on the compiled program:

```
$ gdb signal_sample
(gdb) run
Starting program: /home/avm/book/GDB/signal_sample
.....in alarm_handler()
.....in alarm_handler()
.....in alarm_handler()
```

```
.....in alarm_handler()

ctl-c
(gdb) info signal
Signal    Stop   Print  Pass to program  Description

SIGHUP    Yes    Yes     Yes              Hangup
SIGINT    Yes    Yes     No               Interrupt
SIGQUIT   Yes    Yes     Yes              Quit
SIGILL    Yes    Yes     Yes              Illegal instruction
SIGTRAP   Yes    Yes     No               Trace/breakpoint trap
SIGABRT   Yes    Yes     Yes              Aborted
SIGEMT    Yes    Yes     Yes              Emulation trap
SIGFPE    Yes    Yes     Yes              Arithmetic exception
SIGKILL   Yes    Yes     Yes              Killed
SIGBUS    Yes    Yes     Yes              Bus error
SIGSEGV   Yes    Yes     Yes              Segmentation fault
SIGSYS    Yes    Yes     Yes              Bad system call
SIGPIPE   Yes    Yes     Yes              Broken pipe
SIGALRM   No     No      Yes              Alarm clock
SIGTERM   Yes    Yes     Yes              Terminated
SIGURG    No     No      Yes              Urgent I/O condition
SIGSTOP   Yes    Yes     Yes              Stopped (signal)
...
```

Notice in the preceding output that `SIGALRM` has the Print column set to No. If that is changed to a Yes through the `handle` command, GDB exhibits the following behavior:

```
(gdb) handle SIGALRM print              change SIGALRM Print status to Yes
Signal      Stop   Print  Pass to program Description
SIGALRM     No     Yes    Yes              Alarm clock

(gdb) run
The program being debugged has been started already.
Start it from the beginning? (y or n) y

Starting program: /home/avm/book/GDB/signal_sample
.....
Program received signal SIGALRM, Alarm clock.
in alarm_handler()
.....
Program received signal SIGALRM, Alarm clock.
in alarm_handler()
.....
Program received signal SIGALRM, Alarm clock.
in alarm_handler()
...
```

Notice that after changing the `SIGALRM` print state to Yes, GDB now prints a status message every time the program receives a `SIGALRM`. In the following example, we change the stop state of `SIGALRM` to Yes, which causes GDB to stop when the program receives a SIGALRM:

```
(gdb) handle SIGALRM stop                    change SIGALRM Stop status to Yes
Signal        Stop   Print  Pass to program  Description
SIGALRM       Yes    Yes    Yes              Alarm clock

(gdb) run                                    run the application
The program being debugged has been started already.
Start it from the beginning? (y or n) y

Starting program: /home/avm/book/GDB/signal_sample
.....
Program received signal SIGALRM, Alarm clock.
0x0ff15a30 in __nanosleep_nocancel () from /lib/tls/libc.so.6
(gdb)
```

After the `SIGALRM` stop state was changed to Yes and the program restarted, GDB now stops every time a SIGALRM is generated.

7.1.9 Graphical Front End to GDB

For developers who are more used to graphical debuggers, there is a graphical front end available for GDB called DDD.[3] DDD is available from www.gnu.org/software/ddd/.

For developers who prefer an Integrated Development Environment (IDE), both open-source and commercial products are available. Eclipse[4] and Kdevelop[5] are available as open-source IDEs. Visual Slickedit[6] and Borland Kylix[7] are commercial IDEs available for Linux.

---

3 DDD can also be used as a front end for debuggers other than GDB.

4 www.eclipse.org

5 www.kdevelop.org

6 www.slickedit.com

7 www.borland.com

7.2 strace and ltrace

The `strace` and `ltrace` tools are utility programs that trace program executions. They are a good addition to a programmer's arsenal of debugging tools. Porting engineers find these tools useful for tracking down hard-to-find problems such as timing-related issues.

The `strace` tool traces system calls and signals that happen during program execution. Each line in the `strace` output contains the system call name, followed by its arguments in parentheses and its return value. For example:

```
open("/dev/null", O_RDONLY) = 3
```

Errors display together with the corresponding error return values, as in the following:

```
open("/foo/bar", O_RDONLY) = -1 ENOENT (No such file or directory)
```

As with `strace`, the `ltrace` tool is used to trace program execution for diagnosing timing-related issues. The `ltrace` tool intercepts and records dynamic library calls as well as signals executed and received by the main program, respectively. The `ltrace` tool prints the library call followed by its arguments and its return value, as shown in the following example:

```
strlen("apache-ant-1.6.2")    = 16
```

You can use both `strace` and `ltrace` in lieu of the truss utility present in other UNIX operating platforms.

7.3 cscope Utility

One of the most useful tools available as an open-source project under the BSD license is `cscope`. It is a utility used for interactively locating specified elements of code in C, C++, `lex`, or `yacc` source files. When you are dealing with large porting projects, `cscope` proves useful for finding references to a function, global definitions, functions called by a function, functions calling a function, text strings, regular expression patterns, files, and files including a specific file.

Linux distributions now include `cscope` as part of their standard distribution, but for those who need to download `cscope` and build it themselves, it can be found at http://cscope.sourceforge.net. As of this writing, the latest version is 15.5. The following steps describe how to build `cscope` from scratch, but first you must download `cscope` from http://cscope.sourceforge.net:

```
$ gunzip -c cscope-15.5.tar.gz | tar -xvf -
$ cd cscope-15.5/
$ ./configure --prefix=/usr/local
$ make install
```

To build cscope, flex, bison, and libncurses need to be present and installed on the build system.

Prior to using cscope to browse and search for functions and text, you need to build a cscope database that contains all the searchable symbols in the source code. To do this, cscope needs to be invoked with the necessary switches. An easier way to build the cscope database is to use a script named ocs, which is included in the contrib directory of the cscope source code.

Invoke ocs in the top directory of the source code to be browsed as follows:

```
$ cd $TOP_DIR          $TOP_DIR is the top of the source tree
                       and where the cscope database resides
$ ocs                  executing ocs without any flags runs cscope
                       using the default cscope database
```

The ocs script goes through all the subdirectories and builds a list of files that will eventually be parsed by cscope to build the cscope database. After ocs finishes building the cscope database, it runs cscope using the cscope database, and it is ready for use. To exit cscope, just type ctl-d. The cscope database produced by default is called cscope.out. To update this database in case of code changes or addition to the source code, run ocs again with the -u flag.

7.3.1 Vim and cscope

cscope is a useful tool for searching symbols and functions and invoking the developer's favorite editor to edit a file where these symbols and functions are found. However, cscope is limited such that if the developer wants to search for another symbol found in the current source file opened for editing, the programmer has to exit the editor invoked by cscope to return to the cscope default screen. When back at the cscope default screen, the programmer can then enter the symbol for cscope to do another search. This type of interaction can sometimes be tedious. To alleviate this problem, a number of open-source editors have incorporated support for cscope. The support enables programmers to search and open editing sessions for source code without the need to jump back to the cscope default screen to begin another search.

One such editor that supports `cscope` is Vim. Because some Linux distributions include Vim already compiled without turning on the support for `cscope`, it would be necessary to download the Vim source code and build it. To build Vim with `cscope` support, download Vim from www.vim.org. Then build it as follows:

```
$ bunzip2 vim-6.3.tar.bz2
$ tar -xvf vim-6.3.tar
$ cd vim63/src
$ ./configure --enable-cscope
$ make
$ make install
```

With cscope enabled in Vim,[8] the programmer can use `cscope` through the Vim command `cs`. To add the `cscope` database, cscope.out, to Vim, invoke `cs` by typing `<esc> :cs add cscope.out`. Invoke `cs` again with the `show` argument, as in `<esc> :cs show`, to show whether Vim has any `cscope` connections. If there is a `cscope` connection, Vim shows the following output:

```
# pid   database name  prepend path
0 22212  cscope.out    <none>
```

Invoking `cs` by itself prints the arguments that can be used to invoke `cscope` to do its search features. The `find` argument to `cs` invokes the different search features of `cscope`. For example, `<esc> :cs find g` *`symbol_name`* finds the definition of a symbol.

Here is the help screen printed when `:cs` is invoked by itself:

```
cscope commands:
add : Add a new database         (Usage: add file|dir [pre-path][flags])
find : Query for a pattern       (Usage: find c|d|e|f|g|i|s|t name)
    c: Find functions calling this function
    d: Find functions called by this function
    e: Find this egrep pattern
    f: Find this file
    g: Find this definition
    i: Find files #including this file
    s: Find this C symbol
    t: Find assignments to
help : Show this message         (Usage: help)
kill : Kill a connection         (Usage: kill #)
reset: Reinit all connections    (Usage: reset)
show : Show connections          (Usage: show)
```

---

8 Vim can also be used with `cscope` as the default editor by setting the environment variable `EDITOR=vim`.

The cscope subcommand cs can be invoked using Vim shortcuts, too. This eliminates typing cs commands and enables the programmer to place the cursor on the symbol and press the programmed shortcut key, which expands and executes the command to start the cscope search automatically. Vim shortcuts can be placed in the .vimrc file to automatically program them when Vim is invoked. The following is an example of a .vimrc that programs the F5 and F6 keys to invoke cscope commands to find symbol definitions and find the C symbol in all files, respectively:

```
$ cat .vimrc
if has("cscope")
set csprg=/usr/local/bin/cscope
set csto=0
set cst
set nocsverb
map <F5>  :cs find g <C-R>=expand("<cword>")<CR><CR>
map <F6>  :cs find s <C-R>=expand("<cword>")<CR><CR>
cs add cscope.out
set csverb
endif
```

Vim also keeps track of files that were opened previously during a Vim session. This is called a tag stack. This enables the programmer to back up to previous files using Ctrl-T. For example, if Vim opens foo.c and within the same session the programmer searches for symbol1 and cscope finds it in foo1.c, Vim opens foo1.c for editing. Then in foo1.c the programmer searches for symbol2, and cscope finds it in foo2.c. Vim then opens foo2.c for editing. If the programmer wants to go back to foo.c, all he has to do is press Ctrl-T twice to go back to foo.c. The tag stack is a convenient way to jump back to previously opened files. More information on how to use cscope with Vim is included in the Vim documentation included in the Vim source code distribution.

7.4 glibc Debugging Support

The usual way to examine a back trace of a program is to use an external debugger such as GDB. Sometimes, however, it is useful to obtain back-trace information from within a running program for logging or debugging purposes. The GNU glibc provides support that enables the developer to produce back-trace *printouts* from within the application.

Example 7-4 shows how to use backtrace inside a signal handler and outside a signal handler. The API prototypes for back trace are declared in the header file execinfo.h and should be included in the application.

Example 7-4

Code Listing of sample_backtrace.c

```
#include <execinfo.h>
#include <stdio.h>
#include <signal.h>

void handler()
{
  int i;
  void *trace[128];
  int tr_size;
  char **strings;

  printf("\n########## start backtrace ##########\n\n");
  tr_size = backtrace(trace, sizeof(trace) / sizeof(void *));
  strings = backtrace_symbols(trace, tr_size);
  printf("Number of elements in backtrace: %d\n", tr_size);
  for (i = 0; i < tr_size; i++) {
    printf("%s\n", strings[i]);
  }
  printf("\n########## end backtrace ##########\n");

  free(strings);
}

h()
{
#ifdef _handler_
  abort();
#else
  handler();
#endif
}

void g()
{
  h();
}

void foo()
{
  g();
}

int main(int argc, char **argv)
{
  struct sigaction sigact;

```

```
    sigact.sa_sigaction = handler;
    sigemptyset(&sigact.sa_mask);
    sigact.sa_flags = SA_SIGINFO;
    sigaction(SIGSEGV, &sigact, NULL);
    sigaction(SIGABRT, &sigact, NULL);

    foo();
}
```

Compile the code listing `sample_backtrace.c` with the `_handler_` macro defined to simulate an application program that aborts in the middle of its run:

```
$ gcc sample_backtrace.c -o sample_backtrace -g -rdynamic -D_handler_
$./sample_backtrace


########## start backtrace ##########

Number of elements in backtrace: 9
./main1(handler+0x2d) [0x8048829]
[0xffffe440]
/lib/tls/libc.so.6(abort+0x129) [0x40051f79]
./main1(g+0) [0x80488d2]
./main1(g+0xb) [0x80488dd]
./main1(foo+0xb) [0x80488ea]
./main1(main+0x6a) [0x8048956]
/lib/tls/libc.so.6(__libc_start_main+0xe0) [0x4003e500]
./main1 [0x8048761]

########## end backtrace ##########
Aborted
```

In the preceding example, back-trace information is produced through the `abort` signal handler routine called `handler()`. The same method can be implemented for other signals caught by the application.

In the following, Example 7-4 is compiled without the `_handler_` macro defined. In this example, the `handler()` function is called explicitly by the application to produce a back-trace printout. This method can be used to create back-trace information at certain points of the application for debugging or monitoring reasons.

```
$ gcc sample_backtrace.c -o sample_backtrace -g -rdynamic
$ ./sample_backtrace

########## start backtrace ##########

Number of elements in backtrace: 7
./main1(handler+0x2d) [0x80487f9]
```

```
./main1(h+0xb) [0x80488a2]
./main1(g+0xb) [0x80488af]
./main1(foo+0xb) [0x80488bc]
./main1(main+0x6a) [0x8048928]
/lib/tls/libc.so.6(__libc_start_main+0xe0) [0x4003e500]
./main1 [0x8048731]

########## end backtrace ##########
```

When compiling, notice that the `-rdynamic` flag is used. The `-rdynamic` flag is passed on to the linker to force inclusion of global symbol tables in the final executable.

7.5 Memory-Debugging Tools

Several open-source and commercially sold memory-debugging tools are available on the Linux platform. Some may perform only one specific memory-debugging task but do it very well. An example is Electric Fence, which was created for the purpose of detecting memory overruns and underruns. Some tools are also available to detect memory leaks. Although most of these tools can be used in a multithreaded environment, some may not support it, so be sure to check which one is more suited to your application environment. For further information about how to use these tools, refer to *Linux Programming by Example* (Pearson Education, 2004) and *Linux Application Development,* 2nd Edition (Pearson Education, 2005).

7.5.1 Electric Fence

Available from http://directory.fsf.org/devel/debug/ElectricFence.html, Electric Fence is a memory-debugging tool used in applications suspected of overrunning or underrunning the boundaries of the `malloc`ed buffer. Electric Fence arranges application `malloc`ed memory to be followed or preceded by protected memory using the `mmap` routine. When an application accesses the protected memory, it gets an immediate segmentation fault, stopping the application at the point where it produces a core file. If it's running within a debugger, it stops at the faulting instruction.

Example 7-5 shows how to use Electric Fence given the example program.

Example 7-5

Listing of overrun.c

```

#include <stdio.h>
#include <stdlib.h>

main()
{
  char *p;

  p = malloc(8);

  p[8] = ‘x’;   /* overrun error */
}
```

Compile the program:

```
$ gcc overrun.c -o overrun -L. -lefence -lpthread -g
$ gdb overrun
(gdb) run
Starting program: /home/avm/book/memory/electric-fence-2.1.13/overrun
[Thread debugging using libthread_db enabled]
[New Thread 4160589856 (LWP 12059)]

 Electric Fence 2.1 Copyright (C) 1987-1998 Bruce Perens.

Program received signal SIGSEGV, Segmentation fault.
[Switching to Thread 4160589856 (LWP 12059)]
0x1000089c in main () at overrun.c:11
11        p[8] = ‘x’;
```

In the example, the program was linked to the Electric Fence static library. When an overrun was detected, the electric fence library, through its use of page-protected boundaries, forced the program to segment fault. This produces the exact place of the offending memory operation.

In addition to monitoring for memory overruns and underruns, Electric Fence detects any access to memory that has already been freed.

7.5.2 GNU/Linux mtrace, mcheck, MALLOC_CHECK

`mtrace` is a GNU `glibc` feature that can help in debugging memory-related problems such as memory leaks and freeing unallocated memory. `glibc` exports the APIs `mtrace()` and `muntrace()`, which can be called within the application to turn on and turn off memory checking, respectively. When the `mtrace` function is called, it looks for an environment variable named `MALLOC_CHECK`, which contains a valid filename. The filename is used to log information about calls to `malloc`, `free`, and `realloc`, which can later be parsed and analyzed with a Perl script named `mtrace`.

Example 7-6 shows how to use `mtrace`.

Example 7-6

Listing of leak.c

```
#include <stdlib.h>
#include <mcheck.h> /* Include mtrace functions header */

int main() {
    int *a;

    /* This starts memory tracing. This has to be
    * done before any memory allocation routines
    */

#ifdef _DEBUG
    mtrace(); /* This starts memory tracing. */
#endif

    a = malloc(sizeof(int)); /* Allocate memory */

    *a = 7;

    /* Notice that we did not free allocated
    * memory before we end the program.
    */

#ifdef _DEBUG
    muntrace();
#endif

    return 0;
}
```

```
$ gcc leak.c -o leak -g -D_DEBUG
$ export MALLOC_TRACE=log.txt
$ ./leak

$ cat log.txt
= Start
```

```
@ ./leak:[0x804841b] + 0x804a378 0x4
= End

$ mtrace ./leak log.txt

Memory not freed:
-----------------
   Address     Size     Caller
0x0804a378     0x4 at /tmp/leak.c:15
```

You can find more information about how to use `mtrace` within an application in the `glibc` manual at www.gnu.org/software/libc/manual.

7.5.3 Mpatrol

The source for `mpatrol` is available for download at http://sourceforge.net/projects/mpatrol/. `mpatrol` is a memory-debugging tool in the form of a link library that helps diagnose runtime application errors caused by the improper use of dynamically allocated memory. `mpatrol` can detect application programming errors such as memory leaks and writing to free memory. The documentation from `mpatrol` mentions as one of its features the ability to produce memory allocation profiling information, which can be useful to learn how memory is used by a given application.

After you link the program from Example 7-6 with the `mpatrol` debug library, you should set the `MPATROL_OPTIONS` environment variable to the desired debugging action:

```
$ gcc leak.c -o leak -g -lmpatrol -lbfd
$ export MPATROL_OPTIONS="LOGALL USEDEBUG"
$ ./leak
$ cat mpatrol.log

. . .
ALLOC: malloc (127, 4 bytes, 4 bytes) [main|/tmp/leak.c|15]
  0x0804854B main+31 at /tmp/leak.c:15
  0x40102500 __libc_start_main+224
  0x08048491 _start+33 at ../sysdeps/i386/elf/start.S:102
...
```

In the preceding example, the options `LOGALL` and `USEDEBUG` were used to log memory allocations and display line number information where memory was allocated. Note that the test program was also linked with `libbfd.so`, because `mpatrol` requires symbols from `libbfd`.

7.5.4 dmalloc

Like Electric Fence and `mpatrol`, `dmalloc` is another memory-debugging tool that is freely distributed as open source. You can download the `dmalloc` source code from http://dmalloc.com/. You can use the `dmalloc` library to track memory leaks and fence-post write detections, as well as write detailed reports that contain file and line numbers of routines that use `malloc`, `calloc`, `realloc`, `free`, and other memory management routines.

`dmalloc` debugging features are set with an environment variable that controls the type of memory allocation to be monitored. The level of logging can also be controlled. `dmalloc` generates the values that can be used to set the environment variable:

```
$ gcc leak.c -o leak -g -L. -ldmalloc
$ ./dmalloc high -l logfile
DMALLOC_OPTIONS=debug=0x4f4ed03,log=logfile
export DMALLOC_OPTIONS
```

In the preceding example, the output from `dmalloc` can be placed in a shell startup script that sets the variable `DMALLOC_OPTIONS`. Once set, the application that was linked with the `dmalloc` library can then be run. The output is written to a file named logfile.

The following logfile output shows unfreed memory when the program was run with `dmalloc`:

```
$ DMALLOC_OPTIONS=debug=0x4f4ed03,log=logfile
$ export DMALLOC_OPTIONS
$ ./leak
$ cat logfile
. . .
1126108168: 1: Dumping Not-Freed Pointers Changed Since Start:
1126108168: 1: not freed: '0xf7ffeff8|s1' (4 bytes) from 'leak.c:15'
...
```

7.5.5 valgrind

`valgrind` is a memory-debugging tool available from http://valgrind.org. `valgrind` is free and is open-sourced under the GNU GPL. `valgrind` offers one big advantage over other freely available memory-debugging tools. Whereas other memory-debugging tools require the developer to compile and link the tool library with the program application, `valgrind` allows debugging to happen without the need to compile and link a debug library within the application. `valgrind` "wraps" the application to be debugged and applies one of the error-detection tools to do its core tasks. The tool represents the type and level of debugging tasks that need to be done. valgrind can report on memory allocation usage, heap usage, race condition errors that may exist in multithreaded applications, and on L1 and L2 cache misses.

Using valgrind[9] on the sample program in Example 7-6 yields the following results:

```
$ gcc leak.c -o leak -g
$ valgrind -v --leak-check=full ./leak

. . . output . . .

==25923==
==25923== 4 bytes in 1 blocks are definitely lost in loss record 1 of 1
==25923==  at 0xFFB9794: malloc (vg_replace_malloc.c:130)
==25923==  by 0x10000430: main (leak.c:15)
==25923==
==25923== LEAK SUMMARY:
==25923==  definitely lost: 4 bytes in 1 blocks.
==25923==   possibly lost: 0 bytes in 0 blocks.
==25923==  still reachable: 0 bytes in 0 blocks.

... output ...
```

valgrind found allocated memory on line 15 of Example 7-6 that was not freed after the program exited. Note that the program was compiled with the -g option to allow valgrind to get the proper symbols and addresses within the executable. Also note that there was no need to link any extra libraries with the sample program.

7.5.6 Rational Purify

Rational Purify for Linux is commercially available from IBM. Rational Purify detects memory errors such as memory leaks and invalid memory access. Whereas other memory-debugging tools work only with C and C++ programs, Rational Purify also works with applications written in Java. Rational Purify helps detect Java garbage collection issues that may result in memory being held by object references

9 The valgrind version used in this sample was 2.4.1 for the IBM POWER platform. The valgrind variant for Linux on POWER is available at http://valgrind.org/downloads/variants.html?pmk.

that are no longer needed or other memory issues that can come from the JDK or third-party libraries. When used together with another product called Rational Quantify, it is possible to get accurate profile data that can be used to find performance bottlenecks. Both Rational Purify and Rational Quantify use patented Object Code Insertion (OCI) technology to instrument C/C++ programs that check for logic errors as well as create profiling data. You can find more information about Rational Purify at www.ibm.com/software/awdtools/purifyplus/unix.

7.5.7 Insure++

Insure++ is a commercially available memory-debugging tool from www.parasoft.com. It offers support for Linux running on x86 platforms as well as the POWER (ppc) platform from IBM. Insure++ achieves detailed code coverage when it is used to compile and link application source code. The tool generates instrumented object files that are then passed to the actual compiler, producing instrumented application code. Insure++ detects memory corruption, memory leaks, memory allocation errors, variable initialization errors, variable definition conflicts, pointer errors, library errors, I/O errors, and logic errors.

7.6 Static Program Checker

During application porting, changes to the original code may inject potential errors, such as referencing null pointers or typographical errors (errors that can cause infinite loops and go undetected). These errors may even be left undetected at compile and link time. A tool such as a static code checker[10] that is used in conjunction with the build process can help detect such errors, creating a proactive build environment that can eliminate future problems during functional and systems tests.

7.6.1 Splint

Splint is a tool for statically checking C programs for programming mistakes such as potential memory leaks, referencing of null pointers, unused declarations, type inconsistencies, ignored return values, and likely infinite loops. One important feature that Splint also provides is checking for potential buffer-overflow scenarios in

---

10 Other static program checkers are available, such as Flawfinder (www.dwheeler.com/flawfinder/) and Coverity (www.coverity.com).

an application. Running ported applications through a tool such as Splint creates a more robust application that is less prone to fail during application testing. Splint is available from www.splint.org/.

7.6.2 CodeSonar

CodeSonar is a commercially available source code analyzer that performs a deep static analysis on code and identifies many types of bugs. These include null-pointer dereferences, divide-by-zeros, buffer overruns, buffer underruns, double-frees, use-after-frees, and frees of nonheap memory. CodeSonar does a whole-program analysis, taking into account effects arising from the interaction of different functions in different files. It can detect complex bugs that are difficult to identify through manual analysis. To learn more about CodeSonar, go to www.grammatech.com.

You can find a list of several other static analyzers in both open-source and commercial forms at www.splint.org/links.html.

7.7 Threads trace Tool

A tool to trace thread execution using the New POSIX Threads Library (NPTL) with as few intrusions as possible is available through an open-source project called NPTL trace tool.[11] The tool, designed to help developers of multithreaded applications, can generate a trace that describes the behavior of threads and provide help needed to understand complex situations such as race conditions, deadlocks, and lock contentions.

The `trace` tool starts when the application to be traced starts executing and stops as soon as the application stops. The trace produced can be viewed in text or graphical format. As of this writing, the tool is available only as a beta version (0.8.1). It currently traces 15 of the most common POSIX thread routines and four objects.[12] Platforms currently supported by the `trace` tool are the IA32, IA64, and PowerPC architecture.

---

11 http://nptltracetool.sourceforge.net

12 Condition variables, mutexes, barriers, and threads

The tool requires the user to download the `glibc` source and apply several patches to the NPTL library. These patches are included in the NPTL `trace` tool distribution and add the necessary trace hooks needed to trace thread execution. Although the tool is in its early stages of development,[13] it shows how the open-source community contributes to the advancement of Linux.

7.8 Performance Monitoring Tools

Both application performance and application behavior on the Linux platform need to be checked before the newly ported application is made available. Familiarize yourself with performance monitoring tools available on Linux to find problems or performance bottlenecks. Some of these tools are already available with the standard Linux distributions; others are open-source tools that you can download from the Internet.

We approach application tuning from two views—internal and external. As the names imply, the internal view deals with the functions internal to the application; the external view deals with the environment the application runs on. Both have a direct effect on a customer's perception of the application; a fast-performing application will have more content users than a slow-performing application. We discuss both views next.

7.8.1 Internal View

The first view to application tuning is the internal view. The internal view is where we get to look inside the application. The application is best viewed internally with a profiling tool. A profiling tool tells you where your program spent its time and which functions called which functions. This information can show you which functions of your program are slower than you expected. You can then analyze the code for slow functions to determine whether they can be optimized.

7.8.1.1 gprof

Linux provides a profiling tool called `gprof`.[14] We use Example 7-7 to run `gprof` against and show an example output.

---

13 Use with extreme care at this point.

14 www.gnu.org/software/binutils/manual/gprof-2.9.1/html_mono/gprof.html

Example 7-7

Source Code for gprof_1.c

```
#include <pthread.h>
#include <errno.h>
#include <stdlib.h>

static unsigned int v = 40;
static count = 0;
pthread_mutex_t count_lck;

/*
  A Fibonacci sequence is a sequence of numbers {f0, f1, f2 ....}
  in which the first two values are equal to 1 and each succeeding
  number is the sum of the previous two numbers.
  Here are the first few sequence of numbers of the Fibonacci sequence:
  1 1 2 3 5 8 13 21 ...
*/


/* function to return the kth Fibonacci number */
unsigned long fibonacci(unsigned long k)
{
  unsigned long x, y, z, n;

  x = 1;

  if (k > 1)
  {
    y = z = 1;
    for (n=2; n<=k; n++)
    {
      x = y + z;
      y = z;
      z = x;
    }

  }

  /* return the kth Fibonacci number */
  return x;
}

unsigned long rec_fibonacci(unsigned long k)
{
  unsigned long x;

  x = 1;
  if (k > 1)
```

```
    x = rec_fibonacci(k-1) + rec_fibonacci(k-2);

  /* return the kth Fibonacci number */
  return x;
}

void *compute(void *arg)
{
  pthread_mutex_lock(&count_lck);
  if (count == 0)
  {
    count++;
    pthread_mutex_unlock(&count_lck);
    printf("recursive = %ld\n", rec_fibonacci(v));
  }
  else
  {
    count++;
    pthread_mutex_unlock(&count_lck);
    printf("non recursive = %ld\n", fibonacci(v));
  }
}


main()
{
  int rc;
  int i;
  pthread_t tid[2];

  pthread_mutex_init(&count_lck, NULL);

  for (i=0; i<2; i++)
  {
    if( (rc = pthread_create(&tid[i], NULL, compute, NULL)) != 0)
    {
      printf("pthread_create failed: %d\n", errno);
      exit(1);
    }
  }

  for (i=0; i<2; i++)
  {
    pthread_join(tid[i], NULL);
  }

  pthread_mutex_destroy(&count_lck);

}
```

Compile with the `-pg` flag to turn on profiling:

```
$ gcc gprof_1.c -o gprof_1 -lpthread -D_REENTRANT -pg
```

Run the program:

```
$ ./gprof_1
non recursive = 165580141
recursive = 165580141
```

The program `gprof_1` produces a file named gmon.out. `gprof` interprets gmon.out[15] and prints the profile information in readable form.

Run `gprof` against the application:

```
$ gprof ./gprof_1 > outfile

$ cat outfile


--- some information cut ---

           Call graph (explanation follows)


granularity: each sample hit covers 4 byte(s) no time propagated

index % time  self children  called    name
        0.00  0.00    1/1       compute [10]
[1]    0.0  0.00  0.00    1      fibonacci [1]
-----------------------------------------------
             331160279          rec_fibonacci [2]
        0.00  0.00    1/1       compute [10]
[2]    0.0  0.00  0.00   1+331160279 rec_fibonacci [2]
             331160279          rec_fibonacci [2]

--- some information cut ---
```

Notice that this output indicates the number of times the function `rec_fibonacci()` was called but not how much time was spent on each call. However, it does not give you any number in the self column. Apparently, in some operating system kernels (such as Linux), `gprof` measures only the main thread. Basically, `gprof` uses the internal `ITIMER_PROF` timer, which makes the kernel deliver a signal to the application whenever it expires. This timer data needs to be passed on to all spawned threads. Appendix E, "gprof helper," includes a module to

15 Note that if gmon.out does not exist, `gprof` will complain that it cannot find the file gmon.out.

wrap pthread_create() to pass on the needed timer data. Compile the module to produce a shared library as follows:

```
$ gcc -shared -fPIC gprof_helper.c -o gprof-helper.so -lpthread -ldl
```

This produces a library gprof_helper.so. Run the example gprof_1 application again but this time with the following command:

```
$ LD_PRELOAD=./gprof-helper.so ./gprof_1
pthreads: using profiling hooks for gprof
non recursive = 165580141
recursive = 165580141
```

This produces a new gmon.out file on which we can run gprof:

```
$ gprof ./gprof_1

Flat profile:

Each sample counts as 0.01 seconds.
 %   cumulative   self         self    total
 time   seconds   seconds   calls  s/call   s/call name
100.00   135.95   135.95     1   135.95   135.95 rec_fibonacci

 %      the percentage of the total running time of the
time     program used by this function.

cumulative a running sum of the number of seconds accounted
 seconds   for by this function and those listed above it.

 self    the number of seconds accounted for by this
seconds   function alone. This is the major sort for this
      listing.

calls    the number of times this function was invoked, if
      this function is profiled, else blank.

 self    the average number of milliseconds spent in this
ms/call   function per call, if this function is profiled,
      else blank.

 total    the average number of milliseconds spent in this
ms/call   function and its descendents per call, if this
    function is profiled, else blank.

name     the name of the function. This is the minor sort
      for this listing. The index shows the location of
      the function in the gprof listing. If the index is
      in parenthesis it shows where it would appear in
      the gprof listing if it were to be printed.

           Call graph (explanation follows)
```

```
granularity: each sample hit covers 4 byte(s) for 0.01% of 135.95 seconds

index % time   self children  called    name
                331160280        rec_fibonacci [1]
       135.95  0.00     1/1       compute [2]
[1]  100.0 135.95  0.00     1+331160280 rec_fibonacci [1]
                331160280        rec_fibonacci [1]
-----------------------------------------------
                          <spontaneous>
[2]  100.0  0.00 135.95           compute [2]
       135.95  0.00     1/1       rec_fibonacci [1]
-----------------------------------------------

--- rest of the output cut ---
```

Notice that the self column has been filled up. Because the time for executing the function `fibonacci()` was negligible compared to the time spent executing `rec_fibonacci()`, `gprof` did not print a line for it. Refer to the GNU `gprof` manual[16] for more details about using `gprof` and interpreting its output.

In our simple example, you just saw how slow a recursive function can be. In real applications, `gprof` data can show which functions are called and by whom and how fast these functions perform. This data can help you decide whether there is a need to rewrite some of these functions.

7.8.1.2 OProfile

`OProfile` (http://oprofile.sf.net) is a system-wide profiler capable of profiling all running code, including hardware and software interrupt handlers, kernel modules, kernels, shared libraries, and user-space applications. Unlike `gprof`, `OProfile` does not require code to be compiled with special profiling options or even the `-g` option (unless you want samples to be mapped back to the source code). Therefore, you can profile applications running in production environments using `OProfile`. In addition, `OProfile` collects samples on all processes and threads running on the system and enables the user to examine data from processes that are still running.

`OProfile` can be configured to take samples periodically (time-based samples) to identify which parts of code consumed computing resources. On many architectures, `OProfile` provides access to the performance counter registers, allowing samples to be collected based on other events such as cache misses, TLB misses,

16 www.gnu.org/software/binutils/manual/gprof-2.9.1/html_mono/gprof.html

memory references, and instructions retired. Users can also request reports that have the source trees annotated with the profile information. The generated profiling report enables developers to determine whether performance problems exist in the code and to modify the code accordingly.

Here we show you how to profile the code in Example 7-7 using OProfile. In this example, we use only the time-based event. As mentioned previously, you do not need to compile your code with any special option:

```
# gcc -o oprof1 gprof_1.c -lpthread -D_REENTRANT
```

Execute the following command as root to clear out previous samples:

```
# opcontrol -reset
```

Next, configure and start `OProfile` by running the following two commands:

```
# opcontrol --setup --no-vmlinux --separate=thread \
  --event=CYCLES:1000
# opcontrol --start
Using 2.6+ OProfile kernel interface.
Using log file /var/lib/oprofile/oprofiled.log
Daemon started.
Profiler running.
```

The `-no-vmlinux` option indicates that we do not want samples for the kernel. The `--separate=thread` option gives separation for each thread. The `--event` option specifies measuring the time-based `CYCLES` event with a sample recorded for every 1,000 events. You can issue the command `opcontrol -list-events` to list all supported events on your platform. The `--start` option starts `OProfile`'s data collection.

Now we can start the program:

```
# ./oprof1
non recursive = 165580141
recursive = 165580141
```

To ensure that all the current profiling data is flushed to the sample files before each analysis of profiling data, we issue the following command:

```
# opcontrol -dump
```

Shut down `OProfile` with the following command:

```
# opcontrol --shutdown
Stopping profiling.
Killing daemon.
```

Analysis can be performed on the collected data as a normal user with `opreport` and `opannotate` commands:

```
# opreport -l ./oprof1
CPU: ppc64 POWER5, speed 1650.35 MHz (estimated)
Counted CYCLES events (Processor cycles) with a unit mask of 0x00 (No unit mask)
count 1000
Processes with a thread ID of 15047
Processes with a thread ID of 15048
samples %     samples %     symbol name
1232110 100.000 0       0 rec_fibonacci
0       0 2     100.000 fibonacci
```

The output shows a separate report for each thread. As expected, the function `rec_fibonacci` consumes most of the CPU time (1,232,110 samples, 100 percent) within a thread. Another function, `fibonacci`, received 2 samples, accounting for 100 percent within another thread. If you want to relate samples back to the source code, you need to recompile with the `-g` option. Following is a portion of the output from the `opannotate --source ./oprof1` command:

```
...
             :unsigned long rec_fibonacci(unsigned long k)
0     0  298 27.9288  :{ /* rec_fibonacci total:   0
                     0 1067 100.000 */
             :  unsigned long x;
             :
0     0   1 0.0937   :  x = 1;
0     0  44 4.1237   :  if (k > 1)
0     0  364 34.1143   :  x = rec_fibonacci(k-1) +
                   rec_fibonacci(k-2);
             :
             : /* return the kth Fibonacci number */
0     0  62 5.8107   :  return x;
0     0  298 27.9288   :}

...
```

The first nonzero number on each line is the number of samples; the second nonzero number is the relative percentage of total samples. Refer to the `OProfile` manual[17] for more detailed information about using `OProfile` and interpreting its output.

Here are some white papers that you may find useful to learn more about OProfile:

17 http://oprofile.sourceforge.net/docs/

- Smashing Performance with OProfile (www-128.ibm.com/developerworks/linux/library/l-oprof.html)
- Red Hat: OProfile instruction (www.centos.org/docs/4/html/rhel-sag-en-4/s1-oprofile-configuring.html)
- OProfile for Linux on POWER (www-128.ibm.com/developerworks/library/l-pow-oprofile/)
- Five easy-to-use performance tools for Linux on PowerPC (www-128.ibm.com/developerworks/eserver/library/es-PerformanceInspectoronpLinux.html)
- Tuning Programs with OProfile (http://people.redhat.com/wcohen)

Both `gprof` and `OProfile` have their own niche in application profiling. Depending on the application's profiling requirements, porting engineers and software developers may choose to favor one tool over another. Table 7-2 compares the characteristics of `gprof` and `OProfile`.

TABLE 7-2
Comparison Between gprof and OProfile

gprof	OProfile[18]
Does not require root permission	Requires root permission
Cannot measure hardware effects such as cache misses	Can measure hardware effects such as cache misses
Only profiles at the application level	Can capture performance behavior of entire system
Need to recompile source code with `-pg`	No need to recompile source code with extra flags
Can profile interpreted code (such as Java)[19]	Cannot profile interpreted code[20]
Can profile application and shared libraries (only if shared libraries were compiled with `-pg`)	Can profile application and shared libraries (no need to recompile shared libraries with profiling flags)

18 See http://oprofile.sourceforge.net/doc/introduction.html#applications for more information.

19 Compile your Java code using GNU compiler for Java (gcj).

20 We did not try profiling Java code that was compiled with gcj.

In summary, profiling application code is a way to get an internal view of the application. The internal view gives us an idea about what parts of the code are frequently used and which functions take up the most CPU time. You can use this view to identify *hot spots* within the application that can be optimized to produce a better-performing application.

7.8.2 External View

The second view to application tuning is the external view. This is where we view the application from a systems point of view. When an application runs, it uses system resources. These system resources are small at startup and gradually increase as more users use the application or more functions of the application are utilized. We call the resources used by the application its *resource signature.* The resource signature tells us how much memory, CPU, disk space, and other system resources must be available to the application to function at optimal levels. This view is most useful for system architects, who need to plan for resource capacity, and the view is generally obtained by performing an application benchmark.

During application benchmarking, an environment is set up to simulate application use. Usually, this is done through scripts that simulate users utilizing the application to perform different operations. System tools that monitor memory, CPU, disk I/O, and network traffic are then used to observe the overall resource utilization. Information gathered through these tools helps systems architects plan which resources the application will need. We discuss some of these tools next.

7.8.2.1 vmstat

`vmstat` displays real-time information about processes, memory, paging, block I/O, traps, and CPU activity. The first line provides the average system activity since the last reboot, which can usually be ignored. Additional lines give the information on a sampling period of length *delay* (a user-specified parameter). The output from `vmstat` can be used to identify unusual system behaviors such as high page faults or excessive context switches. A sample output of `vmstat` follows:

```
procs -------memory---------- ---swap-- -----io---- --system-----cpu---
 r b swpd free      buff    cache  si so  bi  bo  in  cs us sy id  wa
 0  0  0  14936464  221040  467720  0  0   0   1  1   9  0  0  100  0
 0  0  0  14936528  221040  467720  0  0   0   6  5  39  0  0  100  0
 0  0  0  14936528  221040  467720  0  0   0   0  3  37  0  0  100  0
 0  0  0  14936528  221040  467720  0  0   0   2  4  40  0  0  100  0
 0  0  0  14936528  221040  467720  0  0   0   0  3  37  0  0  100  0
 0  0  0  14936464  221040  467720  0  0   0   0  3  37  0  0  100  0
```

The output shows the id column as 100 (100 percent idle), which indicates a fairly quiet system. If this were a busy system, we would see the id column at less than 100 and the us (user), sy (system), and wa (wait) columns with significantly high numbers. The us, sy, and id columns indicate the overall usage of the system. And the wa column indicates number of waiting processes to be run.

Consider Example 7-8. In this example, we create four threads that execute the `rec_fibonacci` function. Because we already know that one thread executing the `rec_fibonacci` function uses a significant number of CPU resources, with four threads we can expect the application to put an even higher load on the CPUs. Let's find out whether that is the case.

Example 7-8

Source Code for vmstat_1.c

```
#include <pthread.h>
#include <errno.h>
#include <stdlib.h>

static unsigned int v = 40;

/*
  A Fibonacci sequence is a sequence of numbers {f0, f1, f2 ....}
  in which the first two values are equal to 1 and each
  succeeding number is the sum of the previous two numbers.
  Here are the first few sequence of numbers of the Fibonacci
  sequence:
  1 1 2 3 5 8 13 21 ...
*/


unsigned long rec_fibonacci(unsigned long k)
{
  unsigned long x;

  x = 1;
  if (k > 1)
    x = rec_fibonacci(k-1) + rec_fibonacci(k-2);

  /* return the kth Fibonacci number */
  return x;
}

void *compute(void *arg)
{
```

```
  printf("recursive = %ld\n", rec_fibonacci(v));
}


main()
{
  int rc;
  int i;
  pthread_t tid[2];

  for (i=0; i<4; i++)
  {
    if( (rc = pthread_create(&tid[i], NULL, compute, NULL)) != 0)
    {
      printf("pthread_create failed: %d\n", errno);
      exit(1);
    }
  }

  for (i=0; i<4; i++)
  {
    pthread_join(tid[i], NULL);
  }

}
```

Compile the example:

```
$ gcc vmstat_1.c -o vmstat_1 -lpthread -D_REENTRANT
```

Run the example:

```
$ ./vmstat_1
```

Run `vmstat`:

```
$ vmstat 2
procs -----------memory---------- ---swap-- -----io---- --system-- ----cpu----
 r b   swpd   free   buff   cache  si  so   bi    bo    in    cs   us sy id wa
 0 0   116    23168  69832  522428  0   0    0     0     0     2    0  0  100 0
 0 0   116    23168  69832  522428  0   0    0     4     2    96    0  0  100 0
 0 0   116    22848  69832  522428  0   0    0     0     4   115    0  0  100 0
 7 0   116    22704  69832  522428  0   0    0    18     5   107   19  0   81 1
 6 0   116    22704  69832  522428  0   0    0     0     2    80  100  0    0 0
 4 0   116    22704  69832  522428  0   0    0     0     3    80  100  0    0 0
 4 0   116    22704  69832  522428  0   0    0    14     2    82  100  0    0 0
 4 0   116    22704  69832  522428  0   0    0     0     1    75  100  0    0 0
 6 0   116    22704  69832  522428  0   0    0     0     1    82  100  0    0 0
 0 0   116    22704  69832  522428  0   0    0     0     3   100   42  0   59 0
 0 0   116    22736  69832  522428  0   0    0     0     1    92    0  0  100 0
 0 0   116    22736  69832  522428  0   0    0     0     2   102    0  0  100 0
 0 0   116    22768  69832  522428  0   0    0     0     2    92    0  0  100 0
```

The `vmstat` output shows that the system got really busy when the application was started and went back to an idle state after the application exited. In this case, the user (us) column went up to 100, indicating a busy system in which all the CPU cycles (100 percent) were spent running the application code in the user space. For more information about `vmstat`, consult thc vmstat(8) man pages.

7.8.2.2 iostat

`iostat` generates a report about the system I/O activities. If no display interval is given, `iostat` displays I/O information since the last reboot. If a display interval is given, the first set of output represents total activity since boot time, and the subsequent outputs show only the delta activities. The report is divided into two sections: CPU utilization and device utilization. On multiprocessor systems, CPU statistics are calculated system-wide as averages among all processors:

```
avg-cpu: %user  %nice  %sys %iowait  %idle
           0.21    0.00    0.80      2.07    96.92

Device:        tps     Blk_read/s      Blk_wrtn/s       Blk_read    Blk_wrtn
sda           2.49           0.05         1443.46           2778     9552392
sdb           4.94           0.10         2871.73           5322   158268008
sdc           4.95           0.10         2860.91           5330   157671720
sdd          30.20        1518.55            0.42       83690898       23288
sde          60.25        2902.76            0.92      159978258       50896
sdf           0.00           0.01            0.00            378          24
sdg          59.49        2883.87            0.90      158937034       49520
```

`iostat` can indicate how busy disk devices can be during I/O operations. Depending on where files used by the application are placed, some disks can have more I/O operations than others. A disk that gets too busy can lead to large I/O waits, resulting in poor application performance. `iostat` information can help point out where the disk I/O bottlenecks are. This information can then be used by the application architect to redesign the filesystem layout policies.[21]

In our example printout, we can see that devices sdd, sde, and sdg have done the bulk of read operations, whereas devices sda, sdb, and sdc have done mostly write operations. This example also shows the tps (transaction per second) column of both the read and write operations. While comparing the tps rate of all disks, one can wonder why the write operations have low tps rates compared to the disks

---

21 Filesystems can be designed to be striped across disks to increase throughput.

involved in performing read operations. This question can prompt us to investigate how[22] files in these disks are accessed by the application to give us more clues as to why this is happening. This is just one example of how to use `iostat` to view the profile of the I/O operations of the application. For more information about `iostat`, refer to the iostat(1) man pages.

7.8.2.3 top

`top` provides a continuously updated view of a running system. It displays real-time information on CPU utilization, process statistics, and memory utilization, as shown here:

```
top - 16:23:43 up 27 days,7:07,  2 users,  load average: 0.00, 0.00,0.00
Tasks: 108 total,   1 running, 107 sleeping,   0 stopped,   0 zombie
Cpu0:0.0% us,  0.0% sy,  0.0% ni, 100.0% id,  0.0% wa,  0.0% hi,  0.0% si
Cpu1:0.1% us,  0.1% sy,  0.0% ni, 99.6% id,   0.1% wa,  0.0% hi,  0.0% si
Cpu2:0.0% us,  0.0% sy,  0.0% ni, 100.0% id,  0.0% wa,  0.0% hi,  0.0% si
Cpu3:0.1% us,  0.0% sy,  0.0% ni, 99.9% id,   0.0% wa,  0.0% hi,  0.0% si
Mem:  16190476k total,  2390180k used, 13800296k free,   223624k buffers
Swap: 37760724k total,        0k used, 37760724k free,   912316k cached

5775  root      15   0 31764  12m 2296 S  0.2  0.1 148:53.89 X
21463 root      16   0  2472 1520 1108 R  0.1  0.0   0:00.37 top
    1 root      16   0   628  284  248 S  0.0  0.0   0:04.34 init
    2 root      RT   0     0    0    0 S  0.0  0.0   0:00.00 migration/0
    3 root      34  19     0    0    0 S  0.0  0.0   0:00.00 ksoftirqd/0
    4 root      RT   0     0    0    0 S  0.0  0.0   0:00.00 migration/1
    5 root      34  19     0    0    0 S  0.0  0.0   0:00.00 ksoftirqd/1
    6 root      RT   0     0    0    0 S  0.0  0.0   0:00.01 migration/2
    7 root      34  19     0    0    0 S  0.0  0.0   0:00.00 ksoftirqd/2
```

`top`'s output is divided into two parts. The first part contains useful information related to overall system status such as CPU status, process counts, uptime, load average, and utilization statistics for both memory and swap space. The second part shows process-level statistics.

7.8.2.4 ps

The `ps` command displays information about active processes. Unlike `top`, the output is a single snapshot in time. You can view the information about how the memory and CPU are used by a particular process by using the `ps` command:

---

22 Perhaps the block transfer rates differ.

```
$ps aux
USER     PID   %CPU %MEM VSZ    RSS    TTY   STAT START TIME COMMAND
root     10712 99.9 0.7 119196 118528  pts/4 R+   8:53  2:24  ./ofreqde
root     10720  0.0 0.0   2612   1064  pts/0 R+   8:55  0:00  ps aux
root     10721  0.0 0.0   2172    892  pts/0 S+   8:55  0:00  more
```

The output of the ps aux command shows not only the total percentage of system memory that each process uses, but also its virtual memory footprint (VSZ) and the amount of physical memory that the process is currently using (RSS).

7.8.2.5 nmon

Although primarily used to monitor system performance when benchmarking an application, you can also use nmon to monitor the application's use of system resources. nmon is a free performance tool for Linux running on different supported platforms. You can use it to monitor or gather performance data, including CPU utilization, memory usage, disk I/O rates, network I/O rates, free space on filesystems, and more. Unlike top, nmon can record data to a file that can be analyzed at a later time. A companion tool called nmon analyzer is also available. The nmon analyzer is designed to take input files produced by nmon and turn them into spreadsheets containing high-quality graphs.

At the time of this writing, the nmon tool runs on the following:

- Linux SUSE SLES 9, Red Hat EL 3 and 4, Debian on pSeries p5, and OpenPower
- Linux SUSE, Red Hat, and many recent distributions on x86 (Intel and AMD in 32-bit mode)
- Linux SUSE and Red Hat on zSeries or mainframe
- AIX 4.1.5, 4.2.0 , 4.3.2, and 4.3.3 (nmon version 9a: This version is functionally established and will not be developed further.)
- AIX 5.1, 5.2, and 5.3 (nmon version 10: This version now supports AIX 5.3 and POWER5 processor-based machines, with SMT and shared CPU micropartitions.)

The nmon tool is available at www-128.ibm.com/developerworks/eserver/articles/analyze_aix/.[23]

---

23 Or at www.ibm.com/developer (search for nmon)

We just discussed some of the most commonly used tools that will help the porting engineer gather information about the application's resource signature. For more information about performance tuning on Linux, refer to the following:

- *Performance Tuning for Linux Server,* by Sandra K. Johnson et al. (IBM Press, 2005)
- *Optimizing Linux Performance: A Hands-on Guide to Linux Performance Tools,* by Phillip G. Ezolt (Prentice Hall, 2005)
- Tuning IBM eServer xSeries Servers for Performance, by David Watts et al. (www.redbooks.ibm.com/Redbooks.nsf/RedbookAbstracts/sg245287.html?Open)

With more and more companies relying on their software applications for increased productivity, application performance will play a larger and larger role in contributing to that productivity. Both the internal and external views to application tuning will give us the necessary information we need to help us tune the application to perform to its maximum potential on the Linux platform.

7.8.3 Other Tools

Other open-source tools exist that help in profiling and system performance on Linux that we thought are worth mentioning. They are Performance Inspector, System Tap, and Kprobes. Performance Inspector helps in application profiling; the other two tools deal more with the Linux kernel.

7.8.3.1 Performance Inspector[24]

Performance Inspector (http://sourceforge.net/projects/perfinsp) is a suite of tools that enables you to identify performance problems in your applications and shows you how your application interacts with the Linux kernel. It consists of the following tools:

- TProf is a CPU profiling tool. TProf interrupts the system periodically by time or the hardware performance monitor counters, and then determines the address of the interrupted code along with its process ID and thread ID.

---

24 http://perfinsp.sourceforge.net/

The sampling information is then processed and used to report hot spots in your code.

- PTT collects per-thread statistics, such as the number of CPU cycles, number of interrupts, and number of times the thread was dispatched.
- JLM provides statistics on locks based on the Java 2 technology.
- JProf is a shared library that interfaces with the Java `jvmpi` interface.
- Hdump is used to analyze the live objects in a Java heap. Hdump provides a live object heap usage summary by object class.
- ITrace for PPC64 is a software tracing mechanism that enables you to trace through both application and kernel code. ITrace proves most useful in situations where you have located a specific performance hot spot in your code and would like to optimize that hot spot at the assembly instruction level.

The majority of code within Performance Inspector is released under the GNU General Public License (GPL). Some shared libraries are under the GNU LGPL. At the time of this writing, there are three different packages for the different set of tools and methods for installation, as follows:

- **PerfInsp.** This package uses kernel patches and therefore requires the kernel rebuild. It is for the 2.4 kernel-based distributions.
- **Dpiperf.dynamic.** This package is primarily intended for the 2.6 kernel-based distributions. In this package, TProf and Java tools can be used without rebuilding the kernel. Other tools such as PTT and AI depend on Kprobes. They therefore require a kernel patch until Kprobe is included in the distributions.
- **PerfInsp.ITrace.PPC64.** This package includes the version of ITrace for PPC64 that utilizes the Kprobe kernel feature. The package contains the kernel patch for Kprobe, and therefore requires the kernel rebuild. This package has been tested on SLES9 and RHEL4.

7.8.3.2 SystemTap and Kprobes

SystemTap (http://sources.redhat.com/systemtap) is a dynamic instrumentation system for Linux. SystemTap is built on top of Kprobes, a facility that provides insight into the operation of the Linux kernel without recompiling or rebooting because it is built as a kernel module. Kprobes allows locations in the kernel to be instrumented with code that will be executed when the processor encounters that probe point. After the instrumentation code completes execution, the kernel resumes the normal operation. Kprobes is now included in the mainline 2.6[25] Linux kernel.

Here are some other publications that will help you learn more about SystemTap and Kprobe:

- Kernel debugging with Kprobes (www-106.ibm.com/developerworks/library/l-kprobes.html?ca=dgr-lnxw42Kprobe)
- Gaining insight into the Linux kernel with Kprobes (www.redhat.com/magazine/005mar05/features/kprobes/)
- Architecture of systemtap: a Linux trace/probe tool (http://sourceware.org/systemtap/archpaper-0505.pdf)
- Locating System Problems Using Dynamic Instrumentation, by Vara Prasad et al. Proceeding of Linux Symposium. July 2005, Ottawa, Canada.

SystemTap is safe and lightweight enough to use with live production systems. It is able to instrument both kernel and user space programs even in the absence of source code. SystemTap's probe language will be easy to use, and users will be able to reuse general scripts written by others.

7.9 Summary

Testing and debugging is an iterative process. Whenever a bug is found and then fixed, the application needs to go through another round of testing. Whether the application goes through a complete test cycle or just through a set of regression tests is a matter of choice. The main reason we go through a complete test cycle is to make sure a patch not only fixes the bug it was meant to fix, but that it does not cause other parts of the application to fail. If the patch was applied to a common library that is used by a large number of application functionalities, it is more advisable to run the application through a complete test cycle. If the patch only applies

25 Linux 2.6.12, to be exact

to some self-contained part of the code, however, it is safe to only run the application through a few tests that exercise that part of the code.

The GNU debugger is the debugger of choice on Linux.

`Cscope` is one of the best productivity tools recommended for use when porting or developing software applications. It alleviates the work of finding and cross-referencing symbols and functions used in small to very large application code.

Use of memory-debugging tools is a matter of preference. Some tools come in libraries that need to be linked in with the application; others wrap the application and analyze it without the need to link any libraries with the application.

Two views to application tuning exist. The internal view can help find application functions that can be optimized to perform better. The external view can help find the application's resource signature for systems planning. System utility tools such as `top` display application memory and CPU usage; code profilers such as `OProfile` can pinpoint what part of the application uses the most CPU.

With regard to the list of tools presented in this chapter, any seasoned software developer or porting personnel might say, "The more tools I have, the better." Indeed, to develop or port applications and to do this well, you must have the right tools. Although there may be other debugging and performance tools for Linux we forgot to mention, the tools described here are the most generally available and widely used in the open-source community. The beauty of open source is if a tool does not come standard with a particular Linux distribution, anyone can go to the specific tool's Web site and download it.

A

Solaris to Linux Reference Tables

In this appendix

A.1 Internationalization

Table A-1 compares internationalization application programming interfaces (APIs) between Solaris and Linux.

TABLE A-1
Internationalization APIs

Solaris libc	GNU libc	Functions
iconv, iconv_open, iconv_close	iconv, iconv_open, iconv_close	Translation functions
wcsncat, wcsdup, wcscmp, wcsncmp, wcscpy, wcsncpy, wcschr, wcsrchr, wcslen, wcsol, wcsspn, wcscspn, wcspbrk, wcstok, wcswcs, wcstombs, wctomb, wcwidth, wcswidth, wctob, wcrtomb, wcstoul, wcstod, wcsrtombs, wcscat	wcscat, wcsncat, wcscmp, wcsncmp, wcscpy, wcsncpy, wcslen, wcschr, wcsrchr, wcsstr, wcspbrk, wcsspn, wcscspn, wcswcs, wcstok, wcscoll, wcwidth, wcswidth, wcsxfrm, wcstombs, wctomb, wctob, wcstoul, wcstod, wcsrtombs, wcsdup	Wide-character string functions
btowc, mbrlen, mbsinit, mbrtowc, mbsrtowcs, mblen, mbtowc, mbstowcs	btowc, mbrlen, mbsinit, mbrtowc, mbsrtowcs, mblen, mbtowc, mbstowcs	Multibyte handling
isalpha, isupper, islower, isdigit, isxdigit, isalnum, isspace, ispunct, isprint, iscntrl, isascii, isgraph, isphonogram, isideogram, isenglish, isnumber, isspecial, iswalpha, iswupper, iswlower, iswdigit, iswxdigit, iswalnum, iswspace, iswpunct, iswprint, iswgraph, iswcntrl, iswascii	isascii, isalnum, isalpha, isblank, iscntrl, isdigit, isgraph, islower, isprint, ispunct, isspace, isupper, isxdigit, iswalnum, iswalpha, iswblank, iswcntrl, iswctype, iswdigit, iswgraph, iswlower, iswprint, iswpunct, iswspace, iswupper, iswxdigit	Character classifications

Solaris libc	GNU libc	Functions
getdate, strftime, strptime	getdate, strftime, strptime	Date and time formatting
strcoll, strxfrm, wcscoll, wcsxfrm	strcoll, strxfrm, wcscoll, wcsxfrm	Collation functions
wsprintf, wsscanf, fwprintf, fwscanf, wprintf, wscanf, swprintf, swscanf, vfwprintf, vswprintf	wprintf, fwprintf, swprintf, vwprintf, vfwprintf, vswprintf, fwscanf, swscanf, wscanf	Formatted wide-character input and output
wscasecmp, wsncasecmp, wcsstr, wmemchr, wmemcmp, wmemcpy, wmemmove, wmemset	wcsstr, wmemchr, wmemcmp, wmemcpy, wmemmove, wmemset, wcsncmp, wcsncasecmp	Wide string comparison and filling operations
regcomp, regexec, regerror, regfree, fnmatch	regcomp, regexec, regerror, regfree, fnmatch	Regular expressions

A.2 System Calls

Table A-2 provides the system call comparison between Solaris and Linux.

TABLE A-2
System Calls Comparison

Solaris	Linux	Description
access	access	Check user's permission for a file.
acct	acct	Switch process accounting on or off.
acl, facl	None	Get or set a file's access control list (ACL).
adjtime	adjtimex	Correct the time to allow synchronization of the system clock.
alarm	alarm	Schedule an alarm signal.

Solaris	Linux	Description
audit	None	Write a record to the audit log.
auditon	None	Manipulate auditing.
auditsvc	None	Write audit log to specified file descriptor.
brk	brk	Change data segment size.
chdir	chdir	Change working directory.
chmod	chmod	Change permissions of a file.
chown	chown	Change ownership of a file.
chroot	chroot	Change root directory.
close	close	Close a file descriptor.
creat	creat	Create a new file or rewrite an existing one.
dup	dup	Duplicate a file descriptor.
exec	exec	Execute a file.
exit	exit	Terminate the current process.
fcntl	fcntl	Manipulate file descriptor.
fork, fork1	fork	Create a child process.
fpathconf, pathconf	fpathconf, pathconf	Get configuration values for files.
futimesat	None	Set file access and modification times. It resolves the path relative to the fildes argument.
getacct, putacct, wracct	None	Get, put, or write extended accounting data.
getaudit, setaudit, getaudit_addr, setaudit_addr	None	Get and set process audit information.
getauid, setauid	None	Get and set user audit identity.
getcontext, setcontext	getcontext, setcontext	Get and set current user context.
getdents	getdents	Read directory entries and put in a filesystem-independent format. *Dirent structure on Linux and Solaris differs.*

Solaris	Linux	Description
getgroups, setgroups	getgroups, setgroups	Get or set supplementary group access list IDs.
getitimer, setitimer	getitimer, setitimer	Get or set value of interval timer.
getmsg, getpmsg	getmsg, getpmsg	Get next message off a stream.
getpflags, setpflags	None	Get or set process flags.
getpid, getpgrp, getppid, getpgid	getpid, getpgrp, getppid, getpgid	Get process, process group, and parent process IDs.
getppriv, setppriv	None	Get or set a privilege set.
getrlimit, setrlimit	getrlimit, setrlimit	Control maximum system resource consumption.
getsid	getsid	Get process group ID of session leader.
getuid, geteuid, getgid, getegid	getuid, geteuid, getgid, getegid	Get real user, effective user, real group, and effective group IDs.
getustack, setustack	None	Retrieve or change the address of per-LWP stack boundary information.
ioctl	ioctl	Control device.
issetugid	None	Determine whether current executable is running setuid or setgid.
kill	kill	Send a signal to a process or a group of processes.
link	link	Make a new name for a file.
llseek	_llseek	Move extended read/write file pointer.
lseek	lseek	Move read/write file pointer.
_lwp_cond_signal, _lwp_cond_broadcast	None	Signal a condition variable.
_lwp_cond_wait, _lwp_cond_timedwait, _lwp_cond_reltimedwaid	None	Wait on a condition variable.
_lwp_info	None	Return the time-accounting information of a single LWP.
_lwp_kill	None	Send a signal to an LWP.

Solaris	Linux	Description
_lwp_mutex_lock, _lwp_mutex_unlock, _lwp_mutex_trylock	None	Mutual exclusion.
_lwp_self	None	Get LWP identifier.
_lwp_sema_wait, _lwp_sema_trywait, _lwp_sema_init, _lwp_sema_post	None	Semaphore operations.
_lwp_suspend, _lwp_continue	None	Continue or suspend LWP execution.
memcntl	None	Memory management control.
meminfo	None	Provide information about memory.
mincore	mincore	Determine residency of memory pages.
mkdir	mkdir	Create a directory.
mknod	mknod	Make a directory, a special file, or a regular file.
mmap	mmap	Map pages of memory.
mount	mount	Mount a filesystem. The signatures of this system call on Solaris and Linux differ.
mprotect	mprotect	Set protection of memory mapping.
msgctl	msgctl	Message control operations.
msgget	msgget	Get a message queue identifier.
msgids	None	Discover all message queue identifiers.
msgrcv	msgrcv	Message receive operation. Linux uses `struct msgbuf` type in one of its arguments.
msgsnap	None	Message queue snapshot operation.
msgsnd	msgsnd	Message send operation. Linux uses `struct msgbuf` type in one of its arguments.
munmap	munmap	Unmap pages of memory.

Solaris	Linux	Description
nice	nice	Change priority of a process.
ntp_adjtime	ntp_adjtime	Adjust local clock parameters.
ntp_gettime	ntp_gettime	Get local clock values.
open, openat	open	Open a file. openat() is not available in Linux.
pause	pause	Suspend process until signal.
pcsample	None	Program execution time profile.
pipe	pipe	Create an interprocess channel.
poll	poll	Input/output multiplexing.
p_online	None	Return or change processor operational status.
priocntl	None	Process scheduler control.
priocntlset	None	Generalized process scheduler control.
processor_bind	sched_setaffinity	Bind LWPs to a processor. For more info about sched_setaffinity, see the "CPU Affinity" section in Chapter 4, "Porting Solaris Applications."
processor_info	None	Determine type and status of a processor.
profil	profil	Execution time profile.
pset_bind	sched_setaffinity	Bind LWPs to a set of processors. For more info about sched_setaffinity, see the "CPU Affinity" section in Chapter 4.
pset_create, pset_destroy, pset_assign, pset_info, pset_list, pset_setattr, pset_getattr	None	Manage sets of processors. There is no exact match in Linux, but CPU affinity is supported in Linux. For more information, see the "CPU Affinity" section in Chapter 4.
putmsg, putpmsg	None	Send a message on a stream.
read, readv, pread	read, readv, pread	Read from file.

Solaris	Linux	Description
`readlink`	`readlink`	Read the contents of a symbolic link.
`rename`, `renameat`	`rename`	Change the name of a file. *Linux does not have* `renameat()`.
`resolvepath`	None	Resolve all symbolic links of a path name.
`rmdir`	`rmdir`	Remove a directory.
`semctl`	`semctl`	Semaphore control operations.
`semget`	`semget`	Get set of semaphores.
`semids`	None	Discover all semaphore identifiers.
`semop`, `semtimedop`	`semop`, `semtimedop`	Semaphore operations.
`setpgid`	`setpgid`	Set process group ID.
`setpgrp`	`setpgrp`	Set process group ID.
`setrctl`, `getrctl`	None	Set or get resource control values.
`setregid`	`setregid`	Set real and effective group IDs.
`setreuid`	`setreuid`	Set real and effective user IDs.
`setsid`	`setsid`	Create session and set process group ID.
`settaskid`, `gettaskid`, `getprojid`	None	Set or get task or project IDs.
`setuid`, `setegid`, `seteuid`, `setgid`	`setuid`, `setegid`, `seteuid`, `setgid`	Set user and group IDs.
`shmctl`	`shmctl`	Shared memory control operations.
`shmget`	`shmget`	Get shared memory segment identifier.
`shmids`	None	Discover all shared memory identifiers.
`shmop`, `shmat`, `shmdt`	`shmop`, `shmat`, `shmdt`	Shared memory operation.
`sigaction`	`sigaction`	Detailed signal management.
`sigaltstack`	`sigaltstack`	Set or get signal alternate stack context.

Solaris	Linux	Description
`sigpending`	`sigpending`	Examine signals that are blocked and pending.
`sigprocmask`	`sigprocmask`	Change or examine caller's signal mask.
`sigsend, sigsendset`	None	Send a signal to a process or a group of processes.
`sigsuspend`	`sigsuspend`	Install a signal mask and suspend caller until signal is received.
`sigwait`	`sigwait`	Wait until a signal is posted.
`__sparc_utrap_install`	None	Install a SPARC V9 user trap handler.
`stat, lstat, fstat`	`stat, lstat, fstat`	Get file status.
`fstatat`	None	Get file status.
`statvfs, fstatvfs`	`statvfs, fstatvfs`	Get file system statistics.
`stime`	`stime`	Set system time and date.
`swapctl`	None	Manage swap space.
`symlink`	`symlink`	Make a symbolic link to a file.
`sync`	`sync`	Update super block.
`sysfs`	`sysfs`	Get file system type information.
`sysinfo`	`sysinfo`	Return information on overall system statistics.
`time`	`time`	Get time in seconds.
`times`	`times`	Get process times.
`uadmin`	None	Administrative control.
`ulimit`	`ulimit`	Get and set process limits.
`umask`	`umask`	Set and get file creation mask.
`umount, umount2`	`umount, umount2`	Unmount a file system.
`uname`	`uname`	Get name of current operating system.
`unlink, unlinkat`	`unlink`	Remove directory entry. *Linux does not have* `unlinkat()`.
`ustat`	`ustat`	Get file system statistics.

Solaris	Linux	Description
`utime`	`utime`	Set file access and modification times.
`utimes`	`utimes`	Set file access and modification times.
`vfork`	`vfork`	Spawn new process in a virtual-memory-efficient way.
`vhangup`	`vhangup`	Virtually hang up the current tty.
`waitid`	None	Wait for child process to change state.
`write`, `pwrite`, `writev`	`write`, `pwrite`, `writev`	Write on a file.
`yield`	`sched_yield`	Yield execution to another lightweight process.

A.3 Basic Library Functions

Table A-3 shows Solaris basic library functions and their equivalents on Linux as implemented through the GNU `libc` distribution.

TABLE A-3
Basic Library Function Comparison

Solaris Functions	Linux Equivalent	Description[1,2]
`a64l`	`a64l`	Convert between long integer and base-64 ASCII string.
`abort`	`abort`	Terminate the process abnormally.
`abs`	`abs`	Return absolute value of integer.
`addsev`	None	Define additional severities.
`addseverity`	`addseverity`	Build a list of severity levels for an application for use with `fmtmsg`.
`alloca`	`alloca`	Memory allocator.
`alphasort`	`alphasort`	Scan a directory.
`ascftime`	None	Convert date and time to string.

Solaris Functions	Linux Equivalent	Description
asctime	asctime	Convert date and time to string.
asctime_r	asctime_r	Convert date and time to string.
assert	assert	Verify program assertion.
atexit	atexit	Register a function to run at process termination or object unloading.
atof, atoi, atol, atoll	atof, atoi, atol, atoll	String conversion routines
atomic_add_16, atomic_add_16_nv, atomic_add_32, atomic_add_32_nv, atomic_add_64, atomic_add_64_nv, atomic_add_long, atomic_add_long_nv, atomic_and_32, atomic_and_uint, atomic_ops, atomic_or_32, atomic_or_unit	None	Atomic operations.
attropen	None	Open a file.
basename	basename	Return the last element of a path name.
bcmp	bcmp	Memory operations.
bcopy	bcopy	Memory operations.
bindtextdomain	bindtextdomain	Message handling functions.
bind_textdomain_codeset	bind_textdomain_codeset	Message handling functions.
bsdmalloc	None	Memory allocator.
bsd_signal	bsd_signal	Simplified signal facilities.
bsearch	bsearch	Binary search a sorted table.
bstring	bstring	Memory operations.
btowc	btowc	Single-byte to wide-character conversion.
bzero	bzero	Memory operations.

Solaris Functions	Linux Equivalent	Description
calloc	calloc	Memory allocator.
catclose	catclose	Close a message catalogue.
catgets	catgets	Read a program message.
catopen	catopen	Open a message catalogue.
cfgetispeed	cfgetispeed	Get input and output baud rate.
cfgetospeed	cfgetospeed	Get input and output baud rate.
cfree	cfree	Debugging memory allocator.
cfsetispeed	cfsetispeed	Set input and output baud rate.
cfsetospeed	cfsetospeed	Set input and output baud rate.
cftime	None	Convert date and time to string.
cleanerr	None	Stream status inquiries.
clock	clock	Report CPU time used.
closedir	closedir	Close a directory stream.
closefrom	None	Close or iterate over open file descriptors.
closelog	closelog	Control system log.
cond_broadcast	pthread_cond_broadcast	Condition variables (Solaris thread APIs).
cond_destroy, cond_init, cond_signal, cond_timedwait, cond_wait	pthread_cond_destroy, pthread_cond_init, pthread_cond_signal, pthread_cond_wait, pthread_cond_timedwait	Condition variables.
cond_reltimedwait	None	Blocks on the conditional variable until the specified relative time passes.
confstr	confstr	Get configurable variables.
crypt	crypt	String encoding function.
crypt_genhash_impl, crypt_gensalt, crypt_gensalt_impl	None	Encrypted password functions.

Solaris Functions	Linux Equivalent	Description
cset, csetcol, csetlen, csetno	None	Get information on EUC codeset functions.
ctermid	ctermid	Generate path name for controlling terminal.
ctermid_r	None	Generate path name for controlling terminal.
ctime	ctime	Convert date and time to string.
ctype	None	Character handling.
cuserid	cuserid	Get character login name of the user.
dbm	dbm	Database subroutines.
dbm_clearerr	dbm_clearerr	Database functions.
dbm_close	dbm_close	Database functions.
dbmclose	dbmclose	Database subroutines.
dbm_delete	dbm_delete	Database functions.
dbm_error	dbm_error	Database functions.
dbm_fetch	dbm_fetch	Database functions.
dbm_firstkey	dbm_firstkey	Database functions.
dbminit	dbminit	Database subroutines.
dbm_nextkey	dbm_nextkey	Database functions.
dbm_open	dbm_open	Database functions.
dbm_store	dbm_store	Database functions.
dcgettext	dcgettext	Message handling functions.
dcngettext	dcngettext	Message handling functions.
decimal_to_double, decimal_to_extended, decimal_to_floating, decimal_to_quadruple, decimal_to_single	None	Convert decimal record functions.
delete	delete	Database subroutines.
dgettext	dgettext	Message handling functions.
difftime	difftime	Computes the difference between two calendar times.

Solaris Functions	Linux Equivalent	Description
directio	None	Provide advice to file system.
dirname	dirname	Report the parent directory name of a file path name.
div	div	Compute the quotient and remainder.
dladdr	dladdr	Translate address to symbolic information.
dladdr1	dladdr1	Translate address to symbolic information.
dlclose	dlclose	Close a shared object.
dldump	None	Create a new file from a dynamic object component of the calling process.
dlerror	dlerror	Get diagnostic information.
dlinfo	dlinfo	Dynamic load information.
dlmopen	dlmopen	Gain access to an executable object file.
dlopen	dlopen	Gain access to an executable object file.
dlsym	dlsym	Get the address of a symbol in a shared object or executable.
dngettext	dngettext	Message handling functions.
double_to_decimal	None	Convert floating-point value to decimal record.
drand48	drand48	Generate uniformly distributed pseudorandom numbers.
dup2	dup2	Duplicate an open file descriptor.
econvert	None	Output conversion.
ecvt	ecvt	Convert floating-point number to string.
_edata, edata	None	Last locations in program.
encrypt	encrypt	Encoding function.
_end, end	None	Last locations in program.
endgrent	endgrent	Group database entry functions.

Solaris Functions	Linux Equivalent	Description
endnetgrent	endnetgrent	Get network group entry.
endpwent	endpwent	Get password entry.
endspent	endspent	Get password entry.
endusershell	endusershell	Get legal user shells.
endutent	endutent	User accounting database functions.
endutxent	endutxend	User accounting database functions.
erand48	erand48	Generate uniformly distributed pseudorandom numbers.
errno	errno	Print system error messages.
_etext, etext	None	Last locations in program.
euccol	euccol	Get byte length and display width of EUC characters.
euclen	euclen	Get byte length and display width of EUC characters.
eucscol	eucscol	Get byte length and display width of EUC characters.
exit	exit	Terminate process.
_exithandle	None	Terminate process.
extended_to_decimal	None	Convert floating-point value to decimal record.
fattach	fattach	Attach a STREAMS- or doors-based file descriptor to an object in the file system namespace.
__fbufsize	__fbufsize	Interfaces to stdio FILE structure.
fclose	fclose	Close a stream.
fconvert	None	Output conversion.
fcvt	fcvt	Convert floating-point number to string.
FD_CLR	FD_CLR	Synchronous I/O multiplexing.
fdetach	fdetach	Detach a name from a STREAMS-based file descriptor.

Solaris Functions	Linux Equivalent	Description
FD_ISSET	FD_ISSET	Synchronous I/O multiplexing.
fdwalk	None	Close or iterate over open file descriptors.
FD_ZERO	FD_ZERO	Synchronous I/O multiplexing.
feof	feof	Stream status inquiries.
ferror	ferror	Stream status inquiries.
fetch	fetch	Data base subroutines.
fflush	fflush	Flush a stream.
ffs	ffs	Find first set bit.
fgetc	fgetc, fgets	Input of characters and strings.
fgetgrent, fgetgrent_r	fgetgrent, fgetgrent_r	Group database entry functions.
fgetpos	fgetpos, fseek, fsetpos, ftell	Reposition a stream.
fgetpwent, fgetpwent_r	fgetpwent	Get password entry.
fgets	fgets	Get a string from a stream.
fgetspent, fgetspent_r	fgetspent, fgetspent_r	Get password entry.
fgetwc	fgetwc	Get a wide-character code from a stream.
fgetws	fgetws	Get a wide-character string from a stream.
fileno	fileno	Stream status inquiries.
file_to_decimal	None	Parse characters into decimal record.
finite	finite	Determine type of floating-point number.
firstkey	firstkey	Database subroutines.
__flbf	__flbf	Interfaces to stdio FILE structure.
floating_to_decimal	floating_to_decimal	Convert floating-point value to decimal record.
flock	flock	Apply or remove an advisory lock on an open file.

Solaris Functions	Linux Equivalent	Description
`flockfile`	`flockfile`	Acquire and release stream lock.
`_flushlbf`	`_flushlbf`	Interfaces to `stdio` FILE structure.
`fmtmsg`	`fmtmsg`	Display a message on `stderr` or system console.
`fnmatch`	`fnmatch`	Match filename or path name.
`fopen`	`fopen`	Open a stream.
`fpclass`	`fpclass`	Determine type of floating-point number.
`__fpending`	`__fpending`	Interfaces to `stdio` FILE structure.
`fpgetmask`, `fpgetround`, `fpgetsticky`	None	IEEE floating-point environment control.
`fprintf`	`fprintf`	Print formatted output.
`fpsetmask`, `fpsetround`, `fpsetsticky`	None	IEEE floating-point environment control.
`__fpurge`	`__fpurge`	Interfaces to `stdio` FILE structure.
`fputc`	`fputc`	Put a byte on a stream.
`fputs`	`fputs`	Put a string on a stream.
`fputwc`	`fputwc`	Put wide-character code on a stream.
`fputws`	`fputws`	Put wide-character string on a stream.
`fread`	`fread`	Binary input.
`__freadable`	`__freadable`	Interfaces to `stdio` FILE structure.
`__freading`	`__freading`	Interfaces to `stdio` FILE structure.
`free`	`free`	Memory allocator.
`freopen`	`freopen`	Open a stream.
`fscanf`	`fscanf`	Convert formatted input.
`fseek`	`fseek`	Reposition a file-position indicator in a stream.

Solaris Functions	Linux Equivalent	Description
fseeko	fseeko	Reposition a file-position indicator in a stream.
__fsetlocking	__fsetlocking	Interfaces to stdio FILE structure.
fsetpos	fsetpos	Reposition a file pointer in a stream.
fsync	fsync	Synchronize changes to a file.
ftell	ftell	Return a file offset in a stream.
ftello	ftello	Return a file offset in a stream.
ftime	ftime	Get date and time.
ftok	ftok	Generate an IPC key.
ftruncate	ftruncate	Set a file to a specified length.
ftrylockfile	ftrylockfile	Acquire and release stream lock.
ftw	ftw	Walk a file tree.
func_to_decimal	None	Parse characters into decimal record.
funlockfile	funlockfile	Release stream lock.
fwide	fwide	Set stream orientation.
fwprintf	fwprintf	Print formatted wide-character output.
__fwritable	__fwritable	Interfaces to stdio FILE structure.
fwrite	fwrite	Binary output.
__fwriting	__fwriting	Interfaces to stdio FILE structure.
fwscanf	fwscanf	Convert formatted wide-character input.
gconvert	None	Output conversion.
gcvt	gcvt	Convert floating-point number to string.
getc	getc	Get a byte from a stream.
getchar	getchar	Get a byte from a stream.
getc_unlocked	getc_unlocked	Get a byte from a stream.

Solaris Functions	Linux Equivalent	Description
getcwd	getcwd	Get pathname of current working directory.
getdate	getdate	Convert user format date and time.
getdtablesize	getdtablesize	Get the file descriptor table size.
getenv	getenv	Return value for environment name.
getexecname	None	Return path name of executable.
getextmntent	None	Get mounted device information.
getgrent, getgrent_r	getgrent, getgrent_r	Group database entry functions.
getgrgid, getgrgid_r	getgrgid, getgrgid_r	Group database entry functions.
getgrnam, getgrnam_r	getgrnam, getgrnam_r	Group database entry functions.
gethomelgroup	None	Obtain info on scheduling decisions.
gethostid	gethostid	Get an identifier for the current host.
gethostname	gethostname	Get name of current host.
gethrtime, gethrvtime	clock_getres, clock_gettime, clock_settime	Get high-resolution time.[3]
getloadavg	getloadavg	Get system load averages.
getlogin, getlogin_r	getlogin, getlogin_r	Get login name.
getmntany	None	Get mounted device info.
getmntent	getmntent	Get mounted device info.
getnetgrent, getnetgrent_r	getnetgrent, getnetgrent_r	Get network group entry.
getopt	getopt	Command option parsing.
getopt_clip	None	Parse long command option.
getopt_long	getopt_long	Parse long command option.

Solaris Functions	Linux Equivalent	Description
getopt_long_only	getopt_long_only	Parse long command option.
getpagesize	getpagesize	Get system page size.
getpagesizes	None	Get system supported page size.
getpass	getpass	Read a string of characters without echo.
getpassphrase	None	Read a string of characters without echo.
getpeerucred	None	Get connected socket/ STREAM peer's credentials.
getpriority	getpriority	Get process scheduling priority.
getpw	getpw	Get password entry from UID.
getpwent, getpwent_r	getpwent, getpwent_r	Get password entry.
getpwnam, getpwnam_r	getpwnam, getpwnam_r	Get password entry.
getpwuid, getpwuid_r	getpwuid, getpwuid_r	Get password entry.
getrusage	getrusage	Get info about resource utilization.
gets	gets	Get a string from a stream.
getspent, getspent_r	getspent, getspent_r	Get password entry.
getspnam, getspnam_r	getspnam, getspnam_r	Get password entry.
getsubopt	getsubopt	Parse suboptions from a string.
gettext	gettext	Message handling functions.
gettimeofday	gettimeofday	Get the date and time.
gettxt	None	Retrieve a text string.
getusershell	getusershell	Get legal user shells.
getutent	getutent	User accounting database functions.
getuid	getuid	User accounting database functions.
getutline	getutline	User accounting database functions.
getutmp	getutmp	User accounting database functions.

Solaris Functions	Linux Equivalent	Description
getutmpx	getutmpx	User accounting database functions.
getutxent	getutxent	User accounting database functions.
getutxid	getutxid	User accounting database functions.
getutxline	getutxline	User accounting database functions.
getvfsany, getvfsent, getvfsfile, getvfsspec	None	Get vfstab file entry functions.
getw	getw	Get a byte from a stream.
getwc	getwc	Get a wide character from a stream.
getwchar	getwchar	Get a wide character from a stdin stream.
getwd	getwd	Get current working directory path name.
getwidth	None	Get codeset information.
getws	None	Get a wide-character string from a stream.
getzoneid	None	Map between zone ID and name.
getzoneidbyname, getzonenamebyid	None	Map between zone ID and name.
glob	glob	Generate path names matching a pattern.
globfree	globfree	Generate path names matching a pattern.
gmtime, gmtime_r	gmtime, gmtime_r	Convert date and time to string.
grantpt	grantpt	Grant access to the slave pseudo-terminal device.
gsignal	gsignal	Software signals.
hasmntopt	hasmntopt	Get mounted device information.
hcreate	hcreate	Manage hash search tables.

Solaris Functions	Linux Equivalent	Description
hdestroy	hdestroy	Manage hash search tables.
hsearch	hsearch	Manage hash search tables.
iconv	iconv	Code conversion function.
iconv_close	iconv_close	Code conversion deallocation function.
iconv_open	iconv_open	Code conversion allocation function.
imaxabs	imaxabs	Return absolute value.
imaxdiv	imaxdiv	Return quotient and remainder.
index	index	String operations.
initgroups	initgroups	Initialize the supplementary group access list.
initstate	initstate	Pseudorandom number functions.
innetgr	innetgr	Get network group entry.
insque	insque	Insert/remove element from a queue.
isaexec	None	Invoke ISA-specific executable.
isalnum	isalnum	Character handling.
isalpha	isalpha	Character handling.
isascii	isascii	Character handling.
isastream	isastream	Character handling.
isatty	isatty	Character handling.
isblank	isblank	Character handling.
iscntrl	iscntrl	Character handling.
isdigit	isdigit	Character handling.
isenglish	None	Wide-character code classification functions.
isgraph	isgraph	Character handling.
isideogram	None	Wide-character code classification functions.
islower	islower	Character handling.

Solaris Functions	Linux Equivalent	Description
`isnand`	None	Determine type of floating-point number.
`isnanf`	`isnanf`	Determine type of floating-point number.
`isnumber`	None	Wide-character code classification functions.
`isphonogram`	None	Wide-character code classification functions.
`isprint`	`isprint`	Character handling.
`ispunct`	`ispunct`	Character handling.
`isspace`	`isspace`	Character handling.
`isspecial`	None	Wide-character code classification functions.
`isupper`	`isupper`	Character handling.
`iswalnum`	`iswalnum`	Wide-character code classification functions.
`iswalpha`	`iswalpha`	Wide-character code classification functions.
`iswascii`	None	Wide-character code classification functions.
`iswblank`	`iswblank`	Wide-character code classification functions.
`iswcntrl`	`iswcntrl`	Wide-character code classification functions.
`iswctype`	`iswctype`	Test character for specified class.
`iswdigit`	`iswdigit`	Wide-character code classification functions.
`iswgraph`	`iswgraph`	Wide-character code classification functions.
`iswlower`	`iswlower`	Wide-character code classification functions.
`iswprint`	`iswprint`	Wide-character code classification functions.
`iswpunct`	`iswpunct`	Wide-character code classification functions.

Solaris Functions	Linux Equivalent	Description
iswspace	iswspace	Wide-character code classification functions.
iswupper	iswupper	Wide-character code classification functions.
iswxdigit	iswxdigit	Wide-character code classification functions.
isxdigit	isxdigit	Character handling.
jrand48	jrand48	Generate uniformly distributed pseudorandom numbers.
killpg	killpg	Send signal to a process group.
l64a	l64a	Convert between long integer and base-64 ASCII string.
labs	labs	Return absolute value of integer.
lckpwdf	lckpwdf	Manipulate shadow password database lock file.
lcong48	lcong48	Generate uniformly distributed pseudorandom numbers.
ldiv	ldiv	Compute the quotient and remainder.
lfind	lfind	Linear search and update.
lfmt	None	Display error message in standard format and pass to logging and monitoring services.
llabs	llabs	Return absolute value of integer.
lldiv	lldiv	Compute the quotient and remainder.
lltostr	None	String conversion routines.
localeconv	localeconv	Get numeric formatting information.
localtime	localtime	Convert date and time to string.
localtime_r	localtime_r	Convert date and time to string.

Solaris Functions	Linux Equivalent	Description
lockf	lockf	Record locking on files.
_longjmp	_longjmp	Nonlocal goto.
longjmp	longjmp	Nonlocal goto.
lrand48	lrand48	Generate uniformly distributed pseudorandom numbers.
lsearch	lsearch	Linear search and update.
madvise	madvise	Provide advice to VM system.
major	major	Manage a device number.
makecontext	makecontext	Manipulate user contexts.
makedev	makedev	Manage a device number.
mallinfo	None	Memory allocator.
malloc	malloc	Memory allocator.
mallocctl	None	MT hot memory allocator.
mallopt	mallopt	Memory allocator.
mapmalloc	None	Memory allocator.
mblen	mblen	Get number of bytes in a character.
mbrlen	mbrlen	Get number of bytes in a character (restartable).
mbrtowc	mbrtowc	Convert a character to a wide-character code (restartable).
mbsinit	mbsinit	Determine conversion object status.
mbsrtowcs	mbsrtowcs	Convert a character string to a wide-character string (restartable).
mbstowcs	mbstowcs	Convert a character string to a wide-character string.
mbtowc	mbtowc	Convert a character to a wide-character code.
mctl	None	Memory management control.
memalign	memalign	Memory allocator.
memccpy	memccpy	Memory operations.
memchr	memchr	Memory operations.

Solaris Functions	Linux Equivalent	Description
memcmp	memcmp	Memory operations.
memcpy	memcpy	Memory operations.
memmove	memmove	Memory operations.
memset	memset	Memory operations.
minor	minor	Manage a device number.
mkfifo	mkfifo	Make a FIFO special file.
mkstemp	mkstemp	Make a unique filename from a template and open the file.
mktemp	mktemp	Make a unique filename from a template.
mktime	mktime	Convert a `tm` structure to a calendar time.
mlock	mlock	Lock or unlock pages in memory.
mlockall	mlockall	Lock or unlock address space.
monitor	None	Prepare process execution profile.
mrand48	mrand48	Generate uniformly distributed pseudorandom numbers.
msync	msync	Synchronize memory with physical storage.
mtmalloc	None	MT hot memory allocator.
munlock	munlock	Lock or unlock pages in memory.
munlockall	munlockall	Lock or unlock address space.
nextkey	nextkey	Database subroutines.
nftw	nftw	Walk a file tree.
ngettext	ngettext	Message handling functions.
nice	nice	Change priority of a process.
nlist	None	Get entries from symbol table.
nl_langinfo	nl_langinfo	Language information.
nrand48	nrand48	Generate uniformly distributed pseudorandom numbers.
offsetof	offsetof	Offset of structure member.

Solaris Functions	Linux Equivalent	Description
opendir	opendir	Open directory.
openlog	openlog	Control system log.
pclose	pclose	Initiate a pipe to or from a process.
perror	perror	Print system error messages.
pfmt	None	Display error message in standard format.
plock	None	Lock or unlock into memory process, text, or data.
popen	popen	Initiate a pipe to or from a process.
port_alert, port_associate, port_create, port_dissociate, port_get, port_getn, port_send, port_sendn,	None	Port event functions.
posix_openpt	posix_openpt	Open a pseudo terminal device.
posix_spawn	posix_spawn	Spawn a process.
posix_spawnattr_ destroy	posix_spawnattr_ destroy	Destroy and initialize spawn attributes object.
posix_spawnattr_ getflags	posix_spawnattr_ getflags	Get and set spawn-flags attribute of spawn attributes object.
posix_spawnattr_ getpgroup	posix_spawnattr_ getpgroup	Get and set spawn-pgroup attribute of spawn attributes object.
posix_spawnattr_ getschedparam	posix_spawnattr_ getschedparam	Get and set spawn-schedparam attribute of spawn attributes object.
posix_spawnattr_ getschedpolicy	posix_spawnattr_ getschedpolicy	Get and set spawn-schedpolicy attribute of spawn attributes object.
posix_spawnattr_ getsigdefault	posix_spawnattr_ getsigdefault	Get and set spawn-sigdefault attribute of spawn attributes object.

Solaris Functions	Linux Equivalent	Description
posix_spawnattr_getsigmask	posix_spawnattr_getsigmask	Get and set spawn-sigmask attribute of spawn attributes object.
posix_spawnattr_init	posix_spawnattr_init	Destroy and initialize spawn attributes object.
posix_spawnattr_setflags	posix_spawnattr_setflags	Get and set spawn-flags attribute of spawn attributes object.
posix_spawnattr_setpgroup	posix_spawnattr_setpgroup	Get and set spawn-pgroup attribute of spawn attributes object.
posix_spawnattr_setschedparam	posix_spawnattr_setschedparam	Get and set spawn-schedparam attribute of spawn attributes object.
posix_spawnattr_setschedpolicy	posix_spawnattr_setschedpolicy	Get and set spawn-schedpolicy attribute of spawn attributes object.
posix_spawnattr_setsigfault	posix_spawnattr_setsigfault	Get and set spawn-sigdefault attribute of spawn attributes object.
posix_spawnattr_setsigmask	posix_spawnattr_setsigmask	Get and set spawn-sigmask attribute of spawn attributes object.
posix_spawn_file_actions_addclose	posix_spawn_file_actions_addclose	Add close or open action to spawn file actions object.
posix_spawn_file_actions_adddup2	posix_spawn_file_actions_adddup2	Add dup2 action to spawn file actions object.
posix_spawn_file_actions_addopen	posix_spawn_file_actions_addopen	Add close or open action to spawn file actions object.
posix_spawn_file_actions_destroy	posix_spawn_file_actions_destroy	Destroy and initialize spawn file actions object.
posix_spawn_file_actions_init	posix_spawn_file_actions_init	Destroy and initialize spawn file actions object.
posix_spawnp	posix_spawnp	Spawn a process.
printf	printf	Print formatted output.

Solaris Functions	Linux Equivalent	Description
printstack	None	Walk stack pointed to by ucontext. There is no exact match, but Linux has a command pstack (http://linuxcommand.org/man_pages/pstack1.html) and catchsegv (http://nixdoc.net/man-pages/linux/man1/catchsegv.1.html).
priv_addset, priv_allocset, priv_copyset, priv_delset, priv_emptyset, priv_fillset, priv_freeset, priv_getbyname, priv_getsetbyname, priv_getsetbynum, priv_gettext, priv_ineffect, priv_intersect, priv_inverse, priv_isemptyset, priv_isequalset, priv_isfullset, priv_ismember, priv_issubset, priv_set, priv_set_to_str, priv_str_to_set, priv_union	None	Privilege set manipulation functions.
pselect	pselect	Synchronous I/O multiplexing.
pset_getloadavg	None	Get system load averages for a processor set.
psiginfo	None	System signal messages.
psignal	psignal	System signal messages.
ptrace	ptrace	Allows a parent process to control the execution of a child process.

Solaris Functions	Linux Equivalent	Description
ptsname	ptsname	Get name of the slave pseudo-terminal device.
putc	putc	Put a byte on a stream.
putchar	putchar	Put a byte on a stream.
putchar_unlocked	putchar_unlocked	Put a byte on a stream.
putc_unlocked	putc_unlocked	Put a byte on a stream.
putenv	putenv	Change or add value to environment.
putmntent	None	Get mounted device information.
puts	puts	Put a string on a stream.
putspent	putspent	Write shadow password file entry.
pututline	pututline	User accounting database functions.
pututxline	pututxline	User accounting database functions.
putw	putw	Put a byte on a stream.
putwc	putwc	Put wide-character code on a stream.
putwchar	putwchar	Put wide-character code on a stream.
putws	None	Convert a string of Process Code characters to EUC characters.
qeconvert, qfconvert, qgconvert	None	Output conversion functions.
qsort	qsort	Quick sort.
quadruple_to_decimal	None	Convert floating-point value to decimal record.
raise	raise	Send signal to program.
rand	rand	Simple random-number generator.
random	random	Pseudorandom number functions.

Solaris Functions	Linux Equivalent	Description
rand_r	rand_r	Simple random-number generator.
rctlblk_get_enforced_value, rctlblk_get_firing_time, rctlblk_get_global_action, rctlblk_get_global_flags, rctlblk_get_local_action, rctlblk_get_local_flags, rctlblk_get_privilege, rctlblk_get_recipient_pid, rctlblk_get_value, rctlblk_set_local_action, rctlblk_set_local_flags, rctlblk_set_privilege, rctlblk_set_recipient_pid, rctlblk_set_value, rctlblk_size	None	Manipulate resource control block functions.
rctl_walk	None	Visit registered rctls on current system.
readdir	readdir	Read directory.
readdir	readdir	Read a directory entry.
readdir_r	readdir_r	Read directory.
realloc	realloc	Memory allocator.
realpath	realpath	Resolve path name.
reboot	reboot	Reboot system or halt processor.
re_comp	re_comp	Compile and execute regular expressions.
re_exec	re_exec	Compile and execute regular expressions.
regcmp	None	Compile and execute regular expression. On Linux, use regcomp() instead.
regcomp	regcomp	Regular expression matching.

Solaris Functions	Linux Equivalent	Description
regerror	regerror	Regular expression matching.
regex	regex	Compile and execute regular expression.
regexec	regexec	Regular expression matching.
regfree	regfree	Regular expression matching.
remove	remove	Remove file.
remque	remque	Insert/remove element from a queue.
resetmnttab	None	Get mounted device information.
rewind	rewind	Reset file position indicator in a stream.
rewinddir	rewinddir	Reset position of directory stream to the beginning of a directory.
rindex	rindex	String operations.
scandir	scandir	Scan a directory.
scanf	scanf	Convert formatted input.
schedctl_exit, schedctl_init, schedctl_lookup, schedctl_start, schedctl_stop	None	Preemption control functions.
seconvert	None	Output conversion.
seed48	seed48	Generate uniformly distributed pseudorandom numbers.
seekdir	seekdir	Set position of directory stream.
select	select	Synchronous I/O multiplexing.
setbuf	setbuf	Assign buffering to a stream.
setbuffer	setbuffer	Assign buffering to a stream.
setcat	None	Define default catalogue.
setenv	setenv	Add or change environment variable.

Solaris Functions	Linux Equivalent	Description
`setgrent`	`setgrent`	Group database entry functions.
`sethostname`	`sethostname`	Get or set name of current host.
`_setjmp`	`_setjmp`	Nonlocal goto.
`setjmp`	`setjmp`	Nonlocal goto.
`setkey`	`setkey`	Set encoding key.
`setlabel`	None	Define the label for `pfmt()` and `lfmt()`.
`setlinebuf`	`setlinebuf`	Assign buffering to a stream.
`setlocale`	`setlocale`	Modify and query a program's locale.
`setlogmask`	`setlogmask`	Control system log.
`setnetgrent`	`setnetgrent`	Get network group entry.
`setpriority`	`setpriority`	Get or set process scheduling priority.
`setpwent`	`setpwent`	Get password entry.
`setspent`	`setspent`	Get password entry.
`setstate`	`setstate`	Pseudorandom number functions.
`settimeofday`	`settimeofday`	Get or set the date and time.
`setusershell`	`setusershell`	Get legal user shells.
`setutent`	`setutent`	User accounting database functions.
`setutxent`	`setutxent`	User accounting database functions.
`setvbuf`	`setvbuf`	Assign buffering to a stream.
`sfconvert, sgconvert`	None	Output conversion functions.
`sig2str`	None	Translation between signal name and signal number.
`sigaddset`	`sigaddset`	Manipulate sets of signals.
`sigblock`	`sigblock`	Block signals.
`sigdelset`	`sigdelset`	Manipulate sets of signals.
`sigemptyset`	`sigemptyset`	Manipulate sets of signals

Solaris Functions	Linux Equivalent	Description
sigfillset	sigfillset	Manipulate sets of signals
sigfpe	None	Signal handling for specific SIGFPE codes.
sighold	sighold	Simplified signal management for application processes.
sigignore	sigignore	Simplified signal management for application processes.
siginterrupt	siginterrupt	Allow signals to interrupt functions.
sigismember	sigismember	Manipulate sets of signals.
siglongjmp	siglongjmp	Nonlocal goto.
sigmask	sigmask	Block signals.
signal	signal	Simplified signal management for application processes.
signal	signal	Simplified software signal facilities.
sigpause	sigpause	Simplified signal management for application processes.
sigpause	sigpause	Block signals.
sigrelse	sigrelse	Simplified signal management for application processes.
sigset	sigset	Simplified signal management for application processes.
sigsetjmp	sigsetjmp	Nonlocal goto.
sigsetmask	sigsetmask	Block signals.
sigsetops	None	Manipulate sets of signals.
sigstack	sigstack	Set and/or get alternate signal stack context.
sigstack	sigstack	Set and/or get signal stack context.
sigvec	sigvec	Software signal facilities.
single_to_decimal	None	Convert floating-point value to decimal record.
sleep	sleep	Suspend execution for an interval of time.

Solaris Functions	Linux Equivalent	Description
sleep	sleep	Suspend execution for interval.
snprintf	snprintf	Print formatted output.
sprintf	sprintf	Print formatted output.
sprintf	sprintf	Formatted output conversion.
srand	srand	Simple random-number generator.
srand48	srand48	Generate uniformly distributed pseudorandom numbers.
srandom	srandom	Pseudorandom number functions.
sscanf	sscanf	Convert formatted input.
ssignal	ssignal	Software signals.
stack_getbounds, _stack_grow, stack_inbounds, stack_setbounds, stack_violation	None	Stack manipulation and operation functions.
stdio	stdio	Standard buffered input/output package.
store	store	Database subroutines.
str2sig	None	Translation between signal name and signal number.
strcasecmp, strcat, strchr, strcmp, strcoll, strcpy, strcspn, strdup, strerror, strerror_r	strcasecmp, strcat, strchr, strcmp, strcoll, strcpy, strcspn, strdup, strerror, strerror_r	String operations.
strfmon	strfmon	Convert monetary value to string.
strftime	strftime	Convert date and time to string.
string	string	String operations.
string_to_decimal	None	Parse characters into decimal record.
strlcat, strlcpy, strlen, strncasecmp, strncat, strncmp, strncpy, strpbrk	strlcat, strlcpy, strlen, strncasecmp, strncat, strncmp, strncpy, strpbrk	String operations.

Solaris Functions	Linux Equivalent	Description
strptime	strptime	Date and time conversion.
strrchr	strrchr	String operations.
strsignal	strsignal	Get name of signal.
strspn	strspn	String operations.
strstr	strstr	String operations.
strtod	strtod	Convert string to floating-point number.
strtof	strtof	Convert string to floating-point number.
strtoimax	strtoimax	Convert string to integer type.
strtok	strtok	String operations.
strtok_r	strtok_r	String operations.
strtol	strtol	String conversion routines.
strtold	strtold	Convert string to floating-point number.
strtoll	strtoll	String conversion routines.
strtoul	strtoul	Convert string to unsigned long.
strtoull	strtoull	Convert string to unsigned long.
strtoumax	strtoumax	Convert string to integer type.
strtows	None	Code conversion for Process Code and File Code.
strxfrm	strxfrm	String transformation.
swab	swab	Swap bytes.
swapcontext	swapcontext	Manipulate user contexts.
swprintf	swprintf	Print formatted wide-character output.
swscanf	swscanf	Convert formatted wide-character input.
sync_instruction_memory	None	Make modified instructions executable.
syscall	syscall	Indirect system call.

Solaris Functions	Linux Equivalent	Description
sysconf	sysconf	Get configurable system variables.
syslog	syslog	Control system log.
sys_siglist	None	System signal messages.
system	system	Issue a shell command.
tcdrain	tcdrain	Wait for transmission of output.
tcflow	tcflow	Suspend or restart the transmission or reception of data.
tcflush	tcflush	Flush nontransmitted output data, nonread input data, or both.
tcgetattr	tcgetattr	Get the parameters associated with the terminal.
tcgetpgrp	tcgetpgrp	Get foreground process group ID.
tcgetsid	tcgetsid	Get process group ID for session leader for controlling terminal.
tcsendbreak	tcsendbreak	Send a "break" for a specific duration.
tcsetattr	tcsetattr	Set the parameters associated with the terminal.
tcsetpgrp	tcsetpgrp	Set foreground process group ID.
tdelete	tdelete	Manage binary search trees.
td_event_addset, td_event_delset, td_event_emptyset, td_event_fillset, td_eventisempty, td_eventismember, td_init, td_log	td_event_addset, td_event_delset, td_event_emptyset, td_event_fillset, td_eventisempty, td_eventismember, td_init, td_log	Thread events in libc_db functions.
td_sync_get_info, td_sync_get_stats, td_sync_setstate, td_sync_waiters	None	Operations on a synchronization object in libc_db.

Solaris Functions	Linux Equivalent	Description
td_ta_clear_event (3C_DB)	td_ta_clear_event	Thread events in libc_db.
td_ta_delete(3C_DB)	td_ta_delete	Allocate and de-allocate process handles for libc_db.
td_ta_enable_stats (3C_DB)	td_ta_enable_stats	Collect target process statistics for libc_db.
td_ta_event_addr (3C_DB)	td_ta_event_addr	Thread events in libc_db.
td_ta_event_getmsg (3C_DB)	td_ta_event_getmsg	Thread events in libc_db.
td_ta_get_nthreads (3C_DB)	td_ta_get_nthreads	Get the total number of threads in a process for libc_db.
td_ta_get_ph(3C_DB)	td_ta_get_ph	Allocate and de-allocate process handles for libc_db.
td_ta_get_stats(3C_DB)	td_ta_get_stats	Collect target process statistics for libc_db.
td_ta_map_addr2sync (3C_DB)	None	Get a synchronization object handle from a synchronization object's address.
td_ta_map_id2thr (3C_DB)	td_ta_map_id2thr	Convert a thread ID or LWP ID to a thread handle.
td_ta_map_lwp2thr (3C_DB)	td_ta_map_lwp2thr	Convert a thread ID or LWP ID to a thread handle.
td_ta_new(3C_DB)	td_ta_new	Allocate and de-allocate process handles for libc_db.
td_ta_reset_stats (3C_DB)	td_ta_reset_stats	Collect target process statistics for libc_db.
td_ta_setconcurrency (3C_DB)	td_ta_setconcurrency	Set concurrency level for target process.
td_ta_set_event(3C_DB)	td_ta_set_event	Thread events in libc_db.
td_ta_sync_iter(3C_DB)	None	Iterator functions on process handles from libc_db.
td_ta_sync_tracking_ enable(3C_DB)	None	Operations on a synchronization object in libc_db.

Solaris Functions	Linux Equivalent	Description
td_ta_thr_iter(3C_DB)	td_ta_thr_iter	Iterator functions on process handles from libc_db.
td_ta_tsd_iter(3C_DB)	td_ta_tsd_iter	Iterator functions on process handles from libc_db.
td_thr_clear_event (3C_DB)	td_thr_clear_event	Thread events in libc_db.
td_thr_dbresume(3C_DB)	td_thr_dbresume	Suspend and resume threads in libc_db.
td_thr_dbsuspend (3C_DB)	td_thr_dbsuspend	Suspend and resume threads in libc_db.
td_thr_event_enable (3C_DB)	td_thr_event_enable	Thread events in libc_db.
td_thr_event_getmsg (3C_DB)	td_thr_event_getmsg	Thread events in libc_db.
td_thr_getfpregs (3C_DB)	td_thr_getfpregs	Reading and writing thread registers in libc_db.
td_thr_getgregs(3C_DB)	td_thr_getgregs	Reading and writing thread registers in libc_db.
td_thr_get_info(3C_DB)	td_thr_get_info	Get thread information in libc_db library of interfaces.
td_thr_getxregs(3C_DB)	td_thr_getxregs	Reading and writing thread registers in libc_db.
td_thr_getxregsize (3C_DB)	td_thr_getxregsize	Reading and writing thread registers in libc_db.
td_thr_lockowner (3C_DB)	None	Iterate over the set of locks owned by a thread.
td_thr_set_event (3C_DB)	td_thr_set_event	Thread events in libc_db.
td_thr_setfpregs (3C_DB)	td_thr_setfpregs	Reading and writing thread registers in libc_db.
td_thr_setgregs(3C_DB)	td_thr_setgregs	Reading and writing thread registers in libc_db.
td_thr_setprio(3C_DB)	td_thr_setprio	Set the priority of a thread.
td_thr_setsigpending (3C_DB)	td_thr_setsigpending	Manage thread signals for libc_db.
td_thr_setxregs(3C_DB)	td_thr_setxregs	Reading and writing thread registers in libc_db.

Solaris Functions	Linux Equivalent	Description
`td_thr_sigsetmask (3C_DB)`	`td_thr_sigsetmask`	Manage thread signals for `libc_db`.
`td_thr_sleepinfo (3C_DB)`	None	Return the synchronization handle for the object on which a thread is blocked.
`td_thr_tsd(3C_DB)`	`td_thr_tsd`	Get a thread's thread-specific data for `libc_db` library of interfaces.
`td_thr_validate(3C_DB)`	`td_thr_validate`	Test a thread handle for validity.
`tell`	None	Return a file offset for a file descriptor.
`telldir`	`telldir`	Current location of a named directory stream.
`tempnam`	`tempnam`	Create a name for a temporary file.
`termios`	`termios`	General terminal interface.
`textdomain`	`textdomain`	Message handling functions.
`tfind`	`tfind`	Manage binary search trees.
`times`	`times`	Get process times.
`tmpfile`	`tmpfile`	Create a temporary file.
`tmpnam`	`tmpnam`	Create a name for a temporary file.
`tmpnam_r`	`tmpnam_r`	Create a name for a temporary file.
`toascii`	`toascii`	Translate integer to a 7-bit ASCII character.
`_tolower`	`_tolower`	Transliterate uppercase characters to lowercase.
`tolower`	`tolower`	Transliterate uppercase characters to lowercase.
`_toupper`	`_toupper`	Transliterate lowercase characters to uppercase.
`toupper`	`toupper`	Transliterate lowercase characters to uppercase.
`towctrans`	`towctrans`	Wide-character mapping.

Solaris Functions	Linux Equivalent	Description
towlower	towlower	Transliterate uppercase wide-character code to lowercase.
towupper	towupper	Transliterate lowercase wide-character code to uppercase.
truncate	truncate	Set a file to a specified length.
tsearch	tsearch	Manage binary search trees.
ttyname	ttyname	Find path name of a terminal.
ttyname_r	ttyname_r	Find path name of a terminal.
ttyslot	ttyslot	Find the slot of the current user in the user accounting database.
twalk	twalk	Manage binary search trees.
tzset	tzset	Convert date and time to string.
ualarm	ualarm	Schedule signal after interval in microseconds.
ucred_free, ucred_get, ucred_getegid, ucred_geteuid, ucred_getgroups, ucred_getpflags, ucred_getpid, ucred_getprivset, ucred_getprojid, ucred_getrgid, ucred_getruid, ucred_getsgid, ucred_getsuid, ucred_getzoneid, ucred_size	None	User credential functions.
ulckpwdf	ulckpwdf	Manipulate shadow password database lock file.
ulltostr	None	String conversion routines.
umem_alloc, umem_cache_alloc, umem_cache_create, umem_cache_destroy, umem_cache_free, umem_debug, umem_free, umem_nofail_callback, umem_zalloc	None	Fast, scalable memory operations.

Solaris Functions	Linux Equivalent	Description
`ungetc`	`ungetc`	Push byte back into input stream.
`ungetwc`	`ungetwc`	Push wide-character code back into input stream.
`unlockpt`	`unlockpt`	Unlock a pseudo-terminal master/slave pair.
`unordered`	None	Determine type of floating-point number.
`unsetenv`	`unsetenv`	Remove an environment variable.
`updwtmp`	`updwtmp`	User accounting database functions.
`updwtmpx`	`updwtmpx`	User accounting database functions.
`usleep`	`usleep`	Suspend execution for interval in microseconds.
`utmpname`	`utmpname`	User accounting database functions.
`utmpxname`	`utmpxname`	User accounting database functions.
`valloc`	`valloc`	Memory allocator.
`valloc`	`valloc`	Debugging memory allocator.
`vfprintf`	`vfprintf`	Print formatted output of a variable argument list.
`vfprintf`	`vfprintf`	Formatted output conversion.
`vfscanf`	`vfscanf`	Convert formatted input.
`vfwprintf`	`vfwprintf`	Wide-character formatted output of a `stdarg` argument list.
`vfwscanf`	`vfwscanf`	Convert formatted wide-character input.
`vlfmt`, `vpfmt`	None	Display error message in standard format and pass to logging and monitoring services.

Solaris Functions	Linux Equivalent	Description
vprintf	vprintf	Print formatted output of a variable argument list.
vprintf	vprintf	Formatted output conversion.
vscanf	vscanf	Convert formatted input.
vsnprintf	vsnprintf	Print formatted output of a variable argument list.
vsprintf	vsprintf	Print formatted output of a variable argument list.
vsprintf	vsprintf	Formatted output conversion.
vsscanf	vsscanf	Convert formatted input.
vswprintf	vswprintf	Wide-character formatted output of a stdarg argument list.
vswscanf	vswscanf	Convert formatted wide-character input.
vsyslog	vsyslog	Log message with an stdarg argument list.
vwprintf	vwprintf	Wide-character formatted output of an stdarg argument list.
vwscanf	vwscanf	Convert formatted wide-character input.
wait	wait	Wait for child process to stop or terminate.
wait3	wait3	Wait for process to terminate or stop.
wait4	wait4	Wait for process to terminate or stop.
waitpid	waitpid	Wait for child process to change state.
waitpid	waitpid	Wait for process to terminate or stop.
walkcontext	None	Walk stack pointed to by ucontext.
watchmalloc	None	Debugging memory allocator.

Solaris Functions	Linux Equivalent	Description
`watof`, `watoi`, `watol`, `watoll`	None	Convert wide-character string operations.
`wcrtomb`	`wcrtomb`	Convert a wide-character code to a character (restartable).
`wcscat`	`wcscat`	Wide-character string operations.
`wcschr`	`wcschr`	Wide-character string operations.
`wcscmp`	`wcscmp`	Wide-character string operations.
`wcscoll`	`wcscoll`	Wide-character string comparison using collating information.
`wcscpy`	`wcscpy`	Wide-character string operations.
`wcscspn`	`wcscspn`	Wide-character string operations.
`wcsetno`	None	Get information on EUC codesets.
`wcsftime`	`wcsftime`	Convert date and time to wide-character string.
`wcslen`	`wcslen`	Wide-character string operations.
`wcsncat`	`wcsncat`	Wide-character string operations.
`wcsncmp`	`wcsncmp`	Wide-character string operations.
`wcsncpy`	`wcsncpy`	Wide-character string operations.
`wcspbrk`	`wcspbrk`	Wide-character string operations.
`wcsrchr`	`wcsrchr`	Wide-character string operations.
`wcsrtombs`	`wcsrtombs`	Convert a wide-character string to a character string (restartable).

Solaris Functions	Linux Equivalent	Description
wcsspn	wcsspn	Wide-character string operations.
wcsstr	wcsstr	Find a wide-character substring.
wcstod	wcstod	Convert wide-character string to floating-point number.
wcstof	wcstof	Convert wide-character string to floating-point number.
wcstoimax	wcstoimax	Convert wide-character string to integer type.
wcstok	wcstok	Wide-character string operations.
wcstol	wcstol	Convert wide-character string to long integer.
wcstold	wcstold	Convert wide-character string to floating-point number.
wcstoll	wcstoll	Convert wide-character string to long integer.
wcstombs	wcstombs	Convert wide-character string to character string.
wcstoul	wcstoul	Convert wide-character string to unsigned long.
wcstoull	wcstoull	Convert wide-character string to unsigned long.
wcstoumax	wcstoumax	Convert wide-character string to integer type.
wcstring	None	Wide-character string operations.
wcswcs	wcswcs	Wide-character string operations.
wcswidth	wcswidth	Number of column positions of a wide-character string.
wcsxfrm	wcsxfrm	Wide-character string transformation.
wctob	wctob	Wide-character to single-byte conversion.

Solaris Functions	Linux Equivalent	Description
`wctomb`	`wctomb`	Convert wide-character code to a character.
`wctrans`	`wctrans`	Define character mapping.
`wctype`	`wctype`	Define character class.
`wcwidth`	`wcwidth`	Number of column positions of a wide-character code.
`WIFEXITED`	`WIFEXITED`	Wait for process to terminate or stop.
`WIFSIGNALED`	`WIFSIGNALED`	Wait for process to terminate or stop.
`WIFSTOPPED`	`WIFSTOPPED`	Wait for process to terminate or stop.
`windex`	None	Wide-character string operations.
`wmemchr`	`wmemchr`	Find a wide-character in memory.
`wmemcmp`	`wmemcmp`	Compare wide-characters in memory.
`wmemcpy`	`wmemcpy`	Copy wide-characters in memory.
`wmemmove`	`wmemmove`	Copy wide-characters in memory with overlapping areas.
`wmemset`	`wmemset`	Set wide-characters in memory.
`wordexp`	`wordexp`	Perform word expansions.
`wordfree`	`wordfree`	Perform word expansions.
`wprintf`	`wprintf`	Print formatted wide-character output.
`wrindex`	None	Wide-character string operations.
`wscanf`	`wscanf`	Convert formatted wide-character input.

Solaris Functions	Linux Equivalent	Description
`wscasecmp`, `wscat`, `wschr`, `wscmp`, `wscol`, `wscoll`, `wscpy`, `wscspn`, `wsdup`, `wslen`, `wsncasecmp`, `wsncat`, `wsncmp`, `wsncpy`, `wspbrk`, `wsprintf`, `wsrchr`, `wsscanf`, `wsspn`, `wstod`, `wstok`, `wstol`, `wstostr`, `wstring`, `wsxfrm`	None	Solaris wide-character string operations that do not exist on Linux.

1 Man pages Section 3: Basic Library Functions (http://docs.sun.com/)

2 GNU C Library man page (www.gnu.org/software/libc/manual)

3 On Linux, the resolution of the clocks depends on the implementation and cannot be configured by a particular process. Consult the Linux man page for more information.

B

AIX to Linux Reference Tables

In this appendix

B.1 AIX and Linux C Compiler Options Table

TABLE B-1
AIX XLC/C++ and gcc/g++ Compiler Switches Comparison Table

C/C++ VisualAge for AIX Option[1]	GNU gcc Option[2]	Description (AIX-Based)
-+	-x c++	(C++) Compiles any file, *filename.nnn*, as a C++ language file, where *nnn* is any suffix other than .o, .a, or .s.
-#	-###	Traces the compilation without doing anything.
-q32 -q64	-m32 -m64[3]	Selects 32- or 64-bit compiler mode. Additional -m options for GCC are available. Refer to GNU.
-qlanglvl=<option>	-fstd=<OPTION>	Specifies which language level to use when invoking the compiler.
-qaggrcopy	None	Enables destructive copy operations for structures and unions.
-qalias -qansialias	-fstrict-aliasing	Specifies which type-based aliasing is to be used during optimization.
-qalign	-mstrict-align[3]	Specifies what aggregate alignment rules the compiler uses for file compilation.
-qalloca -ma	None	Substitutes inline code for calls to function alloca as if #pragma alloca directives are in the source code.
-qarch	-mcpu=cpu_type3	Specifies the type of IBM architecture on which the executable program will be run. This refers to the RS6000 and POWER architecture.
-qnoassert	None	Requests the compiler to apply aliasing assertions to your compilation unit.

C/C++ VisualAge for AIX Option	GNU gcc Option	Description (AIX-Based)
`-qattr`	None	Produces a compiler listing that includes an attribute listing for all identifiers.
`-B -t`	`-B`	`-B`: Determines substitute path names for the compiler, assembler, linkage editor, and preprocessor. `-t`: Adds the prefix specified by the `-B` option to designated programs. `-tE` replaces the `CreateExportList` script.

`-bdynamic`
`-bshared`
	`-shared -fpic` (or `-fPIC`)
	`-Bsharable`
	or
	`-Wl -brt -shared`
		Instructs the linker to process subsequent shared objects as either dynamic or shared.

`-bstatic`	`-static`
	`-Bstatic`
	`-dn`
	`-non_shared`
		Links all referenced objects statically, although they may be shared objects.

`-qbitfields`	`-fsigned-bitfields` (default)	Specifies whether bitfields are signed.
`-bmaxdata`	Refer to Large Page Support section 6.13.	Sets the size of the heap in bytes.
`-brtl`	`-shared -Wl`	Enables runtime linking.
`-C`	`-C`	Preserves comments in preprocessed output.
`-c`	`-c`	Instructs the compiler to pass source files to the compiler only.
`-qcache`	None	Specifies a cache configuration for a specific execution machine.
`-qchars=[signed or unsigned]`	`-fsigned-char` `-funsigned-char`	Instructs the compiler to treat all variables of type `char` as either signed or unsigned.

C/C++ VisualAge for AIX Option	GNU gcc Option	Description (AIX-Based)
`-qcheck`	None	Generates code that performs certain types of runtime checking.
`-qcinc`	None	(C++) Include files from specified directories have the tokens extern `" C " {` inserted before the file and `}` appended after the file.
`-qcompact`	`-Os`	When used with optimization, reduces code size where possible, at the expense of execution speed.
`-qcpluscmt`	C++-style comments is turned on automatically in GNU C, unless `-ansi` is turned on.	(C++) Use this option if you want C++ comments to be recognized in C source files.
`-D`	`-D`	Defines the identifier name as in a `#define` preprocessor directive.
`-qdataimported`	None	Marks data as imported. Used to import functions.
`-qdatalocal`	None	Marks data as local.
`-qdbxextra`	None	(C only) Specifies that all `typedef` declarations, `struct`, `union`, and `enum` type definitions are included for debugger processing.
`-qdigraph`	None	Allows the use of digraph character sequences in your program.
`-qdollar`	`-fdollars-in-identifiers` This is the default behavior of GNU on most platforms.	Allows the $ symbol to be used in the names of identifiers.
`-qdpcl`	None	Generates block scopes to support the IBM Dynamic Probe Class Library.

C/C++ VisualAge for AIX Option	GNU gcc Option	Description (AIX-Based)
`-E`	`-E`	Runs the source files named in the compiler invocation through the preprocessor.
`-eLabel`	`-e Label` `—entry=Label` Refer to Linker section	Specifies the entry name for the shared object. Equivalent to using `ld -e` name. See your system documentation for additional information about `ld` options. Used only with `-qmkshrobj`.
`-qeh`	`-fexceptions`	(C++) Controls exception handling.
`-qenum`	Use keyword `__attribute__`[4]	Specifies the amount of storage occupied by the enumerations.
`-qexpfile`	None	Saves all exported symbols in a file.
`-qextchk`	None	Generates bind-time type checking information and checks for compile-time consistency.
`-F`	None	Names an alternative configuration file for `xlC`.
`-f`	None	Names a file to store a list of object files.
`-qfpdr`	None	Collects program information for use with the AIX `fdpr` performance-tuning utility.
`-qflag`	None	Specifies the minimum severity level of diagnostic messages to be reported.
`-qfloat`	None (Accuracy of floating point is different on differing platforms.)	Specifies various floating-point options to speed up or improve the accuracy of floating-point operations.
`-qflttrap`	`-mfp-trap-mode=` `trap mode`	Generates extra instructions to detect and trap floating-point exceptions.

C/C++ VisualAge for AIX Option	GNU gcc Option	Description (AIX-Based)
`-qfold`	None	Specifies that constant floating-point expressions are to be evaluated at compile time.
`-qfullpath`	None	Specifies what path information is stored for files when you use `-g` and the distributed graphical debugger.
`-qfuncsect`	None	Places instructions for each function in a separate object file, control section, or `csect`.
`-G`	`-shared` `-Bshareable`	Linkage editor (`ld` command) option only. Used to generate a dynamic library file.
`-g`	`-g`	Generates debugging information used by a debugger such as the Distributed Debugger.
`-qgenproto`	None	Produces ANSI prototypes from K&R function definitions.
`-qhalt`	None	Instructs the compiler to stop after the compilation phase when it encounters errors of specified severity or greater.
`-qhaltonmsg`	None	Enables debug versions of memory management functions.
`-qhot`	None	Instructs the compiler to perform high-order transformations on loops and array language during optimization, and to pad array dimensions and data objects to avoid cache misses.
`-qhsflt`	None	Speeds up calculations by removing range checking on single-precision float results and on conversions from floating point to integer.

C/C++ VisualAge for AIX Option	GNU gcc Option	Description (AIX-Based)
-qhssngl	None	Specifies that single-precision expressions are rounded only when the results are stored into float memory locations.
-I	-I	Specifies an additional search path if the file name in the #include directive is not specified using its absolute path name.
-qidirfirst	None	Specifies the search order for files included with the #include "file_name" directive.
-qignerrno	None	Allows the compiler to perform optimizations that assume errno is not modified by system calls.
-qignprag	None	Instructs the compiler to ignore certain pragma statements.
-qinfo	None	Produces informational messages.
-qinitauto	None	Initializes automatic storage to a specified two-digit hexadecimal byte value.
-qinlglue	None	Generates fast external linkage by inlining the pointer glue code necessary to make a call to an external function or a call through a function pointer.
-qinline	-finline-functions	Attempts to inline functions instead of generating calls to a function.
-qipa	None	Turns on or customizes a class of optimizations known as interprocedural analysis (IPA).
-qisolated_call	None	Specifies functions in the source file that have no side effects.

C/C++ VisualAge for AIX Option	GNU gcc Option	Description (AIX-Based)
`-qkeepinlines`	`-fkeep-inline-functions`	(C++) Instructs the compiler to keep or discard definitions for unreferenced `extern` inline functions.
`-qkeyword`	None	Controls whether a specified string is treated as a keyword or an identifier.
`-L`	`-L`	Searches the specified directory for library files specified by the `-l` option.
`-l`	`-l`	Searches a specified library for linking.
`-qlanglvl`	`-ansi` `-flang-isoc9x`	Selects the C or C++ language level for compilation.
`-qlargepage`	Refer to Large Page Support section	Instructs the compiler to exploit large page heaps available on POWER4 systems running AIX v5.1D or later.
`-qldbl128` `-qlongdouble`	None	Increases the size of the long double `type` from 64 bits to 128 bits.
`-qlibansi`	None	Assumes that all functions with the name of an ANSI C library function are in fact the system functions.
`-qlinedebug`	None	Generates abbreviated line number and source file name information for the debugger.
`-qlist`	None	Produces a compiler listing that includes an object listing.
`-qlistopt`	None	Produces a compiler listing that displays all options in effect.
`-qlonglit`	None	Makes unsuffixed literals the long type for 64-bit mode.
`-qlonglong`	`-mlong64` (Refer to the `-m` options for your targeted platform)	Allows long long types in your program.

C/C++ VisualAge for AIX Option	GNU gcc Option	Description (AIX-Based)
-M	-M	Creates an output file that contains targets suitable for inclusion in a description file for the AIX make command.
-ma	Refer to alloc	(C only) Substitutes inline code for calls to function alloca as if #pragma alloca directives are in the source code.
-qmacpstr	None	(C only) Converts Pascal string literals into null-terminated strings where the first byte contains the length of the string.
-qmaf	None	Specifies whether the floating-point multiply-add instructions are to be generated.
-qmakedep	-M	Creates an output file that contains targets suitable for inclusion in a description file for the AIX make command.
-qmaxerr	None	Instructs the compiler to halt compilation when a specified number of errors of specified or greater severity is reached.
-qmaxmem	None	Limits the amount of memory used for local tables of specific, memory-intensive optimizations.
-qmbcs, dbcs	LANG[5]	Use the -qmbcs option if your program contains multibyte characters.
-qmkshrobj	-shared or libtool[6]	Creates a shared object from generated object files.
-qnamemangling	None	Selects the name mangling scheme for external symbol names generated from C++ source code.

C/C++ VisualAge for AIX Option	GNU gcc Option	Description (AIX-Based)
`-O` `-qoptimize`	`-O`	Optimizes code at a choice of levels during compilation.
`-o`	`-o`	Specifies a name or directory for the output executable file(s) created by either the compiler or the linkage editor.
`-qobjmodel`	None	(C++) Sets the type of object model.
`-qoldpassbyvalue`	None	(C++) Specifies how classes containing `const` or reference members are passed in function arguments.
`-P`	`-E`	Preprocesses the C or C++ source files named in the compiler invocation and creates an output preprocessed source file for each input source file.
`-p`	None	Sets up the object files produced by the compiler for profiling.
`-qpascal`	None	(C only) Ignores the word `pascal` in in type specifiers and function declarations.
`-qpath`	None	Constructs alternate program and path names.
`-qpdf1` `-qpdf2`	None	Tunes optimizations through Profile-Directed Feedback.
`-pg`	`-fprofile-generate`	Sets up the object files for profiling, but provides more information than is provided by the `-p` option.
`-qphsinfo`	`gcov`[7]	Reports the time taken in each compilation phase.
`-qprint`	None	Suppresses listings.
`-qpriority`	None	(C++) Specifies the priority level for the initialization of static constructors.

C/C++ VisualAge for AIX Option	GNU gcc Option	Description (AIX-Based)
`-qproclocal` `-qprocimported` `-qprocunknown`	None	Marks functions as local, imported, or unknown.
`-qproto`	None	(C only) Assumes all functions are prototyped.
`-Q`	`-O3`	Attempts to inline functions instead of generating calls to a function.
`-r`	`-mrelocatable`	Produces a relocatable object.
`-qreport`	None	Instructs the compiler to produce transformation reports that show how program loops are parallelized and optimized.
`-qrndflt`	None	Controls the compile-time rounding mode of constant floating-point expressions.
`-qrndsngl`	None	Specifies that the result of each single-precision float operation is to be rounded to single precision.
`-qro`	None	Specifies the storage type for string literals.
`-qroconst`	None	Specifies the storage location for constant values.
`-qrrm`	None	Prevents floating-point optimizations that are incompatible with runtime rounding to plus and minus infinity modes.
`-qrtti`	None	(C++) Generates runtime type identification (RTTI) information for the `typeid` operator and the `dynamic_cast` operator.
`-S`	`-S`	Generates an assembly language file (.s) for each source file.

C/C++ VisualAge for AIX Option	GNU gcc Option	Description (AIX-Based)
`-s`	None	Strips the symbol table.
`-qshowinc`	None	If used with `-qsource`, all the include files are included in the source listing.
`-qsmallstack`	None	Instructs the compiler to reduce the size of the stack frame.
`-qsmp`	None	Enables parallelization of IBM SMP-compliant program code.
`-qsource`	None	Produces a compiler listing and includes source code.
`-qspill`	None	Specifies the size of the register allocation spill area.
`-qspnans`	None	Generates extra instructions to detect signaling NaN on conversion from single precision to double precision.
`-qsrcmsg`	None	(C only) Adds the corresponding source code lines to the diagnostic messages in the `stderr` file.
`-qstaticinline`	None	(C ++) Controls whether inline functions are treated as static or `extern`.
`-qstatsym`	None	Adds user-defined, nonexternal names that have a persistent storage class to the name list.
`-qstdinc`	`-nostdinc` (`nostdinc++` for C++ source)	Specifies which files are included with #include <file_name> and #include "file_name" directives.
`-qstrict`	None	Turns off aggressive optimizations of the `-O3` option that have the potential to alter the semantics of your program.

C/C++ VisualAge for AIX Option	GNU gcc Option	Description (AIX-Based)
`-qstrict_induction`	None	Disables loop induction variable optimizations that have the potential to alter the semantics of your program.
`-qsuppress`	None	Specifies compiler message numbers to be suppressed.
`-qsymtab`	None	Sets symbol tables for unreferenced variables or `xcoff` objects.
`-qsyntaxonly`	`-fsyntax-only`	(C only) Causes the compiler to perform syntax checking without generating an object file.
`-qtabsize`	None	Changes the length of tabs as perceived by the compiler.
`-qtbtable`	None	Sets traceback table characteristics.
`-qtempinc`	`-frepo`	(C++) Generates separate include files for template functions and class declarations and places these files in a directory that can be optionally specified.
`-qtemplaterecompile`	`-frepo`	(C ++) Helps manage dependencies between compilation units that have been compiled using the `-qtemplateregistry` compiler option.
`-qtemplateregistry`	`-frepo`	(C++) Maintains records of all templates as they are encountered in the source and ensures that only one instantiation of each template is made.
`-qtempmax`	None	(C++) Specifies the maximum number of template include files to be generated by the `tempinc` option for each header file.

C/C++ VisualAge for AIX Option	GNU gcc Option	Description (AIX-Based)
`-qthreaded`	`-lpthread` `-D_REENTRANT`	Indicates that the program will run in a multithreaded environment.
`-qtmplparse`	None	(C++) Controls whether parsing and semantic checking are applied to template definition implementations.
`-qtocdata`	None	Marks data as local.
`-qtocmerge`	None	Enables TOC merging to reduce TOC pointer loads and improves the scheduling of external loads.
`-qtune`	`-b`	Specifies the architecture for which the executable program is optimized.
`-qtwolink`	None	(C++) Minimizes the number of static constructors included from libraries.
`-U`	`-U`	Undefines a specified identifier defined by the compiler or by the `-D` option.
`-qunique`	None	(C++) Generates unique names for static constructor/deconstructor file compilation units.
`-qunroll`	`-funroll-loops`	Unrolls inner loops in the program.
`-qunwind`	None	Informs the compiler that the application does not rely on any program stack unwinding mechanism.
`-qupconv`	None	Preserves the unsigned specification when performing integral promotions.
`-V`	None	Instructs the compiler to report information on the progress of the compilation in a command-like format.

C/C++ VisualAge for AIX Option	GNU gcc Option	Description (AIX-Based)
`-v`	`-v`	Instructs the compiler to report information on the progress of the compilation.
`-qvftable`	`-fvtable-thunks`	(C++) Controls the generation of virtual function tables.
`-W`	None	Passes the listed words to a designated compiler program.
`-w`	`-w`	Requests that warning messages be suppressed.
`-qwarn64`	None	Enables warning of possible long to integer data truncations.
`-qxcall`	None	Generates code to static routines within a compilation unit as if they were external calls.
`-qxref`	None	Produces a compiler listing that includes a cross-reference listing of all identifiers.
`-y`	None	Specifies the compile-time rounding mode of constant floating-point expressions. See also `rndflt`.

---

1 VisualAge C++ for AIX Compiler Reference (SC09-4959-00)

2 GNU Compiler Collections version 3.4.2 (last updated May 23, 2004)

3 These are all part of the GNU `-m` machine-dependent options. Refer to the following link for specific platform compiler options: http://gcc.gnu.org/onlinedocs/gcc-2.95.3/gcc_2.html.

4 Refer to "Specifying attributes of types" in the GNU documentation: http://hea-www.harvard.edu/MST/simul/software/docs/pkg/gcc/gcc.html#SEC13.

5 Part of GCC environment variables.

6 As an alternative, GNU `libtool` could be used. Similar to the `-qmkshrobj` option, `libtool` is also a script, but it provides a generic interface for building platform-independent libraries. Refer to http://gnu.mirrors.atn.ro/software/libtool/libtool.es.html for more information on using it.

7 `gcov` is a tool you can use in conjuction with GNU CC to test and profile code coverage. For more information on `gcov`, refer to the GNU documentation.

B.2 AIX and Linux Linker Options Comparison Table

Table B-2 only lists the most commonly used linker options.

TABLE B-2
AIX and Linux Linker Switches Comparison Table

AIX	Linux	Description
`-bexpall`	`-E` `--export-dynamic`	When creating a dynamically linked executable, adds all symbols to the dynamic symbol table.
`-bmaxdata:<size>`	`-Gvalue` `--gpsize=value`	Sets the maximum size of objects to be optimized using the GP register to size. This is only meaningful for object file formats such as MIPS ECOFF, which supports putting large and small objects into different sections. This is ignored for other object file formats.
`-eLabel`	`-e entry` `--entry=entry`	Uses entry as the explicit symbol for beginning execution of your program, rather than the default entry point.

`-bdynamic` or
`-bshared`
	`-Bdynamic`
	`-dy`
	`-call_shared`
	
	or
	`-Wl`
	`-brt`
	`-shared`
		Links against dynamic libraries. The different variants of this option are for compatibility with various systems. You may use this option multiple times on the command line. It affects library searching for `-l` options that follow it.

`-bM:SRE` or `-brtl` or `-G`	`-shared` `-Bshareable`	Creates a shared library that is reentrant (runtime linkable).
`-l`	`-larchive`	Adds the archive file `libarchive.a` to the list of files to link. This option may be used any number of times. This option also searches for shared objects (.so) for other platforms; however, when running on a Linux platform, only archives are searched.

AIX	Linux	Description
`-Z`	`-Y`	Specifies a search path for library names.
`-L`	`-rpath path`	Specifies the library search direction for the runtime linker.
`-L`	`-L`	Searches the specified directory for library files specified by the `-l` option.

B.3 I/O Services APIs: AIX to Linux Cross-Reference

TABLE B-3
AIX and Linux System API Comparison: I/O Services

AIX	Linux	ERRNO(s) in AIX Not Implemented in Linux	Description

`access`
`accessx`
`faccessx`
	`access`	`ESTALE`
		`ETIMEDOUT`
			Checks user's permissions for a file.

`fclear` `fclear64`	None		Clears space in a file.

`fseek`
`ftell`
`rewind`
`fgetpos`
`fsetpos`
`fputc`
`fputs`
`putc`
`putchar`
`puts`
	`fseek`
	`ftell`
	`rewind`
	`fgetpos`
	`fsetpos`
	`fputc`
	`fputs`
	`putc`
	`putchar`
	`puts`
		`EAGIN`
		`EFBIG`
		`EINTR`
		`EIO`
		`ENOSPC`
		`EPIPE`
		`ENOMEM`
		`EOVERFLOW`
		`ESPIPE`
			Repositions a stream.
			
			Outputs character and strings.

`scanf`
`fscanf`
`sscanf`
	`scanf`
	`fscanf`
	`sscanf`
		`EAGIN`
		`EBADF`
		`EINTR`
		`EIO`
		`EINVAL`
		`EILSEQ`
		`ENOMEM`
			Inputs format conversion.

AIX	Linux	ERRNO(s) in AIX Not Implemented in Linux	Description
fsync	fsync	EINVAL EINTR	Synchronizes a file's complete in-core state with that on disk.
getutent setutent enutent utmptname getutid getutid_r getutline_r pututline_r setutent_r endutent_r utmpname_r	getutent getutent_r getutid getutid_r gutut line gututline_r putuline setutent endutent utmpname		Provides access user accounting database entries. Entries in the database are described by the definitions and data structures in <utmp.h>.
lseek lseek64 llseek	lseek llseek lseek64	EOVERFLOW	Moves the read-write pointer to an open file.
lockfx lockf flock	lockf flock fcntl		Controls open files' descriptors.
open openx creat	open creat	EAGAIN EDQUOT EFBIG EINTR EIO ENOSR EOVERFLOW ESTALE	Returns a file descriptor and creates files.
pathconf fpathconf	pathconf fpathconf	ESTALE ETIMEDOUT	Retrieves file implementation characteristics.
read readx readv readvx	read, readv	EBADMSG EDEADLK EOVERFLOW ENXIO ESPIPE ETIMEDOUT	Reads from a file descriptor.

AIX	Linux	ERRNO(s) in AIX Not Implemented in Linux	Description
rename	rename	EDQUOT ETIMEDOUT ETXTBSY ESTALE	Changes the name or location of a file.
statx stat fstatx fstat fullstat fullstat	stat fstat lstat	ESTALE ETIMEDOUT EIO	Gets file status.
truncate ftruncate truncate64 ftruncate64	truncate ftrunncate truncate64 ftruncate64	EAGAIN EDQUOT EFBIG EFBIG EINTR EMFILE ENOSPC ESTALE ETIMEDOUT	Truncates a file to a specified length.
umask	umask		Sets file creation mask.
utimes utime	utimes utime	EPERM EACCES EROFS	Changes access and/or modification times of an inode.
write writex writev writevx	write, writev	EDQUOT ENXIO EFBIG ERANGE ESPIPE	Writes to a file descriptor.
chdir	chdir	ESTALE ETIMEDOUT	Changes working directory.
chroot	chroot	ESTALE ETIMEDOUT	Changes root directory.
getwd getcwd	get_current_ dir_name getwd getcwd	ENOMEM	Gets current working directory.

AIX	Linux	ERRNO(s) in AIX Not Implemented in Linux	Description
glob globfree	glob globfree		Finds path names matching a pattern, frees memory from glob().
link	link	EDQUOT ENOSPC ESTALE	Makes a new name for a file.
mkdir	mkdir	EDQUOT ETIMEOUT ESTALE	Creates a directory.
readdir readdir_r	readdir _syscall3		Returns current location in directory stream.
printf fprintf sprintf snprintf vprintf vfprintf vsprintf vsnprintf	printf fprintf sprintf snprintf vprintf vfprintf vsprintf vsnprintf	EAGAIN EABDF EFBIG EINTR EIO ENOSPC EPIPE ELSEQ EINVAL ENOMEM ENXIO	Formats output conversion.
rmdir	rmdir	EEXIST EINVAL ETIMEDOUT ESTALE	Removes a directory.
scandir, alphasort	scandir alphasor versionsort		Scans a directory for matching entries.
readlink	readlink	ERANGE ETIMEDOUT	Reads value of a symbolic link.
remove	remove	EBUSY - ETIMEDOUT ESTALE EEXIST EINVAL	Deletes a name and possibly the file it refers to.

AIX	Linux	ERRNO(s) in AIX Not Implemented in Linux	Description

`symlink`	`symlink`	`EDQUOT`
		`ETIMEDOUT`
		`ESTALE`
			Makes a new name for a a file.

`unlink`	`unlink`	`EBUSY`
		`ETIMEDOUT`
		`ESTALE`
			Deletes a name and possibly the file it refers to.

`fscntl`	None		Manipulates filesystem control operations.

`getfsent_r`
`getfsspec_r`
`getfsfile_r`
`getfstype_r`
`setfsent_r`
`endfsent_r`
	`getfsent`
	`getfsspec`
	`getfsfile`
	`setfsent`
	`endfsent`
			Gets information about a filesystem.
			
			In AIX, `_r` denotes `REENTRANT`, which means functions are threadsafe. In Linux, you must make your modules that are using the equivalent APIs thread safe.

`getvfsent`
`getvfsbytype`
`getvfsbyname`
`getvfsbyflag`
`setvfsent`
`endvfsent`
	None		Gets a (virtual file system) VFS file entry.

`mnctl`	None		Returns mount status information.

`quotacl`	`quotacl`	`ELOOP`
		`ENAMETOOLONG`
		`ENOENT`
		`EOPNOTSUPP`
		`EROFS`
		`EUSERS`
			Manipulates disk quotas.

`statfs`
`fstatfs`
	`statfs`
	`fstatfs`
		`ESTALE`
		`ETIMEDOUT`
		`EIO`
			Gets filesystem statistics.

AIX	Linux	ERRNO(s) in AIX Not Implemented in Linux	Description
`sysconf`	`sysconf`		Provides a way for the application to determine values for system limits or options at runtime. Functions are compatible, but the information they return are specific to the platform they are running on.
`sync`	`sync`		Functions are not compatible. In Linux, `sync` returns an `int`; in AIX, this function returns void. Causes all information in memory that should be on disk to be written out. The information returned and its format differ.
`umask`	`umask`		Sets the `umask` to `mask` and `0777`.
`vmount` `uvmount`	None		AIX-specific. Creates what is known as a virtual file system (VFS). `uvmount` removes a VFS. `umount` can also be used as an alternative to `uvmount`.
`umount`	`umount`	In AIX, `ENOBLK` is returned. In Linux, `ENOTBLK` is returned.	Unmounts a previously mounted filesystem, directory, or file.

B.4 IPC Reference: AIX-Linux

TABLE B-4
AIX and Linux IPC API Comparison: Semaphores

AIX	LINUX	AIX ERRNO(s)	LINUX ERRNO(s)	Description
sem_init	sem_init	EFAULT EINVAL ENFILE ENOMEM ENOSPC ENOTSUP	EINVAL ENOSYS	Initializes the semaphore object.
sem_wait	sem_wait	EACCES EAGAIN (semwait only) EFAULT EIDRM EINTR	Does not set Errno. Always returns 0.	Suspends the calling thread until the semaphore pointed to by sem has nonzero count.
sem_trywait	sem_trywait	EINVAL ENOMEM ENOTSUP	EAGAIN	
sem_post	sem_post	EACCES EFAULT EIDRM EINVAL ENOMEM ENOTSUP	ERANGE	Unlocks a semaphore.
sem_getvalue	sem_getvalue	EACCES EFAULT EINVAL ENOMEM ENOTSUP	Does not set errno. Always returns 0.	Gets the value of a semaphore.
sem_destroy	sem_destroy	EACCES EFAULT EINVAL ENOTSUP	EBUSY	Destroys a semaphore object, freeing the resources it might hold.

AIX	LINUX	AIX ERRNO(s)	LINUX ERRNO(s)	Description
sem_timedwait	sem_timedwait	EFAULT EINVAL ETIMEDWAIT EDEADLK ENTR	EENVAL ETIMEDWAIT EDEADLK ENTR	Advanced real-time wait.
sem_unlink	sem_unlink	EACCES EFAULT ENAMETOOLONG ENOENT ENOTSUP	EACCES ENAMETOLONG ENOENT	Removes a named semaphore.
sem_close	sem_close	EFAULT EINVAL ENOMEM ENOTSUP	EINVAL	Closes a named semaphore.
sem_open	sem_open	EACCES EEXIST EFAULT EINVAL EMFILE ENAMETOOLONG ENOMEM ENOTSUP ENOSPC	EACCES EEXIST EINTR EENVAL EMFILE ENAMETOOLONG ENFILE ENOENT ENOSPC	Opens a named semaphore.

TABLE B-5
AIX and Linux IPC API Comparison: Message Queues

AIX -> Linux	AIX ERRNO(s)	Linux ERRNO(s)	Description
mq_close	EBADF ENOMEM ENOTSUP	EBADF EBUSY	Closes a message queue.
mq_open	EACCES EEXIST EFAULT EINVAL ENOMEM ENOSPC ENOTSUP ENOENT ENFILE ENAMETOOLONG	EACCES EEXIST EINTR EINVAL EMFILE ENOSPC, ENOENT ENFILE ENAMETOOLONG	Opens a message queue.
mq_notify	EBADF EBUSY EFAULT ENOMEM ENOTSUP EINVAL	EBADF EBUSY	Notifies a process that a message is available.
mq_getattr	EBADF EFAULT ENOMEM EINVAL ENOTSUP	EBADF	Gets message queue attributes.
mq_unlink	EACCES EFAULT EINVAL ENAMETOOLONG, ENOTSUP	EACCES ENOENT ENAMETOOLONG	Removes a message queue.

AIX -> Linux	AIX ERRNO(s)	Linux ERRNO(s)	Description
mq_send	EAGAIN EFAULT EBADF EIDRM EINTR EINVAL EMSGSIZE ENOMEM ENOTSUP	EAGAIN EBADF EINTR EINVAL EMSGSIZE	Sends a message to the message queue.
mq_setattr	EBADF EFAULT EINVAL ENOMEM ENOTSUP	EBADF	Sets message queue attributes.
mq_send, mq_timedsend	EAGAIN EBADF EFAULT EIDRM EINTR EINVAL EMSGSIZE ENOTSUP ETIMEDOUT	EAGAIN EBADF EINTR EINVAL EMSGSIZE ETIMEDOUT	Sends a message to a message queue (REALTIME).
mq_receive	EAGAIN EBADF EFAULT EIDRM EINTR EINVAL EMSGSIZE ENOMEM ENOTSUP	EAGAIN EBADF EINVAL EMSGSIZE EINTR EINVAL ETIMEOUT	Receives a message from a message queue.
msgctl	EACCES EPERM EFAULT EINVAL	EACCES EPERM EDIRM EFAULT EINVAL	Provides message control operations.

AIX -> Linux	AIX ERRNO(s)	Linux ERRNO(s)	Description
msgget	EACCES ENOENT EEXIST ENOSPC	ENOMEM EACCES ENOENT EEXIST ENOSPC	Gets a message queue identifier.
msgrcv	E2BIG EACCES ENOMSG EFAULT EINTR EIDRM EINVAL	E2BIG EACCES ENOMSG EFAULT EINTR EIDRM EINVAL	Reads a message from a queue.

TABLE B-6
AIX and Linux POSIX Threads Comparison: APIs Shown to Have Differences

API	Differences
pthread_attr_getschedparam pthread_attr_setschedparm	In AIX, the API takes two parameters: pthread_attr_t* struct sched_param* In Linux, the API takes three parameters: pthread_t int (policy) struct sched_param*
pthread_attr_init	Creates a new thread attribute with default values with the following exceptions. AIX: Contention scope = PTHREAD_SCOPE_PROCESS Sched param.sched_prio = 1 Linux: Contention scope = PTHREAD_SCOPE_SYSTEM Sched param.sched_priority = 0

API	Differences

`pthread_mutex_lock`
`pthread_mutex_trylock`
`pthread_mutex_unlockj`
	Lock mechanism between AIX and Linux is not compatible. The conditions for deadlocking differ, and the attribute values differ.
	AIX: Possible attribute values are as follows:
	`PTHREAD_MUTEX_NORMAL`
	`PTHREAD_MUTEX_ERRORCHECKING`
	`PTHREAD_MUTEX_RECURSIVE`
	`PTHREAD_MUTEX_DEFAULT`
	Linux: Possible attribute values are as follows:
	`#ifdef __USE_GNU`
	`PTHREAD_MUTEX_INITIALIZER`
	`PTHREAD_RECURSIVE_MUTEX_INITIALIZER_NP`
	`PTHREAD_ERRORCHECK_MUTEX_INITIALIZER_NP`
	`#ifdef __USE_UNIX98`
	`PTHREAD_MUTEX_NORMAL`
	`PTHREAD_MUTEX_ERRORCHECKING`
	`PTHREAD_MUTEX_RECURSIVE`
	`PTHREAD_MUTEX_DEFAULT`

`pthread_mutexattr_gettype`
`pthread_mutexattr_settype`
	Gets or sets a mutex type to the following values.
	AIX: Possible attribute values are as follows:
	`PTHREAD_MUTEX_NORMAL`
	`PTHREAD_MUTEX_ERRORCHECKING`
	`PTHREAD_MUTEX_RECURSIVE`
	`PTHREAD_MUTEX_DEFAULT`
	Linux: Possible attribute values are as follows:
	`#ifdef __USE_GNU`
	`PTHREAD_MUTEX_INITIALIZER`
	`PTHREAD_RECURSIVE_MUTEX_INITIALIZER_NP`
	`PTHREAD_ERRORCHECK_MUTEX_INITIALIZER_NP`
	`#ifdef __USE_UNIX98`
	`PTHREAD_MUTEX_NORMAL`
	`PTHREAD_MUTEX_ERRORCHECKING`
	`PTHREAD_MUTEX_RECURSIVE`
	`PTHREAD_MUTEX_DEFAULT`

C

HP-UX to Linux Reference Tables

In this appendix

C.1 HP-UX and Linux C Compiler Options Table

TABLE C-1
HP-UX ANSI cc and gcc Compiler Switches Comparison Table

HP cc Option[1]	GNU gcc Option[2]	Description
`-A[a|c|e]`	`-ansi`	
	`-std=`*`standard`*	Specifies the degree of ANSI compliance.
`-Bextern`	None	Performs the same operation as `+Oextern=sym1,sym2,sym3...` except that symbols are loaded from an existing file, instead of specified on the command line.
`-Bhidden`	None	Hides all the symbols including references except for those prefixed with `__declspec(dllexport)`, `__declspec(dllimport)`.
`-Bhidden_def`	None	Hides all the symbols defined in the module except for those prefixed with `__declspec(dllexport)`.
`-c`	`-c`	Compiles only; does not link.
`-C`	`-C`	Prevents the preprocessor from stripping comments.
`-D_POSIX_C_SOURCE=199506L`		
`-D_REENTRANT -lpthread` or use `-lcma` (for user threads)	`-D_REENTRANT -lpthread`	Compiling with threads.
`-D`*`name`*	`-D`*`name`*	Defines the preprocessor variable name with a value of 1.
`-D`*`name`*`=`*`def`*	`-D`*`name`*`=`*`def`*	Defines the preprocessor variable name with a value of *`def`*.
`-dynamic`	`-Wl,-Bdynamic`	Enables linking of PIC objects.

HP cc Option	GNU gcc Option	Description
`-E`	`-E`	Performs preprocessing only with output to stdout.
`-fast`	None	Expands into a set of compiler options, which results in improved application runtime. Options included are `+O3`, `+Onolooptransform`, `+Olibcalls`, `+FPD`, `+Oentryschedule`, and `+Ofastaccess`. Any of these options can be overridden by placing a subsequent option after `-fast` on the command line.
`-g`	`-g`	Inserts information for the symbolic debugger in the object file.
`-G`	`-pg`	Inserts information required by the gprof profiler in the object file.
`-I`*`dir`*	`-I`*`dir`*	Inserts *`dir`* in the include file search path.
`-l`*`x`*	`-l`*`x`*	Links with the `libx.a` depending on default library paths.
`-L`*`dir`*	`-L`*`dir`*	Links the libraries in *`dir`* before the libraries in the default search path. Adds default linker paths to one specified in the `-L` option before searching the default system library directories.
`-Wl,-Lsearchdir`	`-Wl,-Lsearchdir`	`-Wl` specifies a flag to pass on to the linker. In this case, the `-L` flag is passed on. This has the same effect as the `-L` option.
`-n`	`-shared` `-Bshareable`	Generates shareable code.
`-N`	None	Generates unshareable code.

`-noshared`	`-static`
	`-Bstatic`
	`-dn`
	`-non_shared`
		Creates statically bound executables.

HP cc Option	GNU gcc Option	Description
`-o` *`outfile`*	`-o` *`outfile`*	Places object modules in file *`outfile`*.
`-O`	`-O2`	Optimizes at level 2.
`-p`	`-p`	Inserts information required by the prof profiler in the object file.
`-P`	None	Performs preprocessing only with output to the corresponding .i file.
`-q`	None	Marks the executable as demand-loadable.
`-Q`	None	Marks the executable as not being demand-loadable.
`-s`	`-s`	Strips the symbol table from the executable file.
`-S`	`-S`	Generates an assembly language source file.
`-t` *`x,name`*	None	Substitutes or inserts subprocess *x* with *`name`*.
`-U`*`name`*	`-U`*`name`*	Undefines *`name`* in the preprocessor.
`-v`	`-v`	Enables verbose mode.
None	`-###`	Shows each invoked component; does not execute.
`-V` `-version`	`--version`	Causes subprocesses to print version information to stderr.
`-w`	`-w`	Suppresses warning messages.
`-Wd,-a or +a`	None	Omits HP-provided prefix files required by the linker.
`-W`*`x`*`, arg1 [,arg2,..,argn]`	`-W`*`x,option`*	Passes the arguments to subprocess *x*.
`-y`	None	Generates information used by the HP SoftBench static analysis tool.
`-Y`	None	Enables Native Language Support (NLS).

HP cc Option	GNU gcc Option	Description
`-z`	Default (also see `-fno-delete-null-pointer-checks` `-fdelete-null-pointer-checks`)	Disallows runtime dereferencing of null pointers.
`-Z`	None	Allows dereferencing of null pointers at runtime.
`+DAmodel`	`-b machine` `-m`*`options`* (if GCC is set up as a cross-compiler)	Generates object code for a specific version of the PA-RISC architecture. In the case of GCC, whichever platform it is is set up for cross-compiling.
`+DCapptype`	None	Generates code for portable or embedded applications.
`+DD32`	`-mpa-risc-1-1`	Generates 32-bit code for PA1.1 architecture.
`+DD64` (64-bit)	`-mpa-risc-2-0` (32-bit)	Generates *x*-bit code for PA2.0 architecture.
`+dfname`	None	Specifies the profile database to use with profile-based optimization.
`+DSmodel`	None	Performs instruction scheduling for a specific implementation of PA-RISC.
`+DOosname`	None	Sets the target operating system for the compiler.
`+e`	None	Enables the following HP value-added features while compiling in ANSI C mode: sized enum, long long, long pointers, compiler-supplied defaults for missing arguments to intrinsic calls, and $ in identifier HP C extensions.
`+ESconstlit`	None	Introduces new default behavior. HP C now stores constant-qualified (const) objects and literals in read-only memory.
`+ESfic`	None	Compiles with inline fast indirect calls.

HP cc Option	GNU gcc Option	Description
`+ESlit`	Default	Places string literals and constants into read-only data storage.
`+ESnolit`	None	Disables +ESconstlit, causing HP C to no longer store literals in read-only memory.
`+ESnoparmreloc`	None	Disables parameter relocation for function calls.
`+ESsfc`	None	Replaces function pointer comparison millicode calls with inline code.
`+f`	None	Inhibits the promotion of float to double, except for function calls and returns.
`+FP`*`flags`* Example: `+FPVZO`	None	Controls floating-point traps.
`+help`	None	Launches a Web browser displaying an HTML version of the HP C/HP-UX online help.
`+hugesize`	None	Lowers the threshold for huge data.
`+I`	`-pg`	Prepares the object code for profile-based optimization data collection.
`+k`	None	Generates long-displacement code sequences so a program can reference large amounts of global data physically located in shared libraries.
`+L`	None	Enables any `#pragma` listing directives and the listing facility.
`+m`	None	Prints identifier maps in the source code listing.
`+o`	None	Prints hexadecimal code offsets in the source code listing.
`+[no]objdebug`	None	When used with `-g`, `+objdebug` leaves debug information in the object files.
`+O[0|1|2|3|4]`	`-O[0|1|2|3|s]`	Invokes optimization level.
`+P`	`-fprofile-generate` `-fprofile-use`	Performs profile-based optimization.

HP cc Option	GNU gcc Option	Description
`+pgmname`	None	Specifies the execution profile data set to be used by the optimizer.
`+r`	None	Inhibits the automatic promotion of float to double.
`+sb`	`-fsigned-bitfields` `-fno-unsigned-bitfields`	Makes bit-fields signed by default in both 32- and 64-bit modes.
`+u`*`bytes`*	`-falign-labels=`*`n`* (align branch targets to a power of 2 boundary)	Controls pointer alignment where *`bytes`* is 1, 2, or 4.
`+uc`	`-funsigned-char`	Makes unqualified char data types unsigned.
`+w`*`n`*	`-W`*`options`* (close equivalent) `-Wall` (turns on all warning messages)	Specifies the level of the warning messages where *n* is 1–3 (HP-UX).
`+W n1[,n2,...nN]`	`-Wno`*`options`* (close equivalent)	Suppresses the specified warnings.
`+We n1[,n2,...nN]`	`-Werror` (all warnings, close equivalent) `-pendantic`	Changes the specified warnings to errors.
`+Ww n1[,n2,...nN]`	`-W`*`options`* (close equivalent)	Enables the specified warnings, assuming all other warnings are suppressed with `-w` or `+w3`.
`+z`	`-fpic`	Generates shared library object code (same as +Z in 64-bit mode).
`+Z`	`-fPIC`	Generates shared library object code with a large data linkage table (long-form PIC).

1 HP C/HP-UX Online Help for HP-UX 11i (HP-UX 11.0, HP-UX 11i v1, HP-UX 11i v2). http://docs.hp.com/hpux/onlinedocs/dev/C/B3901BA/c_index.html.

2 GNU Compiler Collections version 3.4.2 (last updated May 23, 2004)

C.2 HP-UX and Linux C++ Compiler Options Table

TABLE C-2
HP-UX aCC and g++ Compiler Switches Comparison Table

HP aCC Option[3]	GNU g++ Option[4]	Description
`-.suffix`	None	The *suffix* parameter represents the character or characters to be used as the output filename suffix.
`-Aa`	`-ansi` `-std=standard`	Instructs the compiler to use Koenig lookup and strict ANSI for scope rules.
`-AA`	`-std=c++98` (closest option found)	Conforms to the ISO C++ standard.
`-AC89`	`-std=c89`	Invokes the compiler in ANSI C89 compilation mode.
`-AC99`	`-std=c99`[5] (also invoke `-pendantic flag` to receive all diagnostics)	Invokes the compiler in ANSI C99 compilation mode with its features.
`-Ae`	`-std=gnu89`	Invokes as an ANSI C compiler, with additional support for HP C or GNU language extensions.
`-AOa` `-AOe`	`-std=iso9899:1990` `-std=iso9899:199409` (invoke with `-Ox flag` for optimization options)	In addition to specifying the ANSI C language dialect, allows the optimizer to aggressively exploit the assumption that the source code conforms to the ANSI programming language C standard ISO 9899:1990.
`-AP`	None	Turns off `-AA` mode and uses the older C++ runtime libraries.
`-b`	None	Creates a shared library rather than an executable file.
`-c`	`-c`	Compiles one or more source files but does not enter the linking phase.

HP aCC Option	GNU g++ Option	Description
`-C`	`-C`	Prevents the preprocessor from stripping comments.
`-dynamic`	`-Wl,-Bdynamic`	Produces dynamically bound executables.
`-D`*`name`*`[=def]`	`-D`*`name`*`=def`	Defines a symbol name (*`name`*) to the preprocessor, as if defined by the preprocessing directive `#define`.
`+d`	`-fno-default-inline` (close but not exact) `-fno-inline`	Prevents the expansion of inline functions.
`+dryrun`	`-###`	Displays the options passed, but does not execute.
`-ext` `+e`	None	Enables platform-dependent C++ standards extensions.
`-E`	`-E`	Runs only the preprocessor on the named C++ files and sends the result to standard output (`stdout`).
`-fast`	None	Selects a combination of optimization options for optimum execution speed for reasonable build times.
`-fpeval=`*`precision`*	None	Specifies the minimum precision to use for floating-point expression evaluation.
`-g[0|1]`	`-g[1|2|3]`	Emits different levels of debug information.
`-G`	`-pg`	Compiles and creates the executable file instrumented for use with `gprof`.
`-I`*`dirs`* `-I-`	`-I`	Indicates an optional list of `-Idirectory` specifications.
`-mt`	`-D_REENTRANT` `-lpthread`	Compiles multithreaded.
`-n`	`-shared` `-Bshareable`	Causes the program file produced by the linker to be marked as sharable.

HP aCC Option	GNU g++ Option	Description
`-N`	None	Causes the program file produced by the linker to be marked as unsharable.
`-o` *`outfile`*	`-o` *`outfile`*	Causes the output of the compilation to be placed in `outfile`.
`-O`	`-O2`	Invokes the optimizer to perform level 2 optimizations.
`-p`	`-p`	Compiles and creates the executable file instrumented for use with `prof`.
`-P`	None	Only preprocesses the files named on the command line without invoking further phases. Leaves the result in corresponding files with the suffix .i.
`-q`	None	Causes the output file from the linker to be marked as demand-loadable.
`-Q`	None	Causes the program file from the linker to be marked as not demand-loadable.
`-r`	`-r`	Retains relocation information in the output file for subsequent relinking.
`-s`	`-Wl,-s`	Causes the executable program file created by the linker to be stripped of symbol table information.
`-S`	`-S`	Compiles the named program and leaves the assembly language output in a corresponding file with an .s suffix.
`-U`*`name`*	`-u` `-undefined=symbol`	*`name`* is the symbol name whose definition is removed from the preprocessor.
`-v`	`-v`	Enables verbose mode, sending a step-by-step description of the compilation process to stderr.
`-V` `-version`	`--version`	Displays the version numbers of the current compiler and linker (if the linker is executed).
`-w`	`-w`	Suppresses all warning messages.

HP aCC Option	GNU g++ Option	Description
`-Wc,-ansi_for_scope,[on][off]`	`-ffor-scope` `-fno-for-scope`	Enables or disables the standard scoping rules for `init` declarations in `for` statements.
`-Wc,-koenig_lookup,[on][off]`	None	Enables or disables standard argument-dependent lookup rules (also known as Koenig lookup).
`-Wx,`*`arg1 [,arg2,..,argn]`*	`-Wx,`*`arg1 [,arg2,..,argn]`*	Passes the arguments *`arg1`* through *`argn`* to the `subprocess x` of the compilation.
`-Y`	None	Enables Native Language Support (NLS) of 8-bit, 16-bit, and 4-byte EUC characters in comments, string literals, and character constants.
`-z`	Default	Disallows dereferencing of null pointers at runtime.
`-Z`	None	Allows dereferencing of null pointers at runtime.
`+help`	None	Invokes the initial menu window of HP `aC++` Online Programmer's Guide.
`+ild`	`-Wl,-i`	Specifies incremental linking.
`+noeh`	None	Disables exception handling.
`+nostl`	None	Eliminates references to the standard header files and libraries bundled with HP `aC++`.
`+O[no]initcheck`	`-Wuninitialized -O`	The initialization checking feature.
`+sb`	None	Specifies unqualified `char/short/int/long/long long` bitfields as signed.
`+tls=[static|dynamic]`	`-ftls-model=model`	Specifies whether references to thread local data items are to be performed according to the mode.
`+ub`	None	Specifies unqualified `char/short/int/long/long long` bitfields as unsigned.
`+uc`	None	Specifying `+uc` causes an unqualified (plain) `char` data type to be treated as unsigned `char`.

HP aCC Option	GNU g++ Option	Description
`+Warg1 [,arg2,..argn]`	None	Selectively suppresses any specified warning messages, where *arg1* through *argn* are valid compiler warning message numbers.
`+We`	`-Werror`	Interprets all warning and future error messages as errors.
`+Wearg1 [,arg2,..argn]`	None	Selectively interprets any specified warning or future error messages as errors. *arg1* through *argn* are valid compiler warning message numbers.
`+Wwarg1 [,arg2,..argn]`	None	Selectively treats compiler warnings as warnings. *arg1* through *argn* are valid compiler message numbers.
`-Wl,+FPVZO`	None	Hardware trap FPEs.

3 HP aC++ Version A.05.50 Programmer's Guide (HP-UX 11i v2) (http://docs.hp.com/hpux/onlinedocs/4310/index.htm)

4 GNU Compiler Collections version 3.4.2 (last updated May 23, 2004)

5 GCC has incomplete support for C99. See http://gcc.gnu.org/gcc-3.4/c99status.html.

C.3 HP-UX and Linux System Calls Comparison Table

TABLE C-3
HP-UX and Linux System Calls Comparison Table

HP-UX System Calls[6]	Linux Equivalent	Description
accept	accept	Accept connection on a socket.
access	access	Determine accessibility of a file.
acct	None	Enable or disable process accounting.
acl	None	Set a file's ACL information.
adjtime	adjtime	Correct the time to synchronize the system clock.
aio_cancel	aio_cancel, aio_cancel64	Cancel asynchronous I/O operation.
aio_error	aio_error, aio_error64	Return error status of asynchronous I/O operation.
aio_fsync	aio_fsync, aio_fsync64	Synchronize asynchronous I/O operations.
aio_read	aio_read, aio_read64	Start asynchronous read operation.
aio_reap	None	Wait for multiple asynchronous I/O requests.
aio_return	aio_return, aio_return64	Return asynchronous I/O operation status.
aio_suspend	aio_suspend, aio_suspend64	Suspend for asynchronous I/O operation.
aio_write	aio_write, aio_write64	Start asynchronous write operation.
alarm	alarm	Set a process's alarm clock.
audctl	None	Start or halt auditing system; set or get audit files.
audswitch	None	Suspend or resume auditing on current process.

HP-UX System Calls	Linux Equivalent	Description
audwrite	None	Write audit record for self-auditing process.
bind	bind	Bind an address to a socket.
brk	brk	Change data segment space allocation.
chdir	chdir	Change working directory.
chmod	chmod	Change file mode access permissions.
chown	chown	Change owner and group of a file.
chroot		Change root directory.
clock_getres	clock_gettime	Clock operations.
clock_gettime	clock_gettime	Clock operations.
clock_settime	clock_gettime	Clock operations.
close	close	Close a file descriptor.
connect	connect	Initiate a connection on a socket.
crashcon	None	Configure system crash dumps.
creat	creat—may return ENODEV in place of ENXIO as specified by SUSv3[7]	Create a new file or rewrite an existing one.
creat64	create64	Non-POSIX standard API interfaces to support large files (HP-UX).
dup	dup	Duplicate an open file descriptor.
dup2	dup2	Duplicate an open file descriptor to a specific slot.
errno	errno (not an API)	Error indicator for system calls.
exec, execl, execle, execlp, execv, execve, execvp	exec, execl, execle, execlp, execv, execve, execvp	Execute a file.
exit	exit	Terminate a process.
fchdir	fchdir	Change working directory.

HP-UX System Calls	Linux Equivalent	Description
`fchmod`	`fchmod`	File mode access permissions.
`fchown`	`fchown`	Change owner and group of a file.
`fcntl`	`fcntl`	File control.
`FD_CLR`, `FD_ISSET` `FD_SET`, `FD_ZERO`	`FD_CLR`, `FD_ISSET` `FD_SET`, `FD_ZERO`	Synchronous I/O multiplexing (see `select`).
`fdatasync`	`fdatasync`	Synchronize a file's in-core state with its state on disk.
`fgetacl`	None	Get access control list (ACL) information.
`fork`	`fork`	Create a new process.
`fpathconf`	`fpathconf`	Get configurable path name variables.
`fsctl`	None	Filesystem control.
`fsetacl`	None	Access control list (ACL) information.
`fstat`	`fstat`	Get file status.
`fstat64`	`fstat64`	Non-POSIX standard API interfaces to support large files.
`fstatfs`	`fstatfs`	Get file status.
`fstatvfs`	`fstatvfs`	Get file status.
`fstatvfs64`	`fstatvfs64`	Non-POSIX standard API interfaces to support large files.
`fsync`, `fdatasync`	`fsync`	Synchronize a file's in-core state with its state on disk.
`ftime`	`ftime`	Get date and time more precisely.
`ftruncate`	`ftruncate`	Truncate a file to a specified length.
`ftruncate64`	`ftruncate64`	Non-POSIX standard API interfaces to support large files.
`getaccess`	None	Get a user's effective access rights to a file.
`getacl`, `fgetacl`	None	Get access control list (ACL) information.

HP-UX System Calls	Linux Equivalent	Description
getaudid	getaudid	Get the audit ID (aid()) for the current process.
getaudproc	None	Get audit process flag for calling process.
getcontext	getcontext	Get and set current user context.
getdirentries	getdirentries	Get entries from a directory in a filesystem-independent format.
getdomainname	getdomainname	Get/set name of current nis domain.
getegid	getegid	Get effective group ID.
geteuid	geteuid	Get effective user group ID.
getevent	None	Get events and system calls currently being audited.
getfh	None	Get file handle for file on remote node.
getgid	getgid	Get real group ID.
getgroups	getgroups	Get group access list.
gethostid	gethostid	Get an identifier for the current host.
gethostname	gethostname	Get name of current host.
getitimer	getitimer	Get value of interval timer.
getksym	None	Get information for a global kernel symbol.
getms	None	Receive next message from a streams file.
getpagesize	getpagesize	Get the current page size.
getpeername	getpeername	Get address of connected peer.
getpgid	getpgid	Get process group ID.
getpgrp	getpgrp	Get process group ID.
getpgrp2	None	Get process group ID of specified process.
getpid, getpgid, getpgrp, getpgrp2, getppid	getpid, getpgid, getpgrp, getppid	Get process, process group, and parent process ID.

HP-UX System Calls	Linux Equivalent	Description
getpmsg	None	Receive next message from a streams file in a priority order.
getpriority, setpriority	getpriority, setpriority	Get or set process priority.
getprivgrp, setprivgrp	None	Get and set special attributes for group.
getrlimit, setrlimit	getrlimit, setrlimit	Control consumption of system resources.
getrlimit64	getrlimit64	Non-POSIX standard API interfaces to support large files.
getrusage	getrusage	Get information about resource utilization.
getsid	getsid	Get session ID.
getsockname	getsockname	Get socket address.
getsockopt	getsockopt	Get or set options on sockets.
gettimeofday	gettimeofday	Get the date and time.
gettune	None	Get value of a kernel tunable parameter.
getuid, geteuid, getgid, getegid	getuid, geteuid, getgid, getegid	Get real user, effective user, real group, and effective group IDs.
gtty	gtty	Bsd terminal modes.
ioctl	ioctl	Control device.
iscomsec	None	Check if system has been converted to a trusted system.
kill	kill—LSB specification says if pid is -1, sig shall not be sent to the calling process.	Send a signal to a process or a group of processes.
killpg, getpgrp, setpgrp	killpg, getpgrp, setpgrp	4.2 BSD-compatible process control facilities.
lilockf	None	Provide semaphores and record locking on files.

HP-UX System Calls	Linux Equivalent	Description
`link`	`link`	Link to a file.
`lio_listio`	`lio_listio`, `lio_listio64`	Start a list of asynchronous I/O operations.
`listen`	`listen`	Listen for connections on a socket.
`loadmod`	None	Load kernel modules on demand.
`lockf64`	`lockf64`	Non-POSIX standard API interfaces to support large files.
`lseek`	`lseek`	Move read/write file pointer; seek.
`lseek64`	`lseek64`	Non-POSIX standard API interfaces to support large files.
`lstat`	`lstat`	Get symbolic link status.
`lstat64`	`lstat64`	Non-POSIX standard API interfaces to support large files.
`madvise`	`madvise`	Advise system of process's expected paging behavior.
`makecontext`, `swapcontext`	`makecontext`, `swapcontext`	Manipulate user contexts.,
`mkdir`	`mkdir`	Make a directory file.
`mknod`	`mknod`	Make directory, special, or ordinary file.
`mlock`	`mlock`	Lock segment of process address space in memory.
`mlockall`	`mlockall`	Lock process address space in memory.
`mmap`	`mmap`[8]	Map object into virtual memory.
`mmap64`	`mmap64`[9]	Non-POSIX standard API interfaces to support large files.
`modpath`	None	Change global search path for dynamically loadable kernel modules.
`modstat`	None	Get information for a dynamically loaded kernel module.
`moduload`	None	Unload a kernel module on demand.

HP-UX System Calls	Linux Equivalent	Description
mount	mount	Mount a filesystem.
mpctl	None	Multiprocessor control.
mprotect	mprotect	Modify memory mapping access protections.
mq_close	mq_close[10]	Close a message queue descriptor.
mq_getattr	mq_getattr	Get status information and attributes associated with a message queue.
mq_notify	mq_notify	Register/cancel a notification request with a message queue.
mq_open	mq_open	Create/open a message queue.
mq_receive	mq_receive	Receive a message from a message queue.
mq_send	mq_send	Send a message to a message queue.
mq_setattr	mq_setattr	Set the blocking status of a message queue associated with a descriptor.
mq_unlink	mq_unlink	Unlink a message queue.
msem_init	None	Initialize semaphore in mapped file or anonymous memory region.
msem_lock	None	Lock a semaphore.
msem_remove	None	Remove semaphore in mapped file or anonymous region.
msem_unlock	None	Unlock a semaphore.
msgctl	msgctl	Message control operations.
msgget	msgget	Get message queue.
msgop	msgop	Message operations.
msgrcv	msgrcv	Receive message from message queue.
msgsnd	msgsnd	Send message to message queue.
msync	msync	Synchronize a mapped file.
munlock	munlock	Unlock segment of process virtual address space.

HP-UX System Calls	Linux Equivalent	Description
munlockall	munlockall	Unlock process virtual address space.
munmap	munmap	Unmap a mapped region.
nanosleep	nanosleep	High-resolution sleep.
nice	nice	Change priority of a process.
O_LARGEFILE	O_LARGEFILE	Non-POSIX standard API interfaces to support large files.
open	open—LSB specifications says open may return ENODEV in place of ENXIO	Open file for reading or writing.
open64	open64	Non-POSIX standard API interfaces to support large files.
pathconf	pathconf	Get configurable path name variables.
pause	pause	Suspend process until signal.
pipe	pipe	Create an interprocess channel.
plock	mlockall	Lock process, text, data, stack, or shared library in memory.
poll	poll	Monitor I/O conditions on multiple file descriptors.
pread	pread	Read from file.
pread64	pread64	Non-POSIX standard API interfaces to support large files.
prealloc	None	Pre-allocate fast disk storage.
prealloc64	None	Non-POSIX standard API interfaces to support large files.
PRI_HPUX_TO_POSIX	None	Return POXIX.4 process priority.
PRI_POSIX_TO_HPUX	None	Return HP-UX process priority.
profil	profil	Execution time profile.
pset_assign	None	Change processor set assignment.

HP-UX System Calls	Linux Equivalent	Description
`pset_bind`	None	Bind a process or a thread to a processor set.
`pset_create`	None	Create a processor set.
`pset_ctl`	None	Processor set control.
`pset_destroy`	None	Destroy processor set.
`pset_getattr`	None	Processor set control API.
`pset_setattr`	None	Processor set control API.
`pstat` `pstat_getcommandline`, `pstat_getcrashdev`, `pstat_getcrashinfo`, `pstat_getdisk`, `pstat_getdynamic`, `pstat_getfile`, `pstat_getfile2`, `pstat_getfiledetails`, `pstat_getipc`, `pstat_getlv`, `pstat_getlwp`, `pstat_getmpathname`, `pstat_getmsg`, `pstat_getnode`, `pstat_getpathname`, `pstat_getpmq`, `pstat_getproc`, `pstat_getprocessor`, `pstat_getprocvm`, `pstat_getpsem`, `pstat_getpset`, `pstat_getsem`, `pstat_getshm`, `pstat_getsocket`, `pstat_getstable`, `pstat_getstream`, `pstat_getswap`, `pstat_getvminfo`, `pstat_static`	None	Get system information.

HP-UX System Calls	Linux Equivalent	Description
ptrace	ptrace	Process trace.
putmsg	None	Send a message on a stream.
putpmsg	None	Send a message on a stream in different priority bands.
pw_getukid, pw_wait, pw_post, pw_postv, pw_getvmax	None	Lightweight synchronization mechanism.
pw_getukid	None	Lightweight synchronization mechanism.
pw_getvmax	None	Lightweight synchronization mechanism.
pw_post	None	Synchronization mechanism.
pw_postv_	None	Lightweight synchronization mechanism.
pw_wait	None	Lightweight synchronization mechanism.
pwrite	pwrite	Write to file.
pwrite64	pwrite64	Non-POSIX standard API interfaces to support large files.
quotactl	None	Manipulate disk quotas.
raise	raise	Send a signal to executing program.
read	read	Read input.
readlink	readlink	Read value of a symbolic link.
readv	readv	Read input.
reboot	reboot[11]	Boot the system.
recv	recv	Receive message from a socket.
recvfrom	recvfrom	Receive message from a socket.
recvmsg	recvmsg	Receive message from a socket.
rename	rename	Change the name of a file.
rmdir	rmdir	Remove a directory file.
rtprio	None	Change or read real-time priority.
sbrk	sbrk	Change data segment space allocation.

HP-UX System Calls	Linux Equivalent	Description
sched_get_ priority_max	sched_get_ priority_max	Return maximum for scheduling policy.
sched_get_ priority_min	sched_get_ priority_min	Return minimum for scheduling policy.
sched_getparam	sched_getparam	Return scheduling parameters.
sched_getscheduler	sched_getscheduler	Return scheduling policy.
sched_rr_ get_interval	sched_rr_ get_interval	Update execution time limit.
sched_setparam	sched_setparam	Set scheduling parameters.
sched_setscheduler	sched_setscheduler	Set scheduling policy.
sched_yield	sched_yield	Force process to relinquish processor.
select	select	Synchronous I/O multiplexing.
sem_close	sem_close	Close a named semaphore.
sem_destroy	sem_destroy	Destroy an unnamed semaphore.
sem_getvalue	sem_getvalue	Read a POSIX semaphore.
sem_init	sem_init	Initialize an unnamed semaphore.
sem_open	sem_open	Open/create a named semaphore.
sem_post	sem_post	Unlock a POSIX semaphore.
sem_trywait	sem_trywait	Lock a POSIX semaphore without blocking.
sem_unlink	sem_unlink	Unlink a named semaphore.
sem_wait	sem_wait	Lock a POSIX semaphore.
semctl	semctl	Semaphore control operations.
semget	semget	Get set of semaphores.
semop	semop	Semaphore operations.
semtimedop	semtimedop	Semaphore operations.
send	send	Send message to a socket.
sendfile	None	Send the contents of a file through a socket.

HP-UX System Calls	Linux Equivalent	Description
`sendfile64`	None	Send the contents of a file through a socket.
`sendmsg`	None	Send message to a socket.
`sendto`	`sendto`	Send message to a socket.
`serialize`	None	Force target process to run serially with other processes.
`setacl`	None	Set access control list (ACL) information.
`setaudid`	None	Set audit ID (`aid()`) for current process.
`setaudproc`	None	Set or clear auditing on calling process.
`setcontext`	`setcontext`	Get and set current user context.
`setevent`	None	Set current events and system calls to be audited.
`setgid`	`setgid`	Set group ID.
`setgroups`	`setgroups`	Set group access list.
`sethostname`	`sethostname` (maximum length of host name may not be equal to POSIX equivalent of `HOST_NAME_MAX`)	Set name of host CPU.
`setitimer`	`setitimer`	Set value of interval timer.
`setpgid`	`setpgid`	Set process group ID for job control.
`setpgrp`	`setpgrp`	Set process group ID.
`setpgrp2`	None	Set process group ID.
`setpgrp3`	None	Create session and set process group ID.
`setpriority`	`setpriority`	Set process priority.
`setprivgrp`	None	Set special attributes for group.
`setregid`	`setregid`	Set the real and effective group IDs.
`setresgid`	`setresgid`	Set real, effective, and saved group IDs.
`setresuid`	`setresuid`	Set real and effective user IDs.

HP-UX System Calls	Linux Equivalent	Description
setrlimit	setrlimit	Control consumption of system resources.
setrlimit64	setrlimit64	Non-POSIX standard API interfaces to support large files.
setsid	setsid	Create session and set process group ID.
setsockopt	setsockopt	Set options on sockets.
settimeofday	settimeofday	Set the date and time.
settune	None	Set value of a kernel tunable parameter.
settune_txn	None	Sets the values of kernel tunable parameters in a transaction.
setuid	setuid	Set user and group IDs.
setuname	None	Set node name (system name).
shm_open	shm_open	Create/open a shared memory object.
shm_unlink	shm_unlink	Unlink a shared memory object.
shmat	shmat	Attach shared memory to data segment.
shmctl	shmctl	Shared memory control operations.
shmdt	shmdt	Detach shared memory from data segment.
shmget	shmget	Get shared memory segment.
shmop	shmop	Shared memory operations.
shutdown	shutdown	Shut down a socket.
sigaction	sigaction	Examine and change signal action.
sigaltstack	sigaltstack	Set and/or get signal alternate stack context.
sigblock	sigblock	Block signals.
sighold, sigrelse	sighold, sigrelse	Signal management.
sigignore	sigignore	Signal management.
siginterrupt	siginterrupt	Allow signals to interrupt functions.
sigpause	sigpause	Signal management.

HP-UX System Calls	Linux Equivalent	Description
`signal`	`signal`	4.2 BSD-compatible process control facilities.
`sigpending`	`sigpending`	Examine pending signals.
`sigprocmask`	`sigprocmask`	Examine and change blocked signals.
`sigqueue`	`sigqueue`	Queue a signal to a process.
`sigsend`	None	Send a signal to a process or a group of processes.
`sigsendset`	None	Send a signal to a group of processes.
`sigsetmask`	`sigsetmask`	Set current signal mask.
`sigspace`	None	Assure sufficient signal stack space.
`sigstack`	`sigstack`	Set and/or get signal stack context.
`sigsuspend`	`sigsuspend`	Wait for a signal.
`sigtimedwait`	`sigtimedwait`	Examine and change signal action.
`sigvec`	`sigvec`	4.2 BSD-compatible process control facilities.
`sigvector`	None	Software signal facilities.
`sigwait`	`sigwait`	Examine and change signal action.
`sigwaitinfo`	`sigwaitinfo`	Examine and change signal action.
`socket`	`socket`	Create an endpoint for communication.
`socketpair`	`socketpair`	Create a pair of connected sockets.
`sprofil`	None	Execution time profile for disjointed text spaces.
`stat`	`stat`	Get file status.
`stat64`	`stat64`	Non-POSIX standard API interfaces to support large files.
`statfs`	`statfs`	Get file system statistics.
`statvfs`	`statvfs`	Get file status.
`statvfs64`	`statvfs64`	Non-POSIX standard API interfaces to support large files.

HP-UX System Calls	Linux Equivalent	Description
`stime`	`stime`	Set time and date.
`stream`	None	Streams enhancements to standard system calls.
`stty`	`stty`	Control terminal device (bell version 6 compatibility).
`swapcontext`	`swapcontext`	Manipulate user contexts.
`swapon`	`swapon`	Add swap device for interleaved paging and swapping.
`symlink`	`symlink`	Make symbolic link to a file.
`sync`	`sync`	Update disk.
`sysconf`	`sysconf`	Get configurable system variables.
`sysfs`	`sysfs`	Get filesystem type info.
`time`	`time`	Get time.
`timer_create`	`timer_create`	Create timer.
`timer_delete`	`timer_delete`	Delete timer.
`timer_getoverrun`	`timer_getoverrun`	Return timer expiration count.
`timer_gettime`	`timer_gettime`	Store timer expiration and reload value.
`timer_settime`	`timer_settime`	Set timer expiration.
`times`	`times`	Get process and child process times.
`truncate`	`truncate`	Truncate a file to a specified length.
`truncate64`	`truncate64`	Non-POSIX standard API interfaces to support large files.
`ttrace`	None	Tracing facility for multithreaded processes.
`ttrace_wait`	None	Wait for `ttrace()` request.
`tuneinfo2`	None	Retrieve detailed information about kernel tunable parameters.
`ualarm`	`ualarm`	Set the interval timer.
`ulimit`	`ulimit`	Get and set user limits.

HP-UX System Calls	Linux Equivalent	Description
umask	umask	Set and get file creation mask.
umount	umount, umount2	Unmount a file system.
uname	uname	Get information about computer system; set node name (system name).
unlink	unlink (may return EISDIR instead of EPERM as specified by SUSv3[12])	Remove directory entry; delete file.
usleep	usleep	Suspend execution for an interval.
ustat	ustat	Get mounted file system statistics.
utime	utime	Set file access and modification times.
utimes	utimes	Set file access and modification times.
vfork	vfork	Spawn new process (use fork() instead).
vfsmount	None	Mount a file system.
wait	wait	Wait for child process to stop or terminate.
wait3, wait4	wait3 (works as specified in SUSv2 except WCONTINUED and WIFCONTINUED are optional) wait4 (waits for process termination, BSD style)	Wait for child process to change state.
waitid	waitid	Wait for child process to change state.
waitpid	waitpid—works as specified in SUSv3 except WCONTINUED and WIFCONTINUED are optional	Wait for child process to stop or terminate.

HP-UX System Calls	Linux Equivalent	Description
`write`	`write`	Write data to a file.
`writev`	`writev`	Write data to a file.

6 HP-UX Reference Section 2: System Calls HP-UX 11i v2

7 www.unix.org/version3/

8 Some flags may not be compatible.

9 This is not documented in the Linux man pages. See /usr/include/mman.h and /usr/include/bits/mman.h.

10 All message queue functions defined in mqueue.h are available only on Linux 2.6 systems that define `_POSIX_MESSAGE_PASSING`. Systems such as SUSE 9.1 do not define it, and hence `mq_*` functions are not available.

11 Takes different arguments.

12 www.unix.org/version3/

C.4 HP-UX and Linux Library API Comparison Table

TABLE C-4
HP-UX and Linux Library API Comparison Table

HP-UX Library Calls	Linux Equivalent	Description
`a64l, l64a`	`a64l, l64a`	Convert between long integer and base-64 ASCII string.
`l64a_r`	None	Convert between long integer and base-64 ASCII string (reentrant).
`abs`	`abs`	Return integer absolute value.
`aclentrystart`	None	Convert string to access control list (ACL) structure.
`aclsort`	None	Sort ACL entries on JFS.
`acltostr`	None	Convert access control list (ACL) structure to string form.
`acos, acosf, acosl`	`acos, acosf, acosl`	Arccosine functions.
`acosw, acosq`	None	Arccosine functions.
`acosd, acosdf, acosdl, acosdw, acosdq`	None	Degree-valued arccosine functions.
`acosh, acoshf, acoshl`	`acosh, acoshf, acoshl`	Arc hyperbolic cosine functions.
`acoshw acoshq`	None	Arc hyperbolic cosine functions.
`add_wch, mvadd_wch, mvwadd_wch, wadd_ch`	`add_wch, mvadd_wch, mvwadd_wch, wadd_ch`	Add a complex character and rendition to a window.
`add_wchstr, mvadd_wchnstr, mvadd_wchstr, mvwadd_wchnstr, mvwadd_wchstr, add_wchnstr, wadd_wchstr`	`add_wchstr, mvadd_wchnstr, mvadd_wchstr, mvwadd_wchnstr, mvwadd_wchstr, wadd_wchnstr, wadd_wchstr (libncurses)`	Add an array of complex characters and renditions to a window.

HP-UX Library Calls	Linux Equivalent	Description
addch, mvaddch, mvwaddch, waddch	addch, mvaddch, mvwaddch, waddch (libncurses)	Add a single-byte character and rendition to a window and advance the cursor.
addmntent	addmntent	Get file system descriptor file entry.
addstr, mvaddnstr, mvaddstr, mvwaddnstr, mvwaddstr, waddnstr, waddstr	addstr, mvaddnstr, mvaddstr, mvwaddnstr, mvwaddstr, waddnstr, waddstr (lincurses)	Add a string of multibyte characters without rendition to a window and advance cursor.
addnwstr, addwstr, mvaddnwstr, mvaddwstr, mvwaddnwstr, mvwaddwstr, waddnwstr, waddwstr	addnwstr, addwstr, mvaddnwstr, mvaddwstr, mvwaddnwstr, mvwaddwstr, waddnwstr, waddwstr (libncurses)	Add a wide-character string to a window and advance the cursor.
alloca	alloca	Allocate space from the stack.
alphasort	alphasort	Sort a directory pointer array.
asctime, asctime_r	asctime, asctime_r	Convert date and time to string.
asin, asinf, asinl, asinw, asinq	asin, asinf, asinl	Arcsine functions.
asinh, asinhf asinhl, asinhw, asinhq	asinh, asinhf asinhl	Arc hyperbolic sine functions.
assert	assert	Verify program assertion.
atan, atanf, atanl, atanw, atanq	atan, atanf, atanl	Arctangent functions.
atan2, atan2f, atan2l, atan2w, atan2q	atan2, atan2f, atan2l	Arctangent-and-quadrant functions.
atan2d, atan2df	None	Degree-valued arctangent-and-quadrant functions.

HP-UX Library Calls	Linux Equivalent	Description
atand, atandf	atand, atandf, atanl	Degree-valued arctangent functions.
atanh, atanhf, atanhl, atanhw, atanhq	atanh, atanhf, atanhl	Arc hyperbolic tangent functions.
atexit	atexit	Register a function to be called at program termination.
atof	atof	Convert string to double-precision number.
atoi	atoi	Convert string to integer.
atol	atol	Convert string to integer.
attr_off, attr_on, attr_set, color_set, wattr_get, wattr_off, wattr_on, wattr_set, wcolor_set	attr_off, attr_on, attr_set, color_set, wattr_get, wattr_off, wattr_on, wattr_set, wcolor_set (libncurses)	Window attribute control functions.
attron, attrset, wattroff, wattron, wattrset	attron, attrset, wattroff, wattron, wattrset (libncurses)	Restricted window attribute control functions.
auth_destroy	auth_destroy	Library routines for client-side RPC authentication.
authdes_getucred	authdes_getucred	Library routines for secure remote procedure calls.
authdes_seccreate	None	Library routines for secure remote procedure calls.
authnone_create	authnone_create	Library routines for client-side RPC authentication.
authsys_create	authunix_create	Library routines for client-side RPC authentication.

HP-UX Library Calls	Linux Equivalent	Description
authsys_create_ default	authunix_create_ default	Library routines for client-side RPC authentication.
basename, dirname	basename, dirname	Extract components of a path name.
baudrate	baudrate (libncurses)	Get terminal baud rate.
bcmp	bcmp	Memory operations, compare bytes.
bcopy	bcopy	Memory operations, copy bytes.
beep	beep (libncurses)	Audible signal.
bgets	None	Read stream up to next delimiter.
bigcrypt	None[13]	Generate hashing encryption on large strings.
bindresvport	bindresvport	Bind a socket to a privileged IP port.
bkgd, bkgdset, getbkgd, wbkgd, wbkgdset	bkgd, bkgdset, getbkgd, wbkgd, wbkgdset (libncurses)	Set or get background character and rendition using a single-byte character.
bkgrnd, bkgrndset, getbkgrnd, wbkgrnd, wbkgrndset, wgetbkgrnd	bkgrnd, bkgrndset, getbkgrnd, wbkgrnd, wbkgrndset, wgetbkgrnd (libncurses)	Set or get background character and rendition using a complex character.
blclose	None	Terminal block-mode library interface.
blget	None	Terminal block-mode library interface.
blopen, blread, blset	None	Terminal block-mode library interface.
box	box	Draw borders from complex characters and renditions.
box_set	box_set	Draw borders from single-byte characters and renditions.
bsd_signal	signal	Simplified signal facilities.
bsearch	bsearch	Binary search a sorted table.

HP-UX Library Calls	Linux Equivalent	Description
bufsplit	None	Split buffer into fields.
		Write records into new wtmps and btmps database.
bwtmpname	None	Write records into new wtmps and btmps database.
byte_status	None	Process 16-bit characters.
byteorder: htonl, htons, ntohl, ntohs	htonl, htons, ntohl, ntohs	Convert values between host and network byte order.
bzero	bzero	Memory operations, clear bytes.
c_colwidth	None	Process 16-bit characters.
cabs, cabsf, cabsl, cabsw, cabsq	cabs, cabsf, cabsl	Complex absolute value functions.
cacos, cacosf, cacosl, cacosw, cacosq	cacos, cacosf, cacosl	Complex arccosine functions.
cacosh, cacoshf, cacoshl, cacoshq, cacoshw	cacosh, cacoshf, cacoshl	Complex arc hyperbolic cosine functions.
calloc	calloc	Allocate memory for array.
can_change_color, color_content, has_colors, init_color, init_pair, start_color, pair_content	can_change_color, color_content, has_colors, init_color, init_pair, start_color, pair_content (libncurses)	Color manipulation functions.
carg, cargf, cargl, cargw, cargq	carg, cargf, cargl	Complex argument functions.
casin, casinf, casinl, casinw, casinq	casin, casinf, casinl	Complex arcsine functions.

HP-UX Library Calls	Linux Equivalent	Description
casinh, casinhf, casinhl, casinhw, casinhq	casinh, casinhf, casinhl	Complex arc hyperbolic sine functions.
catanh, catanhf, catanhl, catanhw, catanhq	catanh, catanhf, catanhl	Complex arc hyperbolic tangent functions.
catgets	catgets	Get a program message.
catopen, catclose	catopen, catclose	Open or close NLS message catalog for reading.
cbreak, nocbreak, noraw, raw	cbreak, nocbreak, noraw, raw (libncurses)	Input mode control functions.
cbrt, cbrtf, cbrtl, cbrtq, cbrtw	cbrt, cbrtf, cbrtl	Cube root function (float, long, and so on).
ccos, ccosf, ccosl, ccosw, ccosq	ccos, ccosf, ccosl	Complex cosine functions.
ccosh, ccoshf, ccoshl, ccoshw, ccoshq	ccosh, ccoshf, ccoshl	Complex hyperbolic cosine functions.
ceil, ceilf, ceill, ceilw, ceilq	ceil, ceilf, ceill	Rounding functions.
cexp, cexpf, cexpl, cexpw, cexpq	cexp, cexpf, cexpl	Complex exponential functions.
cfgetispeed, cfgetospeed	cfgetispeed, cfgetospeed	Get/set tty intput baud rate.
cfsetispeed, cfsetospeed	cfsetispeed, cfsetospeed	Get/set tty output baud rate.
chgat, mvchgat mvwchgat, wchgat	chgat, mvchgat mvwchgat, wchgat	Change renditions of characters in a window.
chownacl	None	Change owner and/or group in access control list.
cimag, cimagf	cimag, cimagf, cimagl	Complex imaginary-part functions.

HP-UX Library Calls	Linux Equivalent	Description
clear, erase, wclear, werase	clear, erase, wclear, werase	Clear a window.
clearenv	clearenv	Clear the process environment.
clearerr	clearerr	Stream status inquiries.
clearerr_unlocked	clearerr_unlocked	Stream status inquiries.
clearok, idlok, leaveok, scrollok setscrreg, wsetscrreg	clearok, idlok, leaveok, scrollok setscrreg, wsetscrreg (libncurses)	Terminal output control functions.
clnt_call	clnt_call	Library routine for client-side calls, rpc.
clnt_control	clnt_control	Library routines for dealing with client handles, rpc.
clnt_create	clnt_create	Library routines for dealing with client handles, rpc.
clnt_create_vers	None	Library routines for dealing with client handles, rpc.
clnt_control, clnt_create, clnt_create_vers, clnt_destroy, clnt_dg_create, clnt_pcreateerror, clnt_raw_create, clnt_spcreateerror, clnt_tli_create, clnt_tp_create, clnt_vc_create, rpc_createerr	clnt_pcreateerror, clnt_geterr	Library routines for dealing with client handles.
clock	clock	Report CPU time used.
clog, clogf, clogl	clog, clogf, clogl	Complex logarithm functions.
closedir	closedir	Directory operations.

HP-UX Library Calls	Linux Equivalent	Description
`closelog`	`closelog`	Control system log.
`clrtobot`, `wclrtobot`	`clrtobot`, `wclrtobot`	Clear from cursor to end of window.
`clrtoeol`, `wclrtoeol`	`clrtoeol`, `wclrtoeol`	Clear from cursor to end of line.
`compile`	None	Regular expression compile and match routines.
`compound`, `compoundf`, `compoundl`, `compoundw`, `compoundq`	None	Compound interest factor.
`confstr`	`confstr`	Get string-valued configuration values.
`conj`, `conjf`, `conjl`, `conjw`, `conjq`	`conj`, `conjf`, `conjl`	Complex conjugate functions.
`copydvagent`	None	Copy device assignment structure.
`copylist`	None	Copy a file into memory.
`copysign`, `copysignf`, `copysignl`, `copysignw`, `copysignq`	`copysign`, `copysignf`, `copysignl`	Copysign functions.
`copywin`	`copywin`	Copy a region of the window.
`cos`, `cosf`, `cosl`	`cos`, `cosf`, `cosl`	Cosine functions.
`cosh`, `coshf`, `coshl`	`cosh`, `coshf`, `coshl`	Hyperbolic cosine functions.
`cpacl`, `fcpacl`	None	Copy access control list (ACL) to another file.
`cpow`, `cpowf`, `cpowl`	`cpow`, `cpowf`, `cpowl`	Complex power functions.
`cproj`, `cprojf`, `cprojl`	`cproj`, `cprojf`, `cprojl`	Complex projection functions.
`cr_close`	None	Close a crash dump descriptor.
`cr_info`	None	Retrieve crash dump information.

HP-UX Library Calls	Linux Equivalent	Description
cr_isaddr	None	Validate whether physical page number was dumped.
cr_open	None	Open crash dump for reading.
cr_perror	None	Print libcrash error or warning message.
cr_read	None	Read from crash dump.
cr_set_node	None	Set crash dump node number.
cr_uncompress	None	Uncompress a file in a crash dump.
cr_verify	None	Verify integrity of crash dump.
creal, crealf, creall	creal, crealf, creall	Complex real-part functions.
crypt, crypt_r, encrypt, encrypt_r, setkey, setkey_r	crypt, crypt_r, encrypt, encrypt_r, setkey, setkey_r	Generate hashing encryption.
csin, csinf, csinl	csin, csinf, csinl	Complex sine functions.
csqrt, csqrtf, csqrtl	csqrt, csqrtf, csqrtl	Complex square root functions.
ctan, ctanf, ctanl	ctan, ctanf, ctanl	Complex tangent functions.
ctermid	ctermid	Generate filename for terminal.
ctime, ctime_r, localtime, localtime_r, difftime, mktime, gmtime, gmtime_r, asctime, asctime_r, timezone, daylight, tzname, tzset	ctime, ctime_r, localtime, localtime_r, difftime, mktime, gmtime, gmtime_r, asctime, asctime_r, timezone, daylight, tzname, tzset	Convert date and time to string.
character classification	character classification	Classify characters.

HP-UX Library Calls	Linux Equivalent	Description
isalpha, isupper, islower, isdigit, isxdigit, isalnum, isspace, ispunct, isprint, isgraph, iscntrl, isascii	isalpha, isupper, islower, isdigit, isxdigit, isalnum, isspace, ispunct, isprint, isgraph, iscntrl, isascii	
cur_term	cur_term (libncurses)	Current terminal information.
curs_set	curs_set (libncurses)	Set the cursor mode.
curscr	curscr (libncurses)	Current window.
cuserid	cuserid	Get character login name of the user.
datalock	None	Lock process into memory after allocating data and stack space.
daylight	daylight	Convert date and time to string.
db_initialize, db_create_table, db_destroy_table, db_first_entry, db_next_entry, db_reset_next_entry, db_list_entries, db_remove_entry, db_add_entry, db_table_exists, db_unload_table, db_checkpoint, db_standby, db_free_result	db_initialize, db_create_table, db_destroy_table, db_first_entry, db_next_entry, db_reset_next_entry, db_list_entries, db_remove_entry, db_add_entry, db_table_exists, db_unload_table, db_checkpoint, db_standby, db_free_result	Write data to a file.
dbminit, fetch, store, delete, firstkey, nextkey, dbmclose	dbminit, fetch, store, delete, firstkey, nextkey, dbmclose (db.h)	Database subroutines.

HP-UX Library Calls	Linux Equivalent	Description
dbm_open, dbm_close, dbm_fetch, dbm_store, dbm_delete, dbm_firstkey, dbm_nextkey, dbm_error, dbm_clearerr	dbm_open, dbm_close, dbm_fetch, dbm_store, dbm_delete, dbm_firstkey, dbm_nextkey, dbm_error, dbm_clearerr (nbdm.h)	Database subroutines.
def_prog_mode, def_shell_mode, reset_prog_mode, reset_shell_mode	def_prog_mode, def_shell_mode, reset_prog_mode, reset_shell_mode (libncurses)	Low-level curses routines.
del_curterm, restartterm, set_curterm, setupterm	del_curterm, restartterm, set_curterm, setupterm (libncurses)	Interfaces to terminfo database.
delay_output	delay_output (libncurses)	Miscellaneous curses utility routine.
delch, mvdelch, mvwdelch, wdelch	delch, mvdelch, mvwdelch, wdelch (libncurses)	Delete character from a window.
deleteln, wdeleteln	deleteln, wdeleteln (libncurses)	Delete lines in a window.
delscreen	delscreen (libncurses)	Free storage associated with a screen.
delwin	delwin (libncurses)	Delete a window.
devnm	None	Map device ID to file path.
dial, undial	None	Establish an outgoing terminal line connection.

HP-UX Library Calls	Linux Equivalent	Description
difftime	difftime	Difference between calendar times.
directory operations	directory operations	Directory operations.
opendir, readdir, telldir, seekdir, rewinddir, closedir	opendir, readdir, telldir, seekdir, rewinddir, closedir	
dirname	dirname	Return path name of parent directory.
div, ldiv	div, ldiv	Integer division and remainder.
dladdr	None	Symbolic information for an address.
dld_getenv	None	Explicit load of shared libraries.
dlerror	dlerror	Get diagnostic information from dynamic linking process.
dlget	None	Retrieve information on loaded module (program or shared library).
dlgetmodinfo	None	Retrieve information on loaded module (program or shared library).
dlgetname	None	Retrieve name of load module.
dlmodadd	None	Register information about dynamically generated functions.
dlmodinfo	None	Retrieve information on loaded module (program or shared library).
dlmodremove	None	Remove information registered using dlmodadd.
dlmodremove	None	Remove information registered using dlmodadd.
dlopen	dlopen	Open a shared library.
dlclose	dlclose	Close a shared library.
dlsym	dlsym	Get address of symbol in shared object.

HP-UX Library Calls	Linux Equivalent	Description
dn_comp, dn_expand, get_resfield, herror, res_init, res_mkquery, res_query, res_search, res_send, set_resfield	dn_comp, dn_expand, herror, res_init, res_mkquery, res_querydomain, res_search, res_send	Resolver routines.
doupdate, refresh, wnoutrefresh, wrefresh	doupdate, refresh, wnoutrefresh, wrefresh	Refresh windows and lines.
drand48, erand48, lrand48, nrand48, mrand48, jrand48, srand48, seed48, lcong48	drand48, erand48, lrand48, nrand48, mrand48, jrand48, srand48, seed48, lcong48	Generate uniformly distributed pseudorandom numbers.
dupwin	dupwin (libncurses)	Duplicate a window.
echo, noecho	echo, noecho	Enable/disable terminal echo.
echo_wchar, wecho_wchar	echo_wchar, wecho_wchar (libncurses)	Write a complex character and immediately refresh the window.
echochar, wechochar	echochar, wechochar (libncurses)	Echo single-byte character and rendition to a window and refresh.
ecvt, fcvt, gcvt	ecvt, fcvt, gcvt	Convert floating-point number to string.
edata	None	Last locations in program.
elf_*	None[14]	Elf object file access library.
encrypt	encrypt	Generate hashing encryption.
end, etext, edata	None	Last locations in program.
endbwent	None	Write records into new wtmps and btmps database.

HP-UX Library Calls	Linux Equivalent	Description
enddvagent	None	Free memory and closes file.
endfsent	endfsent	Get file system descriptor file entry.
endgrent	endgrent	Get group file entry.
endhostent, endhostent_r, gethostbyaddr, gethostbyaddr_r, gethostbyname, gethostbyname_r, gethostent, gethostent_r, sethostent, sethostent_r	endhostent, gethostbyaddr, gethostbyaddr_r, gethostbyname, gethostbyname_r, gethostent, sethostent	Get, set, or end network host entry.
getnetconfig, setnetconfig, getnetconfigent, freenetconfigent, nc_perror, nc_sperror	None	Get network configuration database entry.
getmntent, getmntent_r, setmntent, addmntent, delmntent, endmntent, hasmntopt	getmntent, getmntent_r, setmntent, addmntent, endmntent, hasmntopt	Get file system descriptor file entry.
getnetent, getnetbyaddr, getnetbyname, setnetent, endnetent	getnetent, getnetbyaddr, getnetbyname, setnetent, endnetent	Get network entry.
getnetgrent, setnetgrent, endnetgrent, innetgr	getnetgrent, setnetgrent, endnetgrent, innetgr	Get network group entry.

HP-UX Library Calls	Linux Equivalent	Description
endnetpath	None	Get etc/netconfig entry corresponding to NETPATH component.
endusershell	endusershell	Close legal user shells file.
endutent	endutent	Access utmp file entry.
endutsent	endutsent	Access/update routines for user-accounting database maintained by utmpd.
endutxent	endutxent	Access utmpx file entry.
endwin	endwin	Suspend curses session.
erand48	erand48	Generate pseudorandom numbers.
erase	erase	Clear a window.
erasechar, killchar	erasechar, killchar (libncurses)	Single-byte terminal environment query functions.
erf, erff, erfl, erfw, erfq, erfc, erfcf, erfcl, erfcw, erfcq	erf, erff, erfl, erfc, erfcf, erfcl	Error and complementary error functions.
errno	errno[15]	System error messages.
etext	None	Last locations in program.
exp, expf, expl	exp, expf, expl	Exponential functions.
exp10, exp10f, exp10l	exp10, exp10f, exp10l	Base-10 exponential functions.
exp2, exp2f, exp2l	exp2, exp2f, exp2l	Base-2 exponential functions.
expm1, expm1f, expm1l	expm1, expm1f, expm1l	Exponential minus 1 functions.
fabs, fabsf, fabsl	fabs, fabsf, fabsl	Absolute value functions.
fattach	fattach	Attach a STREAMS file descriptor to an object in the file system name space.
fclose, fflush, fclose_unlocked, fflush_unlocked	fclose, fflush	Close or flush a stream.

HP-UX Library Calls	Linux Equivalent	Description
fcpacl	None	Copy access control list (ACL) to another file.
fcvt	fcvt	Convert floating-point number to string.
fdetach	fdetach	Detach a STREAMS-based file descriptor from a filename.
fdim, fdimf, fdiml	fdim, fdimf, fdiml	Positive difference functions.
fdopen	fdopen	Associate a stream with a file descriptor.
feclearexcept	feclearexcept	Clear floating-point exceptions.
fegetenv	fegetenv	Get floating-point environment.
fegetexceptflag	fegetexceptflag	Get floating-point exception flags.
fegetflushtozero	None	Get floating-point underflow mode.
fegetround	fegetround	Get floating-point rounding mode.
fegettrapenable	None	Get exception trap enables.
feholdexcept	feholdexcept	Save floating-point environment.
feof	feof	Stream status inquiries.
feraiseexcept	feraiseexcept	Raise floating-point exceptions.
ferror, feof, clearer, ferror_unlocked, feof_unlocked, clearerr_unlocked	ferror, feof, clearer, ferror_unlocked, feof_unlocked, clearerr_unlocked	Stream status inquiries.
fesetenv	fesetenv	Set floating-point environment.
feupdateenv	feupdateenv	Set floating-point env.
fetch	fetch[16]	Database subroutines.
fflush, fflush_unlocked	fflush, fflush_unlocked	Close or flush a stream.
ffs	ffs	Memory operations, find first bit set.
fgetc	fgetc	Get character from a stream file.

HP-UX Library Calls	Linux Equivalent	Description
fgetpos, fsetpos	fgetpos, fsetpos	Save or restore file position indicator for a stream.
fopen64, freopen64, fseeko64, fsetpos64, statvfsdev64, ftello64, ftw64, nftw64, statvfsdev64, tmpfile64	fopen64, freopen64, fseeko64, fsetpos64, ftello64, ftw64, nftw64, tmpfile64	File system APIs to support large files.
fgetpwent	fgetpwent	Get password file entry.
fgets, fgets_unlocked	fgets, fgets_unlocked	Get a string from a stream.
fgetspent, fgetspwent, fgetspwent_r	None	Get secure password file entry. Get secure password file entry on trusted systems.
fgetwc, fgetwc_unlocked	fgetwc, fgetwc_unlocked	Get a wide character from a stream file.
fgetws	fgetws	Get a wide string from a stream.
fileno	fileno	Map stream pointer to file descriptor.
filter	filter (libncurses)	Disable the use of certain terminal capabilities.
finite	finite	Floating-point finiteness macro.
firstkey	firstkey	Database subroutines.
firstof2	None	Process 16-bit characters.
flash	flash (lincurses)	Flash the screen.
flockfile, funflockfile	flockfile, funflockfile	Explicit locking of streams within a multithread application.
floor, floorf, floorl floorw, floorq	floor, floorf, floorl	Floor functions.
flushinp		Discard input.

HP-UX Library Calls	Linux Equivalent	Description
fma, fmaf, fmal	fma, fmaf, fmal	Floating multiply-add functions.
fmax, fmaxf, fmaxl	fmax, fmaxf, fmaxl	Maximum value functions.
fmin, fminf, fminl	fmin, fminf, fminl	Minimum value functions.
fmod, fmodf, fmodl	fmod, fmodf, fmodl	Remainder functions.
fmtmsg	fmtmsg	Displays formatted message on standard error and console.
fnmatch	fnmatch	Match filename patterns.
fopen, freopen, fdopen	fopen, freopen, fdopen	Open or reopen a stream file; convert file to stream.
fpclassify	fpclassify	Floating-point classification macro.
fprintf	fprintf	Print formatted output to a file.
fputc	fputc	Put character or word on a stream.
fputs	fputs	Put a string on a stream.
fputs_unlocked	fputs_unlocked	Put a string on a stream.
fputwc	fputwc	Put a wide character on a stream file.
fputwc_unlocked	fputwc_unlocked	Put a wide character on a stream file.
fputws fputws_unlocked	fputws fputws_unlocked	Put a wide-character string on a stream file.
fread, fwrite, fread_unlocked, fwrite_unlocked	fread, fwrite, fread_unlocked, fwrite_unlocked	Buffered binary input/output to a stream file.
free	free	Release allocated block of main memory.
freeaddrinfo	freeaddrinfo	Get hostname and address entry.
freenetconfigent	None	Get network configuration database entry.
freopen	freopen	Reopen a stream file; convert file to stream.
frexp, frexpf, frexpl	frexp, frexpf, frexpl	Extract mantissa and exponent from floating-point number.

HP-UX Library Calls	Linux Equivalent	Description
fscanf	fscanf	Formatted input conversion, read from stream file.
fseek, fseeko, ftell, ftello, rewind, ftell_unlocked, rewind_unlocked	fseek, fseeko, ftell, ftello, rewind	Reposition a file pointer in a stream.
fseek_unlocked	None	Reposition a file pointer in a stream.
fseeko	fseeko	Reposition a file pointer in a stream.
fsetaclentry	None	Add, modify, or delete access control list entry.
fsetpos	fsetpos	Restore file position indicator for a stream.
fstatfsdev	None	Get file system statistics.
ftell	ftell	Reposition a file pointer in a stream.
ftell_unlocked	None	Reposition a file pointer in a stream.
ftello	ftello	Reposition a file pointer in a stream.
ftok	ftok	Create interprocess communication identifier.
ftw, nftw, nftw2	ftw, nftw	Walk a file tree, executing a function.
funflockfile	funflockfile	Explicit locking of streams within a multithread application.
fwide	fwide	Set stream orientation.
fwprintf, wprintf, swprintf	fwprintf, wprintf, swprintf	Print formatted wide-character output.
fwrite, fwrite_unlocked	fwrite, fwrite_unlocked	Buffered binary input/output to a stream file.
fwscanf, wscanf, swscanf	fwscanf, wscanf, swscanf	Convert formatted wide-character input.
gai_strerror	gai_strerror	Get hostname and address entry.
gamma, gammaf, gammal	gamma, gammaf, gammal	Log gamma function.

HP-UX Library Calls	Linux Equivalent	Description
gcvt	gcvt	Convert floating-point number to string.
get_expiration _time	None	Add a specific time interval to the current absolute system time.
get_myaddress	get_myaddress	Obsolete library routines for RPC.
get_resfield	None	Resolver routines.
get_wch, mvget_wch, mvwget_wch, wget_wch	get_wch, mvget_wch, mvwget_wch, wget_wch (libncurses)	Get a wide character from a terminal.
get_wstr	get_wstr	Get an array of wide characters and function key codes from a terminal.
getaddrinfo, getnameinfo, freeaddrinfo, gai_strerror, getipnodebyaddr, getipnodebyname	getaddrinfo, getnameinfo	Get hostname and address entry.
getbegyx, getmaxyx, getparyx	getbegyx, getmaxyx, getparyx (libncurses)	Get additional cursor and window coordinates.
getbkgd	getbkgd (libncurses)	Set or get background character and rendition using a single-byte character.
getbkgrnd	getbkgrnd (libncurses)	Set or get background character and rendition using a complex character.
getbootpent, putbootpent setbootpent, endbootpent parse_bp_htype, parse_bp_hpaddr parse_bp_iaddr	None	Get or put bootptab entry.

HP-UX Library Calls	Linux Equivalent	Description
getbwent	getbwent	Write records into new wtmps and btmps database.
getc, getc_unlocked, getchar, getchar_unlocked, fgetc, getw, getw_unlocked	getc, getc_unlocked, getchar, getchar_unlocked, fgetc, getw, getw_unlocked	Get character or word from a stream file.
getcchar	getcchar	Get a wide-character string.
getch, wgetch, mvgetch, mvwgetch	getch, wgetch, mvgetch, mvwgetch (libncurses)	Get a single-byte character from the terminal.
getchar	getchar	Get character from a stream file.
getclock	None	Get current value of system-wide clock.
getcwd	getcwd	Get pathname of current working directory.
getdate, getdate_r	getdate, getdate_r	Convert user format date and time.
getdiskbyname, getdiskbyname_r	None	Get disk description by its name.
getdvagent, getdvagnam, setdvagent, enddvagent, putdvagnam, copydvagent	None	Manipulate device assignment database entry for a trusted system.
getenv	getenv	Return value for environment name.
getfsent, getfsspec, getfsfile, getfstype, setfsent, endfsent	getfsent, getfsspec, getfsfile, setfsent, endfsent	Get file system descriptor file entry.

HP-UX Library Calls	Linux Equivalent	Description
getgrent, setgrent, endgrent, fgetgrent	getgrent, setgrent, endgrent, fgetgrent	Get group file entry.
getgrgid, getgrnam	getgrgid, getgrnam	Get group file entry.
gethostbyaddr	gethostbyaddr	Get network host entry.
gethostbyname	gethostbyname	Get network host entry.
endhostent_r, gethostbyaddr_r, gethostbyname_r, gethostent_r, sethostent_r	endhostent, gethostbyaddr, gethostbyname, gethostent, sethostent	Get, set, or end network host entry.
gethostent, gethostbyaddr, gethostbyname, sethostent, endhostent	endhostent, gethostbyaddr, gethostbyname, gethostent, sethostent	Get network host entry.
gethrtime	None	Get high-resolution time.
getipnodebyaddr	None	Get hostname and address entry.
getipnodebyname	None	Get hostname and address entry.
getlocale, getlocale_r	None	Get the locale of a program. Get the locale of a program (mt-safe).
getlogin, getlogin_r	getlogin	Get name of user logged in on this terminal.
getmaxyx	getmaxyx	Get additional cursor and window coordinates.
getmntent, setmntent, addmntent, delmntent, endmntent, hasmntopt	getmntent, setmntent, addmntent, delmntent, endmntent, hasmntopt	Get file system descriptor file entry.
getmntent_r	getmntent_r	Reentrant get file system descriptor file entry.

HP-UX Library Calls	Linux Equivalent	Description
getn_wstr, get_wstr, mvgetn_wstr, mvget_wstr, mvwgetn_wstr, mvwget_wstr, wgetn_wstr, wget_wstr	getn_wstr, get_wstr, mvgetn_wstr, mvget_wstr, mvwgetn_wstr, mvwget_wstr, wgetn_wstr, wget_wstr (libncurses)	Get an array of wide characters and function key codes from a terminal.
getnameinfo	getnameinfo	Get hostname and address entry.
getnetbyaddr, getnetbyname	getnetbyaddr, getnetbyname	Get network entry.
getnetbyaddr_r, getnetbyname_r	None	Reentrant get network entry.
getnetconfig, setnetconfig, endnetconfig, getnetconfigent, freenetconfigent, nc_perror, nc_sperror	None	Get network configuration database entry.
getnetent, getnetbyadd, getnetbyname, setnetent, endnetent	getnetent, getnetbyadd getnetbyname, setnetent endnetent	Get network entry.
getnetgrent, setnetgrent, endnetgrent, innetgr	getnetgrent, setnetgrent, endnetgrent, innetgr	Get network group entry.
getnetname	getnetname	Library routines for secure remote procedure calls.
getnetpath, setnetpath, endnetpath	None	Get /etc/netconfig entry corresponding to NETPATH component.

HP-UX Library Calls	Linux Equivalent	Description
getnstr, mvgetnstr, mvwgetnstr, wgetnstr	getnstr, mvgetnstr, mvwgetnstr, wgetnstr	Get a multibyte character-length-limited string from the terminal.
getopt, optarg optind, opterr	getopt, optarg optind, opterr	Get option letter from argument vector.
getparyx	getparyx (libncurses)	Get additional cursor and window coordinates.
getpass	getpass	Read a password.
getprdfent, getprdfnam, setprdfent, endprdfent, putprdfnam	None	Manipulate system default database entry for a trusted system.
getprdfnam	None	Search for file.
getprotoent, getprotobynumber getprotobyname, setprotoent endprotoent	getprotoent, getprotobynumber getprotobyname, setprotoent endprotoent	Get, set, or end protocol entry.
getprpwaid	None	Get protected password database audit ID.
getprpwent, getprpwuid getprpwnam, getprpwaid setprpwent, endprpwent putprpwnam	None	Manipulate protected password database entry.
getprtcent, getprtcnam setprtcent, endprtcent, putprtcnam	None	Manipulate terminal control database entry for a trusted system.

HP-UX Library Calls	Linux Equivalent	Description
getpublickey, getsecretkey publickey	None	Retrieve public or secret key.
getpw	getpw	Get name from UID.
getpwent, getpwuid getpwnam, setpwent endpwent, fgetpwent	getpwent, getpwuid getpwnam, setpwent endpwent, fgetpwent	Get password file entry.
getresuid, getresgid	getresuid, getresgid	Get real, effective, and saved user or group IDs.
getrpcent, getrpcbyname getrpcbynumber	getrpcent, getrpcbyname getrpcbynumber	Get RPC entry.
getrpcport	getrpcport	Get RPC port number.
gets, fgets fgets_unlocked	gets, fgets fgets_unlocked	Get a string from a stream.
getsecretkey	None	Retrieve public or secret key.
getservbyname	getservbyname	Get service entry.
getservbyport	getservbyport	Get service entry.
getservbyport_r, getservbyname_r	None	Reentrant get service entry.
endservent, getservbyname, getservbyport, getservent, setservent	endservent, getservbyname, getservbyport, getservent, setservent	Get, set, or end service entry.
endservent_r, getservbyname_r, getservbyport_r, getservent_r setservent_r	None	Reentrant get, set, or end service entry.

HP-UX Library Calls	Linux Equivalent	Description
getspent, fgetspent getspnam, getspnam_r setspent, endspent	None	Get secure password file entry.
getspwaid getspwaid_r	None	Get secure password file entry on trusted systems.
getspwent, getspwuid getspwaid, getspwnam setspwent, endspwent fgetspwent, getspwent_r getspwuid_r, getspwaid_r getspwnam_r, setspwent_r endspwent_r, fgetspwent_r	None	Get secure password file entry on trusted systems.
getstr, mvgetstr mvwgetstr, wgetstr	getstr, mvgetstr mvwgetstr, wgetstr (libncurses)	Get a multibyte character string from the terminal.
getsubopt	getsubopt	Parse suboptions from a string.
gettimer	None	Get value of a per-process timer.
gettxt	None	Read text string from message file.
getusershell, setusershell, endusershell	None	Get legal user shells.
getutent, getutent_r, getutid, getutid_r, getutline, getutline_r, pututline, setutent, endutent, utmpname	getutent, getutent_r, getutid, getutid_r, getutline, getutline_r, pututline, setutent, endutent, utmpname	Access utmp file entry.

HP-UX Library Calls	Linux Equivalent	Description
pututline_r, setutent_r, endutent_r, utmpname_r	None	Access utmp file entry (reentrant).
getutsent, getutsid, getutsline, pututsline, setutsent, endutsent	None	Access/update routines for user-accounting database maintained by utmpd.
getutxent, getutxid getutxline, pututxline setutxent, endutxent	getutxent, getutxid getutxline, pututxline setutxent, endutxent	Access utmpx file entry.
getwc, getwchar, fgetwc, fgetwc_unlocked	getwc, fgetwc, getwc_unlocked, fgetwc_unlocked	Get a wide character from a stream file.
getwc_unlocked, getwchar	getwc_unlocked, getwchar	Get a wide character from a stream file.
getwd	getwd	Get pathname of current working directory.
getwin, putwin	getwin, putwin (libncurses)	Dump window to, and reload window from, a file.
getyx	getyx (libncurses)	Get cursor and window coordinates.
glob, globfree	glob, globfree (libncurses)	Filename generation function.
gmtime, gmtime_r	gmtime, gmtime_r	Convert date and time to string.
grantpt	grantpt	Grant access to the STREAMS slave pty.
gsignal	gsignal	Software signals.

HP-UX Library Calls	Linux Equivalent	Description
gssapi, gss_accept_sec_context, gss_acquire_cred, gss_add_cred, gss_add_oid_set_member, gss_canonicalize_name gss_*	Supported through the GNU Generic Security Service Library[17]	Generic security sevice application programming interface.
halfdelay	halfdelay	Control input character delay mode.
has_colors	has_colors	Color manipulation functions.
has_ic, has_il	has_ic, has_il (libncurses)	Query functions for terminal insert and delay capability.
hasmntopt	hasmntopt	Get file system descriptor file entry.
hcreate	hcreate	Manage hash search function.
hdestroy	hdestroy	Manage hash search function.
herror	herror	Resolver routines.
hline, mvhline, mvvline, mvwhline, mvwvline, vline, whline, wvline	hline, mvhline, mvvline, mvwhline, mvwvline, vline, whline, wvline (libncurses)	Draw lines from single-byte characters and renditions.
hline_set, mvhline_set, mvvline_set, mvwhline_set, mvwvline_set, vline_set, whline_set, wvline_set	hline_set, mvhline_set, mvvline_set, mvwhline_set, mvwvline_set, vline_set, whline_set, wvline_set (libncurses)	Draw lines from complex characters and renditions.
host2netname	host2netname (rpc/auth.h)	Library routines for secure remote procedure calls.

HP-UX Library Calls	Linux Equivalent	Description
hosts_access, hosts_ctl request_init, request_set	hosts_access, hosts_ctl request_init, request_set	Access control library.
hsearch, hcreate hdestroy	hsearch, hcreate hdestroy	Manage hash search tables.
htonl, htons	htonl, htons	Convert values from host to network byte order.
hypot, hypotf, hypotl	hypot, hypotf, hypotl	Euclidean distance (hypotenuse) functions.
iconv, iconv_open, iconv_close	iconv, iconv_open, iconv_close	Code set conversion routines.
idcok	idcok (libncurses)	Enable or disable use of hardware insert- and delete-character features.
idlok	idlok (libncurses)	Terminal output control functions.
if_freenameindex	if_freenameindex	Interface name to index mapping.
if_indextoname	if_indextoname	Interface name to index mapping.
if_nametoindex, if_indextoname if_nameindex, if_freenameindex	if_nametoindex, if_indextoname if_nameindex, if_freenameindex	Interface name to index mapping.
ilogb, ilogbf, ilogbl	ilogb, ilogbf, ilogbl	Radix-independent exponent functions.
immedok	immedok (libncurses)	Enable or disable immediate terminal refresh.
in_wch, mvin_wch, mvwin_wch, win_wch	in_wch, mvin_wch, mvwin_wch, win_wch (libncurses)	Extract a complex character and rendition from a window.

HP-UX Library Calls	Linux Equivalent	Description
`in_wchnstr`, `in_wchstr`, `mvin_wchnstr`, `vin_wchstr`, `mvwin_wchnstr`, `mvwin_wchstr`, `win_wchnstr`, `win_wchstr`	`in_wchnstr`, `in_wchstr`, `mvin_wchnstr`, `mvin_wchstr`, `mvwin_wchnstr`, `mvwin_wchstr`, `win_wchnstr`, `win_wchstr` (`libncurses`)	Input an array of complex characters and renditions from a window.
`inch`, `mvinch`, `mvwinch`, `winch`	`inch`, `mvinch`, `mvwinch`, `winch` (`libncurses`)	Input a single-byte character and rendition from a window.
`inchnstr`, `inchstr`, `mvinchnstr`, `mvinchstr`, `mvwinchnstr`, `mvwinchstr`, `winchnstr`, `winchstr`	`inchnstr`, `inchstr`, `mvinchnstr`, `mvinchstr`, `mvwinchnstr`, `mvwinchstr`, `winchnstr`, `winchstr` (`libncurses`)	Input an array of single-byte characters and renditions from a window.
`index`	`index`	BSD portability string routine.
`inet_addr`, `inet_lnaof`, `inet_makeaddr`, `inet_netof`, `inet_network`, `inet_ntoa`	`inet_addr`, `inet_lnaof`, `inet_makeaddr`, `inet_netof`, `inet_network`, `inet_ntoa`	Internet address manipulation routines.
`inet_pton`, `inet_nton`, `inet_ntoa_r`	`inet_pton`	Internet address manipulation routines.
`init_colors`, `init_pair`	`init_colors`, `init_pair` (`libncurses`)	Color manipulation functions.
`initgroups`	`initgroups`	Initialize group access list.
`initstate`	`initstate`	Pseudorandom number functions.

HP-UX Library Calls	Linux Equivalent	Description
innstr, instr, mvinnstr, mvinstr mvwinnstr, mvwinstr, winnstr, winstr	innstr, instr, mvinnstr, mvinstr mvwinnstr, mvwinstr, winnstr, winstr (libncurses)	Input a multibyte character string from a window.
ins_nwstr, ins_wstr, mvins_nwstr mvins_wstr, vwins_nwstr mvwins_wstr, wins_nwstr, wins_wstr	ins_nwstr, ins_wstr, mvins_nwstr mvins_wstr, mvwins_nwstr mvwins_wstr, wins_nwstr, wins_wstr (libncurses)	Insert a wide-character string into a window.
ins_wch, mvins_wch, mvwins_wch, wins_wch	ins_wch, mvins_wch, mvwins_wch, wins_wch (libncurses)	Insert a complex character and rendition into a window.
insch, mvinsch, mvwinsch, winsch	insch, mvinsch, mvwinsch, winsch (libncurses)	Insert a single-byte character and rendition into a window.
insdelln, winsdelln	insdelln, winsdelln (libncurses)	Delete or insert lines into a window.
insertln, winsertln	insertln, winsertln (libncurses)	Insert lines into a window.
insnstr, insstr, mvinsnstr, mvinsstr, mvwinsnstr, mvwinsstr, winsnstr, winsstr	insnstr, insstr, mvinsnstr, mvinsstr, mvwinsnstr, mvwinsstr, winsnstr, winsstr (libncurses)	Insert a multibyte character into a window.
insque, remque	insque, remque	Insert or remove an element in a queue.
intrflush	intrflush (libncurses)	Enable or disable flush on interrupt.

HP-UX Library Calls	Linux Equivalent	Description
inwstr	inwstr (libncurses)	Input a string of wide characters from a window.
is_linetouched, is_wintouched, touchline, untouchwin, wtouchln	is_linetouched, is_wintouched, touchline, untouchwin, wtouchln	Window refresh control functions.
isalnum, isalpha, isascii	isalnum, isalpha, isascii	Classify characters.
isastream	isastream	Determine if file descriptor refers to STREAMS device or STREAMS-based pipe.
isatty	isatty	Find name of a terminal.
iscntrl	iscntrl	Classify characters.
isendwin	isendwin (libncurses)	Determine whether a screen has been refreshed.
isfinite, finite	isfinite, finite	Floating-point finiteness macro.
isgraph	isgraph	Classify characters.
isgreater	isgreater	Floating-point quiet comparison macro.
isgreaterequal	isgreaterequal	Floating-point quiet comparison macro.
isinf	isinf	Test for infinity.
isless	isles	Floating-point quiet comparison macro.
islessequal	islessequal	Floating-point quiet comparison macro.
islessgreater	islessgreater	Floating-point quiet comparison macro.
islower	islower	Classify characters.
isnan	isnan	Test for nan.
isnormal	isnormal	Test for normal value.
ispunct, isspace isprint, isupper isxdigit	ispunct, isspace isprint, isupper isxdigit	Classify characters.

HP-UX Library Calls	Linux Equivalent	Description
isunordered	isunordered	Floating-point comparison macro.
iswalpha, iswupper, iswlower, iswdigit, iswxdigit, iswalnum, iswspace, iswpunct, iswprint, iswgraph, iswcntrl, iswctype	iswalpha, iswupper, iswlower, iswdigit, iswxdigit, iswalnum, iswspace, iswpunct, iswprint, iswgraph, iswcntrl, iswctype	Classify wide characters.
jrand48	jrand48	Generate pseudorandom numbers.
keyname, key_name	keyname, key_name (libncurses)	Get name of key.
keypad	keypad (libncurses)	Enable/disable abbreviation of function keys.
killchar	killchar (libncurses)	Single-byte line kill character.
killwchar	killwchar (libncurses)	Current line kill character.
l64a, l64a_r	l64a	Convert between long integer and base-64 ASCII string.
lckpwdf, ulckpwdf	lckpwdf, ulckpwdf (shadow.h)	Control access to /etc/passwd and /etc/shadow files.
lcong48	lcong48	Generate pseudorandom numbers.
ldexp, ldexpf, ldexpl ldexpw, ldexpq	ldexp, ldexpf ldexpl	Scale exponent of a floating-point number.
ldiv	ldiv	Long integer division and remainder.
leaveok	leaveok (libncurses)	Terminal output control functions.
lfind	lfind	Linear search and update.
lgamma, lgammaf, lgammal, lgamma_r, lgammaf_r, lgammal_r	lgamma, lgammaf, lgammal, lgamma_r, lgammaf_r, lgammal_r	Log gamma functions.

HP-UX Library Calls	Linux Equivalent	Description
llrint, llrintf, llrintl	llrint, llrintf, llrintl, llrintw, llrintq	Round to nearest long long function.
llround, llroundf, llroundl	llround, llroundf, llroundl	Round to long long functions.
localeconv	localeconv	Query numeric formatting conventions of current locale.
localtime, localtime_r	localtime, localtime_r	Convert date and time to string.
log, logf, logl, logw, logq	log, logf, logl	Natural logarithm functions.
log10, log10f, log10l	log10, log10f, log10l	Common logarithm functions.
log2, log2f, log2l	log2, log2f, log2l	Logarithm base 2 functions.
logb, logbf, logbl	logb, logbf, logbl	Radix-independent exponent functions.
longname	longname (libncurses)	Get verbose description of current terminal.
lrand48	lrand48	Generate pseudorandom numbers.
lrint, lrintf, lrintl	lrint, lrintf, lrintl	Round to nearest long int functions.
lround, lroundf, lroundl	lround, lroundf, lroundl	Round to long int functions.
lsearch, lfind	lsearch, lfind	Linear search and update.
ltostr, ltostr_r, ultostr, ultostr_r, ltoa, ltoa_r ultoa, ultoa_r	None	Convert long integers to strings.
mallinfo	mallinfo	Display memory space usage.
calloc, free, malloc, mallopt, realloc, valloc	malloc, free, realloc, calloc, mallopt, valloc	Memory allocator routines.

HP-UX Library Calls	Linux Equivalent	Description
alloca	alloca	Memory allocator routines.
mblen	mblen	Multibyte character and string conversions.
mbrlen	mbrlen	Get number of bytes in a character.
mbrtowc	mbrtowc	Convert a character to a wide-character code.
mbsinit	mbsinit	Determine conversion object status.
mbsrtowcs	mbsrtowcs	Convert a string to a wide-character string.
memalign	memalign	Allocate aligned memory.
memccpy, memchr, memcmp, memcpy, memset, bcopy, bcmp, bzero	memccpy, memchr, memcmp, memcpy, memset, bcopy, bcmp, bzero	Memory operations.
meta	meta (libncurses)	Enable/disable meta-keys.
mkdirp, rmdirp	None (see mkdir)	Create, remove directories in a path.
mkfifo	mkfifo	Make a FIFO special file.
mktemp	mktemp	Make a unique filename.
mktime	mktime	Create calendar time value.
mktimer	None	Allocate a per-process timer.
modf, modff, modfl	modf, modff, modfl	Decompose floating-point number.
monitor	None	Prepare execution profile.
mount	mount	Keep track of remotely mounted file systems.
move, wmove	move, wmove	Window cursor location functions.
mrand48	mrand48	Generate pseudorandom numbers.
mblen, mbtowc, mbstowcs, wctomb, wcstombs	mblen, mbtowc, mbstowcs, wctomb, wcstombs	Multibyte character and string conversions.

HP-UX Library Calls	Linux Equivalent	Description
mvaddchnstr, mvwaddchnstr, waddchnstr	mvaddchnstr, mvwaddchnstr, waddchnstr (libncurses)	Add length-limited string of single-byte characters and renditions to a window.
mvaddchstr, mvwaddchstr, waddchstr	mvaddchstr, mvwaddchstr, waddchstr (libncurses)	Add string of single-byte characters and renditions to a window.
mvprintw, mvwprintw, printw, wprintw	mvprintw, mvwprintw, printw, wprintw (libncurses)	Print formatted output in window.
mvscanw, mvwscanw, scanw, wscanw	mvscanw, mvwscanw, scanw, wscanw (libncurses)	Convert formatted input from a window.
mvwin	mvwin (libncurses)	Move window.
nan, nanf, nanl	nan, nanf, nanl	String-to-nan conversion functions.
napms	napms (libncurses)	Suspend the calling process (low-level curses routine).
dbm_open, dbm_close, dbm_fetch, dbm_store, dbm_delete, dbm_firstkey, dbm_nextkey, dbm_error, dbm_clearerr	dbm_open, dbm_close, dbm_fetch, dbm_store, dbm_delete, dbm_firstkey, dbm_nextkey, dbm_error[18]	Database subroutines.
net_aton, net_ntoa	None	Network station address string conversion routines.
netdir_getbyname, netdir_getbyaddr, netdir_free, netdir_options, taddr2uaddr, uaddr2taddr, netdir_perror, netdir_sperror	None	Generic transport name-to-address translation.

HP-UX Library Calls	Linux Equivalent	Description
newpad, pnoutrefresh, prefresh	newpad, pnoutrefresh, prefresh (libncurses)	Pad management functions.
newwin, subwin	newwin, subwin (libncurses)	Window creation functions.
nextafter, nextafterf, nextafterl, nexttoward, nexttowardf, nexttowardl	nextafter, nextafterf, nextafterl, nexttoward, nexttowardf, nexttowardl	Next representable floating-point values.
nis_error, nis_sperrno, nis_perror, nis_lerror, nis_sperror, nis_sperror_r	nis_error, nis_sperrno, nis_perror, nis_lerror, nis_sperror, nis_sperror_r	Display NIS+ error messages.
nis_groups, nis_ismember, nis_addmember, nis_removemember, nis_creategroup nis_destroygroup, nis_verifygroup, nis_print_group_ entry, nis_map_group, _nis_map_group	nis_groups, nis_ismember, nis_addmember, nis_removemember, nis_creategroup nis_destroygroup, nis_verifygroup, nis_print_group_ entry	NIS+ group manipulation functions.
nis_lookup, nis_add, nis_remove nis_modify, nis_freeresult	nis_lookup, nis_add, nis_remove nis_modify, nis_freeresult	NIS+ namespace functions.
nis_objects	nis_objects	NIS+ object formats.

HP-UX Library Calls	Linux Equivalent	Description
nis_ping, nis_checkpoint	nis_ping, nis_checkpoint	NIS+ log administration functions.
nis_mkdir, nis_rmdir, nis_servstate nis_stats, nis_getservlist nis_freeservlist, nis_freetags	nis_mkdir, nis_rmdir, nis_servstate nis_stats, nis_getservlist nis_freeservlist, nis_freetags	NIS+ miscellaneous functions.
nis_leaf_of, nis_name_of nis_domain_of, nis_getnames nis_freenames, nis_dir_cmp nis_clone_object, nis_destroy_object nis_print_object	nis_leaf_of, nis_name_of nis_domain_of, nis_getnames nis_freenames, nis_dir_cmp nis_clone_object, nis_destroy_object nis_print_object	NIS+ subroutines.
nis_list, nis_add_entry nis_remove_entry, nis_modify_entry nis_first_entry, nis_next_entry	nis_list, nis_add_entry nis_remove_entry, nis_modify_entry nis_first_entry, nis_next_entry	NIS+ table functions file.
nl, nonl	nl, nonl (libncurses)	Enable/disable newline translation.
nl_langinfo	nl_langinfo	NLS information about native languages.
nlist	None[19]	Get entries from name list.
noqiflush, qiflush	noqiflush, qiflush (libncurses)	Enable/disable queue flushing.
notimeout, timeout, wtimeout	notimeout, timeout, wtimeout	Control blocking on input.
nrand48	nrand48	Generate pseudorandom numbers.

HP-UX Library Calls	Linux Equivalent	Description
`ntohl`, `ntohs`	`ntohl`, `ntohs`	Convert values from network to host byte order.
`opendir`	`opendir`	Directory operations.
`openlog`	`openlog`	Control system log.
`optarg`, `opterr`, `optind`	`optarg`, `opterr`, `optind`	Get option letter from argument vector.
`overlay`, `overwrite`	`overlay`, `overwrite`	Copy overlapped windows.
`pam`, `pam_acct_mgmt`, `pam_authenticate`, `pam_chauthtok`, `pam_close_session`, `pam_get_user`, `pam_open_session`, `pam_close_session`, `pam_set_data`, `pam_get_data`, `pam_set_item`, `pam_get_item`, `pam_setcred`, `pam_sm`, `pam_sm_acct_mgmt`, `pam_sm_authenticate`, `pam_start`, `pam_end`, `pam_strerror`	`pam (libpam)` `pam_authenticate`, `pam_chauthtok`, `pam_console`, `pam_console_apply`, `pam_end`, `pam_fail_delay`, `pam_get_item`, `pam_krb5`, `pam_krb5`, `pam_localuser`, `pam_open/close_session`, `pam_passwdqc`, `pam_postgresok`, `pam_rps`, `pam_selinux`, `pam_selinux_check`, `pam_set_item`, `pam_setcred`, `pam_stack`, `pam_start`, `pam_strerror`, `pam_succeed_if`, `pam_timestamp`, `pam_timestamp_check`, `pam_xauth`	Pluggable authentication module.
`pathfind`	None	Search for named file in named directories.
`pechochar`, `pecho_wchar`	`pechochar`, `pecho_wchar`	Write a character rendition and immediately refresh the pad.

HP-UX Library Calls	Linux Equivalent	Description
perror, errno, sys_errlist, sys_nerr	perror, errno	System error messages.
pfmt, vpfmt	None	Display message in standard format.
popen, pclose	popen, pclose	Initiate pipe I/O to/from a process.
pow, powf, powl	pow, powf, powl	Power functions.
prcmd	None	Return streams to parallel remote commands.
printf, fprintf, sprintf, snprintf	printf, fprintf, sprintf, snprintf	Print formatted output.
pthread routines (see 6.10 in Chapter 6, "Porting HP-UX Applications")	Native POSIX Threads Library	POSIX Threads implementation.
ptsname, ptsname_r	ptsname	Get the name of a slave pty.
publickey	None	Retrieve public or secret key.
putc, fputc, putchar, putw, putc_unlocked, putchar_unlocked, putw_unlocked	putc, fputc, putchar, putw, putc_unlocked, putchar_unlocked	Put character or word on a stream.
putenv	putenv	Change or add value to environment.
putp, tputs	putp, tputs	Output commands to the terminal.
putpwent	putpwent	Write password file entry.
puts, fputs, puts_unlocked fputs_unlocked	puts, fputs, puts_unlocked fputs_unlocked	Put a string on a stream.
putspent	putspent (shadow.h)	Write shadow password file entry.
putwc, putwchar, fputwc putwc_unlocked, putwchar_unlocked_ fputwc_unlocked	putwc, putwchar, fputwc putwc_unlocked, putwchar_unlocked fputwc_unlocked	Put a wide character on a stream file.

HP-UX Library Calls	Linux Equivalent	Description
qsort	qsort	Quicker sort.
rand, srand	rand, srand	Simple random-number generator.
random, srandom initstate, setstate	random, srandom initstate, setstate	Generate a pseudorandom number.
rcmd, rcmd_af, rresvport rresvport_af, ruserok	rcmd, rresvport, ruserok	Return a stream to a remote command.
re_comp, re_exec	re_comp, re_exec	Compile and execute regular expressions.
realloc	realloc	Change size of allocated memory block.
realpath	realpath	Resolve pathname.
redrawwin, wredrawln	redrawwin, wredrawln	Line update status functions.
regcmp, regex	None	Compile and execute regular expression.
regcomp, regerror, regexec, regfree	regcomp, regerror, regexec, regfree	Regular expression matching routines.
reltimer	None	Relatively arm a per-process timer.
remainder, remainderf, remainderl	remainder, remainderf, remainderl	Remainder functions.
remove	remove	Remove an element in a queue.
remquo, remquof, remquol	remquo, remquof, remquol	Remainder functions with quotient.
res_init, res_mkquery res_query, res_search res_send	res_init, res_mkquery res_query, res_search res_send	Resolver routines.
resetty, savetty	resetty, savetty	Save/restore terminal mode.

HP-UX Library Calls	Linux Equivalent	Description
dn_comp, dn_expand, get_resfield, herror, set_resfield	dn_comp, dn_expand, herror	Resolver routines.
rexec	rexec (netdb.h)	Return stream to a remote command.
rint, rintf, rintl, rintw rintq, nearbyint nearbyintf, nearbyintl nearbyintw, nearbyintq	rint, rintf, rintl nearbyint, nearbyintf, nearbyintl	Round to nearest int functions.
ripoffline	rippoffline (libncurses)	Reserve a dedicated line for a purpose.
rmdirp	None	Remove directories in a path.
rmtimer	None	Free a per-process timer.
rnusers, rusers	None	Return information about users on remote machines.
round, roundf, roundl	round, roundf, roundl	Round to nearest integer, away from 0.
rpc_clnt: auth_destroy, authnone_create authsys_create, authsys_create_ default	 auth_destroy, authnone_create authunix_create, authunix_create_ default	Library routines for client-side remote procedure call authentication.
rpc_services: clnt_call, clnt_freeres clnt_geterr, clnt_perrno clnt_perror, clnt_sperrno clnt_sperror, rpc_broadcast rpc_broadcast exp, rpc_call	 callrpc, clnt_broadcast clnt_call, clnt_destroy, clnt_freeres, clnt_perrno, clnt_spcreeateerror, clnt_sperror	Library routines for client-side calls, RPC.

HP-UX Library Calls	Linux Equivalent	Description
rpc_services: clnt_control, clnt_create clnt_create_vers, clnt_destroy clnt_dg_create, clnt_pcreateerror clnt_raw_create, clnt_spcreateerror clnt_tli_create, clnt_tp_create clnt_vc_create, rpc_createerr	 clnt_control, clnt_create, clnt_destroy, clntraw_create, clnttcp_create, clntudp_create, clntudp_bufcreate	Library routines for dealing with client handles.
rpc_services: svc_dg_enablecache, svc_done, svc_exit, svc_fdset svc_freeargs, svc_getargs svc_getreq_common, svc_getreq_poll svc_getreqset, svc_getrpccaller svc_pollset, svc_run svc_sendreply	 svc_getargs, svc_getcaller svc_getreqset, svc_getreq svc_register, svc_sendreply	Library routines for RPC servers.
rpc_svc_create: svc_control, svc_create svc_destroy, svc_dg_create svc_fd_create, svc_raw_create svc_tli_create, svc_tp_create svc_vc_create	 svc_destroy, svc_freeargs svc_fd_create, svcraw_create, svctcp_create, svc_udpcreate, svcudp_bufcreate	Library routines for the creation of server handles, RPC.

HP-UX Library Calls	Linux Equivalent	Description
rpc_svc_err: svcerr_auth, svcerr_decode svcerr_noproc, svcerr_noprog svcerr_progvers, svcerr_systemerr svcerr_weakauth	svcerr_auth, svcerr_decode svcerr_noproc, svcerr_noprog svcerr_progvers, svcerr_systemerr svcerr_weakauth	Library routines for server-side remote procedure call errors.
rpc_svc_reg: svc_reg, svc_unreg svc_auth_reg, xprt_register xprt_unregister	svc_register, svc_unregister	Library routines for registering servers, RPC.
rpc_xdr: xdr_accepted_reply, xdr_authsys_parms xdr_callhdr, xdr_callmsg xdr_opaque_auth, xdr_rejected_reply, xdr_replymsg	xdr_accepted_reply, xdr_authunix_parms xdr_callhdr, xdr_callmsg xdr_rejected_reply xdr_replymsg	XDR library routines for remote procedure calls.
rpcb_getmaps, rpcb_getaddr, rpcb_gettime, rpcb_rmtcall, rpcb_set, rpcb_unset	pmap_set, pmap_unset, pmap_rmtcall, pmap_getport, pmap_getports	Library routines for RPC bind service.
rsqrt, rsqrtf, rsqrtl	None	Reciprocal square root functions.
rstat, havedisk	None	Get performance data from remote kernel.
ruserok	ruserok	Return a stream to a remote command.
rwall		Write to specified remote machines.

HP-UX Library Calls	Linux Equivalent	Description
scalb, scalbf, scalbl	scalb, scalbf, scalbl	Scale exponent of a radix-independent floating-point number.
scalbln, scalblnf, scalblnl	scalbln, scalblnf, scalblnl	Scale exponent of a radix-independent floating-point number.
scalbn, scalbnf, scalbnl	scalbn, scalbnf, scalbnl	Scale exponent of a radix-independent floating-point number.
scandir, alphasort	scandir, alphasort	Scan a directory.
scanf, fscanf, sscanf	scanf, fscanf, sscanf	Formatted input conversion, read from stream file.
scr_dump, scr_init, scr_restore, scr_set	scr_dump, scr_init, scr_restore, scr_set	Screen file input/output functions.
scrl, wscrl	None	Enhanced scroll curses window functions.
scroll	scroll	Scroll a curses window.
scrollok	scrollok	Terminal output control functions.
secdef	None	Security defaults configuration file routines.
secure_rpc authdes_getucred, authdes_seccreate, getnetname, host2netname, key_decryptsession, key_encryptsession key_gendes, key_setsecret, key_secretkey_is_set, netname2host, netname2user, user2netname	secure_rpc authdes_getucred, getnetname, host2netname, key_decryptsession, key_encryptsession, key_gendes, key_setsecret, key_secretkey_is_set, netname2host, netname2user, user2netname	Library routines for secure remote procedure calls.
set_term	set_term (libncurses)	Switch between screens.

HP-UX Library Calls	Linux Equivalent	Description
setaclentry, fsetaclentry		Add, modify, or delete access control list entry.
setbuf, setvbuf, setvbuf_unlocked	setbuf, setvbuf	Assign buffering to a stream file.
setbwent	None	Write records into new wtmps and btmps database.
setcat	None	Set the default message catalog.
setcchar	setcchar	Set cchar_t from a wide character and rendition.
setclock	None	Set value of system-wide clock.
setkey, setkey_r	None	Generate hashing encryption.
setlabel	None	Define label for formatting routines.
setlocale_r, getlocale, getlocale_r	setlocale	Set and get the locale of a program.
shl_load, shl_definesym, shl_findsym, shl_get, shl_get_r, shl_gethandle, shl_gethandle_r, shl_getsymbols, shl_unload, dld_getenv	dladdr, dlclose, dlerror, dlopen, dlsym, dlvsym	Explicit load of shared libraries.
signbit	signbit	Floating-point sign determination.
sigpause	sigpause	Atomically release blocked signals and wait for interrupt.
sigset, sighold, sigrelse, sigignore, sigpause	sigset, sighold, sigrelse, sigignore, sigpause	Signal management.

HP-UX Library Calls	Linux Equivalent	Description
`sigemptyset, sigfillset, sigaddset, sigdelset, sigismember`	`sigemptyset, sigfillset, sigaddset, sigdelset, sigismember`	POSIX signal set operations.
`sin, sinf, sinl, sinw, sinq`	`sin, sinf, sinl`	Sine functions.
`sincos, sincosf, sincosl, sincosw, sincosq`	`sincos, sincosf, sincosl`	Calculate sin and cos simultaneously.
`sind, sindf`	None	Sine functions of degree argument.
`sinh, sinhf, sinhl`	`sinh, sinhf, sinhl`	Hyperbolic sine functions.
`sleep`	`sleep`	Suspend execution for interval.
`slk_attroff, slk_attr_off, slk_attron, slk_attr_on, slk_attrset, slk_attr_set, slk_clear, slk_color, slk_init, slk_label, slk_noutrefresh, slk_refresh, slk_restore, slk_set, slk_touch, slk_wset`	`slk_attroff, slk_attr_off, slk_attron, slk_attr_on, slk_attrset, slk_attr_set, slk_clear, slk_color, slk_init, slk_label, slk_noutrefresh, slk_refresh, slk_restore, slk_set, slk_touch`	Soft label routines.
`SLPOpen, SLPClose, SLPReg, SLPDereg, SLPDelAttrs, SLPFindSrvs, SLPFindSrvTypes, SLPFindAttrs, SLPParseSrvURL, SLPEscape, SLPUnescape, SLPFree, SLPGetRefreshInterval, SLPFindScopes, SLPGetProperty, SLPSetProperty`	None (refer to OpenSLP[20])	SLP (Service Location Protocol) library routines.

HP-UX Library Calls	Linux Equivalent	Description
spray	None	Scatter data for network checking.
sqrt, sqrtf, sqrtl	sqrt, sqrtf, sqrtl	Square root functions.
ssignal, gsignal	ssignal, gsignal	Software signals facility.
standend, standout, wstandend, wstandout	standend, standout, wstandend, wstandout (libncurses)	Set and clear window attributes.
statfsdev, fstatfsdev	None	Get file system statistics.
statvfsdev, fstatvfsdev	None	Get file system statistics.
stdio	stdio	Standard buffered input/output stream file package.
stdscr	stdscr	Default window.
strerror	strerror	System error messages.
strfmon	strfmon	Convert monetary value to string.
strftime	strftime	Convert date and time to string.
string, strlen	string, strlen	Character string operations.
strord	None	Convert string data order.
strptime	strptime	Date and time conversion.
strtoacl, strtoaclpatt	strtoacl, strtoaclpatt	Convert string to access control list (ACL) structure.
strtod, strtof, strtold_	strtod, strtof, strtold_	Convert string to floating-point number.
strtof	strtof	Convert string to floating-point number (float).
strtoimax, strtoumax	strtoimax, strtoumax	Convert string to integer.
strtol, strtoul, atoll, atoi, strtoll, strtoull	strtol, strtoul, atoll, atoi, strtoll, strtoull	Convert string to integer.

HP-UX Library Calls	Linux Equivalent	Description
subpad	subpad (libncurses)	Enhanced pad management function.
swab	swab	Swap bytes.
syncok, wcursyncup wsyncdown, wsyncup	syncok, wcursyncup, wsyncdown, wsyncup (libncurses)	Synchronize a window with its parents or children.
syslog, openlog, closelog, setlogmask	syslog, openlog, closelog, setlogmask	Control system log.
system	system	Issue a shell command.
t_accept, t_alloc, t_bind, t_close, t_connect, t_error, t_free, t_getinfo, t_getprotaddr, t_getstate, t_listen, t_look_, t_open, t_optmgmt, t_rcv, t_rcvconnect, t_rcvdis, t_rcvrel, t_rcvudata, t_rcvuderr, t_snd, t_snddis, t_sndrel, t_sndudata, t_strerror, t_sync, t_unbind	None	X/open tli-xti.
taddr2uaddr	None	Generic transport name-to-address translation.
tan, tanf	tan, tanf, tanl	Tangent functions.
tand, tandf	None	Tangent functions of a degree argument.
tcgetattr, tcsetattr	tcgetattr, tcsetattr	Control tty device.

HP-UX Library Calls	Linux Equivalent	Description
tcsendbreak, tcdrain, tcflush, tcflow	tcsendbreak, tcdrain, tcflush, tcflow	Tty line control functions.
tcgetpgrp	tcgetpgrp	Get foreground process group ID.
tcgetsid	tcgetsid	Get terminal session ID.
termattrs, term_attrs	termattrs, term_attrs (libncurses)	Get supported terminal video attributes.
tgetent, tgetflag, tgetnum, tgetstr, tgoto, tputs	tgetent, tgetflag, tgetnum, tgetstr, tgoto, tputs (libncurses)	Emulate /usr/share/lib/termcap access routines.
termname	termname (libncurses)	Get terminal name.
tgamma, tgammaf, tgammal	tgamma, tgammaf, tgammal	True gamma functions.
tigetflag, tigetnum, tigetstr, tparm	tigetflag, tigetnum, tigetstr, tparm[21]	Retrieve capabilities from the terminfo database.
timezone	timezone	Convert date and time to string.
tmpnam	tmpnam, tmpnam_r	Create a name for a temporary file.
toupper	toupper	Translate characters to uppercase, lowercase, or 7-bit ASCII.
towlower	towlower	Translate wide characters.
towupper	towupper	Translate wide characters.
trunc, truncf, truncl	trunc, truncf, truncl	Truncation functions.
tsearch, tfind, tdelete, twalk	tsearch, tfind, tdelete, twalk	Manage binary search trees.
ttyname, isatty	ttyname, isatty	Find name of a terminal.
ttyslot	None	Find the slot in the utmpx file of the current user.

HP-UX Library Calls	Linux Equivalent	Description
`typeahead`	None	Control checking for typeahead.
`tzname`, `tzset`	`tzname`, `tzset`	Convert date and time to string.
`unctrl`	`unctrl`	Generate printable representation of a character.
`ungetc`, `ungetc_unlocked`	`ungetc`	Push character back into input stream.
`ungetch`, `unget_wch`	None	Push a character onto the input queue.
`ungetwc`, `ungetwc_unlocked`	`ungetwc`	Push a wide character back into an input stream.
`unlockpt`	None	Unlock a STREAMS pty master and slave pair.
`untouchwin`	`untouchwin` (`libncurses`)	Window refresh control functions.
`updatebwdb`	None	Write records into new `wtmps` and `btmps` database.
`use_env`	None	Specify source of screen size information.
`valloc`	`valloc`	Allocate space on boundary aligned to `sysconf` value.
`vfprintf`	`vfprintf`	Print formatted output of a varargs argument list.
`vfscanf`	`vfscanf`	Formatted input conversion to a `varargs` argument.
`vfwprintf`	`vfwprintf`	Print formatted output to a file.
`vidattr`	`vidattr` (`libncurses`)	Output attributes to the terminal.
`vsprintf`, `vsnprintf`	`vsprintf`, `vsnprintf`	Print formatted output of a varargs argument list.
`vscanf`, `vfscanf`, `vsscanf`	`vscanf`, `vfscanf`, `vsscanf`	Formatted input conversion to a `varargs` argument.

HP-UX Library Calls	Linux Equivalent	Description
vwprintf, vfwprintf, vswprintf	vwprintf, vfwprintf, vswprintf	Print formatted output.
vwprintw	vwprintw (libncurses)	Print formatted output in a window.
vwscanw	vwscanw (libncurses)	Convert formatted input from a window.
wborder	wborder (libncurses)	Draw borders from single-byte characters and renditions.
wcrtomb	wcrtomb	Convert wide-character code to a character.
wcsftime	wcsftime	Convert date and time to wide-character string.
wctob	wctob	Convert between single-byte and wide-character.
wcsrtombs	wcsrtombs	Convert a wide-character string to a string.
wcstod	wcstod	Convert wide-character string to double-precision number.
wcstoimax, wcstoumax	wcstoimax, wcstoumax	Convert wide-character string to long integer.
wcstol, wcstoll, wcstoul, wcstoull	wcstol, wcstoll, wcstoul, wcstoull	Convert wide-character string to integer.
wcscat, wcsncat, wcscmp, wcsncmp, wcscpy, wcsncpy, wcslen, wcschr, wcsrchr, wcsstr, wcspbrk, wcsspn, wcscspn, wcstok, wcstok_r, nl_wcscmp, nl_wcsncmp	wcscat, wcsncat, wcscmp, wcsncmp, wcscpy, wcsncpy, wcslen, wcschr, wcsrchr, wcsstr, wcspbrk, wcsspn, wcscspn, wcstok	Wide-character string operations.

HP-UX Library Calls	Linux Equivalent	Description
iswalpha, iswupper, iswlower, iswdigit, iswxdigit, iswalnum, iswspace, iswpunct, iswprint, iswgraph, iswcntrl, iswctype	iswalpha, iswupper, iswlower, iswdigit, iswxdigit, iswalnum, iswspace, iswpunct, iswprint, iswgraph, iswcntrl, iswctype	Classify wide-character functions.
wmemchr, wmemcmp, wmemcpy, wmemmove, wmemset	wmemchr, wmemcmp, wmemcpy, wmemmove, wmemset	Memory operations based on wide character.
wordexp, wordfree	wordexp, wordfree	Perform word expansions.
wunctrl	wunctrl	Generate printable representation of a wide character.
xdr_control, xdr_getpos, xdr_inline, xdrrec_endofrecord, xdrrec_eof, xdrrec_readbytes, xdrrec_skiprecord, xdr_setpos, xdr_sizeof	xdr_getpos, xdr_setpos, xdr_inline, xdrrec_endofrecord, xdrrec_skiprecord, xdrrec_eof	Library routines for external data representation.
xdr_array, xdr_bytes, xdr_opaque, xdr_pointer, xdr_reference, xdr_string, xdr_string, xdr_vector, xdr_wrapstring	xdr_array, xdr_bytes, xdr_opaque, xdr_pointer, xdr_reference, xdr_string, xdr_string, xdr_vector, xdr_wrapstring	Library routines for external data representation.
xdr_destroy, xdrmem_create, xdrrec_create, xdrstdio_create	xdr_destroy, xdrmem_create, xdrrec_create, xdrstdio_create	Library routines for external data representation stream creation.

HP-UX Library Calls	Linux Equivalent	Description
xdr_bool, xdr_char, xdr_double, xdr_enum, xdr_float, xdr_free, xdr_hyper, xdr_int, xdr_long, xdr_longlong_t, xdr_quadruple, xdr_short, xdr_u_char, xdr_u_hyper, xdr_u_int, xdr_u_long, xdr_u_longlong_t, xdr_u_short, xdr_void	xdr_bool, xdr_char, xdr_double, xdr_enum, xdr_float, xdr_free, xdr_int, xdr_long, xdr_u_int, xdr_u_long, xdr_u_char, xdr_short, xdr_u_short, xdr_void	Library routines for external data representation.
y0, y0f, y1, y1f, yn, ynf	y0, y0f, y1, y1f, yn, ynf	Bessel functions of the second kind.
yp_all, yp_bind, yp_first, yp_get_default_ domain, yp_master, yp_match, yp_next, yp_order, yp_unbind, yperr_string, ypprot_err	yp_all, yp_bind, yp_first, yp_get_default_ domain, yp_master, yp_match, yp_next, yp_order, yp_unbind, yperr_string, ypprot_err[22]	Network Information Service client interface.
yppasswd	yppasswd[23]	Update user password in Network Information Service (NIS).
ypupdate	ypupdate[24]	Changes NIS information.

---

13 Closest equivalent on Linux is `crypt`.

14 See readelf or objdump utilities.

15 Declared as a volatile int in glibc.

16 See rpm/db.h.

17 See http://josefsson.org/gss/manual/.

18 ndbm.h

19 Look at lsof source code for nlist_private example.

20 www.openslp.org/

21 Supported through libncurses library.

22 Undocumented Linux calls. See /usr/include/rpcsvc/ypclnt.h.

23 Undocumented Linux call. See /usr/include/rpcsvc/yppasswd.h.

24 Undocumented Linux call. See /usr/include/rcpsvc/ypupd.h.

D

Linux on POWER

In this appendix

Linux on POWER is the IBM terminology that refers to the Linux operating environment running on systems based on the POWER architecture. **POWER architecture** is an umbrella term for the POWER4, POWER5, and PowerPC processors produced by IBM and other suppliers. This appendix highlights the differences between Linux on POWER and UNIX and Linux environments (specifically, Intel-based platforms), focusing on software migration issues. This appendix covers the following topics:

- Development environment for Linux on POWER
- Porting considerations
- Architecture-specific differences

For more information about Linux software development on POWER4, POWER5, PowerPC architectures, visit www.penguinppc.org and www.ibm.com/servers/enable/linux/power/tech.html.

D.1 Development Environment for Linux on POWER

D.1.1 Compilers

Two compiler sets are available for Linux on POWER: the GNU Compiler Collection (GCC) and the IBM XL C/C++ compiler set. Here is a brief overview of each compiler set and their advantages:

- **GCC.** For projects developed across multiple platforms where a GCC compiler is the original compiler, the GCC compiler is normally used to build applications for Linux on POWER. GCC also allows some code prototypes that only GCC understands, such as GCC-specific macros.
- **XL C/C++ and Fortran.** XL C/C++ and Fortran compilers offer a high-performance alternative to GCC, as well as a number of additional features. XL compilers produce 32- and 64-bit GNU ELF objects, which are fully compatible with the objects GCC compilers produce. This is because the XL C/C++ compilers employ the same GNU libraries, linker, assembler, and binutils as GCC. In fact, functionality formerly exclusively offered by GCC compilers has been ported to XL C/C++ to facilitate source compatibility (for example, some GCC macros and inline functions). Sophisticated XL C/C++ optimization routines have been developed for and tailored to the

POWER architecture. High-performance computing applications, especially those heavily reliant on floating-point operations, often benefit significantly from a simple recompile with XL C/C++. For more information about the XL C/C++ compiler set, visit www.ibm.com/software/awdtools/xlcpp/features/linux/.

D.1.2 Binutils

The GNU binutils are a set of tools for building and working with binaries. The GNU binutils for Linux on POWER conform to the PowerOpen application binary interface (ABI) and the 64-bit PowerPC ELF ABI Supplement guidelines.

D.1.3 Java

Java development for Linux on POWER is supported by the IBM Java Developer Kit for Linux. This developer kit is available in both 32- and 64-bit versions at no cost from IBM at www.ibm.com/developerworks/java/jdk.

D.1.4 64-Bit Linux Distributions

SUSE Linux Enterprise Server

Red Hat Enterprise Linux Advanced Server

Yellow Dog Linux

Debian

Gentoo

OpenSUSE

Fedora

D.2 Porting Considerations

Software professionals porting applications from UNIX or Linux on other platforms to Linux on POWER must remember the following:

- Linux on POWER is a big-endian platform.
- Linux on POWER supports two programming models: ILP32 and LP64.

- The current IBM POWER microprocessor is a 64-bit architecture running a 64-bit Linux OS. However, Linux on POWER provides full binary compatibility with existing 32-bit applications and supports new 64-bit applications.
- Linux on POWER uses the ELF object file format.
- The basic compiler flags used in GCC and XL compilers are generally the same. However, a number of the flags differ. For example, Table D-1 compares the commonly used GNU and XL compiler flags.

TABLE D-1
GNU and XL Compiler Switches

GCC	XL C/C++	Description
`-v`	`-v`, `-V`, `-#`	Turn on verbose mode.
`-p`/`-profile`	`-p`	Set up the object files produced by the compiler for profiling.
N/A	`-q32`, `-q64`, or set the `OBJECT_MODE` environment variable	Create 32- or 64-bit objects. GCC 64-bit compilers are located at /opt/cross/bin.
`-fsyntax-only`	`-qsyntaxonly`	Perform syntax checking without generating object files.
`-fpic`	`-qpic=small`	Generate position-independent code for use in shared libraries. In XL C/C++, the size of the Global Offset Table is no larger than 64K. If `-qpic` is specified without any suboptions, `-qpic=small` is assumed. The `-qpic` option is enabled if the `-qmkshrobj` compiler option is specified.
`-fPIC`	`-qpic=large`	Allows the Global Offset Table to be larger than 64K in size.
`-pthread`	`-qthreaded` or `_r invocation mode`	Create programs running in a multithreaded environment.

GCC	XL C/C++	Description
-fno-rtti	-qnortti	Disable generation of runtime type -qrtti identification (RTTI) for exception handling and for use by typeid and dynamic_cast operators. On XL C/C++, the default is -qnortti.
-static	-qstaticlink	Objects generated with this option do not link with shared libraries.
-static-libgcc	-qstaticlink=libgcc	Instruct the compiler to link with the static version of libgcc.
-shared	-qnostaticlink or -qmkshrobj	Instruct the compiler to produce a shared object.
-shared-libgcc	-qnostaticlink=libgcc	Instruct the compiler to link with the shared version of libgcc.
-Wl, -rpath	-Wl, -rpath, or -R	Pass a colon-separated list of directories used to specify directories searched by the runtime linker.
-fno-implicit-templates, -frepo	-qtempinc, -qtemplateregistry, -qtemplaterecompile	Template instantiation.
-w	-w	Suppress warning messages.
	-warn64	Enables checking for long-to-integer truncation.
	-qinfo=<...>	Produces informational messages.
-fpack-struct	-qalign=bit_packed	Use bit_packed alignment rules.
	-qalign=linuxppc	Uses default GCC alignment rules to maintain compatibility with GCC objects. This is the default.
-O, -O2, -O3	-O, -O2, -O3, -O4, -O5	Optimization levels.
	-qarch, -qtune, -qcache	Optimization options for a particular processor.

D.3 Architecture-Specific Differences

This section addresses some porting issues that arise from architecture-specific differences between POWER/PowerPC architectures and others. For detailed information about the instructions and registers used by application programs for Linux/PPC, consult the PowerPC architecture books available at www.ibm.com/developerworks/eserver/articles/archguide.html.

- **Page sizes.** Currently, the 64-bit POWER and PowerPC platforms (PPC64) support the page sizes of 4K and 16MB. The 32-bit Intel platform (i386) supports 4K and 4MB (2MB in PAE mode) page sizes.
- **Clock and time functions (`clock_getres()`, `clock_gettime()`, `clock_settime()`).** Currently, Linux on POWER implements two types of clocks: CLOCK_REALTIME and CLOCK_MONOTONIC. For Linux on x386, two additional clocks are implemented: CLOCK_PROCESS_CPUTIME_ID and CLOCK_THREAD_CPUTIME_ID. However, PowerPC architecture provides a 64-bit Time Base Register that you can use for the high-resolution timer. You can use existing assembler operations (in your C code) to move to and from this Time Base Register. Consult Section 4 of PPC Book II Virtual Environment Architecture at www.ibm.com/developerworks/eserver/articles/archguide.html.

E

gprof helper

In this appendix

E.1 gprof helper Module for Multithreaded Applications

`gprof`, when used with multithreaded applications on certain kernels (such as Linux), profiles only the main thread. To work around this situation, we include the `gprof helper` module from http://sam.zoy.org/writings/programming/gprof.html. Basically, `gprof` uses the internal `ITIMER_PROF` timer, which makes the kernel deliver a signal to the application whenever it expires. This module passes this timer data to all spawned threads.

To use the module, compile the following:

```
$ gcc -shared -fPIC gprof-helper.c -o gprof-helper.so -lpthread -ldl
```

Type the following in the command line:

```
$ LD_PRELOAD=./gprof-helper.so your_program
```

You should see something like the following on the screen:

```
pthreads: using profiling hooks for gprof
```

```
/* gprof-helper.c -- preload library to profile pthread-enabled programs
 *
 * Authors: Sam Hocevar <sam at zoy dot org>
 *     Daniel Jönsson <danieljo at fagotten dot org>
 *
 * Reprinted with permission from Sam Hocevar.
 *
 * Compilation example:
 * gcc -shared -fPIC gprof-helper.c -o gprof-helper.so -lpthread -ldl
 *
 * Usage example:
 * LD_PRELOAD=./gprof-helper.so your_program
 */

#define _GNU_SOURCE
#include <sys/time.h>
#include <stdio.h>
#include <stdlib.h>
#include <dlfcn.h>
#include <pthread.h>

static void * wrapper_routine(void *);
```

```
/* Original pthread function */
static int (*pthread_create_orig)(pthread_t *__restrict,
                 __const pthread_attr_t *__restrict,
                 void *(*)(void *),
                 void *__restrict) = NULL;

/* Library initialization function */
void wooinit(void) __attribute__((constructor));

void wooinit(void)
{
  pthread_create_orig = dlsym(RTLD_NEXT, "pthread_create");
  fprintf(stderr, "pthreads: using profiling hooks for gprof\n");
  if(pthread_create_orig == NULL)
  {
    char *error = dlerror();
    if(error == NULL)
    {
      error = "pthread_create is NULL";
    }
    fprintf(stderr, "%s\n", error);
    exit(EXIT_FAILURE);
  }
}

/* Our data structure passed to the wrapper */
typedef struct wrapper_s
{
  void * (*start_routine)(void *);
  void * arg;

  pthread_mutex_t lock;
  pthread_cond_t wait;

  struct itimerval itimer;

} wrapper_t;

/* The wrapper function in charge for setting the itimer value */
static void * wrapper_routine(void * data)
{
  /* Put user data in thread-local variables */
  void * (*start_routine)(void *) = ((wrapper_t*)data)->start_routine;
  void * arg = ((wrapper_t*)data)->arg;

  /* Set the profile timer value */
  setitimer(ITIMER_PROF, &((wrapper_t*)data)->itimer, NULL);

  /* Tell the calling thread that we don't need its data anymore */
  pthread_mutex_lock(&((wrapper_t*)data)->lock);
```

```
  pthread_cond_signal(&((wrapper_t*)data)->wait);
  pthread_mutex_unlock(&((wrapper_t*)data)->lock);

  /* Call the real function */
  return start_routine(arg);
}

/* Our wrapper function for the real pthread_create() */
int pthread_create(pthread_t *__restrict thread,
          __const pthread_attr_t *__restrict attr,
          void * (*start_routine)(void *),
          void *__restrict arg)
{
  wrapper_t wrapper_data;
  int i_return;

  /* Initialize the wrapper structure */
  wrapper_data.start_routine = start_routine;
  wrapper_data.arg = arg;
  getitimer(ITIMER_PROF, &wrapper_data.itimer);
  pthread_cond_init(&wrapper_data.wait, NULL);
  pthread_mutex_init(&wrapper_data.lock, NULL);
  pthread_mutex_lock(&wrapper_data.lock);

  /* The real pthread_create call */
  i_return = pthread_create_orig(thread,
                 attr,
                 &wrapper_routine,
                 &wrapper_data);

  /* If the thread was successfully spawned, wait for the data
   * to be released */
  if(i_return == 0)
  {
    pthread_cond_wait(&wrapper_data.wait, &wrapper_data.lock);
  }

  pthread_mutex_unlock(&wrapper_data.lock);
  pthread_mutex_destroy(&wrapper_data.lock);
  pthread_cond_destroy(&wrapper_data.wait);

  return i_return;
}
```

F

Porting Issues Specific to the IBM zSeriesMainframe

In this appendix

Contributed by Wolfgang Gellerich, IBM

Fortunately, there are rather few specific issues to be considered when porting application programs to Linux running on an IBM zSeries mainframe, because the "official" interfaces of the Linux kernel are platform-independent. One important difference, however, concerns the way the Linux system itself executes on a mainframe. Personal computers usually run a native operating system controlling the whole computer system. In contrast, IBM zSeries systems support the concept of virtualization. Any operating system within the zSeries platform executes in a virtual environment, and there may be (and normally are) several instances of several different operating systems running at the same time.

F.1 Linux on IBM zSeries

On an IBM zSeries mainframe, Linux always runs within a virtual environment. The mainframe is divided into *logical partitions* (LPARs) . Each LPAR can directly execute either a Linux kernel (see Figure F-1) or a number of virtual machine (VM) images.

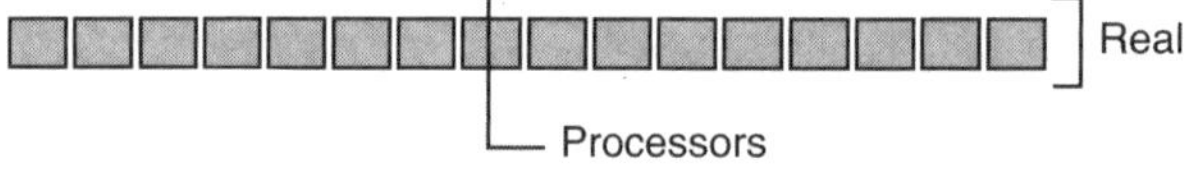

FIGURE F-1
Five LPARs—one running z/OS, and the other four running Linux

Virtual machine is the second way to create a virtual environment executing Linux . Figure F-2 shows several Linux instances running on a VM.

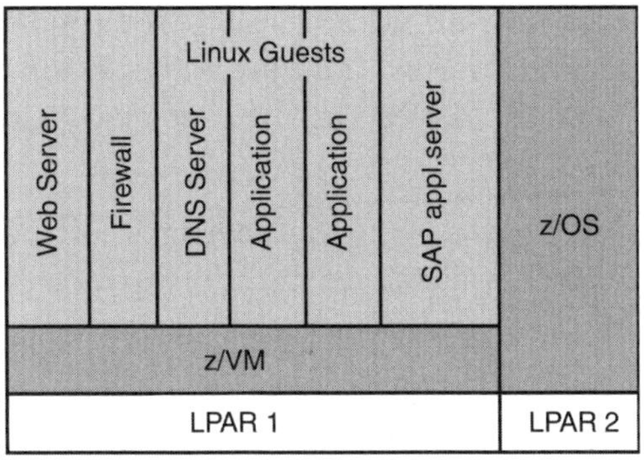

FIGURE F-2
A zSeries mainframe with one LPAR running z/OS, and another LPAR hosting six VM guests, each running Linux

A couple of important features are associated with this strategy, ranging from dynamic load balancing, capacity, and security issues to the issue of a high-speed virtual network between Linux images. In this network, the communicating parties behave as if they send and receive data via a real network. However, the data transfer is much faster and actually is performed by transferring data from one memory location to another. The fact that Linux on zSeries runs in a virtual environment does not affect the actual task of porting an application to Linux. An excellent overview and introduction are given in the book *Linux on the Mainframe.*[1]

F.2 Data Types, Addresses, and Machine Words

When porting applications to Linux on zSeries, it is important to know how the data types and addressing differ on the zSeries platform compared to other hardware platforms.

F.2.1 31-Bit Addresses

Current zSeries models are 64-bit architectures. For historical reasons, the next-smaller address size is 31-bit, not 32-bit. The 31-bit mode might still be in use for compatibility reasons. It is important to note that 31-bit addresses actually do not have a thirty-second bit, so any address 0x80000000 + *n* actually maps onto 0x00000000 + *n*.

---

1 Eilert, John, et al. *Linux on the Mainframe.* Prentice Hall, 2003

Note, however, that casting an integer value to a pointer value does not conform to the language standard. Also, absolute addresses are most likely platform-dependent, so any code actually affected by the problem just mentioned will probably need changes.

Of course, pointer values created using the language's "official" features are always correct. For this reason, the compiler saves the effort to clear the leftmost bit, causing the following expression to yield false:

```
(void*)0x80000000 == (void*)0x00000000
```

F.2.2 Absolute Addresses

A related problem is caused by applications that try to load code at an absolute address by calling `mmap` with the flag `MAP_FIXED`. Such usage of absolute addresses is not portable in general and may need changes.

F.2.3 Numbering Conventions for Bits

In Linux, it is common to denote individual bits by the exponent they would have when interpreted as binary numbers. The bits of a 32-bit word, for example, would be denoted as follows:

```
+--+--+--+-----+--+--+
| 31 | 30 | 29 |  ... 2 | 1 | 0 |
+--+--+--+-----+--+--+
```

Documentation related to the zSeries mainframe, however, counts bits from left to right:

```
+--+--+--+-----+--+--+
| 0 | 1 | 2 | ... 29 | 30 | 31 |
+--+--+--+-----+--+--+
```

Here, the rightmost bit with binary value 2^0 is called "bit 31." On a 64-bit system, this bit is called "bit 63."

F.2.4 Standard Data Type Sizes

Table F-1 shows the standard sizes of C data types.

TABLE F-1
Standard C Data Type Sizes

Type	31-Bit Mode	64-Bit Mode
Char	1	1
Short	2	2
Int	4	4
Float	4	4
Long	4	8
Pointer	4	8
Long long	8	8
Double	8	8
Long double	8	8
size_t	4	8
ptrdiff_t	4	8
wchar_t	4	4

The alignment is always the same as the type size—that is, a variable of type `int` is 4 bytes long and is stored at a 4-byte boundary. Table F-2 shows the standard data types of the Linux kernel.

TABLE F-2
Standard Linux Kernel Data Types

	gid_t	mode_t	pid_t	uid_t
31-bit mode	unsigned int	unsigned int	int	unsigned int
64-bit mode	unsigned int	unsigned int	int	unsigned int

You can find detailed information about data layout in the ELF Application Binary Interface Supplement.[2,3]

2 http://oss.software.ibm.com/linux390/docu/l390abi0.pdf

3 http://oss.software.ibm.com/linux390/docu/lzsabi0.pdf

F.3 Compiling and Linking

F.3.1 Compiler Options

GCC and the binary utilities provide some options supporting zSeries. You can find a detailed description of all GCC options in the manual *Using the GNU Compiler Collection.*[4] This manual provides a section exclusively devoted to the zSeries-specific options. We do not describe these options in full detail but rather give an overview. Also, it is likely that additional compiler options will be provided for new zSeries models and improvements might be offered for existing models. Check the most recent version of the GCC manual (see footnote 4) for details.

Figure F-3 shows a summary of the performance improvements achieved between 1999 and 2004 that suggests it is really worth exploiting GCC's zSeries-specific optimization options. Note that all data given in Figure F-3 was taken on the latest zSeries model available in the particular year and is normalized. Overlapping measurements have been used to scale when the measurements were taken on a new zSeries model. The publication "Contributions to the GNU Compiler Collection"[5] details how the measurements were conducted.

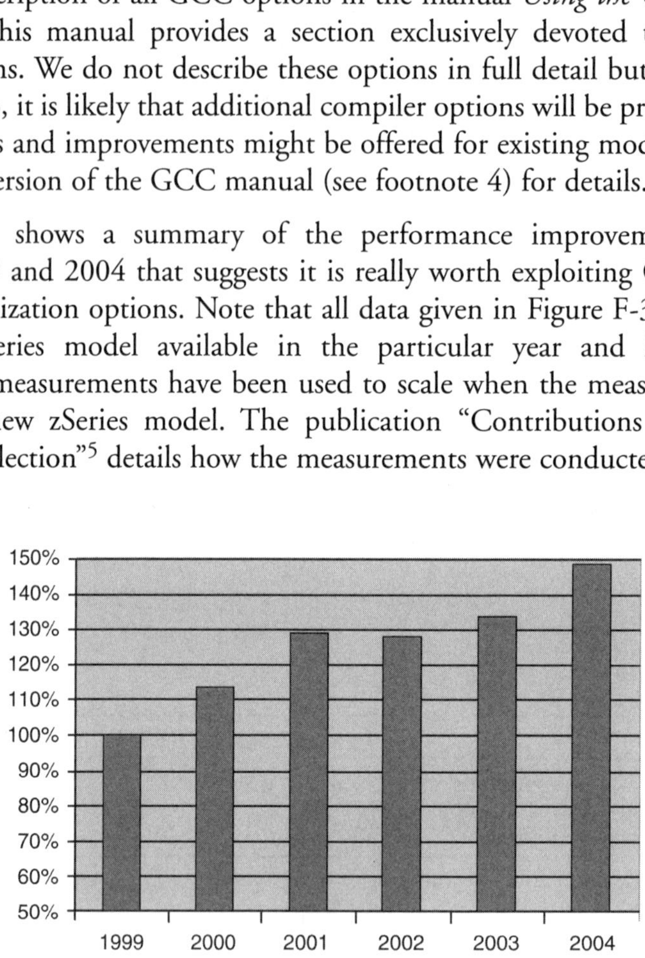

FIGURE F-3
Performance increase due to improved compiler optimization

---

4 GCC manual, www.gnu.org/software/gcc/gcc.html

5 www.research.ibm.com/journal/sj/442/edelsohn.pdf

Table F-3 shows the zSeries-specific code optimization options.

TABLE F-3
zSeries-Specific Code Optimization Compiler Options

Options	Function
`-march=cpu-type`	Exploits all instructions provided by `cpu-type`, including those not available on older models. In general, code compiled with this option does not execute on older CPUs. See the GCC manual (footnote 4) for a list of supported CPU types.
`-mtune=cpu-type`	Schedules instructions to best exploit the internal structure of `cpu-type`. This option does not introduce any incompatibility with older CPUs, but code tuned for a different CPU might execute more slowly.
`-mzarch` and `-mesa`	Generate code exploiting the instruction set of the ESA/390 or the z/Architecture, respectively. See the GCC manual (see footnote 4) for default values and interaction with other options.
`-m64` and `-m31`	Control whether the generated code is compliant to the Linux for S/390 ABI (`-m31`) or the Linux for zSeries ABI (`-m64`).[6,7]
`-msmall-exec` and `-mno-small-exec`	A switch to optimize jump instructions in executables with a total size not exceeding 64K. Some options exist to control and optimize stack growth.

Table F-4 shows some options available to control and optimize stack growth.

6 For details on the ABI, see LINUX for S/390 ELF Application Binary Interface Supplement, http://oss.software.ibm.com/linux390/docu/l390abi0.pdf.

7 For details on the ABI, see LINUX for zSeries ELF Application Binary Interface Supplement, http://oss.software.ibm.com/linux390/docu/lzsabi0.pdf.

TABLE F-4
Compiler Options to Control and Optimize Stack Growth

Options	Function
`-mwarn-framesize=framesize` and `-mwarn-dynamicstack`	Cause a compile-time check of whether a function exceeds a given stack frame size, or uses dynamically sized stack frames. These options help when stack space is rare, as is the case in the Linux kernel, or when application programs fail during a stack overflow.
`-mstack-guard=stack-guard` and `-mstack-size=stack-size`	Help debugging stack size problems. The checks are, however, performed during runtime by executing some extra code inserted into the binary.
`-mpacked-stack` and `-mno-packed-stack`	Control whether the stack frame uses a space-optimized, dense packing scheme for register save slots. See the GCC manual (footnote 4) for details concerning compatibility with other options and for call compatibility with binary code generated by pre-3.0 versions of GCC.
`-mbackchain` and `-mno-backchain`	Control whether the address of the caller's frame is stored as a so-called backchain pointer into the callee's stack frame. See the GCC manual (footnote 4) for details concerning the compatibility with other options, and for details related to debugging.

Linux for zSeries has an important difference from other systems concerning shared libraries. The `-fpic` and `-fPIC` options cause the compiler to generate positioning-dependent code (`pic`) for use in shared or reentrant libraries. On zSeries, `-fpic` causes the Global Offset Table to be rather small, so you should instead use `-fPIC` for large shared libraries.

If the linker reports a "relocation overflow" bug, check whether the project in question uses the `-fpic` option. Changing it to `-fPIC` might fix the problem. Note that you must use the same variant of this option for all compiler runs related to the same project.

Last but not least, the options `-mfused-madd`, `-mno-fused-madd`, `-mhard-float`, and `-msoft-float` control the usage of floating-point operations. See the "Principles of Operation"[8,9] for a complete description of the zSeries instruction set and architecture. In addition, some technical papers describe the internals of how GCC generates code for zSeries, available for download.[10,11,12]

F.3.2 Assembler Code

Any assembler code must, of course, be rewritten. See ESA/390 Principles of Operation[13] and z/Architecture Principles of Operation[14] for a complete description of the zSeries architecture and instruction set.

F.3.3 Stack Frame Layout and Linkage

Although not immediately required for the development of application programs in C and C++, you might occasionally need detailed information about certain implementation issues such as register usage conventions or the stack frame layout. This information is found in the ELF Application Binary Interface Supplement (see footnotes 6 and 7). More conventions used when compiling for zSeries are described in "Porting GCC to the IBM S/390 Platform" (see footnote 11).

---

8 "ESA/390 Principles of Operation," http://publibfp.boulder.ibm.com/cgi-bin/bookmgr/BOOKS/dz9ar007

9 "z/Architecture Principles of Operation," http://publibfp.boulder.ibm.com/cgi-bin/bookmgr/BOOKS/dz9zr001

10 "The GNU 64-bit PL8 compiler: Towards an open standard environment for Firmware development," www.research.ibm.com/journal/rd/483/gellerich.pdf

11 "Porting GCC to the IBM S/390 Platform," www.gccsummit.org/2003/

12 "Contributions to the GNU Compiler Collection," www.research.ibm.com/journal/sj/442/edelsohn.pdf

13 http://publibfp.boulder.ibm.com/cgi-bin/bookmgr/BOOKS/dz9ar007

14 http://publibfp.boulder.ibm.com/cgi-bin/bookmgr/BOOKS/dz9zr001

F.3.4 Predefined Symbols

If some code needs to be platform-dependent, you can use two predefined symbols in preprocessor expressions. `__s390__` is set when compiling for zSeries in 31-bit or 64-bit mode, or when compiling for S/390. `__s390x__` is set when compiling for zSeries in 64-bit mode.

F.3.5 Debugging

Many Linux debugging tools are available on Linux for zSeries. One additional feature is available for Linux running under VM. Using VM's `TRACE` command offers a convenient and powerful way to debug the whole Linux system. See the book *z/VM CP Command and Utility Reference*[15] for a reference on the `TRACE` command. An introduction to debugging is given in Chapter 22 of the book *Linux on the Mainframe.*[16] A detailed description of how to debug is included in most Linux distributions in the file /usr/src/linux/Documentation/s390/debugging390.txt. For debugging more difficult problems, you can find information about register usage, stack frame layout, and other conventions in the ELF Application Binary Interface Supplement (see footnotes 6 and 7).

F.4 Byte Ordering

The term *byte ordering* refers to the order in which the bytes of a word are stored in memory. You can store 32-bit binary values, such as `4A3B2C1D`, in several ways, including the following:

- A big-endian scheme stores the most significant byte (MSB) first, yielding

```
0x4A 0x3B 0x2C 0x1D
```

- A little-endian scheme stores the least significant byte (LSB) first, yielding

```
0x1D 0x2C 0x3B 0x4A
```

The IBM zSeries is big-endian system. When porting source code that was originally developed for a machine that is little-endian, you might occasionally stumble

---

15 IBM publication number SC24-5967

16 Eilert, John, et al. *Linux on the Mainframe.* Prentice Hall, 2003

over subtle problems. The Endianess Checking Tool, provided as part of IBM's Migration Kit for Solaris OS to Linux,[17] can help you locate parts of your code that depend on endianness.

If you need to support multiple platforms with different endianness, you can include the Linux kernel header file asm/byteorder.h, which defines one of the two symbols `__BIG_ENDIAN` and `__LITTLE_ENDIAN`, respectively, depending on the machine's endianness. The header files found in /usr/src/linux/include/linux/byteorder/ provide macros for converting between big- and little-endian representations. If the order is the same, they do nothing. Otherwise, the macros return the converted value.

A set of similar functions handle byte-order issues related to data transferred via the network. These functions, declared in /usr/include/netinet/in.h, convert values between the network and host byte order. Note that networks often use big-endian byte order, so an application running on zSeries does not need a conversion here. It is, however, good programming practice to insert appropriate conversion routines.

F.5 Other Differences

F.5.1 ASCII and EBCDIC Issues

Traditionally, mainframe operating systems use the EBCDIC character set. Given that nonmainframe applications are mostly written in ASCII today, one could expect additional work when porting such programs. However, given that Linux is a pure ASCII environment, such problems are unlikely to arise when migrating applications to Linux on zSeries. Most Linux distributions provide a tool named `recode` to convert files between different character sets. The current version supports about 280 character sets, including 19 EBCDIC variants with national character support. If a program needs to do such conversions, use the `iconv` function declared in /usr/include/iconv.h.

F.5.2 The Format of cpuinfo

The structure of /proc/cpuinfo depends on the particular platform, so any application expecting a particular structure may need further analysis.

---

17 http://www-1.ibm.com/partnerworld/pwhome.nsf/weblook/pat_linux_migrate_solaris.html

F.6 Variable Argument Lists

Normally, C application programs do not need to know how variable argument lists are implemented. Some code might, however, use nonportable assignments, which will fail on Linux for zSeries.

Linux for zSeries implements the `va_list` type as a `struct`. Therefore, a normal assignment such as `va2 = va1`, as shown in the following code snippet, will not work:

```
va_list va1, va2;
va_start (va1);
va2 = va1; /* This assignment will not work. */
```

Instead, use the `__va_copy()` macro for copying, as follows:

```
__va_copy (va2, va1);
```

F.7 Where to Find More Information

Linux on the Mainframe is a 430-page book (footnote 1) that covers most higher-level issues such as reliability, availability, and security; related considerations concerning the total cost of ownership, performance, and capacity planning; and technical overviews of concepts such as virtualization.

You can find a detailed description of the zSeries and architecture in the "Principles of Operation" (see footnote 8). It specifies the zSeries processor's instruction set, register usage, addressing modes, exception handling, and similar issues. At this level, there are also a couple of issues specific to the Linux operating system and its compiler. These have been described in a number of technical articles (see footnotes 10, 11, and 12). See the GCC manual for details about compiler support for zSeries (see footnote 4).

Last but not least, IBM provides a Web page with up-to-date information about porting issues: www.ibm.com/developerworks/eserver/articles/linux_s390/.

F.8 Acknowledgments

Many thanks go to Andreas Herrmann, Andreas Krebbel, Frank Pavlic, Martin Schwidewsky, and Ulrich Weigand (in alphabetical order), who provided information included in this appendix.

G

Solaris to Linux Migration: A Guide for System Administrators

In this appendix

This appendix contains tables from Appendixes A and B, excerpted from the IBM Redbook titled "Solaris to Linux Migration: A Guide for System Administrators," available at www.redbooks.ibm.com/Redbooks.nsf/RedbookAbstracts/sg247186.html?Open, reprinted courtesy of IBM.

As a porting engineer, you may find the need to configure some Linux parameters or devices to be able to run your unit and system tests on the ported application. We include this content to provide you with some technical perspective on Linux system administration. It presents differences in system administration tasks between Solaris and Linux, but as a reference, it will be as useful for AIX and HP-UX as well.

G.1 Packaging Tasks

Table G-1 shows differences in Linux and Solaris packaging tasks.

TABLE G-1*
Packaging Tasks

Units	Solaris	Linux
Smallest installable unit	Package Patch	Package
Single installable image; must be distributed and installed as a unit	Package	Package
Logical grouping of packages	Software cluster Patch cluster	Package
Logical grouping of packages and software clusters	Software configuration clusters For example: Core: Required operating system files End-user system support: Core plus window environment Developer system support: End-user plus the development environment	Workstation install (stand-alone client) Developer install (above, including developer tools, compiler) Server install (server services and software) Full install (all software/ services) Custom (choose packages manually)

Units	Solaris	Linux
	Entire distribution: Developer system plus enhanced features Entire distribution plus OEM: Entire distribution plus third-party hardware drivers (on SPARC only)	

* Table A-1 of IBM Redbook

G.2 Installation and Upgrade Tasks

Table G-2 shows differences in Linux and Solaris installation and upgrade tasks.

TABLE G-2*
Installation and Upgrade Tasks

Task	Solaris	Red Hat	SUSE
Install packages	`pkgadd`	`rpm -i`	
Display installed packages	`pkginfo` or `pkgparam`	`rpm -qa`	
Remove software package	`pkgrm`	`rpm -e`	
Upgrade/install a package	`pkgadd`	`rpm -U`	
Verify correct installation	`pkgchk`	`rpm -V`	
Install a patch	`patchadd`	`rpm -F` (upgrades only if already present)	
List contents of installed package	Look in /var/sadm/install/contents	`rpm -ql`	
Check which file belongs to a package	Look in /var/sadm/install/contents	`rpm -qf`	

Task	Solaris	Red Hat	SUSE
Check package information	Look in /var/sadm/pkg/ PKGNAME/ pkginfo	`rpm -qi`	
Remove a patch	`patchrm`	N/A	
Display installed patches	`showrev -p`	N/A	
Install OS on another disk (alternate disk installation)	Live upgrade	Install different OS on different disk/partition, dual boot using GRUB	
Create an installation server for network installation	`setup_install_server` *`install_dir_path`*	anaconda (see www.tldp.org/HOWTO/Network-Install-HOWTO.html)	autoyast (see www.tldp.org/HOWTO/Network-Install-HOWTO.html)
Create a boot server for network installation	`setup_install_server -b` *`bootdirpath`*	grub (see www.tldp.org/HOWTO/Clone-HOWTO/)	grub (see www.tldp.org/HOWTO/Clone-HOWTO/)
Set up a client for network installation	`add_install_client`	anaconda (see www.tldp.org/HOWTO/Network-Install-HOWTO.html)	autoyast (see www.tldp.org/HOWTO/Network-Install-HOWTO.html)

* Table A-2 of IBM Redbook

G.3 User Management Tasks

Table G-3 shows differences in Linux and Solaris user management tasks.

TABLE G-3*
User Management Tasks

Task/Locations	Solaris	Linux
Run multiple tasks in a GUI environment	`admintool`	In RHEL: `system-config-users` In SLES: `yast2`
Add a user	`useradd`	`useradd`
Remove a user	`userdel`	`userdel`
Change a user	`usermod`	`usermod`
List users	`listusers`	N/A
Password files	/etc/passwd and /etc/shadow	/etc/passwd and /etc/shadow
Group files	/etc/group	/etc/group
Process resource limits for users	N/A	/etc/security/limits.conf
System-wide environment file	N/A	/etc/profile
Configuration information for user authentication	/etc/pam.conf	/etc/login.defs
Profile templates	/etc/skel/	/etc/skel/

* Table A-4 of IBM Redbook

G.4 Network Management and Configuration

Table G-4 shows differences in Linux and Solaris network management and configuration tasks.

TABLE G-4*
Network Management and Configuration Tasks

Task	Solaris	Linux
Run multiple tasks in a GUI environment	N/A	`system-config-network` in RHEL, `yast2` in SLES
Configure TCP/IP	Edit the following files: /etc/hostname.* /etc/inet/* /etc/defaultrouter /etc/defaultdomain /etc/nodename /etc/netmasks	RHEL: /etc/sysconfig/network and /etc/sysconfig/networking/* SLES: /etc/sysconfig/network/*
Display interface settings	`ifconfig`	`ip` `ifconfig`
Display interface status and statistics	`netstat -i`	`netstat -i` `ifconfig`
Configure interface	`ifconfig`	`ip` `ifconfig`
Check various network statistics	`netstat`	`netstat`
Change resolver	vi /etc/resolv.conf	vi /etc/resolv.conf
Configure name services	vi /etc/nsswitch.conf	vi /etc/nsswitch.conf
Display kernel network parameters	`ndd /dev/ip \?` `ndd /dev/tcp \?`	`sysctl -a | grep ^net`
Configure kernel network parameters	`ndd`	`sysctl -w variable=value`
Check for network link	`ndd`	`ethtool` `mii-tool`
Rename a network interface	N/A	`ip`

Task	Solaris	Linux
Check routing table	`netstat -r`	`netstat -r` `route`
Test for connectivity	`ping`	`ping`
Check IP path	`traceroute`	`traceroute`

Capture network packets	`snoop`	`tcpdump`
		`tethereal`
		`ethereal`

* Table A-6 of IBM Redbook

G.5 NFS Management and Configuration

Table G-5 shows differences in Linux and Solaris NFS management and configuration tasks.

TABLE G-5*
NFS Management and Configuration Tasks

Task/Configuration File	Solaris	Linux
Manually start the NFS server	/etc/init.d/nfs.server start	RHEL: /etc/init.d/nfs start SLES: /etc/init.d/nfsserver start
Mount a resource on an NFS client	`mount -F nfs` *`server://resource /mount/point`*	`mount` *`server://resource /mount/point`*
NFS server general config file	/etc/default/nfs	/etc/sysconfig/nfs
NFS logging options config file	/etc/default/nfslogd	/etc/sysconfig/nfs
Share all exported filesystems	`shareall`	`exportfs -a`
Share a new filesystem	`share`	`exportfs -o`
Config file of shared filesystems	/etc/dfs/dfstab	/etc/exports

* Table A-7 of IBM Redbook

G.6 Managing System Resources

Table G-6 shows differences in querying Linux and Solaris systems for general information.

TABLE G-6*
System Information Tasks

Task	Solaris	Linux
List system information	`uname`	`uname`
List processor information	`psrinfo`	`cat /proc/cpuinfo`
List system memory size	`prtconf | grep Memory`	`cat /proc/meminfo | grep MemTotal`
List disk space usage	`df`	`df`
List file space usage	`du`	`du`
List physical disks	`format`	`fdisk -l`
Show the system's host name	`hostname`	`hostname`
List system's network configuration	`ifconfig`	`ifconfig`
List active processes	`prstat`	`ps -e`
List system configuration	`prtconf`	Red Hat: `lshal` SUSE: `hwinfo`
List system diagnostic information	`prtdiag`	Red Hat: `lspci` and `/proc/* files` SUSE: `hwinfo`

* Table A-8 of IBM Redbook

G.7 Disk and Filesystem Management

Tables G-7 and G-8 show differences in Linux and Solaris disk and filesystem management and configuration tasks.

TABLE G-7*
Disk Management Tasks

Task	Solaris	Linux
Create device files for new device	`devfsadm`	`udev`
Create partitions on the disk	`format` or `fmthard`	`fdisk` or `parted`
Display partition table	`prtvtoc`	`fdisk` or `parted`
Maximum usable partitions	7	15 for SCSI 63 for IDE

* Table A-14 of IBM Redbook

TABLE G-8*
Filesystem Management Tasks

Task	Solaris	Linux
Run multiple tasks in a GUI environment	N/A	N/A
Format a disk	`format`	`fdisk`
Check a file system	`fsck`	`fsck`
Mount a filesystem	`mount`	`mount`
Display available filesystem space	`df`	`df`
Partition a disk	`format`	`fdisk`
List a volume's table of contents	`prtvtoc`	`fdisk`
Format a filesystem	`newfs` or `mkfs`	`mkfs`
Unmount a filesystem	`umount`	`umount`
Back up filesystems, files, directories	`ufsdump`	`dump`
Restore filesystems, files, directories	`ufsrestore`	`restore`

Task	Solaris	Linux
Change a filesystem	`tunefs`	RHEL and SLES: `resize2ext` SLES: `resize_reiserfs`
Display filesystem information	`cat /etc/vfstab`	`cat /etc/fstab`
Display filesystem mount table	`/etc/mtab`	`/etc/mtab`

* Table A-15 of IBM Redbook

G.8 Swap Management

Table G-9 shows differences in Linux and Solaris swap management and configuration tasks.

TABLE G-9*
Swap Tasks

Task	Solaris	Linux
Create a swap space	`swap -a`	`mkswap`
Enable a swap space	`swap -a`	`swapon`
Enable all swap spaces	N/A	`swapon -a`
Disable a swap space	N/A	`swapoff`
Disable all swap spaces	N/A	`swapoff -a`
Delete a swap space	`swap -d`	N/A
Display the swap space usage	`swap -s`	`swapon -s`
Display the swap space status	`swap -l`	N/A
Set the swap priority level	N/A	`swapon -p`

* Table A-16 of IBM Redbook

G.9 Logical Volume Management

Tables G-10 and G-11 show differences in Linux and Solaris logical volume management and configuration tasks.

TABLE G-10*
Logical Volume Management

Volume Management Task	Solaris	Linux
Initialize a disk for VM	Create partition area/size: `metainit`	Create partition area/size: `pvcreate` `mkraid, mdadm`

Create a volume or volume group (VG)	`metainit volumename raidtype devices...`	`lvcreate LVname`
		`vgcreate VGname devicename`
		`mkraid, mdadm`

Enable the volume or volume group	N/A	`lvchange -a y LVname`
		`vgchange -a y VGname`
		`raidstart`

Disable the volume or volume group	N/A	`lvchange -a n LVname`
		`vgchange -a n VGname`
		`raidstop, mdadm`

Delete the volume or volume group	`metaclear`	`lvremove LVname` `vgremove VGname`
Add a device to the volume or volume group	`metattach` or `metainit`	`lvextend LVname` `vgextend VGname newdevname`

Delete a device from the volume or volume group	`metadetach`	`lvreduce LVname`
		`vgreduce VGname devicename`
		`raidreconf`

Create a soft partition or logical volume (no RAID)	`metainit -p`	`lvcreate -Lsize -nLVname VGname`
Create a soft partition or logical volume (RAID 0)	`metainit` with RAID 0 on devices first, and then `metainit -p` to create the soft partition volume	`lvcreate -iNumOfStripes -IStripeSize -nLVname VGname` `mdadm, mkraid`

Volume Management Task	Solaris	Linux
Create a soft partition or logical volume on a specific device	Same as above, but the second `metainit -p` has the device name at the end of the command line	Same as above, but add the device name to the end of the command line
Delete a soft partition or logical volume	`metaclear`	`lvremove /dev/VGname/LVname` `raidreconf`
Extend a volume or logical volume	`metattach volume [size or devicename]`	`lvextend -Lsize /dev/VGname/LVname` `raidreconf`
Extend a file system after volume has been grown	`growfs`	Red Hat ext2/ext3: `resize2fs` SUSE ext2: `resize2fs` Red Hat reiser: `resize_reiserfs` Note: View the man pages for unmount requirements, and check whether the online version is available.
Reduce a volume or logical volume	`metadetach` *`Volname devicename`*	ext2: `resize2fs` `lvreduce` reiser: `resize_reiserfs` `lvreduce` Note: View the man pages for unmount requirements.

* Table A-17 of IBM Redbook

TABLE G-11*
Logical Volume Management Commands

Volume Management Task	Solaris	Linux
Set up or display metadb	metadb	vgdisplay, lvdisplay, lsraid
Display metadevice status	metastat	vgdisplay, lvdisplay cat /proc/mdstat
Initialize raw devices to metadevices	metainit	pvcreate
Attach metadevices	metattach	vgchange, lvchange
Detach metadevices	metadetach	vgchange, lvchange
Clear and remove metadevices	metaclear	vgremove, lvremove
Replace a metadevice	metareplace	raidreconf
Rename a volume	metarename	raidreconf
Check metadevice ID configuration	metadevadm	mdadm
Manage hot spares	metahs	mdadm, raidhotadd, raidhotremove
Set submirrors offline	metaoffline	mdadm
Set submirrors online	metaonline	mdadm
Change volume parameters	metaparam	vgchange, lvchange
Back up volume group metadata	N/A	vgcfgbackup
Recover soft partition configuration information	metarecover	vgcfgrestore
Set up root filesystem for mirroring	metaroot	N/A
Administer disk sets for sharing	metaset	N/A
Resynchronize volume during reboot	metasync	N/A
Expand a filesystem size	growfs	vgextend, lvextend, resize2fs, resize_reiserfs, raidreconf

Volume Management Task	Solaris	Linux
Start up the kernel metadevice modules	/etc/system	N/A
Set the default number of available volumes	/kernel/drv/md.conf	/etc/sysconfig/lvm /etc/raidtab

* Table A-18 of IBM Redbook

G.10 General Troubleshooting

Table G-12 provides general troubleshooting information, highlighting differences between methods and configuration file locations between Solaris and Linux (RHEL, SLES).

TABLE G-12*
General Troubleshooting Methods and File Locations

Task/Location	Solaris	Red Hat	SUSE
Change a host name	Minimum change required for the following files: /etc/nodename /etc/hosts /etc/hostname.* /etc/net/*/hosts	`hostname` (while running) or `edit` /etc/sysconfig/network (for permanent change after network restart)	/etc/HOSTNAME and /etc/hosts
List of well-known networking services and port numbers	/etc/services	/etc/services	
List of well-known protocols	/etc/protocols	/etc/protocols	
Display NFS and RPC statistics	`nfsstat`	`nfsstat`	
Display a snapshot of virtual memory	N/A	cat/proc/meminfo	
Display virtual memory statistics	`vmstat`	`vmstat`	

Task/Location	Solaris	Red Hat	SUSE
Display I/O statistics	`iostat`	`iostat`	
Report system activity	`sar`	`sar`	
Display simple and complex lock contention information	N/A	View /var/lock directory	
Report CPU usage	`top`	`top`	
Display system error log	`dmesg`	`dmesg`	
Display paging/ swapping space	`swap -l`	cat/proc/swaps	
Disk crash dump utilities	`dumpadm` `savecore`	/etc/init.d/diskdump `savecore`	`lkcd`
Disk crash config files	/etc/ dumpadm.conf	/etc/sysconfig/ diskdump	/etc/sysconfig/dump
Network crash dump utilities	N/A	/etc/init.d/netdump /etc/init.d/netdump -server	`lkcd`
Network crash config files	N/A	/etc/sysconfig/ netdump /etc/netdump.conf	/etc/sysconfig/dump
Crash-analyzing tools	`mdb`	`crash`	`lcrash`
Crash dump default store directory	/var/crash	/var/crash	/var/log/dump
Specify users who have access to cron (Every user has access to cron if the access file does not exist.)	/etc/cron.d/ cron.allow	/etc/cron.d/cron.allow	
Specify users who have no access to cron	/etc/cron.d/ cron.deny	/etc/cron.d/cron.deny	
Specify remote users and hosts that can execute commands on the local host	/etc/hosts.equiv	/etc/hosts.equiv	

Task/Location	Solaris	Red Hat	SUSE
Default super user log	/var/adm/sulog	/var/log/messages	
Configure syslogd logging	/etc/syslog.conf	/etc/syslog.conf	
Display physical RAM	`prtconf`	cat/proc/meminfo	
Start or stop scripts directory	/etc/init.d	/etc/init.d and /etc/rc.d	/etc/init.d
Devices directory	/dev and /devices	/dev	

* Table A-19 of IBM Redbook

G.11 Network Troubleshooting

Table G-13 provides network troubleshooting information, highlighting differences in methods and configuration file locations between Solaris and Linux (RHEL, SLES).

TABLE G-13*
Network Troubleshooting Methods and File Locations

Tasks	Solaris	Linux
Display interface settings	`ifconfig`	`ip` `ifconfig`
Display interface status and statistics	`netstat -i`	`netstat -i` `ifconfig`
Configure interface	`ifconfig`	`ip` `ifconfig`
Check various network statistics	`netstat`	`netstat`
Check DNS resolver	`more` /etc/resolv.conf	`more` /etc/resolv.conf
Check name services config	`more` /etc/nsswitch.conf	`more` /etc/nsswitch.conf
Display kernel network parameters	`ndd /dev/ip (\?) parameter` `ndd /dev/tcp (\?) parameter`	`sysctl -a | grep ^net`

Tasks	Solaris	Linux
Configure kernel network parameters	`ndd -set driver parameter`	`sysctl -w variable=value`
Check for network link	`ndd driver link_status`	`ethtool` `mii-tool`
Query DNS	`nslookup` `dig`	`nslookup` `dig`
Check routing table	`netstat -r`	`netstat -r` `route`
Check ARP entries	`arp -a`	`arp`
Testing for connectivity	`ping`	`ping`
Check IP path	`traceroute`	`traceroute`

Capturing network packets	`snoop`	`tcpdump`
		`tethereal`
		`ethereal`

* Table A-20 of IBM Redbook

G.12 Configuration and Other Files

Table G-14 provides a quick reference to compare names and locations of configuration files between Solaris and Linux.

TABLE G-14*
Configuration and Other Files

Solaris	Linux	Comments
/etc/auto_master, /etc/auto_home	/etc/auto.master, /etc/auto.home	
/etc/default/login	/etc/securetty	
/etc/default/nfs	/etc/sysconfig/nfs	
/etc/default/nfslogd	/etc/sysconfig/nfs	
/etc/defaultdomain, /var/yp/binding/'domainname'/ypservers	/etc/yp.conf	

Solaris	Linux	Comments
/etc/dfs/dfstab	/etc/exports	
/etc/ftpusers (Solaris 8) /etc/ftpd/ftpusers (Solaris 9)	/etc/vsftpd.ftpusers (vsftpd) /etc/ftpusers (wu-ftpd)	
/etc/inet/ (directory)	/etc/hosts, /etc/HOSTNAME, /etc/sysconfig/network (directory)	
/etc/inet/services	/etc/services	
/etc/inetd.conf	/etc/xinetd.conf, /etc/xinetd.d (directory)	
/etc/krb5/krb5.conf	/etc/krb5.conf	Different format
/etc/logadm.conf	N/A	See Chapter 12, "Monitoring and Performance," on page 173.**
/etc/logindevperm	/etc/logindevperm	Different formats
/etc/mime.types	/etc/mime.types	Different format
/etc/mnttab	/etc/mtab	
/etc/nscd.conf	/etc/nscd.conf	Cache names are different
/etc/pam.conf	/etc/pam.d (directory)	
/etc/printers.conf	/etc/cups/printers.conf	Different format. See Chapter 10, "Printing Services," on page 151
/etc/rmmount.conf	N/A	See Chapter 6, "Device Management," on page 85.

Solaris	Linux	Comments
/etc/security/policy.conf	N/A	See Chapter 11, "Users and Groups," on page 159.
/etc/syslog.conf	/etc/syslog.conf	Slightly different format
/etc/system	/etc/sysctl.conf	
/etc/vfstab	/etc/fstab	
/etc/vold.conf	N/A	See Chapter 6, "Device Management," on page 85.
/usr/share/lib/zoneinfo/*	/usr/share/zoneinfo/*	
/var/adm/messages, /var/log/syslog	/var/log/messages, /var/log/syslog, /usr/adm/messages, /var/log/maillog	
/var/spool/cron/crontabs/root	/etc/crontab, /var/spool/cron	

* Table B-1 of IBM Redbook
** All cross-references in this table refer to the IBM Redbook.

G.13 Comparable Commands

Table G-15 provides a quick reference for *comparable* commands between Solaris and Linux.

TABLE G-15*
Comparable Commands

Solaris	Linux	Usage
/sbin/swapadd	/sbin/swapon	Enable swap devices
`adb`	`gdb`	Debugger
`admintool`	`yast2` (SUSE) /usr/bin/system-* (Red Hat)	Admin GUI

Solaris	Linux	Usage
`apptrace`	`strace` and `ltrace`	Application API tracing
`arch -k`	`uname -m`	List machine type
`cc`	`gcc`	C compiler
`devfsadm`	`modprobe`, `kerneld`, `insmod`, `hotplug`, `cardctl`	Add device without reboot
`df -k`	`df`	Filesystem allocation in units of kilobytes
`getfacl`, `setfacl`	`getfacl`, `setfacl`	Get, set ACLs
`gzcat file | tar -xvf -`	`tar -xzvf file`	Unbundle compressed TAR file
`lpsched`	`lpd`	Printer daemon
`modinfo`	`lsmod modinfo`	List loaded kernel modules
`mountall`	`mount -a`	Mount all entries in fstab
`mvdir`	`mv`	Move a directory
`nawk`	`gawk`	Awk scripting language
`patchadd`	`rpm -U`	Update package
`patchrm`, `pkgrm`	`rpm -e`	Remove package
`pkgadd`	`rpm -i`	Add package
`pkgchk`	`rpm -V`	Verify package
`pkginfo`, `pkgparam`	`rpm -qa`	Query packages
`priocntl -e`, `nice`	`nice`	Start a process with a given priority
`priocntl -s`, `renice`	`renice`	Change the priority of a running process
`prstat`	`top`	Report process statistics
`prtdiag`	`dmesg`	Error reporting tool
`prtvtoc`	`fdisk -l`	Read disk label
`ps -ef`	`ps [-]aux`	List all system processes
`snoop`	`tcpdump`, `ethereal`	Network packets sniffer

Solaris	Linux	Usage
`tip`	`minicom`	Serial port access program
`truss, sotruss`	`strace, ltrace`	Tracing
`umountall`	`umount -a`	Unmount entries in mtab
`useradd`	`adduser`	Add a user account
`who -r`	`/sbin/runlevel`	Show run level
`xterm/dtterm`	`konsole/gnome-terminal`	GUI terminal program

* Table B-2 of IBM Redbook

Index

Symbols

A

B

C

J–K

L

M

N

O

P

Q

U–V

W–Z

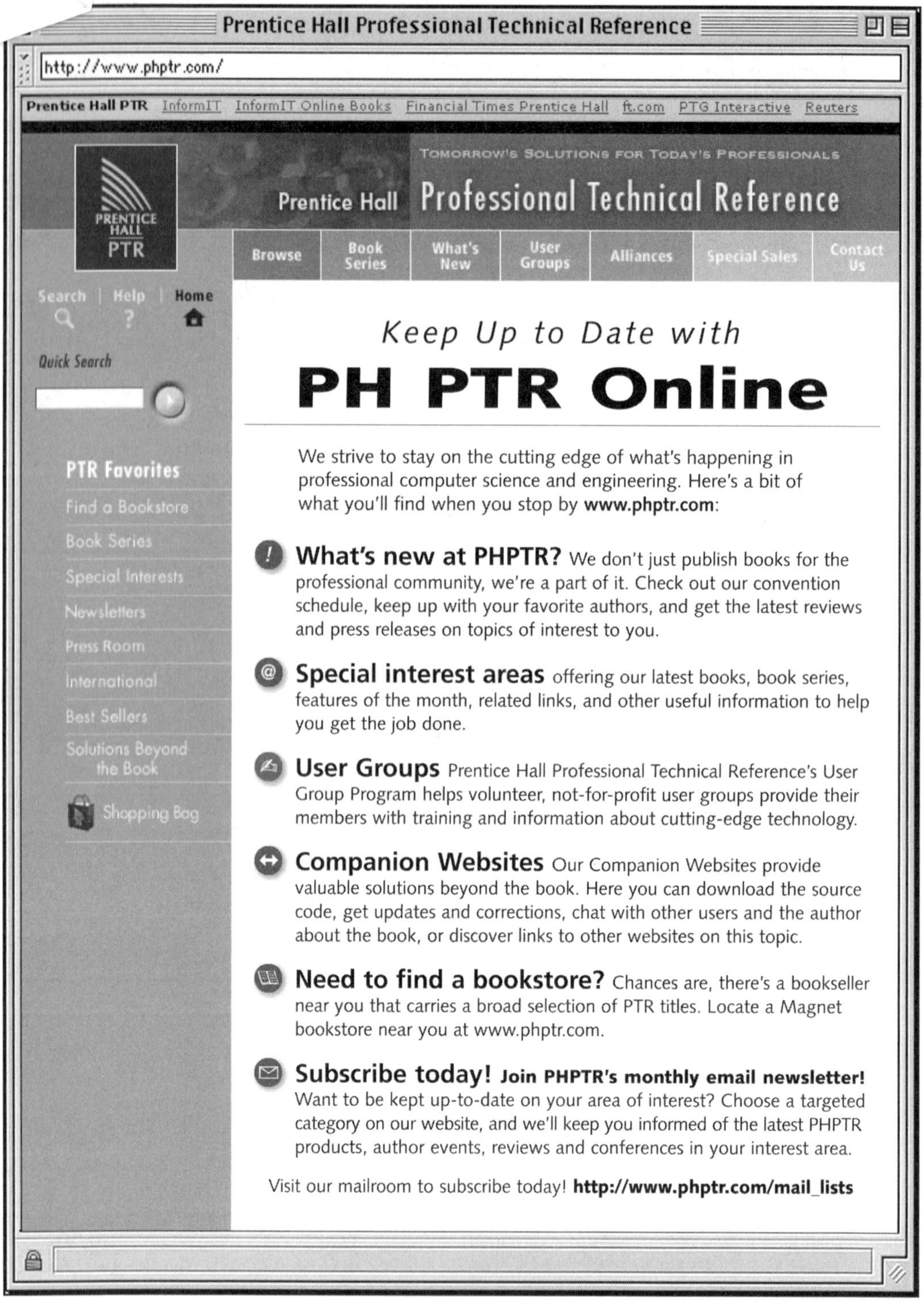

Prentice Hall Professional Technical Reference
http://www.phptr.com/
Prentice Hall PTR InformIT InformIT Online Books Financial Times Prentice Hall ft.com PTG Interactive Reuters
TOMORROW'S SOLUTIONS FOR TODAY'S PROFESSIONALS
Prentice Hall Professional Technical Reference
PRENTICE HALL PTR
Browse
Book Series
What's New
User Groups
Alliances
Special Sales
Contact Us
Search | Help | Home
Quick Search
PTR Favorites
Find a Bookstore
Book Series
Special Interests
Newsletters
Press Room
International
Best Sellers
Solutions Beyond the Book
Shopping Bag
Keep Up to Date with
PH PTR Online
We strive to stay on the cutting edge of what's happening in professional computer science and engineering. Here's a bit of what you'll find when you stop by www.phptr.com:
What's new at PHPTR? We don't just publish books for the professional community, we're a part of it. Check out our convention schedule, keep up with your favorite authors, and get the latest reviews and press releases on topics of interest to you.
Special interest areas offering our latest books, book series, features of the month, related links, and other useful information to help you get the job done.
User Groups Prentice Hall Professional Technical Reference's User Group Program helps volunteer, not-for-profit user groups provide their members with training and information about cutting-edge technology.
Companion Websites Our Companion Websites provide valuable solutions beyond the book. Here you can download the source code, get updates and corrections, chat with other users and the author about the book, or discover links to other websites on this topic.
Need to find a bookstore? Chances are, there's a bookseller near you that carries a broad selection of PTR titles. Locate a Magnet bookstore near you at www.phptr.com.
Subscribe today! Join PHPTR's monthly email newsletter!
Want to be kept up-to-date on your area of interest? Choose a targeted category on our website, and we'll keep you informed of the latest PHPTR products, author events, reviews and conferences in your interest area.
Visit our mailroom to subscribe today! http://www.phptr.com/mail_lists